cooking
through the year
1000 recipes • season by season

cooking
through the year
1000 recipes • season by season

DK

LONDON • NEW YORK
MELBOURNE • MUNICH • DELHI

Consultant Carolyn Humphries
Editors Emma Callery, Susannah Steel

DK UK
Project Editor Shashwati Tia Sarkar
Senior Art Editor Sara Robin
Editorial Assistant Christopher Mooney
Design Assistant Jade Wheaton
Managing Editor Dawn Henderson
Managing Art Editor Christine Keilty
Senior Jackets Creative Nicola Powling
Jackets Assistant Rosie Levine
Pre-Production Senior Producer Tony Phipps
Senior Producer Jen Lockwood
Creative Technical Support Sonia Charbonnier

DK INDIA
Senior Editor Chitra Subramanyam
Senior Art Editor Anchal Kaushal
Editors Ligi John, Janashree Singha
Art Editors Simran Kaur, Divya PR
Assistant Editor Priyanka Chatterjee
Assistant Art Editor Tanya Mehrotra
Managing Editor Glenda Fernandes
Managing Art Editor Navidita Thapa
DTP Designer Satish Chandra Gaur
CTS Manager Sunil Sharma
Picture Researcher Sumedha Chopra

First published in Great Britain in 2012 by
Dorling Kindersley Limited
80 Strand, London WC2R 0RL

Penguin Group (UK)

2 4 6 8 10 9 7 5 3 1
001 – 183117 – Sept/2012

A CIP catalogue record for this book is available from
the British Library.

ISBN 978-1-4093-8409-0

Colour reproduction by Opus Multimedia Services, India

Printed and bound in China by Hung Hing

Discover more at
www.dk.com

contents

All-year **vegetables and fruit**

When thinking of seasonal foods, vegetables and fruit such as asparagus and strawberries are usually the first that come to mind. However, as well as seasonal produce, there are some ingredients that are available all year and can be freely used. Some of these are best at certain times of year, but their availability does not wane. They include exotic ingredients, which can add colour and interest to seasonal dishes.

vegetables   cabbage (different varieties in their season) ▪ carrots ▪ cauliflower ▪ garlic (dried) ▪ lettuce (different varieties in their season) ▪ mushrooms (cultivated) ▪ onions ▪ potatoes (maincrop) ▪ spinach ▪ turnips ▪ watercress

fruit   banana (imported) ▪ lemon (imported) ▪ lime (imported) ▪ mango (imported) ▪ papaya (imported) ▪ passion fruit (imported) ▪ pineapple (imported)

Lemons Extremely popular for flavouring, lemons can be found at all times of year, but are best in winter if you plan to use them as a star ingredient.

Mushrooms Due to their popularity, many mushroom varieties are cultivated throughout the year and their flavour is reliably consistent.

Passion fruit Grown in warm climates globally, exotic fruits such as passion fruit appear in our shops all year and taste great combined with home-grown fruits.

Bananas The banana plant produces crops all year, making it a staple ingredient in many warmer countries and a ubiquitious imported ingredient.

Turnips Young turnips are available in spring but they grow throughout the year, peaking from autumn to late winter.

Carrots Slender young carrots are superb in spring and early summer, but mature carrots are invaluable for hearty autumn and winter dishes.

Cauliflower This vegetable is good at all times of year, making it useful for spring and winter, which are leaner months for produce.

Potatoes Summer new potatoes are delicious, but the fully grown ones are stored throughout winter, making them useful all-year vegetables.

Onion A kitchen essential, onions are never in short supply. In winter, when other vegetables are scarce, they can take a starring role in pastry and casserole dishes.

All-year **meat, poultry, and game**

Most meats are farmed and not affected by seasonal cycles. Lamb is now one of the only farmed animals whose meat can be considered seasonal: best-quality lamb is found in spring, early summer, and autumn. Venison, too, is traditionally best in autumn and winter, although it is farmed all year. Turkeys are often bred for the festive season, making them abundant in winter. For the best flavour and constant variety, cook meat with seasonal vegetables.

ingredients beef ▪ chicken ▪ duck ▪ guinea fowl ▪ lamb ▪ pork ▪ quail ▪ rabbit ▪ turkey ▪ veal ▪ venison ▪ wild boar

Beef joint Hearty beef often works well with cold weather vegetables. Roasting joints are excellent in combination with seasonal squashes and roots.

Veal The delicate flavour of veal chops (above) or diced (below) is excellent in spring and summer with spinach, sorrel and herbs, although Osso Buco, using veal shanks, is a classic winter dish.

Beef steak Cuts that need light, quick cooking are best with a side of seasonal vegetables. Try them in summer with new potatoes, new carrots, beans, or peas.

Diced veal

Chicken This universally farmed bird is justifiably popular as it works with all kinds of flavours in all seasons.

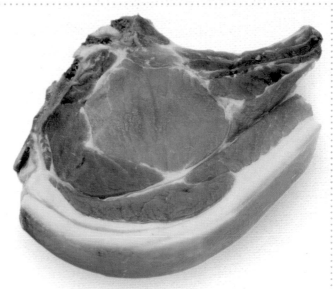

Pork The best flavour pairings for pork include pineapple, plums, aubergines, and tomatoes in spring and summer, and apples, cabbage, and leeks in autumn and winter.

Diced lamb

Lamb Whether you are cooking diced lamb (above) or chops (below), lamb works beautifully with summer and autumnal produce such as beans, artichokes, and fruits.

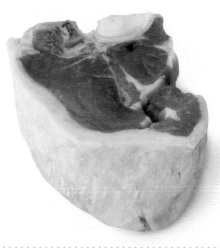

Duck Although wild duck is found only in autumn and winter, farmed birds are available all year. It is great teamed with autumn and winter fare such as apples, turnips, and oranges.

All-year **fish and shellfish**

Fish and shellfish that are caught wild are subject to seasonal fluctuations in availability and, due to sustainability issues, there are sometimes fishing quotas imposed on them as well. However, many of the most popular fish and shellfish are now farmed and therefore easily obtainable all year round. Whether you choose wild fish or farmed fish, ensure that they come from sources that are both sustainable and environmentally sound.

ingredients halibut ▪ herring ▪ monkfish ▪ mussels ▪ Pacific or rock oysters ▪ salmon ▪ king scallops ▪ sea bass ▪ sea bream ▪ brown trout ▪ rainbow trout ▪ sea trout ▪ turbot

Mussels Rope-grown mussels are an excellent sustainable seafood. Farming them in this way means that the traditional avoidance of the summer spawning season doesn't apply.

Scallops Farmed scallops are available all year, but are at their sweetest and best in the spring and summer months.

Salmon A popular fish worldwide, most Atlantic salmon now comes from fisheries. Farmed salmon can be of excellent quality and flavour, with a good balance of oil.

Halibut With its meaty, white flesh, farmed Atlantic halibut is a good fish to steam, pan-fry, grill, poach, and bake, making it suitable for use in all seasons.

▲ **Trout** Farmed trout, such as rainbow trout, are often bigger and have paler flesh than wild trout. The various wild species are best in spring and summer.

spring

at their best

vegetables baby turnips • chicory • forced rhubarb • fresh garlic • morel mushrooms • nettles • new carrots • new potatoes • outdoor rhubarb • pea shoots • radishes • salad onions • sorrel • spinach • spring greens • spring onions • sprouting broccoli • watercress • wild garlic

fruit avocados • pineapple

seafood abalone • brown shrimps • brown trout (wild and farmed) • clams • cold water prawns • common brown crab • king scallops • salmon (wild and farmed) • Dover sole • lemon sole • native oysters • Pacific or rock oysters • sea trout (wild and farmed) • rainbow trout (wild and farmed)

meat, poultry, game baby lamb • wood pigeon • poussins

also available

vegetables asparagus • cabbages • calabrese broccoli • celeriac • cauliflower • Jerusalem artichokes • kale • leeks • lettuce • mushrooms (cultivated) • onions • potatoes (maincrop) • swede **fruit** apples • lemons • limes • kiwi fruit • mangoes • passion fruit • pears **seafood** halibut • herring • John Dory • North Atlantic lobster • monkfish • mussels • red mullet • sardines • sea bass • turbot (farmed) **meat, poultry, game** beef • chicken • duck (farmed) • guinea fowl (farmed) • pork • quail (farmed) • rabbit (farmed) • turkey • veal • venison (farmed) • wild boar (farmed)

spring recipe chooser

ⓥ suitable for vegetarians

Vietnamese spring rolls p17

Pavlova with tropical fruit p62

Flemish vegetable tart p57

Marinated goat's cheese salad p25

Spring rice salad p60

Rhubarb and ginger upside-down cake p65

Vegetables

Asparagus
Spring rice salad p60

Carrot
Flemish vegetable tart p57 ⓥ
Malaysian chicken noodle and spring vegetable soup p28
Vietnamese spring rolls p17

Chicory
Chicken with chicory and bacon p55
Gratin of chicory and ham p60
Italian wedding soup p52
Marinated goat's cheese salad p25 ⓥ
Marmalade-glazed gammon with new potatoes and chicory p54
Turbot with cheese, ham, and chicory p55

Morel mushrooms
Morel and chestnut mushroom orzotto p38 ⓥ

Nettles
Nettle and blue cheese frittata p52 ⓥ
Nettle soup p31 ⓥ

Pea shoots
Warm wood pigeon breast and pea shoot salad p30

Radish
Blinis with smoked salmon p26

Rhubarb
Rhubarb and custard ice cream p67 ⓥ
Rhubarb and ginger upside-down cake p65 ⓥ

Rhubarb and orange yogurt fool p67 ⓥ
Rhubarb brûlée flan p67

Sorrel
Avocado and sorrel soup p16 ⓥ
Sorrel and wild garlic with pine nuts and olives p61 ⓥ

Spinach
Avocado and spinach soup p16 ⓥ
Calzone with cheese, ham, and spinach p51
Cheese gougères and salmon p24
Creamy spinach tart p30 ⓥ
Filo pie with spinach, ricotta cheese, and pine nuts p26 ⓥ
Pizza with spinach and ricotta cheese p58 ⓥ
Sautéed scallops with pancetta and wilted spinach p18
Spinach and coconut prawn curry p34
Spinach and goat's cheese frittata p52 ⓥ
Spinach and goat's cheese tart p18
Spinach sauce p61 ⓥ
Spinach-stuffed veal p55
Spinach with pine nuts and raisins p61 ⓥ

Spring greens
Italian wedding soup p52
Pigeon breasts with spring greens and hoisin p52
Pork and spring greens p52

Spring onion
Blinis with red and black caviar p26
Cheesy bacon and spring onion muffins p19
Flemish vegetable tart p57 ⓥ
Lamb and potato pie p43

Malaysian chicken soup p28
Pad thai p36
Pork with spring onions, soy, and cinnamon p47
Quesadilla with avocado, spring onion, and chilli p59
Singapore noodles with prawns and pork p36
Spaghetti with chilli, broccoli, and spring onion p50 ⓥ
Veggie pad thai p59 ⓥ
Vietnamese spring rolls p17

Sprouting broccoli
Savoury blue cheese and broccoli muffins p19 ⓥ
Spaghetti with chilli, broccoli, and spring onion p50 ⓥ
Steamed broccoli with bagna càuda p28

Turnip
Flemish vegetable tart p57 ⓥ
Lamb and potato pie p43
Malaysian chicken noodle and spring vegetable soup p28
Roast rack of lamb with harissa and baby turnips p46

Watercress
Prawn, avocado, and watercress sandwich p27
Spicy watercress soup p16 ⓥ

Wild garlic
Sorrel and wild garlic with pine nuts and olives p61 ⓥ
Warm wood pigeon breast and pea shoot salad p30

Fruit

Avocado
Avocado and spinach soup p16 ⓥ
Avocado and sorrel soup p16 ⓥ
Prawn, avocado, and watercress sandwich p27
Prawn and guacamole tortilla stacks p31
Quesadilla with avocado, spring onion, and chilli p59 ⓥ

Kiwi
Oriental fruit salad p64 ⓥ
Pavlova with tropical fruit p62 ⓥ

Mango
Oriental fruit salad p64 ⓥ
Pavlova with tropical fruit p62 ⓥ
Tropical angel cake p65 ⓥ
Tropical trifle p64 ⓥ

Pear
Spicy watercress soup p16 ⓥ

Pineapple
Fresh pineapple upside-down pudding p62 ⓥ
Jerk chicken with roasted pineapple p56
Oriental fruit salad p64 ⓥ
Pan-fried gammon with pineapple salsa p54
Pavlova with tropical fruit p62 ⓥ
Pineapple and kirsch floating islands p62 ⓥ
Pineapple broth with halibut p24
Pineapple broth with prawns p24
Pineapple trifle p64 ⓥ
Tropical angel cake p65 ⓥ

Seafood

Abalone
Abalone with oyster sauce p24

Clams
Pan-fried clams with chorizo p37
Pan-fried clams with parsley and garlic p37
Pasta with clams p38
Pork and clam cataplana p42
Shellfish soup p31s

Crab
Crab and prawn saffron tart p23
Minced crab balls p22
Pasta with crab and lemon p32
Seafood and tomato cioppino p32

Halibut
Pineapple broth with halibut p24
Seafood and tomato cioppino p32

Mussels
Pasta with mussels and saffron p38
Seafood and tomato cioppino p32
Shellfish soup p31

Oysters
Oysters skewered with pancetta p16

Prawns
Asian chicken and prawn broth with ginger and coriander p28
Büsumer fish soup p20

Crab and prawn saffron tart p23
Griddled prawns with hot pepper sauce p30
Pad thai p36
Pan-fried prawns with olives p38
Pineapple broth with prawns p24
Prawn and guacamole tortilla stacks p31
Prawn, avocado, and watercress sandwich p27
Prawn makhani p37
Prawn risotto p34
Prawn saganaki p34
Salmon and prawn fish pie p33
Sesame prawn toasts p22
Shellfish soup p31
Singapore noodles with prawns and pork p36
Spinach and coconut prawn curry p34
Thai fish cakes p23
Thai green curry p33
Vietnamese spring rolls p17

Salmon
Baked salmon p41
Blinis with smoked salmon p26
Cheese gougères and salmon p24
Gravadlax p19
Salmon and prawn fish pie p33
Salmon chowder p40

Salmon fish cakes p27
Salmon kedgeree p40
Spring rice salad p60

Scallops
Sautéed scallops with pancetta and wilted spinach p18
Scallops skewered with Parma ham p16
Seafood and tomato cioppino p32
Shellfish soup p31

Sole
Lemon sole with herbs p41
Sole fillets in wine vinegar p39
Sole with butter sauce p51

Red mullet
Shallow-fried red mullet p47

Trout
Baked sea trout with dill p41
Büsumer fish soup p20
Creamy smoked trout soup p20
Instant smoked trout p42
Sautéed trout with hazelnuts p40
Scandinavian-style cured trout p19
Smoked trout with chilli and lime dressing p20
Trout in rice wine vinegar p39
Trout with herbs, caperberries, and olives p41

Meat

Lamb
Flatbreads topped with lamb and hummus p47
Lamb and potato pie p43
Lamb fillet basted with anchovy paste p48
Lamb with lemon and olives p50
Rack of lamb with flageolet beans and herbs p46
Rack of lamb with parsley crumb p49
Roast leg of spring lamb p48
Roast rack of lamb with harissa and baby turnips p46
Skewered lamb with crispy rosemary potatoes p43
Turkish-spiced lamb pizza with pine nuts p48

Pigeon
Pigeon breasts with spring greens and hoisin p52
Warm wood pigeon breast and pea shoot salad p30

Poussin
Poussins glazed with honey and wrapped in bacon p58
Poussins in vine leaves p56
Poussins with mushrooms p56

Salmon and prawn fish pie p33

Lamb fillet basted with anchovy paste p48

Prawn and guacamole tortilla stacks p31

Lemon sole with herbs p41

Flatbreads topped with lamb and hummus p47

Pork and spring greens p52

scallops skewered with parma ham

Fresh, juicy scallops can be served simply. For a meat-free dish, omit the Parma ham and roast for a few minutes less.

🥣 10 MINS   🍲 8 MINS   ❄ FREEZABLE

SPECIAL EQUIPMENT ▪ metal or wooden skewers

SERVES 4

8 scallops, halved

1 tbsp olive oil

juice of 1 lemon

salt and freshly ground black pepper

8 slices of Parma ham, halved

1 If using wooden skewers, soak them in cold water for 30 minutes. Preheat the oven to 190°C (375°F/ Gas 5). Mix the scallops with the oil and lemon juice, and season with salt and pepper.

2 Wrap each scallop half in a piece of Parma ham, then thread onto metal or wooden skewers. You'll probably need 2 scallop halves on each skewer, depending on how big they are.

3 Lay the skewers on a baking sheet, and roast in the oven for 5–8 minutes until the ham starts to crisp. Serve hot with a rocket leaf garnish.

variation

oysters skewered with pancetta

Prepare in the same way but use 16 shucked oysters instead of the scallops. Add a few drops of Tabasco to the oil and lemon juice, and wrap in thin strips of pancetta instead of Parma ham.

avocado and spinach soup

Creamy, slightly nutty avocados and iron-rich spinach blend beautifully for a soup that is great for lunch with some bread.

🥣 15 MINS PLUS CHILLING   ❄ FREEZABLE

SPECIAL EQUIPMENT ▪ blender or food processor

SERVES 4

3 large (or 4 medium) avocados

juice of 1 large lemon

150g (5½oz) baby spinach leaves

900ml (1½ pints) cold light chicken or vegetable stock

½ tsp harissa paste

2 tbsp chopped coriander

salt and freshly ground black pepper

1 Skin the avocados and remove their stones, then chop the flesh and put it in a blender or food processor with the lemon juice. Coarsely chop the spinach and add to the avocados. Pour over the stock. Add the harissa paste, coriander, and seasoning, then pulse until smooth. Transfer to a bowl, cover, and chill in the fridge for at least 1 hour.

2 Pour into bowls or glasses, add an ice cube or two to each, and serve.

variation

avocado and sorrel soup

Prepare in the same way but use 75g (2½oz) sorrel and 75g (2½oz) butterhead lettuce leaves instead of spinach, and swap the coriander for 1 tbsp flat-leaf parsley and 1 tbsp fresh thyme.

spicy watercress soup

Peppery watercress, curry leaf oil, and caramelized pear create a marvellous melange of flavours.

🥣 20 MINS   🍲 30 MINS   ❄ FREEZABLE

SPECIAL EQUIPMENT ▪ blender or food processor ▪ hand-held blender

SERVES 4–6

3 tbsp curry leaves

150ml (5fl oz) olive oil, plus 2 tbsp

1 onion, chopped

2 potatoes, chopped

1 litre (1¾ pints) hot vegetable stock

250g (9oz) watercress

2 tbsp crème fraîche

salt and freshly ground black pepper

For the garnish

1 conference pear, peeled and finely diced

2 tbsp icing sugar

pinch of coarsely ground black peppercorns

1 tbsp crème fraîche

1 First make the curry leaf oil. Drop the curry leaves into a pan of boiling water and cook for about 30 seconds. Remove and refresh with cold water. Pat dry with kitchen paper and transfer to a blender or food processor. Warm the 150ml (5fl oz) of oil and gradually pour into the blender as the leaves are being processed. Pulse to a smooth paste. Line a sieve with kitchen paper and pour the curry leaf mixture into it – the oil will slowly drip through.

2 For the soup, heat the remaining 2 tbsp of oil in a large pan and add the onion and potatoes. Cover and fry over a gentle heat, stirring frequently, until softened but not coloured. Pour in the stock and simmer for another 10 minutes, until the potatoes are cooked. Add the watercress and cook for a further minute. Season, and stir in 2–3 tsp of the curry leaf oil off the heat. Purée with a hand-held blender until smooth and sieve to remove any tough fibres.

3 For the garnish, toss the pear in icing sugar seasoned with pepper. Place a frying pan over a medium heat, add the diced pear, and fry until it has caramelized.

4 Reheat and re-season the soup and whisk in 2 tbsp of crème fraîche. Ladle the soup into bowls, and top with an extra dollop of crème fraîche. Scatter over the pears and finish with an extra drizzle of curry leaf oil.

vietnamese spring rolls

Spring rolls are a great way to celebrate young, new-season produce such as spring onions, carrots, and lettuce. These are wrapped in soft rice paper, unlike the crisp, fried version, and are served with a sweet and spicy dipping sauce.

🍲 50-60 MINS   🍳 25 MINS

SERVES 4

250g (9oz) boneless loin of pork

2 young carrots, scrubbed and cut in julienne strips

1 tsp sugar

60g (2oz) thin rice noodles

8 small lettuce leaves, plus more to serve

75g (2½oz) bean sprouts

12-15 sprigs of mint

15-20 sprigs of coriander

8 round sheets of rice paper, 21cm (8½in) in diameter

4 spring onions, trimmed and cut in julienne strips

16 cooked, peeled cold water prawns

For the dipping sauce

2 garlic cloves, finely chopped

1 small red chilli, finely chopped

2 tbsp sugar

4 tbsp rice vinegar

4 tbsp fish sauce (nam pla)

2 tbsp lime juice

1 For the dipping sauce, in a small bowl, combine the garlic, chilli, sugar, rice vinegar, fish sauce, and 4 tbsp water. Pour in the lime juice and whisk well until thoroughly mixed. Set aside for the flavours to meld together.

2 Half-fill a pan with water and bring to the boil. Add the pork, reduce the heat, cover, and simmer for 15–20 minutes, just until tender. Drain the pork, rinse with cold water and drain again. Cut it across the grain into 3mm (⅛in) slices.

3 In a bowl, toss the carrots with the sugar and set aside. Bring a large pan of water to the boil. Add the noodles and cook for 1–2 minutes, until tender but still slightly chewy. Drain and cut into 7.5cm (3in) lengths.

4 Wash the lettuce leaves. Dry, then tear large leaves into 2–3 pieces. Pick over the bean sprouts, discarding any that are discoloured. Strip the mint and coriander leaves from the stalks, reserving a few sprigs for garnish.

5 Pour about 1cm (½in) of hot water into a shallow dish. Work with 1 sheet of rice paper at a time and keep the remaining sheets wrapped. Dip 1 sheet of rice paper into the hot water for 20–25 seconds, to soften. Remove and spread it out on a dry tea towel.

6 Place a lettuce leaf on the rice paper. Top with one-eighth of the noodles, carrot, spring onion, pork, bean sprouts, and mint and coriander leaves. Roll up the paper, halfway, into a cylinder. Fold both ends over the filling. Place a few more coriander leaves on top, then 2 prawns. Continue rolling the paper into a cylinder and press the end lightly to seal. Place the roll, prawn-side up, on a tray or plate and cover with a dampened tea towel to keep the roll moist. Repeat with the remaining rice papers and filling. Serve with small bowls of the dipping sauce, and sprinkle with the reserved herbs and extra lettuce leaves.

sautéed scallops with pancetta and wilted spinach

The coral on a scallop is usually red and soft. It is edible but some people prefer to only eat the main part of the fish, in which case trim it off first with a sharp knife.

🥣 5 MINS   🍲 15 MINS

SERVES 4

12 fresh scallops, with or without coral (depending on preference)

salt and freshly ground black pepper

1–2 tbsp olive oil

115g (4oz) pancetta, diced

dash of good-quality thick balsamic vinegar

2 handfuls of spinach leaves, stalks removed

juice of 1 lemon

1 Pat dry the scallops with kitchen paper, and season with salt and pepper. Heat the oil in a non-stick frying pan over a medium-high heat. When hot, add the scallops, positioning them around the edge of the pan. Sear for 1–2 minutes on one side, then turn them over, starting with the first one you put in the pan. Once you have completed the circle, remove the scallops from the pan (again starting with the first one), and set aside to keep warm.

2 Add the pancetta to the same pan and cook for a couple of minutes until crispy. Add a generous amount of balsamic vinegar to the pan, increase the heat to high, and allow it to boil for a couple of minutes, stirring to deglaze the pan. Then drizzle the sauce over the reserved scallops.

3 Still using the same pan, tip in the spinach. Cook for 2–3 minutes, moving it around the pan, until it is just wilted. Squeeze over the lemon juice, and serve immediately with the scallops and pancetta sauce.

spinach and goat's cheese tart

Fast becoming a modern classic, this dish can be adapted for vegetarians by substituting pancetta with toasted pine nuts.

🥣 20 MINS   🍲 55–65 MINS   ❄ FREEZABLE

SPECIAL EQUIPMENT ■ 23cm (9in) loose-bottomed tart tin ■ ceramic baking beans

SERVES 6–8

150g (5½oz) ready-made shortcrust pastry

150g (5½oz) pancetta, diced

1 tbsp olive oil

150g (5½oz) baby spinach

100g (3½oz) goat's cheese

sea salt and freshly ground black pepper

300ml (10fl oz) double cream

2 eggs

1 Roll the pastry out on a floured work surface to a large circle, about 3mm (⅛in) thick, and use to line the tart tin, pressing it into the corners. Ensure it overlaps the sides by at least 2cm (¾oz). Prick the bottom with a fork. Line with greaseproof paper and fill with ceramic baking beans. Place the tart tin on a baking sheet and bake for 20–25 minutes. Remove the beans and paper. Bake for a further 5 minutes to crisp the bottom. Remove and leave to cool.

2 In a frying pan, cook the pancetta in the oil for 5 minutes until golden brown. Add the spinach and cook until it wilts. Drain off any water and allow to cool. Spread the spinach and pancetta mixture over the pastry, cube or crumble the goat's cheese on top, and season.

3 Whisk the cream and eggs in a jug. Place the tart tin on a baking sheet and, with the oven door open, rest it half on, half off the middle oven shelf. Hold the sheet with one hand, pour the cream and egg mix into the tart, and slide it into the oven. Bake for 30–35 minutes or until golden. Remove from the oven and leave for 10 minutes. Trim the overhanging pastry with a knife, remove the tart from the tin, and serve warm or cold.

gravadlax

"Gravadlax", a Scandinavian method of preserving salmon, makes a stunning starter. Salt draws moisture from the fish to flavour it and firm its texture. Allow 48 hours for curing.

🥣 **20 MINS PLUS CURING** ❄️ **FREEZABLE**

MAKES 1kg (2¼lb)

85g (3oz) caster sugar

30g (1oz) dill, chopped

1 tbsp lemon juice

75g (2½oz) fine sea salt

1 tsp freshly ground black pepper

2 x 500g (1lb 2oz) thick fillets of very fresh salmon

1 To make the curing mix, put the sugar, dill, lemon juice, salt, and pepper in a small bowl and combine all the ingredients thoroughly.

2 Lay one fillet of salmon, skin-side down, in a large clean tray so it is completely flat. Spread all of the curing mixture evenly over the top of the salmon fillet.

3 Place the other piece of salmon, flesh-side down, on top of the covered fillet. Wrap the fillets tightly together in cling film and weigh them down with a plate and 1–2 cans, or a similar weight. Refrigerate the fillets for 48 hours to cure.

4 Turn the salmon every 12 hours to compress each fillet, and drain off the fluid so the fillets firm up. After 48 hours, remove the fillets from the fridge, unwrap them, and pat them dry with kitchen paper. To serve, cut the salmon into thin diagonal slices with a sharp knife. Serve with brown bread and butter.

variation

scandinavian-style cured trout

For 4 people use 4 very fresh trout fillets and half the Gravadlax cure ingredients. Prepare in pairs. Wrap the pairs separately, press and chill for 24 hours, turning once.

cheesy bacon and spring onion muffins

Spring onions have a milder taste than onion, so they are a perfect addition to these light savoury muffins.

🥣 **15 MINS** 🍲 **25 MINS** ❄️ **FREEZABLE**

SPECIAL EQUIPMENT ▪ 4 x 150ml (5fl oz) metal pudding moulds or ramekins

SERVES 4

150g (5½oz) back bacon rashers

200g (7oz) Cheddar cheese, cut into small pieces

125g (4½oz) fresh breadcrumbs

4 spring onions, trimmed and finely chopped

3 eggs

100ml (3½fl oz) milk

handful of chives, chopped

salt and freshly ground black pepper

1 Preheat the oven to 190°C (375°F/Gas 5). Fry the bacon rashers in a non-stick frying pan over a medium-high heat until they are cooked but not too crispy. Then cut the bacon into bite-sized pieces with a pair of kitchen scissors.

2 Place the Cheddar cheese, breadcrumbs, spring onions, eggs, and milk in a bowl and mix them together. Add the bacon and chives, stir them into the mixture, and season with salt and pepper.

3 Spoon the mixture into non-stick or greased pudding moulds or ramekins and bake in the oven for about 25 minutes until risen and golden.

variation

savoury blue cheese and broccoli muffins

Prepare these muffins in the same way, but use 150g (5½oz) cooked, well-drained, finely chopped purple sprouting broccoli or broccoli rabe instead of bacon rashers (don't use any tough stalks) and use 200g (7oz) mild blue cheese instead of Cheddar (or half and half). For extra flavour, add a few chopped sage leaves to the mixture in addition to the chopped chives.

büsumer fish soup

A delicious variation of this German soup, from a region on the North Sea coast. The original is made with white fish, but this one uses seasonal trout for an extra depth of flavour.

🥣 15 MINS   🍲 20 MINS   ❄ FREEZABLE

SERVES 4

2 large carrots, chopped

1 large floury potato, peeled and diced

1 large onion, diced

1 litre (1¾ pints) hot vegetable stock

1 bay leaf

salt and freshly ground black pepper

juice of 1 lemon

500g (1lb 2oz) trout fillets, skinned, boned, and cut into bite-sized pieces

200g (7oz) button or chestnut mushrooms, sliced

100g (3½oz) cooked, peeled cold water prawns

120ml (4fl oz) double cream

small bunch of dill, chopped

1 Put the carrots, potato, and onion into a saucepan, add the hot stock and bay leaf, and bring to the boil. Reduce the heat, cover, and simmer for 10 minutes until just tender.

2 Sprinkle a little salt, pepper, and half the lemon juice over the fish pieces, then add these to the stock along with the mushrooms. Simmer for another 5 minutes over a low heat.

3 Add the prawns to the pan along with the remaining lemon juice, and simmer gently for 1 minute to just heat through the prawns. Remove the bay leaf and season to taste with salt and pepper. Stir in the cream and half the dill and serve immediately, using the remaining dill to garnish.

creamy smoked trout soup

This comforting soup is based on a simple roux sauce, so it is vital to use very good stock to make it really sing. It makes an excellent light lunch.

🥣 15 MINS   🍲 10 MINS   ❄ FREEZABLE

SERVES 6

50g (1¾oz) butter

4 baby carrots, very thinly sliced

1 small leek, very thinly sliced

35g (1¼oz) plain flour

750ml (1¼ pints) hot vegetable or fish stock

250ml (9fl oz) whipping cream

4 tbsp white wine

2–3 tsp Worcestershire sauce

375g (13oz) hot-smoked trout fillets, skinned and flaked

2 tbsp chopped parsley

salt and freshly ground black pepper

squeeze of lemon juice

1 Melt the butter over a low heat. Add the carrots and leek and stir well. Cover and cook very gently for 5 minutes until soft but not brown, stirring occasionally. Stir in the flour and cook for 1 minute, stirring. Remove from the heat and gradually stir in the stock until smooth. Return to the heat, bring to the boil, and cook for 2 minutes, stirring continuously.

2 Stir in the cream, white wine, Worcestershire sauce, flaked fish, and half the parsley. Heat for 2 minutes. Season to taste with salt, pepper, and the lemon juice. Ladle into soup bowls and garnish with the remaining parsley.

smoked trout with chilli and lime dressing

In-season smoked trout has the fullest flavour. For extra texture, sprinkle over a pinch of toasted sesame seeds.

🥣 10 MINS

SERVES 4

350g (12oz) hot- or cold-smoked trout fillets

large handful of seasonal salad leaves

bunch of spring onions, trimmed and finely sliced

4 radishes, finely sliced

For the chilli and lime dressing

2 tbsp rice wine vinegar

2 tsp light soy sauce

splash of sesame oil

½–1 tsp caster sugar

2 red chillies, deseeded and finely chopped

juice of 1–2 limes

1 Whisk together the dressing ingredients, tasting as you go. Add all of the lime juice, if needed, or use less if the dressing is becoming too sour.

2 Divide the smoked trout among 4 serving plates, then toss together the salad leaves, spring onions, and radishes.

3 When ready to serve, lightly toss the salad with the some of the dressing, and drizzle the remainder over the trout. Serve immediately.

Season's best **trout**

Trout are elegant, oily fish, similar to salmon but with a sweeter, more delicate flavour. Some have pink flesh, others creamy white. They can be farmed all year, but if catching wild, are at their most delicious in spring, though still good through to autumn. They are perfect pan-seared or grilled whole or, if very fresh, gently poached. Try with Hollandaise sauce or orange-flavoured mayonnaise, almonds, watercress, herbs (dill, parsley, and chives), cucumber, and spring onions.

The rainbow trout has a bright, silvery skin with rainbow-hued speckles.

Rainbow trout The North American rainbow trout was introduced into Europe at the end of the 19th century. It grows quickly and is farmed extensively. In European waters, wild fish rarely grow bigger than 10kg (22lb); in the US they can be twice this size. It can be cooked whole or as fillets. Its very fine bones can be difficult to locate.

Trout fillets break into neat flakes when cooked and have a delicate, slightly earthy flavour.

essentials
varieties available

Farmed and wild rainbow trout, brown trout, and sea trout (brown trout that migrate to the sea). Hot- and cold- smoked; salted roe.

buy Whole, gutted, or fillets. Choose ones with slippery skin, bright prominent eyes, and red gills.

store Wrap well and store in the coldest part of the fridge. Eat within 24 hours.

cook Pan-fry, bake, grill, roast.

recipe ideas

Büsumer fish soup p20

Instant smoked trout p42

Sautéed trout with hazelnuts p40

Smoked trout with chilli and lime dressing p20

how to gut fish through the gills

When you plan to poach fish whole (particularly useful with trout or salmon), it is best to gut it through the gills so the stomach is kept intact.

1 Hook your index finger under the gills to lift them from the base of the head. Using a fish knife, cut off the gills and discard. Through the hole so formed, pull out the guts and discard.

2 Make a small slit in the stomach at the ventral (anal) opening. Pull out any remaining guts. Rinse inside and out with cold, running water. Pat dry. Trim and scale as necessary.

sesame prawn toasts

This is a delicious idea for cooking with prawns while they are in season. If necessary, you can make the prawn mix ahead of time, wrap it up, and leave in the fridge until needed.

 15 MINS   10 MINS

SPECIAL EQUIPMENT ▪ blender or food processor

SERVES 4

300g (10oz) cooked, peeled cold water prawns

2 garlic cloves, peeled but left whole

small handful of coriander leaves

1 red chilli, deseeded and finely chopped

juice of 1 lime

salt and freshly ground black pepper

4 slices white bread

125g (4½oz) sesame seeds

1 Preheat the grill to its highest setting. Blitz the prawns, garlic, coriander, chilli, and lime juice to a paste in a blender or food processor. Season well with salt and pepper, and blitz again briefly.

2 Lightly toast the bread on both sides, then spoon the prawn mixture onto one side of each piece of toast.

Spread the mixture evenly, covering the toast completely and pressing the mixture down firmly.

3 Lightly oil a baking sheet, tip the sesame seeds onto it, and spread them in an even layer. Place the toasts, prawn-side down, on top of the seeds, and press them so that the seeds stick to the mixture and coat it. Carefully flip the toasts over on the baking sheet and cut them into triangles.

4 Slide the baking sheet under the hot grill and cook the toasts for a few minutes until the sesame seeds begin to turn golden. Keep a careful eye on them, as they can burn very quickly. Serve immediately.

minced crab balls

When cooking a fresh crab, put it in the freezer 2 hours before boiling it in water. Cook for 15 minutes for the first 500g (1lb 2oz) and 2 minutes per 100g (3½oz) thereafter.

10 MINS   15 MINS

SPECIAL EQUIPMENT ▪ food processor

SERVES 4

250g (9oz) white crab meat

1 red chilli, deseeded

2 garlic cloves, peeled

handful of coriander leaves

grated zest and juice of 1 lemon

1 tsp fish sauce (nam pla)

2 eggs, lightly beaten

salt and freshly ground black pepper

125g (4½oz) fine fresh breadcrumbs

3 tbsp vegetable oil for shallow-frying

dark soy sauce, to serve

sweet chilli sauce, to serve

1 Put the crab meat, chilli, garlic, coriander, lemon zest and juice, and fish sauce in a food processor. Blitz until a rough paste forms, then add the beaten egg and plenty of salt and pepper. Blitz again.

2 Tip the breadcrumbs onto a plate. Scoop the crab mixture up using your hands and roll into 2.5cm (1in) balls. Roll each crab ball in the breadcrumbs until well covered.

3 Heat a little of the oil in a frying pan over a medium heat. Add a few crab balls at a time to the pan and cook them in batches. Shallow-fry the crab balls for about 5 minutes until golden all over, moving them around the pan so that they brown evenly, and topping up with more oil as needed. Drain on kitchen paper and serve hot with soy sauce and sweet chilli sauce for dipping.

crab and prawn saffron tart

The delicate flavours of crab and prawns balance wonderfully with the assertive pungency and musky taste of saffron.

🥣 20 MINS　　🍲 50-65 MINS　　❄ FREEZABLE

SPECIAL EQUIPMENT ▪ 15cm (6in) loose-bottomed tart tin ▪ ceramic baking beans

SERVES 2–4

100g (3½oz) ready-made shortcrust pastry

pinch of saffron

125g (4½oz) white crab meat

100g (3½oz) cooked, peeled cold water prawns

200ml (7fl oz) double cream

1 egg

1 tbsp finely chopped tarragon or chervil

sea salt and freshly ground black pepper

1 Roll the pastry out on a floured work surface to a large circle, about 3mm (⅛in) thick, and use to line the tart tin, pressing it into the corners. Ensure it overlaps the sides by at least 2cm (¾in). Prick the bottom with a fork. Line with greaseproof paper and fill with ceramic baking beans. Place the tart tin on a baking sheet and bake in the centre of the oven for 20–25 minutes. Remove the beans and paper. Bake for 5 minutes to crisp the bottom. Leave to cool.

2 Splash 1 tbsp boiling water over the saffron in a small bowl to allow the colour to develop. Put the crab meat and prawns in a sieve over a sink and press down to remove any excess water. Toss together and scatter over the pastry base.

3 Whisk the double cream and egg in a jug. Add the herbs, the saffron and its soaking water, and seasoning, and mix well. Put the tart tin on a baking sheet and, with the oven door open, rest it half on, half off the middle oven shelf. Hold the sheet with one hand, pour the cream and egg mix into the tart, and slide it into the oven. Bake for 30–35 minutes until golden. Remove from the oven and leave for 10 minutes. Trim off the overhanging pastry edges with a knife, remove the tart from the tin, and serve warm or cold.

thai fish cakes

If you can find Thai basil, which has a spicy, delicate flavour, use it instead of regular basil. It also has a sweeter taste than regular basil, which marries well with fresh prawns.

🥣 15 MINS　　🍲 15 MINS　　❄ FREEZABLE

SPECIAL EQUIPMENT ▪ food processor or blender

SERVES 4

300g (10oz) cooked, peeled cold water prawns

3 garlic cloves, peeled but left whole

small handful of coriander leaves

2 red chillies, deseeded

dash of fish sauce (nam pla)

dash of dark soy sauce

small handful of basil leaves

juice of 2 limes

1 egg

salt and freshly ground black pepper

3-4 tbsp vegetable oil or sunflower oil

sweet chilli sauce, to serve

1 Put all the ingredients except the egg and oil in a food processor or blender and blitz to a rough paste. Add the egg and plenty of salt and pepper, and blitz again.

2 Heat a little of the oil in a frying pan over a medium-high heat. Scoop up a tablespoon of the mixture with a spoon, then carefully slide it into the pan and flatten slightly; it should be about 2cm (¾in) thick. Repeat until all the mixture has been used. Shallow-fry the fish cakes for a minute or two on each side until golden; you may need to cook them in batches, adding more oil as needed. Drain the fish cakes on a plate lined with kitchen paper.

3 Serve the fish cakes hot with a drizzle of sweet chilli sauce and salad leaves, such as rocket.

cheese gougères and salmon

Smoked salmon and spinach give these puffs a luxurious edge.

🥣 40–45 MINS   🫕 30–35 MINS

SERVES 8

For the choux pastry

75g (2½oz) unsalted butter cut into small pieces

¼ tsp salt

150g (5½oz) plain flour, sifted

5–6 eggs

125g (4½oz) Gruyère cheese, grated

For the filling

1kg (2¼lb) spinach, stalks removed

30g (1oz) butter

1 onion, finely chopped

4 garlic cloves, finely chopped

pinch of ground nutmeg

salt and freshly ground black pepper

250g (9oz) cream cheese

175g (6oz) smoked salmon, sliced into strips

4 tbsp milk

1 Preheat the oven to 190°C (375°F/Gas 5) and grease 2 baking sheets. Melt the butter in a pan with 250ml (9fl oz) water and ¾ tsp salt. Bring to the boil. Remove from the heat, add the flour, and beat until smooth. Return the pan to the stove and beat over a very low heat for 30 seconds, to dry. Remove from the heat.

2 Add 4 eggs, one at a time, beating well after each. Beat the fifth egg; add it gradually until the pastry is shiny and soft. Stir in half the cheese. Using 2 spoons, drop eight 6cm (2½in) mounds of dough on to the baking sheets. Beat the last egg and ½ tsp salt and brush over the choux puffs. Sprinkle the remaining cheese over the puffs. Bake for 30–35 minutes until firm. Remove and transfer to a wire rack. Using a serrated knife, slice off the tops and leave to cool.

3 Bring a large pan of salted water to the boil. Add the spinach and wilt for 1–2 minutes. Drain and, when cool, squeeze it to remove the water, then chop finely. Melt the butter in a frying pan. Add the onion and cook until soft. Add the garlic, nutmeg, salt and pepper to taste, and the spinach. Cook, stirring, until any liquid has evaporated. Add the cream cheese and stir until the mix is thoroughly combined. Remove from the heat.

4 Add the smoked salmon, pour in the milk, and stir for 1–2 minutes until piping hot. Mound 2–3 spoonfuls of filling onto each cheese puff. Rest the lid against the side of each filled puff and serve at once, before the choux pastry becomes soft.

pineapple broth with halibut

The astringent quality of pineapple works well in savoury dishes and is a marvellous match for fish and spices.

🥣 30 MINS   🫕 40 MINS   ❄ FREEZABLE

SPECIAL EQUIPMENT ▪ food processor ▪ blender or hand-held blender

SERVES 4

1 onion, diced

50g (1¾oz) raw peanuts, skinned, plus 2 tbsp toasted raw peanuts, roughly chopped, to garnish

2 tbsp desiccated coconut

3cm (1¼in) piece root ginger, chopped

1 tsp coriander seeds

2 tsp sesame seeds

1 tsp cumin seeds

1 tsp poppy seeds

¾ tsp chilli powder

3 tbsp tamarind pulp

½ tsp turmeric

salt and freshly ground black pepper

2 tbsp vegetable oil

1 tsp soft light brown sugar

400ml (14fl oz) fish stock

200ml (7fl oz) pineapple juice

400ml (14fl oz) coconut milk

200g (7oz) halibut, chopped

juice of 1 lime

125g (4½oz) pineapple, chopped

2 tbsp mint leaves, roughly torn

1 Heat the onion, peanuts, coconut, ginger, and seeds in a cast-iron frying pan over a low heat for 5 minutes so the coconut darkens and spices are aromatic. Allow to cool in a bowl, then blitz in a food processor. Add the chilli powder, tamarind, and turmeric. Season and blitz to a smooth paste.

2 Heat the oil in a large saucepan. Fry the paste for 10 minutes on a low heat. Add the sugar. As the paste begins to catch on the base of the pan, add the stock and juice. Simmer for 20 minutes, partially covered.

3 Take the pan off the heat. Purée with a blender or hand-held blender. Add the coconut milk, return to the heat, add the fish, simmer for 3 minutes, then add the lime juice, pineapple, and mint. Serve with the toasted peanuts scattered on top.

variation

pineapple broth with prawns
Replace half the halibut in step 3 with 200g (7oz) cooked, peeled cold water prawns.

abalone with oyster sauce

A type of sea snail with well-flavoured flesh, abalone can be expensive so is often sold canned as well as on the shell.

🥣 5 MINS   🫕 5 MINS   ❄ FREEZABLE

SERVES 2

340g can abalone, drained with the liquid retained

2 tbsp sunflower oil or groundnut oil

bunch of spring onions, trimmed and finely sliced

1 tsp finely grated fresh root ginger

2 tbsp oyster sauce

1 tbsp soy sauce

pinch of sugar

5 tbsp water

2 tsp cornflour

1 Slice the abalone thinly. Heat the oil in a large frying pan, tip in the sliced spring onions and grated ginger, and stir over a low heat for 3–4 minutes. Add the abalone and toss together to heat through.

2 Mix together the oyster sauce, soy sauce, sugar, and water. Stir in the cornflour and the retained abalone liquid. Add this sauce to the abalone and stir over a medium heat until it just comes to the boil and the sauce has thickened. Serve immediately.

marinated goat's cheese salad

In spring, both winter endives and summer lettuces are available; team them with these delightful goat's cheeses marinated in herbs and golden oil. For an eye-catching salad, the goat's cheese should be firm but not dry. For the best flavour, begin marinating it one week ahead of serving.

20-25 MINS PLUS MARINATING

SERVES 4

8 slices of wholemeal bread

a variety of salad leaves, such as chicory, red oakleaf lettuce, and butterhead lettuce

For the marinated goat's cheeses

4 small round goat's cheeses, each weighing about 60-90g (2-3oz), or 1 goat cheese log, weighing about 320g (11oz)

2 bay leaves

2-3 sprigs of thyme

2-3 sprigs of rosemary

2-3 sprigs of oregano

2 tsp black peppercorns

2 small dried red chillies

500ml (16fl oz) olive oil, plus more if needed

For the vinaigrette

2 tbsp red wine vinegar

1 tsp Dijon mustard

salt and freshly ground black pepper

leaves from 5-7 sprigs of thyme

1 Put the goat's cheeses in a large glass jar with the bay leaves, thyme, rosemary, oregano, peppercorns, and chillies. Add enough oil to cover the ingredients generously. Cover and leave for at least 1 week before using. Alternatively, put a goat's cheese log in a non-metallic bowl with the other ingredients, cover with cling film, and marinate for 1-3 days.

2 Remove the cheeses from the marinade with a slotted spoon to drain off any excess oil. Strain the

marinading oil through a sieve into a bowl or wide-mouthed jug and reserve it. You will need 90ml (3fl oz) of the reserved oil to make the vinaigrette, plus a little more for the wholemeal bread.

3 Pour the vinegar into a bowl and add the mustard, salt, and pepper. Whisk the ingredients together. Gradually whisk in the reserved oil so the vinaigrette emulsifies and thickens slightly. Stir in half the thyme and taste for seasoning.

4 Preheat the oven to 200°C (400°F/ Gas 6). Cut each goat's cheese in half horizontally. If you are using a goat's cheese log instead, cut it into 8 equal slices. Using a pastry cutter, cut out a round from each slice of bread.

5 Set the bread rounds on a baking sheet and brush them with a little of the remaining strained olive oil. Bake in the oven for 3-5 minutes until lightly toasted. Heat the grill, put a round of goat's cheese on top of each toasted bread round, and grill for 2-3 minutes until the cheese is bubbling and golden.

6 Arrange the salad leaves on individual plates and drizzle with the vinaigrette. Place 2 cheese toasts on top of each salad, sprinkle with thyme leaves, and serve.

filo pie with spinach, ricotta cheese, and pine nuts

The freshest, tenderest spinach is most easily available in spring and is ideal for this subtly flavoured pie.

🥣 15 MINS   🍲 35 MINS

SPECIAL EQUIPMENT ▪ 20cm (8in) round or square loose-bottomed tart tin

SERVES 4

1 tbsp olive oil

1 onion, finely chopped

salt and freshly ground black pepper

2 garlic cloves, grated or finely chopped

550g (1¼lb) fresh spinach leaves

handful of raisins

75g (2½oz) pine nuts, toasted

200g (7oz) ricotta cheese

1 egg, lightly beaten

12 sheets filo pastry

30g (1oz) butter, melted

1 Preheat the oven to 180°C (350°F/ Gas 4). Heat the oil in a frying pan over a low heat. Add the onion and a little salt, and sweat gently for about 5 minutes until soft and translucent. Add the garlic and cook for a few more seconds until the garlic turns white.

2 Tip in the spinach and cook, stirring, for about 3 minutes until it wilts. Season well with salt and pepper. Remove from the heat, stir through the raisins and pine nuts, and leave to cool. Add the ricotta and beaten egg, and stir well.

3 Lay 2 sheets of filo pastry, one on top of the other, in the cake tin, letting them hang over the edge on two sides. Next, lay 2 more sheets of filo at right angles to the first layer. Continue in this way until you have used 8 sheets for the base of the pie.

4 Spoon the spinach and ricotta mixture into the pie. Fold in the edges of the pastry and top the pie with the remaining 4 sheets of filo pastry, tucking them in neatly. Brush all over with the melted butter and bake in the oven for 20–30 minutes until golden and crisp. Serve warm.

blinis with smoked salmon

Spring radishes add a delightfully peppery punch to this dish, which can be tempered by the soured cream that is a mandatory and delicious traditional accompaniment to blinis.

🥣 25-30 MINS   🍲 8-16 MINS

SERVES 8

2-3 tbsp capers, drained

1 small red onion, very finely diced

8 radishes, thinly sliced

175g (6oz) sliced smoked salmon

1 packet ready-made blinis

175ml (6fl oz) soured cream, to serve

125g (4½oz) butter, to serve (optional)

1 Coarsely chop the capers if they are large, place in a small bowl, and put the onion and radish in separate bowls. Place the slices of smoked salmon on a plate. Cover the plate and all the bowls, or place in the fridge, until needed.

2 Preheat the oven to low. Arrange the blinis on a baking sheet and put them in the oven to warm through. Melt the butter for serving, if using. Arrange the blinis on a serving plate. Place a piece of folded smoked salmon on each blini, top with a couple of radish slices, and garnish with a few chopped capers and onions. Serve with a bowl of soured cream and a separate bowl of melted butter, if you like.

variation

blinis with red and black caviar

Choose lumpfish or beluga caviar, depending on your budget. Omit the capers, red onion, radishes, and smoked salmon accompaniments for this version of the dish. Hard-boil 2 eggs and leave to cool. Peel the eggs, then separate the yolks and whites and finely chop them both. Trim 2 spring onions and cut the green tops into thin diagonal slices. Warm the blinis as directed in step 2. Serve the blinis with 30g (1oz) each red and black caviar (or more to taste), egg yolks and whites, spring onion slices, and a spoonful of soured cream.

prawn, avocado, and watercress sandwich

This winning combination of juicy and colourful spring fare is quick and easy to put together for a tasty instant lunch.

🥣 30 MINS　　🍲 5 MINS

SERVES 4

60g (2oz) cooked, peeled cold water prawns

1 tbsp fresh root ginger, grated or finely chopped

1 small red chilli, finely chopped

1 garlic clove, finely chopped

1 ripe avocado

¼ cucumber, thinly sliced

a few sprigs of mint, leaves picked and roughly torn

1 tbsp dill, finely chopped

1 tbsp capers, chopped, rinsed, and drained

½ small red onion, finely chopped

250ml (9fl oz) soured cream

juice of 1 lime

8 thick slices wholegrain or granary bread

4 handfuls of watercress

1 Mix the prawns with the ginger, chilli, and garlic in a bowl. Set aside.

2 Halve, stone, and peel the avocado. Dice the flesh and put in another bowl. Add the cucumber, mint, dill, capers, onion, soured cream, and lime juice. Tip in the prawns and gently stir through, being careful not to mash the avocado.

3 Spread the mixture evenly over 4 slices of the bread. Arrange the watercress on top so that it will come out over the sides of the sandwich. Cover with the other slices of bread to make 4 sandwiches, cut in half diagonally if you like, and serve.

salmon fish cakes

These herby fish cakes are delicious served on a bed of tender young watercress and spinach leaves.

🥣 15 MINS　　🍲 30 MINS

SERVES 4

900g (2lb) potatoes, peeled and cut into chunks

knob of butter

900g (2lb) salmon, skinned

handful of curly leaf parsley, finely chopped

salt and freshly ground black pepper

a little vegetable oil, for frying

tartare sauce, to serve

lemon wedges, to serve

1 Boil the potatoes in a large saucepan of salted water for about 15 minutes until soft, then drain well and mash. Add the knob of butter and mash again until smooth. Set aside.

2 Put the piece of salmon in a large frying pan and cover it with water. Bring the water just to the boil, turn the heat down, and simmer over a low heat for 5–8 minutes until the salmon turns opaque. Remove with a fish slice and put on a plate. Leave to cool for a minute or two. Using your fingers, flake the fish into pieces.

3 Gently mix the fish with the mashed potato. Add the parsley and season well with salt and pepper. Take a small handful of the mixture in your hands, roll it into a ball, and flatten into a cake. Continue the process until all the mixture has been used – there should be enough for 2 fish cakes per person. Dust the fish cakes with a little flour.

4 Heat just enough oil for shallow-frying in a non-stick frying pan over a medium heat. Cook a few fish cakes at a time, frying them for about 5 minutes on each side until golden. Serve hot with tartare sauce and lemon wedges.

malaysian chicken soup

The poached chicken in this recipe has a silky texture; a generous handful of spring onions adds flavour and crunch. Try adding seasonal greens, noodles, or shrimps at the end.

🥣 15 MINS   🍲 40–50 MINS   ❄ FREEZABLE

SERVES 4–6

1.35kg (3lb) chicken

1 onion, quartered

5cm (2in) piece of fresh root ginger, peeled and sliced

6 garlic cloves, crushed

salt and freshly ground black pepper

splash of soy sauce

splash of fish sauce (nam pla)

250ml (9fl oz) hot vegetable stock (optional)

bunch of spring onions, trimmed and finely sliced

1 Put the chicken, onion, ginger, and garlic in a large pan and cover with water. Season with salt and pepper and bring to the boil. Reduce to a simmer, cover, and cook on a low heat for 30–40 minutes, or until the chicken is cooked and the juices flow clear when pierced with a sharp knife. Remove the chicken from the broth and set aside until it is cool enough to handle.

2 Remove the skin from the chicken and discard, then remove all the meat from the bones. Strain the broth from the pan into a clean heavy-based pan, add the chicken meat, and stir in the soy sauce and fish sauce. Top up with some stock, if necessary, then simmer gently to warm through, taste, and season as required. Ladle into warmed soup bowls and top with the spring onions.

variation

malaysian chicken noodle and spring vegetable soup

For this main meal soup, prepare in the same way but add 2 young carrots, thinly cut in diagonal slices, and 2 finely diced baby turnips to the stock at step 2. Simmer for a few minutes until the vegetables are just tender. Cook 200g (7oz) rice noodles, drain, and toss them in 2 tsp sesame oil. Divide the noodles between 4–6 large bowls and ladle the soup over.

steamed broccoli with bagna càuda

This warm, garlicky dip is delicious with lightly steamed sprouting broccoli but you could also do as the Italians and serve with raw baby carrots and radishes.

🥣 10 MINS   🍲 10 MINS

SERVES 4

500g (1lb 2oz) purple sprouting or young broccoli spears, trimmed

4 chopped anchovies

2 garlic cloves, crushed

100ml (3½fl oz) extra virgin olive oil

25g (scant 1oz) cold butter

1 tsp lemon juice

sea salt and freshly ground black pepper

1 Steam the broccoli for no more than 5 minutes, until it is just al dente.

2 Put the anchovies into a mortar and pestle, and grind them to a paste. Put them in a small saucepan along with the garlic and oil, and heat gently for 2 minutes until the garlic is lightly coloured, but not brown.

3 Remove the pan from the heat and use a wire whisk to add the cold butter in small pieces, beating well between additions.

4 Add the lemon juice and continue to whisk until the mixture emulsifies slightly, then season to taste. Serve the bagna càuda dipping sauce warm with the broccoli.

asian chicken and prawn broth with ginger and coriander

Lots of complex flavours make up this warming broth. The prawns and chicken add plenty of protein, making it a substantial dish.

🥣 15 MINS   🍲 1 HR

SERVES 4–6

1.2 litres (2 pints) hot chicken stock

salt and freshly ground black pepper

1 tbsp dark soy sauce

3 tbsp fish sauce (nam pla)

3 tbsp mirin

1 tsp tahini

2 garlic cloves, finely chopped

5cm (2in) piece of fresh root ginger, peeled and sliced into fine strips

½ tsp dried chilli flakes

225g can bamboo shoots, drained and rinsed

225g can water chestnuts, drained and rinsed

125g (4½oz) button mushrooms, whole or larger ones halved

2 skinless chicken breasts, finely sliced

bunch of spring onions, trimmed and finely chopped

bunch of coriander leaves

250g (9oz) cooked, peeled cold water prawns

1 Put the stock into a large heavy-based pan, season with salt and pepper, and pour in a further 600ml (1 pint) of hot water. Add the soy sauce, fish sauce, mirin, and tahini, and bring to the boil.

2 Reduce to a simmer and add the garlic, ginger, and chilli flakes together with the bamboo shoots, water chestnuts, and mushrooms. Stir, then add the chicken, cover with a lid, and cook gently for 40 minutes. Top up with hot water if necessary.

3 Taste and adjust seasoning as required, then stir through the spring onions and coriander leaves, and simmer on a low heat for a further 10 minutes.

4 Finally, add the prawns and simmer for 5 minutes. Ladle into warmed bowls and serve while piping hot.

Season's best **spring and salad onions**

Thin spring onions and more bulbous salad ones are sold in bunches from spring through summer, usually untrimmed. They have a delicious, mild onion flavour and can be eaten raw or cooked, whole, chopped, or sliced. They enhance dairy-, egg-, and mayonnaise-based dishes and add colour and flavour to rice, pasta, seafood, meat, poultry, pulses, salads, and many Asian dishes.

Spring and salad onions are grown extensively worldwide. They are simply young bulb onions, harvested early while the leaves are still green and the bulbs are not fully formed.

Salad onion More mature than spring onions, they have a slightly stronger flavour but are delicious raw in salads. They can be trimmed and the bulbs cooked whole or pickled, and the greens used for garnish.

The bulbs are large enough to be sliced and separated into rings for salads. Chop the tops and add as well.

Spring onion Also known as green onions or scallions, they just need trimming and then the whole onion can be used to add flavour and colour to dishes.

essentials
varieties available

Thin, spring onions and larger, more bulbous salad ones.

buy They should be crisp with firm stalks, fresh green leaves, and no brown outer skin.

store Both salad and spring onion varieties should be used as soon as possible, but can be stored in the fridge vegetable drawer, wrapped in a plastic bag, for up to 5 days.

cook Stir-fry, sauté; add to salads, soups, and sauces.

preserve Trimmed salad onion bulbs can be pickled.

recipe ideas

Cheesy bacon and spring onion muffins p19

Chicken stir-fried with spring onion, basil, and lemongrass p175

Pork with spring onions, soy, and cinnamon p47

Quesadilla with avocado, spring onion, and chilli p59

how to trim and chop spring onions

You can buy ready-trimmed spring onions as well, but they cost more. Spring onions are very simple to prepare in two steps.

1 Trim off the root ends and tips of the green tops (for the whole bunch, do this with them bound together). Peel off any damaged outer layers.

2 For stir-frying, starting at the white end, cut in diagonal slices, about 2.5cm (1in) long. Alternatively, chop into 5mm (¼in) slices.

creamy spinach tart

Spinach and watercress are a classic spring combination that is enriched here with double cream and a little nutmeg.

🥣 15 MINS   🍲 1 HR

SPECIAL EQUIPMENT ▪ 20cm (8in) round loose-bottomed fluted tart tin ▪ ceramic baking beans ▪ food processor

SERVES 4-6

300g (10oz) ready-made shortcrust pastry

3 eggs, 1 lightly beaten for egg wash

1 tbsp olive oil

1 onion, finely chopped

salt and freshly ground black pepper

2 garlic cloves, grated or finely chopped

450g (1lb) spinach leaves, stalks removed

200g (7oz) watercress

200ml (7fl oz) double cream

pinch of grated nutmeg

1 Preheat the oven to 200°C (400°F/Gas 6). Roll out the pastry on a floured work surface until it is large enough to line the tart tin. Trim away the excess around the edges, line the pastry shell with greaseproof paper, and fill with ceramic baking beans. Bake in the oven for 15–20 minutes until the edges are golden. Remove the beans and greaseproof paper, brush the bottom of the pastry shell with a little of the egg wash, and return to the oven for 2–3 minutes to crisp. Remove from the oven and set aside. Reduce the oven temperature to 180°C (350°F/Gas 4).

2 Heat the oil in a large frying pan over a low heat. Add the onion and a pinch of salt, and sweat gently for about 5 minutes until soft and translucent. Add the garlic and cook for a few more seconds until the garlic turns white. Spoon the mixture into the pastry shell.

3 Put the spinach and watercress in a food processor and pulse a couple of times until broken up, but not mushy. Pour in the cream and the 2 eggs, and pulse again until everything is combined. Season well with salt and pepper, and pulse once more. Carefully pour the mixture into the pastry shell, then sprinkle the nutmeg over, and bake in the oven for 20–30 minutes until set. Leave the tart to cool for 10 minutes before releasing it from the tin.

warm wood pigeon breast and pea shoot salad

Pigeon breasts are best cooked quickly and then left to rest in a warm place to become beautifully tender. You may need to order the pigeon breasts from your local butcher.

🥣 25 MINS   🍲 4 MINS PLUS RESTING

SERVES 4

5 tbsp olive oil

salt and pepper

4 pigeon breasts

For the salad

1 ripe avocado, stoned, peeled, and diced

1 tbsp lemon juice

4 spring onions, trimmed and cut into short diagonal lengths

4 baby or Chantenay carrots, scrubbed and coarsely grated

8 radishes, sliced

75g (2½oz) pea shoots, or watercress and rocket leaves

8 wild garlic leaves, shredded (optional)

For the dressing

2 tbsp white wine vinegar

2 tsp clear honey

½ tsp Dijon mustard

crusty bread, to serve

1 Heat 2 tbsp of the olive oil in a large non-stick frying pan. Season the pigeon breasts lightly and fry for 2 minutes on each side, or until browned but still pink inside. Wrap in foil and leave to rest. Reserve the frying pan for the dressing.

2 In a large bowl, toss the avocado in the lemon juice. Add the other salad ingredients and a grinding of black pepper, and toss gently. Pile the mixture on 4 plates.

3 Reheat the frying pan, add the remaining oil and vinegar, honey, and mustard. Heat, stirring constantly until blended. Season if needed.

4 Cut the pigeon in thick diagonal slices and arrange on top of the salads. Add any remaining juices in the foil to the frying pan. Pour the hot dressing over the salad and serve straight away with the crusty bread.

griddled prawns with hot pepper sauce

If you are lucky enough to find raw cold water prawns, choose them. They take the same time to cook. Peeling hot prawns can be messy, so place finger bowls on the table.

🥣 10 MINS   🍲 10 MINS

SERVES 4

250g (9oz) raw or cooked, unpeeled cold water prawns

1 tbsp olive oil

1 red chilli, deseeded and finely chopped

For the hot pepper sauce

1 tbsp olive oil

1 garlic clove, grated or finely chopped

1 tsp hot chilli powder

1 tsp paprika

pinch of ground cumin

juice of 1 lime

4–5 tbsp mayonnaise

salt and freshly ground black pepper

1 Put the prawns in a medium-sized bowl and add the olive oil and the chilli. Toss the prawns well in the mixture and set aside to marinade for a few minutes.

2 To make the hot pepper sauce, use another bowl to combine the olive oil, garlic, chilli powder, paprika, cumin, lime juice, and mayonnaise, stirring well. Taste and then season accordingly with salt and pepper.

3 Heat a large heavy-based frying pan or ridged cast-iron grill pan over a high heat. Add the prawns and cook for 1–2 minutes on each side until piping hot. Serve the prawns with the hot pepper sauce, a salad, and some crusty bread.

shellfish soup

Mix and match the shellfish to include whatever is seasonal in this delicious tomato-based soup. Add ready-cooked lobster, and use fresh shellfish stock if you can get hold of it.

🥣 20 MINS 🍲 1 HR 15 MINS

SERVES 6

1 tbsp olive oil

2 celery sticks, finely chopped

2 carrots, peeled and finely diced

2 onions, finely diced

175g (6oz) rindless streaky bacon rashers, cut into bite-sized pieces

400g can chopped tomatoes

1 star anise

600ml (1 pint) hot fish stock

about 800g (1¾lb) shellfish, such as scallops, cooked and peeled cold water prawns, clams, and mussels (scrubbed and debearded where necessary; discard any that do not close when tapped, p364)

bunch of flat-leaf parsley, finely chopped

1 Heat the oil in a large flameproof casserole, add the celery, carrots, and onion, and cook for about 10 minutes, or until soft. Add the bacon and cook for about 5 minutes, then stir through the tomatoes and add the star anise. Pour in the stock and bring to the boil. Reduce the heat and simmer gently for about 45 minutes, topping up the stock with a little hot water if it starts to reduce too much.

2 Add the shellfish and cook for 5–10 minutes, or until the clams and mussels have opened (discard any with shells that do not open once cooked). Sprinkle over the parsley and stir it in. Ladle into warmed bowls and serve with crusty bread and some spicy mayonnaise.

nettle soup

This simple soup is a fantastic way to use a much maligned fragrant weed. Choose young, tender nettles or pick nettle tips, and wear a double layer of latex gloves to gather them.

🥣 10 MINS 🍲 20 MINS ❄️ FREEZABLE

SPECIAL EQUIPMENT ▪ hand-held blender

SERVES 4

2 tbsp virgin rapeseed oil or olive oil

4 spring onions, or 1 bunch, trimmed and sliced

3 leeks, roughly chopped

650g (1lb 7oz) potatoes, washed but not peeled, cut into 2cm (¾in) cubes

sea salt and freshly ground black pepper

1 litre (1¾ pints) vegetable stock

100g (3½oz) young nettles or nettle tips (about ¼ carrier bag full), washed

juice of ½ lemon

natural thick yogurt, to serve

1 Heat the rapeseed or olive oil in a large soup pan over a medium heat. Add the spring onions, leeks, and potatoes, along with a little sea salt. Stir, cover with a lid, and cook for 5 minutes, stirring frequently.

2 Add the stock and bring to the boil. Add the nettles, stir, and simmer for 10 minutes, or until the potato is soft. Allow to cool briefly, then purée the soup with a hand-held blender until it is completely smooth. Taste for seasoning, then squeeze in the lemon juice, grind in some black pepper, and give the soup another stir. To serve, pour the soup into bowls, add a dollop of yogurt to each bowl, grind a little more black pepper on top, and serve immediately.

prawn and guacamole tortilla stacks

These tasty Mexican-style canapés are simple to make. Assemble the stacks just before serving to keep them fresh.

🥣 15 MINS 🍲 10-15 MINS

SPECIAL EQUIPMENT ▪ 3cm (1¼in) pastry cutter ▪ piping bag with small plain nozzle

MAKES 50

5 wheat or corn tortillas

1 litre (1¾ pints) sunflower oil

2 ripe avocados, stoned and skinned

juice of 1 lime

Tabasco sauce

4 tbsp coriander, finely chopped, plus extra as a garnish

4 spring onions, trimmed and finely chopped

sea salt and freshly ground black pepper

50 large cooked, peeled cold water prawns

1 Cut at least 100 discs out of the tortillas with a pastry cutter. Heat the oil in a medium-sized saucepan. Drop the tortillas into the oil, a handful at a time, and deep-fry until golden. Do not overcrowd the pan, or the tortillas will not crisp up properly.

Remove them with a slotted spoon, drain on kitchen paper, put aside, and allow to cool.

2 In a bowl, mash the avocados with half the lime juice, a dash of Tabasco, 3 tbsp of the chopped coriander, the chopped onions, and sea salt and pepper to taste.

3 When there are about 30 minutes left before serving, marinate the prawns with the remaining lime juice and the remaining 1 tbsp chopped coriander in a small bowl.

4 To serve, pipe a little guacamole on to a tortilla using a piping bag, top it with another tortilla, pipe more guacamole on top, and finish with a prawn and a little of the remaining coriander as a garnish.

pasta with crab and lemon

There are many ways to cook versatile crab while it is in season; one of the simplest is to stir it through hot pasta together with a few other flavoursome ingredients.

🥣 5 MINS   🍲 10 MINS

SERVES 4

1 tbsp olive oil

1 large onion, cut into quarters, then finely sliced

salt and freshly ground black pepper

2 garlic cloves, finely sliced

grated zest and juice of 1 lemon

handful of flat-leaf parsley, finely chopped

200g (7oz) white crab meat, or canned crab meat, drained

350g (12oz) linguine or spaghetti

chilli oil, to serve (optional)

1 Heat the oil in a large frying pan, add the onion and a little salt, and cook over a low heat for 5 minutes or until the onion is soft and translucent. Stir in the garlic and lemon zest and cook for a few seconds more until the garlic is white.

2 Add the parsley and crab meat to the frying pan and stir, then season well with salt and lots of pepper. Add the lemon juice to taste.

3 Meanwhile, cook the pasta in a large pan of boiling salted water for 6–8 minutes, or until it is tender but still al dente. Drain, keeping back a tiny amount of the cooking water. Return the pasta to the pan and toss together with the reserved cooking water. Add the crab sauce, toss again, drizzle with chilli oil, if using, and serve.

seafood and tomato cioppino

A classic seafood dish from San Francisco.

🥣 45–50 MINS   🍲 20–25 MINS

SERVES 4–6

4 tbsp olive oil

2 large onions, diced

3 garlic cloves, finely chopped

1 tbsp tomato purée

3 x 400g can chopped Italian plum tomatoes

pinch of cayenne pepper

salt and freshly ground black pepper

1 bouquet garni of 5-6 parsley stalks, 2-3 thyme sprigs, and 1 bay leaf

500ml (16fl oz) dry white wine

500g (1lb 2oz) skinned halibut fillets, or other meaty white fish, rinsed

250g (9oz) small scallops

115g (4oz) crab meat and 4-6 large crab claws

750g (1lb 10oz) mussels, scrubbed and debearded (discard any that do not close when tapped) (p364)

leaves from a small bunch of flat-leaf parsley, finely chopped

1 Heat the oil in a saucepan over a low heat, add the onions and cook for 3–5 minutes until soft. Add the garlic, tomato purée, tomatoes, cayenne, salt, pepper, and bouquet garni. Pour in the white wine. Cover the pan and simmer gently, stirring occasionally, for about 20 minutes.

2 Cut the fish into chunky 5cm (2in) pieces. Discard the tough crescent-shaped membrane at the side of each scallop, if not already removed. Make sure the scallops have no black or brownish intestinal vein around the edge; if they do, pull it off and discard.

3 Discard the bouquet garni. Pack the fish into the bottom of a casserole in an even layer, then add the scallops. Arrange the crab and mussels on top. Ladle the hot tomato broth over the seafood and add water, if necessary, so the seafood is just covered. Cover the casserole with the lid and bring to the boil. Simmer for 3–5 minutes, until the mussels have opened and the white fish flakes easily when tested with a fork.

4 Discard any mussels that have not opened. Taste for seasoning. Serve the cioppino immediately in warmed bowls with a crab claw in each bowl and chopped parsley on top. Serve with slices of sourdough bread.

salmon and prawn fish pie

Prawns and salmon are in plentiful supply in spring, so it makes sense to combine them in a tasty dish like this.

🥣 **15 MINS**   🍲 **35 MINS**

SPECIAL EQUIPMENT ▪ 1.2-litre (2-pint) ovenproof dish

SERVES 4

675g (1½lb) potatoes, peeled and quartered

salt and freshly ground black pepper

330ml (11fl oz) milk

350g (12oz) salmon fillet

200g (7oz) cooked, peeled cold water prawns

knob of butter, plus extra for topping

2 tbsp plain flour

1 tbsp wholegrain mustard

1 Preheat the oven to 200°C (400°F/Gas 6). Cook the potatoes in a pan of boiling salted water for about 15 minutes until soft, then drain them. Mash well with 2 tbsp of the milk and set aside.

2 Poach the salmon in the remaining milk in a covered shallow pan over a low heat for 3–5 minutes until just cooked. Drain, reserving the milk.

Flake the fish into chunks, discarding any skin and bones. Place in the ovenproof dish and add the prawns.

3 Rinse out the fish cooking pan and melt the butter in it over a low heat. Remove from the heat and blend in the flour with a balloon whisk or wooden spoon. Gradually blend in the fish cooking milk. Return the pan to the heat, bring to the boil, and cook for 2 minutes, whisking or stirring all the time, until the sauce is thickened and smooth. Stir in the mustard and season to taste.

4 Pour the sauce over the prawns and salmon in the dish and combine. Cover with the mashed potato to make a topping and dot with the extra butter. Bake in the oven for 15–20 minutes until heated through and the topping is crisp and golden.

thai green curry

Succulent, slightly sweet prawns taste divine in this light, fragrantly spiced coconut curry with a kick.

🥣 **10 MINS**   🍲 **30 MINS**

SERVES 4

1 tbsp sunflower oil or vegetable oil

1 onion, finely diced

1-2 tbsp Thai green curry paste (depending on how hot you like it)

400ml can coconut milk

2 tbsp fish sauce (nam pla)

1-2 tsp palm sugar or demerara sugar

2-3 kaffir lime leaves (optional)

salt and freshly ground black pepper

220g can bamboo shoots, drained

200g (7oz) cooked, peeled cold water prawns

1 Heat the oil in a large, deep frying pan or wok over a low-medium heat. Add the diced onion and sauté it for about 5 minutes until it is soft and translucent. Add the green curry paste, stir it around, and cook for a further 2–3 minutes until it gives a fragrant aroma.

2 Pour in the coconut milk, then fill the can with water and add this to the pan or wok. Bring to the boil, reduce the heat slightly, and add the fish sauce, sugar, and lime leaves, if using. Season the sauce with salt and pepper.

3 Simmer over a low heat for about 15 minutes, then stir through the bamboo shoots and prawns. Cook for about 10 minutes, or until the prawns are warmed through. Taste and adjust the seasoning if needed. Serve while still hot.

prawn risotto

Risotto with prawns is perfect food for a cool spring night.

🥣 15–20 MINS　🍲 25–30 MINS

SERVES 6

90ml (3fl oz) olive oil

2 garlic cloves, finely chopped

leaves from a small bunch of flat-leaf parsley, chopped

salt and freshly ground black pepper

4 tbsp dry white wine

1 litre (1¾ pints) fish or chicken stock

1 onion, finely chopped

420g (15oz) arborio rice

500g (1lb 2oz) cooked, peeled cold water prawns

1 Heat a third of the oil in a saucepan and add the garlic, parsley, salt, and pepper. Cook for 1–2 minutes, stirring frequently. Pour in the wine and stir thoroughly. Simmer the liquid in the pan for 2–3 minutes, until reduced by three-quarters. Add the stock and 250ml (9fl oz) water, and bring to the boil. Keep the liquid simmering.

2 Heat half the remaining oil in a large saucepan. Add the onion and cook, stirring, for 2–3 minutes until it is soft and translucent. Add the rice and stir until it is shiny and coated with oil. Ladle in just enough of the simmering liquid to cover the rice.

3 Stir the rice constantly until all the liquid is absorbed. Add more liquid to just cover the rice and simmer, stirring, until completely absorbed. Continue adding liquid to the rice in this way. Stop when the rice is al dente: just tender, but firm to the bite; it should take 25–30 minutes.

4 Stir in the prawns and the remaining oil, allow the prawns to heat until warmed through, and then season to taste with salt and pepper (you may not need much salt). Spoon the risotto into warmed bowls and serve immediately.

prawn saganaki

Try this quick, delicious, and popular Greek one-pot recipe for a simple way to cook with fresh prawns.

🥣 10 MINS　🍲 45 MINS

SERVES 4

1 tbsp olive oil

1 onion, finely chopped

2 garlic cloves, crushed or finely chopped

400g can chopped tomatoes

2 tbsp tomato purée

1 large glass dry white wine

½ tsp sugar

salt and freshly ground black pepper

350g (12oz) large cooked, peeled cold water prawns

125g (4½oz) feta cheese

small handful of thyme leaves

1 Heat half the oil in a large frying pan, add the onion, and cook over a low heat for 8 minutes, or until soft and translucent. Stir through the garlic and cook for a few more seconds, then add the tomatoes, 150ml (5fl oz) water, tomato purée, wine, sugar, and a little salt and pepper. Bring to the boil, reduce the heat, and simmer gently, stirring occasionally for 20–30 minutes until thick and pulpy.

2 Stir the prawns into the sauce, remove from the heat, and crumble over the feta cheese. Pop under the grill until the cheese melts and turns golden brown, then sprinkle over the thyme leaves. Serve with a crisp salad and fresh crusty bread.

spinach and coconut prawn curry

This mild, creamy curry flavoured with coconut is ideal if you have a quantity of spinach to use up. It makes a light and fragrant supper that needs just simple accompaniments.

🥣 15 MINS　🍲 20 MINS

SERVES 4

2 tbsp sunflower oil

2 red onions, finely chopped

4 garlic cloves, finely chopped

large thumb-sized knob of fresh root ginger, grated

¼–½ tsp chilli powder

½ tsp turmeric

2 tsp ground cumin

1 tsp ground coriander

4 large tomatoes, skinned (p197) and finely chopped

400ml (14fl oz) coconut milk

10 fresh or dried curry leaves (optional)

150g (5½oz) spinach, stalks removed and leaves finely shredded

400g (14oz) large cooked, peeled cold water prawns

½ tsp caster sugar

sea salt

1 Heat the sunflower oil in a large, deep frying pan or wok. Add the onions, garlic, and ginger, and cook for 2–3 minutes over a low heat until soft and translucent. Add the spices and cook for a further 1–2 minutes to release their flavours.

2 Add the tomatoes and continue to cook over a low heat for another 2 minutes until their flesh starts to break down. Add the coconut milk and curry leaves (if using), and bring to the boil. Mix in the spinach and lower the heat, continuing to cook until the spinach has wilted. Baby spinach will take 1–2 minutes, bigger leaves up to 4 minutes.

3 Add the prawns, sugar, and a pinch of sea salt, and cook for a further 2–3 minutes until the prawns are heated through. Serve with basmati rice, naan bread, and a couple of lime wedges on the side.

Season's best **prawns**

Northern (cold water) prawns are native to Britain and Europe, and the US. They have sweet, succulent flesh, while the imported large, warm water prawns are meatier and more robust. In season spring and winter, they are a classic for prawn cocktail. They toughen quickly and so are often added towards the end of cooking. They are excellent with mayonnaise, citrus, asparagus, avocados, artichokes, other seafood, and chicken.

Cooked Northern (cold water) prawns You will find them fresh or frozen, ready-cooked, whole, or peeled. They are graded by size.

Raw Northern (cold water) prawns These are small, pinkish-grey, and translucent. They turn bright pink and opaque when cooked.

Buy them shell on, then peel yourself, for the best flavour.

Unpeeled prawns have the most succulent flesh, if you can find them.

essentials
varieties available

Northern (cold water) prawn, occasionally raw whole, but mostly cooked, whole or peeled. Available frozen and canned.

buy Buy from fisheries using sorting grids to reduce by-catch. They should be fresh-smelling and undamaged.

store Eat on day of purchase.

cook Grill, fry, steam, or add to soups, stews, sauces, rice, and pasta dishes. Use cold in salads and sandwiches.

recipe ideas

Asian chicken and prawn broth with ginger and coriander p28

Griddled prawns with hot pepper sauce p30

Prawn and guacamole tortilla stacks p31

Prawn, avocado, and watercress sandwich p27

Salmon and prawn fish pie p33

how to peel prawns

Peeling cooked prawns is a useful skill. It is a fiddly business but worth it as cold water prawns have the sweetest meat of all prawns. If serving whole and unshelled, give your diners finger bowls or damp cloths to wipe their hands on.

1 Hold the prawn firmly in the middle. With the other hand, pinch the head gently and pull it off. Repeat with the tail unless the recipe says otherwise.

2 Turn it upside-down and peel away the back legs and body shell. It will slide off over the back of the prawn. Use the shells for fish stock.

singapore noodles with prawns and pork

Loaded with prawns and spring onions, as well as pork, mushrooms, and fragrant spices, this is a dish for sharing.

🥢 15 MINS PLUS MARINATING   🍲 30 MINS

SERVES 4

450g (1lb) pork tenderloin, cut into 2.5cm (1in) strips

3 tbsp fish sauce (nam pla)

2 tbsp dark soy sauce

2 tbsp rice wine vinegar

2 tsp five-spice powder

225g (8oz) thin rice vermicelli

1½ tsp sunflower oil

1 large garlic clove, finely chopped

½ tsp ground coriander

250g (9oz) chestnut mushrooms, sliced

200g (7oz) large cooked, peeled cold water prawns

1 large onion, finely chopped

2 red chillies, deseeded and finely sliced

salt and freshly ground black pepper

150g (5½oz) bean sprouts

4 spring onions, trimmed and finely chopped

small handful of coriander, chopped

1 Put the pork in a mixing bowl, add the fish sauce, soy sauce, rice wine vinegar, and five-spice powder, and leave to marinate for at least 30 minutes. Meanwhile, put the vermicelli in a bowl, cover with boiling water, and leave for 6 minutes, or until soft. Drain, rinse, and set aside.

2 Put 1 tbsp of the oil in a large wok over a high heat and swirl around the pan. Add the pork and, stirring continuously, cook for 6–8 minutes, or until beginning to turn golden and crisp. Remove with a slotted spoon and set aside. Heat another 1 tbsp of the oil in the wok, then add the garlic and ground coriander and stir. Add the mushrooms and cook for a couple of minutes, then add the prawns and stir-fry over a high heat for 5–8 minutes, or until pink. Remove with a slotted spoon and set aside.

3 Heat the remaining oil in the wok, then add the onions and chillies and stir-fry for 1 minute. Add the vermicelli, season with salt and pepper, then stir in the bean sprouts. Return the pork and prawn mixture to the wok and stir well. Remove from the heat, top with the spring onions and coriander, and serve.

pad thai

There are numerous variations of this classic Thai dish. This version has lovely pieces of omelette, prawns, and chicken.

🥢 15 MINS   🍲 15 MINS

SERVES 4

250g (9oz) medium or thick rice noodles

1½ tbsp sunflower oil

2 eggs, lightly beaten

½ tsp shrimp paste (optional)

2 red chillies, deseeded and finely chopped

3 skinless chicken breasts, cut into 5mm (¼in) slices

1 bunch of spring onions, trimmed and finely chopped

splash of fish sauce (nam pla)

juice of 1 lime, plus lime wedges, to serve

1 tbsp demerara sugar

salt and freshly ground black pepper

115g (4oz) cooked, peeled cold water prawns

150g (5½oz) unsalted peanuts

small handful of coriander, finely chopped

1 Put the noodles in a large bowl, cover with boiling water, and leave for 8 minutes, or until soft. Drain and put to one side. Meanwhile, put ½ tbsp of the oil in a large wok over a high heat and swirl around the pan. Add the beaten egg and whisk it around the wok for about a minute, or until it begins to set – don't let it set completely – then spoon it out and set aside.

2 Add the remaining oil to the pan, then add the shrimp paste (if using) and chillies and stir. With the heat still high, add the chicken and stir vigorously for 5 minutes, or until it is no longer pink. Stir through the spring onions, fish sauce, lime juice, and sugar and toss together well. Cook for a few minutes until the sugar has dissolved, then season well with salt and pepper. Add the prawns and toss for a minute or two to heat through. Return the egg to the pan.

3 Add the noodles to the pan and toss together to coat with the sauce, then add half the peanuts and half the coriander and toss again. Transfer to a large shallow serving bowl and scatter over the rest of the peanuts and coriander. Garnish with lime wedges and serve.

prawn makhani

Cold water prawns are mostly available cooked, so they can simply be stirred in at the end to heat through.

🥣 20 MIN   🍲 40 MINS

SERVES 4

350g (12oz) large, cooked, peeled cold water prawns

salt and freshly ground black pepper

3 garlic cloves, crushed or finely chopped

7.5cm (3in) piece fresh root ginger, peeled and grated or finely chopped

1½ tbsp vegetable oil

1 tsp chilli powder

1 piece of cinnamon stick

2 red chillies, deseeded and finely chopped

3 cardamom pods, crushed

400g can chopped tomatoes

100ml (3½fl oz) thick natural yogurt

60g (2oz) cashew nuts, ground, plus a handful, roughly chopped, to garnish

1 tsp ground fenugreek

100ml (3½fl oz) double cream

1 Season the prawns with salt and pepper and toss with half the garlic, half the ginger, 1 tsp of the oil, and the chilli powder. Set aside.

2 Heat the remaining oil in a large deep frying pan. Add the rest of the garlic and ginger, the cinnamon, chillies, and cardamom pods, and cook over a low heat, stirring occasionally, for 2 minutes. Add the tomatoes and yogurt, bring to the boil, reduce the heat and simmer gently for 10 minutes, or until pulpy (the mixture will curdle at first).

3 Push the tomato mixture through a sieve. Return to the pan, then stir through the ground cashew nuts and fenugreek and simmer for 10 minutes, adding a little hot water if the sauce starts to look too thick. Add the prawns along with the cream, stir, taste, and season, if needed. Cook gently for 5 minutes, then garnish with the chopped cashew nuts and serve with rice.

pan-fried clams with parsley and garlic

Throughout the Mediterranean, garlic and wine are classic partners for the fresh, briny flavour of clams.

🥣 10 MINS   🍲 20 MINS

SERVES 4

1 tbsp olive oil

1 onion, finely chopped

salt

2 garlic cloves, grated or finely chopped

1 green pepper, deseeded and finely chopped (optional)

1 large glass of dry white wine

450g (1lb) clams (discard any with broken shells and any that do not close when tapped)

handful of flat-leaf parsley, finely chopped

1 Heat the oil in a large frying pan over a medium heat. Add the onion and a pinch of salt, and cook for about 5 minutes until soft and translucent. Add the garlic and pepper, if using, and gently sweat until they begin to soften. Increase the heat to high, and add the wine.

Cook for a couple of minutes until the wine begins to evaporate.

2 Add the clams, shaking the pan occasionally, and cook for 5–6 minutes until the clams open (discard any that do not). Add the parsley, and stir to combine.

3 Serve the clams piping hot with a squeeze of lemon and fresh crusty bread to mop up the juices.

variation

pan-fried clams with chorizo

Prepare in the same way, but substitute 1 small leek, quartered lengthways and chopped, for the pepper. Add 70g (2¼oz) chorizo cubes to the pan in Step 1 after the leek has softened. Fry for 2 minutes, stirring, then add the wine and continue with the recipe.

pasta with clams

Fresh seafood can speak for itself. Clams only require the simplest of serving suggestions to delight the palate.

🥣 10 MINS   🍲 15 MINS

SERVES 4

1 tbsp olive oil, plus extra to serve

1 onion, finely diced

3 garlic cloves, finely diced

small handful of flat-leaf parsley, finely chopped

1 small glass dry white wine

450g (1lb) clams (discard any with broken shells and any that do not close when tapped)

350g (12oz) dried linguine or spaghetti

salt and freshly ground black pepper

1 Heat the oil in a large frying pan and cook the onion over a low heat for 2 minutes, or until the onion begins to soften. Add the garlic and parsley and stir for a few seconds.

2 Add the wine, raise the heat, then add the clams and stir. Allow to boil for 5 minutes, or until the shells start to open, and shake the pan from time to time. Then turn the heat off and put a lid on the pan.

3 Meanwhile, cook the pasta in a large pan of boiling salted water for about 6 minutes, or until it is tender, but still al dente. Drain, keeping back a tiny amount of the cooking water. Return the pasta to the pan and toss it in the reserved cooking water. Add a drizzle of oil and season with salt and pepper. Discard any clams that have not opened, then toss the pasta with the clams and serve.

variation

pasta with mussels and saffron

Add 4 baby carrots and ¼ small celeriac, finely chopped, with the onion. Cover and cook gently for 5 minutes until soft, stirring occasionally. Add a good pinch of saffron strands with the wine and use mussels instead of clams.

morel and chestnut mushroom orzotto

Orzo is Italian for barley. If you can't get fresh morels, use 2 dried ones, soaked according to packet directions, and use the soaking water as part of the stock.

🥣 10 MINS   🍲 45 MINS

SERVES 4

15g (½oz) butter

1 onion, chopped

1 garlic clove, crushed

2 large morel mushrooms, cleaned and sliced

225g (8oz) chestnut mushrooms, cleaned and sliced

150ml (5fl oz) dry white wine

200g (7oz) pearl barley

2 tsp chopped thyme, plus a few leaves for garnish

750ml (1¼ pints) chicken or vegetable stock

salt and freshly ground black pepper

2-3 tbsp single cream

Parmesan cheese, grated

1 Melt the butter in a large saucepan over a medium heat, then add the onion and garlic and let them soften for about 2 minutes, stirring often. Add the sliced morels and chestnut mushrooms and the wine, and simmer for 2 minutes. Then stir in the pearl barley and thyme. Add the stock and season well. Bring to the boil, reduce the heat, and simmer for 40 minutes or so, stirring twice. The orzotto is ready when the barley is tender, but still has some bite and the liquid is almost absorbed.

2 Stir in the cream, and taste and re-season if necessary. Serve topped with a little grated Parmesan cheese and a garnish of thyme leaves.

pan-fried prawns with olives

This Spanish-influenced prawn dish makes a quick and easy weeknight supper.

🥣 5 MINS   🍲 15 MINS

SERVES 4

1 tbsp olive oil

1 onion, finely chopped

2 garlic cloves, grated or finely chopped

dash of dry sherry

400g can chopped tomatoes

large handful of mixed olives, pitted

400g (14oz) large cooked, peeled cold water prawns

salt and freshly ground black pepper

small handful of basil, chopped

small handful of flat-leaf parsley, chopped

1 Heat the oil in a large frying pan over a medium heat. Add the onion, and sauté for about 5 minutes until it is soft and translucent. Add the garlic and cook for a few seconds.

2 Add the sherry and continue cooking for 5 minutes, stirring until the alcohol has evaporated. Add the tomatoes and olives, and simmer for 5 minutes until the sauce has thickened slightly. Add the prawns and simmer for a further few minutes to heat through. Stir in the herbs and season to taste. Serve immediately with some crusty bread.

sole fillets in wine vinegar

This is an old Italian dish. Marinate the fish the night before you want to eat it; if you would prefer a milder marinade, use just half the quantity of vinegar and an equal amount of white wine.

🥣 30–35 MINS PLUS MARINATING   🍲 2–4 MINS

SERVES 4–6

90ml (3fl oz) olive oil

1 large onion, thinly sliced

salt and freshly ground black pepper

250ml (9fl oz) red wine vinegar

45g (1½oz) raisins

500g (1lb 2oz) sole fillets

30g (1oz) plain flour

30g (1oz) pine nuts

For the salad

juice of ½ orange

3 tbsp olive oil

250g (9oz) salad leaves, such as rocket

1 Heat a third of the oil in a saucepan over a low heat. Add the onion and season. Cover and cook the onion for 15 minutes until soft. Lift the lid, increase the heat, and cook the onion until it has caramelized. Add the vinegar and raisins and boil for 2 minutes. Set aside.

2 Rinse the fish and pat dry with kitchen paper. Cut each fillet across into 5cm (2in) pieces with a sharp knife. Spread the flour on a large plate and season. Coat the fish pieces in flour.

3 Heat the remaining oil in a frying pan over a medium-high heat. Add the fish fillets and cook them for 1–2 minutes, until browned on one side. Then turn over and fry for another 1–2 minutes, until the flesh just flakes when tested with a fork. Drain the fillets on kitchen paper and allow to cool completely.

4 Place the fish in the base of a baking dish and cover with the onion and vinegar mixture. Sprinkle the pine nuts over the top, then cover the dish tightly and leave to marinate in the fridge for 12 hours, or even up to 24 hours if you have time. Remove it from the fridge 1 hour before serving.

5 Pour the orange juice into a bowl. Gradually whisk in the oil, so the vinaigrette emulsifies and thickens slightly. Taste and season. Add the salad leaves and toss. Serve with the sole, with a little marinade spooned over the top.

variation

trout in rice wine vinegar

Use 500g (1lb 2oz) trout fillets instead of the sole. Prepare in the same way, but use 4 large salad onions instead of the ordinary one. Slice the green tops and add to the salad; slice the bulbs and use as the onion. Use rice wine vinegar instead of red wine vinegar.

sautéed trout with hazelnuts

This recipe is about as quick as cooking gets, and produces a fresh, satisfying, and wholesome family dish. Serve with a rice pilaf for a heartier meal.

🥣 20-25 MINS   🍲 10-15 MINS

SERVES 4

4 whole trout, about 300g (10oz) each, cleaned and scaled

60g (2oz) hazelnuts

2 lemons

30g (1oz) plain flour

salt and freshly ground black pepper

125g (4½oz) butter

2 tbsp chopped flat-leaf parsley

1 Cut the fins from the trout and trim the tails. Rinse inside and out, and pat dry with kitchen paper.

2 Preheat the oven to 180°C (350°F/Gas 4). Spread the hazelnuts on a baking sheet, and toast them in the oven for 8–10 minutes until browned. While still hot, rub them in a tea towel to remove the skins, then set aside.

3 Trim the ends from a lemon, halve it lengthways, and cut into thin semi-circles. Peel the second lemon, removing all the white pith, and cut into thin rounds. Remove any pips.

4 Put the flour on a large plate and season with salt and pepper. Coat each trout in flour, patting to coat evenly. Heat half the butter in a large frying pan until foaming. Add two of the trout to the pan, and brown over a medium heat for 2–3 minutes. Turn the fish over and continue cooking over a low heat for 3–5 minutes. When ready, the trout will be browned and the flesh will flake easily when tested with a fork. Keep the cooked trout warm while you cook the remaining two fish in the rest of the butter.

5 Add the hazelnuts to the pan and sauté them over a medium heat for 3–4 minutes until golden brown, stirring frequently. Then stir in most of the parsley. Serve the fish on warmed plates with the hazelnuts spooned over the top. Decorate each trout with the lemon semi-circles and rounds, and sprinkle over the remaining parsley.

salmon chowder

Chowder makes a hearty and warming lunchtime soup on chilly spring days. If you choose to buy wild salmon, always try to buy it from a sustainable source.

🥣 15 MINS   🍲 25 MINS PLUS RESTING

SERVES 4

2 tbsp olive oil

4 streaky bacon rashers, chopped

6 spring onions, trimmed and cut into 2.5cm (1in) slices

3 sprigs thyme

2 bay leaves

600g (1lb 5oz) small waxy potatoes, thickly sliced

25g (scant 1oz) butter

1 tbsp plain flour

700ml (scant 1¼ pints) fish or chicken stock

400g (14oz) salmon fillets, skinned and cut into chunks

150ml (5fl oz) single cream

2-3 tbsp dill, chopped

grated zest of ½ lemon

salt and freshly ground black pepper

1 Heat 1 tbsp of the oil in a wide, deep sauté pan. Add the bacon and fry until crisp. Drain on kitchen paper and set aside. Pour the remaining oil into the pan, add the spring onions, thyme, and bay leaves, and stir-fry for 1 minute. Then add the potatoes and fry them for 2–3 minutes.

2 In another saucepan, melt the butter and beat in the flour. Cook for 1–2 minutes and then gradually add the stock. Bring to the boil and then simmer gently for 3–4 minutes or until thickened slightly. Add the thickened stock to the potatoes and bring it back to the boil. Cook the potatoes for 10 minutes, without stirring, until they are just tender.

3 Reduce the heat and submerge the salmon chunks into the stock. Simmer them very gently for 3–5 minutes, just until the fish is cooked. Don't stir the chowder, or the fish will break up.

4 Remove the pan from the heat. Without stirring, pour the cream over, and scatter over the dill and lemon zest. Allow the soup to stand for 5–10 minutes for all the flavours to blend. When ready to serve, warm it through gently and briefly, discard the thyme and bay leaves, and add any seasoning if needed. Ladle into bowls and serve scattered with black pepper and the crispy bacon.

salmon kedgeree

Replacing robust smoked haddock with the gentle flavour of salmon turns a traditional rice dish into a light yet filling meal.

🥣 10 MINS   🍲 20 MINS

SERVES 4

50g (1¾oz) butter

1 onion, finely chopped

1 tsp mild curry powder

1 tsp cayenne pepper

350g (12oz) long-grain rice, such as basmati

750ml (1¼ pints) hot vegetable stock

salt and freshly ground black pepper

500g (1lb 2oz) salmon fillet, skinned

fresh mango, sliced, to garnish

1 Melt the butter in a saucepan over a low heat. Add the chopped onion and cook gently for a few minutes until soft.

2 Add the curry powder, cayenne, and the long-grain rice and stir until the grains are well coated in the butter. Gradually add the hot vegetable stock, season, cover the pan (tilt the lid slightly so that steam can escape), and simmer gently for 10 minutes. Lay the salmon on top of the rice, re-cover and cook gently for a further 10 minutes until all the liquid has been absorbed and the salmon and rice are cooked.

3 Gently break up the salmon into large flakes. Lightly fold the fish through the rice, taste and re-season, if necessary. Serve hot with fresh mango slices.

baked salmon

It's vital that the fish you buy is always 100 per cent fresh and never smells "fishy". Use any leftover salmon for a salad or sandwiches.

🥄 **15 MINS**　　🍲 **40-45 MINS**

SERVES 6

1.8kg (4lb) whole salmon, head removed, or a piece cut from a larger fish

125g (4½oz) butter

salt and freshly ground black pepper

handful of flat-leaf parsley, plus extra to garnish (or use watercress)

lemon wedges, to serve

1 Preheat the oven to 180°C (350°F/Gas 4). Lay a large piece of foil (enough to pull up and cover the salmon) over a large baking tray. Sit the salmon on the foil and dot the butter all over it. Season well, then scatter the parsley over the fish, stuffing a little in the cavity, too.

2 Loosely fold the foil over the salmon and seal. Bake in the oven on the baking tray for about 40–45 minutes, calculating the cooking time at 10 minutes per 450g (1lb) of fish. The salmon is cooked when it looks opaque and the flesh flakes easily when tested with a fork.

3 Unwrap the foil, remove any straggly bits of parsley, and carefully transfer the salmon to a warm plate. Garnish with fresh parsley or watercress and the lemon wedges. Serve with sautéed potatoes and salad or grilled asparagus.

variation

baked sea trout with dill

Prepare a large sea trout instead of the salmon, and use dill instead of parsley. Leave the head on or remove as you wish. Cook for 10 minutes per 450g (1lb). You can use small trout and bake in the same way, simply cook for 15–20 minutes instead.

lemon sole with herbs

The white flesh of flat fish is lean, textured, and flavoursome, and should be firm or rigid to the touch when you buy it (if it is soft, it will be past its best).

🥄 **10 MINS**　　🍲 **20 MINS**

SERVES 4

3 tbsp extra virgin olive oil

1 tbsp white wine vinegar

1 tsp Dijon mustard

small handful of fresh mixed herbs such as parsley, thyme, and dill

salt and freshly ground black pepper

4 lemon sole fillets, about 175g (6oz) each, or other flat fish fillets, such as plaice or brill

1 Preheat the oven to 200°C (400°F/Gas 6). Make the herb dressing first: whisk together the oil and vinegar in a jug. Add the mustard and herbs, and mix well. Season well with salt and pepper, and whisk once again.

2 Lay out the fish in a roasting tin and cover them with about 5mm (¼in) water. Season well with salt and pepper. Bake in the oven for 15–20 minutes, until the fish is cooked through and the water has almost evaporated. To check whether the lemon sole is cooked, see if the flesh lifts away from the bone easily. The flesh should also be opaque with no traces of pink.

3 Using a fish slice or spatula, carefully lift the fish onto a serving dish or individual plates. Spoon over some of the herb dressing. Serve hot with sautéed potatoes and sprouting broccoli.

variation

trout with herbs, caperberries, and olives

Use whole, cleaned trout instead of the sole fillets. For the dressing, omit the mustard and add a pinch of sugar, 30g (1oz) pickled caperberries, and 30g (1oz) sliced green olives, stuffed with pimiento, with the herbs.

pork and clam cataplana

This combination of rich pork and salty clams has been enjoyed for centuries in Portugal.

🥣 20 MINS PLUS MARINATING　🍲 30 MINS　❄ FREEZABLE

SERVES 4

450g (1lb) lean pork (leg or tenderloin), cut into bite-sized pieces

2 tbsp dry sherry

2 garlic cloves, finely chopped

1 tsp paprika

1 tsp dried chilli flakes

salt and freshly ground black pepper

3 tbsp olive oil

150g (5½oz) chorizo, diced

1 tbsp tomato purée

1 onion, grated

1 bay leaf

1 glass of dry white wine

1kg (2¼lb) clams (discard any with broken shells and any that do not close when tapped)

small handful of flat-leaf parsley, chopped

1 Put the pork in a bowl with the sherry, half the garlic, paprika, and chillies. Season with salt and pepper and set aside to marinate for 30 minutes, or overnight in the fridge.

2 Heat 1 tbsp of the oil in a large frying pan, add the chorizo, and cook over a medium heat, stirring often, for 5 minutes, or until starting to crisp. Remove with a slotted spoon and set aside. Heat another 1 tbsp of the oil in the pan, add the pork and marinade, and cook for 8–10 minutes, or until the meat is golden all over. Remove with a slotted spoon and set aside.

3 Heat the remaining oil in the pan, add the tomato purée, remaining garlic, onion, and bay leaf and stir well. Leave to simmer over a very low heat for 10 minutes, or until the onion is soft and translucent. Season well.

4 Add the wine, raise the heat, and allow to boil for a few minutes until the alcohol evaporates. Add the clams and cook for 4–5 minutes until the shells open. Discard any that do not. Return the pork and chorizo to the pan, warm through, then transfer to a large serving dish. Sprinkle with the parsley and serve.

instant smoked trout

A wok with a lid makes an admirable instant smoker. It must be well sealed to stop smoke escaping and used over a low heat. Fish and shellfish are perfect for instant smoking.

🥣 15–20 MINS　🍲 25–30 MINS　❄ FREEZABLE

SPECIAL EQUIPMENT ▪ wok with a lid and rack

MAKES 2

1 tbsp light wood chips, such as apple

2 whole trout, gutted and cleaned with heads on

4 fennel fronds or 6–8 sprigs of tarragon (optional)

1 Line the inside of the wok with a double sheet of foil. Place the wood chips in the centre of the foil (so it will smoke evenly) and place the wok rack inside the wok.

2 Wipe the insides of the trout and make 2 or 3 slashes on each side of the fish. Stuff the insides of the fish with the herbs, if you are using them.

3 Place the fish on the rack and put the lid on. Put a foil collar around the edge of the lid to keep the smoke in. Cook over a low heat for 10–15 minutes. Then turn off the heat and leave the sealed wok for 15 minutes to allow the flavours to infuse the fish.

lamb and potato pie

For some great comfort food on cool spring evenings, this is a great way to use up leftover roast lamb.

🥣 20 MINS 🍲 50 MINS

SPECIAL EQUIPMENT ▪ 18cm (7in) round pie dish

SERVES 4

450g (1lb) potatoes, peeled and quartered

1 tbsp olive oil

1 onion, finely chopped

1 leek, trimmed and sliced

4 baby turnips, peeled and quartered

handful of rosemary sprigs, leaves picked and chopped

200g (7oz) leftover roast lamb, roughly shredded or sliced

salt and freshly ground black pepper

1 tbsp plain flour

300ml (10fl oz) hot vegetable stock

2-3 tsp mint sauce

250g (9oz) shortcrust pastry

1 egg, lightly beaten, for egg wash

1 Preheat the oven to 200°C (400°F/ Gas 6). Cook the potatoes in a pan of boiling salted water for about 15 minutes until soft; drain and set aside. Heat the oil in a large pan over a low heat. Add the onion, leek, and turnips, and sweat gently for about 5 minutes until soft and translucent. Stir through the rosemary and add the lamb. Season with salt and pepper.

2 Tip in the flour and stir through, then pour in the stock. Keep stirring for about 10 minutes until the liquid begins to thicken, then add the reserved potatoes and stir in the mint sauce. Simmer for a further 10 minutes. Allow to cool slightly.

3 Divide the pastry into 2 pieces, one a little larger than the other. Roll out the larger piece into a large circle on a floured work surface. Use to line the pie dish, letting the pastry hang over the edges. Roll out the other piece to make the lid for the top of the pie.

4 Spoon the lamb mixture into the pastry shell, then sit the pastry lid on top. Pinch together the edges of the pastry to seal. Trim away the excess. Brush with a little egg wash and bake for 40-50 minutes until the pastry is golden. Leave to cool in the dish for at least 15 minutes before serving. Cut into slices and serve.

skewered lamb with crispy rosemary potatoes

Lamb is at its most succulent and its flavour most subtle at this season, as spring lambs are only aged between 3 and 5 months old.

🥣 15 MINS 🍲 30 MINS

SPECIAL EQUIPMENT ▪ wooden skewers

SERVES 4

675g (1½lb) potatoes, peeled and diced

1-2 tbsp olive oil, plus extra for coating the lamb

handful of rosemary stalks

salt and freshly ground black pepper

900g (2lb) lean lamb steak or neck fillet, cut into bite-sized pieces

juice of 1 lemon

2 tsp paprika

1 Preheat the oven to 200°C (400°F/Gas 6). Soak 8–10 wooden skewers in cold water for at least 30 minutes before using. Put the potatoes, ½ tbsp of the olive oil, rosemary, and some salt in a roasting tin. Using your hands, mix everything together so that the potatoes are evenly coated. Roast towards the top of the oven for 20–25 minutes until golden and crispy.

2 Meanwhile, put the lamb in a bowl and toss with the remaining olive oil, the lemon juice, paprika, some salt, and plenty of pepper. Thread the pieces of lamb onto the skewers until they are tightly packed.

3 Put the lamb skewers in a single layer in a separate roasting tin and roast below the potatoes for 10–15 minutes until cooked to your liking. Serve the skewers with the potatoes and a green salad.

Season's best **lamb**

Lamb comes from sheep less than 1 year old; when aged from 3 to 5 months old, it is called spring lamb. The meat of small spring lambs is pale pink, mild, and highly prized. The meat from older autumn lamb is darker and stronger. Lamb is versatile, and marries well with rosemary, mint, and most herbs, sweet spices, such as cumin and cinnamon, dried fruits, and fresh spring vegetables. Older lamb is good with apricots, berries, squashes, and aubergines.

Rack An elegant dinner party roast, this should have the backbone chined (removed) to allow slices to be cut between the ribs. Allow 2–3 ribs per person.

When the ends of the rib bones are scraped clean and exposed, this is called a French rack.

▼ **Cutlets** These are cut from the best end of the neck (rack) to the fore end of the loin. The eye of the meat is the tender, succulent neck fillet, which is also sold as a separate cut.

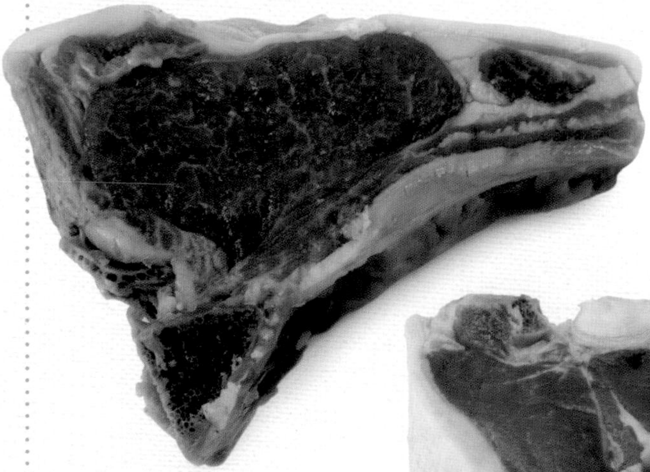

Chump chops These meaty chops are best grilled or fried.

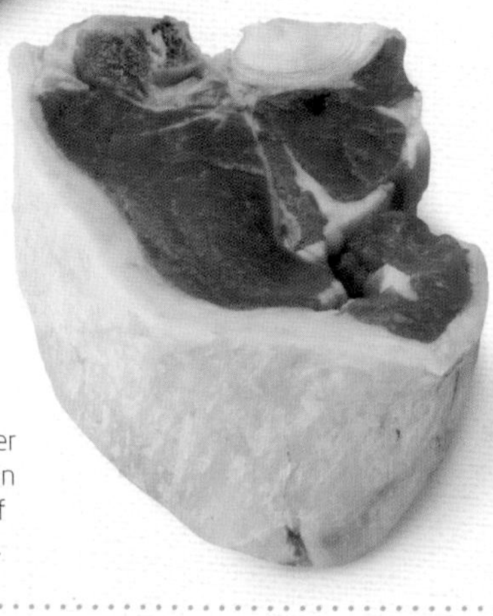

Loin chops Because they are quite thick, loin chops can either be roasted or grilled. Double loin chops have fillet on one side of the bone and loin on the other.

Leg steaks These are cut from the top of the leg of a lamb. Grill or fry.

Lamb shanks very often have the bone end neatly trimmed.

Leg This top-quality joint can be fast- or slow-roasted.

Shanks Slow, moist cooking is required to turn the sinews in the shank to a succulent jelly. Allow one shank per person. Fore-leg shanks are slimmer than those from the back leg.

how to butterfly a leg of lamb

Boning and opening out the lamb is necessary if you wish to stuff and then tie it for roasting, or to marinate it, or to enable it to cook evenly when barbecuing (in a covered barbecue). The leg has 3 bones: the pelvis (the broadest), then the thigh, and the shank. They are cut away systematically, then the boned meat is opened out flat.

1 Place the fleshiest side down on a cutting board. Locate the pelvis at the widest end. Hold it firmly. Use a sharp, boning knife to cut around and expose the leg bone.

2 Cut through the flesh to the bone from the pelvis to the bottom of the leg. Using short, sweeping strokes, work your knife closely around the leg bone, releasing it.

3 When you reach the leg end, cut through the sinew and tendons to release the bone completely. Lift all 3 bones (the pelvis, thigh, and shank) away in one piece.

4 Open out the leg so that the meat lies flat on the cutting board. With short strokes, make cuts downward through the thick meaty pieces on either side.

essentials
cuts available

Leg, leg steaks, shanks, saddle (double loin roast), loin joint, loin chops, rack, cutlets, neck fillets, scrag end of neck, breast, diced meat, mince, and offal. Also available smoked.

buy All lamb should have just a thin covering of white fat. When becoming more mature it can have quite a lot of intramuscular and external fat.

store Keep wrapped, in the bottom of the fridge, for up to 4 days.

cook Roast, grill, fry, stew, or casserole (depending on the cut).

recipe ideas

Lamb with lemon and olives p50

Rack of lamb with flageolet beans and herbs p46

Skewered lamb with crispy rosemary potatoes p43

rack of lamb with flageolet beans and herbs

Flageolet beans are young haricot beans that have been harvested early in the season before they are fully ripe and then dried for preservation. They are small and cream-coloured with a delicate flavour and form the ideal accompaniment to lamb.

15 MINS   **40 MINS**

SERVES 4

1 rack of lamb (8 cutlets)

½ tbsp olive oil

a few sprigs of rosemary leaves, finely chopped

salt and freshly ground black pepper

150ml (5fl oz) hot vegetable stock

1 tsp redcurrant jelly

400g can flageolet beans, drained

handful of mint leaves, finely chopped

1 Preheat the oven to 200°C (400°F/Gas 6). Smother the lamb with the oil, sprinkle over the rosemary, and season well with salt and pepper. Sit the rack in a roasting tin and put in the oven to roast for 40 minutes, or longer if you like your meat well done.

2 Remove the lamb from the tin and keep warm (covered with foil) while you prepare the beans. Sit the roasting tin on the hob over a medium to high heat, add the stock, and bring to the boil. Reduce to a simmer, stir in the redcurrant jelly until dissolved, then stir through the flageolet beans and simmer gently for 5 minutes. Remove from the heat and stir through the mint.

3 Slice the rack into 8 cutlets and serve on warmed plates with the beans and some potatoes.

variation

roast rack of lamb with harissa and baby turnips

Prepare in exactly the same way but before roasting, smear the lamb skin with 1 tbsp harissa paste and omit the rosemary. Boil 6 quartered baby turnips and add to the tin with the flageolet. Stir through 2 tsp tomato purée and a pinch of sugar instead of the redcurrant jelly. Stir in a handful of thyme leaves instead of mint.

pork with spring onions, soy, and cinnamon

Asian flavours successfully perk up pork. Five-spice powder is a favourite Asian ingredient and is made from Szechuan pepper, star anise, fennel seeds, cloves, and cinnamon.

🥣 15 MINS 🍲 2 HRS 15 MINS – 2 HRS 30 MINS

SERVES 4–6

1.1kg (2½lb) pork shoulder or leg, cut into bite-sized pieces

2 tsp five-spice powder

2–3 tbsp olive oil

2 bunches of spring onions, trimmed, white and green parts separated and finely chopped

3 garlic cloves, sliced

5cm (2in) piece of fresh root ginger, peeled and sliced

100ml (3½fl oz) dark soy sauce

2 cinnamon sticks, broken in half

250g (9oz) small button mushrooms, any large ones halved

about 900ml (1½ pints) hot chicken stock

freshly ground black pepper

1 Preheat the oven to 160°C (325°F/Gas 3) and toss the pork in the five-spice powder. Heat half the oil in a large flameproof casserole over a medium-high heat, and cook the pork in batches for 5–6 minutes until it turns golden. Remove and set aside.

2 Heat the remaining oil in the casserole over a medium heat. Add the spring onion whites and cook for a minute, then stir in the garlic and ginger until coated. Stir in the soy sauce, add the cinnamon and mushrooms, and return the pork to the casserole. Finally, add the stock, bring to the boil, then reduce to a simmer and season with black pepper. Cover with the lid and put in the oven for 2 hours.

3 If the sauce is too thin, remove the meat with a slotted spoon and set aside, then sit the casserole on the hob and let it simmer for about 10 minutes, to reduce a little and intensify the flavours. Return the meat, remove the cinnamon sticks, and top with the spring onion greens. Ladle into warmed bowls and serve with noodles or rice.

flatbreads topped with lamb and hummus

Lamb is so popular at this time of year, and this tasty Middle Eastern-style recipe is the perfect use for any leftovers from a roast joint.

🥣 10 MINS 🍲 20 MINS

SERVES 2

1 tbsp olive oil, plus extra for drizzling

1 onion, finely chopped

3 garlic cloves, grated or finely chopped

200g (7oz) leftover roast lamb, shredded

pinch of ground allspice

pinch of ground cinnamon

salt and freshly ground black pepper

2 flatbreads or plain naan

handful of pine nuts, toasted

handful of mint leaves, roughly chopped

hummus, to serve

1 Preheat the oven to 200°C (400°F/Gas 6). Heat the oil in a frying pan over a medium heat, add the onion, and cook for about 5 minutes until the onion is soft and translucent.

2 Stir in the garlic and cook for a few more seconds. Now add the leftover lamb and stir through. Sprinkle over the allspice and cinnamon and cook for a few minutes, stirring occasionally. Season with salt and pepper.

3 Lay the flatbreads or naan on a baking tray and drizzle with a little oil. Spoon over the lamb mixture and cook in the oven for about 10 minutes until the lamb is heated through. Scatter over the pine nuts and mint leaves, and top each flatbread or naan with a dollop of hummus. Serve immediately.

shallow-fried red mullet

Pan-frying, a simple method of cooking, makes the most of the delicate sweetness of red mullet.

🥣 15 MINS 🍲 5 MINS

SERVES 4

4 red mullet, gutted, scaled, trimmed, and heads removed

sea salt and freshly ground black pepper

cornmeal or polenta, for coating

grapeseed oil, for frying

lemon juice, to serve

1 Season the fish with sea salt and pepper, then coat them on both sides with cornmeal or polenta, shaking off any excess. Set a non-stick frying pan over a medium heat and add enough oil to coat the bottom of the pan.

2 Put the prepared fish into the hot oil, presentation-side (the side that will be uppermost when serving)

down. Shallow-fry for 2 minutes, or until the fish is golden brown.

3 Turn the fish using tongs and cook for 2–3 minutes, or until the other side is golden brown. To test for doneness, insert a thin-bladed knife into the centre of the fish, then touch the tip of the knife to your thumb. If the knife is warm, the fish is ready. Drain briefly on kitchen paper and serve with a squeeze of lemon juice together with some boiled potatoes and steamed spring greens.

roast leg of spring lamb

A classic spring dish, roast lamb served with roast potatoes, mint sauce, and seasonal vegetables. Perfection on a plate.

🥣 15 MINS   🍲 1 HR 45 MINS

SERVES 6–8

2kg (4½lb) leg of lamb

4 garlic cloves, peeled but left whole

handful of rosemary sprigs

salt and freshly ground black pepper

600ml (1 pint) hot vegetable stock

1 tsp redcurrant jelly

1 Preheat the oven to 200°C (400°F/Gas 6). Spike the leg of lamb evenly all over with the point of a sharp knife, then stuff the garlic cloves and small sprigs of rosemary into the holes. Season the lamb with salt and pepper.

2 Sit the leg of lamb in a roasting tin and roast in the oven for about 15 minutes, until it begins to brown. Reduce the oven temperature to 180°C (350°F/Gas 4), and continue to roast for a further 1 hour (for rare), basting it with its juices halfway through the cooking time; allow 1½ hours for well done. Transfer the lamb to a large plate, cover with foil, and leave to rest in a warm place for 15 minutes while you make the gravy.

3 To make the gravy, tilt the roasting tin at a slight angle and skim off any fat. Sit the tin over a high heat on the hob. Add the stock and redcurrant jelly and bring to the boil, scraping up any bits from the bottom of the tin with a wooden spoon. Reduce the heat slightly and simmer, stirring all the time, for 5–8 minutes. Taste, and season if needed. Carve at the table and serve with roast or creamy mashed potato, fresh mint sauce, and seasonal vegetables.

lamb fillet basted with anchovy paste

Anchovies give new-season lamb a punchy flavour. You can buy ready-made anchovy paste, but it's not difficult to make, as shown here.

🥣 15 MINS PLUS MARINATING   🍲 40 MINS

SPECIAL EQUIPMENT ▪ blender or food processor

SERVES 4

1 whole lamb neck fillet, about 675g (1½lb)

2 salad onions, trimmed and roughly chopped

150g jar salted anchovies in oil, drained

2 tbsp capers in vinegar, drained

3 tbsp olive oil

1 Score the lamb fillet in a crisscross pattern about 1cm (½in) deep. Put the remaining ingredients in a blender or food processor and blitz to a fine paste. Liberally spread the paste all over the lamb, making sure that it makes its way into the scores. Allow to marinate in the fridge for about 30 minutes.

2 Preheat a grill to medium and sit the lamb fillet on the grill pan. Cook in the lower part of the grill for 15–20 minutes, turning occasionally, until browned and cooked to your liking. Transfer the lamb to a plate and leave it to rest in a warm place for 10 minutes.

3 Cut into 1cm (½in) slices and serve with warm pitta bread, hummus, and seasonal salad leaves.

turkish-spiced lamb pizza with pine nuts

Pine nuts and paprika introduce Turkish flavours that meld perfectly with garlicky lamb on an unusual flatbread base.

🥣 5 MINS   🍲 20 MINS

SERVES 4

1 tbsp olive oil

1 onion, finely chopped

2 garlic cloves, finely chopped

450g (1lb) minced lamb

pinch of chilli powder

juice of 1 lemon

salt and freshly ground black pepper

4 flatbreads, such as pitta or naan

handful of pine nuts

sprinkling of mild paprika

small handful of coriander, to garnish

hummus, to serve

1 Preheat the oven to 200°C (400°F/Gas 6). Heat the oil in a large frying pan over a medium heat, add the onion, and cook for 3–4 minutes until the onion is soft. Then add the garlic and lamb and cook, stirring to break up lumps, until the meat is browned.

2 Add the chilli powder and lemon juice. Season with salt and pepper and stir through. Spoon the lamb mixture onto the flatbreads, scatter over the pine nuts, and sprinkle on the paprika.

3 Place on a baking sheet and cook in the oven for 5–10 minutes until golden. Garnish with the coriander and serve with hummus.

rack of lamb with parsley crumb

A rack of lamb is among the more expensive cuts, so be sure to cook it correctly. Medium is really the best way, to keep the meat at its most succulent. The breadcrumbs mixed with finely chopped parsley give a crisp finish to this dish.

🥣 35-40 MINS   🍲 25-30 MINS

SPECIAL EQUIPMENT • blender or food processor

SERVES 4

2 racks of lamb, weighing 750g-1kg (1lb 10oz-2¼lb) each, chine bones removed

2 garlic cloves, cut into slivers

2 tbsp olive oil

salt and freshly ground black pepper

4 slices of white bread, crusts cut off

45g (1½oz) butter

leaves from a small bunch of flat-leaf parsley, finely chopped

For the gravy

125ml (4fl oz) white wine

250ml (9fl oz) lamb, beef, or chicken stock

1 Set a rack of lamb on a chopping board, ribs upwards, and with a sharp knife, cut out any sinew lying under the ribs. Turn the rack over. Cut away the small crescent of cartilage at one end.

2 Make a small incision under the thin layer of skin covering the fat. Using your fingers, pull off the skin. If you can't get a good grip, use a clean tea towel to help. Score through the fat and meat down to the rib bones, about 5cm (2in) from the ends of the bones.

3 Turn the rack over. Place it over the edge of the board and score down to the bone, about 5cm (2in) from the ends of the bones. Cut out the meat between the bones, using the point of a knife. Scrape the bones clean, being sure to scrape away all skin. Repeat for the second piece of meat.

4 Preheat the oven to 230°C (450°F/Gas 8). Make several incisions in the lamb with the point of a knife and push in the garlic slivers. Transfer the racks to a roasting tin, ribs downwards. Wrap the bones in foil to prevent them from burning. Spoon the oil over the lamb and sprinkle with salt and pepper. Roast in the oven for 25–30 minutes, basting once or twice with the juices in the roasting tin. The meat will shrink away from the bones a little.

5 Test the lamb with a metal skewer: when inserted for 30 seconds, it will feel warm to the touch when withdrawn. A meat thermometer should register 60°C (140°F). This will give medium meat.

6 For the parsley crumb, put the bread in a blender or food processor and pulse to form crumbs. Melt the butter in a frying pan, add the breadcrumbs, and cook for 2–3 minutes, stirring, until just golden. Stir in the parsley and season.

7 When the lamb is cooked to your taste, transfer the racks to a chopping board. Discard the foil used to cover the bones. Insulate the racks with more foil and set aside to rest. This allows all the juices to flow back evenly through the meat, giving juicier lamb. Heat the grill.

8 To make the gravy, discard the fat from the roasting tin. Add the wine and boil until reduced by half, stirring to dissolve the roasting juices from the bottom of the tin. Add the stock and boil for 5–7 minutes, until the gravy is well flavoured. Season to taste. Strain and keep warm until ready to serve. You can stir in 1–2 tsp cornflour, mixed with cold water until smooth, if you want a thicker gravy.

9 Press the breadcrumbs on to the top surface of the lamb and baste with the roasting juices. Grill, breadcrumb-side up, for 1–2 minutes until lightly browned. Watch that the breadcrumb coating does not scorch. Carve and serve on warmed plates with the gravy on the side.

spaghetti with chilli, broccoli, and spring onion

This is a simple way to enjoy fresh greens at their best. You can use other pasta instead if you prefer – try the sauce with bucatini or the large, flat papardelle for a change.

🥣 10 MINS   🍲 12 MINS

SERVES 4

350g (12oz) dried spaghetti

salt and freshly ground black pepper

200g (7oz) sprouting broccoli or broccoli rabe

5 tbsp olive oil

bunch of spring onions, trimmed and chopped

1 tsp dried chilli flakes

1 tbsp lime juice

Parmesan cheese, grated, to serve

1 Cook the spaghetti in boiling salted water according to the packet's instructions. Drain and return to the pan.

2 Meanwhile, trim the broccoli, cut the heads into small florets, and chop the stalks.

3 Heat the oil in a large frying pan or wok. Add the broccoli and spring onions and stir-fry for about 4 minutes until just tender.

4 Tip the contents of the pan into the spaghetti. Add the chilli, lime juice, and seasoning to taste. Toss gently, pile onto plates, and serve with plenty of Parmesan cheese.

lamb with lemon and olives

Using whole lemons, rather than simply the juice, adds a sharpness of flavour to this dish. The addition of olives successfully elaborates on the Mediterranean theme.

🥣 25 MINS   🍲 35 MINS

SERVES 4

3 tbsp olive oil

bunch of spring onions, trimmed and finely chopped

500g (1lb 2oz) lean lamb, cut into bite-sized pieces

6 garlic cloves, finely sliced

1 lemon, cut into eighths

1 tsp chopped rosemary leaves

handful of flat-leaf parsley, chopped

1 tsp paprika

3 tbsp green olives

salt and freshly ground black pepper

1 Preheat the oven to 200°C (400°F/ Gas 6). Heat the oil in a frying pan, add the spring onions, and cook over a medium heat for 5 minutes, or until they are beginning to soften. Add the lamb and cook, stirring occasionally, for 5 minutes, or until no longer pink. Add the garlic and lemon and cook for 1 minute, then add the rest of the ingredients and cook for a further 2 minutes, stirring well.

2 Transfer the mixture to a small baking dish, packing it in tightly. Add 2 tbsp water, mix well, and then bake for 20 minutes.

3 Remove from the oven and allow to rest for 10 minutes before serving with fresh crusty bread and a crisp green salad.

calzone with cheese, ham, and spinach

Calzone is a folded Italian pizza. For a crispy finish, sprinkle the top of the dough with some water before baking.

🥄 15 MINS   🍲 20 MINS

MAKES 1

For the dough

125g (4½oz) strong plain flour

pinch of salt

pinch of caster sugar

¾ tsp easy-blend dried yeast

1 tbsp olive oil

90ml (3fl oz) warm water

For the filling

200g (7oz) spinach leaves, wilted and drained

125g (4½oz) cooked ham, chopped

125g (4½oz) mozzarella, torn into pieces

handful of torn basil leaves

1 Sift the flour, salt, and sugar into a bowl. Add the yeast. Stir in the oil and enough warm water to form a soft but not sticky dough. Knead gently on a lightly floured surface for several minutes until smooth and elastic. Return to the bowl, cover with oiled cling film, and leave in a warm place for about 40 minutes until the dough has doubled in bulk.

2 Preheat the oven to its highest setting. Very lightly oil a baking tray and put it in the oven to get hot. Turn out the dough on a floured surface and knock it back by re-kneading briefly. Roll out thinly to a round, about 25cm (10in) diameter, and transfer to the hot baking tray, spreading it out firmly again.

3 Squeeze any remaining liquid from the spinach and spread it over half the pizza base, leaving about 1cm (½in) around the edge. Top with the ham, mozzarella, and basil, then dampen all around the edge of the pizza with water. Fold one half of the pizza over the other, seal the edges together with your fingers, then sprinkle the top with a little water. Bake for 15–20 minutes, or until golden and crispy.

sole with butter sauce

This sauce is perfect with any flat fish, such as the sole suggested here. Ring the changes by using tarragon (sparingly!) or dill instead of some or all of the parsley.

🥄 15 MINS   🍲 10 MINS   ❄ FREEZABLE

SERVES 4

4 small whole sole, fins and tail trimmed

115g (4oz) butter, diced, plus 30g (1oz) butter, melted

salt and freshly ground black pepper

1 small onion, finely chopped

2 tbsp cider vinegar

2 tbsp chopped parsley

1 Preheat the grill. Lay the fish on the grill rack and brush all over with the melted butter. Season lightly with salt and pepper, and grill for about 5 minutes on each side until lightly golden and cooked through.

2 Meanwhile, put the onion in a small pan with 2 tbsp water and the cider vinegar. Bring to the boil, reduce the heat, and simmer until the onion is soft and the liquid is reduced by half.

3 Whisk in the diced butter, a piece at a time, until the sauce has thickened. Then stir in the parsley and season with more salt and pepper to taste.

4 Transfer the fish to warmed plates, spoon the sauce over, and serve with baby carrots and plain potatoes.

pork and spring greens

Choose your greens with the seasons – this quick stir-fry makes the most of the leafy seasonal produce available.

🥣 10 MINS   🍲 10 MINS

SERVES 4

1 tbsp olive oil

350g (12oz) pork fillet, cut into thin strips

4 garlic cloves, sliced

2 heads of spring greens, shredded

2 tsp onion seeds

salt and freshly ground black pepper

1 Heat the oil in a wok over a medium-high heat. When the oil is hot, add the pork. Stir-fry the pork for about 5 minutes, moving it around the wok as it heats up.

2 Add the garlic and greens. Continue to stir-fry over a medium-high heat for 1 minute, or until the greens have just wilted. Add the onion seeds and stir to combine, then season with salt and pepper. Serve immediately with fluffy rice.

variation

pigeon breasts with spring greens and hoisin

Prepare in the same way but use 8 skinned pigeon breasts, cut into thin strips, instead of the pork. Use sunflower oil instead of olive. Stir-fry for 2 minutes, then add 2 tbsp hoisin sauce and stir-fry for 1 minute more. When cooked, add a dash of soy sauce, to taste.

spinach and goat's cheese frittata

This makes a delicious light lunch or supper dish, served hot or cold. You can use dollops of soft, creamy goat's cheese in place of the cubed pieces if you prefer.

🥣 8 MINS   🍲 12 MINS

SERVES 4

2 tbsp olive oil

knob of butter

4 spring onions, trimmed and chopped

2 large handfuls of baby spinach

6 eggs, beaten

salt and freshly ground black pepper

100g (3½oz) goat's cheese, cut into cubes

6-8 basil leaves, chopped

1 Heat the oil and butter in a large non-stick frying pan. Add the spring onions and fry, stirring, for 2 minutes until soft. Add the spinach and stir for a further 1–2 minutes until wilted. Simmer for a minute or two more to evaporate any juice. Spread the spinach out evenly in the pan.

2 Season the eggs with salt and pepper and pour into the pan. Scatter the goat's cheese and then the basil over. Cook over a low heat, lifting and stirring the mixture gently and tilting the pan to allow the uncooked egg to run underneath. Meanwhile, preheat the grill to medium.

3 Lift the edges of the frittata with a palette knife to check the base. After about 5 minutes, when the base is golden and set but the top is still slightly runny, set the pan under the hot grill for 2–3 minutes to brown. Cut into wedges and serve with fresh crusty bread.

variation

nettle and blue cheese frittata

Prepare in the same way, but use 2 large handfuls of young nettle tops instead of the spinach (use gloves when picking and washing them). Add 2 tbsp water when wilting them in the pan, then evaporate the juice, as before. Substitute 100g (3½oz) soft, creamy blue cheese, such as Dolcelatte, for the goat's cheese and 6–8 chopped sage leaves instead of the basil. Cook and grill as before.

italian wedding soup

The Italian name for this robust, rustic soup is *minestra maritata*, which simply means the flavours marry well together. All this soup needs with it is some crusty bread.

🥣 10 MINS   🍲 1 HR 40 MINS   ❄ FREEZABLE

SERVES 4-5

150g (5½oz) stewing beef, diced

1 boneless belly pork slice, rinded and diced

115g (4oz) piece of salami, diced

1 chicken portion

1 large onion, chopped

1 litre (1¾ pints) beef stock

sprig of rosemary

1 bay leaf

salt and freshly ground black pepper

¼ head spring greens, shredded

1 head of green or red chicory

60g (2oz) soup pasta shapes

Parmesan cheese, grated

crusty bread, to serve

1 Put all the meats in a large pan with the onion, stock, rosemary, and bay leaf, and season well with salt and pepper. Bring to the boil, skim the surface, reduce the heat, cover, and simmer very gently for 1½ hours until the meat is meltingly tender.

2 Discard the herbs. Lift out the chicken, discard the skin, remove all flesh from the bones, cut into neat pieces, and return to the pot. Add the greens, chicory, and pasta. Bring back to the boil, reduce the heat, and simmer for 10 minutes. Taste and adjust the seasoning, if necessary. Ladle into large open soup plates, sprinkle with grated Parmesan cheese, and serve with the bread.

Season's best **spring leafy greens**

All varieties of leafy greens have a sweet flavour with an appealing hint of bitterness. Spinach varieties are delicate, with the new season's large leaves having the best flavour. They add a beautiful green colour to dishes. Spring greens (available late winter through spring) have squeaky leaves and are more robust. Try both with ginger, chilli, garlic, and soy sauce, and also with the more subtle flavours of cream, nuts, and eggs.

True spinach (and baby leaves) needs frequent sowings to provide a sustainable crop. Perpetual varieties re-grow once cut. Spring greens are a hardy crop that can survive harsh winters to become available in spring.

Large leaf spinach Spinach has juicy, tender leaves with a distinctly earthy, acidic flavour. As they are composed mostly of water, they greatly reduce in bulk once cooked.

Spring greens The leaves appear tough, but cook quickly to be sweet and tender, yet retain a pleasing texture.

Tear coarse midribs and stalks from large spinach leaves before cooking.

The stalks and midribs are undeveloped, so the leaves do not need trimming.

essentials
varieties available

Spring greens, baby spinach, large leaf spinach (true and perpetual varieties).

buy Look for glossy leaves with freshly cut stalk ends. Avoid broken or slimy leaves.

store Keep in the fridge in an open plastic bag for 3–4 days.

cook Boil, steam, sauté, stir-fry, or braise all. Wilt any spinach in hot butter or dressing. Eat baby spinach raw in salads.

preserve Blanch and freeze.

recipe ideas

Filo pie with spinach, ricotta cheese, and pine nuts p26

Italian wedding soup p52

Pork and spring greens p52

Baby spinach The mildly flavoured leaves are brittle but soft. They are good in a salad with bacon and avocado, or wilted in an omelette or frittata.

how to trim greens

Spring (and winter) greens need trimming and shredding before cooking. Cut out the thick stalks of large-leaf spinach (or Swiss chard), as in Step 1, then cook and eat with melted butter and Hollandaise sauce, like asparagus.

1 Discard all limp and discoloured leaves. Slice each leaf along both sides of the centre rib, then remove it and discard.

2 Working with a few leaves at a time, roll them loosely into a bunch. Cut across the roll to the desired width, making strips.

pan-fried gammon with pineapple salsa

A contemporary take on a traditional classic. Rather than leaving as whole rings, here the pineapple is chopped very finely for a salsa to serve with the gammon.

🥣 5 MINS   🍲 20 MINS

SERVES 4

1 tbsp olive oil

4 gammon steaks

250g (9oz) peeled pineapple, cored and thinly sliced

1 tbsp honey

knob of butter

3 tomatoes, skinned (p197) and chopped

½ red onion, finely diced

1 Heat the oil in a large non-stick frying pan over a high heat. Add the pieces of gammon and cook for 3–4 minutes on each side, depending on their thickness, until golden and cooked through. Remove from the pan and set aside to keep warm.

2 Smother the pineapple rings in honey. Melt the butter in the same frying pan. Add the pineapple, and cook for a couple of minutes until golden and lightly charred. Remove from the pan, cool slightly, and chop into small pieces.

3 To make the salsa, put the pineapple, tomatoes, and red onion in a bowl, and mix until combined.

4 To serve, transfer the gammon steaks onto warmed plates and serve with the salsa and perhaps some chunky chips or a salad.

marmalade-glazed gammon with new potatoes and chicory

The marmalade gives a wonderfully sticky-sweet finish to this gammon, which is roasted with seasonal chicory.

🥣 15 MINS   🍲 1 HR 45 MINS

SERVES 4-6

1.8kg (4lb) unsmoked gammon joint with no bone

500ml (16fl oz) dry cider

2 bay leaves

3 tbsp marmalade

1 tbsp brown sugar

1.1kg (2½lb) small salad potatoes

1 tbsp olive oil

zest of 1 orange

salt and freshly ground black pepper

4 heads chicory, trimmed and quartered lengthways

1 Sit the gammon in a large pan, add the cider and bay leaves, then top up with enough hot water to cover the joint, if needed. Cover with the lid, bring to the boil, then reduce to a simmer and cook for 40 minutes. Preheat the oven to 180°C (350°F/Gas 4).

2 Remove the gammon from the pan and carefully peel away the outer skin, leaving a layer of fat. Put the marmalade in a pan and heat gently over a low heat until runny. Brush the gammon liberally with the marmalade, then sprinkle over the sugar.

3 Sit the gammon in a roasting tin. Toss the potatoes with the oil and orange zest, season well with salt and pepper, then add to the tin. Put in the oven to roast for 50 minutes to 1 hour. Add the chicory heads for the last 20 minutes of cooking, tossing them in some of the juices.

4 Remove the gammon from the tin and keep warm while it rests for at least 15 minutes. Slice and serve with the potatoes and chicory.

chicken with chicory and bacon

Chicory has a bitter taste, but once roasted it is much more mellow. For added flavour, sprinkle Parmesan cheese over the chicory once it is in the roasting tin, if you like.

🥣 5 MINS   🍲 40 MINS

SERVES 4

knob of butter

pinch of demerara sugar

3 large heads chicory, trimmed and halved lengthways

1 tbsp olive oil

4 large chicken breasts with skin on

12 streaky bacon rashers

1 Preheat the oven to 200°C (400°F/Gas 6). Put the butter and the sugar in a large frying pan over a low heat. Cook until the sugar has dissolved and the butter melted. Add the chicory and cook for 5–8 minutes until golden, then set aside.

2 Increase the heat to medium-high and add the oil to the same pan. When hot, add the chicken, skin-side down, and brown for 3–5 minutes on each side until golden all over. Transfer the chicken to a roasting tin.

3 Wrap the bacon around the reserved chicory and tuck it into the roasting tin, so that it all sits snugly. You want everything tightly packed, so that the dish will produce plenty of juice. Roast in the oven for about 25 minutes until golden. Serve hot with baby roast potatoes.

variation

turbot with cheese, ham, and chicory

Prepare in the same way but use 4 turbot fillets (about 150g/5oz) each instead of the chicken breasts. Bake in the oven for 10 minutes, then top the fish with slices of Gruyère or Cheddar cheese and return to the oven for a further 10 minutes, or until the fish is cooked through and the cheese is golden and bubbling.

spinach-stuffed veal

The rolls can be cooked up to 2 days ahead, covered and refrigerated. Their flavour will mellow.

🥣 45–50 MINS   🍲 30–40 MINS

SERVES 4

500g (1lb 2oz) spinach leaves, trimmed

4 tbsp olive oil, plus more if needed

8 garlic cloves, finely chopped

45g (1½oz) walnuts, chopped

30g (1oz) Parmesan cheese, grated

grated nutmeg

salt and freshly ground black pepper

8 veal escalopes, total weight about 625g (1lb 6oz), pounded between two sheets of baking parchment

1 onion, thinly sliced

1 carrot, thinly sliced

2 celery sticks, thinly sliced

250ml (9fl oz) dry white wine

250ml (9fl oz) chicken stock

1 Bring a saucepan of water to the boil, add the spinach, and simmer for 1–2 minutes, then drain. Squeeze to remove excess water, then chop. Heat 2 tbsp of the oil in a frying pan and add the spinach. Stir until any moisture has evaporated. Remove from the heat and add half the garlic, the walnuts, Parmesan, and nutmeg. Stir and taste for seasoning.

2 Lay one escalope on a work surface and season. Spread an eighth of the spinach stuffing on top. Roll up the meat, tucking in the ends. Repeat with the remaining escalopes and stuffing. Tie up the rolls.

3 Heat the remaining oil in a sauté pan and add the veal rolls. Cook over a high heat for 2–3 minutes, turning occasionally, until browned all over. Transfer to a plate and set aside.

4 Stir the onion and remaining garlic into the pan and cook until softened. Add the carrot and celery. Reduce the heat and cook for 8–10 minutes, until tender. Pour in the wine, bring to the boil, and simmer to reduce by half.

5 Return the veal to the pan and add the stock. Cover and simmer for 30–40 minutes, until tender. Strain the liquid into a saucepan, reserving the vegetables, and boil until reduced to 175ml (6fl oz). Slice the veal rolls and serve with the sauce.

jerk chicken with roasted pineapple

You might choose to use a shop-bought jerk marinade for this recipe instead of making your own.

🥄 10 MINS PLUS MARINATING   🍲 40 MINS   ❄ FREEZABLE

SPECIAL EQUIPMENT ▪ blender or food processor

SERVES 4

For the jerk marinade

1-2 red chillies, deseeded

1-2 green chillies, deseeded

pinch of ground cinnamon

pinch of grated nutmeg

pinch of salt and 1 tsp black pepper

grated zest and juice of 2 limes

3 tbsp soft brown sugar

2 tbsp vegetable oil

handful of flat-leaf parsley

handful of coriander

a few sprigs of thyme, leaves picked

For the chicken

1 whole chicken, jointed (ask your butcher to do this)

1 small pineapple, peeled, cored, thickly sliced, and cut into chunks

1 To make the marinade, put all the ingredients in a blender or food processor. Blitz to a paste and add a little more oil if needed.

2 Deeply slash all the chicken joints, then put in a large plastic freezer bag. Add the jerk marinade and squish everything together until the chicken is well coated. Leave to marinate in the fridge for at least 30 minutes, or preferably overnight.

3 Preheat the oven to 200°C (400°F/ Gas 6). Arrange the chicken pieces in a large roasting tin, making sure that there is plenty of room. Roast in the oven for 35–40 minutes until golden and crisp. Add the pineapple pieces for the last 10 minutes of cooking time. Serve hot with fluffy rice.

poussins with mushrooms

For the best result, use the melted butter for frequent basting.

🥄 30-40 MINS   🍲 35-40 MINS

SERVES 2

85g (3oz) butter

2 poussins, spatchcocked (ask your butcher to do this)

salt and freshly ground black pepper

2½ tbsp Dijon mustard, or to taste

15g (½oz) dried breadcrumbs

15g (½oz) plain flour

150g (5½oz) mushrooms, sliced

2 shallots, finely chopped

1 garlic clove, finely chopped

4 tbsp medium dry white wine

4 tbsp white wine vinegar

375ml (13fl oz) chicken stock

bunch of watercress, to garnish

1 Heat the grill. Brush the grill rack with oil. Melt 30g (1oz) of the butter in a small saucepan and keep it close to hand for basting. Brush the poussins with half the melted butter and sprinkle with salt and pepper.

2 Put the poussins on the grill rack, skin-side up. Grill them about 7.5cm (3in) from the heat for about 15 minutes, basting once with butter during this time. Turn, brush the underside of the birds with the remaining butter and grill for another 10 minutes. Turn again so the birds are breast-side up once more. Brush the skin with 1 tbsp of the mustard, then sprinkle evenly with the breadcrumbs. Grill, skin-side up, for about 10 minutes until tender. If the breadcrumbs threaten to scorch, lower the rack further from the heat.

3 In a shallow dish, mash 30g (1oz) of the remaining butter with the flour. Melt half the remaining butter in a pan, add the mushrooms, and cook, stirring, for 3–5 minutes, until tender and lightly browned.

4 Melt the remaining butter in another pan, add the shallots and garlic, and cook until soft. Add the wine and vinegar and reduce to about 2 tbsp. Stir in the remaining mustard and stock, and then the mushrooms. Simmer for 5 minutes. Whisk in the flour paste a small piece at a time, to slightly thicken the sauce. Season and arrange the birds on warmed plates and serve with the sauce, garnished with watercress.

poussins in vine leaves

Each bird makes a generous portion; perfect for a dinner party.

🥄 45-50 MINS   🍲 1 HR - 1 HR 10 MINS

SERVES 4

6 streaky bacon rashers, sliced

1 shallot, finely chopped

1 chicken liver, coarsely chopped

handful of tarragon leaves, chopped

handful of parsley leaves, chopped

pinch of ground allspice

4 tbsp white breadcrumbs

salt and freshly ground black pepper

4 poussins, seasoned inside and out

8-12 preserved vine leaves, rinsed, drained, and dried in kitchen paper

2 tbsp vegetable oil

250ml (9fl oz) dry white wine

250ml (9fl oz) chicken stock

1 For the stuffing, put 2 of the bacon rashers into a frying pan and cook, stirring, for 3–5 minutes, until crisp. Transfer to a bowl with a slotted spoon. Add the shallot to the pan and cook for 2–3 minutes, until soft. Add the chicken liver and cook, stirring, for 1–2 minutes, until brown.

Combine with the bacon. Stir in the herbs, allspice, and breadcrumbs, and season with black pepper.

2 For each poussin, spoon one-quarter of the stuffing into the cavity, wrap 2 or 3 vine leaves over the breast, top with a folded slice of bacon, and tie with string like a parcel.

3 Preheat the oven to 180°C (350°F/ Gas 4). Heat the oil in a casserole on top of the stove. Add the poussins and brown all over for 5–10 minutes. Cover and bake for 45–55 minutes, until tender and the juices run clear when a metal skewer is inserted.

4 Transfer the poussins to warmed plates. Discard the strings and cover with foil to keep warm. Spoon the fat from the casserole, then add the white wine. Bring to the boil and simmer, stirring, until reduced by half. Add the stock and reduce again by half. Strain and taste for seasoning. Serve the sauce with the poussins.

flemish vegetable tart

A quick brioche dough makes a sumptuous crust for this unusual vegetable tart. You can choose to cook the tart in a frying pan, if you like, for a more rustic effect. Don't be worried about making brioche: this version is very easy indeed, and has the advantage that it can be made the day ahead and refrigerated, wrapped in cling film, overnight.

🥣 50-55 MINS PLUS RISING   🍲 40-50 MINS

SPECIAL EQUIPMENT ▪ 30cm (12in) flan dish

SERVES 8

1½ tsp dried yeast

250g (9oz) strong plain flour, more if needed

salt and freshly ground black pepper

7 eggs

215g (7½oz) unsalted butter, softened

4 carrots, cut in julienne strips

500g (1lb 2oz) mushrooms, stalks removed and caps thinly sliced

2 turnips, cut in julienne strips

8-10 spring onions, trimmed and finely sliced

250ml (9fl oz) double cream

¼ tsp grated nutmeg

1 For the dough, sprinkle the yeast over 2 tbsp lukewarm water in a bowl and let stand for 5 minutes. Oil a medium bowl. Sift the flour on to a work surface with 1 tsp salt. Make a well in the centre and add the yeast and 3 eggs. Work the ingredients until thoroughly mixed. Draw in the flour and work into the other ingredients with your fingertips to form a smooth dough; add more flour if it is sticky.

2 Place the dough on a floured surface and knead for about 10 minutes, lifting it up and throwing it down until it is very elastic. Work in more flour as necessary, so it is slightly sticky but peels easily from the work surface. Add 125g (4½oz) of the butter, and pinch and squeeze

to mix it into the dough. Knead for 3-5 minutes, until smooth again. Shape into a ball and put into the oiled bowl. Cover with cling film and chill for about 1 hour.

3 Melt the remaining butter in a pan. Add the carrots and cook gently for about 5 minutes, stirring occasionally. Add the mushrooms and turnips, and season with salt and pepper. Press buttered foil over the vegetables, cover with a lid, and cook for about 10 minutes until tender, stirring occasionally. Remove from the heat, add the spring onions, and season.

4 Heat the oven to 200°C (400°F/ Gas 6) and butter the flan dish. Place the dough on a floured surface and

lightly knead it to knock out the air. Roll out to a round 7.5cm (3in) larger than the dish. Line the dish and spread the vegetable mixture in the case. Whisk together the cream, salt, pepper, and nutmeg with the remaining eggs, and pour over the vegetables.

5 Fold the top edge of the dough rim over the filling to form a border. Let rise in a warm place for 20-30 minutes until puffed up. Bake for 40-50 minutes until the brioche case is very brown and the custard set but retaining a slight wobble. Serve hot or at room temperature.

poussins glazed with honey and wrapped in bacon

Poussins are young chickens and the best season for them is spring. Wrapping them in bacon keeps the flesh moist.

🥣 20 MINS   🍲 1 HR

SERVES 4

4 poussins

2 onions, roughly chopped

2 tbsp runny honey

12 streaky bacon or pancetta rashers

6 leeks, trimmed and chopped into 5cm (2in) pieces

1 tbsp olive oil

salt and freshly ground black pepper

1 Preheat the oven to 200°C (400°F/Gas 6). Wipe the poussins thoroughly with kitchen paper, then stuff with the onions. Brush all over with the honey, then cover the breast of each poussin with 3 slices of the bacon or pancetta. Sit in a large roasting tin.

2 Toss the leeks with the oil, then add to the tin, tucking them in around the birds. Season with salt and pepper, then put in the oven to roast for 45 minutes to 1 hour, or until the poussins are cooked. To test, pierce them with the tip of a sharp knife – if the juices run clear, they are ready. If the bacon begins to blacken, cover the poussins with foil.

3 Remove the birds from the tin and keep warm. Using a slotted spoon, transfer the leeks to a serving dish and keep warm. Place the tin on the unlit hob and tilt to one side. Skim away any fat, then pour in a little hot water and set over a high heat. Bring to the boil, scraping up any crispy bits from the base of the tin, then simmer for a few minutes. Pour into a gravy boat or jug and serve with the poussins, leeks, and some creamy mashed potatoes.

pizza with spinach and ricotta cheese

It is important to squeeze excess liquid from the spinach to prevent the pizza base from becoming soggy.

🥣 15 MINS PLUS RISING   🍲 10 MINS

MAKES 1

125g (4½oz) strong white flour

pinch of salt

pinch of caster sugar

¾ tsp easy-blend dried yeast

1 tbsp olive oil

90ml (3fl oz) warm water

a little semolina, for sprinkling

2-3 tbsp passata

200g (7oz) spinach leaves, wilted and drained

2-3 tbsp ricotta cheese

1 Sift the flour, salt, and sugar into a bowl. Add the yeast. Stir in the oil and enough warm water to form a soft but not sticky dough.

2 Place the dough on a slightly floured surface, and knead gently for several minutes until smooth and elastic. Return to the bowl, cover with oiled cling film, and place for about 40 minutes, until the dough has doubled in size.

3 Preheat the oven to its highest setting. Place a lightly oiled baking tray in the oven to get hot. Turn out the dough onto a floured surface and briefly re-knead to knock out the air (called knocking back). Roll out thinly into a round, about 25cm (10in) diameter. Sprinkle the hot baking tray with semolina and transfer the pizza base onto it, spreading it out firmly again.

4 Spoon and smooth the passata onto the pizza base, using the back of the spoon. Squeeze any liquid from the spinach, then spread it on the passata. Dot with spoonfuls of ricotta cheese, season with black pepper, and bake for 10 minutes, or until the crust and base are golden and crispy.

quesadilla with avocado, spring onion, and chilli

These wonderfully simple-to-make stuffed tortillas are a useful speedy standby to have ready at hand for a lunch or light supper.

🥣 10 MINS   🍲 5 MINS

MAKES 1

4 spring onions, trimmed and finely chopped

1-2 red chillies, deseeded and finely chopped

juice of ½ lime

salt and freshly ground black pepper

1½ tbsp olive oil

2 wheat tortillas or corn tortillas

½ avocado, stoned, skinned and sliced

50g (1¾oz) Cheddar cheese, grated

1 Place the spring onions, chillies, and lime juice in a bowl, season well with salt and pepper, and mix together. Leave to sit for a couple of minutes to let the flavours develop.

2 Heat the olive oil in a non-stick frying pan, then fry one tortilla for about 1 minute, or until lightly golden. Scatter over the avocado, leaving a little space around the edge, spoon on the spring onion mixture, and sprinkle with the cheese.

3 Top with the other tortilla, pressing it down with the back of a fish slice to sandwich the two together. Scoop up the quesadilla, carefully turn it over, and cook the other side for another minute, or until golden. Slice in half or quarters, and serve.

veggie pad thai

Spring onions are the classic topping for an Asian noodle dish. Make sure they are finely chopped into strips.

🥣 15 MINS   🍲 15 MINS

SERVES 4

250g (9oz) wide or medium rice noodles

3-4 tbsp vegetable oil

200g (7oz) firm tofu, cut into cubes

2 garlic cloves, grated or finely chopped

1 egg, lightly beaten

150ml (5fl oz) hot vegetable stock

juice of 1 lime

1 tsp fish sauce (nam pla) (optional)

2 tsp tamarind paste

2 tsp demerara sugar

1 tbsp dark soy sauce

1 red chilli, deseeded and finely chopped

75g (2½oz) dry-roasted peanuts, roughly chopped

bunch of spring onions, trimmed and finely chopped

75g (2½oz) bean sprouts (optional)

small handful of coriander

1 Soak the noodles in boiling water for 10 minutes, then drain. Meanwhile, heat 1 tbsp of the oil in a wok over a medium-high heat, and swirl it around the pan. Add the tofu and cook for about 10 minutes until golden (you may need to use more oil). Remove with a slotted spoon, and set aside.

2 Add another 1 tbsp of oil to the pan. When hot, add the garlic and cook for 10 seconds, then tip in the egg and cook, stirring and breaking it up with a wooden spoon, until scrambled. Remove from the pan, and set aside.

3 Add another 1 tbsp of the oil. When hot, add the noodles and stir gently to coat with the oil. Pour over the stock, lime juice, fish sauce, tamarind paste, sugar, and soy sauce; toss to combine. Let it simmer for a few minutes, then stir through the chilli.

4 Add half of the peanuts with the spring onions and the bean sprouts, if using, and stir-fry for a minute. Now add the reserved scrambled egg, stir to combine, and transfer to a serving plate. Scatter over the remaining peanuts and a sprinkling of coriander to serve.

spring rice salad

Asparagus spears appear in late spring. The spears are young and slender and don't need peeling.

🍲 20–25 MINS PLUS CHILLING   🍲 15–20 MINS

SERVES 4–6

For the salad

salt and freshly ground black pepper

1 lemon, cut in half

200g (7oz) long-grain rice

250g (9oz) asparagus spears

3 celery sticks, peeled and diced

250g (9oz) smoked salmon, cut into strips

For the vinaigrette

3 tbsp tarragon vinegar

2 tsp Dijon mustard

175ml (6fl oz) vegetable oil

1 Bring a large saucepan of salted water to the boil. Squeeze the juice from one half of the lemon into the water, then drop in the lemon half as well. Add the rice, stir, and bring back to the boil. Simmer for 10–12 minutes until the rice is tender, stirring occasionally.

2 Meanwhile, make the vinaigrette. Put the vinegar and mustard in a small bowl, add seasoning, and whisk together well. Gradually whisk in the oil in a thin stream so the vinaigrette emulsifies and thickens slightly.

3 Drain the rice, discard the lemon half, then place in a sieve and rinse with cold water to wash away the starch. Drain again thoroughly. Repeat a couple of times more. Transfer to a large bowl.

4 Bring a large saucepan of salted water to the boil, add the asparagus, and simmer for 5–7 minutes until tender when pierced with the tip of a knife. Drain and cut the stalks into chunky pieces.

5 Briskly whisk the vinaigrette again and pour it over the rice. Stir the rice well and add the asparagus, celery, smoked salmon, and lemon juice from the reserved half. Toss all the ingredients together and taste for seasoning. Cover and chill for at least 1 hour to allow the flavours to mingle together. Serve at room temperature.

gratin of chicory and ham

Chicory gratin is a marvellous accompaniment to meat and game dishes. This indulgent version includes ham, so you could even serve it as a starter, if you wish.

🍲 15–20 MINS   🍲 1 HR – 1 HR 15 MINS

SERVES 4

8 heads of chicory, trimmed

1 tsp granulated sugar

salt and freshly ground black pepper

500ml (16fl oz) milk

1 slice of onion

1 bay leaf

6 peppercorns

30g (1oz) plain flour

60g (2oz) butter

pinch of grated nutmeg

8 thin slices of cooked ham

45g (1½oz) Gruyère cheese, grated

1 Preheat the oven to 180°C (350°F/Gas 4). Brush a flan dish with butter. Arrange the chicory in the dish and sprinkle with the sugar, salt, and pepper. Press a piece of buttered foil on top. Bake for 45–55 minutes, until tender and slightly caramelized. Transfer to a plate and let cool slightly. Wipe the flan dish.

2 Heat the milk in a saucepan with the onion, bay leaf, and peppercorns to just short of boiling. Cover the pan and set it aside in a warm place off the heat for 10 minutes. Melt the butter in another saucepan over medium heat. Whisk in the flour and cook for 30–60 seconds, whisking all the time, until foaming.

3 Remove the pan from the heat, then strain in the hot milk and whisk. Return to the heat, whisking constantly, until the sauce boils and begins to thicken. Add seasoning and nutmeg, and simmer for 2 minutes more, stirring continuously, to cook out the raw taste of the flour.

4 Increase the oven temperature to 200°C (400°F/Gas 6). Butter the flan dish again. Lay a slice of ham on a work surface. Set a head of chicory on top and roll the ham round to form a cylinder. Repeat with the remaining ham and chicory, arranging them in the dish, seam-side down. Ladle over the béchamel sauce, sprinkle with the cheese, and bake for 20–25 minutes, until bubbling and browned.

spinach sauce

This quick and easy sauce is a perfect accompaniment for chicken, fish, or new potatoes, or stir in a handful of grated Cheddar cheese and serve the sauce stirred into some pasta.

🥣 **15 MINS** 🍲 **20 MINS** ❄ **FREEZABLE**

SERVES 8

4 tbsp olive oil

2 large onions, finely diced

4 garlic cloves, finely sliced

2 red chillies, deseeded and finely chopped

550g (1¼lb) baby spinach leaves, rinsed and roughly chopped

300ml (10fl oz) dry white wine

2 tbsp plain flour

900ml (1½ pints) milk

salt and freshly ground black pepper

1 Heat the oil in a large heavy-based pan over a medium heat, add the onions, and cook for about 5 minutes, until the onions are soft and translucent. Stir in the garlic and chillies and cook for 2 minutes. Add the spinach and cook for 3 minutes, or until wilted.

2 Add the wine and simmer for 5 minutes, or until reduced by half. Add the flour and combine well. Stir in half the milk, and then add the rest of the milk a little at a time, stirring constantly, and cook for 5 minutes, or until you have a creamy sauce. Season well with salt and pepper.

spinach with pine nuts and raisins

This dish can be served hot or cold and adds a piquant flavour to roast chicken alongside a baked potato.

🥣 **5 MINS** 🍲 **10 MINS**

SERVES 4

1 tbsp olive oil

3 tbsp raisins

3 tbsp pine nuts

3 tbsp dry sherry

200g (7oz) spinach leaves, roughly chopped

1 tsp paprika

salt and freshly ground black pepper

1 Put the oil, raisins, and pine nuts in a shallow frying pan over a medium heat. When the raisins and pine nuts start to sizzle, cook for 2 minutes, moving them all the time. Carefully add the sherry and cook until the liquid has reduced by half.

2 Add the spinach and paprika and cook, stirring constantly, for 5 minutes, or until the spinach has wilted. Season with salt and pepper.

variation

sorrel and wild garlic with pine nuts and olives

Prepare in the same way but omit the raisins. Use half sorrel and half wild garlic in place of the spinach (or spinach and 1 small garlic clove, crushed). Add a handful of olives with the leaves. To turn it into a light meal, spoon into bowls, top with poached eggs, and serve with crusty bread.

pavlova with tropical fruit

You'll find that many tropical fruits are good in spring. They add a luscious sweetness to this light, chewy meringue.

🥣 25-30 MINS   🍲 2 HRS - 2 HRS 30 MINS   ❄ FREEZABLE

SPECIAL EQUIPMENT ▪ electric hand whisk or mixer

SERVES 6-8

For the meringue

6 egg whites

salt

350g (12oz) caster sugar

1 tbsp cornflour

1 tsp distilled malt vinegar

375ml (13fl oz) double cream

2 tbsp chopped pistachios, to serve

For the fruit

3 mangoes, total weight about 1kg (2¼lb), cut in half to remove the stone, and the flesh sliced into cubes and then cut away from the skin

5 kiwi fruit, peeled, sliced, and with the slices cut in half

1 pineapple, weighing about 750g (1lb 10oz), peeled, core removed, thinly sliced, and cut into chunks

45g (1½oz) caster sugar

2 tbsp kirsch

1 Preheat the oven to 180°C (350°F/ Gas 4). Line a baking tray with greaseproof paper. Put the egg whites in a large, clean mixing bowl with a little salt. Whisk with an electric hand whisk or mixer until stiff. Whisk in the sugar, 1 tbsp at a time, until the egg whites are stiff and shiny, then whisk in the cornflour and the vinegar.

2 Spoon the meringue on to the baking tray and spread to form a 20cm (8in) circle. Bake for 5 minutes, then reduce the oven temperature to 140°C (275°F/Gas 1) and cook for a further 1 hour and 15 minutes, or until the outside is crisp. Allow it to cool completely before transferring to a serving plate.

3 Whip the cream in a large, clean bowl until it holds its shape, then spoon it onto the meringue base.

4 Put the fruit in a large bowl. Sprinkle over the sugar and kirsch. Stir the fruit gently with a clean, wooden spoon to distribute the flavourings evenly. Arrange the fruit neatly on top of the cream, sprinkle with the chopped pistachios, and serve immediately. Do not leave it to stand, or the cream will make it soggy.

fresh pineapple upside-down pudding

The sweet acidity of fresh pineapple makes this simple sponge dessert taste amazing. It is good enough to eat either straight out of the oven and piping hot, or cold.

🥣 10 MINS   🍲 50 MINS   ❄ FREEZABLE

SPECIAL EQUIPMENT ▪ electric hand whisk or mixer ▪ 1.2-litre (2-pint) ovenproof dish

SERVES 4-6

2-3 tbsp golden syrup

1 small pineapple, peeled, core removed, and cut into 6 slices

150g (5½oz) butter

125g (4½oz) golden caster sugar

2 eggs

175g (6oz) self-raising flour, sifted

1-2 tbsp milk

pouring cream, to serve

1 Preheat the oven to 180°C (350°F/Gas 4). Grease the ovenproof dish. Drizzle in the golden syrup to cover the base, then top with the pineapple rings, and put to one side.

2 Put the butter and sugar in a mixing bowl and whisk with an electric hand whisk or mixer until pale and creamy. Mix in the eggs, one at a time, adding a little of the flour after each egg. Fold in the remaining flour, then add the milk a little at a time until the mixture drops easily off the beaters. Pour the mixture over the pineapple and spread it out evenly. Bake in the oven for 40–50 minutes, or until the sponge is golden brown and springy to the touch.

3 Loosen the edge all round with a round-bladed knife, then carefully turn out, upside-down, onto a serving plate. Serve with pouring cream.

pineapple and kirsch floating islands

Soft meringue islands float on top of pineapple bathed in a creamy, buttery custard laced with Kirsch. Replace the Kirsch with white rum if you like – or omit it altogether.

🥣 25 MINS   🍲 30 MINS PLUS COOLING

SPECIAL EQUIPMENT ▪ 1.4-litre (2½-pint) ovenproof dish ▪ food processor ▪ electric hand whisk or mixer

SERVES 4

1 small pineapple, peeled with the core removed

60g (2oz) butter

115g (4oz) caster sugar

2 large eggs, separated

30g (1oz) cornflour

1 tbsp kirsch

200ml (7fl oz) milk

250ml (9fl oz) single cream

1 Preheat the oven to 150°C (300°F/ Gas 2). Chop the pineapple in a food processor, but don't allow it to become puréed. Strain the chopped pineapple through a fine sieve over a bowl. Reserve the juice and spread the fruit across the base of the dish.

2 Beat the butter and half the sugar together until light and fluffy. Beat in the egg yolks, cornflour, reserved pineapple juice, and the kirsch.

3 Warm the milk and cream until hot but not boiling. Gradually whisk into the egg yolk mixture. Rinse the pan, pour the custard back in, and cook gently, stirring until thickened and smooth. Do not allow it to boil. Pour over the pineapple.

4 Whisk the egg whites until stiff. Add the rest of the sugar and whisk until glossy and peaking. Drop 4 large spoonfuls of meringue over the custard. Bake for 30 minutes, or until the meringues are a pale biscuit colour. Leave to cool, chill, then serve.

Season's best **pineapples**

The rough, knobbly skin of a pineapple is divided into dozens of lozenges, which makes it resemble an enlarged pine cone topped with a grey-green plume of spiky leaves. The firm, rich yellow to pale cream flesh is juicy and sweet with an astringent finish. They are imported all year, but are particularly good in spring. Use in salsas, fruit salads, desserts, smoothies, and preserves. Good flavour pairings include pork, chicken, fish, cottage cheese, ginger, Cointreau, and rum.

Pineapples grow on spiky cactus-like plants. When pollinated, a cluster of flowers fuse to make one fruit. They can be grown in a pot from a cut-off pineapple top.

Pineapple Varieties of pineapple differ slightly in size, shape, and colour – some have a golden shell when ripe, others are dark green or reddish – as well as in their degree of sweetness. All can be eaten fresh or used in salads and desserts.

If you can easily pull out one of the inner leaves, the pineapple is ripe and ready for eating.

how to prepare pineapples

Pineapples have sharp, spiky skin, so handle with care. Use a large, sharp knife for slicing as the central core can be really tough.

1 Top and tail the pineapple. Stand it on its base, and slice the skin from the top down, all the way around the fruit.

2 Quarter it lengthways, cut away the core, then dice; or cut in slices, then cut out the central core, making rings.

essentials
varieties available

Differing sizes from miniature to the size of a torpedo!

buy Pineapples are picked ripe, but colour does not indicate ripeness – some are green, some gold. They should smell sweet but feel firm. Avoid if soft, bruised, or withered.

store Eat soon after purchase, or prepare then store in an airtight container in the fridge for up to 3 days.

cook Prepare and use raw for fruit salads, cold desserts, and smoothies; grill, fry, or bake.

preserve Dry, candy as a sweetmeat, bottle in syrup.

recipe ideas

Fresh pineapple upside-down pudding p62

Jerk chicken with roasted pineapple p56

Pineapple and kirsch floating islands p62

Pineapple broth with halibut p24

pineapple trifle

Refreshing pineapple and spicy ginger are a winning combination, and as pineapple is in abundance in spring, make the most of it with this dessert.

15 MINS PLUS CHILLING

SPECIAL EQUIPMENT ■ electric hand whisk

SERVES 6

250g (9oz) ready-made ginger cake, sliced

100ml (3½fl oz) pineapple juice

250g (9oz) pineapple, finely chopped

300ml (10fl oz) double cream or whipping cream

2-3 tbsp syrup from a jar of stem ginger

2 balls stem ginger in syrup, finely chopped

1 Line the base of a serving bowl with the slices of ginger cake, then pour over the pineapple juice and scatter over the pineapple.

2 Put the cream and ginger syrup in a mixing bowl and whisk with an electric hand whisk until soft peaks form. Spoon the cream mixture over the pineapple, then scatter the chopped stem ginger over. Chill in the fridge for 30 minutes or more, and then serve.

variation

tropical trifle

Use cubed mango or chopped banana instead of the pineapple in step 1, or use a mixture of all three. To prepare the mango, cut it in half to remove the stone, slice the flesh into cubes with a sharp knife, then cut the cubes away from the mango skin.

oriental fruit salad

Although this dessert is quick and simple to prepare, the sharp sweetness of pineapple and kiwi mixed with mango create a stunning and complex explosion of flavours.

15 MINS

SERVES 4

1 mango, peeled and sliced

1 pineapple, peeled, core removed, sliced thinly, and cut into chunks

1 kiwi fruit, skinned and sliced

juice of 1 orange

juice of 1 lime

1 passion fruit, halved

small handful of mint leaves, finely chopped

1 Arrange the mango, pineapple, and kiwi fruit pieces in a shallow serving bowl or platter. Pour over the orange juice and lime juice.

2 Scoop out the flesh and seeds from the passion fruit and spoon over the fruit. Sprinkle with mint leaves and serve.

tropical angel cake

Pineapple and mango crown a deliciously tasty coconut cake.

🥣 15 MINS 🍲 30 MINS

SPECIAL EQUIPMENT ▪ electric hand whisk or mixer ▪ 1.2 x 1.5-litre (2 x 2¾-pints) savarin ring mould

SERVES 6-8

For the cake

4 large egg whites

½ tsp cream of tartar

150g (5½oz) caster sugar

50g (1¾oz) plain flour

10g (¼oz) cornflour

25g (scant 1oz) desiccated coconut

For the topping

200g (7oz) Greek-style yogurt

200g (7oz) mixed peeled and chopped tropical fruit, such as pineapple and mango

seeds and pulp from 2 passion fruits

lime zest, to decorate

1 Preheat the oven to 190°C (375°F/ Gas 5). Put the egg whites, cream of tartar, and 1 tbsp cold water in a large mixing bowl and whisk with an electric whisk or mixer until stiff peaks form. Whisk in 1 tbsp sugar at a time until the mix is stiff and shiny.

2 Sift in the flour and cornflour and gently fold them in together with the coconut until well combined. Carefully spoon the mixture into the ring mould and smooth the top, pressing down gently so there are no air pockets left. Bake in the oven for 15 minutes, then reduce the oven temperature to 180°C (350°F/Gas 4) and bake for a further 15 minutes until the cake is firm to the touch and golden brown.

3 Place the ring mould upside-down on a wire rack and leave until completely cold, then carefully ease the cake out of the mould with a round-bladed knife or small metal spatula and place on a serving plate.

4 To make the topping, beat the yogurt lightly so it is smooth and creamy, then spoon it into the centre of the cake. Top it with the tropical fruit, then drizzle the passion fruit seeds and pulp over the top. Finish by scattering over the lime zest.

rhubarb and ginger upside-down cake

Young rhubarb is cooked into a simple upside-down cake to give a modern twist on a classic dessert.

🥣 40 MINS 🍲 40-45 MINS

SPECIAL EQUIPMENT ▪ 23cm (9in) round springform cake tin ▪ electric hand whisk or mixer

SERVES 6-8

150g (5½oz) unsalted butter, softened

150g (5½oz) dark soft brown sugar

4 tbsp finely chopped, preserved stem ginger

500g (1lb 2oz) young, pink rhubarb, chopped into 2cm (¾in) lengths

3 large eggs

150g (5½oz) self-raising flour

2 tsp ground ginger

1 tsp baking powder

double cream, whipped, or crème fraîche, to serve (optional)

1 Preheat the oven to 180°C (350°F/ Gas 4). Melt a little butter and use to grease the tin with a brush. Line the base and sides of the cake tin with baking parchment.

2 Scatter a little of the sugar evenly over the base of the cake tin. Scatter half of the chopped stem ginger evenly over the sugar. Lay the rhubarb over the sugar and ginger so it is tightly packed and completely covers the base of the cake tin.

3 Place the butter and remaining sugar in a large mixing bowl and whisk with an electric hand whisk or mixer until pale and creamy. Beat in the eggs, one at a time, whisking as much air as possible into the mixture. Gently fold the remaining chopped stem ginger into the batter.

4 In a separate bowl, sift together the flour, ground ginger, and baking powder. Add the sifted ingredients to the bowl containing the cake batter. Gently fold in the dry ingredients, keeping volume in the batter as you do so. Spoon the cake batter into the cake tin, taking care not to disturb the arranged rhubarb, and spread it evenly with a palette knife.

5 Bake the cake in the centre of the oven for 45 minutes until springy to the touch. Remove from the oven and leave to cool for 20–30 minutes before carefully turning the cake out of the tin and onto a serving plate. Serve warm with whipped double cream or crème fraîche.

Season's best **rhubarb**

Rhubarb is technically a vegetable, but is treated like a fruit for the most part. Different varieties offer a range of sizes and colours, but all have a sharp, tangy flavour. Forced in winter to spring, then grown outdoors from late spring through summer, it is popular in pies, crumbles, for ice cream, fools, and mousses. It also makes a delicious sauce to serve with oily fish, particularly mackerel. Ideal flavour pairings include orange, cinnamon, ginger, lavender, and vanilla.

Grown from crowns, rhubarb is planted outdoors in temperate climates, producing thick green and red stalks, but is also forced indoors in the dark to produce tender, pink thinner sticks.

The green leaves are poisonous. Their only use is to boil them in aluminium pans to remove stains.

Forced rhubarb It has slim, pink stalks with a delicious acidic flavour that needs less sugar than outdoor varieties.

Adding a pinch of bicarbonate of soda during cooking reduces the amount of sugar needed to sweeten.

Outdoor rhubarb It has long stalks with a coarse texture. They are best puréed for sauces and desserts. Add a few drops of pink food colouring to the cooked pulp for a pleasing colour.

essentials
varieties available

Coarser red and green outdoor, and thinner, uniformly pink forced rhubarb.

buy Choose firm straight stems that snap easily. Avoid if the stems are very pliable.

store Wrap in moist kitchen paper and store in a plastic bag in the fridge for up to a week.

cook Stew, bake, or roast. Use in pies and jams, and in sauces to accompany oily fish or pork.

preserve Freeze; make into jams, chutneys, or relishes; make wine or cordial.

recipe ideas

Rhubarb and custard ice cream p67

Rhubarb and ginger upside-down cake p65

Rhubarb brûlée flan p67

rhubarb and orange yogurt fool

A quick dessert that takes very little work. You could try using strawberry yogurt instead of plain and, for a special occasion, use half whipped cream and half yogurt.

🥣 5 MINS PLUS CHILLING   🍲 10 MINS

SPECIAL EQUIPMENT ▪ blender or hand-held blender

SERVES 4

450g (1lb) rhubarb, trimmed and cut in short lengths

60g (2oz) caster sugar

grated zest and juice of 1 orange

250ml (9fl oz) Greek-style plain yogurt

4 tsp clear honey, to serve,

1 Put the rhubarb in a pan with the sugar and orange zest and juice. Cook gently, stirring until the juice runs, then cover and continue to simmer for about 10 minutes, stirring occasionally until pulpy.

2 Cool slightly, then purée in a blender (or use a hand-held blender in the pan). Set aside to cool. When completely cold, fold in the yogurt, taste, and add more sugar, if necessary. Spoon into glasses and chill until ready to serve. Drizzle each with a teaspoon of clear honey just before serving.

rhubarb brûlée flan

A delicious make-in-advance dessert. Use digestive biscuits if you prefer and add a couple of pieces of stem ginger in syrup, finely chopped, to the rhubarb pulp for added zest.

🥣 20 MINS PLUS CHILLING   🍲 8 MINS

SPECIAL EQUIPMENT ▪ 20cm (8in) loose-bottomed flan tin or flan dish ▪ electric hand whisk or mixer

SERVES 6

450g (1lb) rhubarb, chopped

85g (3oz) caster sugar

2 tsp powdered gelatine

115g (4oz) gingernuts, crushed

60g (2oz) butter, melted

300ml (10fl oz) double cream, whipped

3-4 tbsp demerara sugar

1 Put the rhubarb in a saucepan with 2 tbsp water and 60g (2oz) of the caster sugar. Bring to the boil, stir, cover, reduce the heat, and cook gently for 5 minutes. Remove the lid and boil rapidly for about 3 minutes, stirring occasionally, until the juice has evaporated and the rhubarb is pulpy.

2 Stir in the gelatine until dissolved and set aside to cool.

3 Mix the crushed biscuits with the melted butter and the remaining caster sugar. Press into the base and sides of a 20cm (8in) flan dish. Chill to firm.

4 When the rhubarb is cold but not set, fold in half the whipped cream and transfer to the flan case. Smooth the surface and chill until set.

5 Just before serving, preheat the grill. Spread the remaining whipped cream over the rhubarb. Sprinkle liberally with the demerara sugar and grill until the sugar melts and bubbles. Serve straight away. Alternatively, use a blow torch to caramelize the sugar.

rhubarb and custard ice cream

If you have an abundance of rhubarb, try this ice cream; it gives a new twist to the traditional rhubarb and custard.

🥣 30 MINS PLUS CHILLING AND FREEZING
🍲 20 MINS   ❄ FREEZABLE

SPECIAL EQUIPMENT ▪ blender or food processor ▪ electric hand whisk or balloon whisk

SERVES 4-6

450g (1lb) pink forced rhubarb, cut into chunks

400g (14oz) caster sugar

5 egg yolks

salt

450ml (15fl oz) milk

150ml (5fl oz) single cream

1 tsp pure vanilla extract

1 Gently stew the rhubarb with 60g (2oz) of the sugar and 2 tbsp water for 10 minutes, or until tender, in a covered pan, stirring occasionally. Purée in a blender or food processor. Leave to cool.

2 Put the egg yolks, the remaining sugar, and a little salt in a large heatproof bowl and whisk with an electric hand whisk or balloon whisk, until pale, thick, and creamy. Gently heat the milk and cream in a pan until hand hot and stir into the egg mix with the vanilla. Put the bowl over a pan of gently simmering water and stir until the custard just coats the back of a wooden spoon. Remove the bowl from the pan and leave to cool.

3 When the custard is completely cold, mix it with the rhubarb purée and freeze in an ice cream maker, following the manufacturer's directions. Alternatively, pour into a shallow, freezerproof container with a lid and freeze for about 2 hours until frozen around the edges. Beat well with a fork to break up the ice crystals, freeze for another 2 hours, beat again, then freeze until firm.

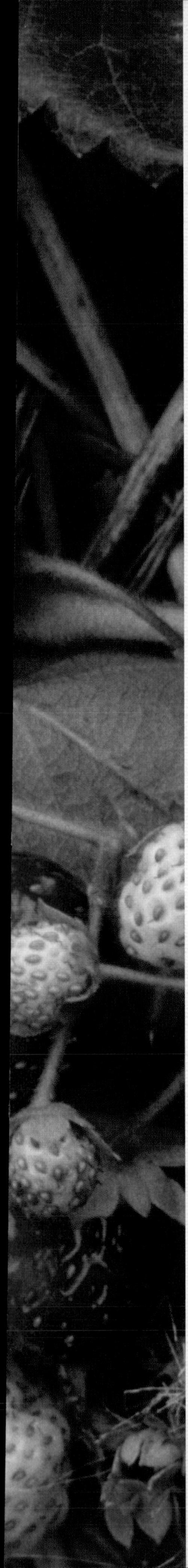

early summer

at their best

vegetables artichokes ▪ asparagus ▪ baby turnips ▪ broad beans ▪ courgettes ▪ cucumber ▪ fresh garlic ▪ lettuce ▪ mangetout ▪ morel mushrooms ▪ nettles ▪ new potatoes ▪ outdoor rhubarb ▪ peas ▪ pea shoots ▪ peppers ▪ radishes ▪ rocket ▪ salad onions ▪ samphire ▪ sorrel ▪ spinach ▪ spring onions ▪ St George's mushrooms ▪ Swiss chard ▪ watercress

fruit cherries ▪ gooseberries ▪ raspberries ▪ strawberries ▪ tayberries ▪ watermelon ▪ wild alpine strawberries

seafood brown shrimps ▪ brown trout (wild and farmed) ▪ common brown crab ▪ crayfish ▪ haddock ▪ herring ▪ king scallops ▪ langoustines ▪ plaice ▪ pollack ▪ rainbow trout (wild and farmed) ▪ red gurnard ▪ salmon (wild and farmed) ▪ sardines ▪ sea bass ▪ sea bream (wild and farmed) ▪ sea trout (wild and farmed) ▪ spider crab ▪ squid

meat, poultry, game spring lamb ▪ wood pigeon

also available

vegetables beetroot ▪ cabbages ▪ calabrese broccoli ▪ carrots ▪ cauliflower ▪ fennel ▪ marrows ▪ mushrooms (cultivated) ▪ okra ▪ onions ▪ potatoes (maincrop) ▪ tomatoes **fruit** avocados ▪ blueberries ▪ lemons ▪ limes ▪ mangoes ▪ melons **seafood** cod ▪ coley ▪ Dover sole ▪ grey mullet ▪ halibut ▪ John Dory ▪ monkfish ▪ mussels ▪ North Atlantic lobster ▪ Pacific or rock oysters ▪ turbot (farmed) ▪ whiting **meat, poultry, game** beef ▪ chicken ▪ duck (farmed) ▪ guinea fowl (farmed) ▪ pork ▪ quail (farmed) ▪ rabbit (farmed) ▪ turkey ▪ veal ▪ venison (farmed) ▪ wild boar (farmed)

early summer recipe chooser

ⓥ suitable for vegetarians

Asparagus frittata on crostini p81

Sliced beef and rocket salad with green olive and raisin salsa p72

Grated courgette and goat's cheese omelette p101

Vegetables

Artichokes
Artichokes, butter beans, and peas p112 ⓥ
Grilled sea bass with roast artichokes and fennel p92
Herb and garlic artichokes p76 ⓥ
Lamb with artichokes, broad beans, and dill p113
Lentils with artichokes and peppers p99
Pepper and artichoke salad p91 ⓥ

Asparagus
Asparagus and herb tart p92 ⓥ
Asparagus and taleggio risotto p92 ⓥ
Asparagus, broccoli, ginger, and mint stir-fry p95 ⓥ
Asparagus frittata on crostini p81 ⓥ
Asparagus in oil p135 ⓥ
Asparagus with lemony dressing p73 ⓥ
Chargrilled asparagus and pancetta p86
Chargrilled asparagus with Gorgonzola cheese p73 ⓥ
Cream of asparagus soup p82 ⓥ
Fresh pea and mint dip with seasonal crudités p84 ⓥ
Pancakes with asparagus, feta cheese, and dill p80 ⓥ
Penne pasta with asparagus and courgettes p112 ⓥ
Risotto primavera p105 ⓥ
Warm pea pancakes with chargrilled asparagus p111 ⓥ
White asparagus with herby mayonnaise p88 ⓥ

Beetroot
Grilled sea bass with roasted baby beetroot and dill p92

Broad beans
Baby broad bean, bacon, and goat's cheese omelette p101
Baby broad bean soup p84 ⓥ
Broad bean and feta panzanella p116 ⓥ
Chicken and chorizo paella p100
Chicken with broad beans p100
Dill and broad bean dip p84 ⓥ
Ham with minted peas and broad beans p116
Hot and spicy lamb with broad beans p96
Lamb with artichokes, broad beans, and dill p113
Lentil, broad bean, and feta salad p114 ⓥ
Niçoise-style salad p81

Pea shoot, ham, broad bean, and Cheddar cheese salad p117
Pork steaks with tomato and broad bean sauce p101
Risotto primavera p105 ⓥ
Sausages with broad beans p100

Broccoli
Asparagus, broccoli, ginger, and mint stir-fry p95 ⓥ
Courgette, herb, and lemon tagine p110 ⓥ

Cabbage
Ham, cabbage, and potato soup p77

Carrot
Curried vegetable pies p83 ⓥ
Fresh pea and mint dip with seasonal crudités p84 ⓥ
Mediterranean vegetable pies p83 ⓥ
Spaghetti primavera p104 ⓥ

Courgette
Cashew and courgette rice p117 ⓥ
Cheddar and courgette soufflés p87 ⓥ
Courgette and pea mini tortillas p86 ⓥ
Courgette cake p130 ⓥ
Courgette fritters with dill tzatziki p87 ⓥ
Courgette, herb, and lemon tagine p111 ⓥ
Courgettes stuffed with preserved lemon, raisins, and spring onion p89 ⓥ
Courgettes stuffed with sultanas, red onion, and pine nuts p89 ⓥ
Curried vegetable pies p83 ⓥ
Grated courgette and goat's cheese omelette p101 ⓥ
Griddled courgettes in oil p135 ⓥ
Mediterranean vegetable pies p83 ⓥ
Penne pasta with asparagus and courgettes p112 ⓥ
Risotto primavera p105 ⓥ
Spaghetti primavera p104 ⓥ

Cucumber
Baked salmon with salsa verde and cucumber p90
Creamy cucumber and spring onion dip p80 ⓥ
Crudités with tapenade p80
Mini chicken tortillas topped with yogurt, cucumber, and mint dip p82
Mini pea tortillas with yogurt, cucumber, and mint dip p82 ⓥ
Raita p117 ⓥ
Salmon salad with mint yogurt dressing p107

Fennel
Grilled sea bass with roast artichokes and fennel p92
Lamb chops in paper with fennel p110

Fresh garlic
Simple garlic confit p135 ⓥ

Lettuce
Caesar salad with poached eggs p97
Chicken caesar salad p97
Lettuce soup with peas p76 ⓥ
Niçoise-style salad p81
Pepper and artichoke salad p91 ⓥ
Potage Saint Germain p82 ⓥ

Mangetout
Asian noodle salad p106
Courgette and pea mini tortillas p86 ⓥ
Fresh pea and mint dip with seasonal crudités p84 ⓥ
Teriyaki chicken with noodles p94

New potatoes
Chicken and pea filo pie p106
Devilled lamb cutlets with crushed potato and mustard seed salad p104
German potato salad p114
Papas arrugadas p115 ⓥ
Roasted new potatoes and sardines p113
Roasted new potatoes and sausages with rosemary and chilli p113
Salmon with new potatoes, flageolet beans, and parsley sauce p96
Stuffed sardines with crushed new potatoes p108

Peas and pea shoots
Artichokes, butter beans, and peas p112 ⓥ
Chicken and pea filo pie p106
Courgette and pea mini tortillas p86 ⓥ
Dressed pea salad p115 ⓥ
Feta and pea salad with watercress mayonnaise p115 ⓥ
Fresh pea and mint dip with seasonal crudités p84 ⓥ
Ham with minted peas and broad beans p116
Lettuce soup with peas p76 ⓥ

Mini pea tortillas with yogurt, cucumber, and mint dip p82 ⓥ
Pasta with pecorino and peas p91 ⓥ
Pea, ham, and potato soup p77
Pea shoot, ham, broad bean, and Cheddar cheese salad p117
Potage Saint Germain p82 ⓥ
Spaghetti primavera p104 ⓥ
Warm pea pancakes with chargrilled asparagus p111 ⓥ

Peppers
Asparagus, broccoli, ginger, and mint stir-fry p95 ⓥ
Chicken and chorizo paella p100
Chicken fajitas with tomato and avocado salsa p99
Crab, radish, and pepper salad p73
Crudités with tapenade p80
Lamb with chickpeas, green peppers, and couscous p111
Lentils with artichokes and peppers p99
Pancakes with peppers and basil p88 ⓥ
Papas arrugadas p115 ⓥ
Pepper and artichoke salad p91 ⓥ
Quesadilla with peppers, green olives, and feta cheese p94 ⓥ
Smoked salmon with radishes and spiced yogurt dressing p73
Veal escalopes with peppers p98

Potato
Curried vegetable pies p83 ⓥ
Ham, cabbage, and potato soup p77
Mediterranean vegetable pies p83 ⓥ
Pea, ham, and potato soup p77

Radish
Crab, radish, and pepper salad p73
Crudités with tapenade p80
Fresh pea and mint dip with seasonal crudités p84 ⓥ
Smoked salmon with radishes and spiced yogurt dressing p73

Rocket
Broad bean and feta panzanella p116 ⓥ
Pasta with pancetta and rocket p90
Quesadilla with Cheddar cheese, rocket, and semi-dried tomatoes p94 ⓥ

Hazelnut torte with berries p122

Cherry jam p132

Stuffed sardines with crushed new potatoes p108

scallops with lemon-herb potatoes

Scallops need to be cooked carefully. If overcooked, they will be dry and rubbery, rather than juicy and silky in texture.

🥣 45-50 MINS   🍲 20 MINS

SPECIAL EQUIPMENT ▪ blender or food processor

SERVES 6

500g (1lb 2oz) potatoes, peeled and cut into pieces

85g (3oz) butter

4-6 sprigs of parsley, leaves removed

4-6 sprigs of tarragon, leaves removed

grated zest and juice of 1 lemon

salt and freshly ground black pepper

75ml (2½fl oz) milk, plus more if needed

30g (1oz) plain flour

500g (1lb 2oz) large scallops (with or without coral, depending on preference), cleaned

2 tbsp olive oil

lemon wedges and rocket leaves

1 Put the potatoes in a saucepan of cold water, cover, and bring to the boil. Simmer for 15–20 minutes, until tender. Meanwhile, put 60g (2oz) of the butter, herb leaves, and lemon zest in a blender or food processor. Blitz to chop the herbs. Drain the potatoes and mash in the pan. Beat in the herb purée until smooth. Season, cover with the milk, and keep warm.

2 Put the flour on a plate and season. Roll the scallops in the flour and pat off the excess. Heat the remaining butter and oil in a frying pan. Sauté the scallops for 2–3 minutes, turning once, until just crisp and brown.

3 Stir the milk into the potatoes, adding 2–3 tsp more if needed. Remove the scallops from the pan and add the lemon juice to taste. Arrange the mashed potatoes and scallops on warmed plates and spoon over the pan juices. Serve with the lemon wedges and rocket leaves.

variation

scallops poached in cider

Put 2 diced shallots and the juice of 2 lemons in a saucepan with 120ml (4fl oz) each cider and white wine and 250ml (9fl oz) water. Add the scallops, heat to simmering, and poach for 30 seconds. Remove from the heat. Reduce the scallop liquid to 250ml (9fl oz) and whisk in 2 tbsp plain flour, then 2 egg yolks beaten with 120ml (4fl oz) double cream. Serve with the lemon-herb potatoes.

sliced beef and rocket salad with green olive and raisin salsa

Rocket leaves start coming into their own in early summer. Their sharp, peppery taste and pretty leaves make them the ideal base for many a fresh salad in the coming months.

🥣 15 MINS

SERVES 4

16–20 green olives, pitted and sliced

large handful of plump raisins

4 tsp capers, rinsed and gently squeezed dry

drizzle of olive oil

handful of flat-leaf parsley, finely chopped

salt and freshly ground black pepper

handful of rocket leaves

350g (12oz) sliced pastrami or other sliced cooked beef

1 For the salsa, mix together the olives, raisins, capers, oil, and parsley in a bowl. Taste and season with a pinch of salt and some black pepper.

2 Arrange the rocket and pastrami or other sliced beef in a shallow serving bowl. Spoon the salsa over and serve at room temperature.

variation

salami and rocket salad with black olives and semi-dried tomato salsa

Prepare the salsa by mixing together 8–10 pitted, sliced black olives, 6 chopped sun-dried tomatoes, 2 tbsp chopped gherkins, a drizzle of olive oil, a small handful of chopped fresh thyme, and a little seasoning. Arrange 24 thin slices of salami on 4 serving plates with a handful of rocket. Spoon the salsa over and serve.

asparagus with lemony dressing

Asparagus needs very little to accompany it as the spears are so particularly flavourful. For a starter like this, some sharp lemon brings out the best of this popular summer vegetable.

🥄 **5 MINS**   🍲 **6 MINS**

SERVES 4

6 tbsp olive oil

2-3 tbsp lemon juice

pinch of caster sugar

1 tsp mayonnaise

salt and freshly ground black pepper

350g (12oz) asparagus spears, trimmed

handful of rocket leaves

1 To make the dressing, put the oil and lemon juice in a small bowl and whisk until combined. Add the sugar and mayonnaise and whisk well. Season with salt and pepper.

2 Cook the asparagus spears in boiling salted water for 2–4 minutes, or until soft. To serve, sit the asparagus on the rocket leaves and dress liberally with the dressing.

variation

chargrilled asparagus with gorgonzola cheese
Cook the asparagus as in step 2, drain, and transfer to a barbecue or griddle pan. Cook over a medium heat for about 5 minutes, brushing the spears with extra virgin olive oil and turning them as they char. Serve hot with 150g (5½oz) Gorgonzola cheese crumbled over, a drizzle of extra virgin olive oil, and a good grinding of black pepper.

smoked salmon with radishes and spiced yogurt dressing

Peppery radishes are a brilliant match with the rich flavour of smoked salmon in this fabulously colourful summer dish.

🥄 **15 MINS**

SERVES 4

3 tomatoes, skinned, deseeded, (p197) and diced

1 tbsp capers, rinsed, gently squeezed dry, and chopped

handful of radishes, diced

1 orange pepper, deseeded and diced

4 spring onions, trimmed and finely chopped

1 red chilli, deseeded and finely chopped

juice of 1 large orange

juice of 1 lime

salt and freshly ground black pepper

250g (9oz) smoked salmon, chopped into bite-sized pieces

For the spiced yogurt dressing

4–6 tbsp Greek-style yogurt

juice of 1 lemon

pinch of five-spice powder

1 In a bowl, mix together the tomatoes, capers, radishes, pepper, spring onions, and chilli. Add the orange and lime juice, and season with salt and pepper. Toss together and leave to stand for about 10 minutes, to allow the flavours to develop.

2 To make the spiced yogurt dressing, mix together the yogurt, lemon juice, and five-spice powder in a small bowl. Season to taste.

3 When ready to serve, add the smoked salmon pieces to the salad mixture and combine well. Serve with the yogurt dip on the side.

variation

crab, radish, and pepper salad
For a less rich version of this dish, use 250g (9oz) white cooked crab meat instead of the smoked salmon.

battered haddock with lemon mayonnaise

The secret behind a successful mayonnaise is having all your ingredients at room temperature and adding the oil as slowly as you possibly can to prevent the sauce from curdling.

🍲 20 MINS 🍳 10 MINS

SPECIAL EQUIPMENT ▪ blender or food processor

SERVES 4

1 egg, plus 1 egg yolk

grated zest and juice of 1 lemon

250ml (9fl oz) olive oil

salt and freshly ground black pepper

125g (4½oz) plain flour

1 tsp bicarbonate of soda

1 tsp paprika

150ml (5fl oz) cold fizzy water

250ml (9fl oz) olive oil, for frying

300g (10oz) haddock fillets, skinned (p75) and cut into 1cm (½in) strips

1 To make the mayonnaise, put the egg, egg yolk, lemon zest and juice in a blender or food processor and blitz for 1–2 minutes, or until a light yellow colour. Reduce the speed and slowly add the oil, a little at a time, until you have a smooth, creamy emulsion. Season with salt and pepper, transfer to a serving dish, and place in the fridge to chill.

2 For the batter, put the flour, bicarbonate of soda, paprika, and fizzy water in a mixing bowl, season with salt and pepper, then whisk until smooth. Put the oil in a deep frying pan and set over a high heat until it reaches 200°C (400°F). To test the heat, pop a cube of bread in the fat. If it sizzles it is ready.

3 Put the fish in the batter one piece at a time and coat. Carefully place in the hot oil. Cook, turning occasionally, for 2–3 minutes, or until the fish pieces are golden. Make sure they don't stick together. Remove with a slotted spoon and place on sheets of kitchen paper to drain. Sprinkle with a little salt and serve hot with the lemon mayonnaise.

variation

haddock in beer batter
Use beer instead of fizzy water in the batter. It will give a rich, dark batter.

skewered lemon and herb haddock

This is a lovely barbecue dish. The freshest haddock will be firm and thread onto skewers easily.

🍲 10 MINS PLUS MARINATING 🍳 4–6 MINS

SPECIAL EQUIPMENT ▪ 12 bamboo or wooden skewers

SERVES 4

500g (1lb 2oz) thick haddock fillets, skinned (p75) and cut into chunks

1 garlic clove, crushed or finely chopped

1 tbsp fresh root ginger, peeled and finely chopped

1 small red chilli, deseeded and finely chopped

1 tsp finely chopped rosemary, plus extra to garnish

4 sprigs of thyme, leaves picked and finely chopped, plus extra to garnish

grated zest and juice of 1 lemon

4 tbsp olive oil

salt and freshly ground black pepper

2 large mangoes, cut in half to remove the stone, and the flesh sliced lengthways and then cut away from the skin

juice of 1 lime

1 Soak 12 bamboo or wooden skewers in cold water for 30 minutes. Put the haddock, garlic, ginger, chilli, rosemary, thyme, lemon zest and juice, and oil in a bowl. Season with salt and pepper, and leave to marinate in the fridge for 20–30 minutes.

2 Put the mango slices in a bowl, add the lime juice, and season with salt and pepper. Stir gently to mix well, and set aside.

3 Heat a grill or barbecue until medium-hot, and brush the grill with oil. Thread the fish onto the skewers. Grill for 2–3 minutes on each side, brushing lightly with the marinade, until the fish is golden and cooked through. Serve the skewers with the mango piled on top, and a scattering of rosemary and thyme.

crab bisque

This creamy soup makes the most of seasonal crab with the addition of some crab butter for extra flavour when serving.

🍲 30 MINS 🍳 50–55 MINS

SPECIAL EQUIPMENT ▪ blender or food processor

SERVES 4–6

1 large fresh cooked crab

1 litre (1¾ pints) fish or chicken stock

75g (2½oz) butter, softened

1 tbsp chopped flat-leaf parsley

bunch of spring onions, trimmed and chopped

5 tbsp dry vermouth

2 tbsp brandy

3 tbsp plain flour

5 tbsp milk

150ml (5fl oz) single cream

salt and freshly ground black pepper

1 Remove all the meat from the crab; keep the dark and light meat separate. Put the crab shell in a pan with the stock and half the dark crab meat. Bring to the boil, reduce the heat, cover, and simmer gently for 45 minutes. Strain, and reserve the stock.

2 Make the crab butter by mashing the remaining dark meat with 45g (1½ oz) of the butter and the parsley. Spoon the butter onto a piece of greaseproof paper, then roll into a log shape. Twist the edges of the paper, and put the roll in the fridge.

3 Fry the spring onions gently in the remaining butter until soft. Add the vermouth and simmer for 5 minutes. Flame the brandy and stir in. Mix the flour with the milk and stir in. Add half the strained stock, bring to the boil, and cook for 2 minutes, stirring. Tip into a blender or food processor and purée with the white crab meat. Return to the pan, stir in the remaining stock and the cream. Season to taste with salt and pepper and heat through. Ladle into warm bowls and top each with a slice of the crab butter. Serve immediately.

Season's best **haddock**

Haddock is found on both sides of the North Atlantic and has a brownish-grey, flecked body. In season from early summer through to winter, it is smaller and sweeter than cod, with delicious, chunky flesh. Cheese and bacon go particularly well with it, as do tomatoes, garlic, white wine, and cider. Smoked haddock is an extremely popular delicacy.

Haddock It has a black lateral line on a grey back and a silver flank. Traditionally used for fish and chips, and preferred in this dish in Scotland, but also commonly used poached, for fish pie. It has a delicate, creamy, and sweet flavour.

The black spot on its shoulder is known as St Peter's mark or thumbprint.

The thick, scaly skin is easy to remove, but can be left on if poaching and removed afterwards.

Haddock fillet Its meaty texture and good, thick flakes make haddock a favourite for frying, grilling, and baking. The fillets are also popular smoked, both dyed and undyed.

Quality haddock will have milky-white flesh.

essentials
cuts available

Loins or fillets, also hot smoked (Arborath smokies) or cold smoked (undyed and dyed fillet and whole Finnan haddock).

buy Firm, moist flesh, must smell pleasantly fishy.

store Best eaten on the day of purchase, or keep wrapped, in the coldest part of the fridge, for up to 24 hours.

cook Fry, grill, bake, steam, poach.

recipe ideas

Baked haddock in white wine with parsley p107

Battered haddock with lemon mayonnaise p74

Portuguese haddock soup p363

Skewered lemon and herb haddock p74

Spiced haddock with coconut, chilli, and lime p176

how to skin a fillet

When skinning, keep the knife in contact with the board, or you will leave too much flesh behind. Dip your fingers in salt for a better grip on the slippery skin.

1 With a flexible boning knife, make a cut between the skin and the flesh at the tail end (the thinnest part), keeping the knife close to the skin.

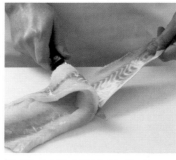

2 With your free hand, grip the flap of skin. Keeping it taut, and the knife at a 30° angle, saw and push along the fillet, separating flesh from skin.

lettuce soup with peas

For the best flavour choose very fresh, crisp lettuces for this refreshing chilled soup. The ginger adds a surprising zing to what might otherwise look like straightforward fare.

🥣 20 MINS PLUS CHILLING

SPECIAL EQUIPMENT ▪ blender or food processor

SERVES 4

125g (4½oz) peas (shelled weight)

1 small garlic clove

sea salt and freshly ground black pepper

2 round lettuces, torn into pieces and solid cores discarded

250ml (9fl oz) natural yogurt

2cm (¾in) piece fresh root ginger, peeled and finely grated

handful of mint leaves

juice of ½ lemon

1 Bring a small amount of water to the boil in a pan, add the peas, and cook for 1 minute. Drain (reserving the cooking water), cool under cold running water, and chill in the fridge.

2 Halve the garlic clove and crush the halves with a pinch of coarse salt. Combine the garlic with all the other ingredients (except the peas) in a blender or food processor, adding just enough of the reserved cooking water to get the blades moving or until the desired consistency is achieved – it is best if you can get it fairly smooth, with a bit of texture.

3 Transfer the soup to a large bowl and chill for 30 minutes. When ready to serve, stir through the cooked peas, leaving a few to garnish.

herb and garlic artichokes

Young globe artichokes with tender stalks are best for this delicious appetizer. Serve warm or at room temperature.

🥣 25–30 MINS 🍲 25–40 MINS

SERVES 6

6 young globe artichokes, stalks trimmed to 4cm (1½in)

2 lemons, halved, plus 1 to garnish

6 garlic cloves, finely chopped

small bunch of flat-leaf parsley, leaves finely chopped

8–10 sprigs of mint, leaves finely chopped, plus more to garnish

salt and freshly ground black pepper

120ml (4fl oz) olive oil

1 Snap the large bottom leaves off the artichokes. Continue to remove the leaves, tearing off about three-quarters of each one so the edible white part remains attached to the heart. Continue until you reach the cone of soft, small leaves in the centre. Trim the cone with a sharp knife and rub the cut edges of the artichoke with a lemon half to prevent discolouration.

2 Peel the stalks, cutting away the tough, fibrous exterior. Trim the green parts of the base to remove any tough, fibrous leaves. Scoop out the hairy choke with a teaspoon and squeeze lemon juice into the hollowed-out centre. Rub the juice around the inside with your finger.

3 Combine the garlic, herbs, and a little salt in a bowl. Put 2–3 spoonfuls in the centre of each artichoke and press it down well against the bottom and sides so they are as full as possible. Keep back 2–3 tbsp to sprinkle on top.

4 Set the artichokes, tops down and stalks up, in a single, tight layer in a large pan. Sprinkle the remaining stuffing over and pour on the oil. Sprinkle with salt and pepper and add enough water to come halfway up the sides, not including the stalks. Bring to the boil, cover, and simmer for 25–45 minutes, until tender. Add more water if necessary, so the artichokes are always half covered. To test if they are cooked, pierce them with the point of a knife; they should be tender.

5 Transfer the artichokes to a large, warmed serving dish with a slotted spoon, arranging them in a single layer, still with their stalks upwards. Take as little as possible of the cooking liquid and then boil it until it is reduced to about 250ml (9fl oz).

6 Squeeze the juice from a lemon half, discard seeds, and add to the cooking liquid. Taste for seasoning. Pour the cooking liquid over the artichokes and leave to cool to room temperature. Serve decorated with lemon wedges and mint sprigs.

grilled sardines on toast

To fillet a sardine, cut off its head, slice along its belly with a knife, and gently flatten it out. Run your fingers along the backbone and then gently lift out the bones.

🥣 10 MINS PLUS MARINATING 🍲 6 MINS

SERVES 4

8 sardines, cleaned, gutted, and filleted

4 tbsp olive oil

3 garlic cloves, finely sliced

1 green chilli, deseeded and finely chopped

juice of 1 lemon

1 tsp fennel seeds, crushed

2 tbsp flat-leaf parsley, finely chopped

salt and freshly ground black pepper

ciabatta, sliced and toasted, to serve

1 Brush the sardines with a little of the oil and cook under a medium grill for 3 minutes on each side. Remove and allow to cool.

2 Meanwhile, put all the remaining ingredients (except for the ciabatta) in a mixing bowl and combine well. Add the sardines, then leave to marinate for 20 minutes, if you have time. Serve on the warm toasted ciabatta.

pea, ham, and potato soup

A firm and traditional favourite with everyone, this soup tastes even better if prepared in advance and reheated to serve the next day. Go easy on the salt when adding seasoning as the ham may be salty enough for most people's taste.

🥣 15 MINS   🍲 2 HRS   ❄ FREEZABLE

SPECIAL EQUIPMENT ▪ hand-held blender

SERVES 4-6

1.1kg (2½lb) unsmoked ham

1 bay leaf

1 tbsp olive oil

1 onion, finely chopped

salt and freshly ground black pepper

1 tbsp Dijon mustard

3 garlic cloves, finely chopped

2 sprigs of rosemary

handful of thyme, leaves only

1.2 litres (2 pints) hot vegetable or chicken stock

450g (1lb) peas (shelled weight)

3 potatoes, peeled and chopped into bite-sized pieces

1 Put the ham and bay leaf in a large pan, cover with 1.2 litres (2 pints) of water, and bring to the boil. Partially cover, reduce the heat, and simmer for about 1 hour, or until the ham is cooked. Skim away any scum that comes to the surface. Discard the ham stock, or strain and reserve a little to add to the soup. Set the ham aside until cool enough to handle.

2 Heat the oil in a large heavy-based pan over a medium heat, add the onion, and cook for 3–4 minutes until the onions are soft. Season with salt and pepper, then stir in the mustard, garlic, and herbs (reserve some thyme leaves for garnish). Add a little stock and bring to the boil, then tip in the peas and remaining stock. Bring to the boil, reduce to a simmer, and cook for 45 minutes, topping up with hot water as needed.

3 About 20 minutes before the end of the cooking time, bring a separate pan of water to the boil. Add the potatoes, bring back up to the boil, and then simmer for 12–15 minutes until soft. Drain and set aside. Remove the rosemary from the soup, then use a hand-held blender to gently purée the peas. Return them to the pan and stir in the potatoes.

4 Remove any fat from the ham, chop into bite-sized pieces, and stir into the soup. Taste and season as needed. Garnish with the reserved thyme leaves and serve with wholemeal bread.

variation

ham, cabbage, and potato soup
Prepare in exactly the same way but use ½ pointed cabbage, shredded, instead of the peas. Cook the potatoes in the soup for the last 20 minutes and do not purée any of it.

Season's best **lettuce**

A delicate vegetable with crunchy leaves, crisp texture, and mild flavour, lettuce is an ideal choice for salads, wraps, and sandwiches. It is a good source of vitamins A and C. Lettuce is available in different shapes, sizes, textures, and colours, in tight heads or with looser leaves. Essentially summer crops, some are grown all year. Ideal flavour pairings include specialty oils and vinegars, with fresh torn herbs and other salad vegetables.

An annual or biennial herbaceous plant, cultivated for centuries and grown in moderate climates worldwide, lettuce thrives in moist, mild weather.

Don't discard the flavoursome outer leaves. Tear them into bite-sized pieces and mix with the heart.

Oakleaf An attractive loose-leaf lettuce with a well-rounded sweet, earthy flavour, this variety has thin, soft leaves and crunchy stalks.

The tender, flavourful leaves are often used in a typical mesclun mix of young leaves and shoots.

Butterhead (Round) Probably the most popular of all lettuce types, butterheads have thick, soft, tender leaves with a mild, sweet flavour.

Cut away the thick stalks from outer leaves as they can be bitter and slightly fibrous.

Cos (Romaine) One of the best tasting varieties of all, Cos is valued for its crunch and full-bodied flavour. The succulent leaves are ideal for burgers, salads, sandwiches, and wraps.

Batavia Bred for continual picking of young leaves, this loose-leaf Mediterranean variety does not form a heart. The attractive, bronze-tinged leaves are tasty and crisp.

Tear the leaves into pieces rather than slicing them, as a knife blade can cause bruising.

Iceberg (Crisphead) Low in flavour but high in crunch, iceberg is the lettuce for sandwiches and burgers. The capacious leaves can also be stuffed with meat or fish, rolled up, and then steamed.

Lollo rosso A mildly flavoured, slightly coarse-textured lettuce, admired for its striking leaves. A few added to a mixed-leaf salad add contrasting texture and colour.

The frilly leaves can harbour dust and soil, so they need careful washing and drying.

Curly leaf lettuce Also known as Green Salad Bowl lettuce, this soft, loose-leaf variety originated in America. It works well in a mixed-leaf salad.

essentials
varieties available

Many types with crisp, firm heads, or soft, looser leaves.

buy Choose fresh-looking leaves with a firm heart, if a tight-headed variety. Avoid if shrivelled, wilted, or discoloured.

store Wrap in moist kitchen paper and keep in a plastic bag in the vegetable box of the fridge for up to 5 days. Ready-prepared leaves should be eaten quickly.

cook Eat raw or braise, steam, or shred and cook. Use in summer soups.

preserve Make into soup, then freeze.

recipe ideas

Chicken Caesar salad p97

Lettuce soup with peas p76

Niçoise-style salad p81

Potage Saint Germain p82

pancakes with asparagus, feta cheese, and dill

A pancake is the most versatile of cases for fillings of all descriptions. Here they are folded around feta cheese and dill, adding salty and sweet flavours to in-season asparagus.

🥣 5 MINS PLUS STANDING   🍲 15 MINS

MAKES 8

125g (4½oz) plain flour

salt and freshly ground black pepper

1 egg

300ml (10fl oz) milk

8–12 fine asparagus spears, trimmed and cut into 3 pieces

handful of dill, finely chopped

250g (9oz) feta cheese, crumbled

drizzle of olive oil, for frying

1 Put the flour in a mixing bowl with a pinch of salt, stir, then make a well in the centre. Crack the egg into the well and add a tiny amount of the milk. Using a wooden spoon, stir the egg and milk, letting the flour gradually tumble in. Add the rest of the milk, little by little, stirring continuously, until all the flour has been incorporated and the mixture is lump-free. Put it in the fridge to stand for 30 minutes, if you have time.

2 Cook the asparagus in boiling salted water for 2–4 minutes, or until soft. Drain, refresh in cold water, and drain again. Transfer to a bowl and mix with the dill, feta cheese, and some black pepper.

3 In a small, flat frying pan or pancake pan, heat a drizzle of olive oil over a high heat, swirling it around the pan, then tipping it out again. Stir the batter mix, then spoon 2 tbsp of it into the pan, swirling it around so it reaches the edges. Cook for a couple of minutes, until a light golden colour, then pull up the edges with a palette knife. Turn the pancake over and cook the other side for 1 minute. Slide it out onto a plate. Repeat witht he remaining batter.

4 Spoon the filling onto the pancakes and either roll or fold them up.

crudités with tapenade

Keep the tapenade for up to 1 week in the fridge by topping it with a thin layer of olive oil and covering.

🥣 30–35 MINS   🍲 10–15 MINS

SPECIAL EQUIPMENT ▪ blender or food processor

SERVES 6–8

6 slices of white bread, crusts cut off

4 garlic cloves, peeled

200g (7oz) pitted black olives

30g (1oz) capers, drained

6 canned anchovy fillets

120ml (4fl oz) olive oil

lemon juice, to taste

freshly ground black pepper

1 baguette, cut into 5mm (¼in) diagonal slices

For the crudités

bunch of spring onions, trimmed and cut into 5cm (2in) pieces

1 cucumber, peeled, quartered, deseeded, and cut into strips

1 red pepper, deseeded and cut into strips

1 green pepper, deseeded and cut into strips

bunch of radishes, trimmed

250g (9oz) cherry tomatoes

1 Tear the bread into pieces and cover with cold water in a bowl. Soak for 5 minutes, squeeze dry, and put into a blender or food processor.

2 Add the garlic, olives, capers, and anchovies and blitz coarsely. With the blades turning, gradually add the oil. Add lemon juice and black pepper to taste and blitz again. It can be a coarse or fairly smooth paste. Transfer to a bowl, cover, and set aside.

3 Preheat the oven to 190°C (375°F/ Gas 5). Bake the baguette on a baking sheet for 10–15 minutes, until crisp. Serve the tapenade with the crudités and toasted bread.

variation

creamy cucumber and spring onion dip

Beat 150ml (5fl oz) thick natural yogurt with 115g (4oz) cream cheese. Stir in 2 finely chopped spring onions and ¼ cucumber, peeled and finely chopped. Add a few drops of Tabasco and season to taste. Serve with the crudités.

asparagus frittata on crostini

Two Italian mainstays – crunchy crostini and the frittata – are combined for a lunchtime snack or evening appetizer. Fine asparagus would be best to ensure they cook successfully.

🥄 **20 MINS**   🍲 **20 MINS**

SERVES 4

4 tbsp olive oil

4 thick slices crusty sourdough bread

salt and freshly ground black pepper

1 garlic clove, peeled but left whole

8 asparagus spears, trimmed

2 tbsp finely chopped onion

4 eggs

120ml (4fl oz) double cream

60g (2oz) Parmesan cheese, grated

handful of flat-leaf parsley, to garnish

1 Preheat the oven to 200°C (400°F/Gas 6). Pour 2 tbsp of the oil onto a baking tray, then gently press the bread into the oil on both sides. Season with salt and pepper. Bake in the oven for 12–15 minutes until golden brown. Remove from the oven and lightly rub each slice of bread with the garlic. Set aside on a wire rack to keep the crostini crisp.

2 Meanwhile, cook the asparagus spears in boiling salted water for 2–4 minutes, or until soft. Drain, refresh in cold water, and drain again. Place on a board and cut each spear in half. Heat the remaining oil in a heavy-based frying pan over a medium heat, add the onion, and cook for 3–4 minutes until the onion is soft and translucent. Add the halved asparagus spears and cook for a further 2 minutes. Preheat the grill to its highest setting.

3 In a bowl, whisk together the eggs, cream, and Parmesan cheese. Season with salt and pepper, and pour the mixture over the asparagus and onion mixture in the pan. As the bottom is cooking, tilt the pan so the uncooked egg mixture from the top runs under the frittata. Continue cooking for 3–5 minutes until almost set.

4 To finish off, place the pan under the grill and cook until the top of the frittata is golden brown. To serve, tear the frittata into 4 rough pieces and sit on top of the crostini. Cut each piece in half, scatter with parsley, and serve immediately.

niçoise-style salad

This dish is an international classic. In its heyday, it included raw red peppers and shallots with artichoke hearts instead of potatoes. Try these seasonal ingredients for variety.

🥄 **15 MINS**

SERVES 4

400g can tuna in olive oil, drained

10 cherry tomatoes, halved

handful of flat-leaf parsley, finely chopped

bunch of chives, finely snipped

salt and freshly ground black pepper

125g (4½oz) broad beans (shelled weight), skinned (p85, optional)

12 black olives, pitted

12 salted anchovies

1 crisp lettuce such as cos, leaves separated

2-3 spring onions, trimmed and finely sliced

For the dressing

6 tbsp extra virgin olive oil

2 tbsp white wine vinegar

2 garlic cloves, grated or finely chopped

1-2 tsp Dijon mustard

salt and freshly ground black pepper

1 To make the dressing, put all the dressing ingredients in a screw-top jar, season well with salt and pepper, cover with the lid, and shake to combine.

2 Put the tuna and tomatoes in a bowl and drizzle over half of the dressing. Sprinkle in half of the fresh herbs and season generously with salt and pepper. Toss together. Add the broad beans, olives, and anchovies and mix gently.

3 Line a shallow serving bowl with the lettuce leaves and arrange the tuna mixture on top. Drizzle with the remaining dressing and sprinkle over the remaining herbs. Top with the spring onions and serve.

cream of asparagus soup

If you are a fan of puréed soups, blitz the mixture in a blender at the end of cooking, then pass it through a sieve and reheat.

🥣 10 MINS   🍲 40 MINS   ❄ FREEZABLE

SERVES 4

salt and freshly ground black pepper

60g (2oz) butter

500g (1lb 2oz) asparagus spears, trimmed, peeled (reserve the trimmings), and cut into 2.5cm (1in) lengths

300ml (10fl oz) milk

30g (1oz) plain flour

pinch of caster sugar

pinch of grated nutmeg

2 egg yolks

2 tbsp whipping cream

1½ tbsp chopped flat-leaf parsley

1 Put 1 litre (1¾ pints) water into a pan with 1 tsp salt and 20g (¾oz) of the butter. Add the asparagus trimmings. Bring to the boil, cover, reduce the heat, and simmer for 15 minutes. Strain through a sieve (reserving the cooking liquid) and discard the trimmings.

2 Cook the asparagus spears in boiling salted water for 2–4 minutes, or until soft, then drain, reserving the cooking liquid. Add enough of the milk to the cooking liquid to make 1 litre (1¾ pints).

3 Melt the remaining butter in a pan, add the flour, and cook over a low heat, stirring, for 2–3 minutes, or until smooth. Gradually add the milk mixture, stirring vigorously with a whisk to make sure there are no lumps. Bring to the boil and cook, uncovered, over a low heat for 5 minutes, stirring occasionally. Add the sugar and nutmeg and season with salt and pepper.

4 Stir the egg yolks into the cream and slowly add the mixture to the soup, stirring to get a smooth texture. Add the asparagus and reheat gently. Do not let the soup boil. Serve garnished with the parsley.

mini chicken tortillas topped with yogurt, cucumber, and mint dip

Tiny morsels to pop into your mouth on a summer evening with a cool, refreshing drink. The fresh flavours of cucumber, mint, and coriander round off the spicy chicken perfectly.

🥣 20 MINS

MAKES 8–10

200ml (7fl oz) Greek-style yogurt

½ cucumber

bunch of mint, leaves picked

salt and freshly ground black pepper

245g packet plain-flavoured corn chips

125–250ml (4½–9fl oz) mango chutney

350g (12oz) cooked chicken tikka pieces, chopped into small pieces

small handful of coriander, to garnish

1 To make the dip, tip the yogurt into a bowl. Trim the ends from the cucumber, peel, cut in half lengthways, and scoop out the seeds with a teaspoon. Finely dice and add to the yogurt with the mint leaves. Season well with salt and pepper. Taste, and season more if needed.

2 Tip the corn chips onto a clean surface and spread out in a single layer. Add 1 tsp of mango chutney to each one.

3 Add some chicken pieces to each corn chip. Spoon on about 1 tsp of the dip and garnish with coriander. Serve immediately.

variation

mini pea tortillas with yogurt, cucumber, and mint dip

Instead of chicken, purée 225g (8oz) cooked shelled peas with 60g (2oz) cream cheese, a pinch of grated nutmeg, and some salt and pepper. Use tomato chutney instead of mango. Assemble with the dip as before.

potage saint germain

Spring onions, peas, and lettuce form the basis for this summery soup; so it is perfect for using up any excess.

🥣 15 MINS   🍲 1 HR   ❄ FREEZABLE

SPECIAL EQUIPMENT ▪ blender or food processor

SERVES 4

1 tbsp olive oil

15g (½oz) butter, plus 25g (scant 1oz) chilled butter, diced

4 large spring onions (white parts only), trimmed and chopped

1.5 litres (2¾ pints) hot vegetable stock

150g (5½oz) split green peas, rinsed and drained

salt and freshly ground black pepper

500g (1lb 2oz) peas (shelled weight)

1 small soft lettuce, leaves snipped

1 large egg yolk

3 tbsp crème fraîche

1–2 tbsp Madeira or port

1 tbsp snipped chervil, to garnish

1 Put a large sauté pan over a medium heat. Add the oil and 15g (½oz) butter. Tip in the spring onions. Reduce the heat and sweat for 5 minutes, stirring frequently. Pour the stock into the pan and then add the split peas. Season it lightly and bring back to a simmer. Reduce the heat a little, cover, and cook for a further 20 minutes, stirring occasionally.

2 Add the peas and lettuce, stir, and cook for 5 minutes. Leave to cool, then pour into a blender or food processor and blitz until smooth. Push the soup back into the pan through a fine sieve, mashing the vegetables with the back of a spoon. Pour 100ml (3½fl oz) water through the sieve to thin the soup, then gently reheat.

3 In a cup or small bowl combine the egg yolk and the crème fraîche with 2–3 tbsp of the hot soup. Whisk this into the pan a little at a time. Continue cooking until the soup is piping hot. Adjust the seasoning. Just before serving, stir in the Madeira or port, whisk in the diced butter, and garnish with the chervil.

curried vegetable pies

A summer vegetable medley of young carrots, courgettes, and spring onions are combined with potatoes in these pies. Their handy size makes them easy to take on a picnic or for a lunchtime snack. Depending on how hot you like your curry, you can buy curry pastes ranging from mild to extra hot. The pastes are a mixture of ground herbs and spices pounded into a vegetable oil.

15 MINS · **45 MINS** · **FREEZABLE**

SPECIAL EQUIPMENT · 15cm (6in) round biscuit cutter

MAKES 4

1 carrot, diced

2 potatoes, peeled and finely diced

salt and freshly ground black pepper

450g (1lb) ready-made shortcrust pastry

1 egg, lightly beaten, for egg wash

1 tbsp curry paste

2 tbsp Greek-style yogurt

1 garlic clove, grated or finely chopped

2.5cm (1in) piece of fresh root ginger, peeled and finely chopped

1 courgette, diced

2 spring onions, trimmed and finely sliced

handful of coriander, finely chopped

juice of ½ lemon

1 Preheat the oven to 200°C (400°F/ Gas 6). Cook the carrot and potatoes in a pan of salted water for about 15 minutes until soft; drain well.

2 Roll out the pastry on a floured work surface, then cut out 4 circles using the biscuit cutter. Put the pastry rounds on a baking tray and brush the edges with a little of the egg wash.

3 Put the carrot and potatoes in a bowl and gently mix with the curry paste and yogurt. Add the garlic, ginger, courgette, spring onions, coriander, and lemon juice, and season well with salt and pepper. Stir in gently until well mixed.

4 Divide the vegetable mixture evenly among the pastry circles, spooning it into the centre of each one. Fold over the pastry to make a half-moon shape, and pinch the edges together to seal. Transfer to a baking sheet. Using a sharp knife, make 2 or 3 slashes in the top of each pie, then brush all over with the remaining egg wash. Bake in the oven for 20–30 minutes until golden. Serve hot or cold.

variation

mediterranean vegetable pies

Prepare in the same way, but substitute 1 tbsp tomato purée and a pinch of sugar for the curry paste. Use a handful of chopped fresh basil instead of the coriander. When the pies are on the baking sheet, brush with egg wash, then sprinkle with a handful of grated Cheddar cheese before baking.

baby broad bean soup

This soup is a perfect summery starter as it makes good use of that early summer vegetable, the broad bean.

🥣 **20 MINS**   🍲 **1 HR**   ❄️ **FREEZABLE**

SPECIAL EQUIPMENT ▪ blender or food processor

SERVES 4–6

3 slices toasting bread, for croûtons

6 tbsp olive oil

3 large mild onions, sliced

4 spring onions, trimmed and chopped

1.5kg (3lb 3oz) broad beans (shelled weight), skinned (p85, optional)

4 garlic cloves, crushed

small handful of chives, snipped

4 new potatoes, peeled and chopped

salt and freshly ground black pepper

leaves from a bunch of radishes

drizzle of extra virgin olive oil

1 To make the croûtons, cut the bread into 1cm (½in) cubes. Heat 3 tbsp of the oil in a large frying pan over a medium-high heat. Add the bread cubes and spread them out. Fry for a minute, then stir and turn them over. Fry for another minute. Spread them on a plate lined with kitchen paper. Pat with more kitchen paper to absorb excess oil. Set aside.

2 Heat the remaining oil in a large heavy-based flameproof casserole over a medium heat. Add the onions and spring onions and cook for 5–7 minutes until they are soft.

3 Add the broad beans with the garlic, chives, and potatoes. Stir, then pour in about 3 litres (5¼ pints) water. Season lightly with salt and pepper and stir in the radish leaves. Increase the heat a little and bring to the boil, then leave to simmer gently for 15–20 minutes.

4 Allow to cool a little, then pour the soup into a blender or food processor and process until smooth. Strain back into the pan. (If you prefer, you can omit the straining, in which case the soup will serve 6–8 people.) Reheat until piping hot before serving. Top with the croûtons and a drizzle of extra virgin olive oil.

dill and broad bean dip

In addition to the in-season broad bean, this dip makes use of Italian large white cannellini beans. Similar in shape and size to haricot beans, they are readily available in cans.

🥣 **30 MINS**   🍲 **45 MINS**

SPECIAL EQUIPMENT ▪ blender or food processor

SERVES 8

3 tbsp olive oil

1 small onion, finely chopped

750g (1lb 10oz) broad beans (shelled weight), skinned (p85, optional)

salt and freshly ground black pepper

400g can cannellini beans, drained

1 tbsp chopped dill

2 spring onions, trimmed and thinly sliced on the diagonal

1 Heat the oil in a heavy-based pan over a medium heat, add the onion, and cook for 3–4 minutes until the onion is soft and translucent.

2 Tip in the broad beans and cook for 10–15 minutes, stirring occasionally. Add 500ml (16fl oz) water, season with salt and pepper, and part-cover the pan with a lid. Reduce the heat and gently simmer for 25 minutes, mashing the beans a little during this time. Drain and allow to cool.

3 Put the cooled broad bean mixture in a blender or food processor. Add the cannellini beans, dill, and spring onions, and blitz to a chunky purée. Season with salt and pepper. Transfer to a serving bowl and serve with fresh crusty bread.

variation

fresh pea and mint dip with seasonal crudités

Prepare in the same way but use 750g (1lb 10oz) peas in their pods. Shell them but no need to remove the skins. Cook, then blend as before but add 1 tbsp chopped fresh mint instead of dill and serve with mangetout, thin asparagus tips, scrubbed baby carrots (or young carrot sticks), and radishes.

Season's best **broad beans**

Before the discovery of the New World, broad beans were the only pulses available, and they are still enjoyed worldwide, fresh and dried. In season throughout the summer, they have a unique meaty, slightly herbaceous flavour, are succulent and sweet when young, becoming floury and more strongly flavoured with age. They are delicious with bacon and cured meats, lamb, meaty white fish, pulses, spices (particularly harissa), potatoes, and spinach.

The first early broad beans are usually prolific, depending on the harshness of the winter, and they are particularly delicious. The later sowing is harvested in high summer.

Broad bean A delicious and nutritious bean at its best when young and tender, but still edible puréed or in soup when old and floury.

Brown speckling on older pods is quite normal and is not a sign of poor quality.

essentials
varieties available

Finger-length immature pods, mature pods; also dried.

buy Choose bright green and firm bean pods, evenly filled but not too swollen.

store Keep unshelled in the vegetable drawer of the fridge for up to 2 weeks (don't worry if the pods go limp).

cook Usually boil or steam; serve hot or cold in salads or in béchamel or parsley sauce. Add to soups, stews, and casseroles. Use the pods for stock.

preserve Blanch and freeze.

Young beans can be eaten raw, drizzled with olive oil, with Pecorino cheese (Italian-style).

recipe ideas

Baby broad bean soup p84

Chicken with broad beans p100

Ham with minted peas and broad beans p116

Hot and spicy lamb with broad beans p96

Lamb with artichokes, broad beans, and dill p113

Pork steaks with tomato and broad bean sauce p101

how to shell and skin broad beans

If pods are smaller than your middle finger, trim and eat whole, pod and all. Broad beans usually need shelling, except for the tiny beans eaten in their pod. For best results, remove the outer skins of the beans after cooking.

1 Snap the stalk end and pull off the string all down the edge. Slit open with your thumbs and slip out the beans.

2 When cooked, drain the beans in a colander. When cool enough to handle, gently pop the beans out of their skins.

courgette and pea mini tortillas

Bursting with fresh green summer vegetables, these mini tortillas make a great appetizer or starter. Alternatively, for a tasty packed lunch, simply wrap them in foil to transport.

 20 MINS   5 MINS

MAKES 20

3 courgettes, grated

50g (1¾oz) baby spinach leaves

grated zest and juice of 1 lemon

250g (9oz) peas (shelled weight)

50g (1¾oz) pine nuts, toasted

salt and freshly ground black pepper

10 wheat tortillas, halved

2 tbsp reduced-fat mayonnaise

large handful of mangetout sprouts

large handful of pea shoots

1 In a large bowl, mix the courgettes, spinach, lemon zest and juice, peas, and pine nuts together. Season well.

2 Heat a frying pan over a high heat. Place 2 tortilla halves in the pan at a time and heat for 15 seconds on each side. Cover the heated tortillas with a tea towel to keep warm.

3 Brush one of the tortilla halves with mayonnaise. Place a little of the filling in the centre. Arrange some mangetout sprouts and pea shoots on top, so that they stick out at one end, then roll up the tortilla. Repeat to make 20 mini tortillas.

chargrilled asparagus and pancetta

Ideal for party food, this simple recipe cleverly combines the sweetness of the new season's asparagus and the salty richness of the pancetta with a zesty dressing.

15 MINS   5 MINS

SERVES 4

12 asparagus spears, trimmed

salt and freshly ground black pepper

24 thin slices of pancetta

1 garlic clove, crushed

4 tbsp olive oil

1 tbsp balsamic vinegar

1 tbsp freshly squeezed orange juice

1 tsp Dijon mustard

1 small radicchio, torn into bite-sized pieces

1 butterhead lettuce, torn into bite-sized pieces

100g (3½oz) rocket leaves

200g (7oz) cherry tomatoes

100g (3½oz) Parmesan cheese, shaved

1 Blanch the asparagus spears in boiling salted water for 2–4 minutes, or until soft. Drain, immediately refresh in a bowl of cold water, and drain again.

2 Heat a ridged cast-iron grill pan or griddle pan until hot. Wrap 2 slices of the pancetta around each asparagus spear. Grill the asparagus spears for about 3–4 minutes until beginning to char, turning once halfway during the cooking time. Set aside.

3 To make the dressing, whisk together the garlic, oil, balsamic vinegar, orange juice, and mustard in a small bowl. Season with salt and pepper and whisk again.

4 Toss the salad leaves, tomatoes, and dressing together in a bowl and divide among 4 serving plates or bowls. Top each serving with 3 of the asparagus and pancetta spears, and sprinkle the Parmesan shavings over the top. Serve immediately.

courgette fritters with dill tzatziki

Courgette is lovely when picked young, but, a member of the concurbit family, it can become watery if left to grow too large. To offset any wateriness, salt larger courgettes before use.

🥣 **20 MINS PLUS DRAINING**   🍲 **10 MINS**

SERVES 4

200g (7oz) courgettes, coarsely grated

sea salt and freshly ground black pepper

100g (3½oz) ricotta cheese

1 large egg

2 tbsp plain flour

3 garlic cloves, crushed

small handful of basil, chopped

small handful of flat-leaf parsley, chopped

light olive oil, for frying

2 tbsp finely chopped dill

200g (7oz) Greek-style yogurt

juice of ½ lemon

1 Sprinkle the courgettes with 1 tsp sea salt and leave to drain in a sieve for 1 hour. Rinse and squeeze dry in a clean tea towel.

2 In a bowl, whisk together the ricotta cheese, egg, and flour. Add 2 of the crushed garlic cloves, the basil, and parsley, and season well. Mix in the courgettes.

3 Fill a frying pan with olive oil to a depth of 1cm (½in) and fry 2 tbsp of the courgette and cheese batter over a medium heat for 2–3 minutes on each side, until golden brown. Drain on kitchen paper.

4 To make the tzatziki, mix the last clove of garlic with the dill, some sea salt and pepper, and the yogurt. Add a squeeze of lemon juice and serve immediately with the hot fritters.

cheddar and courgette soufflés

The courgette mixture for these soufflés can be prepared up to 3 hours ahead, up to the end of step 4. Then, just whisk the egg whites and finish the recipe just before baking.

🥣 **30-35 MINS**   🍲 **30-35 MINS**

SPECIAL EQUIPMENT ▪ 6 x 350ml (12fl oz) ramekins

SERVES 6

60g (2oz) unsalted butter

2 shallots, finely chopped

500g (1lb 2oz) courgettes, coarsely grated

salt and freshly ground black pepper

175ml (6fl oz) milk

20g (¾oz) plain flour

125ml (4fl oz) double cream

pinch of ground nutmeg

4 eggs, separated, plus 2 egg whites

85g (3oz) Cheddar cheese, grated

1 Melt half the butter in a frying pan. Add the shallots and cook until soft. Then add the courgettes, season, and cook for 3–5 minutes until tender. Transfer to a sieve set over a bowl and leave to drain.

2 Scald the milk in a small pan. Melt the remaining butter in a medium pan. Over the heat, add the flour all at once and whisk briskly for 30–60 seconds, until the mixture starts to foam. Remove from the heat, slowly pour in the milk, whisking until mixed.

3 Return to the heat and whisk. When the sauce boils, pour in the cream and whisk again. Season with salt, pepper, and nutmeg. Simmer for 2 minutes. Whisk the egg yolks into the sauce, one at a time, return the pan to the heat, and bring to the boil. Keep whisking, and simmer for 1 minute.

4 Remove the pan from the heat and stir in the Cheddar and courgettes. Preheat the oven to 190°C (375°F/ Gas 5). Brush the ramekins with a little melted butter. Reheat the courgette mixture until hot.

5 Beat the egg whites with a pinch of salt in a metal bowl for 3–5 minutes until stiff peaks form. Add one-quarter to the warm mixture and stir. Add the mixture to the remaining egg whites in the bowl. Fold together until the egg whites are thoroughly incorporated. Spoon into the prepared dishes. Bake for 10–15 minutes until puffed and brown.

6 Serve immediately: the soufflés will lose much of their volume within minutes as they cool.

pancakes with peppers and basil

It is worth leaving the pancake batter to stand for a while as it makes the end result that little bit lighter. For a nutty-tasting version, try buckwheat flour instead of the plain flour.

🥄 10 MINS PLUS STANDING   🍲 20 MINS

MAKES 8

125g (4½oz) plain flour

salt

1 egg

300ml (10fl oz) milk

2 tbsp olive oil, plus a little extra for frying

4 red peppers, deseeded and cut into strips

½ tsp caster sugar

large handful of fresh basil leaves, torn

1 Put the flour in a mixing bowl with a pinch of salt, stir, and make a well in the centre. Crack the egg into the well and add a tiny amount of the milk. Using a wooden spoon, stir the egg and milk, letting the flour gradually tumble in. Add the rest of the milk, little by little, stirring continuously until all the flour has been incorporated and the mixture is lump-free. Put it in the fridge to stand for 30 minutes, if you have time.

2 Heat 1 tbsp of the olive oil in a frying pan, add the peppers, the sugar, and a pinch of salt, and cook over a low heat for 10–15 minutes, or until soft. Stir through the basil.

3 In a small, flat frying pan or pancake pan, heat a drizzle of olive oil over a high heat, swirling it around the pan, then tipping it out again. Stir the batter mix, then spoon 2 tbsp of it into the pan, swirling it around so it reaches the edges. Cook for a couple of minutes until a light golden colour, then pull up the edges with a palette knife. Turn the pancake over and cook the other side for 1 minute. Slide it out onto a plate.

4 Spoon the filling onto the pancakes, then fold them up.

white asparagus with herby mayonnaise

The delicate colour of white asparagus is produced by growing it in the dark, a method known as forcing.

🥄 5 MINS   🍲 10 MINS

SPECIAL EQUIPMENT ▪ blender or food processor

SERVES 4

500g (1lb 2oz) white or thick green asparagus spears, trimmed

2 egg yolks

2 tbsp white wine vinegar

1 tsp Dijon mustard

300ml (10fl oz) light olive oil

juice of ½ lemon

sea salt and freshly ground black pepper

1 garlic clove, crushed

1 tbsp chopped flat-leaf parsley

1 tbsp chopped tarragon

1 Cook the asparagus spears in boiling salted water for 2–4 minutes, or until soft. Drain, refresh in cold water, and drain again.

2 To make the mayonnaise, put the egg yolks, vinegar, and mustard in a blender or food processor and blitz for 1–2 minutes, or until a light yellow colour. Reduce the speed and slowly add the oil, a little at a time, until you have a smooth creamy emulsion.

3 Spoon the mayonnaise into a bowl and stir in the lemon juice. Season to taste with salt and pepper, and stir in the garlic, parsley, and tarragon. Serve as a dip for the cooked asparagus spears.

creamy scallop bisque

A rich broth sets off the sweetness of the scallops perfectly.

🥄 20 MINS   🍲 40 MINS

SPECIAL EQUIPMENT ▪ blender or food processor

SERVES 4

300ml (10fl oz) dry white wine

15g (½oz) butter

1 small onion, finely chopped

1 small shallot, very finely chopped

1 ripe tomato, chopped

300g (10oz) white fish, such as pollack or cod, skinned and cut into chunks

1 tsp anchovy essence (optional)

2 tbsp chopped flat-leaf parsley

2 tsp dill seeds

3 tbsp brandy

salt and freshly ground black pepper

100ml (3½fl oz) single cream

75g (2½oz) chorizo, diced

12 small scallops (white part only)

1 tbsp finely snipped chives, to garnish

1 Boil 750ml (1¼ pints) water with the wine. Heat the butter in a frying pan over a medium heat, add the onion and shallot, and cook for 3–4 minutes, until they are soft and translucent. Stir in the tomato, fish, anchovy essence, if using, parsley, and dill seeds, and cook for 5 minutes. Stir in the brandy and cook for a minute. Pour in the boiling wine mixture and season lightly with salt and pepper. Reduce the heat and simmer for 10 minutes. Take off the heat and leave to cool. Stir and mash down the soup with the back of a spoon. Gently heat the cream in another pan until hot.

2 Transfer the soup to a blender or food processor and blitz until creamy. Strain through a sieve into the pan and stir in the cream. Return to a simmer, then remove from the heat and adjust the seasoning. Cover and keep warm.

3 Put a non-stick frying pan over a medium heat. Add the chorizo and fry for 3–5 minutes until cooked through and crispy. Set aside on a plate lined with kitchen paper and keep warm.

4 Add the scallops to the pan. Cook for 2 minutes on each side. Remove from the heat. Ladle the soup into 4 bowls and add the scallops. Scatter over the chorizo and snipped chives and serve.

courgettes stuffed with sultanas, red onion, and pine nuts

Pine nuts are most frequently used as the basis for pesto sauce as well as scattered over salads. Here they are warmed through with sultanas and topped with feta to add a hint of Middle Eastern flavour to the ever-versatile courgette.

10 MINS **20 MINS**

SERVES 4

8 courgettes

1 tbsp olive oil

1 red onion, finely chopped

pinch of dried chilli flakes

salt

handful of sultanas

handful of pine nuts, toasted

75g (2½oz) feta cheese, crumbled

1 Preheat the oven to 200°C (400°F/ Gas 6). First, prepare the courgettes. Cut in half lengthways. Scoop out the flesh, roughly chop, and set aside with the courgette shells.

2 Heat the oil in a large frying pan over a medium heat, add the onion, and cook for 3–4 minutes until the onion is soft and translucent. Stir in the courgette flesh, chilli flakes, and a pinch of salt, and cook for a couple more minutes.

3 Stir in the sultanas and half of the pine nuts, then remove from the heat. Spoon the mixture into the courgette shells and top with the feta. Sit on a baking tray and roast in the oven for 10–15 minutes until golden.

4 Sprinkle over the remaining pine nuts and serve hot with a simple salad of mixed leaves and tomatoes.

variation

courgettes stuffed with preserved lemon, raisins, and spring onion

At step 2, fry 2 chopped spring onions instead of the red onion. At step 3, stir in a finely chopped preserved lemon and a handful of raisins. Use a handful of pumpkin seeds instead of pine nuts, adding half now and the rest for garnish. Continue as at step 3.

baked salmon with salsa verde and cucumber

Here is a super-fresh cold dish, just right for a light summer's day meal. The salsa verde combines herbs with a caper and anchovy dressing to give some added zing to the meal.

🥄 15 MINS 🍲 5-6 MINS PLUS COOLING

SERVES 4

450g (1lb) salmon fillet

1 bay leaf

1 small glass of white wine

salt and freshly ground black pepper

handful of basil leaves, finely chopped

handful of mint leaves, finely chopped

handful of flat-leaf parsley, finely chopped

2 tbsp white wine vinegar

2 tsp capers, rinsed, gently squeezed dry, and finely chopped

2 garlic cloves, grated or finely chopped

8 anchovies in oil, drained and finely chopped

2 tsp wholegrain mustard

6 tbsp extra virgin olive oil

1 cucumber

1 Put the salmon in a frying pan. Add the bay leaf, wine, and just enough water to cover the fish. Season lightly with salt and pepper. Bring to the boil, reduce the heat, cover, and poach for 4–5 minutes until just cooked through. Remove from the heat and leave to cool in the liquid. Lift out of the poaching liquid and break into bite-sized pieces.

2 To make the salsa verde, put the herbs in a bowl. Drizzle in the vinegar and stir through. Add the capers, garlic, and anchovies, and stir again. Then add the mustard and season well with salt and pepper. Slowly stir in the olive oil. Taste and adjust the seasoning if needed, adding a little more vinegar or oil as required. Transfer to a serving bowl.

3 Trim the ends from the cucumber, peel, cut in half lengthways, and scoop out the seeds with a teaspoon. Dice the flesh and put in a serving bowl.

4 Arrange the cooked salmon on a platter or individual plates. Spoon the salsa verde over the fish, place the cucumber on the side, and serve.

pasta with pancetta and rocket

Rocket leaves have a particularly strong peppery flavour so won't be subsumed by the spicy pancetta. A grating of Parmesan cheese is the essential finishing touch.

🥄 5 MINS 🍲 15 MINS

SERVES 4

1 tbsp olive oil

1 onion, finely chopped

1 red chilli, deseeded and finely chopped

250g (9oz) pancetta, diced

2 garlic cloves, grated or finely chopped

350g (12oz) spaghetti

200g (7oz) rocket leaves

salt and freshly ground black pepper

Parmesan cheese, grated, to serve

1 Heat the oil in a large frying pan over a medium heat, add the onion, and cook for 3–4 minutes until the onion is soft. Add the chilli and cook for a few minutes more. Add the pancetta and cook for 5 minutes, or until crisp and golden, then stir in the garlic and cook for a few more seconds.

2 Meanwhile, cook the pasta in a large pan of boiling salted water for about 12 minutes, or until it is tender but still al dente. Drain, keeping back a tiny amount of the cooking water. Return the pasta to the pan and toss with the pancetta mixture. Add the rocket, season with salt and pepper, and toss gently. Sprinkle with the Parmesan cheese and serve immediately.

pasta with pecorino and peas

Pecorino is a hard Italian cheese made from ewe's milk. In some Italian regions it is used in place of Parmesan cheese. Think of Sicily and sunshine when enjoying this dish.

🥣 **10 MINS**   🍲 **20 MINS**

SERVES 4

1 tbsp olive oil

1 onion, finely chopped

1 garlic clove, grated or finely chopped

1 red chilli, deseeded and finely chopped

salt and freshly ground black pepper

2 tsp plain flour

½ small glass of dry white wine

150ml (5fl oz) milk

150g (5½oz) peas (shelled weight)

125g (4½oz) pecorino cheese, grated, plus extra to serve

350g (12oz) farfalle

1 Heat the oil in a large frying pan over a medium heat, add the onion, and cook for 3–4 minutes until the onion is soft and translucent. Stir in the garlic and chilli, add some salt, and cook for a few seconds more. Stir in the flour, then add the wine and simmer for a couple of minutes. Add the milk and stir.

2 Stir in the peas, then add the pecorino and cook at a low simmer – do not allow to boil – for about 10 minutes, or until the sauce has thickened slightly. Season well with salt and pepper.

3 Meanwhile, cook the pasta in a large pan of boiling salted water for about 12 minutes, or until it is tender but still al dente. Drain, keeping back a tiny amount of the cooking water. Return the pasta to the pan and toss with the sauce. Top with extra pecorino and serve.

pepper and artichoke salad

Artichoke hearts and roasted red peppers are served in this hearty salad with tasty blue cheese wafers.

🥣 **40-45 MINS PLUS CHILLING**   🍲 **25-35 MINS**

SERVES 4

75g (2½oz) Stilton cheese, cut into chunks

75g (2½oz) Cambozola or Bavarian blue cheese, cut into chunks

75g (2½oz) butter, softened

85g (3oz) plain flour

2 tbsp balsamic vinegar

1 tbsp Dijon mustard

salt and freshly ground black pepper

6 tbsp olive oil

leaves from ½ head of lollo rosso

leaves from ½ round lettuce

125g (4½oz) spinach leaves

2 small red peppers, roasted, peeled, and cut into strips (p171) (or from a jar)

30g (1oz) pine nuts, toasted

2 cooked artichoke hearts, quartered (p309) (or from a jar)

1 Beat the cheese into the butter with a wooden spoon until the mixture is creamy and smooth. Stir in the flour until the dough comes together.

2 Shape the dough into a 4cm (1½in) diameter log. Wrap tightly in baking parchment. Twist the ends of the paper to seal and freeze for 1–2 hours until firm.

3 Whisk the vinegar, mustard, and salt and pepper in a small bowl. Slowly whisk in the oil so the vinaigrette emulsifies and thickens slightly.

4 Preheat the oven to 180°C (350°F/ Gas 4). Cut half the cheese wafer dough in 5mm (¼in) thick slices using a thin-bladed knife dipped in hot water. Space out on a baking sheet. Re-wrap the remaining dough and return to the freezer.

5 Bake the wafers for 6–8 minutes until golden. Allow to cool slightly, then transfer to a wire rack lined with kitchen paper. Allow the baking sheet to cool, slice the remaining dough, and bake as before.

6 Put the leaves in a bowl and add the peppers. Toss with the vinaigrette and sprinkle with the pine nuts. Top with the artichoke hearts, add some wafers, and serve the rest separately.

asparagus and taleggio risotto

Taleggio is a mellow, creamy Italian cheese that melts into the rice and complements the asparagus.

🥣 10 MINS   🍲 30–40 MINS

SERVES 4

1 tbsp olive oil

25g (scant 1oz) butter

1 onion, finely chopped

3 garlic cloves, finely chopped

salt and freshly ground black pepper

300g (10oz) arborio rice or carnaroli rice

250ml (9fl oz) white wine

about 900ml (1½ pints) hot chicken or vegetable stock

bunch of asparagus spears, trimmed

75g (2½oz) Taleggio cheese, roughly sliced

1 Heat the oil and butter in a large heavy-based pan over a medium heat, add the onion, and cook for 3–4 minutes until the onion is soft. Stir through the garlic and cook for a further minute. Season with salt and pepper.

2 Stir through the rice and turn it in the oily butter so all the grains are coated. Cook for a few seconds. Increase the heat, add the wine, and let it bubble for 1–2 minutes or until it has been absorbed. In a separate saucepan, simmer the stock. Add a ladleful to the rice and stir until absorbed. Continue doing this for 20–30 minutes until the rice is cooked to al dente and is creamy. You may not need all the stock or you may need a little more.

3 Meanwhile, cook the asparagus spears in boiling salted water for 2–4 minutes, or until soft. Drain, refresh in cold water, and drain again. Slice each spear into three and add to the rice along with the Taleggio cheese. Taste and season, if needed.

asparagus and herb tart

The asparagus laid in neat rows in this rectangular tart makes for a fun and unusual piece of presentation.

🥣 15 MINS   🍲 1 HR

SPECIAL EQUIPMENT ▪ 18 x 30cm (7 x 12in) rectangular loose-bottomed fluted tart tin ▪ ceramic baking beans

SERVES 6–8

250g (9oz) ready-made shortcrust pastry

3 eggs, 1 lightly beaten, for egg wash

350g (12oz) asparagus spears, trimmed

1 tbsp olive oil

bunch of spring onions, trimmed and finely chopped

handful of mint leaves, finely chopped

salt and freshly ground black pepper

125g (4½oz) Cheddar cheese, grated

200ml (7fl oz) double cream

pinch of grated nutmeg

1 Preheat the oven to 200°C (400°F/Gas 6). Roll out the pastry on a floured work surface, and use to line the tart tin. Trim the excess, line the pastry shell with greaseproof paper, and fill with ceramic baking beans. Bake for 15–20 minutes until the edges are golden. Remove the beans and paper, and brush egg wash over the bottom of the shell. Return to the oven for 2–3 minutes to crisp. Remove from the oven and set aside. Reduce the oven temperature to 180°C (350°F/Gas 4).

2 Cook the asparagus spears in boiling salted water for 2–4 minutes, or until soft. Drain, refresh in cold water, and drain again. Heat the oil in a pan over a low heat. Add the spring onions, and sweat for 2 minutes. Remove from the pan with a slotted spoon, and scatter over the bottom of the pastry shell. Arrange the asparagus on top. Scatter over the mint, add seasoning, and sprinkle over the cheese. Mix the cream, 2 eggs, and the nutmeg. Pour the mixture over the tart, and bake for 30–40 minutes until set and golden. Leave in the tin for 10 minutes before serving with a tomato salad.

grilled sea bass with roast artichokes and fennel

Welcome early summer artichokes by pairing them with sea bass. A hot griddle ensures that the fish skin crisps nicely.

🥣 45 MINS   🍲 25 MINS

SERVES 4

6 tbsp extra virgin olive oil

4 sea bass fillets, scaled and pinboned

salt and freshly ground black pepper

8 small or 3–4 large artichoke bottoms

squeeze of lemon juice

1 large fennel bulb, finely sliced

3 garlic cloves, finely sliced

large handful of basil, shredded

1 Preheat the oven to 200°C (400°C/Gas 6). Brush a griddle pan with 2 tbsp of the oil. Slash the skin of each fillet 3 times, and season. Set aside.

2 Cut the artichoke bottoms into quarters and blanch in boiling water with the lemon juice for 3–4 minutes. Drain and put into a large roasting tin with the fennel and garlic. Toss with the remaining olive oil. Season generously and roast in the oven for 15–18 minutes, or until the fennel is roasted and the artichokes are soft.

3 Heat the griddle pan until just smoking, add the fish, skin-side down, and cook for 2–3 minutes on each side: the skin will be charred and the flesh white and firm. Scatter the basil over and serve immediately.

variation

grilled sea bass with roasted baby beetroot and dill

Peel and halve 8 baby beetroots. Put in the roasting tin with the olive oil and garlic instead of the artichokes and fennel. Scatter 1 tbsp chopped dill over. Roast as before. Mix 120ml (4fl oz) crème fraîche with 2 tbsp chopped dill and 1 finely chopped spring onion. Griddle the fish. Serve with the beetroot and the dill cream.

Season's best **asparagus**

The succulent stems of green (and purple) asparagus have a flavour reminiscent of fragrant, freshly cut grass. The fat, white asparagus, prized in Europe, is simply green asparagus blanched by growing under the soil. It has a more delicate taste and creamier texture. All are delicious served with melted butter or Hollandaise sauce, but also go well with olive oil, balsamic vinegar, Parmesan cheese, sun-dried tomatoes, pine nuts, prosciutto, and eggs.

Asparagus grows in temperate zones worldwide where there is regular summer water from either rain or irrigation. Spears can range in thickness from pencil-thin to the size of your thumb.

Green asparagus Of all the asparagus types, green asparagus has the most pronounced flavour. Slender spears are best briefly steamed; fatter ones can be brushed with oil and grilled or roasted.

Spears should be straight and crisp.

essentials
varieties available

Green, purple, and white. Thin asparagus sprue and short, ready-trimmed tips are also sold.

buy Avoid any with woody, dirty stems. The growing tips should be tightly closed.

store Best eaten fresh, or store for up to 3 days wrapped in damp paper in the vegetable box of the fridge.

cook Steam, boil, stir-fry, roast, grill, or chargrill.

preserve Freeze, or preserve in oil.

recipe ideas

Asparagus and herb tart p92

Asparagus and taleggio risotto p92

Asparagus in oil p135

Cream of asparagus soup p82

Penne with asparagus and courgettes p112

White asparagus with herby mayonnaise p88

White asparagus The fat white spears are milder in flavour than the green type. They are deprived of light as they emerge from the ground, which prevents them from becoming green.

The skin of white asparagus can be tough, so it should be pared off before cooking.

how to trim asparagus

The tough stalk bases should always be removed. For thicker spears, it is best to pare off the outer, fibrous sheath to ensure each stem is perfectly tender.

1 With a sharp knife, cut the hard ends from the spears. Alternatively, snap the bottoms off the asparagus spears.

2 Rotating the spear, use a vegetable peeler to remove a thin layer of skin from all sides.

teriyaki fish with noodles

Teriyaki is a Japanese technique for cooking food that has first been marinated in a sweetened soy sauce. Here the sauce is added to coley and then baked until tender.

🥣 **10 MINS PLUS MARINATING**　🍲 **15 MINS**

SERVES 4

1-2 tbsp dark soy sauce

1 tbsp clear honey

2.5cm (1in) piece of fresh root ginger, peeled and grated

pinch of sugar

1 tbsp mirin or dry sherry

4 thick coley fillets, about 150g (5½oz) each

250g (9oz) thick or medium udon noodles

4 spring onions, trimmed and sliced

handful of coriander, leaves only

lime quarters, to serve

1 Preheat the oven to 200°C (400°F/Gas 6). To make the teriyaki sauce, put the soy sauce, honey, ginger, sugar, and mirin or sherry in a bowl, and mix well. Pour this over the fish and leave to marinate for about 10 minutes.

2 Sit the fish pieces with the sauce in a roasting tin and bake in the oven for about 15 minutes until the fish is cooked through.

3 Meanwhile, put the noodles in a bowl and pour over boiling water. Leave for a few minutes, then drain and toss with the spring onions and coriander. Serve with the fish and wedges of lime to squeeze over.

variation

teriyaki chicken with noodles

Prepare in exactly the same way but marinate the chicken for at least 1 hour and bake for about 25 minutes, or until the juices run clear when the chicken is pierced with the tip of a knife. Add a handful of shredded mangetout, steamed for 1 minute, to the noodles and spring onions.

quesadilla with peppers, green olives, and feta cheese

The quesadilla originated from Mexico and is a flour or corn tortilla filled with cheese and other toppings. As the summer progresses, look out for the first peppers to use in this dish.

🥣 **5 MINS**　🍲 **15 MINS**

MAKES 1

2 tbsp olive oil

2 red peppers, deseeded and roughly chopped

salt and freshly ground black pepper

2 wheat tortillas or corn tortillas

handful of pitted green olives, sliced

125g (4½oz) feta cheese, crumbled

1 Heat 1 tbsp of the oil in a frying pan over a low heat, add the peppers, and cook for 10 minutes until the peppers are soft. Season with salt and pepper.

2 Heat the remaining oil in a non-stick frying pan, then fry one tortilla for 1 minute, or until golden. Spoon the peppers onto it, leaving a little room around the edge. Scatter with the olives and feta cheese.

3 Top with the other tortilla, pressing it down with the back of a fish slice to sandwich the two together. Scoop up the quesadilla, carefully turn it over, and cook the other side for another minute, or until golden. Slice in halves or quarters, and serve.

variation

quesadilla with cheddar cheese, rocket, and semi-dried tomatoes

Fry the first tortilla in 1 tbsp olive oil as before. Add a handful of grated Cheddar cheese and spread it out, not quite to the edges. Top with a handful of rocket. Scatter over 2–3 chopped semi-dried tomatoes and 3–4 chopped fresh basil leaves. Continue at step 3.

roasted salmon with swiss chard and herb butter

Swiss chard is a versatile vegetable that can be boiled, steamed, stir-fried, and roasted. Great for ringing the changes when it is growing in abundance throughout the summer.

🥣 **10 MINS**   🍲 **30 MINS**

SERVES 4

4 salmon fillets, about 150g (5½oz) each

1 tbsp olive oil

salt and freshly ground black pepper

2 handfuls of Swiss chard, trimmed

juice of 1 lemon

pinch of dried chilli flakes

For the herb butter

125g (4½oz) butter, softened

handful of curly parsley, finely chopped

handful of dill, finely chopped

1 For the herb butter, put the butter and herbs in a mixing bowl and beat well until everything is combined. Spoon the butter onto a piece of greaseproof paper, then roll into a log shape. Twist the edges of the paper and put the roll in the fridge.

2 Preheat the oven to 200°C (400°F/Gas 6). Sit the salmon fillets in a non-stick roasting tin, drizzle with the oil, and season with salt and pepper. Bake in the oven for 15–20 minutes until the salmon is cooked through.

3 Meanwhile, cook the Swiss chard in a large pan of boiling salted water for 5–8 minutes until it still has a bite to it. Drain well and transfer to a serving dish. Squeeze over the lemon juice and add a pinch of chilli flakes.

4 Divide the Swiss chard between 4 warmed plates. Add a salmon fillet and a slice of the herb butter, and serve immediately.

asparagus, broccoli, ginger, and mint stir-fry

Here is a speedy stir-fry, perfect for using up excess fresh produce. In place of red pepper, consider using mangetout or finely shredded white cabbage leaves.

🥣 **15 MINS**   🍲 **15 MINS**

SERVES 4

1 tbsp sesame oil or vegetable oil

2 red chillies, deseeded and finely chopped

5cm (2in) piece of fresh root ginger, peeled and sliced into thin strips

bunch of spring onions, trimmed and cut into 5cm (2in) lengths

2 garlic cloves, grated or finely chopped

1 red pepper, deseeded and cut into thin strips

300g (10oz) broccoli, cut into florets

bunch of fine asparagus spears, trimmed and halved

1 tbsp caster sugar

salt and freshly ground black pepper

handful of mint leaves

1 Heat the oil in a wok over a medium-high heat and swirl to coat the surface. Add the chillies and ginger, and toss for a few seconds, then add the spring onions, and a few seconds later add the garlic. Stir-fry for 5 minutes until soft.

2 Add the pepper and stir-fry for a few minutes. Add the broccoli and stir-fry for a few minutes more, before adding the asparagus. Continue stir-frying for another minute or two.

3 Sprinkle over the sugar and season well with salt and pepper. Stir-fry for a few seconds until the sugar has dissolved. Remove from the heat and stir through the mint leaves. Serve immediately either on its own, or with some fluffy rice.

salmon with new potatoes, flageolet beans, and parsley sauce

Succulent summer salmon is paired here with a creamy sauce and in-season new potatoes. When serving this dish, you can leave the pieces of salmon whole, if you prefer.

🥣 15 MINS   🍲 30 MINS

SERVES 4

675g (1½lb) new potatoes

salt and freshly ground black pepper

450g (1lb) salmon fillets, skinned

300ml (10fl oz) milk

knob of butter

1 tbsp plain flour

150ml (5fl oz) double cream

handful of curly parsley, finely chopped

400g can flageolet beans, drained and rinsed

handful of dill, finely chopped

1 Cook the potatoes in a pan of boiling salted water for 15–20 minutes until soft. Drain and set aside to keep warm.

2 Meanwhile, put the salmon in a saucepan with the milk. Bring to the boil, reduce the heat, and poach gently for 3–4 minutes until just cooked. Remove from the pan with a slotted spoon and keep warm.

3 Melt the butter in a clean pan over a low heat. Remove from the heat and stir in the flour with a balloon whisk. Add a little of the salmon milk and whisk until smooth. Gradually whisk in the remaining milk and then the cream. Return the pan to the heat, bring to the boil, whisking constantly, then reduce the heat and simmer for 5–8 minutes, whisking all the time. Remove from the heat, season well with salt and pepper, and stir through the parsley.

4 Put the beans in a pan and gently heat through. Season, if you like, and stir through the dill. Break the salmon into neat pieces, if preferred. Place on a platter or individual plates with the flageolet beans and new potatoes on the side and the parsley sauce spooned over the salmon and potatoes.

hot and spicy lamb with broad beans

Broad beans are at their best in early summer and offer a soft, creamy contrast to the spicy lamb in this one-pot dish.

🥣 30 MINS PLUS MARINATING   🍲 2 HRS 10 MINS

SERVES 4

1.1kg (2½lb) lamb (from the leg), cut into bite-sized pieces

2 tbsp olive oil

4 garlic cloves, grated or finely chopped

1–2 tbsp harissa (according to taste)

1 tbsp finely chopped rosemary leaves

6 salted anchovy fillets, finely chopped

3 tbsp Worcestershire sauce

1 tbsp finely chopped thyme leaves, plus a few extra to garnish

juice of 1 lemon

salt and freshly ground black pepper

2 onions, finely chopped

450g (1lb) broad beans (shelled weight), skinned (p85, optional)

900g (2lb) potatoes, peeled and cut into bite-sized pieces

1.2 litres (2 pints) hot vegetable stock

1 Put the lamb in a bowl, add the oil, garlic, harissa, rosemary, anchovies, Worcestershire sauce, thyme, and lemon juice, and mix. Season with salt and pepper, then transfer to a plastic bag and leave to marinate for 30 minutes (or overnight in the fridge).

2 Preheat the oven to 200°C (400°F/Gas 6). Transfer the mixture to a large cast-iron pan and cook over a medium-high heat, turning occasionally, for 10 minutes, or until the lamb is browned. Add the onions and cook for 5 minutes.

3 Add the broad beans and potatoes, pour in the stock, and bring to the boil. Cover and put in the oven for 2 hours, or until tender. If it starts to dry out, top up with hot water. Season with salt and pepper, and serve garnished with a few thyme leaves.

baked salmon in wine with coriander and lime

Sharp lime and fragrant coriander cut through the richness of the salmon in this quick and simple recipe. Cooking the fish in a foil parcel perfectly seals in all the flavour and succulence.

🥣 5 MINS   🍲 25 MINS

SERVES 4

600g (1lb 5oz) side of salmon, descaled and cleaned, but not skinned

handful of coriander sprigs

2 limes, peeled, segmented, and roughly chopped

salt and freshly ground black pepper

½ small glass of dry white wine

1 Cut the side of salmon in half lengthways so that it opens up, but take care not to slice all the way through the skin.

2 Preheat the oven to 200°C (400°F/ Gas 6). Roughly chop a large handful of fresh coriander and mix with the peeled, segmented, and roughly chopped limes. Season with salt and pepper. Spread the herb and lime mixture on the opened salmon, season well once again, then fold over to close.

3 Place the salmon on a large sheet of foil and pour over ½ small glass of dry white wine. Loosely seal the foil to make a parcel. Place on a baking tray and bake in the oven for 25 minutes. Serve hot with boiled new potatoes.

chicken caesar salad

This restaurant classic makes a perfect lunch dish. Although anchovies did not feature in chef Caesar Cardini's original recipe, they add a salty tang and work really well with the sweet young lettuce leaves and the rich Parmesan and chicken. The dressing can be prepared in advance and stored in an airtight container in the fridge overnight.

15 MINS

SERVES 4

2 handfuls of crisp lettuce leaves, such as cos

150g (5½oz) ready-made croûtons

50g (1¾oz) Parmesan cheese, grated

350g (12oz) cooked chicken, sliced

10 salted brown anchovy fillets

For the dressing

2 egg yolks

2 tbsp lemon juice

pinch of English mustard powder

½ tbsp Worcestershire sauce

½ tbsp Tabasco sauce

150ml (5fl oz) sunflower oil

60ml (2fl oz) olive oil

1 First, make the dressing. In a bowl, whisk together the egg yolks, lemon juice, mustard powder, Worcestershire sauce, and Tabasco sauce. As you are whisking, add a tiny amount of the sunflower oil; keep whisking and adding the sunflower oil, then the olive oil, a little at a time, until the dressing emulsifies. If it is too thick, add a little cold water.

2 Put a little of the dressing in a bowl, then add the lettuce leaves, croûtons, and half of the Parmesan. Toss together gently, making sure the leaves are coated. Lay out the leaves on 4 individual serving plates or a serving dish, and top with the chicken and anchovies. Sprinkle with the remaining Parmesan, drizzle over some more dressing, and serve.

variation

caesar salad with poached eggs

Prepare in exactly the same way but omit the chicken. Poach 4 eggs in gently simmering water with 1 tbsp lemon juice for about 3 minutes. Remove with a slotted spoon and place an egg on top of each salad.

chicken stuffed with spinach and gruyère cheese

The mild, clean taste of fresh spinach complements pan-fried chicken perfectly. For an extra depth of flavour, add a splash of balsamic vinegar to the cherry tomatoes as they cook.

🥣 10 MINS   🍲 25 MINS

SERVES 4

200g (7oz) spinach leaves, stalks removed

75g (2½oz) Gruyère cheese, grated

pinch of ground nutmeg

salt and freshly ground black pepper

4 large skinless chicken breasts or chicken thighs

1 tbsp olive oil

8-12 cherry tomatoes

1 Put the spinach in a saucepan with a sprinkling of water, and cook for a few minutes until just wilted. Alternatively, put in a microwave-proof bowl, cover loosely, and wilt in the microwave on medium for about 2 minutes. Drain, and squeeze out any excess water. Mix the spinach with the Gruyère cheese and nutmeg in a mixing bowl, and season well with salt and pepper.

2 Slice each of the chicken breasts lengthways to form a pocket – be careful not to cut all the way through.

Stuff each pocket with some of the spinach and cheese mixture, then fold the top of the breast back over the mixture to seal it.

3 Heat the oil in a large frying pan over a medium-high heat. Add the chicken breasts carefully to the pan, pocket-side down, and leave to cook undisturbed for 6–8 minutes. Gently turn the chicken over, and cook the other side for about the same amount of time until golden and cooked all the way through and the juices run clear when pierced with a sharp knife.

4 Meanwhile, add the tomatoes to the frying pan towards the end of the cooking time. Leave them to cook undisturbed for 5 minutes until they begin to split. Remove the chicken from the pan when it is cooked, and set aside to keep warm. Stir the tomatoes around for a couple of minutes to break them up a little, then serve with the warm chicken.

veal escalopes with peppers

A northern Italian classic. Give the escalopes enough room in the pan, or they will steam instead of developing a crisp crust.

🥣 20-25 MINS   🍲 9-12 MINS

SERVES 6

30g (1oz) plain flour

salt and freshly ground black pepper

2 eggs

60g (2oz) dried breadcrumbs

60g (2oz) Parmesan cheese, grated

6 veal escalopes, about 375g (13oz) in total, and each 3mm (⅛in) thick (place between 2 large pieces of baking parchment and flatten with a mallet or rolling pin, if needed)

4 tbsp olive oil, plus more if needed

1 garlic clove, finely chopped

2 small green peppers, deseeded and cut into strips

2 small red peppers, deseeded and cut into strips

7-10 sprigs of oregano, leaves picked and finely chopped, plus more to serve

30g (1oz) butter

1 lemon, sliced, to serve

1 Season the flour with salt and pepper and sift onto a sheet of baking parchment. Lightly beat the eggs in a shallow dish. Mix the breadcrumbs and Parmesan cheese in a small bowl and spread on another sheet of baking parchment. Coat each side of the veal in the seasoned flour, dip in the egg mix using a fork, then press each side into the breadcrumb and cheese mixture. Put the slices on a plate and refrigerate, uncovered.

2 Heat 2 tbsp of the oil in a frying pan. Add the garlic and peppers, season, and sauté until soft, stirring occasionally. Remove from the heat, add the oregano, and keep warm.

3 Heat the butter and rest of the oil in a large frying pan. Add 2 escalopes and fry over a medium-high heat until golden brown, 1–2 minutes on each side, until no longer pink in the centre. Reduce the heat if the crumbs threaten to burn. Transfer to a plate lined with kitchen paper and keep warm. Fry the remaining veal, adding more oil if necessary; don't add too much, or the veal will be soggy. Serve with the peppers, lemon slices, and a sprig of oregano.

chicken fajitas with tomato and avocado salsa

This is ideal as an easy lunch or for al fresco dining. The punchy salsa is a quicker alternative to guacamole.

🥄 15 MINS 🍲 15 MINS

SERVES 4

1 tbsp olive oil

2 onions, sliced into strips

2 red peppers, deseeded and cut into strips

2 green peppers, deseeded and cut into strips

2 red chillies, deseeded and finely chopped

2 garlic cloves, sliced

4 skinless chicken breasts, cut into strips

1 small glass of dry white wine

handful of coriander, finely chopped

12 soft corn tortillas

For the salsa

1 ripe avocado

handful of cherry tomatoes, chopped

bunch of spring onions, trimmed and finely chopped

handful of flat-leaf parsley, finely chopped

1 tbsp olive oil

1 tbsp white wine vinegar

salt and freshly ground black pepper

1 For the salsa, halve, stone, peel, and chop the avocado. Put in a bowl with the tomatoes, spring onions, and parsley. Drizzle over the oil and vinegar, season with salt and pepper, combine gently, and set aside.

2 Heat the oil in a large frying pan over a low heat. Add the onions and red and green peppers, and sauté for 5 minutes until starting to soften. Stir through the chilli and garlic, and cook for a few seconds.

3 Increase the heat to medium-high, and add the chicken. Keep the mixture moving around the pan so it doesn't burn and the chicken is evenly cooked. Stir-fry for 3–5 minutes until the chicken is no longer pink. Pour in the wine and cook fiercely for 5 minutes. Stir through the coriander.

4 To serve, spoon the chicken mixture onto the tortillas. Top with the salsa, and roll into wraps. Serve with any extra mixture on the side.

lentils with artichokes and peppers

This is a satisfying and filling salad, with artichoke hearts adding a creamy, almost buttery, texture to sweet red peppers and nutty Puy lentils.

🥄 15 MINS

SERVES 4

4–6 cooked artichoke hearts (p309)

4 red peppers, roasted and peeled (p171)

400g can Puy lentils, drained and rinsed

1–2 sprigs of fresh thyme, leaves only

handful of flat-leaf parsley, finely chopped

4 spring onions, trimmed and finely chopped

2–3 tbsp walnut oil

1 tbsp cider vinegar

salt and freshly ground black pepper

4–5 slices of Parma ham, chopped

handful of rocket leaves

1 Halve the artichoke hearts and place in a large bowl. Deseed and cut the roasted peppers into strips. Add to the bowl with the lentils, herbs, and spring onions. Drizzle over the oil and vinegar, season with salt and pepper, and toss gently to combine.

2 Add the Parma ham and rocket, and toss gently once more. Transfer to a serving dish, and serve with a green salad on the side.

chicken with broad beans

Use the freshest baby broad beans you can find to give this dish the maximum amount of flavour.

🥣 **10 MINS** 🍲 **1 HR**

SERVES 4

8 chicken thighs with skin on

salt and freshly ground black pepper

2 tbsp olive oil

1 onion, finely chopped

2 celery sticks, finely chopped

2 garlic cloves, crushed or finely chopped

a few sprigs of rosemary, leaves picked and finely chopped

1 large glass dry white wine

200g (7oz) shelled baby broad beans (shelled weight)

500ml (16fl oz) hot chicken stock

1 Preheat the oven to 200°C (400°F/Gas 6). Season the chicken pieces well with salt and pepper. Heat 1 tbsp of the oil in a large flameproof casserole over a medium-high heat. Add the chicken thighs, skin-side down, and brown for 5–6 minutes on each side until golden all over. Remove from the pan and set aside.

2 Reduce the heat to low and add the remaining oil to the casserole. Add the onion and a little salt, and cook for 5 minutes until soft and translucent. Add the celery, garlic, and rosemary, and cook for a further 5 minutes. Increase the heat, pour in the wine, and simmer the ingredients for about 5 minutes.

3 Stir in the broad beans and return the chicken to the pan, tucking the pieces in and around the beans. Pour over the stock, cover, and cook in the oven for 45–60 minutes. Check halfway through the cooking time, topping up with a little hot water if too dry. Serve with oven-roasted tomatoes and fresh crusty bread.

variation

sausages with broad beans

You could make this dish using 8–12 thick pork sausages instead of the chicken. Add 1 tbsp chopped fresh sage in step 2 instead of the rosemary.

seafood risotto

Squid, sea bass, and scallops make for an impressive rice dish.

🥣 **20 MINS** 🍲 **30 MINS**

SERVES 4

2–3 tbsp olive oil

450g (1lb) baby squid, gutted and cleaned, cut into rings, and tentacles chopped (p263)

salt and freshly ground black pepper

450g (1lb) mixed white fish, such as sea bass, monkfish, and haddock, cut into bite-sized pieces

16 scallops (with or without coral, depending on preference), cleaned

2 knobs of butter

2 onions, finely chopped

4 garlic cloves, grated or finely chopped

675g (1½lb) risotto rice

2 large glasses of white wine

2 litres (3½ pints) hot vegetable stock, or light fish stock

6 tomatoes, skinned (p197) and finely chopped

large handful of flat-leaf parsley, finely chopped

handful of dill, finely chopped

lemon wedges, to serve

1 Heat 1 tbsp of the oil in a frying pan. Add the squid and seasoning, and stir-fry for 1 minute over a medium heat. Remove with a slotted spoon and set aside. Repeat with the fish, adding more oil, if needed. Cook for 2 minutes or until opaque and cooked. Repeat with the scallops.

2 Melt a knob of butter in the pan, add the onion, and cook until soft and translucent. Add the garlic and cook for a few seconds. Add the rice to the frying pan and stir to coat. Season, add the wine, raise the heat a little, and boil for a few seconds. In a separate saucepan, simmer the stock. Add a ladleful to the rice and stir until absorbed. Repeat until the rice is al dente and creamy.

3 Add the tomatoes, return the seafood and fish to the pan, then stir in the herbs and remaining butter. Taste and season if needed, and serve with the lemon wedges.

chicken and chorizo paella

A saffron-flavoured rice dish with baby broad beans, named after the Spanish paellera in which it is traditionally cooked.

🥣 **25 MINS** 🍲 **40–45 MINS PLUS STANDING**

SERVES 4-6

a large pinch of saffron threads

2 tbsp olive oil

8 chicken thighs, on the bone if preferred, cut into neat chunks

salt and freshly ground black pepper

175g (6oz) chorizo sausage, cut in 1cm (½in) slices

1 large onion, diced

1 red pepper, deseeded and sliced

1 green pepper, deseeded and sliced

375g (13oz) paella rice or other short-grain rice

2 garlic cloves, finely chopped

400g can chopped tomatoes

200g (7oz) baby broad beans (shelled weight)

1–2 tbsp chopped flat-leaf parsley

1 Put 3–4 tbsp boiling water in a small bowl and add the saffron. Leave to soak for at least 15 minutes.

2 Heat the oil in a large frying pan. Season the chicken and sauté it, turning, for 10–12 minutes, until brown. Transfer to a plate. Sauté the chorizo for 1–2 minutes on each side, until brown. Transfer to the plate with a slotted spoon. Add the onion and peppers to the pan; cook, stirring occasionally, for 5–7 minutes until soft. Add the rice and cook, stirring, for 2–3 minutes. Add the garlic, the saffron with its soaking liquid, and 750ml (1¼ pints) water. Season, then add the chicken, chorizo, tomatoes, and beans. Bring to the boil.

3 Cover, reduce the heat to low, and simmer very gently for 25 minutes until the liquid has almost evaporated and the rice is tender and al dente. Do not stir or the rice will become sticky. If the rice is undercooked, add a little more water and simmer for a few more minutes. Remove from the heat and stand, covered, for 5 minutes. Sprinkle with parsley and serve.

pork steaks with tomato and broad bean sauce

This dish of tender pork steaks is a delicious way of making the most of the season's crop of broad beans.

🥣 **5 MINS**   🍲 **45 MINS**   ❄️ **FREEZABLE**

SERVES 4

4 pork steaks, about 150g (5½oz) each, trimmed

2 tbsp olive oil

pinch of dried oregano

salt and freshly ground black pepper

1 onion, finely chopped

2 garlic cloves, grated or finely chopped

400g can whole plum tomatoes, chopped

125g (4½oz) broad beans (shelled weight)

handful of flat-leaf parsley, very finely chopped

1 Preheat the oven to 200°C (400°F/ Gas 6). Brush the chops with 1 tbsp of the oil and sprinkle over the oregano. Season well with salt and pepper. Sit the chops in a roasting tin and roast in the oven for 15 minutes until golden. Cut into one of the steaks with a sharp knife to check they are cooked through.

2 Meanwhile, heat the remaining oil in a frying pan over a low heat, and add the onion and a little salt. Cook for 5 minutes until soft and translucent, then add the garlic and stir for a couple of seconds.

3 Tip in the tomatoes, including any juices, and bring to the boil. Reduce the heat slightly and simmer for about 15 minutes. Add the broad beans to the pan and cook for a further 10 minutes, adding a little water if the mixture dries out.

4 Taste the sauce and add more seasoning if needed. Stir through the parsley, sit the chops on the sauce, and serve hot.

variation

pork steaks with peas and tomato sauce

Add 125g (4½oz) shelled peas instead of broad beans in step 3.

grated courgette and goat's cheese omelette

A combination of light, delicate courgette, aromatic thyme, and tangy goat's cheese turns this easy dish into a wonderfully moist, fresh-tasting brunch, lunch, or supper.

🥣 **10 MINS**   🍲 **15 MINS**

MAKES 1

3 eggs, lightly beaten

1 small courgette, grated

salt and freshly ground black pepper

knob of butter

50g (1¾oz) soft goat's cheese, crumbled

small handful of thyme, leaves picked, to garnish (optional)

1 Put the beaten eggs and grated courgette in a jug. Season with salt and pepper and combine.

2 Melt the butter in a small non-stick frying pan over a medium-high heat until foaming. Pour in the egg mixture, swirling it around the pan to cover the base. Lift the edge gently with a palette knife and tilt the pan to allow the raw egg to run underneath.

3 When the omelette is partially set, scatter over the goat's cheese and half of the thyme leaves so that it covers the omelette evenly. Continue

cooking until the centre is almost cooked, but still just a little wet. Remove from the heat, and leave for a couple of minutes to set – the retained heat will continue to cook the omelette a little more.

4 Sprinkle over a little black pepper, and garnish with the remaining thyme leaves (if using). Carefully slide out of the pan and serve immediately.

variation

baby broad bean, bacon, and goat's cheese omelette

Prepare in the same way but use a handful of cooked baby broad beans, popped out of their skins instead of the grated courgette, and scatter a chopped, cooked rasher of streaky bacon over with the goat's cheese.

Season's best **summer squashes**

Summer squashes are harvested young through summer, before their skins harden and the seeds mature. They have a moist, delicate texture and mild flavour. They can absorb different flavourings, from garlic and butter or olive oil to chilli and any other spices or fragrant herbs you can think of. They mix beautifully with other summer vegetables, such as tomatoes, peppers, fennel, and asparagus. The flowers are also edible.

Grown in tropical and warm, temperate regions around the world, summer squashes are a prolific crop. The long, green courgette is the most widely produced.

Green courgette Also known as zucchini, green courgettes are identical in flavour and texture to yellow varieties. Small green courgettes are superior to large ones, which tend to be fibrous and bland.

The edible flowers are fragile, so handle with care when preparing. Nip off the internal stamen before stuffing.

Choose small ones for the best flavour.

Crookneck squash This has tender skin, a firm texture, and a clean, faintly lemony flavour. If the bulbous end is large, halve lengthways before cutting into chunks so that it cooks evenly.

It has a bright yellow, bumpy skin.

Check the cut ends: they should be moist and freshly cut. Trim the stalk before cooking.

Eight ball courgette Identifiable by its mottled pale green stripes, this round variety of summer squash has a subtle but satisfying flavour. It is at its best when only slightly larger than a golf ball.

Yellow courgette Like the green varieties, yellow courgettes have a mild, faintly mushroomy flavour with tender flesh and skin. They make a colourful summer dish when mixed with green courgettes.

If the skin is slightly fuzzy, dipping it in cold water will remove any clinging dirt.

Round squash Related to the elongated courgette, round squash has a similar mild flavour. Its shape makes it ideal for halving and stuffing. Small ones can be stir-fried or steamed whole.

Patty pan squash These flattened, scallop-edged squash, which come in yellow, green, or white, have thin skin and tender flesh. The greater ratio of skin to flesh improves the overall flavour and texture.

Choose firm, young fruits with glossy skin. The skin adds flavour and texture, and does not need peeling.

Yellow one ball courgettes This is another colourful variety of round courgette. It has a good flavour and is excellent halved and stuffed, coated in béchamel sauce, then baked.

essentials
varieties available

The most common are green, yellow, and round courgettes, crookneck squash, and patty pan squash.

buy Choose small, young specimens that feel heavy with unblemished skin.

store Store in the vegetable drawer in the fridge for up to 5 days.

cook Steam, fry, stuff and bake, use in salads, soups, and stews. Grate and use in cakes and muffins. Stuff, batter, and deep-fry the flowers.

preserve Pickle. Freeze griddled slices.

recipe ideas

Cashew and courgette rice p117

Courgette fritters with dill tzatziki p87

Courgette stuffed with sultanas, red onion, and pine nuts p89

Grated courgette and goat's cheese omelette p101

Penne pasta with asparagus and courgettes p112

devilled lamb cutlets with crushed potato and mustard seed salad

New-season lamb, accompanied by sweet, waxy new potatoes, is coated in a tangy marinade and oven-baked.

🥣 10 MINS   🍲 35–45 MINS

SERVES 4

250g (9oz) new potatoes

salt and freshly ground black pepper

8 lamb cutlets

1 tbsp olive oil

1 tbsp mustard seeds

bunch of spring onions, trimmed and finely chopped

For the coating

2 tbsp English mustard

2 tbsp tomato ketchup

1 tbsp cayenne pepper

2 tbsp finely chopped onion

1 tbsp olive oil

1 Preheat the oven to 200°C (400°F/Gas 6). Cook the potatoes in a large pan of boiling salted water for about 15 minutes until soft, then drain.

2 While the potatoes are cooking, mix together all the ingredients for the coating, and season well with salt and pepper. Coat the lamb cutlets evenly in the mixture and place in a roasting tin. Roast in the oven for 20–30 minutes, or until cooked through to your liking.

3 Add the olive oil to the drained potatoes and then crush them gently with a fork. Mix gently with the mustard seeds and spring onions, and season with salt and pepper. Serve the potato salad with the lamb cutlets.

spaghetti primavera

The younger the courgettes, carrots, and peas, the tastier and sweeter this dish will be. Their beautiful pale greens and orange epitomize the colours of early summer.

🥣 45–50 MINS   🍲 15–25 MINS

SERVES 4

2 courgettes, diced

salt and freshly ground black pepper

2 carrots, diced

200g (7oz) peas (shelled weight)

500g (1lb 2oz) spaghetti

45g (1½oz) butter

175ml (6fl oz) double cream

30g (1oz) Parmesan cheese, grated

1 Bring a saucepan of water to the boil. Add the courgettes and some salt and cook for 2–3 minutes, until barely tender to the tip of a knife. Drain well, then blot dry on kitchen paper. Set aside on some fresh kitchen paper to ensure the blanched courgettes are not at all soggy.

2 Put the carrots in a saucepan, cover with cold water, add salt, and bring to the boil. Simmer for about 5 minutes or until just tender, then drain, rinse with cold water, drain again, and set aside. Bring a clean saucepan of salted water to the boil. Add the peas and simmer for 3–8 minutes, depending on their size, until tender. Drain, rinse with cold water, and set aside. It is necessary to blanch the vegetables separately because each must be cooked to be at the peak of their sweetness, and they all cook at a different rate.

3 Cook the spaghetti in a large pan of boiling salted water for about 12 minutes, or until it is tender but still al dente. Drain well.

4 Meanwhile, heat the butter in a large saucepan over a low heat, add the courgette, carrot, and peas, and sauté for 1 minute.

5 Add the cream to the pan of vegetables, stir well, and bring to a simmer. Take the pan from the heat, add the spaghetti, and toss well in the mixture. Add the Parmesan and toss again. Serve on warmed plates, with a good grinding of black pepper.

turkish lamb kebabs

Succulent, grilled minced lamb skewers can be easily whipped up for a relaxed lunch or evening meal.

🍲 **30-35 MINS PLUS DRAINING**   🍲 **10-15 MINS**

SPECIAL EQUIPMENT ▪ 6 wooden or metal skewers ▪ food processor

SERVES 6

1 large onion, cut into chunks

1kg (2¼lb) minced lamb

2 tsp ground cumin

salt and freshly ground black pepper

3 garlic cloves, finely chopped

3-5 sprigs of mint, leaves picked, finely chopped, plus more leaves for garnish

3-5 sprigs of flat-leaf parsley, leaves picked and finely chopped

olive oil

For the yogurt

1 large cucumber, trimmed and grated

1 tsp salt

500ml (16fl oz) Greek-style yogurt

1 garlic clove, finely chopped

1 Soak wooden skewers in cold water for 30 minutes. For the yogurt, mix the cucumber with the salt, and put in a colander. Leave to drain for 10 minutes. Squeeze the excess water from the cucumber. Put the yogurt in a bowl and mix with the cucumber, garlic, and salt to taste. Cover and chill.

2 Put the onion in a food processor and blitz until finely chopped. In a large bowl, mix the lamb, onion, cumin, salt and pepper, garlic, and herbs together. To test for seasoning, fry a spoonful of meat until browned on both sides. Taste, and add more salt and pepper to the raw mix if needed.

3 Heat the grill and set the rack 5cm (2in) from the heat. Wet your hands to make the lamb mixture easier to work with, and divide it into 12. Roll into cylinders about 2.5cm (1in) in diameter.

4 Brush the metal skewers (if using) and the grill rack with oil. Thread the meat cylinders onto the skewers, pressing them into shape, and place on the grill rack. Brush with oil and grill for 5-7 minutes, or until brown.

5 Turn the skewers and grill the other side. The meat should remain juicy in the centre. Serve on a bed of herby bulgur wheat salad, with extra mint leaves and the yogurt sauce.

risotto primavera

This risotto is bursting with the verdant early summer flavours of asparagus, peas, and courgettes.

🍲 **15 MINS**   🍲 **1 HR**

SERVES 4-6

2 tbsp olive oil

50g (1¾oz) butter

1 onion, finely chopped

salt and freshly ground black pepper

3 garlic cloves, finely chopped

300g (10oz) arborio rice or carnaroli rice

250ml (9fl oz) white wine

600ml (1 pint) hot vegetable stock

125g (4½oz) broad beans (shelled weight), skinned (p85, optional)

bunch of asparagus spears, trimmed and chopped into bite-sized pieces

2 small courgettes, diced

30g (1oz) Parmesan cheese, grated, plus extra to serve

1 Heat 1 tbsp of the oil and half of the butter in a large heavy-based saucepan over a medium heat. Add the onion and cook for 3-4 minutes until soft and translucent. Season with salt and pepper, then add the garlic and cook for a minute. Add the rice and stir in the oily butter so that all the grains are coated. Cook for a few seconds. Then increase the heat, add the wine, and boil it for 1-2 minutes until it has been absorbed.

2 In a separate saucepan, simmer the stock. Add a ladleful to the rice and stir. Repeat for 30-40 minutes, or until the rice is cooked and is al dente and creamy. You may not use all the stock, or you may need a little more.

3 While the rice is cooking, add the broad beans to a large pan of boiling salted water. Cook for 3-4 minutes, then drain well and set aside. Heat the remaining oil in another frying pan over a medium heat, add the asparagus and courgettes, and cook for a few minutes until they just begin to colour. When the rice is cooked, stir all the vegetables into the risotto, dot the remaining butter all over, and stir it in. Then stir in the Parmesan cheese, taste, and season, if needed. Serve with more Parmesan and a lightly dressed rocket and tomato salad on the side.

chicken and pea filo pie

This impressive-looking pie of baby new potatoes, peas, and chicken is actually simple and quick to make. Use leftover roast chicken pieces instead of fresh if they need eating up.

🥣 20 MINS   🍲 30 MINS   ❄ FREEZABLE

SPECIAL EQUIPMENT ▪ 18cm (7in) square pie or cake tin

SERVES 6

350g (12oz) skinless chicken breasts

250g (9oz) baby new potatoes, quartered

200ml (7fl oz) chicken stock

125g (4½oz) peas (shelled weight)

12 sheets filo pastry

50g (1¾oz) butter, melted, plus extra if needed

1–2 tbsp mild curry powder

salt and freshly ground black pepper

1 Cook the chicken and the potatoes in the stock in a medium-sized saucepan for about 10 minutes, or until both are tender, adding the peas for the last 5 minutes of cooking time. Drain, reserving the stock. Leave to cool, then cut the chicken into neat pieces.

2 Preheat the oven to 200°C (400°F/ Gas 6). Lightly brush 6 sheets of the filo pastry with the melted butter. Use them to line the bottom of the pie or cake tin, allowing them to overlap the sides.

3 Put the chicken, potatoes, peas, and curry powder in a mixing bowl. Moisten with 3–4 tbsp of the reserved chicken stock, using just enough to wet the mixture and produce a little gravy, but without adding so much that it soaks the pastry. Toss the ingredients together and season well with salt and pepper.

4 Spoon the chicken filling into the filo pastry shell. Fold the pastry edges in towards the middle, and top the pie with the remaining 6 filo sheets, each brushed with a little melted butter. Tuck the edges of the pastry down neatly at the sides, and make sure that the top is well glazed with melted butter. Bake in the oven for 20–30 minutes until the pastry is cooked and golden. Serve hot.

asian noodle salad

A fantastic spicy dressing really lifts this satisfying dish of chicken noodles with mangetout and spring onions.

🥣 30–35 MINS PLUS MARINATING   🍲 6–9 MINS

SERVES 6

2cm (¾in) piece of fresh root ginger, peeled and finely chopped

2 green chillies, deseeded and diced

2 garlic cloves, finely chopped

2 tsp granulated sugar

salt and freshly ground black pepper

4 tbsp rice wine vinegar

120ml (4fl oz) soy sauce

4 tbsp sunflower oil

2 tbsp sesame oil

250g (9oz) thin egg noodles

175g (6oz) mangetout, trimmed

4 spring onions, trimmed and cut into diagonal slices

75g (2½oz) roasted unsalted peanuts, coarsely chopped

small bunch of coriander, chopped

375g (13oz) cooked chicken, cut in neat pieces

1 Put the ginger, chillies, garlic, sugar, pepper, vinegar, and soy sauce in a bowl. Whisk in the oils gradually until the sauce thickens slightly.

2 Cook the noodles in a large pan of boiling salted water for about 4–6 minutes, or until tender but still al dente. Stir occasionally to prevent sticking. Drain, rinse with hot water, and drain again thoroughly. Transfer to a large bowl. Briskly whisk the dressing, pour it over the noodles, and toss until well coated. Set aside for at least 1 hour to marinate.

3 Cook the mangetout in boiling salted water for 2–3 minutes until tender but still crisp. Drain, rinse with hot water, and drain again thoroughly. Cut each diagonally into 2–3 slices. Then add the mangetout, spring onions, two-thirds of the peanuts and the coriander, and all the chicken to the noodles. Toss the ingredients well and taste for seasoning.

4 Mound the noodle salad onto a serving plate, scatter the remaining chopped peanuts and coriander over the top, and serve.

spiced seafood salad

A tangy Thai dish of scallops, squid, and haddock has a delicate and refreshing flavour, just perfect for early summer.

🥣 30–40 MINS   🍲 12–15 MINS

SERVES 4

salt

250g (9oz) small squid, gutted and cleaned and cut into 1cm (½in) wide rings (p263)

250g (9oz) large scallops, trimmed and cut in half horizontally

250g (9oz) thick haddock fillet

250g (9oz) thick salmon fillet

4 kaffir lime leaves, deveined and finely diced, or grated zest of 1 lime

2 garlic cloves, finely chopped

1 green chilli, deseeded and finely chopped

1 stalk of lemongrass, peeled, crushed, and thinly sliced

juice of 3 large limes, plus more if needed

4 tbsp fish sauce (nam pla), plus more if needed

2 tbsp sugar

small lettuce leaves, to serve

1 Fill a large saucepan with 5cm (2in) of water, add salt, and bring to the boil. Reduce the heat, add the squid, and simmer for 2 minutes until opaque and starting to curl. Remove with a fish slice and drain on kitchen paper. Repeat with the scallops and fish.

2 Put the lime leaves, garlic, chilli, lemongrass, lime juice, fish sauce, and sugar in a small bowl. Stir until the sugar dissolves. Put the squid and scallops in a large bowl. Pour the dressing over the seafood and toss. Remove any skin from the haddock and salmon, break into large pieces, then add it, tossing gently to mix. Taste for seasoning, adding more lime juice or fish sauce if needed.

3 Arrange the lettuce on plates, pile some dressed seafood on top, and place a crab claw to one side, if using.

baked haddock in white wine with parsley

Firm-fleshed haddock is at its best at this time of year. It is a versatile fish to cook, and retains its flavour and texture well when baked with white wine and tomatoes.

🥣 5 MINS   🍲 20 MINS

SERVES 4

675g (1½lb) haddock, skinned and cut into 4 pieces

salt

1 large glass of white wine

12 cherry tomatoes

handful of flat-leaf parsley, finely chopped

1 Preheat the oven to 190°C (375°F/ Gas 5). Sprinkle the fish with salt, then lay in an ovenproof dish. Pour over the wine, then add the tomatoes and the parsley.

2 Cover the dish tightly with foil and bake in the oven for 15–20 minutes, until the fish is cooked through and the alcohol has evaporated. Serve with salad and fresh crusty bread or new potatoes.

variation

baked salmon in rosé wine with dill

Use a flameproof dish. Substitute four 175g (6oz) salmon fillets for the haddock, rosé wine for white wine, ½ large cucumber, peeled, deseeded and cut into chunks for the tomatoes, and a handful of chopped dill for the parsley. Once cooked, transfer the salmon to plates. Stir 1–2 tbsp crème fraîche into the cooking juices in the dish, place over a medium heat to warm through, season to taste, then spoon over the fish.

salmon salad with mint yogurt dressing

This is an ideal way to serve succulent salmon on a warm day. Prepare the dressing and cook the salmon in advance, if needed, and then plate up at the last minute.

🥣 15 MINS   🍲 25 MINS

SERVES 4

2 tbsp red wine vinegar

2 tbsp finely chopped mint, plus extra mint leaves, to garnish

4 tbsp Greek-style yogurt

salt and freshly ground black pepper

550g (1¼lb) side of salmon

handful of dill, chopped

1 lemon, sliced

1 cucumber, trimmed and cut into ribbons, to serve

1 Put the red wine vinegar, chopped mint, and Greek-style yogurt in a bowl, season, and whisk together. Set aside.

2 Lay the side of salmon on a large piece of foil. Sprinkle over the handful of chopped dill and overlap a few slices of lemon on top. Season and loosely seal the foil to make a parcel. Place on a baking tray and bake in a preheated 200°C (400°F/Gas 6) oven for 20–25 minutes. Allow to cool.

3 Transfer the cool salmon to a plate, drizzle over the dressing, and scatter a few fresh mint leaves over the top. Serve with a cucumber salad and a slice of lemon on the side.

stuffed sardines with crushed new potatoes

Sardines are best cooked simply to bring out their full flavour. Grill them lightly – on a barbecue or charcoal grill if you have one – and serve them with new potatoes and a plain salad.

15 MINS   **25 MINS**

SERVES 4

600g (1lb 5oz) new potatoes

4 tbsp extra virgin olive oil

salt and freshly ground black pepper

2 tbsp finely chopped flat-leaf parsley

16 fresh sardine fillets

For the hazelnut stuffing

3 tbsp olive oil

1 garlic clove, crushed

50g (1¾oz) hazelnuts, finely chopped

30g (1oz) fresh white breadcrumbs

2 tbsp finely chopped flat-leaf parsley

1 Put the potatoes in a large saucepan and cover with cold water. Bring to the boil and cook for 15–20 minutes until tender. Drain, arrange on a flat tray, and crush slightly with the flat side of a potato masher. Drizzle with the olive oil, season, sprinkle with the parsley, set aside, and keep warm.

2 For the stuffing, heat the oil in a frying pan over a low heat. Add the garlic and cook for 30 seconds. Add the hazelnuts, breadcrumbs, and parsley, and cook for 5 minutes until the breadcrumbs are golden brown. Season with salt and pepper.

3 Heat a barbecue, charcoal grill, or an oven grill until hot and brush with oil. Rinse the sardines, pat them dry with kitchen paper, and season. Grill half the sardines skin-side down over a high heat for about 1 minute on each side. Remove to a plate and keep warm while you grill the remaining fillets.

4 To serve, divide half the sardine fillets among 4 serving plates. Spoon a little of the hazelnut stuffing on top of each fillet, then cover with the remaining fillets. Put the potatoes into a serving bowl for guests to help themselves. Serve immediately with crisp, fresh salad leaves on the side.

mixed fish stew with toasted croûtons

This is an easy-to-cook stew for relaxed dining. Choose fish and shellfish in season for the best flavour, and serve with a garlicky mayonnaise sauce (rouille), if you like.

15 MINS   **30 MINS**

SERVES 4

1.1kg (2½lb) mixed seasonal fish such as pollack, whiting or coley, sea bass, smoked haddock, salmon, and squid

1½ tbsp olive oil

2 garlic cloves, crushed or finely chopped

1 tbsp tomato purée

1 small onion, finely chopped

4 tomatoes, skinned (p197) and chopped

½ tsp fennel seeds

a few strands of saffron

pinch of paprika

600ml (1 pint) light fish stock

salt and freshly ground black pepper

½ baguette

75g (2½oz) Gruyère cheese, grated

handful of flat-leaf parsley, finely chopped, to garnish

1 Wash the fish, then cut it into chunky bite-sized pieces and set aside. Put the oil in a large wide pan, add the garlic, tomato purée, and onion, and cook over a very low heat for 5–8 minutes, or until the onion is soft and translucent.

2 Add the tomatoes, fennel seeds, saffron, and paprika, pour in the stock, and season with salt and pepper. Bring to the boil, then reduce to a simmer and cook for 10 minutes. Add all the fish and simmer for a further 5–8 minutes, or until the fish is cooked.

3 Slice the bread diagonally and toast. Serve the stew in shallow bowls with the toasted croûtons and a sprinkle of cheese on top, and finish with a garnish of parsley.

grilled herring with mustard butter

Many breakfast herring recipes use bacon and oatmeal, but the mustard here makes this recipe a special way to start the day. Enjoy this with hot buttered toast.

10 MINS   **4–6 MINS**

SERVES 4

8 herrings, scaled, gutted, and trimmed; heads removed

1 tbsp vegetable oil

salt and freshly ground black pepper

115g (4oz) watercress, to garnish

lemon wedges, to garnish

For the mustard butter

75g (2½oz) butter, softened

1 tbsp wholegrain mustard

1 tsp thyme leaves

squeeze of lemon juice

1 Preheat the grill on its highest setting. Pat the herrings dry with kitchen paper, brush with oil, and season lightly. Place on a large sheet of lightly buttered foil on a baking sheet.

2 Mix the butter, mustard, and thyme together. Add a little lemon juice and season. Grill the herrings for 2–3 minutes on each side, or until cooked: it will be firm to the touch.

3 Lift the herrings onto a large, warmed serving dish and dot with the mustard butter to melt over the fish. Garnish with watercress and lemon wedges.

Season's best **herrings and sardines**

Members of the same family, herrings and sardines are both sustainable, oily fish, making them excellent choices for both health and ethical reasons. Sardines are at their best in summer, but herrings can be fished all year. They move in huge shoals to warmer waters through the summer months, so are a fine catch then. Delicious simply with lemon or fresh herbs, they are also good with stronger Mediterranean flavours, too.

Atlantic herring Also known as sea herrings, these are found on both sides of the Atlantic. They can grow up to 46cm (18in) long, but most are caught much smaller. They have a lot of fine bones but, when fresh, the flavour is good and sweet and not too oily.

Sardine This fast-growing fish is rounded, oil-rich, and high in omega-3 essential fatty acids. It has a greeny-blue back, bright silvery sides and belly, and loose scales. It has a lot of bones, a coarse texture, and is meaty with a robust flavour. Large sardines are called pilchards.

how to bone a herring

Herrings are full of tiny bones and the majority can be removed with the backbone using this method. You will need to feel over the flesh and pull out any remaining bones with tweezers, too. The butterflied fillets can be egged, then crumb- or oat-coated and fried, or they can be stuffed and re-shaped, then baked, or rolled and soused. Sardines and pilchards are usually cooked whole and eaten straight off the bone, but can be filleted first (though it is a bit fiddly).

1 Lay the fish on a board and cut off the head with a sharp knife; also cut off the tail.

2 Clean the fish, if not already gutted, then open the fish out and lay it, skin-side up, on the board.

3 Hold the fish and firmly run your thumb up and down the backbone several times to loosen the bones.

4 Turn the fish over and gently lift the backbone and attached bones away. Remove any loose bones, too.

essentials
varieties available

Atlantic herring (whole or fillets), sardine, pilchard (Cornish sardine). Herrings are also sold pickled, cold smoked as kippers (split) and bloaters (whole), and hot smoked as buckling. Sardines and pilchards are also popular canned (in olive oil or tomato sauce).

buy Choose shiny, firm fish with a fresh smell of the sea and, if whole, with bright eyes.

store Best eaten fresh. Wrap and store in the coldest part of the fridge for up to 24 hours.

cook Pan-fry, grill, or barbecue. Herrings are also good roasted and soused.

recipe ideas

Grilled sardines on toast p76

Rollmops p135

Stuffed sardines with crushed new potatoes p108

lamb chops in paper with fennel

Chops enclosed in baking parchment steam in their own juices, using minimum fat for maximum flavour. The paper parcels puff up and turn golden brown in the oven and, when opened, release wafts of delicious, gentle aniseed aroma.

🥣 25-30 MINS   🍲 35-40 MINS

SERVES 4

1kg (2¼lb) fennel bulbs

4 tbsp olive oil

2 garlic cloves, finely chopped

400g can chopped tomatoes

3 tbsp pastis

salt and freshly ground black pepper

4 lamb loin chops, each 2.5cm (1in) thick, about 625g (1lb 6oz) total weight

melted butter, to brush

1 egg

1 Trim off and discard the fennel stalks and root, along with any tough outer layers from the bulb. Reserve some green fronds for garnish. Thinly slice each fennel bulb.

2 Heat half the oil in a frying pan over a medium heat, add the fennel and garlic, and fry for 6–8 minutes until the fennel begins to soften.

3 Add three-quarters of the tomatoes, the pastis, and salt and pepper to the pan and cook, stirring occasionally, for 20–25 minutes until the mixture is thick and most of the moisture has evaporated. Taste for seasoning.

4 Meanwhile, cut the "tail" from each chop and season. Heat the remaining oil in another frying pan over a high heat, add the chops and tails, and cook for 1–2 minutes until well browned. Turn and brown the other side.

5 Fold a large sheet of baking parchment measuring about 30 x 37.5cm (12 x 15in) in half, and draw a curve to make a heart shape when unfolded, large enough to leave a 7.5cm (3in) border around a chop. Cut out the heart shape with scissors. Repeat to make 4 paper hearts. Open out and brush each one with melted butter, leaving a border of about 2.5cm (1in) unbuttered.

6 Beat the egg with ½ tsp salt. Brush the egg glaze on the unbuttered border of each paper heart.

7 Heat the oven to 190°C (375°F/ Gas 5). Spoon a bed of the fennel mixture on 1 half of a paper heart. Set a lamb chop and tail on top of the fennel mixture. Spoon a little of the reserved tomato over and lay a fennel frond on top. Fold the paper over the filling and run your fingers along the edge to stick the 2 sides of the heart together. Make small pleats to seal the edges of the paper case.

8 Twist the ends of the paper case to finish. Repeat the process with the remaining ingredients to make 4 paper parcels. Place on a baking sheet and bake for 10–14 minutes until puffed and brown. Serve at once with steamed asparagus or other seasonal vegetables, allowing each diner to open their own parcel.

courgette, herb, and lemon tagine

If you have an earthenware tagine dish then do use it; otherwise, a large heavy-based pan does the job just as well.

🥄 25 MINS 🍲 40 MINS

SERVES 4

2 tbsp olive oil

1 red onion, finely chopped

salt and freshly ground black pepper

2 garlic cloves, grated or finely chopped

pinch of fennel seeds

pinch of ground cinnamon

1–2 tsp harissa paste

2 preserved lemons, halved, pith removed, and halved again

400g can plum tomatoes, chopped

1 head of broccoli, broken into florets

3 courgettes, sliced

juice of 1 lemon

handful of dill, finely chopped

handful of flat-leaf parsley, chopped

1 Heat half the oil in a large heavy-based pan over a medium heat, add the onions, and cook for 3–4 minutes until soft. Season well with salt and pepper. Stir through the garlic, fennel seeds, cinnamon, harissa, and preserved lemons. Add the tomatoes and crush them with the back of a wooden spoon. Bring to the boil, then reduce the heat and simmer for 30–40 minutes. If the sauce starts to dry out, top up with a little hot water.

2 Cook the broccoli in a pan of boiling salted water for 3–5 minutes or until tender, then drain and refresh in cold water. Drain again and set aside. Heat the remaining oil in a frying pan over a low heat, add the courgettes, and cook over a low heat, stirring, for 5 minutes until they start to colour. Add the lemon juice, some seasoning, and stir through the dill.

3 Add the broccoli and courgettes to the sauce and stir through the parsley. Serve hot with some fluffy couscous and lemon wedges to squeeze over.

warm pea pancakes with chargrilled asparagus

A deceptively simple dish to prepare, this recipe showcases early summer produce. The bright colours of the peas and asparagus contrast beautifully with the golden yolk of the egg.

🥄 10 MINS 🍲 30 MINS

SPECIAL EQUIPMENT ▪ food processor

SERVES 4

400g (14oz) fresh peas (shelled weight)

large handful of mint leaves, chopped

50g (1¾oz) melted butter, plus extra for frying

4 tbsp plain flour

4 tbsp double cream

2 tbsp Parmesan cheese, grated

6 large eggs

salt and freshly ground black pepper

1 large bunch of asparagus spears, trimmed

1 tsp extra virgin olive oil

1 Put the peas in a pan and blanch in boiling water for 1–2 minutes, then drain and leave to cool.

2 Put the peas and mint into a food processor and blitz together to get a rough texture. Add the melted butter, flour, cream, Parmesan, and 2 eggs, and season. Process the mixture to a stiff paste.

3 Heat some butter or oil in a large frying pan and add 1 or 2 tbsp of the mixture for each pancake. Cook over a medium heat and use the back of a spoon to smooth the top of the mixture. After 3–4 minutes, the edges of the pancakes will change colour. Carefully turn them over and cook for another 1–2 minutes.

4 Meanwhile, bring a large pan of water to the boil and lightly poach the remaining eggs until just set. Remove them with a slotted spoon.

5 Meanwhile, chargrill the asparagus in a hot griddle pan with a little olive oil, seasoning while cooking, until golden. Serve on the side with an egg on top of the pancakes.

lamb with chickpeas, green peppers, and couscous

Lamb and cousous: quintessential north African food.

🥄 10 MINS 🍲 30 MINS

SERVES 4

1 tbsp olive oil

1 onion, finely chopped

2 garlic cloves, grated or finely chopped

900g (2lb) lean lamb, cut into bite-sized pieces

1 tsp ground cinnamon

1 tsp paprika

salt and freshly ground black pepper

2–3 green peppers, deseeded and roughly chopped

400g can chickpeas, drained and rinsed

900ml (1½ pints) hot vegetable stock

175g (6oz) couscous

50g (1¾oz) pine nuts, toasted

handful of flat-leaf parsley, chopped

1 Heat the oil in a large frying pan over a medium heat, add the onion, and cook for 3–4 minutes until the onion is soft. Add the garlic, lamb, cinnamon, and paprika, and season with salt and pepper.

2 Tip in the peppers and chickpeas, and cook, stirring occasionally, until the meat is browned on all sides. Pour over 600ml (1 pint) of the hot stock, cover the pan, and simmer gently for 20 minutes. Top up with a little hot water if the mixture starts to dry out.

3 Meanwhile, tip the couscous into a bowl and pour over enough of the remaining stock just to cover. Leave for about 5 minutes, then fluff up with a fork and season with salt and pepper. To serve, sprinkle the lamb mixture with the pine nuts and parsley, and serve immediately with the couscous.

penne pasta with asparagus and courgettes

Choose smaller courgettes for better flavour and young asparagus with tender stalks for this quick, lemony pasta.

🥣 10 MINS   🍲 20 MINS

SERVES 4

1 tbsp olive oil

1 onion, finely chopped

salt

4 small courgettes, 2 diced and 2 grated

3 garlic cloves, grated or finely chopped

bunch of fine asparagus spears, trimmed and stalks cut into 3 pieces

1 small glass of white wine

1-2 tsp capers, rinsed and chopped

zest of 1 lemon

350g (12oz) penne pasta

handful of flat-leaf parsley, finely chopped

Parmesan cheese, grated, to serve

1 Heat the oil in a large frying pan, add the onion and salt, and cook over a low heat for 5 minutes, or until soft and translucent. Add all the courgettes and cook for 10 minutes, or until they have softened. Don't allow them to brown.

2 Stir in the garlic and asparagus. Add the wine, raise the heat, and allow to boil for 2-3 minutes, then return to a simmer. Cook for a further 2-3 minutes, or until the asparagus has softened, then stir in the capers and lemon zest.

3 Meanwhile, cook the pasta in a large pan of boiling salted water for about 10 minutes, or until it is tender but still al dente. Drain, keeping back a tiny amount of the cooking water. Return the pasta to the pan and toss with the cooking water. Add the courgette mixture and parsley, then toss again. Sprinkle with Parmesan cheese and serve.

artichokes, butter beans, and peas

This is a substantial vegetarian dish. The artichokes and butter beans give it a wonderful creamy finish, and breadcrumbs are stirred through at the last minute to add some texture.

🥣 15 MINS   🍲 1 HR 30 MINS

SERVES 4-6

1 tbsp olive oil

1 onion, finely chopped

3 garlic cloves, finely chopped

250g (9oz) small button mushrooms, larger ones halved

2 x 400g cans butter beans, drained

pinch of ground nutmeg

juice of ½ lemon

salt and freshly ground black pepper

600ml (1 pint) hot vegetable stock

125g (4½oz) peas (shelled weight)

8 cooked artichoke hearts (p309), halved or quartered (or a large jar, drained)

60g (2oz) breadcrumbs, toasted

a few sprigs of flat-leaf parsley, finely chopped, to serve

1 Heat the oil in a large heavy-based pan over a medium heat, add the onion, and cook for 3-4 minutes until soft and translucent. Then stir in the garlic and mushrooms and cook for about 5 minutes until the mushrooms are tender.

2 Stir in the butter beans, add the nutmeg and lemon juice, and season with salt and pepper. Pour over the stock and bring to the boil. Boil for about 10 minutes, then reduce to a simmer, partially cover with a lid, and cook for 45 minutes. Check occasionally that there is enough stock in the pan and it's not drying out, and top up with a little hot water if necessary.

3 Stir in the peas and artichokes and cook gently for a further 15-20 minutes, or until the butter beans are completely soft. Spoon over the breadcrumbs and carefully fold some in, then top with the parsley. Serve with some freshly baked crusty bread.

roasted new potatoes and sausages with rosemary and chilli

Flavoursome new potatoes roasted in their skins with sprigs of rosemary taste simply delicious. Choose sausages that have a high percentage of meat and a low percentage of fat.

🥣 **15 MINS**   🍲 **40 MINS**

SERVES 4

8-12 pork sausages

2 red onions, peeled and cut into eighths

pinch of chilli flakes

handful of rosemary sprigs

1.1kg (2½lb) new potatoes, large ones halved

salt and freshly ground black pepper

1 tbsp olive oil

1 Preheat the oven to 200°C (400°F/ Gas 6). Put the sausages in a roasting tin with the onion, sprinkle over the chilli flakes and rosemary, then add the new potatoes. Season well with salt and pepper, drizzle over the oil, and combine together well.

2 Put the tray in the oven to roast for 30–40 minutes, turning the sausages and potatoes halfway

through cooking. When the sausages are golden all over and cooked through, remove from the oven and serve on warmed plates.

variation

roasted new potatoes and sardines

Prepare the potatoes and onions in the same way, place in the roasting tin with a handful of thyme leaves instead of rosemary and seasoning as before. Drizzle with olive oil and toss. Roast for 30 minutes, turning once. Lay 8 cleaned and descaled sardines on top, drizzle with a little more olive oil, season and roast for a further 10 minutes or until the fish and vegetables are cooked.

lamb with artichokes, broad beans, and dill

This is a light stew that is full of early summer flavours.

🥣 **15 MINS**   🍲 **1 HR 45 MINS**   ❄ **FREEZABLE**

SERVES 4-6

1.25kg (2¾lb) lamb shoulder, with bones, trimmed and cut into bite-sized pieces

salt and freshly ground black pepper

2 tbsp olive oil

2 onions, roughly chopped

3 carrots, peeled and roughly chopped

1 tbsp plain flour

120ml (4fl oz) dry white wine

900ml (1½ pints) hot vegetable stock

a few sprigs of rosemary

grated zest of ½ lemon and juice of 1 lemon

4 large cooked artichoke hearts (p309), quartered

350g (12oz) broad beans (shelled weight), skinned (p85, optional)

bunch of dill, finely chopped

1 Preheat the oven to 180°C (350°F/ Gas 4). Season the meat with salt and pepper. Heat half the oil in a large flameproof casserole over a high heat, add the lamb (in batches, if necessary), and cook for 6–8 minutes until no longer pink. Remove from the casserole and set aside.

2 Heat the remaining oil in the casserole over a medium heat, add the onions, and cook for 3–4 minutes until soft. Season with salt and pepper, add the carrots, and cook for a further 5 minutes. Sprinkle over the flour, stir, and cook for a couple of minutes. Add the wine, increase the heat, and cook the sauce for a minute.

3 Add the stock, rosemary, lemon juice and zest, and lamb. Bring to the boil, cover, and put in the oven for 1 hour. Check occasionally that it's not drying out and top up with a little hot water if needed. Stir through the artichokes and broad beans and cook for a further 30 minutes, or until the vegetables are tender. Taste and season as required and add the dill to taste. Serve with crusty bread.

german potato salad

The piquant caraway dressing on this salad is inspired by recipes that came from the Black Forest in Germany, where few dishes are complete without ham or sausage, or both.

🥣 25–30 MINS PLUS CHILLING   🍲 15–20 MINS

SERVES 6–8

1.35kg (3lb) red-skinned new potatoes

salt and freshly ground black pepper

1 small red onion, very finely chopped

3 tbsp red wine vinegar

3 tbsp soured cream

2 tbsp hot mustard

2 tsp caraway seeds

250ml (9fl oz) vegetable oil

150g (5½oz) thinly sliced smoked ham

7-10 sprigs of parsley, leaves picked and chopped

1 Scrub the potatoes under cold, running water but do not peel. Cut any larger potatoes into 2–4 pieces. Put in a large saucepan with plenty of cold, salted water, cover, and bring to the boil. Simmer for 15–20 minutes, just until tender, then drain.

2 Put the onion in a bowl with the vinegar, soured cream, mustard, and salt and pepper. Sprinkle in the

caraway seeds. Whisk together just until mixed, then gradually whisk in the oil so the dressing emulsifies and thickens slightly. Taste for seasoning and set aside.

3 While still warm, cut the potatoes into 1cm (½in) slices. Transfer to a large bowl. Briskly whisk the dressing, then pour it over the warm potatoes. Stir gently to thoroughly coat and leave to cool.

4 Trim the fat from the ham, then cut into 1cm (½in) strips. Add the ham to the potatoes. Sprinkle three-quarters of the parsley over the top. Stir, taste for seasoning, cover, and place in the fridge for at least 1 hour.

5 Transfer the salad to a large platter, or individual plates or shallow bowls, and sprinkle evenly with the remaining chopped parsley. Serve at room temperature.

lentil, broad bean, and feta salad

The lentils in this salad can be whatever colour you happen to have to hand: green, brown, or anything else. The broad beans and feta cheese add further colour to the finished dish.

🥣 15 MINS

SERVES 4

85g (3oz) baby broad beans (shelled weight), skinned (p85, optional)

400g can lentils in water, drained and rinsed

salt and freshly ground black pepper

bunch of spring onions, trimmed and finely chopped

1 green chilli, deseeded and finely chopped

175g (6oz) feta cheese, cut into cubes

handful of flat-leaf parsley, finely chopped

For the dressing

3 tbsp olive oil

1 tbsp white wine vinegar

2.5cm (1in) piece of fresh root ginger, peeled and grated

pinch of caster sugar (optional)

1 Cook the broad beans in boiling, lightly salted water for 4–5 minutes until just tender. Drain, rinse with cold water, and drain again.

2 Put the lentils in a serving bowl and season with salt and pepper. Add the spring onions, chilli, and drained broad beans and stir well.

3 To make the dressing, put the oil, vinegar, and ginger in a jug or small bowl. Season with salt and pepper and a pinch of sugar, if using, and whisk until well combined. Drizzle over the salad and leave to stand for 10 minutes, to allow the flavours to develop. When ready to serve, stir through the feta cheese and parsley.

papas arrugadas

Going by the delightful name of "wrinkly potatoes", this dish originates in the Canary Islands. Serve as tapas with other dishes, or as a light lunch with a crisp green salad.

🥣 15 MINS   🍲 45 MINS

SPECIAL EQUIPMENT ▪ blender or food processor

SERVES 4-6

1kg (2¼lb) new potatoes, scrubbed

sea salt and freshly ground black pepper

100ml (3½fl oz) extra virgin olive oil

1 red pepper

juice of 1 lemon

2 heaped tbsp tomato purée

1 tsp smoked paprika

½ tsp ground cumin

pinch of chilli powder, or to taste

1 garlic clove, crushed

2 tbsp chopped flat-leaf parsley or coriander (optional)

1 Preheat the oven to 200°C (400°F/Gas 6). Place the potatoes on a baking tray, toss in some sea salt and 1 tbsp of the oil, and roast whole for about 45 minutes or until golden brown, turning occasionally.

2 Meanwhile, rub the pepper in olive oil and roast in the same oven for around 30 minutes, turning occasionally, until tender and soft. Remove the pepper from the oven, place it in a plastic bag for 2–3 minutes to loosen the skin, then cool, peel, and deseed. Roughly chop the cooked pepper.

3 Put the pepper, lemon juice, tomato purée, spices, and garlic in a blender or food processor, together with the remaining oil. Blitz to form a thick dipping sauce, adding a little more oil if needed. Check the seasoning, add the parsley or coriander, if using, and serve with the potatoes.

feta and pea salad with watercress mayonnaise

This recipe features a mayonnaise with a difference: blitzing watercress with some horseradish into the sauce introduces quite a kick to the usual creamy condiment.

🥣 15 MINS

SPECIAL EQUIPMENT ▪ blender or food processor

SERVES 4

handful of watercress, roughly chopped

3-4 tbsp mayonnaise

1 tsp creamed horseradish

salt and freshly ground black pepper

175g (6oz) feta cheese, cut into cubes

125g (4½oz) peas (shelled weight)

2 handfuls of baby spinach leaves

small handful of mint leaves

lemon wedges, to serve

1 Put the watercress, mayonnaise, and horseradish sauce into a blender or food processor and blitz until well combined. Taste and season with salt and pepper.

2 Put the feta, peas, spinach, and mint leaves in a bowl and gently mix together. Season with a little black pepper if you wish. Transfer to a serving bowl and serve with the mayonnaise and lemon wedges on the side.

variation

dressed pea salad

For a less elaborate side dish, omit the watercress, mayonnaise, and feta. Simply assemble the peas, spinach, and mint, and drizzle with olive oil and white balsamic vinegar. Season and toss gently. Divide between 4 bowls and serve.

ham with minted peas and broad beans

This easy dish is big on summer produce and makes a quick, tasty meal. Serve it with chunks of good bread, or include it as one of a selection of warm and cold salads at a meal.

🥣 10 MINS   🍲 20 MINS

SERVES 4

1 tbsp olive oil

1 onion, finely chopped

2 garlic cloves, finely chopped

150g (5½oz) broad beans (shelled weight), skinned (p85, optional)

75g (2½oz) peas (shelled weight)

150ml (5fl oz) hot chicken stock

handful of mint leaves, chopped

175g (6oz) cooked ham, cut into cubes

1 Heat the oil in a large frying pan over a medium heat, add the onion, and cook for 3–4 minutes until the onion is soft. Add the garlic cloves and stir in the broad beans and peas.

2 Pour in the hot chicken stock and bring to the boil. Reduce the heat slightly and simmer for 15 minutes. Add the mint leaves and ham and stir well. Serve immediately.

broad bean and feta panzanella

Inspired by the classic Italian bread salad, panzanella, this unusual green version is redolent of the fresh colours and flavours of summer, cut with the salty tang of crumbled feta.

🥣 25 MINS PLUS STANDING   🍲 10 MINS

SERVES 4

150g (5½oz) ciabatta, diced into 2cm (¾in) cubes

180ml (6fl oz) extra virgin olive oil

sea salt and freshly ground black pepper

2 tbsp white wine vinegar

1 large garlic clove, crushed

400g (14oz) broad beans (shelled weight), skinned (p85, optional)

4 spring onions, green parts removed, and finely chopped

200g (7oz) feta cheese, diced into 1cm (½in) cubes or roughly crumbled

handful of mint, chopped

2 tbsp chopped dill (optional)

4 handfuls of rocket leaves, watercress, or baby lettuce leaves

juice of 1 lemon

1 Preheat the oven to 220°C (425°F/ Gas 7). Toss the diced bread in 4 tbsp of the oil, sprinkle with a little sea salt and pepper, and cook at the top of the hot oven for about 8 minutes, turning once, until the bread is golden brown and crispy.

2 In a large serving bowl, whisk together the remaining oil with the vinegar and garlic, then season with plenty of black pepper and just a little sea salt (the feta is salty). Add the broad beans, toasted bread, chopped spring onions, feta, and herbs, and toss well to coat everything.

3 Leave the salad for 30 minutes to develop the flavours and soften the bread. To serve, add the salad leaves, pour the lemon over, and check again for seasoning.

raita

A cooling, yogurt-based dipping sauce that makes use of the cucumbers that are coming into their own early in the summer. It is traditionally served with most Indian meals.

10 MINS PLUS STANDING

MAKES 300ml (10fl oz)

1 cucumber, peeled

½ tsp salt

½ tsp cumin seeds, dry-roasted

120ml (4fl oz) natural full-fat yogurt

½ tsp caster sugar

1 garlic clove, crushed

1 tbsp chopped mint

1 tbsp chopped coriander

1 Finely grate the cucumber. Toss with the salt and leave for 1 hour.

2 Squeeze out as much liquid from the cucumber as you can.

3 Crush the cumin seeds to a fine powder in a mortar with a pestle. Add to the cucumber with the remaining ingredients, mix, and chill before serving.

watercress, flageolet bean, and smoked cheese salad

Don't feel that you have to use the Applewood smoked cheese listed in the ingredients; experiment with, say, a smoked Gruyère or Gouda to ring the changes.

15 MINS

SERVES 4

400g can of flageolet beans, drained and rinsed

1 tsp Dijon mustard

handful of flat-leaf parsley, finely chopped

salt and freshly ground black pepper

½ red onion, finely chopped

2 large handfuls of watercress, trimmed, and roughly chopped

juice of 1 lemon

125g (4½oz) lightly smoked cheese, such as Applewood, diced

1 Put the beans in a large bowl. Add the mustard and parsley, and stir through. Season with salt and pepper. Tip in half of the chopped onion and stir through well.

2 Arrange the watercress on a large platter or individual plates. Drizzle over the lemon juice and sprinkle over a pinch of salt. Spoon over the bean mixture, then scatter over the remaining onion, top with the smoked cheese, and serve.

variation

pea shoot, ham, broad bean, and cheddar cheese salad

Cook 225g (8oz) shelled broad beans and pop them out of their skins (p85). Mix with 2 chopped spring onions instead of the red onion. Omit the mustard. Drizzle the beans with a little olive oil and the lemon juice. Add the chopped parsley and season to taste. Pile onto pea shoots instead of watercress and scatter over 2 slices of cooked ham, diced, and some diced Cheddar cheese instead of Applewood.

cashew and courgette rice

You can serve this nutty, gingery pilaf on its own or with grilled lamb or fish. Grated root ginger freezes well, so wrap small quantities in cling film and you'll always have some to hand.

15 MINS   **40 MINS**

SERVES 4

1–2 tbsp olive oil

1 onion, finely chopped

salt and freshly ground black pepper

10cm (4in) piece of fresh root ginger, peeled and grated

4 courgettes, sliced into quarters lengthways and chopped into bite-sized pieces

3 garlic cloves, finely chopped

1 tbsp cider vinegar

pinch of cayenne pepper

200g (7oz) easy-cook basmati rice

about 900ml (1½ pints) hot vegetable stock

75g (2½oz) cashew nuts, roughly chopped

bunch of spring onions, green parts only, thinly sliced

bunch of coriander, leaves only, chopped

1 Heat 1 tbsp of the oil in a large heavy-based pan over a medium heat, add the onion, and cook for 3–4 minutes until soft. Season with salt and pepper, increase the heat, and stir through the ginger and courgettes. Cook for 2–5 minutes until the courgettes are lightly golden (adding more oil, if necessary), then add the garlic and cook for a further 3 minutes.

2 Increase the heat, add the vinegar, and let it cook for a minute, then stir through the cayenne pepper and rice. Add a little stock and turn it so all the grains are coated. Bring to the boil, add enough stock to cover, cover with a lid, and simmer gently for about 20 minutes, or until the rice is tender. Top it up with more stock when needed.

3 Stir through the cashew nuts, spring onions, and half the coriander. Taste and season as needed. Sprinkle with the remaining coriander to serve.

strawberry and raspberry granita

Lemon juice really brings out the vivid flavours of the early summer berries in this refreshing frozen dessert.

🥣 **10 MINS PLUS FREEZING** ❄ **FREEZABLE**

SPECIAL EQUIPMENT ▪ blender or food processor

SERVES 6

125g (4½oz) icing sugar

1 tbsp lemon juice

150ml (5fl oz) boiling water

250g (9oz) raspberries

250g (9oz) strawberries, hulled

single cream, to serve (optional)

1 Put the icing sugar and lemon juice in a blender or food processor with the boiling water and blitz until the sugar has completely dissolved. Add the raspberries and strawberries, and blitz to a purée.

2 Transfer the mixture to a shallow freezerproof plastic container, cover, and place in the freezer for 4 hours.

3 Remove from the freezer every 2 hours and stir with a fork, breaking the mixture up into small pieces.

When the mixture has completely broken up into frozen, gravelly pieces, leave in the freezer until ready to serve. It will keep for up to 1 month. Serve straight from the freezer on its own, or with a drizzle of single cream.

variation

strawberry and watermelon granita

Prepare the syrup in the same way but use the grated zest and juice of 1 lime instead of the lemon juice. Add 250g (9oz) strawberries and 250g (9oz) peeled, cubed, and deseeded watermelon instead of raspberries. Freeze as before.

raspberry soufflés with kirsch custard

For the very best flavour, choose freshly picked, sweet and juicy raspberries for these pretty pink soufflés.

🥣 **15 MINS** 🍲 **20–22 MINS**

SPECIAL EQUIPMENT ▪ food processor

SERVES 6

375ml (13fl oz) milk

150g (5½oz) caster sugar

5 eggs, separated

1 tbsp cornflour

2–3 tbsp kirsch

500g (1lb 2oz) raspberries

icing sugar, sifted, to serve

1 For the custard, pour the milk into a heavy-based saucepan and bring to the boil. Set aside 90ml (3fl oz) milk. Add 50g (1¾oz) of the sugar to the remaining milk, stirring until dissolved. In a bowl, whisk the egg yolks and cornflour until smooth. Add the sweetened milk to the egg yolks, whisking until smooth. Cook the custard over a medium heat, stirring constantly, until it comes to the boil and thickens enough to coat the back

of a spoon. Remove from the heat and stir in the reserved milk. Strain and cool. Stir in the kirsch, cover, and chill.

2 Brush 6 ramekins with melted butter, coat evenly with a little sugar, and place on a baking sheet. Preheat the oven to 190°C (375°F/Gas 5).

3 Purée the raspberries with half the remaining sugar in a blender or food processor. Sieve the purée into a large bowl. Whisk the egg whites until stiff. Add the remaining sugar and whisk until glossy. Add one-quarter of the meringue to the purée and stir. Return this to the remaining meringue; fold together. Spoon the mixture into the ramekins. Bake for 10–12 minutes, until puffed. Dust with icing sugar and serve immediately with the custard.

cherry strudel

Walnuts add extra crunch to luscious ripe cherries in this quick-to-make version of the Viennese classic.

🥣 **15 MINS** 🍲 **30–40 MINS**

SERVES 6–8

500g (1lb 2oz) cherries

1 lemon

75g (2½oz) walnuts

6 large sheets filo pastry

60g (2oz) butter, melted

100g (3½oz) light soft brown sugar

1 tsp ground cinnamon

icing sugar, for dusting

1 Stone all the cherries. Grate the zest from the lemon onto a plate. Coarsely chop the walnuts; nuts are best chopped by hand to control the finished texture, although this will always be uneven.

2 Preheat the oven to 190°C (375°F/Gas 5). Place 3 sheets of filo pastry overlapping by about 5cm (2in), side

by side on a clean cloth. Brush with melted butter, then lay the last three sheets on top in the same way. Brush with more butter.

3 Sprinkle the buttered strudel dough with the stoned cherries, chopped walnuts, brown sugar, lemon zest, and cinnamon. Using the cloth to help, roll up from a long side to form a long, filled roll. Carefully lift onto a buttered baking sheet in a horseshoe shape. Brush all over with the remaining butter.

4 Bake for 30–40 minutes until crisp and golden brown. Dust with icing sugar and serve hot or cold, with cream or crème fraîche.

bavarian raspberry gâteau

Tart, fresh raspberries are enlivened with the kirsch in the rich custard cream filling of this elegant dessert.

🥄 55-60 MINS   🍲 20-25 MINS

SPECIAL EQUIPMENT ▪ 23cm (9in) round springform cake tin ▪ electric hand whisk ▪ blender or food processor

SERVES 8

60g (2oz) unsalted butter

125g (4½oz) plain flour

pinch of salt

4 eggs, beaten

135g (5oz) caster sugar

2 tbsp kirsch

For the Bavarian raspberry cream

500g (1lb 2oz) raspberries

3 tbsp kirsch

200g (7oz) caster sugar

250ml (9fl oz) double cream

1 litre (1¾ pints) milk

1 vanilla pod, split,
   or 2 tsp vanilla extract

10 egg yolks

3 tbsp cornflour

10g (¼oz) powdered gelatine

1 Preheat the oven to 220°C (425°F/ Gas 7). Grease the cake tin with a little butter and line the base with buttered parchment. Sprinkle in 2–3 tbsp flour to prevent the cake from sticking. Melt the butter in a pan and set aside to cool. Sift the flour and salt into a bowl. In a separate bowl, beat the eggs and sugar, using an electric hand whisk for 5 minutes. Sift one-third of the flour over the egg mixture and fold. Add the remaining flour in 2 batches, then the melted butter and fold. Pour into the tin and bake for 20–25 minutes until risen.

2 Turn the cake out onto a wire rack to cool. Remove the parchment. Trim the top and bottom so that they are flat. Cut the cake horizontally in half. Clean, dry, and re-grease the tin. Put a cake round in the tin and sprinkle with 1 tbsp of kirsch.

3 Purée three-quarters of the berries in a blender or food processor, then work through a sieve to remove the pips. Stir in 1 tbsp of kirsch with 100g (3½oz) of the sugar. Whip the cream until it forms soft peaks.

4 Pour the milk in a pan. Add the vanilla pod or extract and bring to the boil. Remove the pan from the heat, cover, and set aside for 10–15 minutes. Remove the pod. Set aside one-quarter of the milk, then stir the remaining sugar into the milk in the pan. Beat the egg yolks and cornflour in a bowl. Add the hot milk and whisk until smooth. Pour the yolk mixture back into the pan and cook over a medium heat, stirring, until the custard boils. Stir in the reserved milk.

5 Strain the custard equally into 2 bowls. Stir 2 tbsp of kirsch into one bowl and set aside to serve with

the finished dessert. Sprinkle the powdered gelatine over 4 tbsp of water in a small pan and leave for 5 minutes. Heat until melted. Stir into the bowl of unflavoured custard, along with the raspberry purée. Set the bowl in a pan of iced water and stir the mixture until thickened, then remove the bowl. Fold the raspberry custard into the whipped cream. Pour half into the cake tin and sprinkle a few reserved raspberries over. Pour the remaining Bavarian cream on the berries. Sprinkle 1 tbsp of kirsch over the second cake round.

6 Lightly press the cake round, kirsch-side down, on the cream. Cover with cling film and refrigerate for 4 hours until firm. To serve, remove the side of the tin, decorate the top of the cake with the reserved raspberries, and serve with the kirsch custard sauce.

Season's best **strawberries**

Plump and juicy, the many hybrids of this gorgeous fruit vary in colour from scarlet to pinkish-orange, and can be conical, globular, oval, or heart-shaped. The aroma and flavour of the first summer outdoor berries are delightful, but they are available from late spring right through to autumn. Fragrant wild strawberries are also cultivated. All taste heavenly with chocolate, cream, and other fruits, and chilli or black pepper enhances their flavour.

Strawberries are grown in all temperate regions. Their season is extended by growing in hothouses in cooler regions. Wild strawberries are found in woods and shady pastures.

Chandler This large, firm variety has a typically flat, wedge shape. It is a good all-purpose strawberry with a brilliant, glossy colour and excellent berry flavour.

Elsanta One of the most popular commercial varieties in the UK, Elsanta has glossy good looks, but muted flavour. It is a useful berry for cold desserts, such as fools and mousses.

how to hull strawberries

Hull strawberries before adding to desserts, but if serving with melted chocolate or cream to dip, leave the stalk on as a natural handle, then bite the fruit off.

1 Wash the fruit and drain well. If ripe, hold the fruit in one hand and twist off the green calyx between your thumb and forefinger.

Driscoll These berries were developed in 1904 in California. They are now internationally renowned for their excellent shape, colour, and flavour. The Kent Driscoll Jubilee is shown here.

2 If the fruit is not very ripe, cut off the stalk end with a small, sharp knife, but don't take too much fruit.

Wild strawberry Also known as *fraises des bois*, these are found in the wild as well as cultivated (when they are often called Alpine strawberries). The tiny, fragile red or white fruit has an exquisite, fragrant taste. Use in tarts or as a special dessert.

The wild strawberry is small in size, but big in flavour.

Albion A modern Californian variety with a long growing season, Albion is an extra-large, dark red conical berry with a lush, very sweet taste. It makes quite an impact in desserts and cakes.

The berries look like red spinning tops with a bright green hull.

Mieze Schindler A classic German variety, the berries are plump and heart-shaped, and have a delicious, full-fruit flavour. Enjoy them fresh or make into excellent jam.

The flesh is red throughout.

Evie These strawberries are dark red and full-flavoured and can crop three times in a season, making them very productive.

Sonata This is a mid-season fruit with large uniform berries, sweet, firm flesh, and a stunning aroma. It is a cross between the popular Elsanta and Polka.

The fruit keeps well without darkening in colour.

essentials
varieties available

Hundreds of cultivated strawberry varieties of varying shape, colour, and size, plus wild ones that are now also grown commercially.

buy Choose firm, fragrant berries. Avoid if bruised or the juice is running. The calyces should be fresh and green.

store Use as soon as possible. Discard mouldy or squashed berries, then cover loosely and keep at the bottom of the fridge.

cook Eat unadorned or dipped in chocolate. Top cheesecakes and tarts. Purée for coulis, cold and iced desserts, and milkshakes. Use in pie fillings.

preserve Bottle in syrup; make jam or flavoured vinegar.

recipe ideas

Strawberry baked Alaska p123

Hazelnut torte with berries p122

Strawberry and cream Victoria sandwich p131

Strawberries and cream whoopie pies p126

Strawberry conserve p133

summer fruit millefeuilles

This beautiful, appetizing dessert with soft berries suits any occasion, from a dinner party to a buffet or garden tea party.

🍲 2 HRS PLUS CHILLING   🍳 25-30 MINS

SPECIAL EQUIPMENT ▪ electric hand whisk

SERVES 8

600g (1lb 5oz) ready-made puff pastry

250ml (9fl oz) double cream

1 quantity crème pâtissière (p229)

400g (14oz) mixed summer fruits, such as strawberries (hulled and diced) and raspberries

icing sugar, for dusting

1 Preheat the oven to 200°C (400°F/Gas 6). Sprinkle a baking sheet evenly with cold water. Roll out the pastry on a floured work surface to a rectangle larger than the baking sheet and about 3mm (⅛in) thick. Roll around the rolling pin and unroll onto the baking sheet so the edges overhang. Chill for 15 minutes.

2 Prick the pastry all over with a fork. Cover with baking parchment, then set a wire rack on top of it. Bake for

15–20 minutes until it just begins to brown. Gripping the sheet and rack, invert the pastry. Slide the baking sheet back under and continue baking for 10 minutes until both sides are browned. Remove from the oven and slide the pastry onto a chopping board. While still warm, trim the edges, then cut lengthways into 3 equal strips. Allow to cool.

3 Whip the double cream in a mixing bowl with an electric hand whisk until stiff peaks form. Fold into the pastry cream. Spread half the pastry cream filling over 1 pastry strip. Sprinkle with half the fruit. Repeat with another pastry strip to make 2 layers. Put the last pastry strip on top and press down gently. Sift the icing sugar thickly over the top of the millefeuilles and serve.

hazelnut torte with berries

A layered cream tower with strawberries and raspberry coulis.

🍲 40-45 MINS PLUS CHILLING   🍳 15-18 MINS

SPECIAL EQUIPMENT ▪ food processor ▪ electric hand whisk

SERVES 8

250g (9oz) hazelnuts

140g (5oz) caster sugar plus 1½ tbsp for the cream

125g (4½oz) plain flour

½ tsp salt

150g (5½oz) unsalted butter

1 egg yolk

500g (1lb 2oz) raspberries

2–3 tbsp icing sugar, or to taste

1–2 tbsp kirsch (optional)

750g (1lb 10oz) strawberries, hulled

375ml (13fl oz) double cream

1 tsp vanilla extract

1 Preheat the oven to 180°C (350°F/Gas 4). Spread the nuts on a baking sheet. Toast for 8–10 minutes, until lightly browned. Rub in a clean tea towel to remove the skins. Leave to cool, then blitz with the sugar to a fine powder in a food processor. Put the mix on a work surface and sift the flour and salt on top. Make a well in the centre, add the butter and egg yolk, and with your fingers work the ingredients together in the well until a soft dough ball forms. Knead until smooth on a floured work surface. Wrap in cling film. Chill for 30 minutes.

2 Preheat the oven to 200°C (400°F/Gas 6). Divide the dough ball into 3. Press each into a 20cm (8in) round on a baking sheet and set 2.5cm (1in) apart. Bake for 15–18 minutes until the edges are brown. While still warm, trim into neat rounds with a knife and cut 1 of the layers into 8 equal wedges. Then transfer to wire racks to cool completely.

3 Blitz the raspberries in the food processor. Stir in icing sugar to taste, and the kirsch, if using, then work the purée through a sieve to remove the pips. Set aside 8 small strawberries for decoration, and halve or quarter the rest. Pour the cream into a chilled mixing bowl. Whip with an electric hand whisk until soft peaks form. Then add the sugar and vanilla, and whip again until stiff peaks form.

4 Set a pastry round on a serving plate, cover with a quarter of the cream, and put half the strawberries on top. Repeat with the second pastry round, half the remaining cream, the rest of the strawberries, and more cream. Top with the pastry wedges arranged at an angle and the whole strawberries on top. Serve in wedges, drizzled with the coulis.

strawberry baked alaska

This clever dessert is a festive way to conclude a celebration.

🥣 45-50 MINS   🍲 30-40 MINS

SPECIAL EQUIPMENT ▪ electric hand whisk ▪ blender or food processor ▪ 20cm (8in) square cake tin

SERVES 8-10

4 eggs, beaten

135g (5oz) caster sugar

1 tsp vanilla extract

salt

125g (4½oz) plain flour, sifted

60g (2oz) unsalted butter, melted

300g (10oz) strawberries, hulled

2-3 tbsp icing sugar, to taste

450g (1lb) caster sugar

9 egg whites

1.5 litres (2¾ pints) vanilla ice cream

1 Preheat the oven to 180°C (350°F/ Gas 4). Butter the tin and line the base with buttered baking parchment. Coat the bottom and sides in 2 tbsp flour and tap out the excess. Put the eggs and sugar in a large bowl. Whisk until pale, thick, and creamy. Beat in the vanilla. Add salt to the flour, add a third of the flour to the bowl, and fold in. Fold in another third, then the remaining flour and butter, and pour into the tin. Bake for 30–40 minutes until just firm to the touch. Transfer to a wire rack, peel off the paper, and allow to cool.

2 Purée the strawberries in a food processor and pour into a bowl. Add the icing sugar to taste. Dissolve the sugar in a pan with 250ml (9fl oz) water and boil without stirring until a sugar thermometer registers 120°C (248°F), or test if the syrup forms a pliable ball in your finger and thumb. Meanwhile, whisk the egg whites until stiff peaks form. Gradually pour in the hot syrup, whisking constantly until the egg whites are cool and stiff.

3 Trim the cake to 15cm (6in) square, split horizontally into 2 layers, and arrange to form a rectangle on a greased heatproof serving plate. Blitz the cake trimmings in a processor. Add 250ml (9fl oz) of the strawberry coulis, and pulse. Spread the rest of the coulis over the cake. Arrange two layers of scooped ice cream balls over the cake and smooth with a palette knife. Cover with strawberry crumbs, then spoon the meringue all over the top and sides. Freeze for 2 hours. Preheat the oven to 220°C (425°F/ Gas 7). Sprinkle the alaska with sugar and let stand for 1 minute. Bake for just 3–5 minutes. Serve at once.

gooseberry tart

Tangy gooseberries quiver in smooth, just-set custard, in a light sweet pastry crust for a sublime seasonal treat.

🥣 30 MINS PLUS CHILLING   🍲 1 HR

SPECIAL EQUIPMENT ▪ electric hand whisk ▪ 25cm (10in) round loose-bottomed fluted tart tin ▪ ceramic baking beans

SERVES 6-8

175g (6oz) plain flour

75g (2½oz) butter

75g (2½oz) caster sugar

2 egg yolks, plus 2 eggs

250ml (9fl oz) double cream

400g (14oz) gooseberries, topped and tailed

thick cream, to serve (optional)

1 In a large bowl, rub together the flour and butter until they resemble crumbs. Stir in 25g (scant 1oz) of the sugar, add the egg yolks, then bring the ingredients together to form a dough. Wrap in cling film and chill for 30 minutes.

2 Preheat the oven to 180°C (350°F/ Gas 4). To make the custard, put the double cream, eggs, and the remaining sugar in a mixing bowl and whisk together with an electric hand whisk. Then leave to chill in the fridge.

3 Roll out the pastry on a floured work surface to a circle a little larger than the tin. Line the tin with the pastry, pressing it into the corners. Prick the bottom with a fork. Line the pastry shell with greaseproof paper and fill with baking beans. Bake in the oven for 20 minutes. Remove the beans and paper and return to the oven for 5 minutes more to crisp. Remove from the oven and set aside.

4 Arrange a layer of gooseberries over the base of the pastry shell. Pour the custard over and bake for 35 minutes until set and golden. Allow to cool slightly before removing from the tin and serving with thick cream, if you like.

raspberry tart with chocolate cream

A chocolate-lined pastry is a perfect partner for raspberries.

40 MINS PLUS CHILLING   **20-25 MINS**

SPECIAL EQUIPMENT ■ 23cm (9in) round loose-bottomed fluted tart tin ■ ceramic baking beans

SERVES 6-8

125g (4½oz) plain flour

20g (¾oz) cocoa powder

100g (3½oz) unsalted butter, diced

150g (5½oz) caster sugar

1 egg yolk, plus 2 eggs

1½ tsp vanilla extract

50g (1¾oz) cornflour, sifted

450ml (15fl oz) whole milk

175g (6oz) dark chocolate, in pieces

400g (14oz) raspberries

1 Rub together the flour, cocoa, and butter to resemble breadcrumbs. Stir in 50g (1¾oz) of the sugar. Beat the egg yolk with ½ tsp of the vanilla and add to the flour mixture, bringing it together to form a soft dough. Add a little extra water if it seems too dry. Wrap in cling film and chill for 1 hour.

2 Preheat the oven to 180°C (350°F/ Gas 4). Roll the pastry out on a floured surface to 3mm (⅛in) thick and use to line the tin, pressing it into the corners and overlapping the edges by 2cm (¾in). Prick the bottom with a fork. Line the

shell with greaseproof paper and fill with baking beans. Place on a baking sheet and bake for 20 minutes. Remove the beans and paper, and return to the oven for 5 minutes. Then trim the overlapping pastry.

3 Beat 100g (3½oz) of the sugar, the eggs, cornflour, and 1 tsp of the vanilla in a bowl. In a pan, bring the milk and 100g (3½oz) of the chocolate to the boil, whisking all the time. Take off the heat as it starts to bubble. Pour onto the egg mixture, whisking. Return to the cleaned-out pan and bring to the boil over a medium heat, whisking. Reduce the heat to its lowest when it thickens and cook for 2-3 minutes, whisking. Pour into a bowl, cover with cling film, and cool.

4 Melt the remaining chocolate in a bowl set over a pan of simmering water, and brush around the inside of the tart case. Leave to set. Beat the chocolate cream with a wooden spoon and pour into the case. Arrange the raspberries on top, remove from the tin, and serve dusted with icing sugar.

chocolate decadence with raspberry coulis

A tart raspberry coulis cuts through this deliciously rich cake.

30-40 MINS PLUS CHILLING   **20 MINS**

SPECIAL EQUIPMENT ■ food processor ■ electric hand whisk ■ 23cm (9in) round springform tin

SERVES 8

500g (1lb 2oz) plain chocolate

150g (5½oz) unsalted butter

6 eggs, separated

2 tbsp caster sugar

1 tbsp plain flour

750g (1lb 10oz) raspberries, plus more to serve

2-3 tbsp icing sugar

crème fraîche or whipped double cream, to serve

1 Preheat the oven to 200°C (400°F/ Gas 6). Butter the tin and line with greaseproof paper. Coat the base and sides in 2 tbsp flour and tap out the excess. Pulse the chocolate coarsely into pieces in a food processor. Cut the butter into pieces and put in a heatproof bowl with the chocolate. Set over a pan of hot, but not simmering, water. Stir until melted and smooth. Let cool, stirring occasionally.

2 Beat the egg yolks into the cooled chocolate with a wooden spoon. Put the egg whites in a clean bowl and whisk until stiff peaks form.

Add the sugar and continue whisking for about 20 seconds until glossy. Stir the flour into the chocolate mix, then fold in one-third of the egg whites to lighten it. Fold in the rest of the whisked egg whites in 2 batches, then transfer to the tin.

3 Bake for about 20 minutes until crusty on top. Let cool completely in the tin, then set on a wire rack. When cold, chill for 2 hours. Then remove from the tin and peel off the paper.

4 Blitz the raspberries in a food processor. Add icing sugar to taste, pulse briefly, then work the puréed raspberries through a sieve into a bowl to remove all the pips.

5 Using a serrated knife, cut the cake into 8 wedges. Set 1 wedge in the centre of each plate. Ladle a small pool of raspberry coulis onto each plate near the tip of the wedge of cake. Decorate each plate with a few whole raspberries and serve with crème fraîche or whipped double cream.

strawberries and cream macarons

This delectable dessert is a creative twist on the traditional English combination of strawberries and cream. The art of macaron making may seem complex, but these little almond-flavoured meringues are in fact easy to make, and this recipe is ideal to try at home. Unfilled macaron shells can be stored for up to 3 days.

🥄 30 MINS　　🍲 18-20 MINS

SPECIAL EQUIPMENT ▪ food processor with blade attachment ▪ electric hand whisk ▪ piping bag with small, plain nozzle

MAKES 20

75g (2½oz) ground almonds

100g (3½oz) icing sugar

2 large egg whites, at room temperature

75g (2½oz) granulated sugar

For the filling

200ml (7fl oz) double cream

5-10 very large strawberries, preferably the same diameter as the macarons

1 Preheat the oven to 150°C (300°F/ Gas 2). Line 2 baking sheets with silicone paper. Trace 20 x 3cm (1¼in) circles with a pencil onto the paper, allowing 3cm (1¼in) between the circles. Then invert the paper.

2 Blitz the almonds and icing sugar in a food processor. Then put the egg whites in a mixing bowl and whisk with an electric hand whisk until stiff peaks form. Add the granulated sugar to the egg whites, a little at a time, whisking as you do so and whisking well between each addition. At this point the meringue mixture should be very stiff (more so than for a regular meringue). Gently fold in the almond mixture, a spoonful at a time, until just incorporated into the meringue.

3 Transfer the macaron mixture to the piping bag, placing the bag into a bowl to aid you. Using the pencil guidelines, pipe the mix into the centre of each circle, holding the bag vertically. Try to keep the discs equal in size and volume; the mix will spread only very slightly. Bang the baking sheets down a few times if there are any peaks left in the centre. Bake in the middle of the oven for 18-20 minutes until the surface is set firm. Test one macaron shell: if you give it a firm prod with a finger, the top of the macaron should crack. Leave for 15-20 minutes, then transfer to a wire rack and allow to cool completely.

4 Pour the cream into a large mixing bowl and whisk with the electric hand whisk until stiff peaks form; a soft whip would ooze out of the sides of the macarons and soften the shells. Transfer the cream into the (cleaned) piping bag used earlier, with the same nozzle. Pipe a blob of the whipped cream onto the flat surfaces of half the macarons.

5 Slice the strawberries widthways into thin slices so they are the same diameter as the macarons. Put a slice of strawberry on top of the cream filling of each macaron, put the remaining macaron shells on top, and sandwich together gently. The fillings should peek out at the sides. Arrange on a serving plate or cake dish and serve immediately.

tiramisu cherry bombe

It's best to make this decadent treat a day in advance, as a well-chilled bombe is easiest to unmould without breaking.

20 MINS PLUS CHILLING

SPECIAL EQUIPMENT ▪ 1.2-litre (2-pint) pudding basin ▪ electric hand whisk

SERVES 8

175g packet sponge fingers

2–3 tbsp brandy

small cup of strong coffee, cooled

600ml (1 pint) double cream

2 tbsp cocoa powder, plus more to dust

2 tbsp icing sugar, plus more to dust

300g (10oz) cherries, stoned and halved

3 whole cherries, to decorate

125g (4½oz) dark chocolate, grated

1 Lightly grease the basin and line the base with a circle of greaseproof paper. Dip all but 5 sponge fingers in the brandy and then the coffee. Line the base with halved sponge fingers (sugar-side out), then line the sides with whole ones.

2 Put the cream in a bowl and whisk with an electric hand whisk until soft peaks form. Transfer half of the cream to another bowl. Stir the cocoa powder and icing sugar into one bowl. Add the stoned cherries to the other.

3 Spoon the separate mixtures into the basin in alternate layers, and top with the remaining sponge fingers, pressing them down well. Chill in the fridge for at least 2 hours.

4 To serve, place a plate on top of the basin and turn the tiramisu upside-down. Remove the basin, then dust with cocoa powder and icing sugar, and top with the whole cherries and grated chocolate.

strawberries and cream whoopie pies

Best served immediately, these strawberry-layered whoopie pies make a lovely addition to a traditional afternoon tea.

40 MINS　**12 MINS**

SPECIAL EQUIPMENT ▪ electric hand whisk

MAKES 10 PIES

175g (6oz) unsalted butter, softened

150g (5½oz) light soft brown sugar

1 large egg

1 tsp vanilla extract

225g (8oz) self-raising flour

75g (2½oz) cocoa powder

1 tsp baking powder

150ml (5fl oz) whole milk

2 tbsp Greek-style yogurt or thick natural yogurt

150ml (5fl oz) double cream, whipped

250g (9oz) strawberries, hulled and thinly sliced

1 Preheat the oven to 180°C (350°F/ Gas 4). Line several baking sheets with greaseproof paper. Put the butter and sugar in a mixing bowl and whisk with an electric hand whisk until pale and creamy. Beat in the egg and vanilla. Sift the flour, cocoa, and baking powder into another bowl. Mix these dry ingredients and the milk,

alternately, into the creamed mixture, a spoonful at a time. Then fold in the yogurt. Place heaped tablespoons of the batter onto the baking sheets, leaving space for the mix to spread. Dip a spoon in warm water and use the back to smooth over the surface of the pies. Bake for 12 minutes until well risen. Leave for a few minutes, then turn out onto a wire rack to cool.

2 Spread the cream onto half the cakes. Top with a layer of strawberries and a second cake. Dust with icing sugar and serve.

variation

black forest whoopie pies

Substitute the strawberries for 225g (8oz) black cherries. Chop half the cherries and fold into the cake batter and bake as normal. To make the filling, purée the remaining cherries and mix with 2 tbsp caster sugar and 250g (9oz) mascarpone.

raspberry cream meringues

These mini meringues are filled with fresh raspberries and whipped cream; perfect for a summer buffet.

🥣 **20 MINS**   🍲 **1 HR**

SPECIAL EQUIPMENT ▪ piping bag with plain nozzle ▪ electric hand whisk

MAKES 8–10

4 egg whites, at room temperature

about 250g (9oz) caster sugar

100g (3½oz) raspberries

300ml (10fl oz) double cream

1 tbsp icing sugar, sifted

1 Preheat the oven to around 130°C (250°F/Gas ½). Line a baking sheet with greaseproof paper. Weigh the egg whites, then measure out exactly double the weight of sugar to egg whites.

2 Put the egg whites in a mixing bowl and whisk with an electric hand whisk until stiff peaks form. Slowly add half the sugar, a couple of tablespoons at a time, whisking the mixture in between. Then gently fold in the remaining sugar.

3 Pipe the meringue mixture onto the baking sheet using a plain nozzle (or spoon the mixture onto the sheet) leaving 5cm (2in) gaps in between each. Bake for 1 hour. The meringues are ready when they lift easily from the greaseproof paper and sound hollow when tapped.

4 Put the raspberries in a bowl and crush them with the back of a fork. Pour the double cream into a separate bowl and whisk with the electric hand whisk until stiff peaks form. Gently fold together the cream, raspberries, and icing sugar. Spread the raspberry mixture onto half the meringues. Top with the remaining meringue halves, gently press together to form meringue sandwiches, and serve.

strawberry-raspberry tart

This heavenly summer tart is nothing more than fresh fruits, whipped cream, and hazelnuts on a pastry base.

🥣 **35–40 MINS PLUS CHILLING**   🍲 **30–35 MINS**

SPECIAL EQUIPMENT ▪ 23–25cm (9–10in) round springform fluted tart tin ▪ electric hand whisk ▪ food processor

SERVES 6–8

140g (5oz) hazelnuts

melted butter, for brushing

500g (1lb 2oz) ready-made sweet shortcrust pastry

250ml (9fl oz) double cream

3–4 tbsp icing sugar, plus more to dust

2 tbsp Marsala wine

125g (4½oz) raspberries

300g (10oz) strawberries, hulled and cut in half or into quarters if large

1 Preheat the oven to 180°C (350°F/Gas 4). Spread the nuts on a baking sheet. Toast for 8–10 minutes until lightly browned. Rub in a clean tea towel to remove the skins. Leave to cool, roughly chop 60g (2oz) of the nuts and reserve, and blitz the rest to a powder in a food processor.

2 Leave the oven on. Brush the tart tin with melted butter. Roll out the pastry on a floured work surface to a circle larger than the tin and about 3mm (⅛in) thick, and use it to line the tin, pressing it into the corners. Chill for at least 15 minutes in the fridge until firm. Bake for 30–35 minutes until golden brown and shrinking slightly from the tin. Cool, then remove the sides of the tin.

3 Pour the cream into a mixing bowl and whisk with an electric hand whisk until soft peaks form. Add the ground hazelnuts, icing sugar, and Marsala wine. Continue whisking until stiff peaks form.

4 Ensuring the pastry is completely cold, spread two-thirds of the Marsala and hazelnut whipped cream evenly over the pastry shell, just to the edge. Arrange most of the fruit evenly over the cream. Top with the remaining Marsala cream, then scatter with the remaining fruits and the reserved chopped nuts. Chill in the fridge, then dust with icing sugar before serving.

cherry clafoutis

Tart cherries give the most flavour, and contrast very successfully with the sweet batter they are cooked in.

🥣 20-25 MINS   🍲 30-35 MINS

SPECIAL EQUIPMENT ▪ 2-litre (3½-pint) round baking dish

SERVES 6-8

melted butter, for brushing

625g (1lb 6oz) cherries, stoned

45g (1½oz) plain flour

salt

150ml (5fl oz) milk

75ml (2½fl oz) double cream

4 eggs, plus 2 egg yolks

100g (3½oz) caster sugar

3 tbsp kirsch

2 tbsp icing sugar

1 Brush the baking dish with melted butter. Sprinkle some caster sugar into the dish. Turn the dish around and shake it, to coat the bottom and side evenly. Turn the dish upside-down and tap the base with your knuckles to remove any excess sugar. Spread the cherries in an even layer over the bottom of the dish.

2 Sift the flour and a pinch of salt into a bowl. Make a well in the centre with your fingers. Pour the milk and cream into the well at the same time and stir with a whisk, gradually drawing in the flour and whisking constantly, to make a smooth paste and work out any lumps. Add the eggs, egg yolks to add richness, and caster sugar, and continue whisking to make a smooth batter.

3 Preheat the oven to 180°C (350°F/Gas 4). Just before baking, ladle the batter evenly over the cherries – it should partially cover them – then drizzle over the kirsch.

4 Bake the clafoutis in the heated oven for 30–35 minutes, until puffed up and beginning to turn golden brown. If it threatens to scorch before it is cooked, cover with foil. When cooked, the clafoutis will begin to pull away slightly from the sides of the baking dish. Just before serving, sift icing sugar over the top. Serve warm or at room temperature, with a serving of crème fraîche or whipped cream, if desired.

cherry pie

Cherry pie is an all-American favourite that can be made with sweet or sour cherries, or hybrids; whichever you prefer.

🥣 20 MINS PLUS CHILLING   🍲 35-45 MINS

SPECIAL EQUIPMENT ▪ shallow 23cm (9in) round pie dish

SERVES 6

100g (3½oz) butter

75g (2½oz) lard

300g (10oz) plain flour

salt

3 tbsp demerara sugar

750g (1lb 10oz) cherries, stoned

1 tbsp cornflour

½ tsp ground cinnamon

2 drops of almond extract

1 tbsp lemon juice

1 egg white, beaten with 1 tbsp water

milk and caster sugar, to glaze

1 Preheat the oven to 200°C (400°F/Gas 6) and grease the pie dish. To make the pastry, rub 75g (2½oz) of the butter with the lard into the flour with a pinch of salt until the mixture resembles crumbs. Bind the pastry with 2–3 tbsp water. Chill in the fridge for 30 minutes.

2 For the filling, dissolve the demerara sugar in 300ml (10fl oz) water in a heavy-based saucepan, then boil rapidly for 3–4 minutes.

Add the cherries to the syrup and bring back to the boil. Drain the cherries and allow to cool.

3 Gently mix together the cherries, cornflour, cinnamon, almond extract, and lemon juice. Roll out two-thirds of the pastry on a floured work surface and use it to line the pie dish. Brush the pastry case with the egg white to prevent sogginess. Spoon in the cherry mixture and dot with the remaining butter.

4 Roll out the remaining pastry and lay it over the pie. Trim the overhang to about 2cm (¾in). Moisten the edges where they meet, then press together lightly and turn under. Crimp the edge decoratively and make small snips in the top crust so steam can escape. Brush with milk and dust with caster sugar.

5 Place the pie dish on a baking sheet and bake for 30–40 minutes, or until the crust is golden brown. Cool on a wire rack before serving warm or at room temperature.

summer fruit meringue roulade

Stuffed with seasonal fruits, this delicious roulade makes an ideal dessert for a summer buffet.

🥣 25 MINS   🍲 15 MINS   ❄ FREEZABLE

SPECIAL EQUIPMENT ▪ 25 x 35cm (10 x 14in) Swiss roll tin ▪ electric hand whisk

SERVES 8

5 egg whites

225g (8oz) caster sugar

½ tsp white wine vinegar

1 tsp cornflour

½ tsp pure vanilla extract

250ml (9fl oz) double cream, whipped

icing sugar, for dusting

250g (9oz) mixed berry fruit, such as strawberries, raspberries, and blueberries, any large fruit chopped

1 Preheat the oven to 180°C (350°F/Gas 4) and line the baking tin with baking parchment. Whisk the egg whites with an electric hand whisk until stiff peaks form, then gradually whisk in the caster sugar. Fold in the vinegar, cornflour, and vanilla extract. Spread the mixture into the tin and bake for 15 minutes. Remove from the oven and allow to cool.

2 Place the roulade on a piece of parchment dusted with icing sugar. Spread the cream over the roulade and then the fruits, then roll the meringue up around the cream filling. Place seam-side down on a serving plate, cover, and chill. Sift over icing sugar to serve.

Season's best **cherries**

There are two kinds of cherries ripening now through summer: plump, sweet ones that are either firm and crisp or soft and juicy, delicious raw; and the usually smaller, sour ones, which range from almost sweet to bitter, but taste great when cooked. They vary in colour from pale creamy-yellow with a pink blush, to deep red, or purple-black. They are delicious in sauces with duck and game, and are brilliant with chocolate, almonds, brandy, and amaretto.

Native to western Asia, cherries are now cultivated in many countries. The trees are often trained along walls to protect the fruit from birds.

essentials

varieties available

Several varieties of red/black, yellow, or sour ones. Look out for wild, too. Available dried and glacéed.

buy Best bought on the stalk, they should be plump, firm, and shiny with pliant green stems. Avoid if too soft, split, or shrivelled.

store Keep (unwashed and on the stem) in an open paper bag in the fridge for a few days.

cook Use in cakes, pies, compôtes, soups, salads, and sweet or savoury sauces.

preserve Make jam; preserve in brandy or syrup; pickle or crystallize; freeze.

recipe ideas

Cherry and cassis conserve p132

Cherry clafoutis p128

Cherry pie p128

Cherry strudel p118

Tiramisu cherry bombe p126

Red cherries There are several popular varieties – all sweet, round, and different shades of reddish-purple with a slightly crisp texture. Delicious raw or cooked.

Sour cherries Sour cherries such as Morello have a very short midsummer season. They have clear juice and a fresh, tart flavour. Unpalatable raw, but when cooked and sweetened they taste outstanding.

Sour cherries are bright to dark red in colour.

how to stone cherries

Eating raw cherries is a pleasure and no one minds spitting out the stones. However, when cooking for desserts, the flavour and texture is ruined if they are left inside.

1 Wash the cherries and remove the stalks. Place a cherry, stalk end up, in a stoner chamber and hold over a bowl (to catch the stones and juice).

2 Press the handle down so the blunt spike goes through the cherry, forcing the stone out. Repeat until all the cherries are stoned.

Yellow cherries Golden-skinned, often with a pink blush, there are several varieties, including Rainier, pictured here. They are rich and juicy but bruise easily, so tend to be expensive.

courgette cake

This intriguing alternative to carrot cake makes an unusual use of courgettes when they are at their most plentiful.

🥣 20 MINS ◻ 45 MINS ❄ FREEZABLE

SPECIAL EQUIPMENT ▪ 23cm (9in) round springform cake tin

SERVES 8-10

100g (3½oz) hazelnuts

225ml (7½fl oz) sunflower oil

3 large eggs

1 tsp vanilla extract

225g (8oz) caster sugar

200g (7oz) courgettes, grated

200g (7oz) self-raising flour

75g (2½oz) wholemeal self-raising flour

pinch of salt

1 tsp cinnamon

grated zest of 1 lemon

1 Preheat the oven to 180°C (350°F/ Gas 4). Oil the base and sides of the tin and line the base with baking parchment. Spread the hazelnuts on a baking tray and cook for 5 minutes until lightly browned. Put the nuts on a clean tea towel and rub them to get rid of any excess skin. Roughly chop and set aside.

2 Pour the oil and eggs into a bowl, then add the vanilla and sugar. Whisk the oil mixture until lighter in colour and thickened. Squeeze moisture from the courgettes and fold in with the nuts. Sift over the flour. Add the salt, cinnamon, and lemon zest, and fold.

3 Pour the batter into the tin. Bake for 45 minutes, or until springy to the touch. Turn out onto a wire rack to cool completely.

chocolate strawberry shortcakes

These delightful little cakes are perfect served with afternoon tea. For a party canapé, cut smaller versions, sandwich with a single slice of strawberry, and serve to your guests.

🥣 15 MINS ◻ 10 MINS

SPECIAL EQUIPMENT ▪ 7.5cm (3in) round cutter

SERVES 6

200g (7oz) plain flour

30g (1oz) cocoa powder

2 tsp baking powder

60g (2oz) butter, softened

60g (2oz) caster sugar, plus extra for sweetening

1 large egg

1 tsp vanilla extract

6 tbsp milk

225g (8oz) strawberries

150ml (5fl oz) double cream, whipped

1 Preheat the oven to 230°C (450°F/ Gas 8). Sift the flour, cocoa, and baking powder into a bowl. Add the butter and rub in with fingertips. Stir in the sugar. Beat the egg with the vanilla and stir in. Add enough milk to form a soft, but not sticky, dough. Knead gently until smooth.

2 Pat out the dough to about 1cm (½in) thick. Cut into 6 rounds using a 7.5cm (3in) cutter. Place on a lightly greased baking sheet. Bake in the oven for about 10 minutes until risen and the bases sound hollow when tapped. Transfer to a wire rack to cool for 5-10 minutes.

3 Halve 3 strawberries for decoration, leaving the calyces intact, and reserve. Hull and slice the remaining strawberries in half, and sweeten with a little caster sugar, if necessary.

4 Split the shortcakes and sandwich with the sliced strawberries and some of the cream. Top with the remaining cream and decorate with the reserved, halved strawberries.

rhubarb and strawberry pie

Tart rhubarb and sweet strawberries go into this wonderful pie, which is delicious served warm with ice cream.

🥣 20 MINS PLUS CHILLING ◻ 50-55 MINS

SPECIAL EQUIPMENT ▪ 23cm (9in) pie dish

SERVES 6-8

melted butter, for brushing

500g (1lb 2oz) ready-made shortcrust pastry

1kg (2¼lb) rhubarb, sliced

grated zest of 1 orange

250g (9oz) caster sugar

¼ tsp salt

30g (1oz) plain flour

375g (13oz) strawberries, hulled

15g (½oz) unsalted butter, diced

1 tbsp milk

1 tbsp caster sugar

1 Brush the pie dish with melted butter. On a lightly floured surface roll out two-thirds of the pastry into a round, 5cm (2in) larger than the dish. Using the rolling pin, drape the pastry over the dish and press it into the bottom and sides.

2 Lift the dish and trim the pastry at the outer edge of the dish, using a table knife. Reserve the trimmings. Chill the pastry shell for about 15 minutes until firm.

3 In a bowl, combine the rhubarb, orange zest, sugar, salt, and flour, and stir to mix. Add the strawberries and toss gently. Spoon the fruit into the lined pie dish and dot the butter over.

4 Brush the edge of the pastry with cold water. Roll out the remaining dough into a 28cm (11in) round and drape over the filling. Trim the top crust to be even with the bottom. Press the edges together to seal.

5 Cut steam vents around the top crust of the pie. Brush with milk and sprinkle with sugar. Chill for about 15 minutes. Preheat the oven to 220°C (425°F/Gas 7). Put a baking sheet in the centre of the oven to heat.

6 Bake the pie on the baking sheet for 20 minutes. Reduce the oven temperature to 180°C (350°F/Gas 4). and bake for 30-35 minutes longer, or until the rhubarb is tender.

double chocolate raspberry tart

This impressive dessert uses the classic combination of raspberries and chocolate, but is quick and simple to make with a good quality ready-made pastry case.

40 MINS PLUS COOLING

SERVES 6-8

100g (3½oz) white chocolate, broken into pieces

75g (2½oz) dark chocolate, broken into pieces

1 ready-made chocolate pastry case

250ml (9fl oz) double cream

400g (14oz) raspberries

icing sugar, for dusting

1 Melt the white chocolate in a heatproof bowl by setting over a pan of barely simmering water. Leave to cool.

2 Melt the dark chocolate in a separate bowl in the same way, and use a pastry brush to paint the inside of the tart case with a layer of chocolate. This will keep the pastry case from becoming soggy once it is filled with the raspberry and chocolate cream. Leave to set.

3 Whip the cream until it forms stiff peaks. Fold the cooled white chocolate into the whipped cream. Crush half the raspberries and gently fold them through the cream mixture. Pile the filling into the case evenly. Decorate the top with the remaining raspberries, dust with icing sugar, and serve.

gooseberry fool with elderflower

An all-time favourite way to serve gooseberries, this chilled, creamy dessert is the epitome of summer eating.

20 MINUTES PLUS CHILLING   **10 MINUTES**

SPECIAL EQUIPMENT ▪ blender or food processor

SERVES 4-6

350g (12oz) gooseberries, topped and tailed

100g (3½oz) caster sugar

1 tbsp elderflower cordial

250g (9oz) good-quality ready-made custard

200ml (7fl oz) double cream

1 Put the gooseberries, sugar, and elderflower cordial into a pan and stir to dissolve the sugar. Cover and cook over a low heat for 5 minutes until the gooseberries have given out some water and started to swell. Remove the lid and cook for another 5 minutes.

2 Mash the gooseberries lightly with a potato masher to break up a few of the bigger ones. Alternatively, if you prefer a smoother fool, purée the fruit in a blender or food processor. Leave the mixture to cool completely then chill in the fridge.

3 In a large bowl, whip the double cream until it forms fairly stiff peaks.

4 Once the purée is completely cold, fold it into the cream, and then fold in the custard to make a light, fluffy fool. Spoon into a serving dish or individual glasses and chill in the fridge for a few hours, or overnight, before serving.

variation

gooseberry and strawberry summer fool

Substitute half the gooseberries with ripe, hulled strawberries. Do not stew them. Stew 175g (6oz) gooseberries in 60g (2oz) sugar and 2 tsp water. Purée with 175g (6oz) strawberries until smooth, then leave to cool and continue at step 3. Decorate the tops with a little grated dark chocolate before serving.

strawberry and cream victoria sandwich

A traditional afternoon tea favourite, instead of buttercream and jam, this version makes the most of luscious strawberries when they are at their juicy peak.

20 MINS   **25 MINS**   ❄ **FREEZABLE**

SPECIAL EQUIPMENT ▪ 2 x 20cm (8in) round sandwich tins ▪ electric hand whisk

SERVES 8

225g (8oz) butter, softened

225g (8oz) caster sugar

4 large eggs, lightly beaten

225g (8oz) self-raising flour

For the strawberry and cream filling

100ml (3½oz) double cream

175g (6oz) strawberries, hulled and sliced

1 Preheat the oven to 180°C (350°F/ Gas 4). Line the bases of the sandwich tins with baking parchment. In a bowl, mix the butter and sugar with an electric hand whisk until light and creamy. Whisk in the eggs a little at a time, adding in a little of the flour if the mixture looks as if it is going to curdle. Sift in the remaining flour and fold in gently with a large metal spoon. Divide the mixture between the tins and bake for 25 minutes, or until risen and firm to the touch. Leave to cool in the tins for 5 minutes, then transfer to a wire rack to cool completely.

2 To make the filling, place the cream in a bowl and whisk with an electric hand whisk until soft peaks form. Spread over one of the cakes, then top with the strawberries. Place the other cake on top, then dust thickly with icing sugar.

cherry jam

This jam has just a hint of brandy to help cut through the sweetness of the cherries.

🥣 15 MINUTES   🍲 30-35 MINUTES

SPECIAL EQUIPMENT ▪ preserving pan ▪ muslin

MAKES APPROX 1kg (2¼lb)

500g (1lb 2oz) dark cherries, stoned, with the stones reserved

juice of 2 lemons

500g (1lb 2oz) jam sugar

2 tbsp brandy or cherry brandy

1 Place the cherry stones in a small square of muslin, gather into a small bag, and tie with string. Put the cherries in a preserving pan or a large heavy-based saucepan and pour in 300ml (10fl oz) of water. Bring to the boil and simmer for 10–15 minutes, or until the cherries are tender and begin to soften. Discard the stones. Pour in the lemon juice and add the sugar. Heat gently, stirring until the sugar has all dissolved. Bring to the boil and keep at a rolling boil, stirring occasionally, for 10 minutes or until it reaches the setting point.

2 Remove from the heat. Test for a set with a sugar thermometer or a wrinkle test (chill a saucer in the fridge before cooking). If you use a thermometer, the temperature must reach 105°C (220°F); the mixture will also thicken around the sides of the pan, boil sluggishly, and the bubbles "plop" rather than froth. Or put 1 tsp jam on the chilled saucer, allow to cool for a moment, then push it with a finger. If it leaves a trail and wrinkles slightly, it is set.

3 Stir in the brandy, then ladle into warm sterilized jars, cover with discs of waxed paper, seal, and label. Store in a cool, dark place for up to nine months and refrigerate after opening.

gooseberry and raspberry jam

The flavour of ripe gooseberries and raspberries comes through distinctly in this jam.

🥣 10 MINS   🍲 45-50 MINS

SPECIAL EQUIPMENT ▪ preserving pan

MAKES APPROX 1.1kg (2½lb)

450g (1lb) gooseberries, topped and tailed

grated zest of ½ lemon

225g (8oz) raspberries

675g (1½lb) granulated sugar

small knob of butter

1 Put the gooseberries in a preserving pan or a heavy-based saucepan with 150ml (5fl oz) of water and the lemon zest. Bring to the boil, reduce the heat, cover, and cook for 30 minutes until soft and pulpy. Add the raspberries and cook just until their juices run.

2 Add the sugar and stir over a gentle heat until it has dissolved. Bring to the boil and boil rapidly for about 15 minutes, or until the setting point is reached. Remove from the heat and test for a set with a sugar thermometer or a wrinkle test (chill a saucer in the fridge before cooking). If you use a thermometer, the temperature must reach 105°C (220°F); the mixture will also thicken around the sides of the pan, boil sluggishly, and the bubbles "plop" rather than froth. Or put 1 tsp jam on the chilled saucer, allow to cool for a moment, then push it with a finger. If it leaves a trail and wrinkles slightly, it is set.

3 Use a skimmer to skim off the surface scum, then stir in the butter to disperse any residual scum. Ladle into warm sterilized jars, cover with discs of waxed paper, seal, and label. Store in a cool, dark place and refrigerate after opening.

cherry and cassis conserve

It's worth preparing a rich cherry conserve such as this to make the most of the short cherry season. It should be a soft-set texture, so don't overcook it or it will turn sticky.

🥣 20 MINS PLUS STANDING   🍲 30 MINS

SPECIAL EQUIPMENT ▪ preserving pan

MAKES APPROX 1.1kg (2½lb)

600g (1lb 5oz) cherries, stoned

300g (10oz) jam sugar

1 tsp vanilla extract

juice of 2 lemons

4 tbsp cassis

1 Layer the fruit and sugar in a large bowl, cover, and leave for several hours or overnight at room temperature.

2 Put the fruit, sugar, vanilla, and lemon juice in a preserving pan or a large heavy-based saucepan and cook gently for 15 minutes, or until the cherries are soft.

3 Turn up the heat until the conserve reaches a rolling boil and cook for 5–8 minutes, or until it reaches the setting point. Remove from the heat and test for a set with a sugar thermometer or a wrinkle test (chill a saucer in the fridge before cooking). If you use a thermometer, the temperature must reach 105°C (220°F); the mixture will also thicken around the sides of the pan, boil sluggishly, and the bubbles "plop" rather than froth. Or put 1 tsp jam on the chilled saucer, allow to cool for a moment, then push it with a finger. If it leaves a trail and wrinkles slightly, it is set.

4 Stir in the cassis, ladle into warm sterilized jars, cover with waxed paper discs, seal, and label. Store in a cool, dark place. Refrigerate after opening.

strawberry conserve

This ever-popular soft-set conserve is best made with freshly picked juicy strawberries. Serve with thick cream and scones for a classic summer afternoon tea.

🥣 20 MINUTES PLUS STANDING　　🍲 20-25 MINUTES

SPECIAL EQUIPMENT ▪ preserving pan ▪ muslin

MAKES APPROX 1kg (2¼lb)

900g (2lb) juicy strawberries, hulled

900g (2lb) granulated sugar

juice of 1 lemon

juice of 1 lime

1 Layer the strawberries and sugar in a large bowl, cover, and leave for several hours or overnight.

2 Tip the fruit and sugar into a preserving pan or a large heavy-based saucepan, and cook over a low heat, stirring continuously, until the sugar has dissolved. Then boil gently for

about 5 minutes, just enough for the fruit to soften but not break up. Remove the pan from the heat, cover it loosely with some muslin, and leave the cooked fruit overnight.

3 Remove the muslin, put the pan back on the heat, stir in the lemon and lime juice, and bring to the boil. Boil gently for 5–10 minutes, or until thickened and the setting point is reached, skimming any scum off the surface as needed. Remove from the heat and test for a set with a sugar thermometer or a wrinkle test (chill a saucer in the fridge before cooking).

If you use a thermometer, the temperature must reach 105°C (220°F); the mixture will also thicken around the sides of the pan, boil sluggishly, and the bubbles "plop" rather than froth. Or put 1 tsp jam on the chilled saucer, allow to cool for a moment, then push it with a finger. If it leaves a trail and wrinkles, it is set.

4 Ladle into warm sterilized jars, cover with discs of waxed paper, seal, and label. Store in a cool, dark place for up to six months. Refrigerate after opening.

variation

three-fruit conserve

Prepare in exactly the same way but use 300g (10oz) strawberries, hulled; 300g (10oz) raspberries, picked over and any calyces removed; and 300g (10oz) red cherries, stoned. Cook and pot as before.

rhubarb and rose petal syrup

The rose gives this syrup an aromatic kick. Dilute to taste with still or sparkling water, or drizzle over ice cream.

🍲 20 MINUTES   🍲 25–35 MINUTES

SPECIAL EQUIPMENT ▪ jelly bag or muslin-lined sieve

MAKES APPROX 500ml (16fl oz)

450g (1lb) pink or red-stemmed rhubarb, cut into short lengths

350g (12oz) granulated sugar

8 scented pink rose petals

2 tbsp rosewater

1 tsp citric acid

1 Put enough water in a heavy-based saucepan to just cover the base. Add the rhubarb, sugar, and rose petals. Bring to the boil, stir gently, cover, reduce the heat, and cook gently for 20–30 minutes until really pulpy, stirring once or twice.

2 Strain the pulp in a jelly bag or a muslin-lined sieve set over a measuring jug or bowl. Press the pulp to extract maximum juice. Return the juice to the pan and bring back to the boil.

3 Remove from the heat and stir the rosewater and citric acid into the strained juice. Pour immediately into warm sterilized bottles using a sterilized funnel. Seal, label, and leave to cool, then store in the fridge for up to 1 month. Shake before use.

bottled watermelon in ginger syrup

Watermelon needs lemon juice added to it to make it suitable for bottling, so don't omit it.

🍲 20 MINS   🍲 10 MINS

SPECIAL EQUIPMENT ▪ melon baller ▪ mandoline

MAKES 1 LITRE (1¾ PINTS)

1 small watermelon

2.5cm (1in) piece fresh root ginger

140g (5oz) granulated sugar

2 tbsp lemon juice

1 Cut the melon in half, remove the seeds, and either scoop the flesh into balls using a melon baller, or remove the skin and cut the flesh into bite-sized cubes.

2 Peel the ginger and cut into wafer-thin slices using either a mandoline, the slicer blade on a grater, or a sharp knife.

3 Make the syrup using 300ml (10fl oz) water and the ginger, sugar, and lemon juice. Add the melon and boil for 2 minutes. Place the warm sterilized jars on a wooden board or cloth. Using a slotted spoon, pack the fruit tightly into the jars without squashing it, leaving 1cm (½in) of space at the top. Fill the jars to the brim with the hot syrup, then tap the jars lightly on a board to remove air bubbles. Top up with extra syrup if needed to cover the fruit completely. Fit the rubber band or metal lid seal and clamp on the lid. If using screw-band jars, loosen by a quarter of a turn.

4 Preheat the oven to 150°C (300°F/ Gas 2), place the jars on a baking sheet lined with newspaper, and heat-process in the centre of the oven for 40–50 minutes. Tighten the lids or put on the screw-band, leave for 24 hours, then test for a seal. (If using kilner jars with metal lids, you will know immediately or soon after processing if you have a seal, as the lid becomes slightly concave and is firm with no "give" when pressed. You may even hear a "pop" as the seal forms.) Store in a cool, dark place, and then refrigerate after opening.

raspberry and vanilla syrup

Combine this syrup with milk, stir well, and top with raspberry ice cream for a delicious milkshake.

🍲 15 MINUTES   🍲 20 MINUTES

SPECIAL EQUIPMENT ▪ muslin-lined sieve

MAKES APPROX 500ml (16fl oz)

450g (1lb) ripe raspberries

1 vanilla pod, split

250g (9oz) caster sugar

1 tsp citric acid

1 Put the raspberries and 200ml (7fl oz) water in a saucepan. Heat gently over a low heat until the juices run. Crush the fruit with a potato masher or the back of a large spoon.

2 When the fruit is really soft, strain through a muslin-lined sieve (or use a new clean disposable kitchen cloth) into a clean bowl. Squeeze or press to extract the maximum juice. Return the juice to the rinsed-out pan. Add the vanilla pod to the pan with the sugar. Stir, then heat gently, without stirring, until the sugar dissolves. Bring to the boil and boil for 5 minutes, or until syrupy. Remove from the heat, discard the vanilla pod, and stir in the citric acid.

3 Pour immediately into warm sterilized bottles using a sterilized funnel. Seal, label, and leave to cool, then store in the fridge for up to two months. Shake before use.

simple garlic confit

This is a heavenly way to eat and preserve newly harvested garlic. Simply squeeze the cloves from their skins and use for garlic toast, in mashed potato, roast meats, and other dishes.

🥣 1 MIN   🍲 45 MINS–1 HOUR

MAKES APPROX 225g (8oz)

2 large plump garlic bulbs, with the cloves separated

90–150ml (3–5fl oz) extra virgin olive oil, plus extra as needed

1 sprig of thyme

1 bay leaf

sea salt

2 tbsp balsamic or sherry vinegar

1 Pack the unpeeled cloves of garlic into a small snug-fitting ovenproof dish, pour in enough olive oil to cover the garlic, tuck in the thyme and bay leaf, and sprinkle over the salt.

2 Cook in a low oven at 150°C (300°F/Gas 2) for 45–60 minutes or until the garlic cloves are soft (this will depend on the size of the cloves).

3 To store, allow to cool, transfer the cooked cloves to a sterilized jar, and add the vinegar, stirring to ensure all the cloves are well coated. Fill the jar with the garlic-infused oil they were cooked in, topping up with extra fresh oil if needed. Store in the fridge, ensuring that the cloves are always completely covered in oil, and use within 1 month.

asparagus in oil

Since the season for asparagus is so short, it makes sense to preserve them in oil for a little longer. Asparagus has a unique flavour that is greatly intensified when griddled.

🥣 15 MINS   🍲 15 MINS

MAKES APPROX 500ml (16fl oz)

350g (12oz) medium asparagus spears, trimmed to the height of your jar

200ml (7fl oz) extra virgin olive oil, plus extra if needed for coating and topping up

sea salt and freshly ground black pepper

juice of 2 lemons in a small bowl

1 Smother the asparagus in 3 tbsp olive oil, using your hands to coat them, and season them well with salt and pepper.

2 Heat a griddle pan until hot, then add the asparagus spears in batches and turn occasionally. Cook each batch for about 5 minutes, or until they begin to char slightly and soften but are not limp.

3 Toss the asparagus spears in the lemon juice and leave to cool in the juice. Then stand them upright in a sterilized jar, tips upright. Pack them in tightly and top up with the oil to cover them completely. Seal, label, and store in the fridge. Once opened, keep refrigerated, top up with oil if necessary so the asparagus spears are always covered, and use within 3 weeks.

variation

griddled courgettes in oil
Replace the asparagus spears with 450g (1lb) baby courgettes, sliced thinly lengthways. Put the slices in a large bowl with the olive oil and seasoning and toss them together with your hands until the slices are evenly covered. Then follow step 2, cooking the courgettes for about 3 minutes on each side, or until golden. Layer the slices in a sterilized jar in step 3 and press them down lightly to remove any air bubbles once you have covered them in oil.

rollmops

Pickling herrings in vinegar in effect "cooks" the fish and dissolves tiny bones. Make the flavourings as mild or sharp as you want (for a mild pickle, use half the quantity of vinegar).

🥣 20–25 MINS PLUS SALTING AND MATURING

SPECIAL EQUIPMENT ▪ preserving jar or crock ▪ cocktail sticks

MAKES APPROX 750ml (1¼ PINTS)

6–8 very fresh herring fillets, with any visible bones removed

60g (2oz) sea salt per 450ml (15fl oz) cold water

450ml (15fl oz) cider or white wine vinegar

1 tbsp light soft brown sugar

6 black peppercorns

6 allspice berries

1 mace blade

3 bay leaves

1 dried chilli

1 red onion, peeled, halved, and finely sliced

6–8 pickled gherkins

1 Put the fillets in a glass dish. Dissolve the sea salt in the water, pour the brine over the fish, and leave to soak for 2–3 hours. Then drain and pat dry with kitchen paper.

2 Put the vinegar, sugar, and spices into a stainless steel saucepan, bring slowly to the boil, simmer for 1–2 minutes, and then set the mixture aside to cool.

3 Lay the fillets skin-side down on a clean board. Place a slice of onion and gherkin at the tail end of each and roll them up. Secure each rollmop with a cocktail stick. Pack into a snug-fitting sterilized preserving jar or crock. Pour the cold, spiced vinegar and its spices over the rollmops so they are completely submerged.

4 Top up with vinegar if needed. Seal and store in the fridge for 3–4 days to mature. Always keep the fish submerged in vinegar.

high summer

at their best

vegetables artichokes ▪ aubergine ▪ beetroot ▪ cep mushrooms ▪ chillies ▪ courgettes ▪ cucumbers ▪ fennel ▪ green beans ▪ kohlrabi ▪ lettuce ▪ mangetout ▪ new potatoes ▪ outdoor rhubarb ▪ peas ▪ peppers ▪ radishes ▪ rocket ▪ runner beans ▪ samphire ▪ sorrel ▪ spinach ▪ sweetcorn ▪ Swiss chard ▪ sugarsnap peas ▪ tomatoes ▪ watercress

fruit apricots ▪ blackcurrants ▪ blueberries ▪ cherries ▪ damsons ▪ figs ▪ gooseberries ▪ grapes ▪ greengages ▪ loganberries ▪ melons ▪ nectarines ▪ peaches ▪ plums ▪ raspberries ▪ redcurrants ▪ strawberries ▪ tayberries ▪ watermelon ▪ white currants ▪ wild alpine strawberries

seafood brown trout (wild and farmed) ▪ common brown crab ▪ Dover sole ▪ haddock ▪ herring ▪ John Dory ▪ king scallops ▪ langoustines ▪ lemon sole ▪ mackerel ▪ North Atlantic lobster ▪ pollack ▪ rainbow trout (wild and farmed) ▪ red mullet ▪ sardines ▪ sea bass ▪ sea bream (wild and farmed) ▪ sea trout (wild and farmed) ▪ spider crab

meat, poultry, game grouse ▪ quail (farmed) ▪ rabbit (wild and farmed) ▪ wood pigeon

also available

vegetables broad beans ▪ cabbages ▪ calabrese broccoli ▪ carrots ▪ cauliflower ▪ chanterelle mushrooms ▪ marrows ▪ mushrooms (cultivated) ▪ nettles ▪ okra ▪ onions ▪ pak choi ▪ pea shoots ▪ salad onions ▪ spring onions ▪ turnips **fruit** avocados ▪ apples ▪ blackberries ▪ crabapples ▪ lemons ▪ limes ▪ mangoes **seafood** cod ▪ coley ▪ crayfish (farmed) ▪ halibut ▪ monkfish ▪ mussels ▪ Pacific or rock oysters ▪ plaice ▪ salmon (farmed) ▪ turbot (farmed) ▪ whiting **meat, poultry, game** beef ▪ chicken ▪ duck (farmed) ▪ guinea fowl (farmed) ▪ lamb ▪ pork ▪ rabbit (farmed) ▪ turkey ▪ veal ▪ venison (farmed) ▪ wild boar (farmed)

high summer recipe chooser

ⓥ suitable for vegetarians

Spicy chicken balls with chilli and ginger sauce p143

Roasted red pepper tart p153

Vegetables

Aubergine
Aubergine and chickpea pâté p164 ⓥ
Aubergine, potato, and feta cheese
 frittata p185 ⓥ
Aubergines stuffed with tomato rice
 p187 ⓥ
Baba ganoush p164 ⓥ
Chargrilled aubergine with spiced
 tomato sauce p194 ⓥ
Chicken, aubergine, and tomato tagine
 p184
Chorizo with aubergine and courgettes
 p160
Fish with courgettes, aubergines, and
 tomatoes p168
Griddled Mediterranean vegetables
 p202 ⓥ
Hot-spiced aubergine chutney p244 ⓥ
Moroccan-style pancakes p164 ⓥ
Pasta with aubergine sauce p187 ⓥ
Roasted tomato and aubergine soup
 p148 ⓥ
Roasted sardines with vegetable medley
 p168
Spicy stuffed aubergines with feta
 cheese p187 ⓥ
Stuffed aubergine rolls with salsa p165 ⓥ
Summer frittata with ratatouille p185 ⓥ
Tabbouleh with griddled aubergine dip
 p199 ⓥ

Beetroot
Goat's cheese, beetroot, and pistachios
 p151 ⓥ
Spiced beetroot pickle p245 ⓥ
Tomato borscht p159 ⓥ

Carrot
Gado gado p181 ⓥ
Malaysian-style pickled vegetables p205
 ⓥ
Mixed vegetable pickle p237 ⓥ

Cauliflower
Malaysian-style pickled vegetables p205
 ⓥ
Mixed vegetable pickle p237 ⓥ

Chilli
Baked eggs with tomatoes and peppers
 p170 ⓥ

Caribbean stew with allspice and ginger
 p173
Chicken, aubergine, and tomato tagine
 p184
Chicken stir-fried with spring onion,
 basil, and lemongrass p175
Chilli beef and bean soup p142
Chilli cornbread p203 ⓥ
Chipotle chicken p184
Crispy beef and vegetables p182
Cucumber-chilli salad p201 ⓥ
Cucumber, chilli, and roasted pepper
 salad p201 ⓥ
Escabeche p152
Fish tagine p191
Fiery pepper noodles p173 ⓥ
Gado gado p181 ⓥ
Greek stuffed tomatoes p172
Hot chilli sauce p198 ⓥ
Lemongrass chicken p180
Malaysian-style pickled vegetables
 p204 ⓥ
Mini chicken burgers with tomato and
 chilli sauce p142
Mixed vegetable pickle p237 ⓥ
Paneer and sweet pepper curry
 p181 ⓥ
Pan-fried salmon with coconut, chilli,
 and lime p176
Pan-fried scallops with chilli, ginger, and
 an anchovy dressing p165
Potato and pea curry p187 ⓥ
Salmon jungle curry p191
Sardines with sweet chilli and chive
 sauce p160
Scallops with sweet chilli sauce p160
Spiced haddock with coconut, chilli,
 and lime p176
Spicy chicken balls with chilli and
 ginger sauce p143
Spicy stuffed aubergines with feta
 cheese p187 ⓥ
Tomato and chilli jam p232 ⓥ
Tortilla bean salad p202 ⓥ
Whipped yogurt soup with sautéed
 courgette p146 ⓥ
Vietnamese beef soup p174

Courgette
Chicken and courgette mousse p163

Tomato and harissa tart p145

Chorizo with aubergine and courgettes
 p160
Courgette and hazelnut bread p202 ⓥ
Courgette and potato soup p146 ⓥ
Courgette tian p204 ⓥ
Fiery pepper noodles p173 ⓥ
Fish with courgettes, aubergines, and
 tomatoes p168
Griddled Mediterranean vegetables
 p202 ⓥ
Mediterranean sweetcorn soup p154 ⓥ
Pancakes with courgettes and Emmental
 p147 ⓥ
Pancakes with courgettes, tomatoes, and
 mozzarella p147 ⓥ
Roasted sardines with vegetable medley
 p168
Runner bean and courgette chutney
 p245 ⓥ
Summer frittata with ratatouille p185 ⓥ
Whipped yogurt soup with sautéed
 courgette p146 ⓥ

Cucumber
Cucumber-chilli salad p201 ⓥ
Cucumber, chilli, and roasted pepper
 salad p201 ⓥ
Cucumber and dill soup p148 ⓥ
Cucumber pickle p244 ⓥ
Gado gado p181 ⓥ
Greek salad p195 ⓥ
Hot cucumber and tarragon soup
 p162 ⓥ
Lemongrass chicken p180

Egg and fennel potato salad p200

Malaysian-style pickled vegetables
 p205 ⓥ
Marinated cucumber and dill salad
 p201 ⓥ
Pickled gherkins p236 ⓥ
Pickled gherkins with salad onions
 p236 ⓥ
Smoked chicken with basil mayonnaise
 on cucumber rounds p162
Smoked trout with horseradish
 mayonnaise on cucumber rounds p162
Summer vegetable bread salad p195 ⓥ
Tabbouleh with cacik p199 ⓥ
Tabbouleh with griddled aubergine dip
 p199 ⓥ
Tomato and cucumber pilaf p205 ⓥ

Fennel
Chicken roasted with fennel and lemon
 p183
Egg and fennel potato salad p200 ⓥ
Smoked trout, fennel, and mascarpone
 crostini p158

Green beans
Gado gado p181 ⓥ
German chicken broth p154
Green bean, red onion, and Camembert
 salad p151 ⓥ
Malaysian-style pickled vegetables
 p205 ⓥ
Rocket, green bean, and pesto salad
 p204 ⓥ
Spiced haddock with coconut, chilli,
 and lime p176

Scallop and sweetcorn chowder p157

Baked eggs with tomatoes and peppers p170

Gado gado p181

Mediterranean burgers p189

Paneer and sweet pepper curry p181

high summer recipe chooser continued

(v) suitable for vegetarians

Génoise cake with raspberries and cream p231

Blueberry-ripple cheesecake p226

Figs with cassis mascarpone p220

Apricots with amaretti biscuits and mascarpone p210

Cold raspberry soufflés p210

Raspberry and almond bake p213

Greek salad p195 (v)
Greek stuffed tomatoes p173
Green bean, red onion, and Camembert salad p151 (v)
Hot chilli sauce p198 (v)
Lamb fillet with tomato and basil salad p191
Mediterranean sweetcorn soup p154 (v)
Melon and tomato salad p194 (v)
Mini chicken burgers with tomato and chilli sauce p142
Mixed vegetable pickle p237 (v)
Moroccan-style pancakes p164 (v)
Pancakes with courgettes, tomatoes, and mozzarella p147
Paneer and sweet pepper curry p181 (v)
Pasta with aubergine sauce p187 (v)
Pasta with no-cook tomato sauce p192 (v)
Pasta with yellow pepper sauce p187 (v)
Pizza with tomatoes, olives, and capers p193 (v)
Pork and fennel sausages with fresh tomato salsa p144
Roast lamb with cherry tomatoes and new potatoes p188
Roasted sardines with vegetable medley p168
Roasted tomato and aubergine soup p148 (v)
Roasted tomato soup p148 (v)
Rocket and tomato pasta salad p204 (v)
Rocket, green bean, and pesto salad p204 (v)

Sausage and tomato pie p192
Salted cod and roasted pepper dip p146
Spaghetti with cherry tomato, rocket, and black olive sauce p158 (v)
Spanish pepper and tomato soup p166 (v)
Spiced pork, apricot, and tomato skewers p145
Spicy sausage and tomato skewers p145
Stuffed aubergine rolls with salsa p165 (v)
Stuffed lamb, Greek style p182
Summer frittata with ratatouille p185 (v)
Summer vegetable bread salad p195 (v)
Sweetcorn fritters with tomato salsa p167 (v)
Tabbouleh with cacik p199 (v)
Tabbouleh with griddled aubergine dip p199 (v)
Tomato and chilli jam p232 (v)
Tomato and cucumber pilaf p205 (v)
Tomato and harissa tart p145 (v)
Tomato and roasted pepper chutney p233 (v)
Tomato and tarragon pilaf p205 (v)
Tomato borscht p159 (v)
Tomato, red onion, and mozzarella salad p151 (v)
Tomato salad with butter beans and lime p198 (v)
White fish with Swiss chard, harissa, tomatoes, and pumpkin seeds p169

Fruit

Apricot
Apricots and almonds in amaretto p237 (v)
Apricot and champagne conserve p237 (v)
Apricot clafoutis p224 (v)
Apricot conserve p238 (v)
Apricot crumble shortbread p230 (v)
Apricot friands p218 (v)
Apricot meringue roulade p208 (v)
Apricot pastries p208 (v)
Apricots with amaretti biscuits and mascarpone p210 (v)
Rumtopf p242 (v)
Spiced pork, apricot, and tomato skewers p145

Blackberries
Berry syrup p234 (v)
Boozy berries with mint and elderflower cream p220 (v)
Chilled rice pudding with warm berry sauce p227 (v)
Gratin of fresh berries with sabayon p230 (v)
Mixed berries with white chocolate sauce p226 (v)
Mixed berry flan p228 (v)
Mixed berry pancakes with white chocolate sauce p226 (v)

Blackcurrants
Blackcurrant and rosemary cheesecake p212 (v)

Chilled rice pudding with warm berry sauce p227 (v)

Blueberries
American blueberry pancakes p211 (v)
Berry friands p218 (v)
Blueberry and almond bake p213 (v)
Blueberry and raspberry freezer jam p243 (v)
Blueberry muffins p218 (v)
Blueberry-ripple cheesecake p226 (v)
Blueberry upside-down cake p206 (v)
Boozy berries with mint and elderflower cream p220 (v)
Chilled rice pudding with warm berry sauce p227 (v)
Gratin of fresh berries with sabayon p230 (v)
Mixed berries with white chocolate sauce p226 (v)
Mixed berry jam p239 (v)
Mixed berry pancakes with white chocolate sauce p226 (v)

Currants
Boozy berries with mint and elderflower cream p220 (v)
Rumtopf p242 (v)

Cherries
Cherries in brandy p242 (v)
Cherry and almond cake p213 (v)
Cherry and chocolate brownies p228 (v)
Cherry and white chocolate trifle p212 (v)

Seafood

Sole bonne femme p193

Strawberry shortcakes p211

**Peach and nectarine puff pastry
tart** p215

**Fish with courgettes, aubergines,
and tomatoes** p168

Scallops with sweet chilli sauce p160

chilli beef and bean soup

Ideal for bringing a little heat to a cooler summer evening, this hearty soup makes the most of peppers, spicy chillies, and fragrant summer parsley.

🥣 **20 MINS** 🍲 **2 HRS** ❄️ **FREEZABLE**

SERVES 8

2 tbsp olive oil

2 onions, finely chopped

salt and freshly ground black pepper

2 red peppers, deseeded and finely chopped

2-3 red chillies, deseeded and finely chopped

550g (1¼lb) braising steak, cut into 2.5cm (1in) cubes

1 tbsp plain flour

2.3 litres (4 pints) hot beef stock

2 x 400g cans kidney beans, drained, rinsed, and drained again

handful of flat-leaf parsley, finely chopped, to serve

1 Heat the oil in a large heavy-based pan, add the onions, and cook over a low heat for 6–8 minutes, or until soft and translucent. Season with salt and pepper, then stir through the peppers and chillies and cook for 5 minutes. Add the meat and cook, stirring frequently, for 5–10 minutes, or until beginning to brown all over.

2 Sprinkle in the flour, stir well, and cook for 2 minutes. Add the stock, bring to the boil, then cover with a lid and reduce to a simmer. Cook for 1½ hours, or until the meat is tender. Add the kidney beans and cook for 10 minutes more, then season to taste with salt and pepper. Stir through the parsley and serve.

mini chicken burgers with tomato and chilli sauce

These mini chicken patties are infused with fragrant Middle Eastern spices and are served elegantly on a bed of peppers. They are complemented by a refreshing tomato sauce.

🥣 **30 MINS PLUS CHILLING** 🍲 **30 MINS**

SPECIAL EQUIPMENT ▪ food processor

SERVES 12

800g (1¾lb) skinless chicken breast, chopped into pieces

1 tbsp finely chopped flat-leaf parsley

1 tsp finely sliced sage leaves

2 garlic cloves, 1 finely chopped, 1 peeled but left whole

100g (3½oz) dates, chopped

50g (1¾oz) hazelnuts, roughly chopped

2 tsp Middle Eastern spice mix (dukkah)

2 eggs

2 tbsp olive oil, plus extra for brushing

75g (2½oz) fresh breadcrumbs

salt and freshly ground black pepper

400g jar tomato sauce

1 red chilli, finely chopped (optional)

handful of basil leaves, torn

baguette, cut into 12 thick slices

2 yellow peppers, grilled, deseeded, and sliced

2 red peppers, grilled, deseeded, and sliced

1 Mince the chicken in a food processor for 10–15 seconds; be careful not to blend into a paste. Transfer to a bowl and add the herbs, chopped garlic, dates, hazelnuts, dukkah, eggs, olive oil, and breadcrumbs. Mix thoroughly and season with salt and pepper. Cover with cling film and chill for about 1 hour.

2 Preheat the grill to low. Shape the chilled chicken mixture into 12 burger-style portions, then brush with a little oil. Grill the chicken burgers for 6–8 minutes on each side until cooked through. Set aside for 15 minutes in a warm place.

3 Warm through the tomato sauce, adding the chilli and basil. Brush the baguette slices with some oil and toast on both sides under the grill. Rub each slice with the whole garlic clove. To serve, layer the grilled yellow and red peppers on each bread slice, then top with a burger on top and spoon over a little sauce.

chilled melon and ginger soup

This is a soup to make in a hurry. All that's needed to bring out its fruity flavour is a seriously good chill – and a perfectly ripe melon.

🥄 **15 MINS PLUS CHILLING**   ❄️ **FREEZABLE**

SPECIAL EQUIPMENT ▪ blender or food processor

SERVES 4

1 ripe Galia melon, peeled and deseeded

2.5cm (1in) piece of fresh root ginger, peeled

1 tsp fennel seeds

200g (7oz) white seedless grapes

grated zest and juice of 1 lime

1 tsp dried mint

4 tbsp Greek-style yogurt, beaten

salt and freshly ground black pepper

For the garnish

2 tbsp mint leaves

pinch of sugar

25g (scant 1oz) crystallized ginger, finely chopped

1 Roughly chop three quarters of the melon flesh into bite-sized chunks. Finely chop the remainder and set aside. Grate the root ginger and squeeze any juice over the melon chunks. Discard the leftover ginger.

2 Heat a heavy-based frying pan or griddle over a gentle heat and lightly toast the fennel seeds for about 30 seconds, until you smell an aniseed-like aroma. Grind the seeds to a coarse powder using a mortar and pestle.

3 Put the ground fennel seeds into a blender or food processor with the roughly chopped melon and ginger juice. Add the grapes, lime juice and zest, and dried mint. Blitz until smooth and push through a sieve to remove the skins.

4 Stir in the yogurt, season, and chill thoroughly – it's best to half-freeze this soup, then give it a good whisk just before serving. Spoon into bowls, adding a small pile of the reserved melon to each one. Shred the fresh mint, mix with the sugar and crystallized ginger, and scatter over the soup. Serve immediately.

spicy chicken balls with chilli and ginger sauce

Crisp, spicy chicken enriched with honey, dried apricots, and macadamia nuts is well-matched with a zesty sauce in which the chilli is given an extra kick by the addition of fresh lime.

🥄 **20 MINS**   🍲 **30 MINS**

SPECIAL EQUIPMENT ▪ food processor

SERVES 8

50g (1¾oz) dried apricots

1 tbsp honey

3 tbsp brandy

4 skinless chicken breast, about 200g (7oz) each, coarsely chopped

50g (1¾oz) macadamia nuts, chopped

60g (2oz) cooked and cooled rice

2 garlic cloves, grated or finely chopped

2 tbsp finely chopped sage leaves

1 tbsp finely chopped basil leaves

1 tbsp finely chopped flat-leaf parsley

2 small red chillies, deseeded and chopped

1 egg

salt and freshly ground black pepper

light olive oil, for deep-frying

cress, to serve

For the sauce

juice of 4 limes

2 small red chillies, deseeded and chopped

2 tbsp olive oil

1 tbsp finely chopped fresh root ginger

1 spring onion, finely sliced

1 Put the apricots, honey, and brandy in a small pan. Simmer for about 15 minutes until the apricots soften and the liquid has been absorbed. Leave to cool.

2 Mince the chicken in a food processor for 15–20 seconds; be careful not to turn it into a paste. Transfer to a bowl and add the cooled apricots, nuts, rice, garlic, herbs, chillies, and egg. Season with salt and pepper and mix well. Using wet hands, shape the mixture into walnut-sized balls; you should end up with 36–40.

3 Heat enough oil for deep-frying over a medium-high heat. Cooking in batches, deep-fry the balls for about 15 minutes, or until golden brown. Drain on kitchen paper and keep warm.

4 To make the sauce, put all the sauce ingredients in a bowl and mix well. Arrange the spicy chicken balls on a platter, pour over the sauce, and scatter some cress over the top. Serve immediately.

chilled tomato and red pepper soup

A variation on the Spanish classic gazpacho, this nutritious soup retains all the vitamins and vivid colour from the raw vegetables. Chopped boiled egg is also good as a topping.

15 MINS

SPECIAL EQUIPMENT ▪ blender or food processor

SERVES 4

3 slices white bread, crusts removed

1 garlic clove, roughly chopped

1 tbsp sherry vinegar or red wine vinegar

1 tbsp olive oil

6 very ripe tomatoes, roughly chopped

2 red peppers, halved, deseeded, and roughly chopped

1 red chilli, deseeded and roughly chopped

salt and freshly ground black pepper

For the garnish

1 tomato, finely diced

¼ cucumber, finely diced

1 spring onion, finely diced

1 Using the blender or food processor, purée the bread, garlic, and vinegar until smooth. With the motor running, gradually pour in the oil and continue to purée until incorporated. Add the tomatoes, peppers, and chilli, and blend until well combined.

2 Keep the motor running and slowly add about 500ml (16fl oz) iced water, checking the consistency of the soup as you go – it should be like a gazpacho. Taste and season with a pinch of salt and some pepper. Add a dash of vinegar if the soup needs it. Chill until required.

3 Make the garnish just before serving. Put the tomato, cucumber, and spring onion in a small bowl and stir to combine. Serve the soup well chilled, topped with the garnish.

pork and fennel sausages with fresh tomato salsa

If you feel like having a barbecue, then this is the recipe to use. The salsa is a summery mix of tomatoes and olives and is a refreshing sauce to serve alongside the herby sausages.

10 MINS PLUS MARINATING   **15 MINS**

SERVES 4

4 Italian-style pork and fennel sausages

3 tbsp olive oil

2 garlic cloves, grated or finely chopped

4 sprigs of dill

salt and freshly ground black pepper

4 thick slices of Italian-style crusty ciabatta, toasted to serve

For the tomato salsa

4 ripe tomatoes, deseeded and diced

115g (4oz) kalamata olives, pitted and diced

large handful of basil leaves, torn

2 tbsp extra virgin olive oil

1 Put the sausages in a shallow glass or ceramic dish. Add the oil, garlic, and dill, and season with a little salt and pepper. Stir the sausages around so that they are well coated. Cover with cling film and leave to marinate in the fridge for at least 1 hour.

2 Meanwhile, to make the salsa, combine all the ingredients in a bowl and mix well. Season with salt and pepper.

3 Heat a grill, barbecue, or heavy-based frying pan until hot. Grill the sausages for 10–15 minutes until cooked through, turning halfway during cooking to brown both sides.

4 Divide the sausages between 4 warmed plates, and serve immediately on a piece of toasted ciabatta, with the tomato salsa spooned over.

spicy sausage and tomato skewers

Cherry tomatoes are ideal for skewers, as they hold their shape far more successfully than quartered or halved larger tomatoes. Team them with chilli or paprika flavoured sausages.

🥄 15 MINS   🍲 20 MINS

SPECIAL EQUIPMENT ▪ wooden or bamboo skewers

SERVES 4

12 spicy sausages, cut into large pieces

12 cherry tomatoes

a few bay leaves

a little olive oil

large sprig of rosemary, leaves picked and finely chopped

sea salt and freshly ground black pepper

1 If you are using wooden or bamboo skewers, soak them in cold water for 30 minutes.

2 Thread the spicy sausages and cherry tomatoes alternately onto the skewers, interspersing them with a few bay leaves. Brush each sausage and tomato skewer with oil, sprinkle over the chopped rosemary leaves, and season.

3 Heat a barbecue, ridged cast-iron grill pan, or griddle until hot. Add the skewers and grill for 5–8 minutes on each side until the sausages are well cooked and lightly charred.

variation

spiced pork, apricot, and tomato skewers
Cut 350g (12oz) pork fillets in 2.5cm (1in) chunks. Add 8 cherry tomatoes and 4 halved and stoned apricots. Toss in 2 tbsp olive oil mixed with 1 crushed garlic clove, 1 tsp smoked paprika, 1 tsp ground cinnamon, and some salt and pepper. Marinate for 2 hours. Thread alternately on skewers with a few bay leaves. Griddle as before, brushing with any remaining marinade.

tomato and harissa tart

Harissa paste is a thick chilli sauce that includes chilli peppers as well as garlic, coriander, chilli powder, and caraway blended with olive oil. Use as much of the paste as suits your taste.

🥄 10 MINS   🍲 15 MINS

SERVES 6

400g (14oz) ready-made puff pastry

2 tbsp red pepper pesto

6 tomatoes, halved

2–3 tbsp harissa paste

1 tbsp olive oil

a few sprigs of thyme, leaves picked

1 Preheat the oven to 200°C (400°F/ Gas 6). Roll out the pastry on a floured work surface into a large rectangle or square. Lay on a baking tray, then use a sharp knife to score a border about 5cm (2in) in from the edges all the way around, being careful not to cut all the way through the pastry. Next, using the back of the knife, score the pastry around the outer edges – this will help it to puff up.

2 Working inside the border, smother the pastry with the pesto. Arrange the tomatoes on top, cut-side up. Mix the harissa paste with the oil and drizzle over the tomatoes. Scatter over the thyme leaves.

3 Bake in the oven for about 15 minutes until the pastry is cooked and golden. Serve hot.

salt cod and red pepper dip

Salt cod used to be dried outdoors in the sun and wind, but now, it is far more usually dried with electric heaters.

🥣 25 MINS   🍲 1 HR   ❄ FREEZABLE

SPECIAL EQUIPMENT ▪ blender or food processor

SERVES 12

2 red peppers

2 garlic cloves, peeled

1 small red onion, finely chopped

4 tbsp olive oil

salt and freshly ground black pepper

2 tbsp finely chopped Spanish onion

450g (1lb) plum tomatoes, skinned (p197) and chopped (or a 400g can whole plum tomatoes)

500g (1lb 2oz) salt cod

2 tbsp finely chopped marjoram

2 tbsp finely chopped dill

handful of basil leaves, finely chopped

handful of flat-leaf parsley, finely chopped

juice of 1 lemon

Turkish bread or crostini, grilled to serve

1 Preheat the oven to 200°C (400°F/Gas 6) and line a baking tray with baking parchment. Slice the tops off the peppers and remove the seeds and membrane. Put a garlic clove and half of the chopped red onion in the cavity of each pepper. Sit the peppers on the baking tray. Drizzle with 1 tbsp of the oil and season with salt and pepper. Roast in the oven for about 1 hour. Remove from the oven and set aside to cool.

2 While the peppers are roasting, heat the remaining oil in a heavy-based frying pan over a medium heat. Add the Spanish onion and sweat for 3–4 minutes until soft. Tip in the chopped tomatoes, including any juices, and cook for a further 10 minutes, stirring from time to time. Season with salt and pepper.

3 Meanwhile, slice the skin off the salt cod and flake the flesh into chunks. Add to the tomato sauce after the 10 minutes' cooking time and cook gently for a further 10 minutes. Set aside to cool.

4 Put the cooled, roasted peppers in a blender or food processor with the cooled tomato and cod mixture. Blitz until smooth, then transfer to a serving bowl, and season with salt and pepper. Add the herbs and lemon juice, and stir to mix well. Serve with grilled Turkish bread or crostini.

courgette and potato soup

A very simple soup that is easy to make and with very few ingredients. The courgettes and potatoes are lifted out of the ordinary by the gentle aniseed tang of dill.

🥣 10 MINS   🍲 15 MINS   ❄ FREEZABLE

SPECIAL EQUIPMENT ▪ food processor or hand-held blender

SERVES 4

2 large potatoes, peeled and diced

500ml (16fl oz) hot chicken stock

salt and freshly ground white pepper

1 tbsp olive oil

3 courgettes, peeled and finely diced or grated

1 onion, finely diced or grated

100ml (3½fl oz) double cream

300ml (10fl oz) milk

small bunch of dill, chopped

1 Put the potatoes in a pan with the hot stock and 1 tsp salt, bring to the boil, and simmer for about 5 minutes, or until tender. Remove the pan from the heat and using a food processor or hand-held blender, purée until smooth. Return to the pan.

2 In another saucepan, heat the oil, add the courgettes and onion, and fry over a gentle heat for 2–3 minutes, or until slightly softened but not coloured. Stir in a dash of the white pepper, the cream, milk, and puréed potato broth, and simmer gently for 5 minutes, or until the courgettes have softened. Add the dill and season to taste. Serve hot.

whipped yogurt soup with sautéed courgette

This spin on a popular Indian curry makes an innovative first course. The crackling curry leaves, toasted spices, and tangy tamarind work well with the yogurt base.

🥣 30 MINS PLUS STANDING   🍲 25 MINS

SERVES 4

3 tbsp vegetable oil

2 dried red chillies

1 tsp mustard seeds

¼ tsp fenugreek seeds

1 tsp cumin seeds

12 curry leaves

3 tbsp gram flour

½ tsp turmeric

400ml (14fl oz) Greek-style yogurt

salt

2 tbsp tamarind pulp

2 tbsp chopped coriander leaves, to garnish

For the sautéed courgette topping

2 tbsp vegetable oil

1 small red onion, diced

1 courgette, finely diced

1 green chilli, deseeded and finely chopped

sea salt

1 Heat the oil in a wok over a medium heat. Toss in the chillies and mustard seeds and swirl around for a few seconds before adding the fenugreek, cumin, and curry leaves. Reduce the heat and stir-fry for a few seconds. Sprinkle in half the flour and stir-fry for 2–3 minutes, or until lightly toasted. Remove from the heat, add the turmeric, and leave to cool slightly.

2 Whisk the remaining flour with the yogurt and 400ml (14fl oz) water and add to the wok. Return to the heat and, whisking all the time, bring to a simmer and cook for 3–4 minutes. Add more water, if needed, to loosen the consistency. If you wish, you can sieve the soup at this stage. Season with salt and tamarind to sharpen.

3 For the sautéed courgette topping, heat the oil in a frying pan over a medium heat. Add the onion and cook for 3–4 minutes until the onion is soft. Add the courgette and green chilli and continue cooking for a further minute. Season with sea salt and add to the hot soup. Garnish with the chopped coriander.

pancakes with courgettes and emmental

If you can't get hold of Emmental (also known as Swiss cheese), there are other cheeses that you can use here in its place. Try the Dutch Leerdammer or Norwegian Jarlsberg, which are also hard cheeses with a similar mild and slightly sweet flavour that don't overwhelm the delicate flavour of courgettes in these light stuffed pancakes.

🥣 10 MINS PLUS RESTING　　🍲 15 MINS　　❄️ FREEZABLE

MAKES 8

125g (4½oz) plain flour

salt and freshly ground black pepper

1 egg

300ml (10fl oz) milk

1 tbsp olive oil, plus a little extra for frying

2 small courgettes, grated

125g (4½oz) Emmental cheese, grated

1 Put the flour in a mixing bowl with a pinch of salt, stir, and make a well in the centre. Crack the egg into the well and add a tiny amount of the milk. Using a wooden spoon, stir the egg and milk, letting the flour gradually tumble in. Add the rest of the milk, little by little, stirring continuously until all the flour has been incorporated and the mixture is lump-free. Put it in the fridge to rest for 30 minutes, if you have time.

2 Heat 1 tbsp of the oil in a frying pan over a medium heat, add the courgettes, and cook for 5–8 minutes, or until golden. Season well with salt and pepper, then remove from the heat and stir in the Emmental.

3 In a small flat frying pan or pancake pan, heat a drizzle of oil on a high heat, swirling it around the pan, then tipping it out again. Stir the batter mix, then spoon in 2 tbsp of it, swirling it around the pan so it reaches the edges. Cook for a couple of minutes, then pull up the edges with a palette knife. Turn the pancake over and cook the other side for 1 minute. Slide it out onto a plate.

4 Spoon the filling onto the pancakes, sprinkle with black pepper, then either roll or fold them up.

variation

pancakes with courgettes, tomatoes, and mozzarella

Prepare in the same way, but use 1 courgette and 2 chopped, ripe tomatoes. Stir-fry for 5 minutes. Add 1 tbsp tomato purée, a pinch of sugar, and 6 chopped, fresh basil leaves. Season to taste. Substitute mozzarella for Emmental. Don't mix in, but sprinkle over the filling before rolling.

cucumber and dill soup

This refreshing soup makes an elegant starter. For a lunch or dinner party, try serving it with smoked salmon.

🥣 30 MINS PLUS CHILLING

SPECIAL EQUIPMENT ▪ blender or food processor

SERVES 4

2 medium cucumbers

salt and freshly ground black pepper

1 litre (1¾ pints) whole or semi-skimmed milk

small bunch of dill

150ml (5fl oz) natural yogurt

1 Peel the cucumbers, leaving one or two strips of skin on for colour. Slice, put into a colander, and sprinkle with a teaspoon of salt. Toss and leave to stand over a bowl for one hour. Meanwhile, pour the milk into another bowl, add a few whole dill fronds, stir, and chill in the fridge for 1 hour to allow the flavours to infuse slightly.

2 Rinse the cucumber slices under the cold water tap, then press down on them with your hand to extract as much moisture as possible. Remove the dill fronds from the milk. Put the milk and cucumber in a blender or food processor. Add a few more fronds of dill and some black pepper and blend well. Pour into a bowl and chill in the fridge for 3 hours.

3 Place a sieve over a second bowl, pour the chilled soup through the sieve and push the pulp through with the back of a wooden spoon. Add 100–150ml (3½–5fl oz) chilled water to the soup and return to the fridge until ready to serve.

4 Stir in the yogurt, taste, and adjust the seasoning if necessary. Whisk until frothy with a hand-held or balloon whisk, then pour into cups, bowls, or glasses. Decorate with a little more dill and serve.

minted pea and ham soup

If you have a glut of fresh peas, this is a delicious soup to make with them. If they are not cooked soon after picking, you may need to add a little sugar.

🥣 15 MINS 🍲 20-25 MINS ❄ FREEZABLE

SPECIAL EQUIPMENT ▪ blender or hand-held blender

SERVES 4-6

40g (1¼oz) butter

2 shallots, finely chopped

1 potato, peeled and chopped

300ml (10fl oz) hot vegetable stock

500g (1lb 2oz) peas (shelled weight)

2 handfuls of mint leaves

150g (5½oz) cooked ham, diced

salt and freshly ground black pepper

150ml (5fl oz) crème fraîche, to serve

1 Melt the butter in a saucepan over a low heat, add the shallots, and cook for 2–3 minutes until soft. Add the potato and continue cooking, covered, for another 7–10 minutes, or until the potato is tender. Pour over the hot stock and simmer for 10–15 minutes.

2 In a separate pan, boil 400ml (14fl oz) water and cook the peas for 4–5 minutes, or until tender. Add the mint leaves for the last 20 seconds of cooking. Tip the peas and mint into a sieve over a bowl, reserving the cooking liquid in the bowl. Add the peas and mint to the potato and onion stock. Purée the soup until smooth in a blender, or in the pan using a hand-held blender, pouring in enough reserved cooking liquid from the peas to loosen the consistency. Stir in the diced ham.

3 Reheat the soup and season with salt and pepper, to taste. Serve in bowls with a dollop of crème fraîche in the centre.

roasted tomato soup

For home-made food in a jiffy, roast the plum tomatoes up to 3 days in advance and store them in the fridge.

🥣 10 MINS 🍲 30 MINS ❄ FREEZABLE

SPECIAL EQUIPMENT ▪ blender or hand-held blender

SERVES 4

8 plum tomatoes, about 675g (1½lb) in total, quartered

1 red onion, cut into 8 wedges

2 garlic cloves, unpeeled

3 tbsp olive oil

sea salt and freshly ground black pepper

1 litre (1¾ pints) hot vegetable stock

3 tbsp sun-dried tomato paste

1 Preheat the oven to 190°C (375°F/Gas 5). Put the tomatoes, onion, and garlic on separate baking trays lined with greaseproof paper. Drizzle with the oil and season well with sea salt and pepper. Roast until they are soft, caramelized, and slightly browned – allow 10–15 minutes for the garlic, 15–20 minutes for the onion, and about 25 minutes for the tomatoes. Squeeze the garlic cloves from their skins once they have cooled slightly.

2 Transfer to a blender, or to a pan if you are using a hand-held blender, add the stock and tomato paste, and purée until smooth but still slightly chunky. Season to taste, reheat gently, and serve hot in bowls.

variation

roasted tomato and aubergine soup

Prepare in exactly the same way, but substitute 4 of the tomatoes with a small aubergine. Roast the aubergine for about 40 minutes until really soft; the other vegetables as before. Halve the aubergine and scoop out the flesh. Put all the vegetables in the blender as before, and add ½ tsp dried oregano. Blend until smooth. Season and serve in bowls and drizzle with a little chilli oil before serving.

Season's best **peas**

From the humble garden pea, shelled for eating, two varieties have been cultivated that have tender edible pods: mangetout and sugarsnap peas. Freshly picked, all are wonderfully sweet, but lose their sweetness rapidly if stored. A classic summer vegetable, they pair perfectly with mint, chilli, garlic, and ginger, and complement ham, bacon, duck, and seafood.

Originally from the Middle East, peas are now grown in warm climates worldwide. One of the most difficult tasks for the farmers is to protect the plants from birds.

Garden peas Plump, juicy garden peas have a uniquely sweet, grassy flavour and a tender-crisp texture. They should be lightly cooked to prevent them from becoming starchy.

The tiny peas need only a minute or two in boiling water.

▲ **Petits pois** A naturally small-seeded variety, petits pois are the sweetest of all peas. They are delicious eaten raw or lightly cooked.

essentials
varieties available

Essentially two varieties: peas for shelling and those eaten pod and all.

buy Pods should be evenly green, with no brown, yellow, or decay spots. Look for plump garden peas that are not quite touching in the pod; avoid fat pods with oversized peas. Mangetout and sugarsnap peas should be crisp and moist.

store Eat as soon as possible to preserve their sweetness. Keep them in a closed plastic bag in the fridge for no more than 1–2 days.

cook Boil or steam until just tender. Also stir-fry or tempura-fry mangetout and sugarsnap peas.

preserve Blanch and freeze.

recipe ideas

Minted pea and ham soup p148

Pea and mint risotto p184

Pea and pancetta tart p183

▶ **Mangetout** Also called snow peas, the flat, edible pods and minuscule seeds have a sweet, herbaceous flavour. They add crisp texture and brilliant colour to stir-fries.

Sugarsnap peas Rounder and fatter than mangetout, the edible, fleshy pods and seeds are crunchy and wonderfully sweet. Eat them whole or thickly sliced.

pea soup with mint gremolata

Growing peas is one of the greatest pleasures, but discarding the pods can seem like such a waste. Here, the pods as well as the peas are used to make a vibrant summer soup.

10 MINS   35 MINS

SPECIAL EQUIPMENT ▪ food processor or hand-held blender

SERVES 6

30g (1oz) butter

1 onion, finely chopped

1 potato, peeled and roughly chopped

550g (1¼lb) peas in their pods, roughly cut up

1.2 litres (2 pints) hot chicken or vegetable stock

1 tsp caster sugar

sprig of mint

sea salt and freshly ground black pepper

single cream, to serve

For the mint gremolata

2 tbsp finely chopped flat-leaf parsley

2 tbsp finely chopped mint

2 tsp grated lemon zest

1 garlic clove, finely chopped

1 Melt the butter in a pan over a low heat, add the onion, and cook for 7–10 minutes until the onion is soft. Add the remaining soup ingredients, apart from the cream. Bring to the boil, reduce the heat, partly cover, and simmer for 20 minutes until the peas and potato are soft. Discard the mint.

2 Remove the soup from the heat and using a food processor or hand-held blender, purée until smooth. Pass through a sieve to remove any tough bits of pod and pea skins. Taste and season again, if necessary. Reheat to serve.

3 To make the gremolata, mix together all the ingredients. Ladle the soup into bowls. Add a swirl of cream and sprinkle with a little gremolata.

roasted red pepper soup

Sweet red peppers spiced up with some dried chilli flakes and served with summery basil leaves is a delicious soup to be making and eating at this time of year.

15 MINS   1 HR   ❄ FREEZABLE

SPECIAL EQUIPMENT ▪ food processor or hand-held blender

SERVES 8

2 tbsp olive oil

2 onions, finely chopped

3 garlic cloves, grated or finely chopped

pinch of dried chilli flakes

salt and freshly ground black pepper

10 red peppers, roasted, peeled (p171), and deseeded

2.3 litres (4 pints) hot vegetable stock

large handful of basil leaves, torn, to serve

drizzle of extra virgin olive oil, to serve

1 Heat the oil in a large heavy-based pan over a medium heat, add the onions, and cook for 3–4 minutes until the onion is soft. Stir through the garlic and chilli flakes and season with salt and pepper. Add the roasted peppers and juices, pour in the stock, and bring to the boil. Reduce the heat and simmer for 15 minutes.

2 Remove the soup from the heat and using a processor or hand-held blender, purée until smooth. Season to taste with salt and pepper. Stir through the basil, drizzle with oil, and serve with fresh crusty bread.

tomato, red onion, and mozzarella salad

Packed wth strong Mediterranean flavours, this colourful salad combines peppery rocket and sweet, spicy basil to bring out the juiciness of the ripe tomatoes.

10 MINS

SERVES 4

8 ripe plum tomatoes, sliced

6 cherry tomatoes, halved

1 small red onion, peeled and sliced

handful of basil leaves, torn

extra virgin olive oil, for drizzling

salt and freshly ground black pepper

2 handfuls of rocket leaves

balsamic vinegar, for drizzling

2 balls of mozzarella cheese, torn

1 Put the tomatoes, red onion, and half of the basil leaves in a bowl. Drizzle over plenty of the oil, season well with salt and pepper, and toss until well mixed.

2 Arrange the rocket leaves on a serving platter and drizzle over a little oil and some balsamic vinegar.

Season with salt and pepper, and spoon over the tomato and basil mixture. Add the torn mozzarella. Scatter over the remaining basil leaves and drizzle again with a little oil and balsamic vinegar. Serve immediately.

variation

green bean, red onion, and camembert salad

Substitute the plum tomatoes with 175g (6oz) lightly cooked green beans, topped, tailed, and cut in thirds. Place in a bowl with the cherry tomatoes. Chop the onion instead of slicing and dress in the same way, but add a squeeze of lemon juice with the oil. Place on the rocket and top with 115g (4oz) Camembert, cut in thin wedges, instead of mozzarella.

goat's cheese, beetroot, and pistachios

Beetroot starts fattening up well at this time of the year. It introduces a burst of purple-red colour and brings a smooth texture and flavour to a dish.

15 MINS PLUS STANDING

SERVES 4

For the salad

2 handfuls of rocket leaves

4-6 large beetroots, cooked, peeled (p255) and roughly chopped

175g (6oz) goat's cheese, sliced

handful of shelled pistachio nuts, roughly chopped

For the dressing

3 tbsp extra virgin olive oil

1 tbsp white wine vinegar

2 shallots, finely chopped

1 tsp grainy mustard

pinch of sugar

salt and freshly ground black pepper

1 To make the dressing, put the oil, vinegar, and shallots in a jug or small bowl, and whisk together thoroughly. Add the mustard and sugar, and season well with salt and pepper. Whisk again, then taste. Season again as needed, then let the dressing stand for a while, to allow the flavours to develop.

2 Arrange the rocket leaves on a large platter or 4 individual plates, then top with the beetroot and goat's cheese. Drizzle over a little of the dressing, then sprinkle over the pistachio nuts. Add more dressing, if you wish. Serve with crusty bread.

fresh tomatoes stuffed with fruity couscous

Large but firm summer tomatoes are ideal for this quick-to-make starter. Alternatively, for a light lunch, serve the tomatoes on top of any extra couscous.

🥣 30 MINS PLUS STANDING

SERVES 4

4 large beefsteak tomatoes

150ml (5fl oz) tomato juice

125g (4½oz) couscous

50g (1¾oz) sultanas

handful of basil leaves, chopped

handful of flat-leaf parsley, chopped

salt and freshly ground black pepper

1 Slice the tops off the tomatoes and reserve. Scoop out the seeds and flesh from the tomatoes, so that you are left with a "shell", and put in a large bowl with the tomato juice. Set the tomato shells aside.

2 Put the couscous in a separate bowl, pour over 150ml (5fl oz) hot water so that it just covers the couscous, and leave to stand for 10 minutes. Use a fork to fluff up the grains, then tip in the tomato seeds and flesh. Mix together and leave to stand for a further 10 minutes.

3 Stir the couscous well, breaking up any bits of tomato. Add the sultanas, basil, and parsley, and mix again. Taste and season with salt and pepper as needed. Spoon the mixture into the reserved tomato shells and put the tops on to serve.

escabeche

Escabeche means "pickled" in Spanish, and oily fish are often prepared this way. Try using white, meaty fish, as the result has a cleaner, less rich flavour.

🥣 30 MINS PLUS MARINATING   🍲 15 MINS

MAKES 4-6 SERVINGS

675g (1½lb) thick coley fillet, skinned

3 tbsp plain flour

salt and freshly ground black pepper

2 tsp chopped thyme, plus a few leaves for garnishing (or 1 tsp dried thyme, and garnish with a little chopped parsley)

6 tbsp olive oil, plus extra for drizzling

1 onion, thinly sliced into rings

1 large garlic clove, crushed

1 large carrot, cut into thin matchsticks

1 red pepper, halved, deseeded, and cut into thin strips

1 celery stick, cut into thin matchsticks

2.5cm (1in) piece fresh root ginger, peeled and grated

2-4 large green chillies, deseeded and sliced

250ml (9fl oz) white wine vinegar

¼ tsp sea salt

½ tsp caster sugar

1 Cut the coley into 5cm (2in) pieces. Mix the flour with a little salt and pepper and the herbs. Use this mix to coat the fish.

2 Heat half the oil in a frying pan and fry the fish quickly on all sides until brown and just cooked – about 4 minutes. Place in a large, shallow serving dish.

3 Wipe out the pan, heat the remaining oil, and fry the onion, garlic, carrot, pepper, and celery gently for 5 minutes, stirring until just tender, but still with some "bite". Remove from the pan with a slotted spoon and set aside.

4 Add the remaining ingredients to the pan, bring to the boil, reduce the heat, and simmer for 5 minutes. Stir in the vegetables, then spoon the mixture over the fish. Allow to cool slightly, then cover and leave to marinate overnight.

5 Serve the same day at room temperature, drizzled with oil and sprinkled with a few fresh thyme or parsley leaves. It can also be stored in the fridge for up to 3 days (bring back to room temperature before garnishing and serving).

kohlrabi soup with pesto

If you are a fan of smooth soups, you can blitz this recipe in a blender at the end of step 1, and then swirl the pesto through the resulting delicate, light green purée.

🥣 5 MINS   🍲 15 MINS   ❄ FREEZABLE

SERVES 6

25g (scant 1oz) butter

3-4 kohlrabi, cut into bite-sized cubes

1 litre (1¾ pints) hot vegetable stock

2 tbsp crème fraîche

salt and freshly ground black pepper

6 tsp pesto, to garnish

1 Melt the butter in a frying pan, add the kohlrabi, and fry for 5 minutes, or until light golden brown. Pour in the stock and bring to the boil. Add the crème fraîche and season with salt and pepper. Cook for 8–10 minutes, or until the kohlrabi is tender, but not mushy.

2 Taste and adjust the seasoning, then ladle the soup into warm bowls and garnish each with a teaspoon of pesto.

roasted red pepper tart

Red pesto and mascarpone add depth to this sweet pepper filling. Preheat a baking sheet in the oven and place the tart tin on top to achieve a really crisp pastry base.

🥣 15 MINS　　🍲 1 HR　　❄ FREEZABLE

SPECIAL EQUIPMENT ▪ 23cm (9in) square loose-bottomed fluted tart tin ▪ ceramic baking beans ▪ food processor

SERVES 6–8

4 large red peppers

1 tbsp olive oil

300g (10oz) ready-made shortcrust pastry

3 eggs, 1 lightly beaten for egg wash

1 tbsp mascarpone

handful of basil leaves, plus extra to garnish

salt and freshly ground black pepper

1 tsp red pesto

1 Preheat the oven to 200°C (400°F/ Gas 6). Put the peppers in a roasting tin. Using your hands, smear each one with the oil. Roast in the oven for about 20 minutes until lightly charred. Transfer to a plastic bag and leave until cool enough to handle, before skinning and deseeding.

2 Meanwhile, roll out the pastry on a floured work surface and use to line a tart tin. Trim away the excess, line the pastry shell with greaseproof paper, and fill with ceramic baking beans. Bake in the oven for 15–20 minutes until the edges are golden. Remove the beans and paper, brush the bottom of the shell with the extra egg wash, and return to the oven for 2–3 minutes to crisp. Remove from the oven and set aside. Reduce the oven temperature to 180°C (350°F/Gas 4).

3 Put the roasted peppers, the 2 eggs, mascarpone, and the basil leaves in a food processor and blitz until combined. Season well with salt and pepper. Spread the pesto evenly over the bottom of the pastry shell, then carefully pour in the pepper mixture. Bake in the oven for 25–35 minutes until set. Leave to cool for 10 minutes before releasing from the tin. Garnish with extra basil leaves and serve with a wild rocket and fennel salad.

german chicken broth

Based on a Thuringian vegetable soup, this recipe uses kohlrabi, beans, and mangetout. It benefits from a well-flavoured chicken stock, so prepare your own, if you prefer.

🥣 10 MINS   🍲 25 MINS   ❄ FREEZABLE

SERVES 4-6

1.2 litres (2 pints) chicken stock

150g (5½oz) green beans, topped, tailed, and strings removed

2 large carrots, sliced

200g (7oz) kohlrabi, diced

150g (5½oz) mangetout or sugar snap peas, topped and tailed

salt and freshly ground black pepper

single or double cream, to serve

1 bunch of chervil, finely chopped

1 Bring the stock to the boil in a medium-sized saucepan, add the green beans, and simmer for 5 minutes. Add the carrots and kohlrabi and cook for 5 minutes, then add the mangetout or sugar snap peas and cook for a further 5 minutes – be careful not to overcook these or they will lose their delightful crunchiness.

2 Season with salt and pepper and remove the pan from the heat. Ladle into serving bowls, add a swirl of cream to each, and sprinkle with chervil before serving.

mexican sweetcorn soup

A flavourful soup of sweetcorn and red pepper. If you don't have chilli-flavoured olive oil, stir a little piquant pimentón, harissa, or smoked paprika into fruity olive oil.

🥣 15 MINS   🍲 20 MINS   ❄ FREEZABLE

SPECIAL EQUIPMENT ▪ blender or hand-held blender

SERVES 4

3 tbsp olive oil

1 Spanish onion, finely chopped

1 red pepper, deseeded and finely chopped

1 garlic clove, crushed

1 tsp fennel seeds

1 tsp fresh thyme leaves

3–4 sweetcorn cobs, kernels removed (about 400g/14oz kernels, p155)

salt and freshly ground black pepper

100ml (3½fl oz) single cream

1½ tbsp chilli-flavoured olive oil, to serve

1 Heat the oil in a large sauté pan over a moderate heat, add the onion, red pepper (reserving a scant tablespoon of the pepper as a garnish), garlic, fennel seeds, and thyme, and stir-fry for 3 minutes. Add the sweetcorn and season lightly. Continue stirring and cooking for 2 minutes, then pour in 500ml (16fl oz) hot water, stir, and bring to a simmer. Lower the heat, cover, and simmer for 15 minutes, or until the vegetables are tender and cooked through. Stir in the cream and leave to cool for a few minutes.

2 Purée the soup until smooth in a blender (you may need to do this in batches), or in the pan using a hand-held blender. Return to the pan and reheat the soup gently, stirring occasionally. Taste and adjust the seasoning if necessary. Ladle into warmed bowls and add the reserved red pepper as a garnish. Drizzle over a little chilli-flavoured olive oil and serve immediately.

variation

mediterranean sweetcorn soup

Use the kernels from 2 corn cobs. Add 4 skinned and chopped tomatoes, and a finely chopped courgette with the pepper. Add 750ml (1¼ pints) chicken or vegetable stock instead of water. Do not purée. Omit the cream, and stir in 1 tbsp chopped, fresh basil when adjusting the seasoning. Serve topped with grated Parmesan instead of drizzling with chilli oil.

sweetcorn and pepper filo triangles

Canned or frozen corn doesn't quite compare to the crisp, succulent kernels from a fresh corn cob. Combined with red peppers, they make these pastries crunchy and slightly sweet.

🥣 20 MINS   🍲 20 MINS   ❄ FREEZABLE

SERVES 2

1 tbsp olive oil

1 onion, finely chopped

salt and freshly ground black pepper

3 red peppers, deseeded and diced

4 sweetcorn cobs, kernels removed (about 450g/1lb kernels, p155)

175g (6oz) feta cheese, cut into small cubes

200g (7oz) filo pastry

a little butter, melted, plus extra for glazing

1 Preheat the oven to 200°C (400°F/Gas 6). Heat the oil in a large frying pan over a low heat. Add the onion and a little salt, and cook gently for about 5 minutes until soft and translucent. Tip in the peppers and corn, cover, and continue cooking gently for a further 10 minutes until the peppers are soft and the corn is tender, stirring occasionally. Stir through the feta and season well with black pepper.

2 Lay out the filo sheets into four piles of 3 or 4 layers about 30 x 10cm (12 x 4in), brushing each pile with a little melted butter. Divide the pepper mixture between each pile of pastry, spooning it onto the bottom right-hand corner of every one. Fold this corner so that it makes a triangle, then fold the top right-hand corner down. Repeat until you have made 5 folds in all for each one and you end up with 4 large triangles.

3 Brush the triangles all over with a little melted butter and put them on an oiled baking tray. Bake in the oven for about 20 minutes until crisp and golden. Serve hot.

Season's best **sweetcorn**

True to its name, sweetcorn is a type of maize with the sweet, golden or white kernels set in rows along the central cob. The kernels can be eaten on the cob or cut off before cooking. Harvested in high summer through to early autumn, they have a short season. Best paired with melted butter or bacon, they also taste amazing with Cheddar cheese, fish, chicken, chillies, and peppers.

essentials
varieties available

Whole cobs; baby cobs; kernels; fresh, frozen, or canned. Other products include cornflour, cornmeal, polenta, and popcorn.

buy The cut end of the cob should not be dry and the leaves should be fresh and bright. Choose well-filled cobs; if you puncture a kernel with the thumbnail, the fluid should be milky, not clear or paste-like.

store Best eaten on day of purchase or store, wrapped in damp kitchen paper, in the fridge for 1–2 days at most.

cook Roast whole in the husk, or shuck (remove husk and silk) and then boil, roast, or grill. Boil, braise, bake, or sauté kernels.

preserve Kernels and shucked cobs can be frozen.

recipe ideas

Mexican sweetcorn soup p154

Scallop and sweetcorn chowder p157

Sweetcorn and pepper filo triangles p154

Native to Mexico and Guatemala, but grown all over the world from the tropics to any northern region with a sufficient growing season, sweetcorn is an important staple crop.

Baby corn Unlike full-grown ears, baby corn is completely edible, including the central cob. With its mild flavour and crunchy texture, it is a useful ingredient in stir-fries, as a colourful vegetable crudité, and cut in pieces in soups, stews, and salads.

The tiny cobs are no more than 10cm (4in) long.

Deep yellow kernels will not be sweet. Choose pale, creamy-yellow ones.

Yellow sweetcorn Classic corn varieties have differing sugar contents: "normal", "sugar enhanced", and "super sweet".

White sweetcorn The flavour is not as sweet as yellow corn but is still delicious. It is a popular vegetable in farmers' markets. Look for mixed white and yellow cobs.

how to remove sweetcorn kernels

One of the sweetest vegetables, the flavour of fresh sweetcorn easily beats that of canned or frozen ones. Preparing the cobs to eat whole or removing the kernels is very straightforward.

1 Remove the husks and all the silk threads from the corn-on-the-cob. Rinse the husked corn under cold running water.

2 Place the blunt end on the cutting board. Use a sharp chef's knife and slice straight down the cob. Rotate the cob and repeat.

chicken and sweetcorn soup

Sweetcorn comes into its own in high summer, as it ripens on the cob. Its sweet flavour complements the chicken in this soup most deliciously.

🥣 10 MINS   🍲 30 MINS

SPECIAL EQUIPMENT ▪ blender or food processor

SERVES 4

1 tbsp olive oil

25g (scant 1oz) butter

1 onion, finely chopped

2 garlic cloves, crushed

1 large potato, peeled and sliced

1.2 litres (2 pints) hot chicken stock

4 sweetcorn cobs, kernels removed (about 450g/1lb kernels, p155)

2 skinless chicken breasts, cut into thin strips

salt and freshly ground black pepper

handful of flat-leaf parsley, finely chopped

1 Heat the oil and butter in a large pan over a medium heat, add the onion, and cook for 3–4 minutes until the onion is soft. Add the garlic and potato and fry, stirring, for 1 minute.

2 Add the stock and corn cobs. Bring to the boil, lower the heat, and simmer for 15 minutes until the vegetables are really tender. Remove the corn cobs, then pour the soup into a blender or food processor and purée until smooth. Return to the pan.

3 Add the chicken and corn kernels. Bring to the boil, reduce the heat, and simmer for 10 minutes until the chicken is cooked and the corn is tender. Taste and season if needed. Stir through the flat-leaf parsley just before serving.

brandied lobster chowder

Serve this delightful soup with some nutty rye bread and chilled unsalted butter. If you like, you can use crab as a less expensive alternative to the lobster.

🥣 20 MINS   🍲 1 HR

SERVES 4

1 small cooked lobster

150ml (5fl oz) dry white wine

1 bay leaf

knob of unsalted butter

2 shallots, finely chopped

4 tbsp brandy

1 large tomato, skinned (p197) and diced

2 tsp anchovy essence

4 large new potatoes, peeled and diced

8 baby corn, cut in short lengths

salt and freshly ground black pepper

60g (2oz) mangetout, cut in short lengths

5 tbsp single cream

4 thick slices of lemon

4 sprigs of parsley

1 Twist the legs and claws off the lobster. Cut the body in half lengthways and remove the dark vein that runs along it. Lift out the tail meat and cut in small pieces. Crack the large claws, remove the meat, and dice. Set all the meat aside. Leave the remaining bits of meat in the shell. Roughly chop it

up and put it in a saucepan with the claws and legs. Add 800ml (scant 1½ pints) water with the wine and bay leaf. Bring to the boil, reduce the heat, cover, and simmer for 30 minutes. Strain and reserve the stock.

2 Melt the butter in another large saucepan over a low heat. Add the shallots and fry gently, stirring, for 1 minute. Add the brandy, ignite, and shake the pan until the flames subside. Add the tomato, anchovy essence, potatoes, and corn. Return the stock to the pan. Season and bring to the boil. Reduce the heat, cover, and simmer gently for 20 minutes until the potatoes are tender.

3 Meanwhile, blanch the mangetout in a little boiling water for 2 minutes until just tender. Drain, rinse with cold water, and drain again. Then add to the soup along with the cream and lobster meat. Taste and season again. Reheat the soup but do not boil it. Ladle into warmed bowls. Serve with a slice of lemon and a small sprig of parsley in each bowl.

rocket and parmesan soup

This makes good use of peppery late-season rocket that may have become a bit leathery.

🥣 10 MINS   🍲 30 MINS   ❄ FREEZABLE

SPECIAL EQUIPMENT ▪ food processor or hand-held blender

SERVES 4

2 tbsp olive oil

2 onions, chopped

650g (1lb 7oz) potatoes, washed but not peeled, cut into 2cm (¾in) cubes

sea salt and freshly ground black pepper

4 small or 2 large garlic cloves, crushed

1 litre (1¾ pints) hot vegetable stock

1 Parmesan rind, about 3 x 9cm (1¼ x 3½in), cut into tiny cubes

125g (4½oz) rocket leaves, chopped

Parmesan cheese, grated to serve

1 Heat the oil in a pan over a medium heat, add the onion, and cook for 3–4 minutes until the onion is soft. Stir in the potatoes with a little sea salt, cover, and cook for 5 minutes, stirring.

2 Add the garlic and stir for a few seconds until fragrant, then pour in the stock. Bring to the boil, add the Parmesan rind, then reduce the heat and simmer for about 10 minutes, stirring occasionally, until the potato is soft. Add the rocket, stir, and cook for 3–5 minutes until tender but still bright green.

3 Remove the soup from the heat and using a food processor or hand-held blender, purée until smooth. Taste for seasoning. Serve each bowl with grated Parmesan.

scallop and sweetcorn chowder

A luxurious American classic. A wonderful dish for a special occasion that marries the sweetness of both the shellfish and sweetcorn with salty bacon. Oyster crackers, available from specialist delicatessens, are the traditional accompaniment. If you can find them, serve on the side to allow diners to crumble them over their own bowl.

25-30 MINS 15-20 MINS

SERVES 4

2 sweetcorn cobs, about 225g (8oz) kernels

375g (13oz) small scallops, cleaned

125g (4½oz) streaky bacon, cut into strips

1 onion, thinly sliced

250g (9oz) new potatoes, scraped and diced

1 bay leaf

salt and freshly ground black pepper

375ml (13fl oz) hot fish stock

120ml (4fl oz) double cream

250ml (9fl oz) milk

paprika, for sprinkling

1 Hold each sweetcorn cob vertically on a chopping board and cut from the tip down to remove the kernels. Put them in a small bowl. Working over the bowl, with the back of the knife, scrape the pulp and milk from each cob.

2 If necessary, discard the tough, crescent-shaped membrane at the side of each scallop. Make sure there is no black intestinal vein running around the edge of the shellfish. If you find one, peel it off and discard.

3 Heat a large saucepan, add the bacon, and fry for 3–5 minutes, stirring until the fat has rendered. With a

slotted spoon, transfer the bacon to a plate lined with kitchen paper.

4 Reduce the heat, then add the onions and cook, stirring frequently, for 3–4 minutes until soft and translucent. With a slotted spoon, transfer the onions to the lined plate. Discard any remaining fat from the pan.

5 Add the potatoes to the pan with the bay leaf, salt, and pepper. Pour in the stock. Bring to the boil, then reduce the heat and simmer gently for 7–10 minutes, until the potatoes are slightly soft.

6 Return most of the bacon and onions to the pan with the sweetcorn kernels and pulp, cream, and milk. Bring to the boil, then reduce the heat and simmer for 7–10 minutes until the potatoes are tender. Add the scallops. Bring back just to the boil to cook the scallops. Taste and re-season if necessary. Discard the bay leaf, ladle into warmed bowls, and sprinkle with paprika and the reserved onion and bacon.

rocket, ricotta cheese, and black olive dip

A member of the mustard family, rocket leaves are abundant at this time. They add an extra peppery dimension to this quick-to-make dip and pep up the mild ricotta and rich olives.

15 MINS

SPECIAL EQUIPMENT ▪ blender or food processor

SERVES 4

100g (3½oz) rocket leaves

2 garlic cloves, grated or finely chopped

100g (3½oz) black olives, pitted

grated zest and juice of 1 lemon

90ml (3fl oz) olive oil

250g (9oz) ricotta cheese

freshly ground black pepper

1 Put the rocket leaves, garlic, olives, lemon zest and juice, and oil in a blender or food processor, and blitz or blend until smooth.

2 Transfer the rocket and olive mixture to a bowl, add the ricotta cheese, and season with black pepper. Mix well.

3 Serve with torn chunks of warm sourdough bread, thick toasted slices of baguette, or grilled flatbread.

variation

spaghetti with cherry tomato, rocket, and black olive sauce

This makes a great pasta sauce, but you only need half the ingredients for four people. Simply cook 350g (12oz) spaghetti according to the packet directions. Drain and return to the pan. Add 12 halved cherry tomatoes and then half the rocket dip. Toss over a gentle heat until the dip has melted and coats the spaghetti. The tomatoes should have softened just slightly, but retained their shape. Pile into bowls and serve hot with some freshly grated Parmesan sprinkled over. Store the rest of the dip in the fridge in an airtight container and use within 3 days.

smoked trout, fennel, and mascarpone crostini

In this easy appetizer, the richness of the trout and mascarpone is nicely balanced by the fresh, light flavour and crunch of the summer fennel.

25 MINS   **15 MINS**

SERVES 4

2 tbsp olive oil

4 thick slices of crusty sourdough bread

salt and freshly ground black pepper

1 garlic clove, peeled but left whole

2 smoked trout, about 300g (10oz) each

150g (5½oz) fennel bulb, trimmed, halved, and thinly sliced

120ml (4fl oz) mascarpone

30g (1oz) flaked almonds, toasted

juice of ½ lemon

sprigs of chervil, to garnish

1 lemon, cut into wedges, to serve

1 Preheat the oven to 200°C (400°F/Gas 6). Pour the oil onto a baking tray, then gently press the bread into the oil on both sides. Season with salt and pepper. Bake in the oven for 12–15 minutes until golden brown. Remove from the oven and lightly rub each slice with the garlic. Set aside on a wire rack to keep the crostini crisp.

2 Meanwhile, remove the skin from the smoked trout and gently remove the flesh from the bones in big chunks.

3 Put the trout, fennel, mascarpone, flaked almonds, and lemon juice in a bowl. Season with black pepper and gently mix together.

4 To serve, arrange the trout mixture over the crostini, season with some more pepper, and garnish with the chervil. Serve immediately with lemon wedges for squeezing over.

tomato borscht

In Russia and the Ukraine, borscht often includes tomatoes as well as beetroot. This version may seem unusual, but you will love its rich colour and fantastic taste.

🥣 25 MINS   🍲 25 MINS   ❄ FREEZABLE

SPECIAL EQUIPMENT ▪ food processor or hand-held blender

SERVES 4

2 tbsp olive oil

1 small onion, finely chopped

1 garlic clove, chopped

225g (8oz) raw beetroot, peeled and finely grated

1 tsp freshly ground toasted cumin seeds, plus unground to serve

¼ tsp ground cinnamon

225g (8oz) ripe tomatoes, skinned (p197) and roughly chopped

250ml (9fl oz) tomato juice

1 tbsp sun-dried tomatoes, very finely chopped

600ml (1 pint) vegetable stock

1 tbsp light soy sauce

salt and freshly ground black pepper

soured cream or crème fraîche, to serve

1 Heat the oil in a heavy-based pan over a medium heat, add the onion and garlic, and cook for 3–4 minutes until the onion is soft. Then add the beetroot and sweat gently for a further 10 minutes, stirring occasionally, until softened.

2 Add the ground spices, tomatoes, tomato juice, and sun-dried tomatoes, then pour in the stock. Bring to the boil. Reduce the heat slightly, cover, and simmer very gently for 15 minutes, or until all the vegetables are soft. Remove the soup from the heat and using a processor or hand-held blender, purée until smooth. Check the seasoning, adding the soy sauce, salt, and pepper to taste.

3 Serve chilled, at room temperature, or slightly warm. If you reheat the soup, do so gently over a low heat. To serve, spoon into serving bowls and garnish with toasted cumin seeds and a spoonful of soured cream or crème fraîche.

watermelon salad with feta and pumpkin seeds

This salad is fast becoming a modern classic. The sweetness of the ripe melon contrasts wonderfully with the salty feta and the nuttiness of the pumpkin seeds.

🥣 10 MINS   🍲 5 MINS

SERVES 4

60g (2oz) pumpkin seeds

sea salt and freshly ground black pepper

¼ tsp chilli powder

4 tbsp light olive oil

juice of 1 lemon

500g (1lb 2oz) watermelon, peeled, deseeded if preferred, and cut into 2cm (¾in) squares

½ red onion, finely sliced

4 large handfuls of mixed salad leaves, such as watercress, rocket, or baby spinach

300g (10oz) feta cheese, cut into 1cm (½in) squares

1 Dry-fry the pumpkin seeds for 2–3 minutes until they start to pop. Add a pinch of sea salt and the chilli powder, stir, and cook for another minute. Set aside to cool.

2 In a large bowl, whisk together the oil, lemon juice, and sea salt and pepper to taste. Add the watermelon, red onion, and salad leaves, and toss well to coat with the dressing.

3 Scatter the feta cheese and the seeds over the top of the salad and serve immediately.

scallops with sweet chilli sauce

Red chillies are relatively high in capsaicin, the chemical that creates a fiery sensation in the mouth, and this chilli sauce is designed to give sweet-flavoured scallops a little bit of a kick.

🥣 10 MINS PLUS MARINATING   🍲 5 MINS

SERVES 4

4 garlic cloves, grated or finely chopped

3 red chillies, deseeded and finely chopped

3 tbsp dry sherry

1 tsp caster sugar

2 tbsp olive oil, plus a little extra for frying

12 large scallops (with or without coral, depending on preference), cleaned

1 Put the garlic, chillies, sherry, and sugar in a bowl and mix well until the sugar dissolves. Add the oil and scallops, toss together, then leave to marinate for at least 30 minutes.

2 Transfer the scallops to a plate, using a slotted spoon. Reserve the marinade. Heat a little oil in a non-stick frying pan and cook the scallops over a high heat for 1 minute on each side. Remove from the pan and pour in the marinade. Bring to the boil, stirring all the while, then pour over the scallops. Serve with a crisp green salad.

variation

sardines with sweet chilli and chive sauce

Substitute 12 cleaned sardines for the scallops and prepare in exactly the same way. Add 2 tbsp snipped chives to the marinade when heating, and serve with lemon wedges to squeeze over.

chorizo with peppers

Spicy chorizo sausage needs just the addition of some chunky mixed peppers and seasonings to turn it into a tasty tapas dish or starter. Serve with crusty bread.

🥣 10 MINS   🍲 10 MINS

SERVES 4

2 tbsp olive oil

2 red peppers, deseeded and cut into 2cm (¾in) squares

2 green peppers, deseeded and cut into 2cm (¾in) squares

3 garlic cloves, crushed

300g (10oz) chorizo cut into 2cm (¾in) cubes

2 tbsp dry sherry

1 tbsp chopped oregano

salt and freshly ground black pepper

1 Heat the oil in a frying pan, add the peppers, and cook over a medium heat, stirring occasionally, for 5 minutes. Add the garlic, chorizo, and sherry and cook for 5 more minutes.

2 Sprinkle over the oregano, season with salt and pepper, and serve.

variation

chorizo with aubergine and courgettes

Substitute the peppers with 1 diced aubergine and 2 diced courgettes, then prepare in exactly the same way. Add 2 tbsp chopped parsley along with the oregano, and try crumbling 85g (3oz) feta cheese over just before serving.

feta-stuffed peppers

A speciality in northern Spain, these piquant little peppers take on a smoky-sweet flavour once roasted, and taste divine stuffed with tangy feta cheese.

🥣 15 MINS   🍲 20 MINS

SERVES 4

150g (5½oz) feta cheese

3 garlic cloves, crushed

1 tbsp finely chopped flat-leaf parsley

1 tsp freshly ground black pepper

12 piquillo peppers

4 tbsp olive oil

1 Preheat the oven to 200°C (400°F/Gas 6). Put the feta, garlic, parsley, and black pepper in a mixing bowl and mash them with the back of a fork to form a smooth paste.

2 Cut the stalk end off each pepper and discard. Carefully deseed them (p171), then stuff with the feta cheese mixture. Brush with oil, then pack tightly into a small baking dish. Spoon over the remaining oil and bake in the oven for 20 minutes, or until the peppers are soft. Serve hot with fresh crusty bread.

variation

cream cheese and sweetcorn stuffed peppers

Prepare and cook the peppers in the same way, and replace the feta cheese filling with 115g (4oz) cream cheese mixed with the kernels of 1 corn cob (p155), 1 crushed garlic clove, 1 tbsp chopped thyme, and seasoning to taste.

bruschetta with tomato and basil

These tasty appetizers of toasted ciabatta topped with juicy tomatoes and fragrant basil are ideal for serving with a drink outdoors, or before an evening meal.

🥣 10 MINS   🍲 4-5 MINS

MAKES 8

6 ripe tomatoes, roughly diced

handful of basil leaves, roughly torn

4 tbsp extra virgin olive oil

salt and freshly ground black pepper

1 loaf ciabatta

3 garlic cloves, peeled but left whole

1 Put the tomatoes, basil, and oil in a bowl. Season really well with salt and pepper. Set aside to allow the flavours to develop.

2 Preheat the grill to its highest setting. Slice the ciabatta horizontally lengthways, then cut each piece into quarters so that you have 8 pieces of bread in total. Toast both sides of the ciabatta until golden.

3 Immediately rub each piece of toasted bread with the garlic. Spoon over the tomato and basil mixture, and serve immediately.

variation

bruschetta with roasted peppers and olives

Substitute 4 of the tomatoes with 1 small roasted red pepper and 1 small roasted green pepper, peeled, deseeded, and diced (p171), and 2 tbsp stoned, sliced black olives.

hot cucumber and tarragon soup

Cooked cucumber has a subtle flavour that combines well with the more assertive but still delicate tarragon.

🥣 15 MINS   🍲 20 MINS

SPECIAL EQUIPMENT ▪ blender or food processor

SERVES 4

2 medium-large or 3 small cucumbers

1 tbsp sunflower or rapeseed oil

50g (1¾oz) chilled butter, diced

2 tbsp chopped tarragon

750ml (1¼ pints) light vegetable or chicken stock

salt and freshly ground black pepper

2 tbsp cornflour

4 heaped tsp cream cheese (optional)

1 Peel the cucumbers, cut crossways in half, then cut each half lengthways. With a pointed teaspoon, scoop out and discard all the seeds and chop the flesh coarsely.

2 Place a sauté pan over a moderate heat. Add the oil and 15g (½oz) of the butter. Once the butter has melted, add the cucumber and half the tarragon. Stir for 2 minutes, then pour in the stock and season lightly.

3 Bring to a simmer, reduce the heat a little, then cover and simmer gently for 10–15 minutes. Stir in the cornflour and cook for a further 2 minutes. Take off the heat and leave to cool a little.

4 Transfer to a blender or food processor and blitz until smooth. Return to the pan and whisk in the remaining butter. Taste and adjust the seasoning, stir in the rest of the tarragon, and serve hot. If you like, add a dollop of cream cheese (if using) to each bowl when serving.

smoked chicken with basil mayonnaise on cucumber rounds

A slice of succulent cucumber is the perfect size for eating in a single bite, and so is the ideal base for an *hors d'oeuvre*. Serve these tasty appetizers before dinner or at a party.

🥣 20 MINS

SERVES 6–8

approx 250g (9oz) smoked chicken breast

3 tbsp mayonnaise

1 tbsp ready-made pesto

freshly ground black pepper

approx 300g (10oz) cucumber, cut into 5mm (¼in) thick slices

1 Remove the skin from the chicken. Slice across the breast into thin slices and finely chop into small cubes. Put the chicken, mayonnaise, and pesto in a mixing bowl. Season with black pepper and mix well.

2 Spoon 1 heaped teaspoon of the smoked chicken mixture onto a slice of cucumber and arrange on a platter. Repeat with the remaining mixture and cucumber slices.

variation

smoked trout with horseradish mayonnaise on cucumber rounds

Prepare in the same way, but use smoked trout fillets, skinned and flaked (but not too finely) instead of chicken, and horseradish sauce instead of the pesto. Garnish each with a slice of cherry tomato and a tiny sprig of parsley.

samphire soup with poached eggs

For absolute decadence, top each bowl with a little chopped hard-boiled egg, instead of poached, and a shucked oyster.

🥣 10 MINS   🍲 30 MINS   ❄ FREEZABLE

SPECIAL EQUIPMENT ▪ blender or food processor

SERVES 4

200g (7oz) young samphire, washed

knob of unsalted butter

1 large leek, sliced

1 large potato, peeled and diced

1 thick slice of lemon

small handful of parsley

900ml (1½ pints) light vegetable or chicken stock

freshly ground black pepper

a little milk (optional)

1 tbsp white wine vinegar

4 eggs

1 Boil the samphire in a little water for 3–5 minutes, or until tender. Drain, rinse in cold water, and drain again.

2 Melt the butter in a large saucepan. Add the leek and potato and fry gently, stirring, for 2 minutes, or until soft but not browned. Add the lemon, parsley, stock, and black pepper. Bring to the boil, reduce the heat, cover, and simmer gently for 20 minutes, or until soft. Discard the lemon and blitz in a blender with the samphire flesh. Return to the pan, taste, and add more black pepper if necessary. If freezing, cool and freeze at this point, then defrost and continue. Thin with a little milk, if desired, then reheat gently.

3 Meanwhile, bring a large pan of water to the boil and add the vinegar. Swirl around to make an eddy and break in the eggs one at a time. Poach until cooked to your liking, then remove with a slotted spoon. Ladle the soup into wide, shallow soup plates, then rest a poached egg in the centre of each one to serve.

chicken and courgette mousse

This smooth, creamy mousse wrapped in fine slices of courgette makes an impressive hot first course. The trick to success is to butter the ramekin dishes well to make sure that the prettily arranged courgette slices do not stick when unmoulding.

🥣 25-35 MINS PLUS CHILLING 🍲 20-30 MINS

SPECIAL EQUIPMENT ▪ food mincer or food processor ▪ 6 x 350ml (12fl oz) ramekins

SERVES 4

500g (1lb 2oz) skinless chicken breasts

2 egg whites

salt and freshly ground black pepper

pinch of grated nutmeg

175ml (6fl oz) double cream

2 courgettes

melted butter, for brushing

For the sauce

125g (4½oz) butter

2 garlic cloves, finely chopped

2 shallots, finely chopped

4 tbsp Madeira

1 tbsp double cream

1 Cut the chicken into chunks and work it through the fine blade of a food mincer, or process in a food processor until minced. It should not be too fine but remain a coarsely minced mixture. Whisk the egg whites until frothy. Gradually add them to the chicken, beating with a wooden spoon until smooth and firm after each

addition. Season with salt, pepper, and nutmeg. Beat in the cream, a little at a time. Chill the mixture for about 15 minutes, or until firm. It should hold its shape. To test for seasoning, fry a little piece in a frying pan and taste. Adjust the seasoning if necessary.

2 Cut the courgettes into very thin slices. Bring a saucepan of salted water to the boil. Add the courgettes and simmer for 1–2 minutes until softened. Drain in a colander, rinse under cold water to stop the cooking, then drain on kitchen paper.

3 Using a ramekin as a guide, cut out 6 circles of baking parchment. Butter the ramekins. Lay a parchment paper circle in the base of each and brush it, too, with butter. Be sure to cover all the paper to prevent the courgette slices from sticking. Meanwhile, preheat the oven to 180°C (350°F/ Gas 4). Line the bottoms and sides of the ramekins with overlapping slices of courgette.

4 Spoon the chicken mousse mixture into the ramekins, smoothing the top, then put in a baking dish. Pour in boiling water to come more than halfway up the sides. Cover the dish with baking parchment and bake for 20–30 minutes, or until a skewer inserted in the centre is hot to the touch. During baking, do not let the water boil or the mousse will separate.

5 For the sauce, heat about 30g (1oz) of the butter in a small saucepan, add the garlic and shallots, and cook, stirring, for 2–3 minutes. Make sure the garlic does not brown, or the sauce will taste bitter. Add the Madeira and bring to the boil, stirring to dissolve the pan juices, for 2–3 minutes, or until it has reduced to a syrupy glaze. Add the cream and boil again until reduced to a glaze. Remove from the heat and add the remaining butter, a few pieces at a time, whisking constantly and moving the pan on and off the heat to make sure the sauce does not become too hot (or it will separate).

6 Run a fine, sharp knife around the edge of each ramekin. Unmould the chicken mousses onto warm plates, carefully rearranging any slices of courgette which have become displaced. Spoon the warm Madeira sauce around each mousse.

variation

chicken mousse with tomato and mint coulis

Prepare and cook the mousse as directed in the main recipe. Leave to cool. Omit the butter sauce and make a tomato coulis instead: skin, deseed, and roughly chop 250g (9oz) fresh tomatoes (p197), then purée in a food processor until very smooth. With the motor running, gradually add 1 tbsp of olive oil to make an emulsion. Serve the mousses with the tomato coulis spooned around them and sprinkle evenly with chopped fresh mint.

baba ganoush

Thought to originate from India, aubergine has long been popular in Western dishes, too. Smoky baba ganoush, with its garlicky overtones, is one of the most inviting ways to eat it.

🥣 15 MINS   🍲 45 MINS

SPECIAL EQUIPMENT ▪ blender or food processor

SERVES 6

2 large aubergines

4 garlic cloves, crushed

small handful of oregano, leaves picked (optional)

grated zest and juice of 1 lemon

90ml (3fl oz) olive oil

150g (5½oz) pine nuts, toasted and chopped

120ml (4fl oz) Greek-style yogurt

salt and freshly ground black pepper

1 Heat the grill of a barbecue or a ridged cast-iron grill pan until very hot. Add the whole aubergines and grill, turning every so often, for 30–45 minutes until their skin is charred and blistered all over; it will become quite black. Remove from the heat and leave to cool a little before peeling away the skin and roughly chopping the flesh.

2 Put the chopped aubergine, garlic, oregano (if using), lemon zest and juice, and oil in a blender or food processor, and blend to a chunky spread. Transfer to a bowl and add the pine nuts and yogurt. Season with salt and pepper and mix the ingredients well.

3 Serve with torn chunks of sourdough bread, or toasted slices of baguette.

variation

aubergine and chickpea pâté
Prepare in the same way, but use 1 aubergine instead of 2, substitute a drained 400g can of chickpeas for the pine nuts, and add a good pinch of dried chilli flakes with the other ingredients. Blend until chunky, stopping and scraping down the sizes as necessary. Serve in chunks of cucumber, halved, and the seeds scooped out, topped with dried mint.

moroccan-style pancakes

Modern aubergines are less bitter than in the past, and rarely need salting. But if first salted, left in a colander for half an hour, washed, then dried, they absorb less oil during cooking.

🥣 5 MINS   🍲 25 MINS

MAKES 2–4

125g (4½oz) plain flour

salt and freshly ground black pepper

1 egg

300ml (10fl oz) milk

1 tbsp olive oil, plus a little extra for frying

1 aubergine, diced

2 tomatoes, finely chopped

pinch of ground cinnamon

small handful of mint leaves, finely chopped

lemon wedges, to serve

1 Put the flour in a mixing bowl with a little salt, stir, and make a well in the centre. Crack the egg into the well and add a tiny amount of the milk. Using a wooden spoon, stir the egg and milk, letting the flour gradually tumble in. Add the rest of the milk, little by little, stirring continuously until all the flour is incorporated and the mixture is lump-free. Put in the fridge to rest for 30 minutes, if you have time.

2 Heat the oil in a frying pan, add the aubergine, and cook over a medium heat for 5–8 minutes, or until golden. Add the tomatoes and cook for a further 5 minutes, or until they start to break down a little. Season well with salt and pepper, then add the cinnamon and mint and stir well.

3 In a small, flat frying pan or pancake pan, heat a drizzle of oil over a high heat, swirl it around the pan, then tip it out. Stir the batter, then spoon 2 tbsp of the mix into the frying pan, swirling it around so it reaches the edges. Cook for a couple of minutes, then pull up the edges with a palette knife. Turn the pancake over and cook the other side for 1 minute. Slide the pancake out onto a plate and keep warm. Repeat with the rest of the batter.

4 Spoon the filling onto the pancakes and either roll or fold them up, or simply place the aubergine mixture on top. Serve with lemon wedges.

pan-fried scallops with chilli, ginger, and an anchovy dressing

In general, the smaller the chilli, the hotter its flavour. If you enjoy something truly hot, look for habañero chillies.

🥣 10 MINS 🍲 30 MINS

SERVES 4

For the scallops

2–3 tbsp olive oil

675g (1½lb) waxy potatoes, peeled and thinly sliced

12 scallops (with or without coral, depending on preference), cleaned

salt and freshly ground black pepper

1 red chilli, deseeded and finely chopped

2.5cm (1in) piece of fresh root ginger, peeled and grated

1 lemon, halved

handful of flat-leaf parsley, finely chopped

For the anchovy dressing

3 tbsp extra virgin olive oil

1 tbsp white wine vinegar

8 anchovies in oil, drained and finely chopped

pinch of sugar (optional)

1 Heat 1–2 tbsp of the oil in a large non-stick frying pan over a medium-high heat. Add the potatoes and sauté for 15–20 minutes until the potatoes are golden and cooked through. Drain on kitchen paper and set aside to keep warm.

2 Meanwhile, make the anchovy dressing. In a jug, whisk together the oil, vinegar, and anchovies until well combined. Taste and add a pinch of sugar if it needs it. Season with black pepper.

3 Pat dry the scallops with kitchen paper and season with salt and pepper. Put the remaining oil in the frying pan over a high heat. When hot, add the scallops. Sear for about 1 minute on one side, then turn them over. Add the chilli and ginger, and squeeze over the lemon juice, being careful as it may spit. Remove the pan from the heat and sprinkle over the parsley.

4 Serve immediately with the sautéed potatoes and a drizzle of the anchovy dressing.

stuffed aubergine rolls with salsa

Fried aubergine slices cleverly become wraps, with creamy ricotta cheese and pesto centres and a tangy tomato salsa.

🥣 20 MINS 🍲 20 MINS

SPECIAL EQUIPMENT ▪ cocktail sticks

SERVES 4

1 large aubergine, cut lengthways into eight 5mm (¼in) thick slices

125g (4½oz) fresh toasted breadcrumbs

1 tbsp chopped flat-leaf parsley

1 garlic clove, crushed

2 tbsp grated Parmesan cheese

salt and freshly ground black pepper

2 eggs, lightly beaten

175g (6oz) plain flour

120ml (4fl oz) olive oil

250g (9oz) ricotta cheese

1 tbsp ready-made pesto

For the salsa

3 tomatoes, finely chopped

small handful of flat-leaf parsley, finely chopped

1 tbsp olive oil

1 Put the aubergine slices in a colander, rinse well, and drain. Pat dry with kitchen paper. Put the breadcrumbs, parsley, garlic, and Parmesan cheese in a large flat dish. Season, and mix thoroughly until well combined. Put the beaten eggs in another flat dish and the flour in a third. Dip the aubergine slices first in the flour, then in the beaten egg, and finally in the breadcrumbs, coating evenly.

2 Heat the oil in 2 large heavy-based frying pans over a medium heat, using half of the oil in each one. Divide the aubergine slices among the 2 pans and shallow-fry for 2–4 minutes on each side until golden. Alternatively, cook in 2 batches. Drain on a baking tray lined with kitchen paper and keep warm.

3 Meanwhile, put the ricotta cheese and pesto in a bowl and lightly mix together with a fork. To make the tomato salsa, put the tomato, parsley, and oil in a separate bowl. Season with salt and pepper and stir through gently.

4 To serve, put 1 tbsp of the ricotta mixture towards the end of each of the aubergine slices. Roll and secure with a cocktail stick. Place 2 rolls in the centre of each of 4 serving plates and pile the tomato salsa on top.

salade lyonnaise

A dressing of red wine vinegar and bacon peps up this warm spinach salad. For a more sizable dish, top with a warm poached egg, breaking the yolk into the dressing as you eat.

🥣 30–35 MINS   🍲 20–25 MINS

SERVES 6

½ baguette

3 tbsp olive oil

1 garlic clove

2 eggs

500g (1lb 2oz) spinach leaves

250g (9oz) lardons or streaky bacon rashers, chopped

75ml (2½fl oz) red wine vinegar

1 Preheat the oven to 200°C (400°F/ Gas 6). Cut the baguette into 5mm (¼in) slices. Brush both sides of each slice with oil and set on a baking sheet. Bake for 7–10 minutes, until toasted and golden brown, turning once. Cut the garlic clove in half. Rub one side of each slice of toasted bread with the cut side of the garlic. Set the croûtes aside.

2 Hard-boil and shell the eggs. Tear the spinach leaves into large pieces and put in a bowl. Separate the egg yolks from the whites by gently pulling the whites apart. Chop the whites. Put the yolks in a sieve set over a bowl and work them through with the back of a metal spoon.

3 Heat a frying pan, add the bacon, and cook, stirring, for 3–5 minutes, until it is crisp and the fat is rendered. Add to the spinach and toss vigorously for 30 seconds, until the spinach is slightly wilted.

4 Pour the vinegar into the frying pan. Bring it to the boil, stirring, and boil it for about 1 minute, until reduced by one-third. Pour the vinegar over the spinach and bacon and toss together well.

5 Pile the salad onto 6 individual plates. Sprinkle each serving evenly with the chopped egg whites and sieved yolks, and serve immediately, with a pile of the croûtes on the side.

chinese egg drop soup

This can be a simple chicken broth with just the drizzled egg, but it's more tasty and filling with the addition of summery sweetcorn and baby leaf spinach, and Chinese seasonings.

🥣 5 MINS   🍲 25 MINS

SERVES 4

1 litre (1¾ pints) hot chicken stock

1 garlic clove, grated or finely chopped

½ tsp grated fresh root ginger

2 spring onions, trimmed and chopped

2 tbsp soy sauce

½ tsp Chinese five-spice powder

2 sweetcorn cobs, kernels removed (about 225g/8oz kernels, p155)

2 large handfuls of baby leaf spinach

2 tbsp cornflour

2 eggs, beaten

1 Put the stock in a pan with the garlic, ginger, spring onions, soy sauce, and five-spice powder. Add the sweetcorn kernels and bring to the boil. Reduce the heat, cover, and simmer gently for 20 minutes.

2 Add the spinach, bring back to the boil, reduce the heat, and simmer for 1 minute or until the spinach has just wilted. Taste and add more soy sauce if necessary.

3 Mix the cornflour with 4 tbsp water and stir into the soup. Bring back to the boil and simmer, stirring, for 1 minute to thicken slightly. Gradually trickle in the beaten eggs, stirring gently, so that it forms thin strands. Serve in warmed soup bowls.

spanish pepper and tomato soup

Just a touch of chilli and paprika enlivens this soup and the slow cooking of the peppers enhances their sweet flavour. You could add canned chickpeas for a more substantial soup.

🥣 20 MINS   🍲 1 HR 15 MINS – 1 HR 30 MINS   ❄️ FREEZABLE

SPECIAL EQUIPMENT ▪ food processor or hand-held blender

SERVES 4–6

1 tbsp olive oil

1 onion, finely chopped

salt and freshly ground black pepper

2 celery sticks, roughly chopped

3 garlic cloves, finely chopped

1 large carrot, chopped

pinch of dried chilli flakes

pinch of paprika

6 red peppers, deseeded and roughly chopped

3 tomatoes, roughly chopped

1.4 litres (2½ pints) hot vegetable stock

85g (3oz) feta cheese, crumbled, to serve (optional)

1 Heat the oil in a large heavy-based pan over a medium heat, add the onion, and cook for 3–4 minutes until soft. Season with salt and pepper, add the celery, garlic, and carrot, and cook for 5–10 minutes until soft, stirring occasionally.

2 Stir in the chilli flakes and paprika and cook for a minute, then add the peppers and tomatoes. Cook on a very low heat for about 20 minutes, stirring so they don't stick. Pour in half of the stock and bring to the boil, then reduce to a simmer and partially cover with the lid. Cook on a low heat for 45–60 minutes, topping up with the reserved stock as the cooking liquid reduces.

3 Remove the soup from the heat and, using a food processor or hand-held blender, purée until smooth. Add a ladleful of hot water if it is too thick. Pour the soup into a clean pan, taste, season as needed, and heat through. Serve with a little feta cheese on top, if using, together with some crusty bread.

sweetcorn fritters with tomato salsa

Home-grown sweetcorn is so tender that there is no need to cook it before making these fritters. The generous flavours used here will turn your cobs into something the whole family will enjoy. A fresh tomato salsa is the perfect partner.

20 MINS   **10 MINS**

SPECIAL EQUIPMENT ▪ blender or food processor

MAKES 14-16

100g (3½oz) self-raising flour

1 tsp baking powder

2 large eggs

4 tbsp milk

2 sweetcorn cobs, kernels removed (about 225g/8oz kernels, p155)

1 tsp smoked paprika

2 spring onions, trimmed, finely chopped, and green and white parts separated

4 tbsp chopped coriander

1 red chilli, deseeded and finely chopped (optional)

salt and freshly ground black pepper

2 tbsp sunflower oil

2 ripe tomatoes, skinned (p197) and roughly chopped

2 tbsp extra virgin olive oil

dash of Tabasco or chilli sauce

1 Sift the flour and baking powder into a bowl. Mix the eggs and milk together in a jug, then gradually whisk them into the flour to make a thick batter.

2 Add the sweetcorn kernels, paprika, the white parts of the spring onions, 2 tbsp of the coriander, and the chilli, if using. Mix well and season with salt and pepper.

3 Heat the sunflower oil in a large frying pan and add the batter mixture in tablespoons. Use the back of the spoon to spread the fritters out slightly, and fry for 2–3 minutes on each side until puffed up and golden brown. Batch-fry until all the mixture is cooked, adding a little more sunflower oil as necessary.

4 For the salsa, put the tomatoes, the remaining coriander and spring onion, olive oil, and Tabasco or chilli sauce into a blender or food processor, and blitz until blended but still quite chunky. Check the salsa for seasoning and serve the hot fritters with the salsa on the side.

butterflied sardines stuffed with tomatoes and capers

If you would rather barbecue these sardines, first bake the tomato mix, then lightly oil the grill, and barbecue the fish until golden and cooked through. Combine to serve.

🥣 15 MINS 🍲 10 MINS

SERVES 4

4–6 tomatoes, skinned (p197) and finely chopped

2 tsp capers, rinsed and gently squeezed dry

handful of flat-leaf parsley, finely chopped, plus extra to garnish (optional)

2 garlic cloves, grated or finely chopped

salt and freshly ground black pepper

12 sardines, butterflied

a little olive oil

juice of 1 lemon

1 Preheat the oven to 200°C (400°F/ Gas 6). Put the tomatoes, capers, parsley, and garlic in a bowl. Season with salt and pepper and stir well to combine.

2 Lay the sardines out flat, skin-side down, and spoon on the tomato mixture. Either roll up the sardines lengthways or just fold them over, then sit them all in a baking tray. Drizzle the sardines with the oil and lemon juice.

3 Bake in the oven for 10–15 minutes until the sardines are cooked through. Garnish with extra parsley, if you wish, and serve with a crisp green salad.

fish with courgettes, aubergines, and tomatoes

Roasted aubergine marries well with full-bodied ingredients like tomatoes and lemon. Either haddock or pollack (a sustainable choice) are good seasonal options for this dish.

🥣 15 MINS 🍲 35 MINS

SERVES 4

675g (1½lb) white fish loins, such as haddock or pollack, skinned and cut into chunky pieces

2 tbsp olive oil

1 tsp fennel seeds, crushed

grated zest of 1 lemon

salt and freshly ground black pepper

4 small to medium courgettes, sliced

2 aubergines, cut into bite-sized pieces

12 cherry tomatoes

handful of dill, finely chopped

lemon wedges, to serve

1 Preheat the oven to 200°C (400°F/ Gas 6). Toss the fish pieces with half the oil, half the fennel seeds, and half the lemon zest. Season well with salt and pepper, then cover and set aside.

2 Meanwhile, put the courgettes and aubergines in a roasting tin with the remaining oil, fennel seeds, and lemon zest and toss together well.

Season with salt and pepper, then put the vegetables in the oven to roast for 20 minutes, or until they begin to soften.

3 Stir and turn the vegetables well. Add the fish and the tomatoes and cook for a further 15 minutes, or until the fish is cooked through. Sprinkle over the dill and serve with the lemon wedges and some fresh crusty bread.

variation

roasted sardines with vegetable medley

Prepare in a similar way, but use 8 cleaned, large sardines (pilchards) instead of the white fish. Stuff them with some sprigs of thyme and omit the fennel seeds. Drizzle the fish with olive oil before baking. When cooked, scatter over a few fresh thyme leaves instead of the dill.

white fish with spinach and pine nuts

Haddock, pollack, and turbot are all excellent, flaky white fish substitutes for cod, and are full of flavour.

🥄 **10 MINS**   🍲 **15 MINS**

SERVES 4

4 haddock fillets or other white fish such as pollack, turbot, or sustainable cod, about 150g (5½oz) each

salt and freshly ground black pepper

2 tbsp olive oil

1 onion, finely chopped

handful of plump raisins

handful of pine nuts, toasted

1-2 tsp capers, rinsed and gently squeezed dry

2 large handfuls of spinach, rinsed and drained

1 Season the fish with salt and pepper. Heat 1 tbsp of the oil in a large non-stick frying pan over a medium heat. Add the fish and cook gently for 5–6 minutes on one side. Turn over and cook on the other side until cooked through – this will depend on the thickness of the fish, but be careful not to overcook. Remove from the pan and set aside to keep warm.

2 Carefully wipe out the pan with kitchen paper, then add the remaining oil. Sauté the onion for about 5 minutes until soft and translucent. Add the raisins, pine nuts, and capers and cook for a few minutes more, breaking up the capers with the back of a fork. Add the spinach and cook until just wilted. Taste and season if needed. Serve the fish on a bed of the wilted spinach mixture.

variation

white fish with swiss chard, harissa, tomatoes, and pumpkin seeds

Prepare in the same way, but use 6 sun-dried tomatoes in oil, drained and chopped, instead of the raisins, pumpkin seeds instead of the pine nuts, and add 1 tbsp harissa paste. Use 350g (12oz) Swiss chard leaves instead of the spinach, thickly shredded. Add 12 halved cherry tomatoes along with the Swiss chard.

chicken jambalaya

Jambalaya, a traditional southern American dish from Louisiana, combines the summer flavours of peppers, peas, and herbs and adds a little heat with some cayenne pepper.

🥄 **15-20 MINS**   🍲 **1 HR 30 MINS**

SERVES 4-6

2 tbsp olive oil

6 boneless chicken pieces (thigh and breast), cut into large chunky pieces

salt and freshly ground black pepper

2 tbsp chopped oregano

2 tsp cayenne pepper

1 red onion, finely chopped

3 garlic cloves, finely chopped

1 green pepper, deseeded and finely chopped

1 red pepper, deseeded and finely chopped

200g (7oz) thick slices cooked ham, roughly chopped

900ml (1½ pints) hot chicken stock

175g (6oz) easy-cook long-grain rice

140g (5oz) peas (shelled weight)

small handful of coriander, finely chopped (optional)

1 Heat half the oil in a large flameproof casserole over a medium-high heat. Season the chicken pieces with salt and pepper, toss in the oregano and cayenne pepper, then add to the casserole (in batches, if necessary) and cook for 6–10 minutes until golden brown. Remove and set aside.

2 Heat the remaining oil in the casserole over a medium heat, add the onion, garlic, and peppers and cook for 5–8 minutes, stirring, until soft. Return the chicken to the casserole and stir in the ham. Pour in the stock and bring to the boil, then reduce to a simmer, season well, partially cover with the lid, and cook gently for about 40 minutes. Check occasionally that it's not drying out and top up with a little hot water if needed. Stir in the rice, turning it so it absorbs all the stock, and cook for about 15 minutes or until the rice is cooked, topping up with more stock if necessary. Add the peas for the last 5 minutes.

3 Taste and add seasoning, if needed, and stir in the coriander, if using. Try serving with a green salad, green beans, plain yogurt or soured cream, and some crusty bread.

baked eggs with tomatoes and peppers

This dish is instantly enlivened by colourful peppers, tomatoes, and chillies. Omit or reduce the quantity of chillies slightly if you don't like too much heat in your food.

🥣 10 MINS   🍲 20 MINS

SERVES 4

1 tbsp olive oil

1 red onion, sliced

salt and freshly ground black pepper

2 red peppers, deseeded and sliced

2 yellow peppers or orange peppers, deseeded and sliced

2 red chillies, deseeded and finely chopped

3 tomatoes, skinned (p197) and roughly chopped

2 handfuls of spinach leaves

pinch of paprika

4 eggs

1 Preheat the oven to 200°C (400°F/ Gas 6). Heat the oil in a large ovenproof frying pan over a low heat. Add the onion and a little salt. Cook for 5 minutes until the onion is soft, then add the peppers and chillies. Cook for a further 5 minutes until the peppers soften.

2 Stir through the tomatoes and cook, stirring well until they begin to soften. Add the spinach and paprika and cook for a few minutes more until the spinach begins to wilt.

3 Make a little pocket in the mixture for each of the eggs, then carefully break an egg into each pocket. Slide the pan into the oven and cook for about 5 minutes until the eggs are baked. Be careful not to let them overcook – the residual heat will keep cooking them after you have removed them from the oven. Sprinkle with black pepper and serve immediately.

calzone with peppers, capers, and olives

A family crowd-pleaser with sweet peppers and salty capers. All you need to accompany this is a fresh, seasonal salad.

🥄 15 MINS   🍲 20 MINS   ❄ FREEZABLE

MAKES 1

125g (4½oz) strong plain flour

salt and freshly ground black pepper

pinch of sugar

¾ tsp easy-blend dried yeast

1 tbsp olive oil

4 red peppers, roasted, peeled, and chopped (p171)

handful of pitted black olives, roughly chopped

1-2 tsp capers, rinsed

2-3 tbsp ricotta cheese or mozzarella, torn into pieces

1 Sift the flour, a pinch of salt, and the sugar into a bowl and add the yeast. Stir in the oil and add up to 90ml (3fl oz) warm water to form a soft, but not sticky, dough. Knead gently on a floured work surface for several minutes until smooth and elastic. Return to the bowl, cover with oiled cling film, and leave in a warm place (you can preheat the oven and leave the bowl on top of the hob above) for 30–40 minutes, or until doubled in size.

2 Turn the dough out onto a floured work surface again and knock it back by re-kneading briefly. Preheat the oven to its highest setting and heat a lightly oiled baking sheet. Roll out the dough thinly to a round, about 25cm (10in) in diameter. Transfer the pizza base to the baking sheet, spreading it out firmly again.

3 Spoon the peppers, olives, capers, and ricotta cheese or mozzarella onto half the pizza base, leaving about 1cm (½in) around the edge. Season well with salt and pepper. Dampen the edges of the pizza with a little water, then fold one half of the pizza over the other and seal together with your fingers. Sprinkle the top with a little water and bake in the oven for 15–20 minutes, or until golden and crispy. Serve while hot.

Season's best **peppers**

Members of the capsicum family, sweet peppers are usually bell-shaped, or long and flat. They range in colour from green when unripe to yellow, orange, or red, getting sweeter as they change colour. You may also find purple, brown, or near black ripe varieties. At their best in high summer and autumn, they are particularly delicious with garlic, onions, tomatoes, and other Mediterranean vegetables and fragrant rosemary, basil, and oregano.

Peppers are native to the tropical Americas, but are now grown worldwide. They need heat and light so, in cooler climates, are grown under glass or in polytunnels.

essentials
varieties available

Bell-shaped or long and pointed, there are many varieties ranging in colour from green through red to almost black.

buy Choose fruits that are glossy and firm, with no soft spots or mould. They should have some heft to them, rather than feel light.

store Keep in paper bags or open-topped plastic bags in the fridge for up to 2 weeks. Once cut, use within 24 hours.

cook Stuff and bake, roast, grill, or barbecue. Stew, sauté, stir-fry, or use raw as crudités or in salads.

preserve Pickle in vinegar or in oil.

recipe ideas

Chilled tomato and red pepper soup p144

Mixed peppers in oil p232

Three-pepper pizza with cheese p172

Red bell pepper As they ripen, bell peppers turn from green to red, and become sweeter and fleshier. With their boxy shape, they are ideal for stuffing or roasting whole.

Green bell pepper Unripe green bell peppers have thinner walls than ripe bell peppers, and a distinct herbaceous flavour that mellows as they mature.

Romano (Ramiro) pepper The Italian heirloom variety Nardello has a mild flavour when green, becoming intensely sweet when red. It is ideal stuffed, or fried with slices of Italian sausage.

how to roast and peel peppers

Bell peppers can have thick skins, which are easiest to remove by char-roasting. The technique also imparts a delicious, slightly smoky taste and enhances the sweetness of the pepper flesh. The same roasting and peeling method can be used for chilli peppers as well as for tomatoes and even garlic.

1 Using long-handled tongs, hold each pepper over an open flame, rotating slowly to char the skin on all sides until black all over.

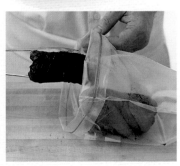

2 While they are still hot, place the charred peppers into a plastic bag and seal tightly. Set aside to allow steam to loosen the skin.

3 After about 10 minutes, and once cooled, peel away the charred skin from each pepper with your fingers. Slice or chop the flesh as needed.

three-pepper pizza with cheese

Choose brightly coloured, firm peppers with no soft spots, and add finely sliced chillies instead of cayenne, if you prefer.

🥄 1 HR 15 MINS PLUS STANDING   🍲 20-25 MINS

SERVES 4-6

125g (4½oz) strong plain flour

salt and freshly ground black pepper

pinch of sugar

¾ tsp easy-blend dried yeast

5 tbsp olive oil

2 onions, thinly sliced

2 red peppers, deseeded and cut into strips

1 green pepper, deseeded and cut into strips

1 yellow pepper, deseeded and cut into strips

3 garlic cloves, finely chopped

small bunch of any herb, such as rosemary, thyme, basil, or parsley, or a mixture, leaves finely chopped

cayenne, to taste

175g (6oz) mozzarella cheese, sliced

1 Sift the flour, a pinch of salt, and the sugar into a bowl and add the yeast. Stir in 1 tbsp of the oil and add up to 90ml (3fl oz) warm water to form a soft, but not sticky, dough. Knead gently on a floured work surface for several minutes until smooth and elastic. Return to the bowl, cover with oiled cling film, and leave in a warm place (you can preheat the oven and leave the bowl on top of the hob above) for 30–40 minutes, or until doubled in size.

2 Heat 1 tbsp of the oil in a frying pan, add the onions, and stir for 2–3 minutes until soft. Transfer to a bowl and set aside. Add the remaining oil to the pan, then add the peppers, garlic, and half the herbs. Season with salt and cayenne. Sauté, stirring, for 7–10 minutes until soft. Taste for seasoning; it should be quite spicy.

3 Preheat the oven to 230°C (450°F/ Gas 8). Put a baking sheet near the bottom of the oven to heat up and generously flour a second baking sheet. Turn the dough out onto a floured work surface again and knock it back by re-kneading briefly. Roll out the dough thinly to a round, about 25cm (10in) in diameter. Transfer the pizza base to the floured baking sheet and press up the edge to form a shallow rim, if you like.

4 Spread the onions and then the peppers, evenly over the pizza base, leaving a 2cm (³⁄₄in) border all around the edge (if you haven't made a shallow rim), so it can become golden in the oven. Spoon any remaining oil from the frying pan over the peppers and top them evenly with the slices of mozzarella. Let the assembled pizza stand in a warm place for

10–15 minutes, until the dough has puffed up well around the edges. Don't leave it for any longer, as it should be baked as soon as possible to retain maximum flavour.

5 With a sharp, jerking movement, slide the pizza onto the heated baking sheet at the bottom of the oven. Bake for about 20–25 minutes, or until brown all over and the cheese has melted. If you are using finely sliced chilli instead of cayenne, add it 5 minutes before the end of the cooking time. Remove from the oven, scatter the reserved herbs over the top of the pizza, and serve.

caribbean stew with allspice and ginger

Fiery Scotch Bonnets are the quintessential Caribbean chilli.

🥣 30 MINS PLUS MARINATING   🍲 30 MINS   ❄ FREEZABLE

SPECIAL EQUIPMENT ▪ blender or food processor

SERVES 8

1–2 Scotch Bonnet chillies (according to taste), deseeded

2 tsp allspice

handful of thyme leaves

2 tsp tamarind paste

5cm (2in) piece of fresh root ginger, peeled and roughly chopped

salt and freshly ground black pepper

3 tbsp olive oil

4 large skinless chicken breasts, cut into bite-sized pieces

1 tbsp plain flour

1.4 litres (2½ pints) hot chicken stock

4 mixed peppers, deseeded and roughly chopped

5 tomatoes, skinned (p197) and chopped

1 Put the chillies, allspice, thyme, tamarind, ginger, and seasoning in a food processor and blitz to a paste. Add a little of the oil and blitz again.

Pour into a plastic bag, add the chicken, and marinate for 30 minutes, or overnight in the fridge.

2 Heat the remaining oil in a large cast-iron pan or flameproof casserole, add the chicken and marinade, and cook, stirring often, over a medium heat for 10 minutes, or until the chicken is golden. Stir in the flour, add a little of the stock, and stir to scrape up any crispy bits from the bottom of the pan. Pour in the rest of the stock and stir until the flour has blended in.

3 Stir in the peppers and tomatoes and season well with salt and pepper. Bring to the boil, then reduce to a simmer and cook over a low heat for 30 minutes, or until the sauce has begun to thicken slightly. Taste and season again if needed. Serve piping hot with baked sweet potatoes or sweet potato mash.

fiery pepper noodles

A wonderfully spicy vegetarian dish, where lime and chilli work brilliantly well with peppers, spring onions, and peanuts.

🥣 30 MINS   🍲 4–5 MINS

SERVES 4

1 red pepper

1 green pepper

1 tbsp sunflower oil

4 spring onions, chopped

1 garlic clove, finely chopped

1 courgette, finely chopped

1 or 2 green jalapeño or poblano chillies, deseeded and chopped

1 tsp grated fresh root ginger

1 tbsp chopped flat-leaf parsley

1 tbsp chopped coriander, plus a few torn leaves, to serve

grated zest and juice of 1 lime

4 tbsp crunchy peanut butter

3 tbsp soy sauce

1 tbsp dry sherry

500g (1lb 2oz) fresh egg noodles

60g (2oz) chopped roasted peanuts, to serve

1 Preheat the oven to 200°C (400°F/Gas 6). Put the peppers in a roasting tin and cook for 25–30 minutes until they begin to char. Remove from the oven, put in a plastic bag, and leave to cool before removing the stalks and skin, deseeding, and roughly chopping.

2 Heat the oil in a wok or large frying pan. Add the spring onions, garlic, and courgette and stir-fry for 1 minute. Add the peppers, chillies, ginger, herbs, lime zest and juice, peanut butter, soy sauce, sherry, and 9 tbsp water. Stir the ingredients until the peanut butter melts.

3 Add the noodles and toss for 2 minutes until piping hot. Pile into warm bowls and sprinkle with peanuts and a few torn coriander leaves.

greek stuffed tomatoes

With their thick, plump flesh, large beefsteak tomatoes make ideal "containers" within which to bake other ingredients. This recipe also includes medium-hot chillies for added flavour.

🥣 10 MINS   🍲 1 HR 30 MINS

SERVES 4

4 large beefsteak tomatoes

½ tbsp olive oil

400g (14oz) lamb mince

pinch of paprika

pinch of ground cumin

pinch of ground cinnamon

2 green chillies, deseeded and finely chopped

1 tbsp tomato purée

1 tbsp harissa paste

handful of mint leaves, chopped

150ml (5fl oz) hot vegetable stock

sea salt and freshly ground black pepper

1 Slice the tops off the tomatoes and scoop out the flesh. Reserve the shells and "lids", and roughly chop and reserve the scooped-out flesh (including juices and seeds). Preheat the oven to 200°C (400°F/Gas 6).

2 Heat the oil in a large frying pan over a medium heat. Add the lamb mince and cook, stirring to break up any lumps, until the meat is browned and no longer pink.

3 Add the reserved chopped tomato flesh and the paprika, ground cumin, and ground cinnamon. Cook, stirring, for a couple of minutes.

4 Add the chillies, tomato purée, harissa, and mint leaves, and stir. Pour in the hot vegetable stock and bring to the boil. Simmer for 15 minutes until the mixture has thickened, then season with sea salt and pepper.

5 Spoon the mixture into the reserved tomato shells, put their lids on, and sit the stuffed tomatoes on a roasting tin. Cover with foil and bake in the oven for 1 hour, then serve.

vietnamese beef soup

It's the slow-cooked beef stock, flavoured with gentle spices that really makes this dish. Add extra spring onions, chillies, or julienned carrots and bean sprouts, if you wish.

🥣 15 MINS   🍲 1 HR 15 MINS

SERVES 4-6

about 675g (1½lb) beef bones, rinsed and dried

1 tbsp dark soy sauce

1 tbsp olive oil

1 star anise

1 tsp black peppercorns

1 cinnamon stick

½ tbsp fish sauce (nam pla)

1 onion, finely chopped

3 garlic cloves, finely chopped

1 chilli, deseeded and finely chopped

1 lemongrass stalk, trimmed, tough outer leaves removed, and finely chopped

2.5cm (1in) piece of fresh root ginger, peeled and finely sliced

salt and freshly ground black pepper

350g (12oz) fillet steak, very finely sliced across the grain

60g (2oz) vermicelli noodles, soaked in hot water for 5 minutes (or as per packet's instructions) and drained

bunch of green spring onions, trimmed and finely sliced

1 First make the beef stock. In a bowl, toss the beef bones with the soy sauce. Heat a little of the oil in a large heavy-based pan over a medium-high heat, add the bones, and cook, stirring, for about 15 minutes until the meat is no longer pink.

2 Transfer them to a large stock pan, pour over 1.4 litres (2½ pints) water, and add the star anise, peppercorns, cinnamon stick, and fish sauce. Bring to the boil, then partially cover with the lid, reduce to a simmer, and cook for 1 hour. Strain the stock through a sieve into a clean pan, topping up with water to 900ml (1½ pints), if necessary, and reserve.

3 Heat the remaining oil in a large heavy-based pan, add the onion, and cook for 3–4 minutes until soft. Do not brown. Stir in the garlic, chilli, and lemongrass and cook for a minute. Then pour in the beef stock, add the ginger, and taste, adding seasoning if needed. Gently simmer for a few minutes, then add the sliced steak to the stock and cook for 2–3 minutes. Stir through the noodles and spring onions and ladle into warmed bowls.

lacquered chicken salad

A chicken salad with crunchy lettuce and baby sweetcorn.

🥣 25-30 MINS PLUS MARINATING   🍲 10-15 MINS

SERVES 4

4 boneless, skinless chicken breasts, total weight about 750g (1lb 10oz)

1cm (½in) piece of fresh root ginger, peeled and finely chopped

1 garlic clove, finely chopped

45g (1½oz) soft brown sugar

2 tbsp Dijon mustard

3 tbsp rice wine

3 tbsp sesame oil

salt and freshly ground black pepper

4 tbsp soy sauce

120ml (4fl oz) vegetable oil

125g (4½oz) bean sprouts

leaves from 1 cos lettuce, shredded

85g (3oz) baby sweetcorn, halved lengthways

1 Lightly score the top of each chicken breast and set them in a shallow, non-metallic dish.

2 Combine the ginger, garlic, soft brown sugar, mustard, 1 tbsp each of the rice wine and sesame oil, and black pepper in a bowl. Pour in the soy sauce and stir. Remove and reserve 4 tbsp of the marinade, then pour the rest over the chicken, cover, and chill in the fridge for 1–2 hours, turning 3–4 times during that period.

3 Add the remaining rice wine and sesame oil to the reserved marinade and mix. Gradually whisk in the vegetable oil until the dressing emulsifies and thickens slightly. Taste for seasoning and set aside, or chill in the fridge, tightly sealed, for up to 12 hours if you have time. Put the bean sprouts in a bowl. Cover generously with boiling water and leave to stand for 1 minute. Drain, rinse with cold, running water, and drain again.

4 Heat the grill and oil the grill rack. Put the chicken on the rack and brush with the marinade. Grill about 7.5cm (3in) from the heat, brushing often with the marinade, for 5–7 minutes on each side until well browned and glossy, but still tender. Put chicken on a chopping board and cut diagonally into slices.

5 Put the shredded lettuce in a mixing bowl and add the bean sprouts and sweetcorn. Briskly whisk the dressing again and pour it over the salad. Toss and taste for seasoning. Arrange the salad on a serving plate, top with the chicken, and serve while still warm.

sea bass with herb butter sauce

An impressive dish of superbly flavoured sea bass to share.

🥣 40–45 MINS 🍲 30–40 MINS

SPECIAL EQUIPMENT ▪ food processor

SERVES 4

bunch of watercress, half reserved as a garnish

8 spinach leaves

10–12 sprigs of parsley, leaves picked

10–12 sprigs of chervil, leaves picked

1 garlic clove, peeled

2 anchovy fillets

2 tsp capers, drained

1 small gherkin

75g (2½oz) butter

3 tbsp olive oil

1 lemon, cut in half lengthways, one half cut crossways into thin slices, and the other half squeezed

1 tsp Dijon mustard

salt and freshly ground black pepper

1 whole sea bass, about 2kg (4½lb)

3–5 sprigs of thyme

30g (1oz) butter

120ml (4fl oz) dry white wine

1 Bring a pan of well-salted water to the boil. Add half the watercress, spinach, parsley, and chervil, and

simmer for 1–2 minutes until tender. Drain, rinse with cold water, and drain again. Squeeze the leaves with your hand to remove all excess water.

2 Preheat the oven to 190°C (375°F/Gas 5). Blitz the garlic, anchovies, capers, and gherkin in a food processor. Add the butter, piece by piece, and pulse to a purée. Tip in the greens and pulse again. With the blade turning, slowly pour in the oil. Add the lemon juice, mustard, and seasoning, and blitz briefly. Transfer to a serving dish.

3 Slash the fish, about 1cm (½in) deep, diagonally 3–4 times on each side. Set in a roasting tin and tuck a sprig of thyme and a slice of lemon into each slash. Dot with the butter and sprinkle with white wine, salt, and pepper. Roast, basting occasionally, for about 30 minutes, until it just flakes easily when tested with a fork and is no longer translucent in the centre. Be careful not to overcook. Serve with the sauce and reserved watercress.

chicken stir-fried with spring onion, basil, and lemongrass

Stir-frying is such a quick way to cook food that it's best to chop and prepare all your ingredients first.

🥣 10 MINS 🍲 15 MINS

SERVES 4

2–3 skinless chicken breasts, sliced into strips

salt and freshly ground black pepper

1 tbsp cornflour

2 tbsp sesame oil or vegetable oil

bunch of spring onions, trimmed and sliced diagonally

3 garlic cloves, sliced

1 lemongrass stalk, trimmed, tough outer leaves removed, and chopped

2 red chillies, deseeded and sliced

1 tbsp Chinese rice wine

handful of basil leaves

1 Season the chicken with salt and pepper. Put the cornflour on a plate and toss the chicken strips in it until very well coated.

2 Heat 1 tbsp of the oil in a wok over a high heat. Swirl it around the wok, then add the chicken and stir-fry quickly, moving the chicken around for 3–5 minutes until golden and cooked through. Remove with a slotted spoon and keep warm.

3 Carefully wipe out the wok with kitchen paper, reduce the heat to medium-high, and add the remaining oil. When hot, add the spring onions, garlic, lemongrass, and chillies. Stir-fry for a couple of minutes, then increase the heat to high once again, add the rice wine, and boil for a few minutes.

4 Return the chicken to the wok to just heat through, then stir in the basil and serve immediately with some fluffy rice.

spiced haddock with coconut, chilli, and lime

Chopped red chilli and lime juice add intensity and heat to this Thai-inspired dish of mild, creamy coconut and white fish.

🥣 10 MINS   🍲 20 MINS

SERVES 4

4 haddock fillets, about 675g (1½lb) in total

salt and freshly ground black pepper

400ml can coconut milk

1 red chilli, deseeded and finely chopped

juice of 1 lime

splash of fish sauce (nam pla)

pinch of sugar (optional)

150g (5½oz) fresh green beans, trimmed

1 tbsp groundnut oil or sunflower oil

For the spice mixture

1–2 tsp cayenne pepper, to taste

1 tsp paprika

1 tsp ground cinnamon

1 tsp ground coriander

1 tbsp cornflour

1 To make the spice mixture, combine the spices and the cornflour in a bowl. Season the haddock, then coat well with the spice mixture. Set aside.

2 Pour the coconut milk into a wide pan, add the chilli, and bring to the boil. Reduce the heat to a simmer and add the lime juice, fish sauce, and a pinch of sugar (if using). Throw in the green beans and simmer for about 5 minutes.

3 Meanwhile, heat the oil in a non-stick frying pan over a high heat. Add the fish and fry for about 5 minutes on each side until golden. To serve, add the fish to the sauce and serve hot. Alternatively, serve the sauce on the side.

variation

pan-fried salmon with coconut, chilli, and lime

Replace the haddock with 4 salmon fillets, about 675g (1½lb) in total, in step 1.

sausage and chicken jambalaya

This is a highly flavoured, gutsy dish with okra and mixed peppers. Serve with a salad and crusty bread.

🥣 15 MINS   🍲 2 HRS 15 MINS   ❄ FREEZABLE

SERVES 6

1–2 tbsp olive oil

4 chicken thighs, chopped in half

250g (9oz) smoked sausage, cut into bite-sized pieces

250g (9oz) chorizo, chopped into thick slices

2 onions, diced

1 green pepper, deseeded and diced

1 red pepper, deseeded and diced

salt and freshly ground black pepper

3 garlic cloves, finely chopped

2 tsp Cajun seasoning

1 tbsp plain flour

900ml (1½ pints) hot chicken stock

2 tbsp Worcestershire sauce

300g (10oz) easy-cook white rice

2 bay leaves

250g (9oz) okra, sliced

handful of flat-leaf parsley, chopped

1 Preheat the oven to 150°C (300°F/Gas 2). Heat the oil in a large flameproof casserole over a medium-high heat, add the chicken, and fry quickly, turning, until browned all over. Remove with a slotted spoon and set aside. Add the sausages and cook for 5–8 minutes until golden. Remove and set aside.

2 Reduce the heat to medium, add the onions, and cook for 3–4 minutes until soft. Add the peppers and cook for a few minutes. Season, add the garlic and Cajun seasoning, and cook for 1 minute. Stir in the flour, ladle in a little stock, and stir well. Return the chicken and sausages to the pan and add the Worcestershire sauce.

3 Stir through the rice and bay leaves, then pour over the remaining stock. Mix well, cover, and put in the oven for 1½ hours. Occasionally check it's not drying out and top up with a little hot water if needed. Stir in the okra, re-cover, and cook for a further 30 minutes. Remove the bay leaves, taste and season if needed, then stir in the parsley and serve.

fish with tomatoes, potatoes, and onions

Red mullet, haddock, or sea bass are the best seasonal choices for this summery all-in-one meal.

🥣 30 MINS   🍲 15 MINS

SERVES 8

3 tbsp olive oil

5 large potatoes, cut into bite-sized pieces

salt and freshly ground black pepper

4 garlic cloves, grated or finely chopped

handful of flat-leaf parsley, finely chopped

550g (1¼lb) cherry tomatoes, halved

2 glasses of dry white wine

675g (1½lb) mixed firm-flesh fish, such as red mullet, haddock, and sea bass, cut into bite-sized pieces

16 anchovy fillets in oil, drained

1 Heat the oil in a large, shallow heavy-based pan, add the potatoes, and season well with salt and pepper. Cook over a medium heat, stirring frequently, for 10–15 minutes, or until beginning to turn golden brown. Lower the heat, then stir through the garlic and parsley, and cook for a few seconds before adding the tomatoes.

2 Cook for 6–8 minutes, or until the tomatoes begin to split, then raise the heat, add the wine, and allow to boil for a couple of minutes while the alcohol evaporates. Turn the heat to low, add the fish and the anchovies, cover, and cook for 10–15 minutes, or until the fish is tender. Transfer to a large, shallow serving dish and serve with a crisp dressed salad and some fresh crusty bread.

cobb salad

This Californian classic is a wonderful main course salad. With its smooth textures of avocado and Roquefort cheese mixed with crispy bacon bits, cooked chicken, and crunchy cos lettuce leaves, it is bound to satisfy. A tarragon vinaigrette helps to bring the whole dish together.

20-25 MINS   **5 MINS**

SERVES 4-6

1.8kg (4lb) whole cooked chicken or 500g (1lb 2oz) cooked skinless, boneless chicken

6 unsmoked back bacon rashers, sliced

2 avocados

juice of 1 lemon

1 shallot, finely chopped

500g (1lb 2lb) large cos lettuce or Little Gem lettuces, leaves sliced into strips

2 large tomatoes, cored and sliced

85g (3oz) Roquefort or other blue cheese, crumbled

For the vinaigrette

4 tbsp red wine vinegar

2 tsp Dijon mustard

½ tsp salt

¼ tsp pepper

175ml (6fl oz) vegetable oil

3 sprigs of tarragon, leaves picked and finely chopped

1 If using a whole cooked chicken, remove the meat from the bones, discarding all skin and any gristle, and cut into thin slices.

2 To make the vinaigrette, put the vinegar, mustard, salt, and pepper in a small bowl and whisk together. Add the oil in a steady stream, whisking constantly. The dressing will emulsify and thicken slightly. Stir the chopped tarragon into the dressing and taste for seasoning, adjusting it if needed.

3 Heat a small frying pan over a medium heat and cook the bacon strips until golden and crispy and the fat has rendered. Remove with a slotted spoon and drain on kitchen paper to blot off any excess fat.

5 Cut lengthways around the avocados, remove the stone, peel, and thinly slice. Toss the avocado slices gently in the lemon juice to prevent any discolouration.

6 Toss the chicken, shallot, and lettuce with a little of the dressing. Arrange in bowls with all the other ingredients added, and drizzle more vinaigrette on top before serving.

variation

sweetcorn, avocado, and bacon salad

Omit the chicken. Blanch 4 shucked corn cobs in boiling, lightly salted water for 3–4 minutes. Drain, cool, then cut off the kernels (p155). Make the rest of the salad in the same way, adding the corn at step 6 instead of the chicken.

Season's best **chillies**

Chillies come in hundreds of varieties, colours, shapes, and sizes, and ripen in high summer. They can add a tingle or an explosive fieriness. Chilli lovers don't just taste heat, but can detect the complex flavours of each variety. Chillies go wonderfully with cheeses, seafood, meats, poultry, and game. Add them to pasta and pulses, or to enhance many fruit and vegetable dishes.

Native to tropical regions, chillies are in such huge demand worldwide, they are now also grown in temperate areas, in polytunnels to protect them from the elements.

Jalapeño These are green, some with dark patches, torpedo-shaped, and quite fat with crisp, thick flesh. Sometimes roasted and peeled, they have a light flavour and are medium-hot. They are sweeter and less hot when red and fully ripe. Also sold *en escabeche* (pickled), they are widely used as a table condiment.

Piri piri This fiery chilli is used in Portuguese piri piri sauce, made with lemon, spices, and herbs.

Scotch bonnet Yellow-green to orange-red, with a wrinkled top and flattened base, the Scotch bonnet chilli is very hot and has a deep, fruity, smoky flavour, similar to the habanero. It is used in many Caribbean hot sauces and in jerk seasoning.

how to deseed and cut chillies

Choose a type of chilli to suit your recipe, but if you are not a fan of heat, removing the seeds and membranes may reduce some potency. Although some chillies are added whole, they are usually shredded or chopped before use.

1 Cut the chilli lengthways in half. Using the tip of your knife, scrape out the seeds and remove the membrane and stem.

2 Flatten each chilli half with your hand and slice lengthways into thin strips. Use like this, or chop.

3 To chop, hold the strips firmly together and slice crossways to make equal-size pieces. The hotter the chilli, the finer it is chopped.

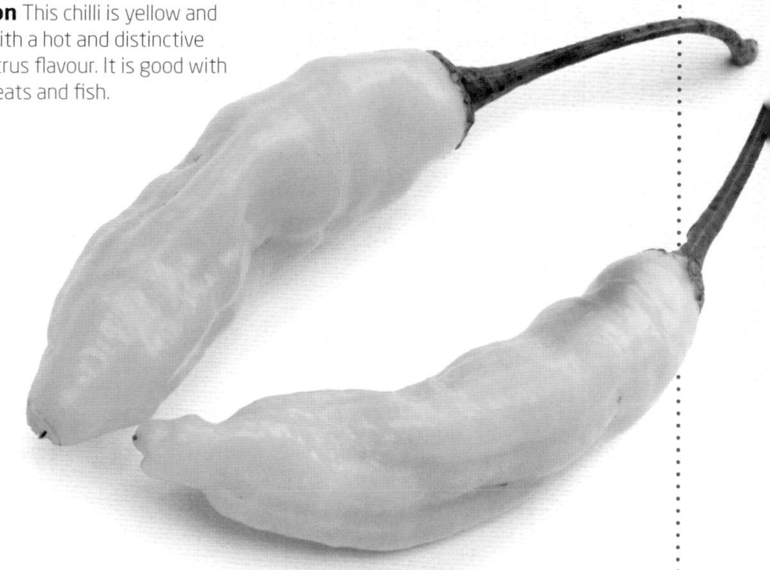

Aji Limon This chilli is yellow and crinkly with a hot and distinctive herby, citrus flavour. It is good with white meats and fish.

Serrano has a distinctive bullet shape.

Serrano This Mexican chilli is mid-green, cylindrical, and crisp-textured, with a concentrated, fresh, grassy flavour and very pungent seeds and veins. It ripens to bright red, and is commonly used in sauces.

Thai Used fresh and dried, this slender chilli is bright red or green, with a lingering heat. Add whole to curries and stir-fries or chop for pastes and dips.

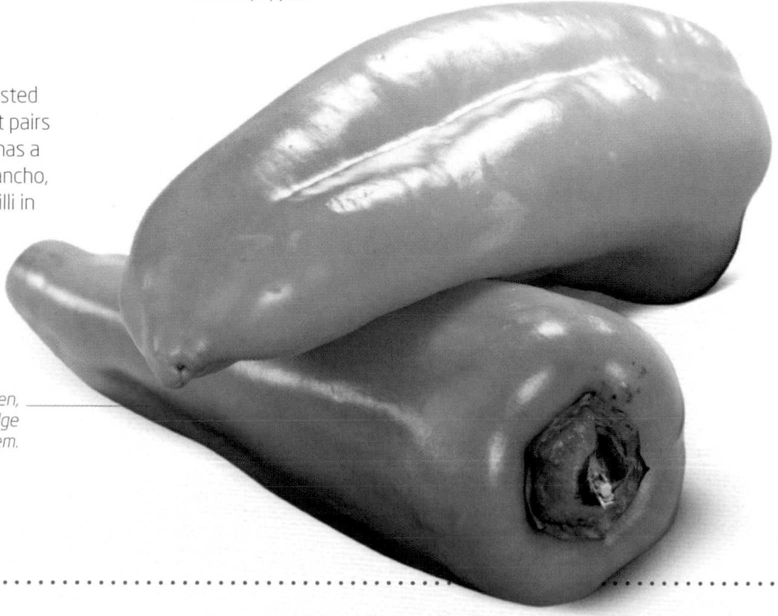

In Thailand, these are offered chopped in fish sauce instead of salt and pepper.

Poblano This chilli is delicious roasted and peeled, then stuffed or fried. It pairs well with corn and tomatoes, and has a rich flavour. The dried form is the ancho, which is the most popular dried chilli in Mexico and the US.

Poblanos are large, green, and triangular, with a ridge around the base of the stem.

essentials
varieties available
Hundreds of varieties, from fairly mild poblanos and moderately hot jalapeños to extremely hot Scotch Bonnets. Also available dried (whole, flakes, or powder).

buy They should be shiny, smooth-skinned, and firm.

store They can be refrigerated for a week or two.

cook In curries, stews, casseroles, salsas, rubs, marinades, and sauces. Stuff and roast or grill large ones. Good in chocolate desserts, and also in some fruit ones.

preserve Freeze, dry, or preserve in oil.

recipe ideas
Chipotle chicken p184

Cucumber-chilli salad p201

Hot chilli sauce p198

Scallops with sweet chilli sauce p160

Spicy chicken balls with chilli and ginger sauce p143

Tomato and chilli jam p232

chicken with pancetta, peas, and mint

Fresh peas and mint are a perfect match, and epitomize the flavours and aromas of summer. Here they are incorporated into a tasty chicken stew that requires minimal effort.

🥣 15 MINS   🍲 1 HR 45 MINS

SERVES 4

2 tbsp olive oil

4 large or 8 smaller chicken pieces, such as thighs and breasts, skin on

2 onions, finely chopped

200g (7oz) pancetta, diced, or bacon lardons

2 garlic cloves, grated or finely chopped

2 glasses of dry white wine

600ml (1 pint) hot chicken stock

salt and freshly ground black pepper

225g (8oz) peas (shelled weight)

handful of flat-leaf parsley, finely chopped

handful of mint leaves, finely chopped

1 Preheat the oven to 150°C (300°F/ Gas 2). Heat 1 tbsp of the oil in a large flameproof casserole (preferably cast-iron) over a medium heat. Add the chicken pieces and cook for about 8 minutes until golden all over. Remove from the casserole and set aside.

2 Reduce the heat to low and add the remaining oil and onions to the casserole. Cook gently for about 5 minutes until soft and translucent, then add the pancetta or bacon. Increase the heat a little and cook for a further 5 minutes until the pancetta or bacon is golden. Stir in the garlic, then pour in the wine. Increase the heat to high and simmer for a few minutes until the alcohol has evaporated.

3 Add the stock and bring to the boil once again. Season with salt and pepper, tip in the peas, and stir through. Return the chicken pieces to the casserole. Stir through the parsley and mint, cover with a lid, and transfer to the oven to cook for 1½ hours. Check the level of liquid occasionally while cooking – it needs to be fairly dry, but if it does need topping up, just add a little hot water. Serve hot with fresh crusty bread or sautéed potatoes.

lemongrass chicken

A delicious, warm Southeast Asian salad with chillies, spring onions, and cucumber. As chillies can vary wildly in strength, choose ones as mild or as fiery as you dare for this dish.

🥣 45-55 MINS PLUS MARINATING   🍲 10 MINS

SERVES 4

2 lemongrass stalks, trimmed, tough outer leaves removed and finely chopped

2 garlic cloves, finely chopped

3 tbsp fish sauce (nam pla), more if needed

¼ tsp freshly ground black pepper

8 large skinless, boneless chicken thighs, about 1.1kg (2½lb) total weight, cut into 2.5cm (1in) cubes

1 small cucumber

leaves from ½ head of round lettuce

125g (4½oz) bean sprouts

leaves from 1 small bunch of basil, preferably Asian basil

2 tbsp oil

2 red chillies, finely sliced

1 tsp sugar

3 spring onions, trimmed and sliced

30g (1oz) roasted unsalted peanuts

1 Combine the lemongrass, garlic, 2 tbsp of the fish sauce, and the black pepper in a large bowl and mix well. Add the chicken and toss until well coated. Cover the bowl tightly and chill in the fridge for at least 1 hour and up to 24 hours.

2 Trim the cucumber and, with a vegetable peeler, remove strips of skin to create a striped effect. Slice the cucumber in half lengthways, then slice each half finely. Arrange the lettuce, bean sprouts, half the basil, and the cucumber in piles on plates. Cover tightly and chill.

3 Heat a wok over a high heat until hot. Drizzle in the oil to coat the bottom and sides. Continue heating until the oil is hot. Add the chicken and marinade and stir-fry, stirring and tossing frequently, for 8–10 minutes, until the chicken is golden.

4 Add the remaining fish sauce, the chillies, sugar, and spring onions. Stir-fry for about 1 minute. Add the remaining basil and toss quickly to mix. Taste for seasoning, adding more fish sauce, if necessary. Serve the chicken on the salads and scatter a few peanuts over each serving.

paneer and sweet pepper curry

Paneer is a very mild, unsalted cheese with a dense, crumbly texture and fresh flavour that benefits from the stronger flavours of pepper, chilli, tomato, and spices in this curry.

🥣 15 MINS   🍲 40 MINS

SERVES 8

4 tbsp ghee or vegetable oil

2 x 250g packets paneer, cubed

10cm (4in) piece of fresh root ginger, peeled and sliced

3 red chillies, deseeded and finely chopped

2 tbsp dried curry leaves, crushed

2 tsp cumin seeds

4 tsp garam masala

2 tsp ground turmeric

8 red peppers, deseeded and sliced

8 tomatoes, skinned (p197) and roughly chopped

salt and freshly ground black pepper

bunch of coriander, finely chopped

1 Heat half of the ghee or oil in a large wide pan over a medium-high heat, add the paneer, and cook for 5–8 minutes, or until golden all over. Keep turning the pieces so they don't turn too brown. Remove with a slotted spoon and set aside.

2 Heat the remaining oil or ghee in the pan. Add the ginger, chillies, curry leaves, cumin, garam masala, and turmeric, and stir well to coat with the oil or ghee. Add the peppers and cook over a low heat for 10 minutes, or until they begin to soften.

3 Add the tomatoes and cook for 10 minutes. Return the paneer to the pan, season with salt and pepper, then simmer gently for 10–15 minutes. Stir through the coriander and serve with rice, chapati, or naan bread.

gado gado

This tasty Indonesian dish is a combination of both cooked and uncooked ingredients – including chilli, sweetcorn, green beans, and cucumber – and literally means "mix mix".

🥣 20 MINS   🍲 20 MINS

SPECIAL EQUIPMENT ▪ food processor

SERVES 8

4 corn on the cob

350g (12oz) green beans, trimmed

550g (1¼lb) potatoes, unpeeled

450g (1lb) roasted peanuts

4 garlic cloves

3 red chillies, deseeded

salt and freshly ground black pepper

2 tsp demerara sugar

juice of 1 lime

4 carrots, finely sliced

200g (7oz) bean sprouts

half a cucumber, chopped into bite-sized pieces

6 eggs, hard-boiled, shelled, and quartered

handful of coriander, chopped

1 Cook the corn on the cob in a pan of boiling salted water for 6–8 minutes, or until soft. Add the green beans for the last 5 minutes of cooking time. Drain, slice the corn on the cob into chunky rings, and place them and the green beans in a large, shallow serving bowl. Meanwhile, cook the potatoes in a pan of boiling salted water for about 15 minutes, or until just beginning to soften. Drain and set aside to cool, then slice and add to the sweetcorn and beans.

2 Put the peanuts, garlic, and chillies in a food processor and blitz until finely ground. Season with salt and pepper. Add a little water and blitz again to make a paste. Add the sugar and lime juice and blitz again, adding more water if needed – the paste should be smooth, but not too runny.

3 Add the carrots, bean sprouts, and cucumber to the cooked vegetables, then pour over the sauce and toss together. Top with the hard-boiled eggs and coriander, and serve.

crispy beef and vegetables

Use fat red chillies, which are relatively mild, for this dish – it's their colour and gentle heat you want, so they won't mask the flavours of the spring onions, sugarsnap peas, and Swiss chard.

 15 MINS 　　 30 MINS

SERVES 4

1½ tbsp cornflour

1 large egg

salt and freshly ground black pepper

2 tbsp vegetable oil

550g (1¼lb) beef topside, cut into thin strips

4 spring onions, trimmed and sliced in four lengthways

1-2 red chillies, finely shredded

1 large garlic clove, finely sliced

200g (7oz) sugarsnap peas, shredded

4-6 Swiss chard leaves, shredded

1½ tbsp dark soy sauce

1½ tbsp rice wine or dry sherry

2 tsp sugar

1 Put the cornflour and egg in a mixing bowl, season with salt and pepper, and mix together well. Heat 1 tbsp of the oil in a wok, dip the beef into the cornflour mixture, coat well, and add a few pieces at a time to the wok. Add more oil, if you need to. Cook for 2 minutes, or until crispy and golden. Remove with a slotted spoon and set aside.

2 Wipe out the wok with kitchen paper and heat the remaining oil. Add the spring onions, chillies, and garlic and cook for a few seconds, stirring all the time. Add the sugarsnap peas and Swiss chard and stir-fry for 2–3 minutes. Add the soy sauce, rice wine or sherry, and sugar, and cook until the sugar has dissolved and the alcohol has evaporated. Return the meat to the pan, toss together well, and serve with rice.

stuffed lamb, greek style

Olives, feta cheese, and thyme are all synonymous with Greek cuisine. Here they are combined with a succulent leg of lamb stuffed with red peppers and served with roasted tomatoes.

🥣 30 MINS 　　 🍲 2 HRS 15 MINS - 2 HRS 45 MINS

SERVES 4-6

1 leg of lamb, boned and butterflied (about 1.8kg/4lb after boning) (p45), ask your butcher to do this, or use a boneless shoulder

salt and freshly ground black pepper

2 tbsp olive oil

1 tbsp dried oregano

2 red peppers, deseeded and finely chopped

60g (2oz) stoned black olives, finely chopped

175g (6oz) feta cheese, finely chopped

3 red onions, roughly chopped

4-6 tomatoes, roughly chopped

450ml (15fl oz) red wine

a few sprigs of thyme

1 Preheat the oven to 160°C (325°F/ Gas 3). Lay the lamb out flat and season well. Rub both sides all over with the oil and oregano. Cover one side of the lamb with the red peppers, then the olives, and then the feta. Starting from one end, roll up the lamb, tucking in any loose pieces to neaten it. Tie it up with butcher's string, so it is secure.

2 Heat a large flameproof casserole over a medium heat, add the lamb, and cook for 4-6 minutes on each side until it begins to colour. Add the red onions and tomatoes to the pan, and cook for a minute more, then pour in the wine. Bring to the boil, then reduce to a simmer and add some seasoning and the thyme. Cover with the lid and put in the oven for 2–2½ hours, or until cooked to your liking. Check occasionally that it's not drying out, and top up with a little hot water, if needed.

3 Remove from the oven, cover the meat loosely with foil, and leave to rest for 15 minutes. Remove the string and carve into slices. Serve with some of the sauce, together with baby roast potatoes with rosemary and wilted spinach.

pea and pancetta tart

The delicate aroma and crisp texture of freshly shelled peas translates into a sweet burst of flavour in this creamy tart.

🥣 **10 MINS**   🍲 **1 HR 15 MINS**   ❄️ **FREEZABLE**

SPECIAL EQUIPMENT ▪ 18cm (7in) round loose-bottomed straight-sided tart tin ▪ ceramic baking beans

SERVES 4–6

300g (10oz) ready-made shortcrust pastry

3 eggs, 1 lightly beaten, for egg wash

1 tbsp olive oil

1 onion, finely chopped

salt and freshly ground black pepper

125g (4½oz) pancetta, diced

6 sage leaves, roughly chopped

225g (8oz) peas (shelled weight)

150ml (5fl oz) double cream

1 Preheat the oven to 200°C (400°F/Gas 6). Roll out the pastry on a floured work surface to a large circle about 3mm (⅛in) thick and use to line a tart tin, pressing it into the corners. Trim away the excess and prick the bottom with a fork. Line the pastry shell with greaseproof paper and fill with ceramic baking beans. Bake in the oven for 15–20 minutes until the edges are golden. Remove the beans and paper, brush the bottom of the shell with a little of the egg wash, and return to the oven for 2–3 minutes to crisp. Remove from the oven and set aside. Reduce the oven temperature to 180°C (350°F/Gas 4).

2 Meanwhile, heat the oil in a large frying pan over a low heat. Add the onion and a pinch of salt, and cook gently for about 5 minutes until soft and translucent. Add the pancetta and sage, increase the heat a little, and cook for 6–8 minutes until the pancetta is golden and crispy. Stir through the peas, and then season well with salt and pepper.

3 Spoon the onion and pancetta mixture into the pastry shell and level the top. Mix together the cream and eggs, season, and carefully pour the mixture over the filling to cover. Bake in the oven for 20–30 minutes until set and golden. Leave to cool for 10 minutes before releasing from the tin. Serve warm with a tomato salad.

chicken roasted with fennel and lemon

If you want to cook something easy, then one-pot recipes such as this are perfect. Creamy mashed potatoes are all that's needed to complement these sharp, tangy flavours.

🥣 **15 MINS PLUS MARINATING**   🍲 **1 HR**

SERVES 4

4 large chicken thighs, with skin on

sea salt and freshly ground black pepper

drizzle of extra virgin olive oil

juice of 1 lemon, and 2 small lemons, quartered

a few sprigs of thyme, leaves picked

1 large fennel bulb, roughly chopped

handful of green olives, pitted

1 large glass of dry white wine

1 Season the chicken thighs generously with salt and pepper. Drizzle over the oil and lemon juice, scatter over the thyme leaves, then transfer to a large bowl or plastic bag and leave to marinate for 30 minutes. Preheat the oven to 200°C (400°F/Gas 6).

2 Using a slotted spoon, transfer the chicken to a small roasting tin and add the fennel and lemon quarters. Season well and bake for 20 minutes.

3 Remove the roasting tin from the oven and add the olives and wine. Return to the oven and cook for a further 20 minutes, then turn the heat down to 180°C (350°F/Gas 4), cover the tin with foil, and cook for another 20 minutes, so the alcohol evaporates but the chicken remains moist. Check if the chicken is ready to eat by piercing the plumpest thigh with the tip of a sharp knife; if the juices run clear, it is cooked. Allow the chicken to rest for 5 minutes, then serve.

chicken, aubergine, and tomato tagine

Originally from North Africa, a tagine is a wonderfully aromatic stew that is cooked slowly and gently so that the meat and vegetables are richly flavoured and tender.

🥣 30 MINS   🍲 25 MINS

SERVES 8

3-4 tbsp olive oil

8 chicken pieces (thighs and breasts)

salt and freshly ground black pepper

2 aubergines, cut into bite-sized cubes

1 tsp ground cinnamon

2 onions, grated

3 red chillies, deseeded and finely chopped

2 tsp ground cumin

2 bay leaves

1.8kg (4lb) tomatoes

1 tbsp tomato purée

4 preserved lemons, halved and pith discarded

handful of coriander, finely chopped

1 Heat 1 tbsp of the oil in a large, wide heavy-based pan, season the chicken with salt and pepper, and add to the pan. Cook for 8 minutes, or until golden, stirring occasionally, then remove and set aside. Toss the aubergines in the cinnamon and add to the pan with 1 tbsp of the oil. Cook over a medium heat, stirring occasionally, for 10 minutes, or until golden. Add more oil if needed. Remove and set aside.

2 Add 1 tbsp of the oil to the pan, then add the onions, chillies, cumin, and bay leaves. Season well with salt and pepper and cook over a low heat for 5 minutes. Return the chicken and aubergine to the pan along with the tomatoes and tomato purée. Cover with a lid and simmer over a low heat for 25 minutes, topping up with hot water if it begins to look too dry.

3 Stir through the preserved lemon halves and coriander, and serve with plenty of fluffy couscous and some harissa on the side.

chipotle chicken

Hot and spicy, with the flavours of Mexico; add some deseeded and finely chopped chipotle chillies if you like it really hot. Serve with plain boiled rice, some soured cream, and tortilla bread.

🥣 15 MINS   🍲 1 HR 45 MINS   ❄ FREEZABLE

SERVES 4-6

1 tbsp olive oil

8 chicken thighs, with skin on

salt and freshly ground black pepper

1 onion, finely chopped

3 garlic cloves, finely chopped

½ tsp cumin seeds

2 red peppers, deseeded and roughly chopped

4 tbsp chipotle paste or salsa

grated zest of ½ lime and juice of 1 lime

1 tbsp white wine vinegar

2 x 400g cans whole tomatoes

600ml (1 pint) hot chicken stock

400g can black beans, drained and rinsed

1 cinnamon stick

handful of coriander, leaves roughly chopped

1 avocado, stoned, peeled, and chopped into bite-sized pieces (optional)

1 Preheat the oven to 180°C (350°F/Gas 4). Heat the oil in a large flameproof casserole over a medium to high heat. Season the chicken with salt and pepper and cook for 6–8 minutes until golden. Remove and set aside. Lower the heat, add the onion, garlic, and cumin seeds, and cook for 1 minute. Add the peppers and cook for 5 minutes. Return the chicken to the casserole and stir in the chipotle paste. Add the lime zest, juice, and vinegar, increase the heat, and let the sauce bubble for a few minutes.

2 Add the tomatoes and a little stock and bring to the boil. Pour in the remaining stock and add the beans. Boil for 2–3 minutes then reduce to a simmer. Add the cinnamon stick and some pepper, cover with a lid, and put in the oven for 1½ hours. Top up with water occasionally if needed. Remove the cinnamon stick, stir in most of the coriander, and top with avocado, if using. Sprinkle over the remaining coriander leaves to serve.

pea and mint risotto

Risotto is the perfect foil for delicate flavours and this one is beautifully scented with summer herbs.

🥣 10 MINS   🍲 25 MINS   ❄ FREEZABLE

SERVES 4

1.1 litres (2 pints) light vegetable stock

1 tbsp olive oil

knob of butter

1 onion, finely chopped

salt and freshly ground black pepper

350g (12oz) risotto rice, such as Arborio

1 large glass of dry white wine

150g (5½oz) peas (shelled weight)

50g (1¾oz) Parmesan cheese, grated

handful of mint leaves

handful of basil leaves

1 First, pour the stock into a large pan and heat to a gentle simmer.

2 Heat the oil and butter in a large non-stick frying pan over a low heat. Add the onion and a pinch of salt.

Sweat for 5 minutes until soft and translucent, then stir through the rice, making sure that the grains are completely coated. Increase the heat to medium-high, pour in the wine, and let it simmer for a couple of minutes until the alcohol has evaporated.

3 Reduce the heat slightly and add the simmering stock a ladleful or two at a time, stirring frequently with a wooden spoon; when each addition of stock has been absorbed, add some more. Continue like this for about 20 minutes until the rice is cooked; it should be slightly al dente so that it still has a bite to it.

4 Stir through the peas, Parmesan, mint, and basil. Season well with salt and pepper and serve hot.

summer frittata with ratatouille

While the eggs cook slowly in this Italian-style omelette, you can sit back and enjoy a glass of wine. Use any vegetables you have to hand to make the filling, which can be prepared up to 24 hours ahead and kept, tightly covered, in the fridge. Cook the frittata just before serving.

🥣 20-25 MINS 🍲 20-25 MINS

SERVES 3-4

1 small aubergine

1 courgette

salt and freshly ground black pepper

4 tbsp olive oil, plus more if needed

1 green pepper, sliced into strips

1 onion, thinly sliced

250g (9oz) tomatoes, skinned (p197), deseeded and chopped, or 200g can chopped tomatoes

2 garlic cloves, finely chopped

5-7 thyme sprigs, leaves picked, plus a few sprigs to decorate

½ tsp ground coriander

1 large bouquet garni (10-12 sprigs of parsley, 4-5 sprigs of thyme, and 2 bay leaves)

6 eggs

15-30g (½-1oz) butter

1 Trim the aubergine and cut into 1cm (½in) chunks. Cut the courgette into 1cm (½in) slices. Put the aubergine and courgette on a tray and sprinkle generously with salt. Leave for 30 minutes, then place in a colander, rinse, and pat dry with kitchen paper.

2 To make the ratatouille, heat about half the oil in a frying pan. Add the aubergine to the pan and stir-fry for 3-5 minutes, until browned. Transfer to a bowl with a slotted spoon. Repeat with the courgette slices.

3 Add the green pepper to the pan with a little more oil and stir-fry until it is softened; remove to the bowl. Heat about 1 tbsp more oil in the pan, add the onion, and sauté for 2-3 minutes, until soft and slightly translucent.

4 Return the aubergine, courgette, and pepper to the pan, and add the tomatoes, garlic, salt, pepper, thyme, coriander, and the bouquet garni. Stir until well mixed. Cover and cook for 10-15 minutes, until tender. Remove and discard the bouquet garni. Leave to cool.

5 Whisk the eggs in a bowl until completely mixed. Stir in the ratatouille mixture thoroughly and season well with salt and pepper.

6 Wipe the frying pan; melt the butter over a medium heat until foaming, then add the egg mixture. Reduce the heat, cover, and cook very gently for 20-25 minutes, until the centre is set and the base is cooked and lightly browned when you lift the edge with a palette knife. Invert the

frittata onto a large warmed plate and decorate with the reserved thyme sprigs. Cut the frittata into wedges and serve.

variation

aubergine, potato, and feta cheese frittata

Omit the courgette, pepper, and tomatoes. Fry 1 large, diced aubergine with 1 finely sliced onion in 6 tbsp olive oil for 5 minutes, stirring until soft. Add 350g (12oz) cooked, sliced new potatoes. Cook, stirring gently, for 2 minutes, season with ½ tsp ground cinnamon and the thyme leaves, then tip into a bowl. Continue at step 5 but scatter 115g (4oz) crumbled feta cheese over the egg mix before covering and cooking. Slide out onto a plate, don't invert.

Season's best aubergine

Aubergine is also known as eggplant, eggfruit, and brinjal. It was named *mala insana* (apple of insanity) by the Ancient Romans, who thought it was poisonous. It has slightly bitter, tender flesh. It is at its best in high summer, but is in season throughout summer and autumn. Its flesh acts like a sponge, soaking up flavours and liquid, and works well with sweet spices, oregano, ham, lamb, mushrooms, cheeses, peppers, olives, and tomatoes.

Aubergine is grown all over the world in many shapes and sizes. Native to tropical Asia, it needs plenty of warmth so, in some areas, is grown in glasshouses and polytunnels.

Baby aubergine Perfect for curries and South-Eastern dishes, they have thinner skins than their larger relative and have a sweet, delicate flavour.

Oval deep purple aubergine
The familiar, fat, elongated aubergine develops a complex flavour and silky texture when cooked. It is good thickly sliced and grilled, or roasted whole and then puréed with spices.

The skin keeps its attractive mottled stripes even when cooked.

Italian striped aubergine
Rosa Bianca, an heirloom variety, has firm, creamy flesh, which makes it a choice ingredient for melanzane alla parmigiana.

essentials
varieties available
Oval deep purple, baby purple, and Italian striped (round and long white ones).

buy Look for relatively small, firm aubergines with glossy skin and bright green cap and stalk.

store Use it on the day of purchase, or at least by the next day. Keep in a cool spot until needed.

cook Bake or roast, braise, grill, barbecue or chargrill, stir-fry, sauté, coat in batter and deep-fry, curry, or stew.

preserve Griddle slices, then freeze.

recipe ideas
Aubergine massaman curry p289

Aubergines stuffed with tomato rice p187

Baba ganoush p164

Hot-spiced aubergine chutney p244

Melanzane alla parmigiana p304

potato and pea curry

Here is a vegetarian curry that puts summer vegetables to good use; spicing up peas, tomatoes, and new potatoes. It doesn't take long to make either.

🥣 10 MINS 🍲 30 MINS

SERVES 4

1 tbsp sunflower oil

2.5cm (1in) piece of fresh root ginger, peeled and finely chopped

2–3 green chillies, deseeded and finely chopped

1 tsp cumin seeds

1 tsp mustard seeds

small handful of curry leaves

6 tomatoes, skinned (p197) and chopped

675g (1½lb) new potatoes, peeled and cubed

1 tsp ground turmeric

300ml (10fl oz) hot vegetable stock

75g (2½oz) peas (shelled weight)

salt and freshly ground black pepper

handful of coriander, finely chopped

1 Heat the oil in a large frying pan over a medium heat. Add the ginger, chillies, cumin seeds, and mustard seeds, and crumble in the curry leaves. Cook for a couple of minutes until the mustard seeds start to pop. Add the tomatoes, stir through, and cook for a few more minutes.

2 Add the potatoes and turmeric, and pour in the stock. Bring to the boil, reduce the heat slightly, cover, and simmer for about 15 minutes.

3 Tip in the peas, stir through, and cook for a further 5–10 minutes. Season well with salt and pepper, and stir through the coriander. Serve hot with rice or naan bread.

pasta with aubergine sauce

Aubergines have a mild smoky flavour and spongy flesh that softens when cooked. This recipe calls for a bulbous, deep purple variety to accompany tomatoes and pesto sauce.

🥣 10 MINS 🍲 25 MINS

SERVES 4

1 large aubergine, cut into cubes

salt and freshly ground black pepper

2–3 tbsp olive oil

½ small glass of red wine

1 onion, finely diced

2 garlic cloves, grated or finely chopped

6 ripe tomatoes, skinned (p197) and chopped

pinch of dried oregano

1 tsp red pesto

350g (12oz) large pasta shells

Parmesan cheese, grated, to serve (optional)

1 Place the aubergine cubes in a colander and sprinkle well with salt. Cover with a plate, then place a heavy weight on top for 10 minutes to extract the bitter juices.

2 Heat the oil in a large frying pan over a medium heat, add the aubergine cubes, and cook for 4–6 minutes, or until they turn golden. Add the wine, increase the heat, and allow to boil for a couple of minutes. Stir in the onion and garlic and cook for a few seconds, then add the tomatoes and stir. Add the oregano and pesto, part-cover and simmer very gently for 10–15 minutes, stirring occasionally.

3 Meanwhile, cook the pasta in a large pan of boiling salted water for about 12 minutes, or until it is tender but still al dente. Drain, keeping back a tiny amount of the cooking water. Return the pasta to the pan. Thin the sauce with a little of the pasta water if necessary. Taste the sauce and season with salt and pepper. Toss with the pasta, sprinkle with grated Parmesan cheese, if using, and serve.

variation

pasta with yellow pepper sauce

Prepare in the same way, but substitute 2 large yellow peppers for the aubergine. Omit step 1.

aubergines stuffed with tomato rice

Stuffed aubergines are popular in the Middle East. Use a larger variety so that when you scoop out the centre flesh there is enough left around the edge to keep its shape.

🥣 10 MINS 🍲 30 MINS

SERVES 4

4 aubergines, halved lengthways

2 tbsp olive oil, plus extra for brushing

200g (7oz) long-grain rice, rinsed

300ml (10fl oz) tomato juice

1 tsp sugar

salt and freshly ground black pepper

1 onion, finely chopped

small handful of dill, finely chopped

1 Preheat the oven to 200°C (400°F/ Gas 6). Scoop out the flesh from the aubergines, chop the flesh into bite-sized chunks, and set aside. Sit the shells in a roasting tin and brush with olive oil. Cover with foil and roast in the oven for 10–15 minutes while you cook the rice.

2 Cook the rice in a pan of boiling salted water for about 10 minutes, or until it is tender. Drain if needed, then pour over the tomato juice. Sprinkle over the sugar and season well with salt and pepper. Stir the rice until the tomato juice is absorbed.

3 Heat 1 tbsp of the oil in a large frying pan over a medium heat, add the onion, dill, and a pinch of salt, and cook for 3–4 minutes until the onion is soft and translucent. Then add the reserved aubergine flesh and cook for a further 5 minutes. Season with black pepper, add the tomato rice mixture, and stir well.

4 Remove the aubergine shells from the oven and carefully spoon the mixture into them. Drizzle over the remaining oil and return to the oven for a further 5 minutes. Serve hot with a crisp green salad.

variation

spicy stuffed aubergines with feta cheese

Prepare in the same way, but add 2 deseeded, chopped red chillies to the tomato rice and crumble over 200g (7oz) feta cheese before drizzling with oil at step 4.

roast lamb with cherry tomatoes and new potatoes

A little redcurrant jelly brings out the sweetness of these summer tomatoes roasted on the vine. Cooking the baby potatoes in their skins helps to retain all their flavour, too.

15 MINS   1 HR 30 MINS

SERVES 4

1 tbsp olive oil

900g (2lb) butterflied leg of lamb (p45)

1.1kg (2½lb) baby new potatoes

salt and freshly ground black pepper

handful of thyme sprigs

12–16 cherry tomatoes on the vine

1–2 tsp redcurrant jelly

1 Preheat the oven to 190°C (375°F/ Gas 5). Pour half the oil into a large roasting tin and set over a high heat. When very hot, add the lamb and cook for 4–6 minutes, or until browned, then turn and brown the other side for 4–6 minutes.

2 Toss the new potatoes with the remaining oil and add to the tin. Season well with salt and pepper, and add the thyme. Put into the oven to cook for 45 minutes, if you like your lamb rare, 1 hour for medium, and 1¼ hours for well done. Add the tomatoes for the last 15 minutes

of cooking. Remove the lamb and cover with foil to keep warm while it rests.

3 Meanwhile, make the gravy. Using a slotted spoon, transfer the potatoes and tomatoes to a serving dish and keep warm. Place the tin on the unlit hob and tilt to one side. Skim away any fat, then add the redcurrant jelly and set over a high heat. Stir well, adding a little boiling water until the gravy reaches the required consistency. Allow to boil, then reduce to a simmer and cook for a couple of minutes. Slice the lamb and serve with the potatoes, tomatoes, gravy, and some mint sauce or jelly on the side.

swiss chard and gruyère cheese tart

Select young, tender stalks of Swiss chard with unblemished dark green leaves. Its slightly bitter, assertive flavour works well with the rich cheese filling of this tart.

15 MINS   1 HR   ❄ FREEZABLE

SPECIAL EQUIPMENT ▪ 23cm (9in) round loose-bottomed fluted tart tin ▪ ceramic baking beans

SERVES 6

300g (10oz) ready-made shortcrust pastry

3 eggs, 1 lightly beaten for egg wash

1 tbsp olive oil

1 onion, finely chopped

salt and freshly ground black pepper

2 garlic cloves, grated or finely chopped

a few sprigs of rosemary, leaves picked and finely chopped

250g (9oz) Swiss chard, stalks trimmed

125g (4½oz) Gruyère cheese, grated

125g (4½oz) feta cheese, cubed

200ml (7fl oz) double cream or whipping cream

1 Preheat the oven to 200°C (400°F/ Gas 6). Roll out the pastry on a floured work surface and use to line a tart tin. Trim away the excess, line the pastry shell with greaseproof paper, and fill with ceramic baking beans. Bake in the oven for 15–30 minutes until the edges are golden. Remove the beans and paper, and brush the bottom of the shell with a little of the egg wash. Return to the oven for 1–2 minutes to crisp. Remove

from the oven and set aside. Reduce the oven temperature to 180°C (350°F/Gas 4).

2 Heat the oil in a pan over a low heat. Add the onion and salt and sweat gently for about 5 minutes until soft and translucent. Add the garlic and rosemary and cook for a few seconds, then roughly chop the Swiss chard and add to the pan. Stir for about 5 minutes until it wilts.

3 Spoon the onion and chard mixture into the pastry shell. Scatter evenly with the Gruyère and feta cheeses, and season. Mix together the cream and the 2 eggs until well combined, then carefully pour over the tart filling. Bake in the oven for 30–40 minutes until set and golden. Leave to cool for 10 minutes before releasing from the tin. Serve warm.

variation

spinach and gruyère tart

Substitute the Swiss chard for 250g (9oz) spinach, cooking until just wilted in step 2. Continue with the recipe.

mediterranean burgers

The chopped red peppers in these well-seasoned gourmet burgers give a delicious crunch and hint of sweetness. You could also barbecue the burgers for extra flavour.

🥣 **10 MINS**　🍲 **15 MINS**

SERVES 4

500g (1lb 2oz) beef mince

1 onion, finely chopped

2 garlic cloves, finely chopped

1 tbsp dried oregano

2 red peppers, deseeded and finely chopped

handful of basil leaves, finely chopped

handful of flat-leaf parsley, finely chopped

sea salt and freshly ground black pepper

splash of red wine

knob of butter

1 In a large bowl, combine the beef mince, onion, garlic, dried oregano, red peppers, basil leaves, and parsley. Season and add a splash of red wine.

2 Using your hands, mix the ingredients together until well combined. Divide the mixture into 4 large balls and flatten into burgers.

3 Melt the butter in a frying pan over a medium-high heat, and fry the burgers for 3–5 minutes on each side until browned and cooked through. Serve sandwiched in a fresh bun or roll, with fresh salad leaves and tomato.

oriental halibut en papillote

Noodles and stir-fried crisp vegetables would be excellent alongside this fragrant dish.

🥣 **15-20 MINS**　🍲 **10-12 MINS**

SERVES 4

125g (4½oz) mangetout, trimmed

4 garlic cloves, finely chopped

2.5cm (1in) piece of fresh root ginger, peeled and finely chopped

2 tbsp black bean sauce

3 tbsp light soy sauce

2 tbsp dry sherry

½ tsp granulated sugar

1 tbsp sesame oil

2 tbsp vegetable oil, for brushing

1 egg

salt

4 x 175g (6oz) skinned halibut fillets or steaks

4 spring onions, trimmed and thinly sliced

1 Bring a pan of salted water to the boil. Add the mangetout and simmer for 1–2 minutes. Combine the garlic, ginger, black bean sauce, soy sauce, sherry, sugar, and sesame oil in a bowl. Set aside.

2 Fold a sheet of baking parchment (about 30 x 34.5cm/12 x 15in) in half and draw a curve with a pencil to make a heart shape when unfolded. It should be large enough to leave a 7.5cm (3in) border around a fish fillet.

Cut out the heart shape with scissors. Repeat to make 4 paper hearts. Open each out and brush with the vegetable oil, leaving a border about 2.5cm (1in) wide at the edges.

3 Put the egg and ½ tsp salt in a small bowl and beat together. Brush this egg glaze evenly on the border of each of the paper hearts.

4 Preheat the oven to 200°C (400°F/ Gas 6). Rinse the fish fillets and pat dry with kitchen paper. Arrange a quarter of the mangetout on one side of each paper heart and set a halibut fillet on top.

5 Spoon a quarter of the oriental seasoning on top of each fillet and sprinkle with a quarter of the spring onions. Fold the paper over the fish and run your finger along the edge to stick the 2 sides of paper together. Make small pleats to seal the edges.

6 Twist the "tails" of each paper case to seal them, so that the filling does not ooze out during baking. Lay the cases on a baking sheet and bake for 10–12 minutes, until puffed and brown. Transfer to warmed plates, allowing each guest to open their own aromatic fish package.

sweet and sour duck with cherries

Really tart cherries are key to this dish from Limousin, central France, where cherries grow wild in the hedgerows.

🥣 30–35 MINS   🍲 1 HR 15 MINS – 1 HR 30 MINS

SPECIAL EQUIPMENT ▪ trussing needle and string

SERVES 2-3

1 duck, weighing about 1.8kg (4lb)

salt and freshly ground black pepper

1 tbsp vegetable oil

60g (2oz) granulated sugar

75ml (2½fl oz) red wine vinegar

375ml (13fl oz) rich chicken stock

375g (13oz) tart cherries, stoned

sprigs of flat-leaf parsley, to serve (optional)

1 Wipe the inside of the duck with kitchen paper and season inside and out. Pull off and discard any loose bits of fat. With a small knife, remove the wishbone to make the duck easier to carve later. Set the duck breast-side up. Push the legs back and down. Push a trussing needle into the flesh at the knee joint, through the bird and out, through the other knee joint. Turn the duck over. Pull the neck skin over the neck cavity and tuck the wing tips over it. Push the needle through one of the wings into the neck skin. Continue under the backbone of the duck to the other side. Repeat with the second wing.

2 Preheat the oven to 220°C (425°F/Gas 7). Turn the duck onto its side. Pull the ends of the string firmly together, and tie them together securely. Turn the duck breast-side up. Tuck the tail into the cavity of the bird and fold over the top skin. Push the needle through the skin. Loop the string around one of the drumsticks, under the breastbone, and over the other drumstick. Tie the ends of the string together.

3 Heat the oil in a roasting tin. Set the duck on its side and roast in the oven for 15 minutes. Turn the duck over and roast for another 15 minutes. Spoon the fat from the roasting tin and discard. Prick the skin all over to release the fat. Reduce the temperature to 190°C (375°F/Gas 5). Turn the duck on to its breast and roast for another 15 minutes. Discard any melted fat. Finally, set the duck on its back and continue roasting for a further 15–20 minutes, until the juices run clear. Transfer to a warmed platter and cover with foil to rest and keep warm.

4 Put 75ml (2½fl oz) water and the sugar into a small heavy-based saucepan and heat gently, until the sugar is dissolved, stirring occasionally. Increase the heat and boil, without stirring, until the syrup starts to turn golden. Reduce the heat and cook to a deep golden caramel. Remove from the heat and let the bubbles subside. Pour in the vinegar. Simmer, stirring occasionally, for 3–5 minutes, until the caramel is dissolved and the mixture is reduced by half. Remove from the heat and set aside.

5 In a medium saucepan, combine the caramel vinegar and the stock. Add the cherries to the pan and simmer for 3–5 minutes, until just tender. Transfer the cherries to a bowl with a slotted spoon. Discard any remaining fat from the duck roasting tin. Add the caramel sauce and bring to the boil, stirring to dissolve the pan juices. Simmer until this sweet-sour sauce is reduced by half.

6 Discard the trussing string and carve the duck. Arrange the meat on warmed plates and spoon over some of the cherry sauce. Decorate with parsley sprigs, if you like, and serve at once. Serve the remaining cherry sauce separately.

fish tagine

This light dish of potatoes, red peppers, and sea bass has a lively mix of herbs and spices.

🍲 20 MINS PLUS MARINATING 🍲 1 HR 30 MINS

SPECIAL EQUIPMENT ▪ food processor

SERVES 4–6

1–2 tbsp olive oil

2 onions, sliced into rings

2 celery sticks, finely chopped

salt and freshly ground black pepper

3 garlic cloves, chopped

1 tsp ground ginger

1 tsp ground cumin

1 tsp sweet paprika

1 red chilli, deseeded and roughly chopped

1 preserved lemon, flesh only, finely chopped, or use grated zest of ½ lemon

2 carrots, sliced

2 red peppers, deseeded and roughly chopped

6 new potatoes, halved

about 600ml (1 pint) hot fish stock

900g (2lb) sea bass, cut into chunky pieces

3 tomatoes, deseeded and chopped into thin slices

squeeze of lemon juice

coriander leaves, to serve (optional)

1 Heat the oil in a large flameproof casserole or tagine over a medium heat, add the onions and celery, season, and cook for 5–6 minutes until soft. Stir in the garlic, ginger, cumin, paprika, chilli, lemon flesh or zest and cook for a few minutes. Then add the carrots and peppers and cook for 5 more minutes.

2 Add the potatoes and stock, bring to the boil, cover with the lid, and cook at a very low simmer for about 45 minutes, topping up with a little hot water if needed. Then add the fish and layer the tomatoes over the top, re-cover, and bring up to a simmer once again. Cook for a further 15–30 minutes until the fish is opaque and cooked through. Taste and season, if needed, add a squeeze of lemon juice, and stir through the coriander leaves, if using. Serve with fluffy couscous and lemon wedges to squeeze over.

salmon jungle curry

This is a hot fish curry with baby sweetcorn. Small green pea aubergines are a classic Thai ingredient that are each about the size of a grape and give a slightly bitter burst of flavour.

🍲 10 MINS 🍲 20 MINS

SERVES 4

2 tbsp vegetable oil

2 tbsp Thai green curry paste

3 garlic cloves, crushed

5cm (2in) piece fresh root ginger

2 red chillies, deseeded and cut into fine strips

400ml (14fl oz) coconut milk

splash of fish sauce (nam pla)

200g can bamboo shoots, drained

2 heaped tbsp pea aubergines (optional)

100g (3½oz) baby sweetcorn, halved diagonally

400g (14oz) skinned salmon, cut into 4cm (1½in) chunks

small handful of Thai basil leaves

1 Heat the oil in a large frying pan until hot. Add the Thai green curry paste and stir it around the pan to combine it with the oil.

2 Throw in the garlic, ginger, and chillies. Stir constantly for 2–3 minutes. Pour in the coconut milk, bring to the boil, then add a good splash of fish sauce, the bamboo shoots, pea aubergines (if using), and baby corn. Reduce the heat slightly and simmer for 5 minutes.

4 Add the salmon chunks and Thai basil leaves. Simmer for a further 5–10 minutes until the salmon is opaque and cooked through when tested with a fork. Season and serve hot with sticky Thai jasmine rice.

lamb fillet with tomato and basil salad

Garlic, chilli, rosemary, and parsley combine to add piquancy to this flash-grilled marinated lamb.

🍲 15 MINS PLUS MARINATING 🍲 20 MINS

SPECIAL EQUIPMENT ▪ barbecue or charcoal grill

SERVES 4

165g (1½lb) lamb fillet

3 tbsp olive oil

1 large garlic clove, crushed

1½ tbsp finely chopped flat-leaf parsley, plus extra to garnish

sprig of rosemary, leaves picked

small pinch of dried chilli flakes

salt and freshly ground black pepper

drizzle of extra virgin olive oil

For the tomato and basil salad

2 ripe plum tomatoes, cut into quarters lengthways

250g (9oz) cherry tomatoes on the vine, separated but still with their stems

125g (4½oz) yellow bell or cherry tomatoes, halved

small handful of basil leaves

1 small garlic clove, crushed

½ small red onion, thinly sliced into rings

1½ tbsp extra virgin olive oil

1 Trim the lamb of any fat. Mix together the olive oil, garlic, parsley, rosemary, and chilli flakes in a large bowl and season with salt and pepper. Add the lamb, massaging the marinade into the meat. Allow to marinate in the refrigerator for at least 1 hour.

2 Heat the barbecue or charcoal grill until hot. Grill the lamb over a medium heat for 8–10 minutes on each side for medium-rare, or until cooked to your liking. Remove to a plate, cover with foil, and leave to rest in a warm place for 20 minutes.

3 To make the salad, put all the ingredients in a bowl, season with salt and pepper, and toss gently. When ready to serve, slice the lamb diagonally and arrange on a serving platter. Scatter with the parsley leaves and a drizzle of extra virgin olive oil and serve accompanied by the salad.

pasta with no-cook tomato sauce

For a sauce that is this simple, you should select really ripe, plump tomatoes and pungent basil. Prepare it before you cook the pasta and the flavours will have time to develop.

5 MINS   **10 MINS**

SERVES 4

6 tomatoes, deseeded and roughly chopped

2 garlic gloves, grated or finely chopped

handful of basil leaves, torn

pinch of dried chilli flakes

3 tbsp extra virgin olive oil

salt and freshly ground black pepper

350g (12oz) farfalle

1 Put the tomatoes, garlic, basil, chilli flakes, and oil in a large bowl and season well with salt and pepper. Stir well to combine, then set aside while you cook the pasta – the flavours will develop.

2 Cook the pasta in a large pan of boiling salted water for 10 minutes, or until it is cooked but is still al dente. Drain well, then toss with the tomato sauce and serve.

sausage and tomato pie

Complemented by the oregano, sweet, plump tomatoes release their juices into this pie as it cooks, keeping the lightly spiced sausagemeat wonderfully moist.

15 MINS   **40 MINS**   **FREEZABLE**

SPECIAL EQUIPMENT ▪ 20cm (8in) square pie dish or fluted tart tin ▪ ceramic baking beans

SERVES 4

225g (8oz) ready-made shortcrust pastry

1 egg, lightly beaten

½ tbsp olive oil

1 onion, finely chopped

salt and freshly ground black pepper

400g (14oz) good-quality pork sausages, skinned

1 tsp dried oregano

4 tomatoes, sliced

1 Preheat the oven to 200°C (400°F/Gas 6). Roll out the pastry on a floured work surface and use to line a pie dish or tart tin. Trim away any excess, line the pastry shell with greaseproof paper, and fill with ceramic baking beans. Bake in the oven for 15–20 minutes until the edges are golden. Remove the beans and paper, brush the bottom of the pastry with a little of the beaten egg, and return to the oven for 2–3 minutes to crisp.

Remove from the oven and set aside. Reduce the oven temperature to 180°C (350°F/Gas 4).

2 Meanwhile, heat the oil in a large frying pan over a low heat. Add the onion and a pinch of salt and sweat gently for about 5 minutes until soft and translucent. Add the sausagemeat, breaking it up with a fork or the back of a spatula. Season well with salt and pepper and sprinkle over the oregano. Cook, stirring regularly, over a low-medium heat for about 10 minutes until no longer pink. Leave to cool, then mix in the remaining egg.

3 Spoon the sausage mixture into the pastry shell, then layer the tomatoes over the top. Bake in the oven for about 20 minutes until lightly golden. Leave to cool for about 10 minutes, then slice in the dish or tin. Serve with a crisp green salad.

sea bass in a salt crust

This classic dish from northern Italy is traditionally made using sea bass (known locally as branzino) but you could also use sea bream as an excellent alternative.

15 MINS   **22–25 MINS**

SERVES 4

1 whole sea bass (1.35–2kg/3–4½lb) trimmed and gutted, but not scaled

1kg (2¼lb) coarse sea salt

1–2 egg whites

1 Preheat the oven to 220°C (425°F/Gas 7). Gut the fish, making the smallest incision possible. Clean well and rinse – do not scale.

2 Spread a layer of salt over a large piece of foil on a baking tray. Arrange the fish on top. Moisten the remaining salt with the egg whites and a splash of water, if necessary. Pack this mixture on the fish to completely encase it.

3 Bake in the oven for 22–25 minutes. Lift the fish onto a serving dish. Take to the table and carefully chip off any remaining salt crust. Carefully peel away the skin and serve the fish straight from the bone. Accompany the fish with some aïoli or mayonnaise and a green salad.

pizza with tomatoes, olives, and capers

This thin-based Italian-style pizza is ideal for using up a glut of homegrown summer tomatoes.

🥣 **10 MINS PLUS RISING**   🍲 **15 MINS**   ❄ **FREEZABLE**

MAKES 1

2-3 tbsp passata

3 tomatoes, sliced

handful of pitted black olives

1-2 tsp capers, rinsed

pinch of freshly ground black pepper

For the pizza dough

125g (4½oz) strong white flour

pinch of salt

pinch of caster sugar

¾ tsp easy-blend dried yeast

1 tbsp olive oil

a little semolina, for sprinkling

1 Sift the flour, salt, and sugar into a bowl. Add the yeast. Stir in the oil and enough warm water to form a soft but not sticky dough (about 90ml/3fl oz).

2 Place the dough on a slightly floured surface and knead gently for several minutes until smooth and elastic. Return to the bowl, cover with oiled cling film, and leave in a warm place for about 40 minutes, until the dough has doubled in size.

3 Preheat the oven to its highest setting. Very lightly oil a baking tray and put it in the oven to get hot. The baking tray and the oil both need to be really hot before cooking the pizza.

4 Place the dough on a floured surface and roll it out as thinly as you can; about 25–30cm (10–12in) in diameter. Sprinkle the hot baking tray with a little semolina and transfer the pizza dough onto it.

5 Spoon the passata onto the pizza base, using the back of the spoon to smooth it out evenly. Top with the tomato slices, then arrange the olives and capers on top. Bake for 10–15 minutes, or until the crust and base are crisp and golden. Season with black pepper and serve.

sole bonne femme

The bones from the filleted sole are used to make the stock, which itself is the basis for this recipe's creamy sauce.

🥣 **30-35 MINS**   🍲 **25-30 MINS**

SPECIAL EQUIPMENT ▪ 20cm (8in) square baking dish

SERVES 4

15g (½oz) butter

250g (9oz) mushrooms, sliced

salt and freshly ground black pepper

2 shallots, finely chopped

2 Dover sole, 1kg (2¼lb) each, filleted, heads and bones reserved for the stock

For the fish stock

heads and bones from 2 Dover sole

1 onion, sliced

1 tsp peppercorns

3-5 sprigs of parsley

250ml (9fl oz) white wine or juice of 1 lemon

For the velouté sauce

30g (1oz) butter

2 tbsp plain flour

3 tbsp double cream

3 egg yolks

juice of ½ lemon, or to taste

1 Cut the washed fish heads and bones into 4–5 pieces. Put in a pan with the onion, 500ml (16fl oz) water, peppercorns, and parsley. Add the wine. Boil, then simmer for 20 minutes. Pour through a sieve into a second pan.

2 Preheat the oven to 180°C (350°F/ Gas 4). Melt the butter in a frying pan and add the mushrooms, salt, pepper, and 3–4 tbsp water. Cover with buttered foil and cook for 5 minutes.

3 Butter a baking dish and add the shallots. Fold each fillet in half, skin-side inwards, and place on the shallots. Season and half cover with stock. Top with buttered foil and cook in the oven for 15–18 minutes. Reserve the liquid.

4 Add the liquid and shallots to the stock and boil until reduced to 375ml (13fl oz). For the sauce, melt the butter in another pan and whisk in the flour. Cook for 1–2 minutes. Remove from the heat and cool. Strain the stock into the butter and flour, and boil, whisking until thickened, then simmer for 5 minutes. Remove from the heat and add the mushrooms and liquid.

5 Whisk the cream and egg yolks in a bowl, add a little of the hot sauce, and whisk to mix. Stir the cream mixture into the sauce in the pan. Return to the heat and cook gently for 2–3 minutes. Remove from the heat. Add lemon juice, salt, and pepper. Heat the grill. Arrange the fillets on flameproof plates, ladle the sauce over, and grill for 1–2 minutes. Serve at once.

chargrilled aubergine with spiced tomato sauce

Paprika, a spice made from dried sweet pepper pods, adds a lively flavour to this tomato sauce and complements the creamy flesh of the plump, ripe aubergines.

15 MINS   20 MINS

SERVES 4

2 large aubergines, cut into slices 1cm (½in) thick

salt and freshly ground black pepper

4 tbsp olive oil

2 garlic cloves, sliced

½ tsp paprika

4 large, ripe tomatoes, skinned (p197) and chopped

1 tbsp tomato purée

good pinch of sugar

1 Put the aubergines in a colander, sprinkle with salt, and weigh down with a plate. Leave to drain for 15 minutes, rinse, and pat dry with kitchen paper.

2 Meanwhile, heat 1 tbsp of the oil in a pan over a very low heat. Add the garlic and paprika and cook gently for a few seconds. Stir in the tomatoes, tomato purée, and sugar and cook fairly gently, stirring frequently, for about 10 minutes until pulpy. Season with salt and pepper.

3 Place a ridged cast-iron grill pan or a griddle pan over a medium-high heat until hot. Brush the aubergine slices with the remaining oil, then griddle for 3 minutes on each side until golden. Serve immediately with the sauce drizzled over, or in a bowl on the side.

melon and tomato salad

This refreshing salad, with its sweet and savoury dressing, can be made up to 6 hours ahead and kept, covered and without the dressing, in the fridge.

15–20 MINS PLUS CHILLING

SERVES 6

2 small orange- or yellow-fleshed melons, such as cantaloupe, about 1.35kg (3lb) total weight

1 medium green-fleshed melon, such as galia, about 1.35kg (3lb)

375g (13oz) cherry tomatoes

handful of mint

For the dressing

75ml (2½fl oz) port

juice of 2 lemons

2 tbsp honey

salt and freshly ground black pepper

1 Halve the melons, scoop out the seeds with a spoon, and discard.

2 Using a melon baller, cut balls from the flesh of each melon and place into a large bowl.

3 Remove the stalks from the cherry tomatoes. Immerse in a saucepan of boiling water very briefly, just until

the skins start to split, then plunge into a bowl of cold water. When cold, peel off the skins. Add the tomatoes to the melon.

4 Strip the mint leaves from the stalks, reserving some sprigs for garnish. Pile the mint leaves on a board and coarsely chop. Add the mint to the melon and tomatoes.

5 For the dressing, put the port in a bowl. Add the lemon juice, honey, salt, and pepper and whisk. Taste for seasoning. Pour the dressing over the melon, tomatoes, and mint. Stir gently and taste for seasoning, adding more of the dressing ingredients, if you like. Cover the bowl and refrigerate for about 1 hour, so the flavours mellow. Serve decorated with the reserved mint sprigs. It complements cold or cured meats especially well.

bread salad

This traditional Italian recipe (known as panzanella) is not only a great way to use up any leftover bread, but adds another dimension to the classic combination of tomatoes and basil.

15 MINS

SERVES 4

3 slices ciabatta or other rustic country-style bread, toasted and cut into chunky bite-sized cubes

2-3 tbsp olive oil

handful of basil leaves, torn

salt and freshly ground black pepper

2 red peppers, roasted, peeled (p171), and sliced

4 tomatoes, roughly chopped

handful of toasted pine nuts

125g (4½oz) Dolcelatte or other mild blue cheese, cut into bite-sized cubes

1 Put the bread cubes in a large bowl and drizzle over the oil. Add the basil and season with salt and pepper. Toss together and leave to stand for about 10 minutes, to allow the flavours to develop.

2 Add the peppers, tomatoes, pine nuts, and cheese and toss gently until everything is evenly mixed. Serve with cold cooked meats.

variation

summer vegetable bread salad

Prepare and dress the bread in the same way but with a small handful of fresh mint leaves instead of basil. Add 1 avocado, stoned, peeled, and diced, and tossed in lemon juice instead of the peppers. Add the tomatoes, roughly chopped, a large handful of raw, shelled peas, ¼ diced cucumber, and a handful of rocket. Season and toss gently. Serve with poached eggs or grilled gammon.

greek salad

A classic, deeply refreshing combination that needs very ripe, flavourful tomatoes. Make sure you use very tasty, pungent black olives, and an aromatic, strong extra virgin olive oil.

25-30 MINS PLUS STANDING

SERVES 6-8

2 small cucumbers

1kg (2¼lb) tomatoes

1 red onion

2 green peppers, cored, deseeded, and diced

125g (4½oz) Kalamata or other Greek olives

175g (6oz) feta cheese, cubed

For the herb vinaigrette

3 tbsp red wine vinegar

salt and freshly ground black pepper

120ml (4fl oz) extra virgin olive oil

3-5 sprigs of mint, leaves picked and finely chopped

3-5 sprigs of oregano, leaves picked and finely chopped

7-10 sprigs of parsley, leaves picked and finely chopped

1 To make the vinaigrette, whisk together the vinegar, salt, and pepper. Gradually whisk in the oil, so the vinaigrette emulsifies and thickens slightly. Add the herbs, then whisk again and taste for seasoning.

2 Peel the cucumbers and cut each in half lengthways. Scoop out the seeds with a teaspoon. Discard the seeds. Cut the cucumbers lengthways into 2-3 strips, then into 1cm (½in) slices.

3 With the tip of a small knife, core the tomatoes. Cut each one into 8 wedges, then cut each wedge in half. Peel and trim the red onion and cut into very thin rings. Gently separate the concentric circles within each ring with your fingers.

4 Put the cucumbers, tomatoes, onion rings, and peppers in a large bowl. Briskly whisk the dressing, pour it over, and toss thoroughly. Add the olives (they may be either left whole or stoned) and feta and gently toss again. Taste for seasoning. Allow the flavours to mellow for about 30 minutes before serving.

Season's best **tomatoes**

The myriad varieties of this quintessential ingredient range in colour from near black through red, yellow to almost white; in size from that of a pea to a huge sphere; and in taste from sweet to spritely acid. Best in high summer and autumn, they suit all cheeses. Good flavourings are garlic, herbs (basil, coriander, oregano, or thyme), orange, vodka, or chilli. Onions, peppers, meat, fish, or eggs are also perfect partners.

Tomatoes grow in almost all temperate climates, even Siberia. They are grown either outdoors, or in polytunnels or hothouses, but ripened in the sun in summer they have the scent and flavour everyone desires.

Red Cherry These small-fruited varieties are usually more flavoursome than larger ones. Handy to eat whole as a snack, or when lightly crushed and warmed in oil, they make a colourful pizza topping.

Uniform bright red, glossy skin and sweet, juicy flesh.

Brandywine A gourmet-quality tomato, Brandywine is highly praised for its distinctive, well-balanced acidity and sweetness.

Moneymaker A prolific cropper with a rich tomato flavour. It is a popular all-rounder for salads, grilling or frying in halves, or for sauces.

The yellow pear tapers at the top, making it stand out from other cherry varieties.

With its generous diameter, Brandywine is ideal for slicing, to use in salads and sandwiches.

Beam's yellow pear An attractive little yellow tomato with a distinctive shape. It looks great halved in salads.

Most of the flavour is in the jelly surrounding the seeds, so do not discard them.

Green Zebra A good-sized tomato with greenish-gold stripes and spots, this variety has an excellent, tangy flavour. It is good used raw in salads and salsas.

San Marzano With its superior, rich tomato flavour and meaty interior, this is the classic variety for canning and paste-making. Many consider it to be the best sauce tomato in the world.

Gardener's delight A very popular cherry tomato with a bright red colour and a sweet flavour.

If the fruit turns too yellow, it is overripe.

White beauty This is a rarer tomato, with creamy white flesh all the way through. It has a delicate flavor and is very sweet.

essentials
varieties available
Tomberries, cherry, cocktail (larger than cherry), baby plum, plum, standard, beefsteak.

buy Choose ones that smell of the vine, not too soft, with fresh, bright green calyces.

store Keep at room temperature, not in the fridge, unless they are very ripe. Arrange so tomatoes don't touch each other.

cook Bake whole, roast, grill, fry, sauté, or stew. Make into sauce or soup. Add to casseroles and stews.

preserve Oven-dry and pack in olive oil; make ketchup or chutney; pickle green (unripe) tomatoes.

recipe ideas
Fresh tomatoes stuffed with fruity couscous p152

Roasted tomato soup p148

Sausage and tomato pie p192

how to peel and deseed tomatoes
Tomatoes are best skinned and deseeded if you plan to use them for sauces or soups. When using cold for salads or for stuffing, this isn't necessary.

1 Remove the green stem, score an "X" in the skin of each tomato, at the base, then immerse it in a pan of boiling water for 20 seconds, or until the skin loosens.

2 With a slotted spoon, remove the tomato from the boiling water and place it immediately into a bowl of iced water to cool quickly.

3 Lift out of the water and, using a paring knife, peel away the loosened skin. To deseed, halve the tomato, then gently squeeze out the seeds over a bowl to catch them.

tomato salad with butter beans and lime

If it's a light lunch that you're after, then this fresh, zingy salad is just the thing to accompany whatever else you have in the fridge, whether cold meats, cheese, or bread.

🥣 **20 MINS**

SERVES 4

400g can butter beans, drained and rinsed

8 tomatoes, skinned (p197) and roughly chopped

2 limes, peeled, segmented, and chopped

salt and freshly ground black pepper

drizzle of extra virgin olive oil

1 Put the beans, tomatoes, and lime segments in a bowl and gently toss together. Season well with salt and pepper.

2 Drizzle over the oil. Serve with crusty bread and a selection of sliced cooked meats.

concentrated tomato sauce

Sauces and purées are the ideal use for a glut of tomatoes, especially if they are overripe. This thick version is great for pizzas and in other savoury dishes.

🥣 **15 MINS**　🍲 **1 HR**　❄ **FREEZABLE**

MAKES 1 LITRE (1¾ PINTS)

2.5–3kg (5½–6½lb) very ripe tomatoes, roughly chopped

1 large onion, sliced

1 large sprig of parsley, basil, and/or celery leaves

1 bay leaf

1 large garlic clove

1 Put all the ingredients into a large heavy-based saucepan and bring to the boil. Reduce the heat to very low and simmer for about 1 hour, or until the mixture becomes thick and concentrated. Stir frequently. The sauce is ready when there is no discernible liquid left.

2 Remove and discard the bay leaf and garlic and sieve the sauce through a metal sieve into a bowl, pressing hard to extract as much of the sauce as possible. Leave the sauce to cool.

3 Pour the concentrated tomato sauce into small, clean freezer pots, then seal, label, and freeze. Thaw before using.

hot chilli sauce

This blend of ingredients gives an extra kick to everything from cold meat to kebabs, scrambled eggs to cheese on toast. The tamarind paste adds sharpness to the sauce, but it's optional.

🥣 **15–20 MINS**　🍲 **45–60 MINS**　❄ **FREEZABLE**

SPECIAL EQUIPMENT ▪ preserving pan (optional) ▪ blender or food processor

MAKES 600ml (1 PINT)

4 red bird's eye (thin) chillies, stalks removed

1 dried chipotle chilli

4 ripe tomatoes, quartered

1 carrot, chopped

1 small onion, chopped

1 celery stick, chopped

2 tbsp agave syrup or clear honey

1 tbsp tomato purée

2 tbsp red wine vinegar

1 tsp tamarind paste (optional)

150ml (5fl oz) apple juice

salt and freshly ground black pepper

1 Put all the ingredients except the salt and pepper (and the tamarind paste if you aren't using it) in a large heavy-based, stainless steel saucepan or a preserving pan. Bring to the boil, reduce the heat, cover, and simmer gently, stirring occasionally, for 45 minutes or until pulpy.

2 Pour the sauce into a blender or food processor with 5 tbsp water and blitz until smooth, stopping and scraping down the sides as necessary. Then run through a sieve into a bowl. Season to taste with salt and pepper.

3 Pour the sauce into warm sterilized jars with non-metallic or vinegar-proof lids, top with waxed paper discs, seal, label, and refrigerate for up to 1 month after opening.

tabbouleh and cacik

Warmed pitta bread makes a fitting and delicious accompaniment to these mezze salads. Mezze are little dishes of vegetables, salads, olives, and such like that are standard features for meals all over the Middle East.

35–40 MINS PLUS SOAKING AND CHILLING

SERVES 4

- 100g (3½oz) bulghur wheat
- 1 small cucumber
- salt and freshly ground black pepper
- 250g (9oz) tomatoes, peeled (p197), deseeded, and chopped
- 2 spring onions, trimmed and chopped
- small bunch of flat-leaf parsley, leaves chopped
- 3 tbsp lemon juice
- 4 tbsp olive oil
- 1 bunch of mint, leaves chopped
- 1 large garlic clove, finely chopped
- ¼ tsp ground coriander
- ¼ tsp ground cumin
- 250ml (9fl oz) natural yogurt
- 3–4 pitta breads

1 Put the bulghur wheat in a large bowl and pour over enough cold water to cover generously. Let it soak for 30 minutes, then drain through a sieve and squeeze out any remaining water with your fist.

2 Trim the ends from the cucumber, cut in half lengthways, and scoop out the seeds with a teaspoon. Dice the cucumber halves, put in a colander, sprinkle with salt, and stir to mix. Leave for 15–20 minutes, to draw out the bitter juices, then rinse under cold, running water and drain.

3 For the tabbouleh, in a large bowl, combine the bulghur, tomatoes, spring onions, parsley, lemon juice, oil, two-thirds of the mint, and plenty of salt and pepper. Mix and taste for seasoning, then cover and chill in the fridge for at least 2 hours.

4 To make the cacik, put the cucumber in a bowl and add the garlic, remaining mint, ground coriander, ground cumin, and salt and pepper. Pour in the yogurt. Stir to combine and taste for seasoning. Chill in the fridge for at least 2 hours, to allow the flavours to blend.

5 Warm the pitta breads in a low oven for 3–5 minutes, then remove and cut into strips. Take the salads from the fridge and allow to come to room temperature, then arrange them in separate bowls with the warm pitta bread fingers alongside.

variation

tabbouleh with griddled aubergine dip

Make the tabbouleh the same way, but substitute chopped coriander for the flat-leaf parsley. For the dip, trim and slice an aubergine, brush with olive oil, and griddle the slices for 2–3 minutes on each side until soft and striped brown. Cool, finely chop, and mix with the 250ml (9fl oz) yogurt and the spices as before. Serve with individual Little Gem lettuce leaves to use as receptacles for the tabbouleh and dip as well as the pitta breads.

rocket pesto

Rocket is one of the fastest growing salad crops. To use up the glut, make batches of this pesto sauce and freeze it in ice cube trays to be used as and when you need it.

🥣 **10 MINS**   🍲 **2-3 MINS**   ❄ **FREEZABLE**

SPECIAL EQUIPMENT▪ blender or food processor

MAKES ABOUT 200g (7oz)

50g (1¾oz) pine nuts

50g (1¾oz) rocket leaves

10g (¼oz) basil leaves (optional)

30g (1oz) Parmesan cheese, grated

1 small garlic clove, crushed

salt and freshly ground black pepper

100ml (3½fl oz) extra virgin olive oil

1 In a dry frying pan, over a low heat, gently toast the pine nuts for 2–3 minutes, moving them all the time, until they are golden brown all over. Set aside to cool.

2 Put the rocket and basil leaves, if using, with the cooled pine nuts, Parmesan, garlic, salt, and a good grinding of pepper into a blender or food processor. Add 2–3 tbsp of the oil and process to a thick paste. If you are serving it with pasta,

you can add a little more garlic and Parmesan, but use less if you are using it as an accompaniment to grilled chicken or fish.

3 Reduce the speed and continue to add the oil, in a thin stream, until the pesto becomes a thin paste. Taste and adjust the seasoning if needed. If you prefer a coarser texture, pulse in the food processor until you reach the desired consistency. Serve on warmed plates mixed into cooked pasta, such as pappardelle.

variation

rocket, almond, and blue cheese pesto

In place of the pine nuts, use blanched almonds and replace the Parmesan cheese with an equal quantity of blue cheese, crumbled or diced. Omit the basil leaves. Follow the recipe as written.

egg and fennel potato salad

The mild aniseed flavour of fennel gently enlivens this potato salad. Look for a small, blemish-free, pale-green bulb that is firm and tightly packed to ensure you buy the freshest fennel.

🥣 **10 MINS**   🍲 **15 MINS**

SERVES 4

4 eggs

250g (9oz) new potatoes, scrubbed and cut into bite-sized pieces

drizzle of olive oil

sea salt and freshly ground black pepper

handful of flat-leaf parsley, finely chopped

1 fennel bulb, trimmed and finely chopped

1 Boil the eggs in a small saucepan of water for 6 minutes; less if you prefer a runnier yolk.

2 Cook the new potatoes in lightly salted boiling water in a large pan for 15–20 minutes until soft, then drain. Drizzle some olive oil over the potatoes while they are still hot and season with sea salt and pepper.

3 Mix in the parsley and the fennel bulb. Then tip the potato mixture into a serving bowl.

4 Shell and quarter the hard-boiled eggs and add them to the potato salad. Serve immediately.

variation

egg, pea, and potato salad

Cook the eggs as before. At step 2, add 175g (6oz) shelled peas and a sprig of mint to the potatoes after 10 minutes of cooking. Discard the mint after cooking. Add a splash of white balsamic condiment with the olive oil. Mix in the parsley but omit the fennel.

marinated cucumber and dill salad

This beautifully simple Scandinavian dish is an elegant accompaniment to a piece of grilled or cold poached salmon. The cooling cucumber adds colour as well as crunch.

🥣 **10 MINS PLUS STANDING**   ❄ **FREEZABLE**

SPECIAL EQUIPMENT ▪ mandoline or food processor

SERVES 4–6

2 cucumbers, thinly sliced using a mandoline or food processor

2 tbsp coarse sea salt

2 tbsp caster sugar

4 tbsp rice wine vinegar, or white wine vinegar

freshly ground black pepper

handful of dill, finely chopped

juice of ½ lemon (optional)

1 Put the sliced cucumber in a colander and toss in the sea salt. Place a slightly smaller bowl on top of the cucumber and weigh down with weights, or a few unopened cans of food. Leave over a sink for 1 hour to allow the cucumber to lose any excess water.

2 Remove the weighted bowl, wrap the cucumber carefully in a clean tea towel, and squeeze out the excess water. Transfer to a bowl, cover, and leave in the fridge for at least 1 hour, until completely chilled.

3 Meanwhile, put 2 tbsp boiling water into a bowl and stir in the sugar to dissolve. Add the vinegar, a generous grinding of black pepper, and the dill, then place the bowl in the fridge to cool. Once the dressing and cucumber are completely cold, mix the two together. Adjust the seasoning to taste before serving. If using rice wine vinegar, add the lemon juice.

cucumber-chilli salad

Delicious with grilled or barbecued dishes, the longer this salad is left to marinate, the spicier it will be. Even if you like a milder dish, give it at least 1 hour for the flavours to meld.

🥣 **15–20 MINS PLUS MARINATING**

SERVES 4

125g (4½oz) caster sugar, plus extra to taste

salt

120ml (4fl oz) rice vinegar, plus extra to taste

1 cucumber

1 red chilli, deseeded and cut into very thin strips

1 Pour 120ml (4fl oz) water into a small pan and tip in the sugar and ½ tsp salt. Place over a medium heat and stir until the sugar has dissolved, then bring to the boil. Remove from the heat, stir in the vinegar, and set aside to cool.

2 Trim the ends from the cucumber, peel, cut in half lengthways, and scoop out the seeds with a teaspoon. Cut the halves lengthways into long thin slices.

3 Combine the cucumber, chilli, and vinegar mixture in a bowl. Cover and marinate in the fridge for at least 1 hour and up to 4 hours. Taste just before serving, adding more salt, sugar, or vinegar to taste.

variation

cucumber, chilli, and roasted pepper salad

Roast 1 red, 1 yellow, and 1 green pepper, deseed, and slice (p171). Use only ½ cucumber but prepare in the same way as before. Use 1 green (preferably jalapeño) chilli instead of the red one.

tortilla bean salad

For an even more dramatic-looking bowlful, you could use black beans. Don't be timid with the chillies, as beans can take a lot of seasoning and will soak up much of the heat.

🥣 25–30 MINS PLUS CHILLING   🍲 1 HR – 1 HR 30 MINS

SERVES 6–8

2 x 400g cans red kidney beans, rinsed

4 sweetcorn cobs, kernels removed (about 450g/1lb kernels, p155)

750g (1lb 10oz) tomatoes, skinned (p197) and coarsely chopped

1 red pepper, deseeded and diced

1 green pepper, deseeded and diced

1 yellow pepper, deseeded and diced

6 corn tortillas

¼ tsp cayenne pepper

For the dressing

120ml (4fl oz) cider vinegar

½ tsp ground cumin

salt and freshly ground black pepper

3 green chillies, deseeded and finely diced

120ml (4fl oz) vegetable oil, plus more for tortillas and baking sheet

small bunch of coriander, leaves finely chopped

1 For the dressing, whisk together the vinegar and cumin, and season with salt and pepper. Add the chillies, then gradually whisk in the oil, so the vinaigrette emulsifies and thickens slightly. Stir in the coriander, reserving a little for garnish. Taste for seasoning.

2 In a large bowl, combine the kidney beans, sweetcorn, tomatoes, peppers, and dressing. Gently toss the salad and taste for seasoning. Cover and chill in the fridge for at least 1 hour.

3 Just before serving, heat the grill and oil a baking sheet. Brush the tortillas with oil and season with salt and cayenne pepper, then slice them into triangles.

4 Spread the tortilla triangles on the baking sheet. Grill, 10cm (4in) from the heat, for 4–6 minutes, until golden brown and crisp, stirring occasionally so they colour evenly.

5 Divide the salad among 6–8 deep plates and top with the tortilla triangles. Sprinkle the reserved chopped coriander over the top. Serve chilled or at room temperature.

courgette and hazelnut bread

Hazelnuts add taste and texture to this quick and easy bread.

🥣 20 MINS   🍲 50 MINS PLUS RESTING   ❄ FREEZABLE

MAKES 1 LOAF

300g (10oz) plain flour

100g (3½oz) wholemeal self-raising flour

1 tsp bicarbonate of soda

salt

50g (1¾oz) hazelnuts, roughly chopped

150g (5½oz) courgette, coarsely grated

250ml (9fl oz) buttermilk

1 Preheat the oven to 220°C (425°F/Gas 7). Line a baking sheet with parchment. In a bowl, mix the plain flour, wholemeal flour, bicarbonate of soda, ½ tsp salt, and hazelnuts. Add the grated courgette, mixing it in well.

2 Make a well in the centre of the dry ingredients and stir in the buttermilk, bringing the mixture together to form a loose dough. Use your hands to bring the mixture together into a ball, then turn it out onto a floured surface and knead for 2 minutes, until it forms a smooth dough. You may need to add a little extra flour at this stage.

3 Shape the dough into a round about 15cm (6in) in diameter. With a sharp knife, slash a cross in the top of the dough to help it to rise easily when baking.

4 Place the dough on the baking sheet and cook in the middle of the oven for 30 minutes. Reduce the temperature to 200°C (400°F/Gas 6) and bake for 20 minutes until well risen, golden brown, and a skewer inserted into the middle emerges clean. Transfer to a wire rack and allow it to rest for at least 20 minutes before serving.

griddled mediterranean vegetables

As well as being perfect to serve as a side dish, chop up these vegetables and layer them between sheets of lasagne and top with a cheese sauce for something more substantial.

🥣 15 MINS   🍲 10–15 MINS   ❄ FREEZABLE

SPECIAL EQUIPMENT ▪ griddle pan or electric griddle

MAKES ABOUT 1.35kg (3lb)

2 small aubergines, trimmed and cut into strips lengthways, about 5mm (¼in) thick

4 courgettes, trimmed and cut into strips lengthways, about 5mm (¼in) thick

a drizzle of olive oil, plus extra for brushing

4 red peppers, deseeded and cut into 6–8 strips

1 Preheat a griddle pan. Prepare 3–4 baking sheets with a layer of greaseproof paper or baking parchment.

2 Brush the aubergines and courgettes with oil on both sides. Put the peppers in a shallow dish, drizzle with a little oil, and toss with your hands to coat them completely.

3 When the griddle is very hot, but not smoking, add a single layer of vegetables (don't overcrowd them). Press them down firmly with a fish slice, until the undersides are nicely striped. Turn the vegetables over and cook for a further 2–3 minutes, until just cooked and striped. Don't overcook them, or they will become too soft. Transfer to the prepared baking sheets to cool.

4 Repeat for the remaining vegetables, reheating the griddle between each batch. Serve with grilled fish or chicken, or mix in with flageolet beans, haricot beans, or chickpeas, and dress with pesto.

cornbread

Cornbread is a traditional American loaf that makes a quick and easy accompaniment to soups and stews. The name is given to any bread that is made with corn rather than wheat and leavened with baking powder, instead of yeast. To ring the changes , for a non-vegetarian cornbread, add finely diced grilled bacon rashers with the corn.

🥄 **15-20 MINS**   🍲 **20-25 MINS**

SPECIAL EQUIPMENT ▪ 23cm (9in) flameproof cast-iron frying pan or similar-sized round loose-bottomed cake tin

SERVES 8

150g (5½oz) fine yellow cornmeal or polenta

125g (4½oz) strong white bread flour

50g (1¾oz) caster sugar

1 tbsp baking powder

salt

2 sweetcorn cobs, kernels removed (about 225g/8oz kernels, p155)

2 eggs

60g (2oz) unsalted butter or bacon dripping, melted and cooled

250ml (9fl oz) milk

1 Preheat the oven to 220°C (425°F/ Gas 7). Grease the frying pan or round cake tin with butter or dripping. Place in the oven.

2 Sift the cornmeal or polenta, flour, sugar, baking powder, and 1 tsp salt into a bowl. Add the kernels.

3 In a bowl, whisk together the eggs, melted butter or bacon dripping, and milk. Pour three-quarters of the milk mixture into the flour mixture and stir. Draw in the dry ingredients, adding the remaining milk mixture. Stir just until smooth.

4 Carefully take the hot pan or cake tin out of the oven and pour in the batter; it should sizzle. Quickly brush the top with butter or bacon dripping, return the pan or cake tin to the oven, and bake for 20–25 minutes. The bread should shrink away from the sides of the pan and a skewer inserted into the middle should come out clean.

5 Let the cornbread cool slightly on a wire rack. Serve warm, with soup, chilli con carne, or fried chicken. The cornbread does not keep well, but leftovers can be used as a stuffing for roast poultry.

variation

chilli cornbread

Prepare in exactly the same way but add 2 red chillies, deseeded and finely chopped to the mixture. For extra kick, sprinkle the surface with 1tsp dried chilli flakes after brushing with butter or bacon drilling before baking at step 4.

courgette tian

This is an excellent side dish for roast lamb or chicken or good on its own as a vegetarian dish. Try to use small courgettes as they have a more concentrated flavour than larger varieties.

🥣 30–35 MINS 🍲 20–30 MINS

SPECIAL EQUIPMENT ▪ 1.5-litre (2¾-pint) baking dish

SERVES 6

75ml (2½fl oz) olive oil

1kg (2¼lb) small courgettes, cut into 5mm (¼in) thick slices

salt and freshly ground black pepper

65g (2¼oz) long-grain rice

2 onions, thinly sliced

3 garlic cloves, finely chopped

5–7 sprigs of flat-leaf parsley, leaves picked and finely chopped

60g (2oz) Parmesan cheese, grated

3 eggs

1 Heat one-third of the oil in a large frying pan over a medium heat. Add the courgettes and salt and pepper, and cook, stirring occasionally, for 10–15 minutes, until tender and evenly browned. Spread the slices out over a large plate to cool.

2 Cook the rice in a pan of boiling salted water for about 10 minutes, or until it is tender. Drain the rice in a colander, rinse with cold water to remove some of the starch, and drain again thoroughly. Let the rice cool for 8–10 minutes, then stir with a fork.

3 Heat half the remaining oil in the frying pan over a medium heat, add the onions and garlic, and cook, stirring occasionally, for 3–5 minutes until soft but not coloured.

4 Preheat the oven to 180°C (350°F/ Gas 4). Brush the baking dish with oil. Coarsely chop the cooled courgettes.

5 In a large bowl, combine the courgettes, onion mixture, parsley, rice, and Parmesan. Stir to mix, then taste for seasoning. Crack the eggs into a bowl and beat to mix. Stir them into the vegetable mixture with the wooden spoon.

6 Spread the mixture in the baking dish and sprinkle with the remaining oil. Bake the tian for 10–15 minutes, until set. Increase the temperature to 200°C (400°F/Gas 6) and bake for a further 10–15 minutes, until brown. Serve hot, or at room temperature, from the baking dish.

rocket and tomato pasta salad

Rocket leaves and tomatoes are a classic combination. Tossed together with pasta and mayonnaise, the end result is a creamy dish, perfect for a light summer's day lunch.

🥣 15 MINS 🍲 10 MINS

SERVES 4

225g (8oz) pasta, such as penne, fusilli, or farfalle

2 tbsp mayonnaise

handful of rocket leaves

125g (4½oz) fresh or cooked garden peas (shelled weight)

6 cherry tomatoes, finely chopped

salt and freshly ground black pepper

1 Cook the pasta in a large pan of boiling salted water for about 12 minutes, or until it is tender but still al dente. Drain, keeping back a tiny amount of the cooking water, then return the pasta to the pan.

2 Mix the pasta with the mayonnaise, rocket leaves, peas, and tomatoes. Season well with salt and pepper. When cool, cover with cling film, and keep in the fridge. Serve at roomtemperature.

variation

rocket, green bean, and pesto salad

Use 125g (4½oz) green beans, cut in short lengths instead of the peas and cook them with the pasta for the last 4–5 minutes. Flavour the mayonnaise with green pesto to taste. Garnish with some black olives.

malaysian-style pickled vegetables

This assortment of vegetables tossed in a golden turmeric sauce will enliven any stir-fry, curry, or Asian noodle dish.

🥣 35–45 MINS 🍲 10 MINS PLUS STANDING

SPECIAL EQUIPMENT ▪ blender or food processor (optional)

SERVES 4

½ cucumber

2 carrots

florets from ¼ small cauliflower

15 green beans, trimmed

125g (4½ oz) wedge of green cabbage, cored and finely shredded

30g (1oz) roasted unsalted peanuts

For the pickling sauce

3 roasted unsalted macadamia nuts

1 garlic clove, finely chopped

3 shallots, diced

2cm (¾in) piece of fresh galangal or root ginger, peeled and finely chopped

1 tsp ground turmeric

1 red chilli, deseeded and finely chopped

2 tbsp vegetable oil

50g (1¾oz) sugar

salt

60ml (2fl oz) rice vinegar

1 Trim the ends from the cucumber, peel, cut in half lengthways, and scoop out the seeds with a teaspoon. Cut lengthways into 5mm (¼in) strips, then into 5cm (2in) sticks. Cut the carrots into sticks as well. Cut any large cauliflower florets in half.

2 Fill a wok 5cm (2in) deep with water and bring to the boil. Add the carrots, cauliflower, and beans. Simmer for 2–3 minutes, until tender but still crisp, then add the cucumber and cabbage for 1 minute. Drain well.

3 For the pickling sauce, finely chop the macadamia nuts. Then pound the nuts, garlic, shallots, galangal, turmeric, and chilli in a mortar and pestle, adding one ingredient at a time and pounding well after each addition. Alternatively, work the ingredients to a paste in a blender or food processor.

4 Heat a wok over a medium heat until hot. Drizzle in the oil to coat the sides and bottom. When the oil is hot, add the chilli-nut paste and stir for 3–5 minutes, until slightly thickened and the spices are fragrant.

5 Stir in the sugar, a pinch of salt, and vinegar and bring to the boil. Remove the wok from the heat and add the vegetables, tossing to coat. Transfer to a bowl and cover. Let stand for about 1 hour at room temperature, or at least 2 hours in the fridge. To serve, coarsely chop the peanuts and sprinkle on top.

tomato and tarragon pilaf

A pilaf is a Turkish dish with rice cooked in a seasoned stock. It is made in one pot so saves on the washing up, as well as being a quick and easy dish to cook for a midweek supper.

🥣 10 MINS 🍲 25 MINS

SERVES 4

1 tbsp olive oil

knob of butter

1 onion, finely chopped

salt and freshly ground black pepper

2 garlic cloves, grated or finely chopped

250g (9oz) basmati rice

500ml (16fl oz) hot vegetable stock

450g (1lb) tomatoes, quartered

2 or 3 sprigs of tarragon, leaves picked and torn

1 Heat the oil and butter in a large frying pan over a medium heat, add the onion, and cook for 3–4 minutes until soft and translucent. Add some salt and stir in the garlic and rice, making sure the rice is well coated and soaks up the butter.

2 Pour over the hot stock, stir, reduce the heat as low as possible, cover, and cook for 15 minutes or until the rice is cooked and has absorbed the stock. If the pilaf starts to dry out, add a little more hot water.

3 Remove the lid, leave to stand for a few minutes, season well with salt and pepper, then stir through the tomatoes and tarragon. Serve the pilaf hot with a crisp green salad.

variation

tomato and cucumber pilaf
Substitute half the tomatoes with a peeled, deseeded, and diced cucumber, and add a handful each of toasted pine nuts and currants.

blueberry upside-down cake

This is an unusual yet delicious way of turning a punnet of blueberries and a few storecupboard essentials into a quick and delicious dessert for a crowd.

🥣 15 MINS   🍲 40 MINS

SPECIAL EQUIPMENT ▪ 23cm (9in) round springform cake tin
▪ electric hand whisk

SERVES 8-10

150g (5½oz) unsalted butter, softened

150g (5½oz) caster sugar

3 eggs

1 tsp vanilla extract

100g (3½oz) self-raising flour

1 tsp baking powder

50g (1¾oz) ground almonds

250g (9oz) blueberries

1 Preheat the oven to 180°C (350°F/ Gas 4) and place a baking sheet inside to heat up. Grease the cake tin and line the base with baking parchment.

2 Cream together the butter and sugar using an electric hand whisk, until light and fluffy. Gradually beat in the eggs and vanilla extract, whisking well between each addition, until well combined. Sift together the flour and baking powder, add the ground almonds, and fold into the batter.

3 Tip the blueberries into the tin and spread the batter gently over them. Bake the cake on the baking sheet in the centre of the oven for 35–40 minutes until golden brown and springy to the touch; a skewer should come out clean when inserted in the centre. Leave the cake to cool for a few minutes, before removing from the tin.

4 Place the cake on a serving plate. Serve warm as a dessert, topped with cream or light vanilla custard; or serve cold, dusted with icing sugar.

cherry crumble

Ground almonds in the topping are a classic combination with the cherries in the filling of this crumble. They grow on related species of tree, so perhaps this isn't surprising.

🥣 15 MINS   🍲 40 MINS   ❄ FREEZABLE

SPECIAL EQUIPMENT ▪ 2-litre (3½-pint) baking dish

SERVES 6

125g (4½oz) butter, diced

125g (4½oz) plain flour

125g (4½oz) ground almonds

50g (1¾oz) caster sugar

For the filling

550g (1¼lb) cherries, stoned

2 tbsp caster sugar

2 tbsp apple juice

1 Preheat the oven to 180°C (350°F/ Gas 4). In a bowl, rub the butter into the flour and ground almonds with your fingertips until the mixture resembles rough breadcrumbs. Stir in the caster sugar.

2 Place the cherries in the baking dish and scatter over the sugar and apple juice. Sprinkle the crumble mixture over the cherries and bake for 35–40 minutes, or until the crumble is golden brown.

variation

raspberry and peach oaty crumble

Prepare in the same way, but for the crumble use 75g (2½oz) rolled oats and 60g (2oz) plain flour, instead of all flour. For the filling, use 3 peaches, skinned, stoned, and sliced, and 350g (12oz) raspberries.

raspberry crème brûlée

Little individual pots of crème brûlée is a most attractive way to serve this dessert. The raspberries add some sharpness.

🥣 10 MINS PLUS SETTING   🍲 30 MINS   ❄ FREEZABLE

SPECIAL EQUIPMENT ▪ 6 x 160ml (5½fl oz) ramekins ▪ electric hand whisk
▪ grill or cook's blowtorch

MAKES 6

200g (7oz) raspberries

4 large egg yolks

8 tbsp golden caster sugar

560ml (18fl oz) double cream

1 tsp vanilla extract

1 Divide the raspberries among the ramekins. Put the egg yolks and 2 tbsp of the sugar in a large bowl and whisk with an electric hand whisk until the mixture begins to thicken and becomes pale and creamy.

2 Heat the cream gently in a pan for 5 minutes. Do not let it boil. Remove from the heat, stir in the vanilla extract, and allow to cool for 5 minutes.

3 Slowly add the warm cream to the egg mixture a little at a time, whisking constantly. Pour the mixture back into the pan and cook over a low heat for a couple of minutes, stirring all the time with a wooden spoon until thick. Do not allow to boil. Pour the custard into the ramekins and allow to cool completely. Transfer to the fridge to set for a couple of hours or overnight.

4 When ready to serve, preheat the grill to hot. Sprinkle the tops of the custards evenly with the remaining sugar and place under the grill until the sugar bubbles and turns golden brown. Alternatively, use a cook's blowtorch, making sweeping movements with the flame until the sugar starts to caramelize. Allow the topping to harden for 20 minutes before serving.

variation

peach crème brûlée

Use 200g (7oz) ripe peaches, skinned, stoned, and chopped, instead of the raspberries.

almond and raspberry lattice tart

This is the Viennese speciality Linzertorte made with almond lattice pastry.

🍲 30-35 MINS PLUS CHILLING   🍲 40-45 MINS

SPECIAL EQUIPMENT ▪ 23cm (9in) round loose-bottomed fluted tart tin ▪ food processor ▪ fluted pastry wheel (optional)

SERVES 6-8

125g (4½oz) plain flour

pinch of ground cloves

½ tsp ground cinnamon

175g (6oz) ground almonds

125g (4½oz) unsalted butter, softened and diced

1 egg yolk

100g (3½oz) caster sugar

salt

grated zest of 1 lemon, and juice of ½ lemon

For the filling

125g (4½oz) caster sugar

375g (13oz) raspberries

1-2 tbsp icing sugar, for dusting

1 Sift the flour into a bowl. Mix in the cloves, cinnamon, and almonds, and make a well in the centre.

2 In a separate bowl and using your fingers, mix together the butter, yolk, sugar, ¼ tsp salt, and lemon zest and juice. Place in the well. Then draw in the flour and work it until coarse crumbs form. Mix the dough into a ball. Knead the dough for 1–2 minutes until smooth, then wrap in cling film and chill in the fridge for 1–2 hours.

3 For the filling, put the sugar and raspberries in a pan over a low heat and gently cook for 10–12 minutes until thick. Leave to cool, then with the back of a wooden spoon, press half of the fruit pulp through a sieve. Stir in the remaining pulp.

4 Preheat the oven to 190°C (375°F/ Gas 5) and butter a tart tin. Flour the work surface and roll out two-thirds of the dough into a 28cm (11in) round. Use the dough to line the tin and cut off any excess overhanging the sides. Spread the filling in the case.

5 Roll the rest of the dough to a 15 x 30cm (6 x 12in) rectangle. Using a fluted wheel, for a decorative edge (if you have one, or a sharp knife if you don't), cut the dough into 12 x 1cm (5 x ½in) wide strips. Arrange half the strips from left to right over the tart, 2cm (¾in) apart. Turn the tart through 45 degrees. Lay the other strips diagonally over the top. Trim the overhang, roll out the trimmings, and cut 4 more strips.

6 Brush the edge of the tart with water and fix the edge strips. Leave to chill in the fridge for 15 minutes. Bake for 15 minutes. Reduce the temperature to 180°C (350°F, Gas 4) and bake for a further 25–30 minutes. Take the tart out of the oven, leave it to cool, then remove from the tin. About 30 minutes before serving, lightly dust the top with icing sugar.

apricot meringue roulade

Don't be put off by the thought of rolling the meringue base to make the roulade. Using the parchment paper that it is cooked on helps prevent your fingers from getting sticky.

🥄 **30 MINS**　🍲 **15-20 MINS**　❄️ **FREEZABLE**

SPECIAL EQUIPMENT ▪ 32.5 x 23cm (13 x 9in) Swiss roll tin
▪ electric hand whisk

SERVES 8

4 large egg whites

salt

225g (8oz) caster sugar

25g (scant 1oz) flaked almonds

icing sugar, for dusting

4 apricots, halved and stoned

150ml (5fl oz) apple juice

300ml (10fl oz) double cream

seeds and pulp from 2 passion fruits

1 Preheat the oven to 190°C (375°F/ Gas 5). Line a Swiss roll tin with baking parchment. Place the egg whites in a bowl with a pinch of salt and whisk with an electric hand whisk until soft peaks form. Whisk in the sugar 1 tbsp at a time until the mixture is stiff and shiny. Spoon into the Swiss roll tin and smooth into the corners. Scatter the flaked almonds over the top, then bake for 15–20 minutes, or until just firm to the touch and golden. Turn

the meringue out onto a sheet of baking parchment dusted with icing sugar, and leave to cool.

2 Meanwhile, poach the apricots gently in the apple juice in a covered pan for about 5 minutes until tender. Set aside to cool. Drain the fruit halves on kitchen paper, then cut into neat pieces.

3 Place the cream in a bowl and whisk with an electric hand whisk until soft peaks form. Spread the cream over the meringue, then scatter over the apricots and passion fruit seeds. Roll up the meringue, starting from one short end and using the parchment to help you. Wrap tightly in the baking parchment and chill until ready to serve.

4 To serve the roulade, unwrap it and place on a serving plate. Dust with a little more icing sugar and serve cut in thick slices.

apricot pastries

What better than a fresh pastry with a steaming cup of coffee?

🥄 **30 MINS PLUS CHILLING AND RISING**　🍲 **15-20 MINS**

MAKES 8

75ml (2½fl oz) warm milk

1 tsp dried yeast

15g (½oz) caster sugar

1 egg, plus 1 egg for glazing

225g (8oz) strong white bread flour

salt

125g (4½oz) chilled butter, cut into 4 slices

100g (3½oz) apricot jam

8 apricots, halved and stoned

1 Mix the milk, yeast, and 1 tbsp of the sugar in a bowl. Cover for 20 minutes, then beat in the egg. Sift the flour into a bowl and add a pinch of salt and remaining sugar. Make a well and pour in the yeast mix. Mix into a soft dough. Knead for 15 minutes until soft. Place in an oiled bowl, cover with cling film, and chill for 15 minutes. On a floured surface, roll the dough into a square 1cm (½in) thick. Lay the butter slices on one-half, leaving a border all around. Fold the other half over the top, pressing the edges with a rolling pin to seal.

2 Generously flour and roll it into a rectangle 3 times as long as it is wide and 1cm (½in) thick. Fold the top third into the middle, then the bottom third back over it. Wrap; chill for 15 minutes. Repeat Step 2 twice.

3 Roll the dough on a well-floured work surface to a 30cm (12in) square. Trim the edges and cut out eight 10cm (4in) squares.

4 Spread 1 tbsp of the jam over each square using the back of a spoon and leaving a border of about 1cm (½in). Place an apricot half in 2 opposite corners of each square. Take the 2 corners without apricots and fold them into the middle. Place on lined baking sheets, cover, and leave in a warm place for 30 minutes to rise. Preheat the oven to 200°C (400°F/ Gas 6). Brush the pastries with egg and bake for 15–20 minutes until golden. Melt the remaining jam and brush over the pastries, to glaze. Transfer to a wire rack.

Season's best **apricots**

Apricots are small and sweet but with a hint of tartness. They are in season throughout the summer, but best now. With golden-orange, velvety skin often flushed with red, they exude a delicious fragrance when ripe. They are not as juicy as other stone fruits, but blossom when cooked. Apricots are brilliant poached in amaretto, and with almonds or coconut. Team them with lamb, ham, poultry, or venison, too.

Apricots need well-drained soil and sun but don't require much attention. They are often picked unripe, but since they don't ripen any further, it may result in disappointing fruit.

Royal Blenheim This is a delicate, exquisite heritage variety with a musky perfume and soft, downy skin, which resembles golden suede lightly speckled with pink. It is a rare find, so if you are lucky, savour it fresh.

Goldstrike This large, meaty apricot has an attractive orange colour with a red blush. You can eat these fresh or make into delicious jam.

essentials
varieties available
Numerous varieties: either pure orange, green-tinged, or with pink specks or a red blush.

buy Select plump, smooth, slightly soft apricots with a rich colour. Reject pale, dull, or hard fruit.

store Can be kept at room temperature (for a few days) or in an open paper bag at the bottom of the fridge.

cook Bake stuffed or in tarts and pastries, poach, purée for desserts and sauces.

preserve Bottle in liqueur or syrup; make jam or chutney.

recipe ideas

Apricots and almonds in amaretto p237

Apricot clafoutis p224

Apricot conserve p238

Apricot crumble shortbread p230

Apricot meringue roulade p208

Patterson A popular, widely grown variety, Patterson scores highly in terms of durability and shelf life. It is plump, well shaped, and soft to the touch when ripe. It is an excellent choice for baking and cooking.

how to stone apricots
Apricots are very easy to prepare if ripe, so always check before buying and cutting. Unlike peaches, their skin is seldom removed before cooking.

1 Choose ripe apricots. To test, place in the palm of the hand and squeeze gently. It should give slightly. Wash and dry with kitchen paper before cutting.

2 Cut in halves and the stones will come away easily with the point of a knife. If they don't, the fruit is not ripe.

cold raspberry soufflés

An elegant recipe like this shows raspberries at their best. This fragrant dessert is a perfect finale to a summer meal.

🥣 30 MINS

SPECIAL EQUIPMENT ▪ ramekins ▪ food processor

SERVES 4

2 tbsp rosewater

1 tbsp powdered gelatine

350g (12oz) raspberries

1 tbsp lemon juice

85g (3oz) icing sugar, sifted

450ml (15fl oz) double cream

4 egg whites

mint leaves, to garnish (optional)

1 Wrap double-layered bands of greaseproof paper around the outsides of 4 ramekins, so they sit 5cm (2in) above the rim. Secure with adhesive tape. Brush the inside rim of the paper lightly with oil.

2 Place the rosewater in a small bowl, sprinkle with the gelatine, and leave to soak for 2 minutes, or until it becomes spongy. Set the bowl in a larger bowl, half filled with boiling water, and stir to dissolve the gelatine. Remove from the heat and allow to cool slightly.

3 Place all but 8 of the raspberries in a food processor and blend to a purée. Sieve, discarding any pips. Stir in the lemon juice and sugar, then stir in the gelatine mixture. Leave in a cool place until just beginning to set.

4 Whip the cream to soft peaks and fold into the raspberry mixture. In a separate bowl, whisk the egg whites until stiff and fold into the raspberry mixture. Pour into the ramekins and chill in the fridge until set.

5 Remove from the fridge, peel off the greaseproof paper from each ramekin, and decorate with the reserved whole raspberries and mint leaves (if using).

apricots with amaretti biscuits and mascarpone

Apricots and amaretti are a food pairing made in heaven, but as amaretti is made from almonds (a close relation to the apricot) or ground apricot kernels, it's not really surprising.

🥣 15 MINS

SERVES 4

8 amaretti biscuits

200g tub mascarpone cheese

16 ripe apricots, halved and stoned

handful of blanched almonds, halved

1 Lightly crush the amaretti biscuits with a rolling pin, then divide among 4 individual glass dishes. Lightly beat the mascarpone with a wooden spoon until thickened.

2 Layer the apricots and mascarpone on top of the amaretti biscuits, finishing with a layer of mascarpone. Sprinkle with the almonds and serve.

variation

amaretti, peaches, and mascarpone

Use 8 ripe, skinned peaches instead of the apricots and follow the recipe exactly as above.

strawberry shortcakes

Made with a scone-like dough and filled with strawberries and a tangy coulis, the shortcakes are perfection.

🥣 15-20 MINS   🍲 12-15 MINS

SPECIAL EQUIPMENT ▪ 7.5cm (3in) pastry cutter ▪ blender or food processor

SERVES 6

250g (9oz) plain flour, sifted

1 tbsp baking powder

½ tsp salt

85g (3oz) caster sugar, plus 2-3 tbsp

60g (2oz) unsalted butter, diced

450ml (15fl oz) double cream

1kg (2¼lb) strawberries, hulled

2-3 tbsp icing sugar

1 tsp vanilla extract

1 Preheat the oven to 220°C (425°F/ Gas 7). Butter a baking sheet. In a bowl, mix the flour, baking powder, salt, and caster sugar. Rub in the butter with your fingertips to form fine crumbs. Add 175ml (6fl oz) of the cream and toss to form larger crumbs; add a little more cream if dry. Lightly press the crumbs together to form a ball of dough.

2 On a floured surface, lightly knead the dough for a few seconds. Pat out to 1cm (½in) thick and cut out 6 rounds with the pastry cutter. Transfer to the baking sheet. Bake for 12–15 minutes until lightly browned, then transfer to a wire rack to cool.

3 Purée half the strawberries in a blender or food processor. Transfer to a bowl and stir in the icing sugar. It should be thick enough to coat the back of a spoon. Slice the remaining strawberries, reserving some for decoration. Sprinkle the sliced berries with the 2–3 tbsp caster sugar and let stand for 5–10 minutes.

4 Whip the remaining cream until soft peaks form. Add 2–3 tbsp caster sugar and the vanilla extract. Whip until stiff. Cut the cakes in half with a serrated knife. Spoon the strawberries on the bottom halves. Pile on the cream and top each with its lid and the reserved sliced strawberries. Serve with the coulis.

american blueberry pancakes

Dropping the blueberries on top of the half-cooked pancakes stops the juice from leaking out into the pan and burning.

🥣 10 MINS   🍲 15-20 MINS

MAKES 30

200g (7oz) self-raising flour

1 tsp baking powder

40g (1¼oz) caster sugar

250ml (9fl oz) milk

2 large eggs

1 tsp vanilla extract

30g (1oz) unsalted butter, melted, plus extra for frying and to serve

150g (5½oz) blueberries

maple syrup, to serve

1 Sift the flour and baking powder into a bowl, then stir in the sugar until evenly mixed with the flour. Form a well in the centre with a spoon.

2 In a jug, lightly beat together the milk, eggs, and vanilla extract until well blended. Pour a little of the egg mixture into the well and start to whisk it in. Wait until each addition of the egg mixture has been incorporated before whisking in more. Then whisk in the melted butter until the mixture is entirely smooth.

3 Melt a knob of butter in a large non-stick frying pan over a medium heat. Pour 1 tbsp of the batter into the pan to form a round pancake. Continue to add tablespoons of batter, leaving space in between for them to spread.

4 As they begin to cook, sprinkle a few blueberries over the uncooked surface. They are ready to turn when small bubbles appear and pop, leaving little holes. Turn the pancakes over carefully with a palette knife and continue to cook for 1–2 minutes until golden brown on both sides.

5 Remove the pancakes from the pan and drain briefly on kitchen paper. Then place them on a plate and transfer to a warm oven. Wipe out the frying pan with kitchen paper and add another knob of butter. Repeat for all the batter and wipe between batches. The pan should not get too hot.

6 Remove the pancakes from the oven and serve warm in piles, with butter and maple syrup.

raspberry and white chocolate trifle

Make the most of the raspberries in this trifle by squashing them lightly so they release some of their juices.

🥣 25 MINS PLUS CHILLING   ❄ FREEZABLE

SERVES 6-8

300g (10oz) Madeira cake or plain sponge cake, cut into 2cm (¾in) slices

700g (1lb 9oz) raspberries

2 x 250g tubs mascarpone cheese

300ml (10fl oz) double cream

200g (7oz) white chocolate

1 Line the base and sides of the glass bowl or individual glass dishes with the cake. Spoon half the raspberries over and place in the fridge for at least 15 minutes while the sponge soaks up the juices.

2 Meanwhile, put the mascarpone and cream in a bowl and beat with a wooden spoon. Break three-quarters of the chocolate into pieces and place in a small heatproof bowl. Sit the bowl over a pan of barely simmering water and stir occasionally until the chocolate has melted. Remove from the heat. Spoon half over the raspberries and mix half with the mascarpone and cream.

3 Add the cream mixture and the remaining raspberries to the trifle(s) in layers, ending with a cream topping. Grate over the remaining chocolate. Chill in the fridge for 15–30 minutes, then serve.

variation

cherry and white chocolate trifle

Replace the raspberries with 700g (1lb 9oz) ripe cherries. Stone and halve the cherries and place them in a bowl. Squash slightly to release some of their juices. Add 2 tbsp kirsch to the cherries and set aside while you prepare the cake in step 1. Continue with the recipe, layering the trifle with the cherries and kirsch, instead of the raspberries.

blackcurrant and rosemary cheesecake

Summer blackcurrants are always a treat. Here, the delicate fragrance of rosemary enhances this sweet, sharp, and creamy dessert that is simple to put together.

🥣 20 MINS PLUS CHILLING   🍲 1 HR - 1 HR 15 MINS

SPECIAL EQUIPMENT ▪ 20cm (8in) round loose-bottomed cake tin

SERVES 8-10

200g (7oz) digestive biscuits

85g (3oz) butter

1 tbsp chopped rosemary

675g (1½lb) cream cheese

225g (8oz) caster sugar

2 eggs

1 tsp vanilla extract

For the topping

225g (8oz) blackcurrants

caster sugar, to taste

1 tsp arrowroot

1 Preheat the oven to 150°C (300°F/Gas 2). Grease the cake tin. Put the biscuits in a plastic bag and crush with a rolling pin. Melt the butter in a pan, then add the biscuit crumbs and rosemary, and stir until coated. Press the crumbs into the base of the tin.

2 Beat the cream cheese with the sugar, eggs, and vanilla extract. Spoon into the prepared tin, level the surface, and bake for up to 1¼ hours, until set. Turn off the oven and leave the cheesecake there until cold. Transfer to the fridge to chill.

3 Meanwhile, stew the blackcurrants in 4 tbsp water until the juices run but the currants still hold their shape. Sweeten to taste. Blend the arrowroot with 1 tsp water and stir in. Cook, stirring, until thickened and clear. Leave to cool.

4 Remove the cheesecake from the tin and place on a serving plate. Spoon the blackcurrant topping over so that the fruits trickle down the sides a little and serve.

plum and marzipan clafoutis

This stunning version of a clafoutis is equally good made with damsons or cherries, but instead of putting the marzipan in the fruit cavities, dot pieces between each fruit.

🥣 30 MINS   🍲 50 MINS   ❄ FREEZABLE

SPECIAL EQUIPMENT ▪ 2-litre (3½-pint) shallow baking dish

SERVES 6

675g (1½lb) plums, halved and stoned

4 eggs, plus 1 egg yolk

115g (4oz) caster sugar

60g (2oz) butter, melted

85g (3oz) plain flour, sifted

450ml (15fl oz) milk

150ml (5fl oz) single cream

For the marzipan

115g (4oz) ground almonds

60g (2oz) caster sugar

60g (2oz) icing sugar, plus extra for dusting

dash of almond extract

½ tsp lemon juice

1 egg white, lightly beaten

1 Preheat the oven to 190°C (375°F/Gas 5). Mix the marzipan ingredients with enough of the egg white to form a stiff paste. Push a tiny piece into each plum half.

2 Grease the baking dish and arrange the plums cut-side down in a single layer in the dish, with the marzipan pieces underneath.

3 Add any leftover egg white from the marzipan to the eggs and egg yolk. Add the sugar and whisk until thick and pale. Whisk in the melted butter, flour, milk, and cream to form a batter. Pour over the plums and bake in the oven for about 50 minutes until golden and just set. Serve warm, dusted with icing sugar.

cherry and almond cake

A classic combination of flavours and a traditional cake that is always popular with guests.

🥄 20 MINS   🍲 1 HR 30 MINS – 1 HR 45 MINS   ❄ FREEZABLE

SPECIAL EQUIPMENT ■ 20cm (8in) round deep springform cake tin
■ electric hand whisk or mixer

SERVES 8–10

150g (5½oz) unsalted butter, softened

150g (5½oz) caster sugar

2 large eggs, lightly beaten

250g (9oz) self-raising flour, sifted

1 tsp baking powder

150g (5½oz) ground almonds

1 tsp vanilla extract

75ml (2½fl oz) whole milk

400g (14oz) cherries, stoned

25g (scant 1oz) blanched almonds, chopped

1 Preheat the oven to 180°C (350°F/Gas 4). Grease the tin and line the base with baking parchment. Put the butter and sugar in a mixing bowl and whisk with an electric hand whisk or mixer until pale and creamy. Whisk in the eggs one at a time, adding 1 tbsp of flour to the mixture before adding the second egg.

2 Mix in the remaining flour, baking powder, ground almonds, vanilla extract, and milk. Mix in half the cherries, then spoon the mixture into the tin and smooth the top. Scatter the remaining cherries and all the almonds over the surface.

3 Bake for 1½–1¾ hours, or until golden brown and firm to the touch. A skewer inserted into the centre should come out clean. If the surface of the cake starts to brown before it is fully cooked, cover with foil. When cooked, leave to cool in the tin for a few minutes, then remove the foil and parchment, and transfer to a wire rack to cool completely before serving.

raspberry and almond bake

This fruity cake is enhanced by lemon to bring out the raspberry taste. The ground almonds help to keep the cake moist as well as adding some contrasting flavour.

🥄 20 MINS   🍲 40 MINS   ❄ FREEZABLE

SPECIAL EQUIPMENT ■ 20cm (8in) square loose-bottomed cake tin

SERVES 8

125g (4½oz) plain flour

1 tsp baking powder

75g (2½oz) ground almonds

150g (5½oz) butter, diced

200g (7oz) caster sugar

juice of 1 lemon

1 tsp vanilla extract

2 large eggs

200g (7oz) raspberries

icing sugar, for dusting (optional)

1 Preheat the oven to 180°C (350°F/Gas 4). Grease the tin and line the base and sides with baking parchment. Sift the flour into a bowl, add the baking powder and ground almonds, and mix well. In a pan, melt the butter, then add caster sugar and lemon juice, stirring until well combined.

2 Stir this syrupy mixture into the dry ingredients, then mix in the vanilla extract and the eggs, one at a time, until the mixture is smooth and well combined. Pour into the tin, then scatter the raspberries over the top. Bake for 35–40 minutes, or until golden and a skewer inserted into the centre comes out clean.

3 Cool in the tin for 10 minutes, then turn out and cool completely on a wire rack. Dust with icing sugar before serving, if using. To serve, cut into rectangles.

variation

blueberry and almond bake

This cake also works well with blueberries, or a mix of soft berries, instead of the raspberries. Swap the raspberries for an equal quantity of blueberries or a mixture of soft berries and bake as instructed.

baked peaches with amaretti

A classic from northern Italy, as delicious as it is easy to prepare, this can be served hot or cold. Choose fruits that feel heavy for their size, showing they contain lots of juice.

🥣 15–20 MINS   🍲 1 HR – 1 HR 15 MINS

SPECIAL EQUIPMENT ▪ blender or food processor

SERVES 6

7 large peaches, about 1kg (2¼lb) total weight

8-10 amaretti biscuits

60g (2oz) caster sugar, plus 1-2 tbsp

1 egg yolk

120ml (4fl oz) double cream

1-2 tbsp amaretto liqueur

1 Immerse 1 peach in boiling water for 10 seconds, then plunge into iced water. Cut the peach in half, using the indentation on one side of the peach as a guide. Using both hands, give a sharp twist to each half to loosen it from the stone. Scoop out the stone with a small knife. Peel the skin from the peach halves. Discard the stone and skin.

2 Preheat the oven to 180°C (350°F/ Gas 4). Crush the amaretti in a plastic bag with a rolling pin and pour them into a bowl. Put the 2 peeled peach halves in a blender or food processor,

and blitz to a thick, smooth purée.

3 Transfer the peach purée to a large bowl, scraping it from the food processor with a spatula. Add the sugar, egg yolk, and amaretti crumbs to the peach purée and mix well.

4 Butter a baking dish. Halve and remove the stone from the remaining peaches, without peeling them. If necessary, spoon out a little of the flesh from the centre of each, so the cavity is large enough for the filling.

5 Set the peach halves, cut-side up, in the baking dish. Spoon some filling into each. Bake for 1–1¼ hours, until tender. Meanwhile, whip the cream with the 1–2 tbsp sugar and liqueur until stiff peaks form. Transfer the hot peaches to individual serving plates and spoon any juices over. Serve the flavoured cream in a separate bowl.

peach pie

Less famous than its cherry cousin but no less tasty, this American classic with a latticed top is a splendid summer dessert. Choose perfectly ripe peaches full of juice.

🥣 40–45 MINS PLUS CHILLING   🍲 40–45 MINS

SPECIAL EQUIPMENT ▪ 23cm (9in) pie dish

SERVES 8

280g (9½oz) plain flour

salt

125g (4½oz) lard or white vegetable fat, chilled

75g (2½oz) unsalted butter, chilled

4-5 ripe peaches

150g (5½oz) granulated sugar

1-2 tbsp lemon juice, to taste

1 egg

1 Sift 250g (9oz) of the flour and ½ tsp salt into a bowl. Dice the lard and butter, and rub into the flour with your fingers until crumbs form. Sprinkle with 3 tbsp water and mix until the dough turns into a ball. Wrap in cling film and chill for 30 minutes.

2 Preheat the oven to 200°C (400°F/ Gas 6) and put in a baking sheet. On a floured surface, roll out two-thirds of the dough and use to line the dish with some overhang. Press the dough into the dish and chill for 15 minutes.

2 Immerse the peaches in boiling water for 10 seconds, then plunge into iced water. Halve the peaches, remove the stones, and peel off the skins. Cut into 1cm (½in) slices and put in a large bowl. Sprinkle with the remaining flour, sugar, salt, and lemon juice. Stir, then transfer to the pastry case with their juices.

3 Roll out the remaining dough into a rectangle. Cut out 8 strips, each 1cm (½in) wide, and arrange them in a lattice-like pattern on top of the pie; trim the pastry. Beat the egg with ½ tsp salt and use this to glaze the lattice and secure the strips to the edge of the pie. Bake for 40–45 minutes until the pastry is golden brown. Serve at room temperature or chilled, with a dollop of cream.

creamy rice pudding with peaches

Both the rice and the peaches can be prepared one day ahead and kept covered in the fridge. Let the rice come to room temperature, or warm it in a low oven, before serving.

🍲 15–20 MINS PLUS MACERATING AND STANDING 🍲 3 HRS

SERVES 4–6

4 ripe peaches

60g (2oz) caster sugar, plus more if needed

250ml (9fl oz) dry red wine, plus more if needed

For the rice pudding

65g (2¼oz) short-grain rice

1 litre (1¾ pints) milk, plus more if needed

5cm (2in) cinnamon stick

50g (1¾oz) caster sugar

salt

1 To prepare the peaches, put them in a non-metallic bowl and sprinkle with the sugar; they may need more or less sugar than specified, depending on their sweetness. Pour over enough red wine to cover the fruit completely. Set a plate on top and leave to macerate in the fridge for at least 2 hours and up to 24 hours.

2 Strain the liquid into a saucepan, bring to the boil, and simmer for 2 minutes until syrupy. Stir it back into the peaches.

3 Preheat the oven to 150°C (300°F/ Gas 2). Put the rice, milk, cinnamon stick, sugar, and a pinch of salt into an ovenproof dish, and stir. Transfer to the oven and bake for 3 hours, uncovered, stirring gently every 30 minutes until the pudding is thick and creamy. Cover the dish with foil if it starts to brown too much.

4 Remove the pudding from the oven. Carefully slip a spoon down the side and stir from the bottom. Let it stand for 1 hour. Discard the cinnamon stick, ladle into serving bowls, and serve with the peaches and wine syrup, which can be either warmed or cold.

peach and nectarine puff pastry tart

If you don't have time to make puff pastry at home, ready-made versions are just as good. You can buy it in a block or ready-rolled, as suggested for this recipe.

🍲 20 MINS PLUS CHILLING 🍲 20 MINS ❄️ FREEZABLE

SPECIAL EQUIPMENT ▪ electric hand whisk

SERVES 8

1 large egg, plus 1 large egg yolk

50g (1¾oz) golden caster sugar

25g (scant 1oz) plain flour

300ml (10fl oz) milk

juice of 1 lemon

375g packet ready-rolled puff pastry

1 egg yolk, beaten, to glaze

4 ripe peaches, halved and stoned

4 ripe nectarines, halved and stoned

icing sugar, for dusting

1 Put the egg, egg yolk, sugar, and flour in a mixing bowl and whisk with an electric hand whisk until well combined. Heat the milk in a pan until almost boiling, then slowly whisk into the egg mixture with the lemon juice. Return the mixture to the pan and slowly bring to the boil, stirring continuously. Cook for a couple of minutes, then transfer to a bowl. Sit a piece of greaseproof paper on the surface so the custard doesn't form a skin, then leave to cool.

2 Meanwhile, on a lightly floured work surface, roll the pastry out into a 23 x 30cm (9 x 12in) rectangle and place on a lightly oiled baking sheet. With a knife, score a rectangle on it, leaving a 2cm (¾in) border all round the edge. Press the back of the knife into the border to make horizontal lines – these will ensure the pastry rises. Prick the base of the rectangle with a fork and place in the fridge for 20 minutes. Preheat the oven to 200°C (400°F/Gas 6).

3 Once the pastry has chilled, brush the border with the beaten egg yolk, then bake for 20 minutes, or until the pastry is cooked and golden. Push the inner rectangle down slightly, then leave to cool for 30 minutes.

4 Spoon in the custard, then top with the fruit, dust with icing sugar, and serve.

Season's best **peaches and nectarines**

Peaches have a downy skin with a fragrant, sweet delicate flavour, whereas nectarines, which are close relatives, are smooth-skinned with a sweet but sharper, more intense flavour. They are the classic summer fruits and perfect partners with raspberries and strawberries, almonds, soft white cheeses, chilli and sweet spices, brandy and amaretto, and also pair well with bacon, pork, and chicken.

Peach and nectarine trees are grown in hot and temperate climates. They can be trained on south-facing walls to protect them from the wind and for maximum sunlight, which ripens and sweetens the fruit.

The downy skin of peaches is best removed before eating.

Red Baron Large and richly coloured, this freestone peach has firm yet juicy yellow flesh. Its fine flavour makes it an all-round winner, to be enjoyed both fresh and cooked.

Donut So named because it is shaped like a doughnut with a sunken middle, this peach has mildly sweet flavour with a hint of almonds. Eat fresh, use in salsas, or halve and grill.

The flesh of this variety does not adhere to the stone, hence the term "freestone".

Snow Pearl Round in shape with warmly coloured skin, this nectarine has firm, white flesh that clings around the stone. It is a good choice for pies and baking.

Flavortop This is an excellent firm, sweet nectarine with yellow flesh. It is ideal for both eating and cooking.

Yellow-fleshed fruit has more robust flavour suited to baking, grilling, sautéing, or poaching.

Babcock A small- to medium-sized peach, this has fuzz-free, blushed skin. The white flesh is tender, juicy, and tangy sweet. Eat fresh or use to make perfect Bellini.

White-flesh peaches and nectarines have fragrant, low-acid flesh that is best eaten raw.

essentials
varieties available

Numerous varieties of peaches and nectarines with either yellow or white flesh. Varieties depend on local conditions.

buy Select by touch, but handle carefully: when ripe, the fruit should yield to gentle pressure and have a sweet fragrance. Look for fruit with unblemished skin.

store Keep at room temperature for a couple of days, or in an open paper bag at the bottom of the fridge for up to a week. Both peaches and nectarines are suitable for freezing.

cook Eat raw; slice and sauté; or halve, stuff, and bake for hot desserts. Halve and grill to serve with savoury dishes.

preserve Bottle in syrup or alcohol; make jams and jellies; or use underripe fruit for chutney; dry.

recipe ideas

Peach Melba ice cream p221

Peach pie p214

Peach tarte tatin p219

Sweet and sour nectarine and cherry relish p242

how to skin peaches

Peaches need skinning before use as their downy skin can be tough and unpalatable. Nectarines have smooth skin but can be treated the same way.

1 Starting at the base, with a sharp-pointed knife, make a cut crossways around the middle, just through the skin. Then repeat the cut in the other direction.

2 Place in a heatproof bowl and pour over boiling water. Leave to stand for 30 seconds. Remove with a slotted spoon. Plunge in cold water. Drain and remove the skin.

peaches with meringue and raspberry sauce

Eton mess goes light! Instead of double cream mixed in with the broken meringue shells, here is a variation that pours a drizzle of single cream over the top just before serving.

🥣 15 MINS

SPECIAL EQUIPMENT ▪ hand-held blender

SERVES 4

350g (12oz) raspberries

4 meringue shells

4 ripe peaches, stoned and roughly chopped or sliced

zest of 1 lime, to decorate

single cream, to serve

1 Put the raspberries in a bowl, then purée with a hand-held blender. Pass them through a sieve so you have a smooth purée.

2 Break the meringues up with your hands, then scatter the pieces in one large shallow serving dish or 4 individual ones. Top with the peaches, spoon over the raspberry purée, and decorate with lime zest. Serve with a drizzle of cream.

variation

nectarine meringue melba

Make the raspberry sauce. Halve and stone 2 nectarines. Skin if liked. Sit each half in a meringue nest in a glass dessert dish. Top each half with a scoop of vanilla ice cream then drizzle the sauce over.

berry friands

A friand is a small, light, and moist cake flavoured with ground nuts, usually almond. They can be dressed up with berries or stone fruits, but make sure they are really ripe and juicy.

🥣 15 MINS   🍲 35 MINS

SPECIAL EQUIPMENT ▪ electric hand whisk ▪ 6-cup muffin tin

MAKES 6

100g (3½oz) icing sugar

45g (1½oz) plain flour

75g (2½oz) ground almonds

3 large egg whites

75g (2½oz) unsalted butter, melted

150g (5½oz) mixed berries, such as blueberries and raspberries

1 Preheat the oven to 180°C (350°F/ Gas 4). Line the muffin tin with muffin cases. Sift the sugar and flour into a bowl, then stir in the ground almonds. In another bowl, whisk the egg whites with an electric hand whisk until soft peaks form.

2 Gently fold the flour mixture and the melted butter into the egg whites to make a smooth batter. Spoon the batter into the muffin cases, then scatter over the berries, pressing them down slightly into the batter so they all fit in. Bake for 30–35 minutes, or until risen and golden. Leave to cool in the tin for 5 minutes, then serve warm or leave to cool.

variation

apricot friands

Prepare in the same way, but substitute the berries for 150g (5½oz) ripe apricots. Halve and stone the apricots, then chop into small pieces. Add the apricot pieces to the muffin cases in step 2 and bake as in the recipe.

blueberry muffins

You can whip up a batch of muffins in next to no time, ready for serving as a dessert or to accompany a cup of coffee at a mid-morning break. Blueberries are the classic addition.

🥣 15 MINS   🍲 20 MINS

SPECIAL EQUIPMENT ▪ 12-cup muffin tin

MAKES 12

250g (9oz) self-raising flour

1 tsp baking powder

75g (2½oz) caster sugar

grated zest of 1 lemon (optional)

salt

250g (9oz) natural yogurt

2 large eggs, lightly beaten

50g (1¾oz) butter, melted and cooled

250g (9oz) blueberries

1 Preheat the oven to 200°C (400°F/ Gas 6). Line the muffin tin with muffin cases. Sift the flour into a large bowl, mix in the baking powder, sugar, lemon zest, if using, and a pinch of salt, then make a well in the centre with a spoon.

2 Mix the yogurt, eggs, and cooled, melted butter together in a large jug, then pour into the well of the dry ingredients, along with the blueberries. Mix until just combined, but don't over-mix or the muffins will be heavy. Don't worry if there are a few lumps left in the mixture.

3 Spoon evenly into the muffin cases and bake for 20 minutes, or until risen and golden. Leave to cool in the tin for 5 minutes, then serve warm or leave to cool.

variation

raspberry muffins

Use raspberries in place of blueberries, and orange zest instead of the lemon.

peach tarte tatin

This is an unusual tarte tatin as it is made with peaches rather than apples, which makes it a good choice for a high summer dessert when peaches are in season. Choose firm peaches to ensure the fruit holds its shape as it cooks.

🥣 40-45 MINS PLUS CHILLING 🍲 35-40 MINS

SPECIAL EQUIPMENT ▪ 25cm (10in) round baking dish

SERVES 6

3 egg yolks

½ tsp vanilla extract

215g (7½oz) plain flour

60g (2oz) caster sugar

salt

85g (3oz) unsalted butter, diced

For the filling

200g (7oz) caster sugar

1kg (2¼lb) peaches

1 In a small bowl, mix the egg yolks with the vanilla extract. Mix together the flour, sugar, and ¼ tsp salt in a large bowl. Add the butter and, with your fingertips, mix to form crumbs. Add the egg mix and bring together to form a dough. Knead until smooth and chill for 30 minutes.

2 For the filling, place the sugar in a saucepan and heat gently until dissolved, stirring occasionally. Boil, without stirring, until the mixture starts to turn golden around the edge. Do not stir, or it may crystallize. Reduce the heat and continue cooking, swirling the saucepan once or twice so the syrup colours evenly, until the caramel is golden. Cook the

caramel only until medium gold; if it gets too dark, it will become bitter.

3 Remove the saucepan from the heat and immediately plunge the base of the saucepan into a bowl of cold water, until cooking stops. Stand back in case of splashes; there are few things hotter than caramel. Pour the caramel into the bottom of the baking dish. Working quickly, tilt the dish so the bottom is coated with a thin, even layer. Let it cool.

4 Immerse the peaches in a pan of boiling water for 10 seconds, then plunge them into cold water. Cut them in half, remove the stones, and peel off the skin. Cut the peach halves lengthways into two. Tightly

pack the peach wedges on top of the caramel, rounded-side down, in concentric circles.

5 On a lightly floured work surface, roll out the dough to a 28cm (11in) round. Wrap it around the rolling pin and drape over the dish. Tuck the edge of the dough down around the peaches. Chill for 15 minutes. Preheat the oven to 200°C (400°F/Gas 6).

6 Bake for 30–35 minutes. Let the tart cool to tepid. To unmould, set a platter on top of the baking dish. Hold the dish and platter firmly together and invert them, then remove the baking dish. Serve at once, cut into wedges.

boozy berries with mint and elderflower cream

Mint leaves add such a great fresh taste to a dessert and combine especially well with the summer berries. If you don't have crème de cassis, use a sweet dessert wine instead.

10 MINS PLUS CHILLING

SPECIAL EQUIPMENT ▪ electric hand whisk

SERVES 4–6

450g (1lb) mixed summer berries, such as strawberries, blackberries, raspberries, and redcurrants

150ml (5fl oz) crème de cassis

200ml (7fl oz) double cream or whipping cream

1 tbsp finely chopped mint leaves

1-2 tbsp elderflower cordial, depending on taste

1 Put the berries in a shallow serving dish, pour over the cassis, then chill for 30 minutes, or overnight, stirring now and again.

2 Put the cream in a mixing bowl and whisk with an electric hand whisk until soft peaks form. Fold in the mint and elderflower cordial, and serve with the berries.

variation

boozy wild strawberries with elderflower cream

Use a mixture of wild and baby cultivated strawberries instead of the mixed berries. Use strawberry liqueur instead of cassis. Top with the elderflower cream as before.

figs with cassis mascarpone

The sweet blackcurrant flavour and dark red colour of crème de cassis adds an unusual twist to the figs in this otherwise classically simple dessert. It's quick to make, too!

15 MINS

SERVES 4

12 plump figs

drizzle of crème de cassis

200g tub mascarpone cheese

1 Make a cross at the top of each fig (but don't cut all the way to the bottom), then gently prise them open. Place 3 figs in each of 4 dessert dishes and drizzle with crème de cassis.

2 Mix the mascarpone with a drizzle of cassis and stir gently until lightly marbled. Add a spoonful of mascarpone to each dish and serve.

variation

figs and raspberries with framboise

Prepare in the same way but use raspberry liqueur to drizzle over the figs and to flavour the mascarpone instead of cassis. Add a handful of crushed raspberries to the mascarpone with the liqueur and scatter a few on each plate with the figs.

peach melba ice cream

The classic peach Melba is a delightful combination of vanilla ice cream, fresh peaches, and a raspberry sauce. The three flavours marry to make a deliciously fragrant ice cream.

30 MINS PLUS FREEZING   **15 MINS**

SPECIAL EQUIPMENT ▪ hand-held blender ▪ ice cream maker

SERVES 4–6

300ml (10fl oz) double cream

300ml (10fl oz) whole milk

3 large egg yolks

1 tsp vanilla extract

150g (5½oz) caster sugar

100g (3½oz) raspberries

4 ripe peaches, stoned, peeled, and diced

1 Heat the cream and milk gently in a saucepan until it almost boils, then take off the heat. In a bowl, whisk together the egg yolks, vanilla extract, and 100g (3½oz) of the sugar until fluffy. Pour the cream and milk over the egg mixture, whisking continuously. Return the mixture to the cleaned pan. Bring to the boil, reduce the heat, and simmer for 6–8 minutes, stirring continuously, until the custard thickens. Transfer the mixture to a bowl and leave it to cool, stirring occasionally to prevent skin forming.

2 Put the raspberries and 25g (scant 1oz) of the sugar in a bowl. Purée with a hand-held blender, pass through a sieve, and pour into a jug. Purée the peaches and the remaining sugar and pour into another jug.

3 When cold, process the custard in an ice cream maker for 20–30 minutes until nearly frozen. Transfer to a plastic container. Alternatively, pour in a plastic container with a lid and freeze for about 2 hours until half-frozen. Whisk with a fork to break up the ice crystals and freeze until nearly firm. Drizzle the raspberry purée over. Use a skewer to draw the purée through the ice cream to make a ripple effect. Freeze for a few hours before serving.

minted melon with vodka

Using contrasting colours of melons makes for an attractive dessert. Honeydew and watermelon also taste quite different, the honeydew being the sweeter of the two.

15 MINS PLUS MARINATING

SERVES 6–8

1 galia or honeydew melon, cut in quarters lengthways, rind and seeds removed, and flesh sliced

1 small watermelon, cut in half, rind and seeds removed, and flesh sliced

1–2 tbsp vodka

1–2 tbsp orange juice without bits

handful of mint leaves, roughly torn

1 Arrange the melon slices in a large flat serving bowl or platter, drizzle with the vodka and orange juice, then leave to sit for 15 minutes while the fruit absorbs the juices.

2 Sprinkle with the mint and serve.

variation

triple melon cocktail

Use 1 galia, 1 cantaloupe, and ½ small watermelon. Cube or ball the flesh instead of slicing. Place in a bowl. Add 4 tbsp orange liqueur instead of vodka and orange juice. Leave to sit for at least 15 minutes then toss again. Spoon into glasses and top each with a scoop of orange or raspberry sorbet and sprinkle with the roughly torn mint.

Season's best **melons**

Sweet and succulent, melons can be round, oblong, or ovoid. Smaller summer ones have smooth or netted rind, with orange, green, or yellow flesh. Large dark green-skinned watermelons have pink-red flesh dotted with black seeds. Imported all year but some are homegrown; both are best in summer and autumn; when yellow or green ridged-skinned honeydews are also good. Enjoy them with raspberries and other fruits, seafood, prosciutto, ginger, and mint.

Members of the gourd family, melons used to be cultivated only in hot, sunny regions (both tropical and subtropical), but are now grown in temperate climates too, such as the UK.

The soft, juicy flesh is at its best when eaten chilled.

Galia A honeydew-cantaloupe cross, the Galia is larger than the cantaloupe and has creamy, light green flesh. It is spicy-sweet with a lovely aroma.

Charentais (French cantaloupe) The green ribs on the rind of this round summer melon make it look as if it comes ready-sectioned. With its tender, apricot-orange flesh and its heady and delicious fragrance, this is a gorgeous dessert melon.

The rind has the typical lacy net pattern.

The vivid orange flesh is honeyed and perfumed.

Cantaloupe A small, round summer melon, also known as muskmelon, this has pale orange flesh with a sweet, slightly musky scent.

Watermelon It is round or oblong with dark green skin and super-sweet red flesh. The "icebox" variety (Sugar Baby pictured here) makes a fabulous sorbet.

The vivid, slightly granular flesh is scattered with black seeds.

essentials

varieties available

Many varieties of summer melons, watermelons, and honeydews.

buy Summer melons should feel heavy for their size and give off a pleasant aroma through the skin. Watermelons should be firm and evenly coloured, and feel heavy. They should not sound empty when tapped, but give out a ringing sound.

store Whole melons are best kept in a cool, airy place, but when cut should be stored in the fridge.

cook Eat halved, or in balls, chunks, or wedges; purée for soups and sorbets; or briefly sauté in savoury dishes.

preserve Make into jams. Chunks of watermelons can be pickled. Roast and salt seeds.

recipe ideas

Chilled melon and ginger soup p143

Melon and tomato salad p194

Watermelon and lime sorbet p224

Watermelon salad with feta and pumpkin seeds p159

how to deseed and cut melons

Halve and deseed melons before serving. Fill halves with seafood, berries, or some ginger wine for a starter, or further prepare in wedges or chunks as required.

1 Halve the melon and hold it over a bowl. With a spoon, scoop out the seeds into the bowl and discard.

2 Cut each half in wedges, then firmly holding a wedge with one hand, cut the flesh away from the rind in one piece with a chef's knife.

3 Serve in wedges with proscuitto or prawns for a starter, or cut into chunks of desired size to add to fruit salads or fruit kebabs.

watermelon and lime sorbet

This is very simple to prepare and is really refreshing on a hot summer's day. The little round watermelons often have very few black seeds, which saves time and effort.

🥣 **20 MINS PLUS FREEZING**

SPECIAL EQUIPMENT ▪ blender or food processor ▪ ice cream maker (optional) ▪ electric hand whisk (optional)

MAKES 1 LITRE (1¾ PINTS)

175g (6oz) caster sugar

1 small watermelon, about 1.75kg (3¾lb) in weight

grated zest and juice of 1 lime

1 Put the sugar in a small heavy-based pan with 120ml (4fl oz) water. Heat gently, stirring occasionally until the sugar dissolves, then bring to the boil and cook for 1 minute. Leave to cool.

2 Cut the melon into wedges, remove any black seeds then the rind and cut the flesh into chunks. Purée in a blender or food processor. Stir in the cold syrup and lime zest and juice.

3 Either freeze in an ice cream maker until set then transfer to a freezerproof container with a lid and freeze for up to 3 months, or place in the freezerproof container and freeze for about 2 hours until firm around the edges. Whisk with a fork or electric hand whisk to break up the ice crystals. Freeze and whisk twice more before freezing until firm. Transfer to the fridge 15 minutes before serving to soften slightly.

apricot clafoutis

A clafoutis is a baked French dessert with a flan-like batter covering fresh fruit. Usually black cherries, here apricots are used. It can be enjoyed warm or at room temperature.

🥣 **10 MINS**   🍲 **35 MINS**

SPECIAL EQUIPMENT ▪ 1.2-litre (2-pint) shallow ovenproof dish

SERVES 4

250g (9oz) ripe apricots, halved and stoned

1 egg, plus 1 egg yolk

25g (scant 1oz) plain flour

50g (1¾oz) caster sugar

150ml (5fl oz) double cream

¼ tsp vanilla extract

thick cream or crème fraîche, to serve (optional)

1 Preheat the oven to 200°C (400°F/ Gas 6). Lightly butter the ovenproof dish. Place the apricots cut-side down in a single layer in the dish; there should be a small amount of space between them.

2 In a bowl, whisk together the egg, egg yolk, and the flour. Whisk in the sugar. Finally, add the cream and vanilla extract, and whisk thoroughly to form a smooth custard-like batter.

3 Pour the batter around the apricots, so the tops of a few are just visible. Bake on the top shelf of the oven for 35 minutes until puffed up and golden brown in places. Remove and let cool for at least 15 minutes. Serve warm, with thick cream or crème fraîche, if using.

melon and raspberry baskets with ginger chantilly

These look prettiest with green-fleshed melon but you can use orange ones too. You could serve this as a starter for 6 people (spooned in glasses) but without the topping.

🥣 **20 MINS PLUS CHILLING**

SERVES 4

2 small, ripe Galia melons

2 tbsp orange liqueur

225g (8oz) raspberries

For the ginger Chantilly

300ml (10fl oz) double cream

3 tbsp ginger syrup from the jar

2 pieces of stem ginger in syrup, drained and finely chopped

1 Halve the melons and scoop out the seeds. Use a melon baller to scoop out the flesh, or score it in cubes using a sharp knife (taking care not to cut through the rind), then scoop out with a teaspoon. Reserve the shells.

2 Place the melon in a plastic container with a lid, add the orange liqueur, toss gently, cover, and chill in the fridge until ready to serve.

3 To make the Chantilly, whip the cream until softly peaking, then whisk in the ginger syrup until softly peaking again. Fold in the chopped ginger. Chill until ready to serve.

4 Just before serving, put the melon shells in small glass dishes (if they don't sit firmly upright, cut a thin slice off the base rind (but not right through to the flesh). Gently mix the raspberries with the macerated melon and spoon into the shells. Top each with a good dollop of the Chantilly cream and serve immediately.

bavarian plum tart

Bavaria is famous for its cakes and tarts. In this recipe, a quick version of brioche forms the base. Juice from the fruit mingles with the custard filling to bring about a deliciously moist result. Apricots are also delicious in this tart.

🥄 **35–40 MINS PLUS RISING AND STANDING**　　🍲 **50–55 MINS**

SPECIAL EQUIPMENT ▪ 28cm (11in) round quiche dish

SERVES 8–10

1½ tsp dried yeast, or
　9g (⅓oz) fresh yeast

375g (13oz) plain flour, more if needed

2 tbsp caster sugar

1 tsp salt

3 eggs

125g (4½oz) unsalted butter, softened

For the filling

2 tbsp dried breadcrumbs

875g (1lb 15oz) purple plums, stoned
　and quartered

2 egg yolks

60ml (2fl oz) double cream

100g (3½oz) caster sugar

1 Sprinkle or crumble the yeast over 60ml (2fl oz) lukewarm water in a small bowl. Let stand for 5 minutes, until dissolved. Lightly oil a medium bowl. Sift the flour onto a work surface, make a well in the centre, and add the sugar, salt, yeast mixture, and eggs.

2 With your fingertips, work the ingredients in the well until they are thoroughly mixed. Work in the flour to form a soft dough; adding more flour if it is very sticky. Knead on a floured work surface for 10 minutes, until very elastic. Work in more flour as needed, so that the dough is slightly sticky, but peels easily from the work surface.

3 Add the butter to the dough, pinch and squeeze to mix it in, then knead until smooth. Shape into a ball and put it into the oiled bowl. Cover, and let rise in the fridge for 1½–2 hours, until doubled in size.

4 Brush the quiche dish with melted butter. Knead the dough lightly to knock out the air. Flour a work surface; roll out the dough into a 32cm (13in) round. Wrap it around the rolling pin and drape it over the dish. Press it into the bottom and up the side of the dish. Trim off the excess and sprinkle the breadcrumbs over the bottom. Preheat the oven to 220°C (425°F/Gas 7). Put a baking sheet in the oven to heat.

5 Arrange the plum wedges, cut-side up, in circles on the brioche shell. Let stand at room temperature for 30–45 minutes, until the edge of the dough is puffed. Put the egg yolks, double cream, and two-thirds of the sugar into a bowl. Whisk together. Sprinkle the plum wedges with the remaining sugar and bake the tart on the baking sheet for 5 minutes. Reduce the heat to 180°C (350°F/Gas 4).

6 Ladle the custard mixture over the fruit, return the tart to the oven, and continue baking for 45–50 minutes longer, until the dough is browned, the fruit is tender, and the custard is set. Let the tart cool on a wire rack. Serve warm or at room temperature.

blueberry-ripple cheesecake

In this classic baked cheesecake recipe, the blueberries are puréed and then swirled into the cheese mixture, before the whole dish is put in the oven to cook.

20 MINS　　**45 MINS PLUS COOLING**

SPECIAL EQUIPMENT ■ 20cm (8in) round deep loose-bottomed cake tin ■ blender or food processor

SERVES 8

125g (4½oz) digestive biscuits

50g (1¾oz) butter

150g (5½oz) blueberries

150g (5½oz) caster sugar, plus 3 tbsp

400g (14oz) cream cheese

250g tub mascarpone cheese

2 large eggs, plus 1 large egg yolk

½ tsp vanilla extract

2 tbsp plain flour

1 Preheat the oven to 180°C (350°F/ Gas 4). Grease the cake tin. Put the biscuits in a large food bag and crush with a rolling pin. Melt the butter in a pan, then add the biscuit crumbs and stir until well coated. Press the crumbs into the base of the tin.

2 Put the blueberries and the 3 tbsp of caster sugar in a blender or food processor and blitz until smooth, then push the mixture through a nylon sieve into a small pan. Bring to the boil, then allow to simmer for 3–5 minutes, or until thickened and jammy. Set aside. Rinse the goblet of the blender or food processor.

3 Put all the remaining ingredients into the blender or food processor and blitz until well combined. Pour the mixture onto the biscuit base and smooth the top. With a teaspoon, carefully drizzle the blueberry mixture over the cream cheese mixture in a swirly pattern.

4 Bake the cheesecake for 40 minutes, or until it has set, but still has a slight wobble in the middle when you shake the tin. Leave to cool in the oven for an hour, then cool completely and serve.

mixed berries with white chocolate sauce

The chocolate sauce is made extra rich here through the addition of double or whipping cream. It is the perfect complement to the mixture of fresh summer berries.

5 MINS　　**5 MINS**

SERVES 4

400g (14oz) mixed berries, such as raspberries, strawberries, blackberries, and redcurrants

125g (4½oz) white chocolate, plus extra to grate (optional)

140ml (4½fl oz) double cream or whipping cream

1 Divide the berries among 4 serving bowls. Break the chocolate into pieces and place in a pan with the cream. Slowly bring almost to the boil, stirring continuously until the chocolate has melted and is well combined.

2 Pour the chocolate mixture over the frozen berries and serve topped with grated white chocolate, if you wish.

variation

mixed berry pancakes with white chocolate sauce

Make a batch of pancakes (see Swedish pancake stack opposite). Whisk 200ml (7fl oz) each of double cream and plain yogurt. Roughly crush 300g of the berries. Fold in and sweeten to taste. Add the grated zest of a small lemon. Make the chocolate sauce as before. Fold the pancakes into cones and fill with the fruit mixture. Arrange on plates. Spoon the sauce over and scatter with the remaining berries.

swedish pancake stack cake

Make sure you use only the thinnest of crêpes for this sumptuous dessert. It makes a perfect summer birthday cake and is a children's favourite.

🥣 **10 MINS**　🍲 **15 MINS**

SERVES 6-8

200ml (7fl oz) double cream

250ml (9fl oz) crème fraîche

3 tbsp caster sugar

¼ tsp vanilla extract

250g (9oz) raspberries

icing sugar, for dusting

For the pancakes

85g (3oz) plain flour, sifted

2 tsp caster sugar

salt

2 eggs

200ml (7fl oz) milk

1 For the pancakes, mix the flour, sugar, and a pinch of salt in a mixing bowl. Make a well in the centre. Crack the eggs into the well and add a little of the milk. Mix to a smooth batter using a wooden spoon or balloon whisk. Gradually stir in the rest of the milk. Chill in the fridge for 30 minutes, if you have time.

2 Heat a little oil in a small frying pan. Pour off the excess. Add 2–3 tbsp of batter and swirl round to coat the pan base. Cook for about 2 minutes until brown underneath. Flip over and quickly cook the other side. Slide onto a plate. Repeat to make 8 pancakes. Leave to cool.

3 Whip the double cream, crème fraîche, caster sugar, and vanilla extract until stiff peaks form. Reserve about 4 tbsp for decoration.

4 Set aside a handful of raspberries. Lightly crush the remaining fruit and roughly fold into the remaining cream mixture to create a ripple effect.

5 Layer the pancakes with the raspberry cream on a platter. Decorate the top with the reserved cream mixture, scatter the remaining raspberries over the top, dust with icing sugar, and serve.

chilled rice pudding with warm berry sauce

A creamy dessert that works so well with the sharpness of the warm berry sauce. Use whatever fresh berries you have available, but make sure they are well sweetened.

🥣 **10 MINS PLUS CHILLING**　🍲 **20 MINS**

SPECIAL EQUIPMENT ▪ hand-held blender

SERVES 4-6

800ml (1¼ pints) whole milk

150g (5½oz) long grain or basmati rice

100g (3½oz) caster sugar

250ml (9fl oz) double cream

85g (3oz) blanched almonds, toasted and finely chopped

1 tbsp sweet sherry

1 tsp vanilla extract

300g (10oz) mixed berries, such as blackcurrants, raspberries, and blackberries

1 Mix the milk, rice, and half the sugar in a large heavy-based pan and bring to the boil, stirring frequently to prevent the rice from sticking. Reduce the heat and simmer for 15 minutes, or until the rice is soft, stirring frequently. Turn the rice out into a bowl and leave to cool.

2 While the rice cools, whip the cream to form soft peaks, then fold it into the cooled rice.

3 Dry-fry the almonds in a frying pan over a low heat until golden. Leave to cool, and then chop. Fold the chopped almonds, sherry, and vanilla extract into the rice and leave in the fridge for 3–4 hours or overnight to chill before serving.

4 To make the sauce, heat the berries gently with the remaining sugar and 1 tbsp water, and simmer on a low heat for 3–4 minutes until they are cooked through. Purée the sauce with a hand-held blender and pass through a sieve. To serve, pour the hot sauce over the chilled pudding.

knickerbocker glory

If you love ice cream with strawberries, this is the perfect dessert. It's best to serve it with extra long spoons so you can reach all the layered ingredients in the tall glasses.

🥣 15 MINS

SPECIAL EQUIPMENT ▪ hand-held blender or food processor ▪ electric hand whisk

SERVES 2

200g (7oz) strawberries, hulled

drizzle of strawberry liqueur, or other liqueur of your choice

150ml (5fl oz) double cream

2 slices plain sponge cake

6 scoops good-quality vanilla ice cream

50g (1¾oz) blanched almonds, roughly chopped

1 Roughly slice the strawberries, reserving 2 whole ones. Put the sliced berries in a bowl, drizzle with liqueur, then purée with a hand-held blender. Alternatively, use a food processor and pulse to a purée. Pour the cream into a mixing bowl and whisk it with an electric hand whisk until soft peaks form.

2 Sit the sponge cake slices neatly in the base of two tall dessert glasses, then spoon over 1 tbsp of the strawberry sauce. Add a scoop of ice cream, followed by a spoonful of whipped cream. Add another drizzle of strawberry sauce, then continue building up in layers, finishing with ice cream at the top. Sprinkle with the almonds and top with the reserved strawberries.

mixed berry flan

This is a truly instant dessert, comprising a ready-made sponge base filled with soft ice cream, juicy raspberries, strawberries, blackberries, and redcurrants.

🥣 10 MINS

SERVES 6

3–4 scoops soft chocolate ice cream

3–4 scoops soft vanilla ice cream

20cm (8in) ready-made round plain sponge base

500g (1lb 2oz) mixed summer berries, such as raspberries, blackberries, strawberries (hulled and quartered), and redcurrants

drizzle of crème de cassis, or other liqueur of your choice (optional)

1 Spoon the ice cream onto the sponge base, arranging it in a small mound in the centre of the base, if you like, then pile the fruit on top and around the edges of the base.

2 Drizzle over the crème de cassis, or other liqueur (if using), and serve the flan immediately

cherry and chocolate brownies

Dense chocolate brownies become luxuriously rich with the addition of sweet, ripe cherries. Use a cherry pitter or stoner to remove the cherry stones.

🥣 15 MINS   🍲 30–35 MINS

SPECIAL EQUIPMENT ▪ 20 x 25cm (8 x 10in) brownie tin

MAKES 16

150g (5½oz) unsalted butter, diced

150g (5½oz) dark chocolate, broken into pieces

250g (9oz) light soft brown muscovado sugar

3 eggs

1 tsp vanilla extract

150g (5½oz) self-raising flour, sifted

115g (4oz) cherries, stoned and quartered

1 tbsp cocoa powder

1 Preheat the oven to 180°C (350°F/Gas 4). Grease a brownie tin and line with baking parchment. Melt the butter and chocolate pieces in a heatproof bowl over a pan with a small amount of simmering water. Remove from the heat, add the sugar, and stir well to combine thoroughly. Allow to cool slightly.

2 Mix the eggs and vanilla extract into the melted chocolate mixture. Pour the wet mixture into the sifted flour and fold together, being careful not to over-mix. Mix the cherries with the cocoa powder and gently fold into the mixture.

3 Pour the brownie mixture into the tin and bake in the centre of the oven for 20–25 minutes. The brownies are ready when the edges are firm, but the middle is still slightly soft under the crisp top when gently pressed.

4 Leave the brownies to cool in the tin for 5 minutes. Then turn out, cut into squares, and place on a wire rack to cool completely.

strawberry tart

Master the basics of this fresh fruit tart and you can adapt it easily by replacing the strawberries with other soft fruits.

🥄 40 MINS PLUS CHILLING   🍲 25 MINS

SPECIAL EQUIPMENT ▪ 23cm (9in) round loose-bottomed fluted tart tin ▪ ceramic baking beans

SERVES 6-8

150g (5½oz) plain flour

100g (3½oz) unsalted butter, chilled and diced

50g (1¾oz) caster sugar

1 egg yolk

½ tsp vanilla extract

6 tbsp redcurrant jelly, for glazing

300g (10oz) strawberries, hulled and thickly sliced

For the crème pâtissière

100g (3½oz) caster sugar

50g (1¾oz) cornflour

2 eggs

1 tsp vanilla extract

400ml (14fl oz) whole milk

1 Put the flour and butter in a mixing bowl and rub them together with your fingertips to form fine crumbs. Stir in the sugar. Beat together the egg yolk and vanilla extract, and add them to the flour mixture. Then combine all the ingredients together to form a dough, adding a little water if it seems dry. Wrap tightly in cling film and chill in the fridge for 1 hour.

2 Preheat the oven to 180°C (350°F/ Gas 4). Roll out the pastry on a floured work surface to a large circle about 3mm (⅛in). If the pastry starts to crumble, bring it together with your hands and gently knead. Use it to line the tart tin, pressing it into the corners and leaving an overlapping edge of 2cm (¾in). Use a pair of scissors to trim any excess pastry that hangs down further than this point.

3 Prick the bottom of the pastry shell all over with a fork, to prevent air bubbles forming as it bakes, then line the bottom with greaseproof paper and fill with baking beans. Place on a baking sheet and bake in the oven for 20 minutes until the edges are golden. Remove the beans and paper, and bake for 5 more minutes. Remove from the oven and trim the excess pastry. Melt the jelly with 1 tbsp water and brush a little over the pastry shell. Leave to one side to cool, and reserve the melted jelly.

4 For the crème pâtissière, beat the sugar, cornflour, eggs, and vanilla extract in a mixing bowl.

5 Pour the milk into a heavy-based saucepan, bring it to the boil, and take it off the heat just as it begins to bubble. Pour the hot milk onto the egg mixture, whisking all the time. Return the crème to a pan and bring to the boil over a medium heat, whisking constantly. When the crème thickens, reduce the heat to low and continue to cook for 2–3 minutes. Transfer to a bowl, cover with cling film, and leave to cool completely.

6 Beat the crème pâtissière once more and spread it over the pastry case. Top with the sliced strawberries arranged in a circular pattern. Heat the jelly glaze again and brush over the strawberries, then leave to set. When you are ready to serve the tart, remove it from the tart tin.

apricot crumble shortbread

This variation on classic shortbread has a buttery crumb topping and a chunky, lemony apricot layer beneath – a delicious, fruit-filled teatime treat.

🥄 20 MINS PLUS CHILLING   🍲 1 HR 15 MINS

SPECIAL EQUIPMENT ▪ 12.5 x 35.5cm (5¼ x 14¼in) baking tin
▪ electric hand whisk or mixer

MAKES 10 BARS OR 20 SQUARES

200g (7oz) butter, softened

100g (3½oz) caster sugar

200g (7oz) plain flour

100g (3½oz) cornflour

250g (9oz) apricots, skinned, stoned and roughly chopped

grated zest of ½ lemon

For the crumble topping

75g (2¹/₂oz) butter, diced

150g (5¹/₂oz) plain flour

75g (2¹/₂oz) demerara sugar or caster sugar

1 Line the baking tin with baking parchment. Cream the butter and sugar together in a bowl with an electric hand whisk or mixer until pale and creamy. Sift in the flour and cornflour and combine well so that the mix comes together to form a dough. (You'll probably need to use your hands to bring it together at the end.) Knead the dough lightly until smooth, then push it evenly into the base of the tin and smooth the top. Chill in the fridge for at least 1 hour, or until firm.

2 Preheat the oven to 180°C (350°F/Gas 4). To make the crumble topping, put the butter and flour into a mixing bowl. Rub the butter into the flour with your fingertips until the mixture resembles breadcrumbs. Add the sugar and stir it in. Scatter the apricots and lemon zest evenly over the chilled shortbread base, then top with the crumble mixture, pressing it down quite firmly.

3 Bake for 1¼ hours, or until a skewer inserted into the centre comes out clean with no uncooked mixture on it (it might be a bit damp from the fruit, though). Leave to cool in the tin. When cold, remove from the tin and divide into either 10 bars or 20 squares.

variation

plum crumble shortbread

Replace the apricots with 300g (10oz) plums, stoned and roughly chopped, and the lemon zest with the grated zest of 1 lime. In step 2, scatter the plums and lime zest over the chilled shortbread base, top with the crumble mixture, and bake as instructed.

gratin of fresh berries with sabayon

Be sure to choose berries – such as strawberries, raspberries, blackberries or blueberries – that are plump and full of flavour to partner this fluffy sabayon sauce with lemon zest.

🥄 15-20 MINS PLUS CHILLING   🍲 1-2 MINS

SPECIAL EQUIPMENT ▪ balloon whisk or electric hand whisk
▪ blow torch (optional)

SERVES 4

375g (13oz) mixed berries, such as raspberries, strawberries, blackberries, or blueberries

1 lemon

3 egg yolks

50g (1¾oz) caster sugar

90ml (3fl oz) Grand Marnier or Marsala

1 Pick over the berries, washing them only if they are dirty. Hull the strawberries. Cut any large berries into halves or quarters. Divide the berries evenly among 4 individual gratin dishes or heatproof dessert plates, and chill in the fridge.

2 Heat the grill, or if you own a blow torch, have it ready to hand. Grate the zest from half the lemon. Put the egg yolks, sugar, and Grand Marnier or Marsala in a large heatproof bowl, and whisk them together with a balloon whisk or electric hand whisk.

Set the bowl over a saucepan half-filled with hot, but not simmering, water (the base of the bowl must not touch the water), and start to whisk the mixture again.

3 Continue whisking for 5–8 minutes, until the mixture is frothy and thick enough to leave a ribbon trail when the whisk is lifted and has almost doubled in size. Remove from the pan of hot water, whisk in the zest, and continue whisking for 1–2 minutes until slightly cooled.

4 Arrange the gratin dishes on a baking sheet and spoon the sabayon over and around the berries. Grill about 15cm (6in) from the heat for 1–2 minutes, or use a blow torch, until the sabayon is golden brown and the fruit is warm. Put each of the hot dishes onto small plates to prevent burning you or your guests' hands and serve immediately.

cherry cheesecake

Beautiful whole cherries in a sweet cherry sauce arranged on top of a lemony filling turn this unbaked cheesecake into a delightful fresh summer treat for a hot day.

🥣 **30 MINS PLUS CHILLING**　🍲 **5 MINS**

SPECIAL EQUIPMENT ▪ 20cm (8in) round springform cake tin
▪ electric hand whisk

SERVES 6

75g (2½oz) unsalted butter

200g (7oz) digestive biscuits, crushed

2 x 250g tubs ricotta cheese

75g (2½oz) golden caster sugar

grated zest and juice of 4 lemons

140ml (4½fl oz) double cream

6 gelatine leaves, cut into small pieces

350g (12oz) cherries, stoned

200ml (7fl oz) apple juice

2 tbsp redcurrant jelly

1 Grease and line the cake tin. Melt the butter in a pan, add the crushed biscuits, and stir until coated. Transfer the mixture to the tin, pressing it down firmly with the back of a spoon.

2 Mix together the ricotta, sugar, and zest. In a separate bowl, whisk the cream with an electric hand whisk until it forms soft peaks.

Add the ricotta mixture to the whipped cream and beat with a wooden spoon until well combined.

3 In a pan, soak the gelatine in the lemon juice for 5 minutes to soften. Then gently heat, but do not boil, stirring to dissolve. Set aside. Add to the ricotta mixture and stir well. Then pour the mixture on top of the biscuit base, spreading it out evenly. Place in the fridge for at least 2 hours or until set and firm.

4 Put the cherries in a pan with the apple juice and stir for 2–3 minutes until the juices run. Carefully lift out the cherries with a slotted spoon. Stir in the redcurrant jelly until dissolved. Bring to the boil, then simmer until reduced by about three-quarters. Leave to cool, then arrange the cherries on top of the cheesecake, spoon over the sauce, and serve.

génoise cake with raspberries and cream

A sumptuous whisked sponge with a delicate raspberry filling.

🥣 **30 MINS**　🍲 **25–30 MINS**　❄ **FREEZABLE**

SPECIAL EQUIPMENT ▪ 20cm (8in) round springform cake tin
▪ electric hand whisk

SERVES 8–10

45g (1½oz) unsalted butter

4 large eggs

125g (4½oz) caster sugar

125g (4½oz) plain flour

1 tsp vanilla extract

grated zest of 1 lemon

450ml (15fl oz) double or whipping cream

325g (11oz) raspberries, plus extra to decorate

1 tbsp icing sugar

1 Melt the butter in a saucepan and reserve. Preheat the oven to 180°C (350°F/Gas 4). Grease the baking tin and line the base with baking parchment.

2 Put the eggs and caster sugar in a large heatproof bowl. Bring a pan of water to the boil, remove from the heat, then set the bowl over the top. Whisk using an electric hand whisk for 5 minutes until the whisk leaves a trail when lifted; the mixture will expand up to 5 times its original volume. Remove the bowl from the pan and whisk for 1 minute to cool. Sift in the flour and fold it in. Fold in the vanilla extract, lemon zest, and melted butter. Put the mixture into the tin. Bake for 25–30 minutes, or until the top is springy and light golden brown. A skewer inserted into the centre should come out clean.

3 Leave the cake in its tin for a few minutes, then turn out onto a wire rack. Remove the parchment. When cold, cut it horizontally into three equal pieces with a serrated knife.

4 In a large bowl, whisk the cream until stiff peaks form. Lightly crush the raspberries with the icing sugar and fold into the cream, leaving any juice behind. Place the bottom slice of cake on a serving plate and spread with half the cream mix. Top with the second slice, spread with the rest of the cream, and place the final slice on top. Decorate with raspberries, if using, dust with icing sugar, and serve.

mixed peppers in oil

This is one of the best ways to enjoy ripe peppers. Roasting them amplifies their sweetness and concentrates their flavour, while the olive oil enhances their unctuous texture.

🥣 10–15 MINS   🍲 25–30 MINS

MAKES 750ml (1¼ PINTS)

3 red peppers

3 orange peppers

3 yellow peppers

1 tsp dried oregano

sea salt and freshly ground
    black pepper

2 tbsp extra virgin olive oil, plus extra
    to top up

2 tbsp cider vinegar

1 Preheat the oven to 200°C (400°F/ Gas 6). Put the peppers in a roasting tin and cook for about 25–30 minutes until they begin to char slightly. Remove from the oven, put in a plastic bag (to make the skins easier to remove), and leave to cool.

2 Pull away the stalks, remove the skin, deseed, and tear or slice the peppers into chunky strips. Put into a bowl with the oregano and season with sea salt and pepper. Mix the oil with the vinegar, then pour over the peppers and stir carefully.

3 Spoon the peppers into sterilized jars and add all the juices. Top up with oil to cover completely. Seal, label, and store in the fridge. Once opened, keep refrigerated, top up with oil if necessary so the peppers are always covered, and use within 1 month.

tomato and chilli jam

Tomato jam is traditionally a sweet jam, but here it has been adapted slightly to give it a savoury note. If you prefer a simple sweet tomato jam, omit the chilli and mixed herbs.

🥣 10–15 MINS   🍲 25–30 MINS

SPECIAL EQUIPMENT ▪ preserving pan ▪ sugar thermometer

MAKES 350g (12oz)

500g (1lb 2oz) tomatoes, skinned
    (p197) and roughly chopped

1 tsp chilli flakes

1 tsp dried mixed herbs

juice of 1 lemon

salt

250g (9oz) granulated sugar

1 Put all the ingredients except the sugar into a preserving pan or a large heavy-based saucepan. Bring to the boil and simmer gently for about 8 minutes, or until the tomatoes break down and soften.

2 Add the sugar and heat gently, stirring until it has all dissolved. Turn up the heat and bring to the boil. When the jam reaches a rolling boil, cook for 10–15 minutes, or until it starts to thicken and become glossy and reaches the setting point (stir occasionally to prevent the jam from sticking or burning). Remove the pan from the heat while you test for a set.

3 Test for a set with a sugar thermometer or using a wrinkle test (chill a saucer in the fridge before cooking). If you use a thermometer, the temperature must reach 105°C (220°F); the mixture will also thicken around the sides of the pan, boil sluggishly, and the bubbles "plop" rather than froth. Or put 1 tsp jam on the chilled saucer, allow to cool for a moment, then push it with a finger. If it leaves a trail and wrinkles slightly, the jam is set.

4 Ladle into a warm sterilized jar, cover with a disc of waxed paper, seal, and label. Store in a cool, dark place and refrigerate after opening.

damson cheese

This glossy fruit cheese is packed with flavour. Serve sliced with cold meats and cheeses or as an after-dinner sweetmeat.

🥣 25–45 MINS PLUS MATURING   🍲 1 HR 5 MINS – 1 HR 45 MINS

SPECIAL EQUIPMENT ▪ preserving pan ▪ ramekins

MAKES 400g (14oz)

1kg (2¼lb) damsons, stoned
    and chopped

granulated sugar (see method)

15–30g (½–1oz) butter (optional)

1 Put the fruit in a preserving pan or a large heavy-based saucepan with 300ml (10fl oz) of water. Bring to the boil and simmer for 30–40 minutes until the fruit is reduced to a thick, syrupy pulp. Crush the fruit occasionally with a potato masher or fork as it cooks.

2 Sieve the fruit in batches and collect the juices and fruit purée in a clean bowl. Measure the purée and add the sugar (for every 600ml/1pint of damson purée, allow 450g/1lb of sugar. If the purée seems tart, use 600g/1lb 5oz of sugar).

3 Return the purée to the pan and add the butter if you wish (it mellows the sharpness of the damsons). Stir over a low heat to dissolve the sugar, then bring to a gentle boil.

4 Simmer gently for 35–45 minutes or longer, stirring often, until the pulp reduces to a black-purple glossy paste that "plops" and sticks to the wooden spoon, or leaves a clear trail if the spoon is drawn across the bottom of the pan.

5 Lightly oil warm sterilized pots, ramekins, or moulds. Spoon in the cheese and level the top. Cover with discs of waxed paper and seal with cellophane covers if leaving in their pots. Or cool, turn out using a palette knife, and wrap in waxed paper or cling film. Store in a cool, dark place for at least 6–8 weeks before eating.

tomato and roasted pepper chutney

This sweet, jammy, mild-flavoured chutney is an ideal accompaniment to Brie, goat's cheese, or other soft cheeses. Stir a teaspoon or two of chilli flakes into the mixture at the end of cooking if you want to give it added spice.

🥣 20 MINS PLUS MATURING   🍲 1 HR 30 MINS - 2 HRS

SPECIAL EQUIPMENT ▪ food processor ▪ preserving pan

MAKES 1.35kg (3lb)

1 red pepper

1 orange pepper

1 yellow pepper

1.35kg (3lb) ripe tomatoes, skinned (p197)

2 onions, roughly chopped

450g (1lb) granulated sugar

600ml (1 pint) white wine vinegar

1 Preheat the oven to 200°C (400°F/Gas 6). Put the peppers in a roasting tin and cook for about 25–30 minutes until they begin to char slightly. Remove from the oven, put in a plastic bag (to make the skins easier to remove), and leave to cool.

2 Pull away the stalks from the peppers, remove the skin, deseed, and roughly chop. Put the skinned tomatoes, roasted peppers, and onions in a food processor and pulse briefly until chopped but not mushy. Alternatively, chop by hand.

3 Tip the mixture into a preserving pan or a large heavy-based, stainless steel saucepan with the sugar and vinegar. Cook on a low heat, stirring continuously, until the sugar has dissolved. Bring to the boil, then reduce to a simmer and cook for about 1–1½ hours, stirring occasionally, until it starts to thicken and turn jammy. You may need to increase the heat a little towards the end of cooking. Stir continuously near the end so the chutney doesn't catch on the base of the pan.

4 Ladle into warm sterilized jars with non-metallic or vinegar-proof lids, making sure there are no air gaps. Cover each pot with a waxed paper disc, seal, and label. Store in a cool, dark place. Allow the flavours to mature for 1 month, then refrigerate after opening.

plums in brandy

You can also use this method for preserving damsons and greengages. If you like sweet spices, try adding a cinnamon stick or a star anise to the jar as you pot up the fruit.

🥣 10 MINS PLUS MATURING

MAKES 1 LITRE (1¾ PINTS)

approx 500g (1lb 2oz) plums

approx 175g (6oz) granulated sugar

approx 350ml (12fl oz) brandy

1 Prick the fruits with a fork or darning needle. If the plums are quite large, halve them and stone them instead. Pack the fruits into sterilized jars, adding as many fruits as you can without squashing or bruising them.

2 Add enough sugar to fill about one-third of the jar. Pour over enough brandy to fill the jar completely. Tap the jars gently on a wooden board and turn them to and fro to release any air bubbles, then seal. Invert the jars a few times to mix the sugar around a bit.

3 The sugar will gradually dissolve. Give the jars a quick shake to help this process whenever you remember. Store in a cool, dark place for 2–3 months to allow the flavours to mature. Refrigerate after opening and eat within 2 weeks.

plum and rum jam

Rum enhances the flavour of plums superbly. Although most of the fruit will disintegrate as it cooks, the occasional piece of succulent plum may remain, adding welcome texture.

🥣 30–35 MINS   🍲 45–55 MINS

SPECIAL EQUIPMENT ▪ preserving pan ▪ sugar thermometer

MAKES 1.5kg (3lb 3oz)

1kg (2¼lb) plums, washed, halved, and stoned

1kg (2¼ lb) granulated sugar

3 tbsp dark rum

1 Place the plums in a preserving pan or a large heavy-based saucepan with 250ml (9fl oz) of water and bring to the boil.

2 Simmer for 30 minutes until the plums have softened, then add the sugar and heat gently, stirring until the sugar has all dissolved.

3 Bring to the boil. When it reaches a rolling boil, cook for 5–10 minutes, or until the setting point is reached. Remove the pan from the heat while you test for a set.

4 Test for a set with a sugar thermometer or using a wrinkle test (chill a saucer in the fridge before cooking). If you use a thermometer, the temperature must reach 105°C (220°F); the mixture will also thicken around the sides of the pan, boil sluggishly, and the bubbles "plop" rather than froth. Or put 1 tsp jam on the chilled saucer, allow to cool for a moment, then push it with a finger. If it leaves a trail and wrinkles slightly, the jam is set.

5 Add the rum and mix well, then ladle into warm sterilized jars, cover with discs of waxed paper, seal, and label. Store in a cool, dark place and refrigerate after opening.

berry syrup

This homemade blackberry syrup tastes much fruitier than a bought version. Use it to flavour milkshakes and smoothies, as a sauce for ice cream, and stir into fruit salads.

🥣 20 MINS   🍲 5 MINS   ❄ FREEZABLE

SPECIAL EQUIPMENT ▪ jelly bag or muslin

MAKES 500ml (16fl oz)

450g (1lb) ripe blackberries or loganberries, washed if needed

approx 350g (12oz) caster sugar

1 tsp citric acid

1 Place the fruit in a saucepan with a thin film of water at the bottom, and simmer very gently for the shortest time possible to extract the juice (3–5 minutes). Squash the fruit with a potato masher or the back of a wooden spoon as it cooks.

2 Strain the purée through a jelly bag or muslin-lined sieve into a clean bowl (to give a clearer syrup). Press the pulp in the sieve very gently to extract any remaining juice.

3 Pour the juice into a measuring jug. Calculate and measure the amount of sugar needed (350g/12oz of sugar per 500ml/16fl oz of juice), then add it to the juice with the citric acid. Stir until the sugar has dissolved.

4 Once the sugar has completely dissolved, immediately pour the fruit syrup into warm sterilized bottles using a sterilized funnel, then seal the bottles.

5 Store in the fridge if consuming immediately. Syrups can also be frozen in freezerproof containers, in which case, leave 2.5cm (1in) of space at the top of each container. Refrigerate after opening.

Season's best **plums**

One of the most versatile fruits, plums vary greatly in colour, from green through yellow to red and purple; in size, large or small; and shape, round or tear-shaped. Some are sweet, others are tart, and they also differ in juiciness. Most of them ripen in high summer, and the rest in early autumn. Some are better eaten fresh, others are better cooked. All blend beautifully with other stone fruits, nuts, cheeses, rich meats, spirits, and wines.

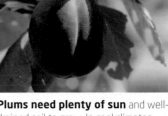

Plums need plenty of sun and well-drained soil to grow. In cool climates, later-flowering varieties fare better when the risk of frost has passed.

essentials

varieties available

Many varieties, but essentially two types – the large, round Japanese and the European ones, which include all the gages and damsons. Also dried (often called prunes).

buy They should be firm, yet give slightly when pressed, and have a slight bloom.They should not feel squashy. Avoid hard, wrinkled, or shrivelled plums, and ones with brown patches.

store Ripe plums can be kept for several days in an open paper bag in the fridge vegetable drawer. Soften fruit that is slightly underripe in a paper bag at room temperature.

cook Leave the skin on for dishes in which they need to keep their shape. Purée for soufflés, mousses, and sauces. Poach or bake in syrup. Use in pies, tarts, crumbles, dumplings, and batter puddings. Add to stews. Halve and grill. Enjoy raw.

preserve Bottle in syrup or brandy; dry; make into jam or chutney.

recipe ideas

Bavarian plum tart p225

Cinnamon and plum cobbler p337

Greengage wine p243

Plum and marzipan clafoutis p212

Plum and rum jam p234

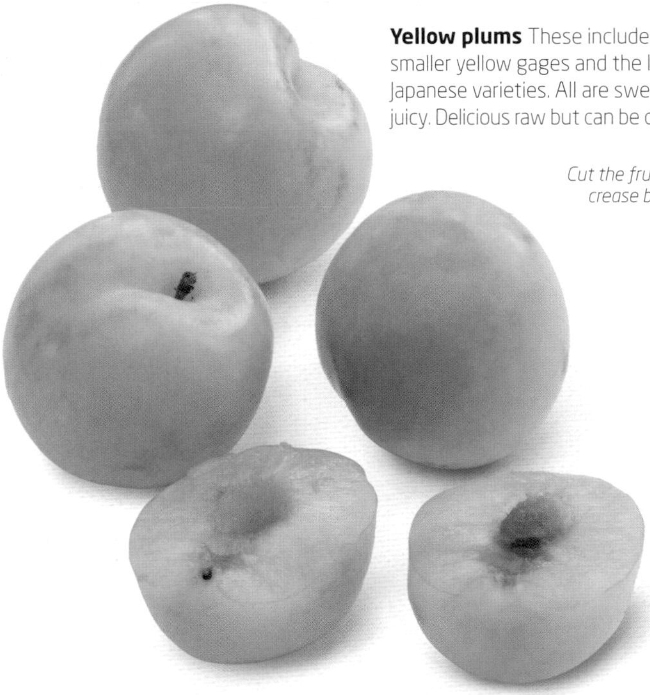

Yellow plums These include the smaller yellow gages and the larger Japanese varieties. All are sweet and juicy. Delicious raw but can be cooked.

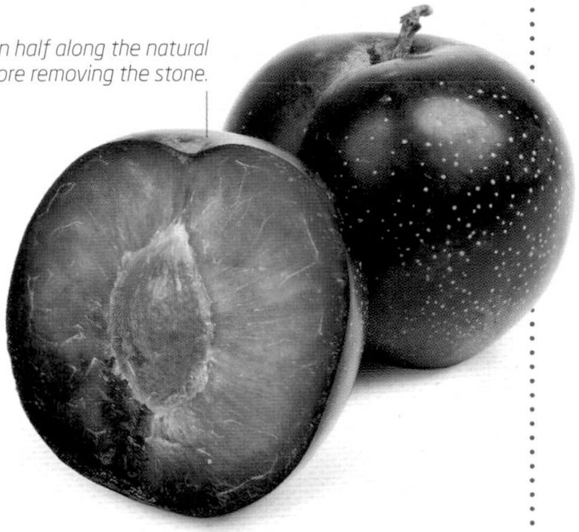

Cut the fruit in half along the natural crease before removing the stone.

Red plums These include the large, round Japanese varieties (Santa Rosa pictured here), with red, purple, or almost black skins and red or yellow flesh.

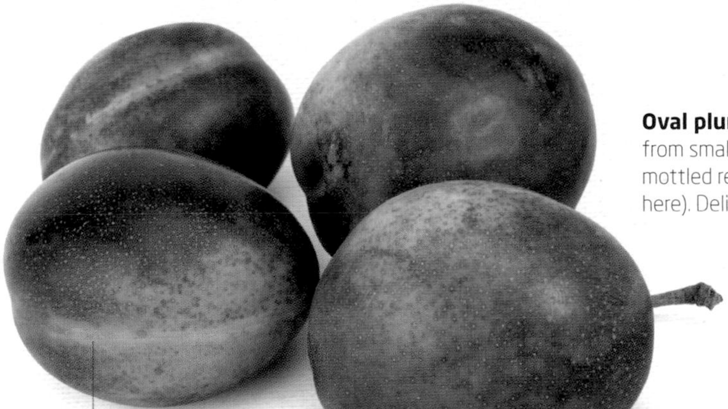

Oval plums European varieties varying from small purple ones to larger red or mottled red/yellow ones (Victoria shown here). Delicious raw, cooked, or in preserves.

Green patches mean it is not quite ripe.

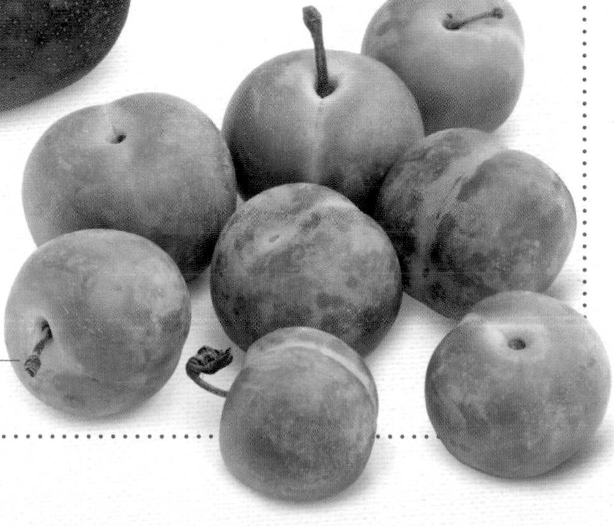

Greengage Distinctively sweet and fragrant, these are best eaten fresh, although they also make excellent jam and tarts.

Greengages are oval and green-yellow, yellow, or acid green, with a dusty white bloom.

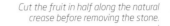

pickled gherkins

Cold pickling is a simple process: vegetables are first salted to draw out moisture to avoid diluting the vinegar and thus keep them crisp, and then they are pickled in cold vinegar. Use pickling cucumbers or cornichons for this recipe.

🥄 10 MINS PLUS SALTING AND MATURING   🍲 1 HR 20 MINS - 1 HR 30 MINS

MAKES 1kg (2¼lb)

500g (1lb 2oz) small pickling cucumbers, 5-6cm (2-2½in) long

125g (4½oz) sea salt

3-4 peeled shallots

1-2 peeled garlic cloves (optional)

2-3 dried chillies (optional)

2-3 cloves (optional)

½ tsp coriander seeds, peppercorns, dill seeds, or 1 crumbled dried bay leaf

2 sprigs of tarragon, dill, or thyme

1 washed vine leaf (optional)

approx 750ml (1¼ pints) white wine vinegar

1 Snip off the stalks and any dried blossom from the end of the cucumbers. Wash the skins thoroughly, then rub each with a cloth to dry and remove its fine down. If your jars are large enough, leave the cucumbers whole, otherwise cut them into quarters lengthways, or into 3mm (⅛in) slices.

2 Put a layer of sea salt in a bowl, add a layer of cucumbers, then another layer of salt. Repeat the layers until all the cucumbers are used up, finishing with a layer of salt. Leave at room temperature for 24 hours.

3 Wash the cucumbers to remove all the salt and pack into clean, sterilized jars, leaving 1cm (½in) of head space. Add the shallots or garlic cloves, if using, spices, and herbs. Include fresh dill if you want a traditional flavour and a vine leaf to keep the pickles crisp and crunchy. Fill the jars with enough vinegar to cover the cucumbers completely.

4 Seal the jars with non-metallic or vinegar-proof lids and label. Store in a cool, dark place for 3–4 weeks to mature before eating (remove the pickles with wooden tongs). Refrigerate after opening.

variation

pickled gherkins with salad onions

Use 300g (10oz) pickling cucumbers and 2 bunches of salad onions, bulbs only, trimmed and peeled, instead of all cucumbers. Salt in the same way. Omit the shallots. Flavour with 2 large bay leaves instead of the tarragon, dill, or thyme.

apricot and champagne conserve

The addition of a little Champagne transforms this classic apricot conserve into a premium preserve.

🥄 15 MINS PLUS STANDING 🍲 25–30 MINS

SPECIAL EQUIPMENT ▪ preserving pan ▪ sugar thermometer

MAKES 675g (1½lb)

500g (1lb 2oz) ripe apricots, stoned and chopped

300g (10oz) jam sugar

juice of 1 lemon

200ml (7fl oz) Champagne or dry sparkling wine

1 Layer the fruit and sugar in a bowl, cover, and leave for several hours or overnight at room temperature.

2 Put the fruit, sugar, lemon juice, and champagne in a preserving pan or a large heavy-based saucepan and simmer gently for 10–12 minutes, or until the apricots become quite soft.

3 Turn up the heat and bring to a rolling boil, cook for about 10 minutes, or until it reaches the setting point. It will begin to set very quickly, so test frequently. Remove the pan from the heat and test for a set with a sugar thermometer or using a wrinkle test (chill a saucer in the fridge before cooking). If you use a thermometer, the temperature must reach 105°C (220°F); the mixture will also thicken around the sides of the pan, boil sluggishly, and the bubbles "plop" rather than froth. Or put 1 tsp jam on the chilled saucer, allow to cool for a moment, then push it with a finger. If it leaves a trail and wrinkles slightly, the jam is set.

4 Ladle into warm sterilized jars, cover with discs of waxed paper, seal, and label. Store in a cool, dark place and refrigerate after opening.

mixed vegetable pickle

This crunchy, sharp cold pickle requires no cooking and could not be simpler to make. Try it with cheese sandwiches, as part of a mixed hors d'oeuvres, or with vegetarian dishes.

🥄 30 MINS PLUS STANDING AND MATURING

MAKES 500g (1lb 2oz)

60g (2oz) sea salt

1 small cauliflower, chopped into florets

1 large onion, roughly chopped

2 carrots, sliced

10 cherry tomatoes

5 jalapeño peppers, left whole (optional)

600ml (1 pint) ready-spiced pickling vinegar

1 tsp coriander seeds

1 tsp mustard seeds

1 Put the sea salt in a large bowl, add 600ml (1 pint) water, and mix thoroughly. Add all the vegetables, cover the bowl, and leave to stand overnight. If you find that your prepared vegetables weigh more than 500g (1lb 2oz), you may need to make up more brine: always use a ratio of 60g (2oz) salt per 600ml (1 pint) water.

2 Mix the vinegar in a jug with the coriander and mustard seeds and set aside.

3 Rinse the vegetables under cold water, drain, and dry well with a clean tea towel or kitchen paper. Layer and pack them into a sterilized jar with a non-metallic or vinegar-proof lid and pour over the spiced vinegar to cover them completely. Top up with more of the vinegar mix if needed, then seal and label. Keep at room temperature for 2 days, then put in the fridge and leave for at least 1 week before eating. Refrigerate after opening.

apricots and almonds in amaretto

Apricots seeped in almond liqueur taste heavenly. If you want to preserve them whole, prick them with a darning needle and poach in a single layer in the syrup for 1–2 minutes.

🥄 10–15 MINS PLUS MATURING 🍲 20 MINS

MAKES 1 LITRE (1¾ PINTS)

85g (3oz) granulated sugar

450g (1lb) apricots, halved and stoned

60g (2oz) blanched almonds

approx 250ml (9fl oz) almond liqueur

1 Put the sugar and 150ml (5fl oz) cold water in a large saucepan. Heat gently, stirring continuously until the sugar has dissolved.

2 Remove half the apricots and reserve, then place the remaining apricots in a single layer in the pan. Bring the syrup and fruit to the boil and boil for 1 minute until the fruit has softened slightly, but still holds its shape well. Remove with a slotted spoon and place in a warm sterilized jar. Add half the almonds. Repeat with the remaining apricots and nuts.

3 Bring the syrup back to the boil, then pour it over the fruit. Top up with liqueur to cover completely. Leave to cool, cover tightly, and invert gently a few times to mix the syrup and liqueur. Store in a cool, dark place for 4 weeks for the flavours to develop. Refrigerate after opening.

apricot conserve

Conserves differ from jams in that they contain large pieces of fruit or whole fruits, which are steeped in sugar first to firm them up, and boiled more gently than jam.

🥣 10-15 MINS PLUS STANDING   🍲 12-15 MINS

SPECIAL EQUIPMENT ▪ preserving pan ▪ sugar thermometer

MAKES 675g (1½lb)

500g (1lb 2oz) ripe apricots, halved and stoned

350g (12oz) granulated sugar

juice of 1 lemon

1 Layer the fruit and sugar in a bowl, cover, and leave for several hours or overnight at room temperature.

2 Put the fruit and sugar in a preserving pan with the lemon juice. Heat gently, stirring to dissolve the sugar. Raise the heat and bring to a steady – rather than a fast – boil for 7–10 minutes until the setting point is reached. Don't stir unless necessary. Remove the pan from the heat to test for a set with a sugar thermometer or using a wrinkle test (chill a saucer in the fridge before cooking). If you use a thermometer, the temperature must reach 105°C (220°F); the mixture will also thicken around the sides of the pan, boil sluggishly, and the bubbles "plop" rather than froth. Or put 1 tsp conserve on the chilled saucer, allow to cool for a moment, then push it with a finger. If it leaves a trail and wrinkles slightly, it is set.

3 Leave the conserve to cool slightly so a thin skin forms and the fruit is evenly distributed throughout, then ladle into warm sterilized jars. Cover with discs of waxed paper, seal, and label. Store in a cool, dark place and refrigerate after opening.

peaches in syrup

Bottled peaches in a light syrup have a charm and appeal of their own, and are a wonderful way to capture the flavours of summer. They also make excellent gifts.

🥣 10 MINS   🍲 2 MINS PLUS HEAT-PROCESSING

MAKES 450ml (15fl oz)

approx 115g (4oz) granulated sugar

4-5 just-ripe peaches, skinned (p217)

cracked peach kernels (optional)

1 Preheat the oven to 150°C (300°F/ Gas 2). Put the sugar and 600ml (1 pint) water into a pan, bring gently to the boil, and boil for 1–2 minutes.

2 Place some warm sterilized jars in a deep roasting tray lined with newspaper. Pack the peaches into the jars, leaving 1cm (½in) of head space at the top. Add the peach kernels, if using, and fill the jars to the brim with the hot syrup. Bang the jars lightly and swivel them to remove air bubbles. Top up with more syrup, then fit the rubber-sealed or screw lids (loosen the screw lids by a quarter of a turn).

3 Put the roasting tray of filled jars in the centre of the oven for 50–60 minutes to heat-process (remove the remaining air in the jars). Then remove from the oven and tighten the clips or lids (or screw on plastic screw-band lids) immediately. Leave for 24 hours, then unscrew or unclip and test the lids are firmly sealed, before refastening and storing. (If using kilner jars with metal lids, you will know if you have a seal as the lid becomes slightly concave and is firm with no "give" once pressed.) Store the jars in a cool, dark place and refrigerate after opening.

raspberry jam

Jams are the simplest of preserves: fruit cooked with sugar over a high heat until set. This method, suitable for all soft-skinned berries, such as raspberries, produces a soft-set jam.

🥣 5 MINS   🍲 10–15 MINS

SPECIAL EQUIPMENT ▪ preserving pan ▪ sugar thermometer

MAKES 450g (1lb)

675g (1½lb) raspberries

juice of ½ lemon

500g (1lb 2oz) granulated sugar

1 Wash the fruit only if needed and put in a preserving pan or a large saucepan. Add the lemon juice and pour in 150ml (5fl oz) water.

2 Simmer gently for 3–5 minutes to soften and release the juices from the fruit. Add the sugar, stir it in over a gentle heat until it has dissolved, then turn up the heat.

3 Bring the jam to a rolling boil. Boil for 5–10 minutes or until a setting point is reached. Remove the pan from the heat while you test for a set with a sugar thermometer or using a wrinkle test (chill a saucer

in the fridge before cooking). If you use a thermometer, the temperature must reach 105°C (220°F); the mixture will also thicken around the sides of the pan, boil sluggishly, and the bubbles "plop" rather than froth. Or put 1 tsp jam on the chilled saucer, allow to cool for a moment, then push it with a finger. If it leaves a trail and wrinkles slightly, the jam is set.

4 Ladle the jam into warm sterilized jars using a sterilized jam funnel, filling the jars almost to the brim. Cover with discs of waxed paper, seal with cellophane covers and elastic bands, or metal lids, and label. Store the jam in a cool, dark place and refrigerate after opening.

mixed berry jam

Sometimes called jumbleberry jam, this can be made with any summer fruits, so choose what is plentiful. Blackberries, blackcurrants, redcurrants, or cherries are also good.

🥣 5 MINS   🍲 10–15 MINS

SPECIAL EQUIPMENT ▪ preserving pan ▪ sugar thermometer ▪ skimmer

MAKES 350g (12oz)

450g (1lb) mix of strawberries, raspberries, and blueberries, hulled if needed

450g (1lb) granulated sugar

juice of 2 lemons

1 Put the fruits in a preserving pan or a large heavy-based saucepan and lightly crush them with the back of a wooden spoon.

2 Add the sugar and heat gently, stirring until the sugar has all dissolved. Turn up the heat and bring to the boil. When the jam reaches a rolling boil, cook for 5–10 minutes or until it reaches the setting point. Remove the pan from the heat while you test for a set with a sugar thermometer or using a wrinkle test

(chill a saucer in the fridge before cooking). If you use a thermometer, the temperature must reach 105°C (220°F); the mixture will also thicken around the sides of the pan, boil sluggishly, and the bubbles "plop" rather than froth. Or put 1 tsp jam on the chilled saucer, allow to cool for a moment, then push it with a finger. If it leaves a trail and wrinkles slightly, the jam is set.

3 Use a skimmer to skim off any surface scum. Leave the jam to cool slightly so that a thin skin forms and the berries are evenly distributed throughout the jam. Ladle into warm sterilized jars, cover with waxed paper discs, seal, and label. Store the jam in a cool, dark place and refrigerate after opening.

Season's best **summer berries**

The pleasant sight of colourful soft berries and currants ripening on the bushes marks the beginning of summer for most people. Abundant in high summer, berries picked and eaten fresh have an intense, sweet flavour, usually found missing from the supermarket varieties. They team incredibly well with rich meats, such as duck, pork, and game, are great combined in many desserts, and are also delicious juiced.

Easy to grow and quick to bear fruit, even in cool climates, berries (such as blueberries pictured here) are tolerant to most soil types and will even grow in the shade.

Blackberry Cultivated blackberries – larger and sweeter than their wild cousins and ripening earlier – should look firm, plump, and glossy. Although most are midnight-black, it is also possible to find red blackberries.

Raspberry Soft and delicate, raspberries have an intense, slightly sharp, perfumed flavour. The leaves can be used to make a popular curative tisane.

Raspberries are made up of dozens of tiny drupelets, each one bursting with juice.

Blueberry Small, plump, and round, blueberries are sweet and mild with a tart edge and a firm texture. While delicious raw, their flavour is enhanced when cooked.

The blue-black skin has a distinctive silvery bloom.

Redcurrant The shiny crimson berries are slightly smaller and more fragile than blackcurrants and have a tangy kick. They make good jellies, syrups, and decorations for cakes and desserts. Also good with lamb.

Whitecurrant These translucent, delicate berries have a pearl-like, pinkish blush. They are a bit smaller and sweeter than redcurrants, and can be served fresh or used for preserves. They can also be frosted with egg white and sugar.

These small, round, purple-black berries are full of juice.

Blackcurrant These have an intense, tart flavour, and are a classic choice for pies, sauces, and jam. The fragrant leaves are used to flavour ice cream.

essentials
varieties available
Many varieties of early-, mid-season-, and late-cropping fruits. Blueberries are also sold dried.

buy Avoid any with brown patches. They should all be bright, shiny, and have a rich uniform colour. Running juices indicate they are overripe.

store Enjoy raw, on their own, or to decorate gâteaux, flans, pavlovas, and trifles. Purée for sauces, fools, and creams, or stew for compôtes.

cook Ideally eat or cook freshly picked, or store in the fridge for several days (depending on ripeness).

preserve Freeze; make into jam, jelly, cordials, wine, or fruit vinegar; bottle in syrup.

recipe ideas

how to freeze soft fruits

Freezing preserves the flavour and nutritional content of fruit, but breaks down the cell walls so the fruit is soft when thawed – but the flavour will be just as delicious as fresh. The thawed fruit is particularly good puréed.

1 Discard any berries that are overripe or blemished. Spread out in a single layer on baking trays. Sprinkle liberally with caster sugar.

2 Freeze the trays for about 1 hour until the berries are frozen. Once hard, scrape them off and put them into portion-sized freezer bags.

3 Label and date the freezer bags and return the berries to the freezer for up to 12 months, until they are needed.

raspberry and mint conserve

The addition of a little mint adds a subtle hint of flavour to this deep-red raspberry conserve.

🥣 10 MINS PLUS STANDING   🍲 10–15 MINS

SPECIAL EQUIPMENT ▪ preserving pan ▪ sugar thermometer

MAKES 900g (2lb)

675g (1½lb) raspberries

500g (1lb 2oz) granulated sugar

handful of mint, very finely chopped

juice of 1 lemon

1 Layer the fruit and sugar in a bowl, cover, and leave for several hours or overnight at room temperature.

2 Put the fruit and sugar, mint, and lemon juice in a preserving pan or a large heavy-based saucepan and cook gently for 5–8 minutes. Increase the heat until the jam reaches a rolling boil and cook for 5–10 minutes, or until it reaches the setting point. Keep a close eye on it, as it will set very quickly. Remove the pan from the heat while you test for a set with a sugar thermometer or using a wrinkle test (chill a saucer in the fridge before cooking). If you use a thermometer, the temperature must reach 105°C (220°F); the mixture will also thicken around the sides of the pan, boil sluggishly, and the bubbles "plop" rather than froth. Or put 1 tsp conserve on the chilled saucer, allow to cool for a moment, then push it with a finger. If it leaves a trail and wrinkles slightly, it is set.

3 Ladle into warm sterilized jars, cover with discs of waxed paper, seal, and label. Store in a cool, dark place and refrigerate after opening.

cherries in brandy

Juicy cherries preserved in alcohol taste deliciously boozy. Serve with coffee, or with the fragrant liquor on ice cream.

🥣 10 MINS PLUS MATURING

SPECIAL EQUIPMENT ▪ sterilized preserving jars

MAKES 750ml (1¼ PINTS)

500g (1lb 2oz) just-ripe cherries (sweet or Morello) in perfect condition, washed and de-stalked

approx 175g (6oz) caster sugar

approx 350ml (12fl oz) brandy

1 Carefully place the cherries in some wide-necked, sterilized preserving jars, packing them in tightly. Take care not to squash or bruise them.

2 Add enough sugar to fill one-third of the jar and top up with alcohol. (As a general guide, use ¼–⅓ sugar and ¾–⅔ alcohol to fruit.)

3 Tap the jar gently on a board, turn it to and fro to release any air bubbles, and seal. The sugar will gradually dissolve – give the jar an occasional shake or turn it upside down to help it dissolve. Store in a cool, dark place for 2–3 months to mature before opening.

variation

rumtopf

Use a rumtopf jar or a sterilized earthenware jar with a lid. Instead of only cherries, choose a selection of fresh soft, ripe fruits, such as halved and stoned apricots, peaches, plums, and cherries, and whole strawberries, raspberries, grapes, and currants. Weigh the fruits and measure out half their weight in granulated sugar. Put the fruit and sugar in the jar and mix well. Leave to stand for 1 hour. Instead of brandy, pour in just enough rum to cover the fruit. Use a small, sterilized plate, or similar, to weigh down the fruit and keep it submerged. Cover the jar opening with cling film, replace the lid, and store in a cool, dark place for at least 1 month to mature. It tastes best after 3 months of maturing.

sweet and sour nectarine and cherry relish

This tangy relish is full of fresh, fruity flavours and warm aromatic spices. The cherries provide texture, the nectarines give a soft base, and the onion delivers crunch.

🥣 20 MINS PLUS MATURING   🍲 50 MINS – 1 HR 10 MINS

SPECIAL EQUIPMENT ▪ preserving pan

MAKES APPROX 800g (1¾lb)

1 tbsp olive oil

2 red onions, finely chopped

sea salt

1 tsp chilli flakes

450g (1lb) nectarines, stoned and chopped

125g (4½oz) dried sour cherries or cranberries

1 tsp coriander seeds

pinch of ground cinnamon

pinch of allspice

300g (10oz) light soft brown sugar

150ml (5fl oz) white wine vinegar

1 Heat the oil in a preserving pan or a large heavy-based, stainless steel saucepan. Add the onions and a little sea salt and cook until soft.

2 Stir in the chilli flakes. Add the nectarines and cherries, spices, sugar, and vinegar, and stir until the sugar has dissolved. Bring to the boil, stirring occasionally, then reduce to a simmer and cook on a low heat for 40 minutes to 1 hour, until the mixture begins to thicken. Stir frequently towards the end of the cooking time so the mixture doesn't stick to the bottom of the pan. Add a little hot water if it becomes too dry.

3 Ladle into warm sterilized jars with non-metallic or vinegar-proof lids, seal, and label. Store in a cool, dark place. Allow the flavours to mature for at least 1 month and refrigerate after opening.

greengage wine

An excellent pale yellow dessert wine.

🥣 2 HRS PLUS FREEZING, BREWING, AND STORING

SPECIAL EQUIPMENT ▪ fermenting bin ▪ muslin cloth ▪ sterilized siphon ▪ sterilized demijohn ▪ sterilized airlock

MAKES 4.5 LITRES (1 GALLON)

2kg (4½lb) greengages, washed

juice of 1 lemon

1 tsp pectolase

1 tsp wine yeast

1.5kg (3lb 3oz) unrefined cane sugar

1 Put the fruit in the freezer overnight, then defrost (to destroy the pectin that turns wine cloudy).

2 Stone and mash the defrosted fruit and add the lemon juice. Place in a sterilized fermenting bin or other suitable container and cover with 3.5 litres (6 pints) boiling water. When cool, add the pectolase. Leave for 24 hours at room temperature (15–25°C/59–77°F).

3 Add the yeast to the fruit mash, cover, and leave for 4–5 days at room temperature (15–25°C/59–77°F) in a dark place.

4 Strain the pulp through a muslin cloth into a sterilized container to remove the skins. Put the sugar into a large jug and add hot water to cover, stirring until it has dissolved. Stir it into the mash, mixing well.

5 Using the siphon, transfer the liquid into the demijohn and fit the airlock. Pour a little water into the airlock and let the liquid ferment at room temperature for 2 months.

6 When there are no air bubbles in the airlock, use the siphon to transfer the wine into sterilized bottles, leaving 2cm (¾in) space at the top. Seal and store in a cool, dark place for 6 months before opening and drinking.

variation

plum wine

Replace the greengages with 2kg (4½lb) red or purple plums to make a fruity red wine.

peach and raspberry conserve

Ripe peaches and raspberries produce a beautifully red-orange-coloured, soft-set conserve. Its relatively low sugar content produces a lovely fresh flavour.

🥣 10 MINS PLUS STANDING   🍲 25 MINS

SPECIAL EQUIPMENT ▪ preserving pan ▪ sugar thermometer

MAKES 900g (2lb)

675g (1½lb) just-ripe peaches, stoned and diced

175g (6oz) raspberries

400g (14oz) jam sugar

juice of 1 lemon

1 Layer the fruit and sugar in a bowl, cover, and leave for several hours or overnight at room temperature.

2 Put the fruit, sugar, and lemon juice in a preserving pan or a large heavy-based saucepan and cook at a gentle simmer for 15 minutes until the fruit softens.

3 Turn up the heat and bring to the boil. When the jam reaches a rolling boil, cook for about 10 minutes or

until it reaches the setting point. Remove the pan from the heat while you test for a set with a sugar thermometer or using a wrinkle test (chill a saucer in the fridge before cooking). If you use a thermometer, the temperature must reach 105°C (220°F); the mixture will also thicken around the sides of the pan, boil sluggishly, and the bubbles "plop" rather than froth. Or put 1 tsp conserve on the chilled saucer, allow to cool for a moment, then push it with a finger. If it leaves a trail and wrinkles slightly, it is set.

4 Ladle into warm sterilized jars, cover with discs of waxed paper, seal, and label. Store in a cool, dark place and refrigerate after opening.

blueberry and raspberry freezer jam

This deliciously tangy combination of berries makes a healthy instant dessert served with natural yogurt and granola or on top of sliced, perfectly ripe peaches.

🥣 6–8 MINS PLUS STANDING   🍲 7–9 MINS   ❄ FREEZABLE

SPECIAL EQUIPMENT ▪ freezer pot

MAKES 500g (1lb 2oz)

225g (8oz) blueberries

225g (8oz) raspberries

2 tsp lemon juice

1 tbsp agar flakes or 1 tsp agar powder

115g (4oz) caster sugar

1 Make sure the fruit is at room temperature. Put it in a bowl with the lemon juice and roughly crush with a potato masher or fork; you want to leave some texture, not reduce the berries to a smooth pulp.

2 Put 200ml (7fl oz) water in a small saucepan, sprinkle the agar flakes or powder over it, and leave to soften for 2–3 minutes. Give the pan a gentle swirl, then bring the water slowly to the boil over a low heat without stirring it. Simmer gently for 3–5 minutes, stirring occasionally to make sure all the agar has dissolved. Add the sugar and stir for 2–3 minutes, until dissolved over a low heat. Remove the pan from the heat.

3 Pour the hot agar syrup over the fruit in the bowl, constantly stirring the fruit gently until the ingredients are well mixed.

4 Pour into clean freezer pots, leaving 1cm (½in) of space at the top. Leave to cool, then seal and label. Leave overnight in the fridge to thicken fully, then freeze. To use, thaw in the fridge, then keep refrigerated and use within 2 weeks.

fresh figs in honey syrup

Although figs lose their vibrant colour and turn greener when bottled, being macerated in honey syrup with lemon zest enhances their flavour.

10 MINS   5 MINS PLUS HEAT-PROCESSING

MAKES 1 LITRE (1¾ PINTS)

250ml (9fl oz) clear honey

2 thinly pared strips of washed lemon zest about 1cm (½in) wide

juice of 1 lemon

approx 16 small ripe figs (or 12 larger ones), washed and dried

1 Put the honey, 500ml (16fl oz) cold water, and the lemon zest and juice in a saucepan. Heat gently, stirring until the honey has dissolved. Bring to the boil and cook for 3 minutes. Then add the figs to the syrup and boil for 2 minutes.

2 Place some warm sterilized jars in a deep roasting tray lined with newspaper. Using a slotted spoon, pack the fruit tightly into jars without squashing them in too much. Lift the zest from the syrup and discard. Pour the hot syrup over the figs to cover them completely. Tap each jar gently on a wooden board or work surface to remove any air bubbles.

3 Fit the rubber band or metal lid seal and clamp on the lid. If using screw-band jars, loosen by a quarter of a turn.

4 Put the roasting tray of filled jars in the centre of the oven for 50–60 minutes to heat-process (remove the remaining air in the jars). Then remove from the oven and tighten the clips or lids (or screw on plastic screw-band lids) immediately. Leave for 24 hours, then unscrew or unclip and test the lids are firmly sealed before refastening and storing. (If using kilner jars with metal lids, you will know if you have a seal as the lid becomes slightly concave and is firm with no "give" once pressed.) Store the jars in a cool, dark place and refrigerate after opening.

cucumber pickle

This sweet cucumber pickle is an all-time American favourite. The cucumbers are pickled in hot vinegar, which makes them soft rather than crunchy.

 10 MINS PLUS STANDING AND MATURING   10 MINS

SPECIAL EQUIPMENT ▪ preserving pan

MAKES 1.25kg (2¾lb)

1 large cucumber, diced or sliced

1 large onion (white), peeled and chopped or sliced

1 small green pepper, finely sliced

1 tsp sea salt

300ml (10fl oz) cider vinegar

225g (8oz) light soft brown sugar

¼ tsp celery seeds

¼ tsp mustard seeds

¼ tsp ground cloves

¼ tsp dill

1 Put the cucumber, onion, and pepper in a large bowl, add the sea salt and mix thoroughly. Cover the bowl and leave to stand for 2 hours.

2 Rinse the vegetables under cold water, drain, and put into a preserving pan or a large heavy-based, stainless steel saucepan. Add the vinegar and bring to the boil. Turn off the heat.

3 Add the remaining ingredients and stir to dissolve the sugar. Then leave to cool. Ladle into warm sterilized jars with non-metallic or vinegar-proof lids, seal, and label. Store in a cool, dark place. Allow the flavours to mature for at least 1 month and refrigerate after opening.

hot-spiced aubergine chutney

Tender aubergine pieces, onion seeds, and a gingery mix gives this chutney an authentic flavour. Serve with lamb or Indian food such as curries or snacks.

10 MINS PLUS MATURING   1 HR 20 MINS – 1 HR 30 MINS

SPECIAL EQUIPMENT ▪ preserving pan

MAKES 1.5kg (3lb 3oz)

900g (2lb) aubergines, cut into cubes

2 red onions, roughly chopped

sea salt

1 tbsp tomato purée

500ml (16fl oz) cider vinegar

450g (1lb) light soft brown sugar

175g (6oz) sultanas

pinch of dried chilli flakes

1 cinnamon stick

2 tsp onion seeds (nigella seeds)

5cm (2in) piece of fresh root ginger, peeled and finely chopped or grated

1 Put the aubergine in a preserving pan or a large heavy-based, stainless steel saucepan. Add the red onions and a little sea salt. Stir to combine, then stir in the tomato purée.

2 Pour in the vinegar and sugar and stir, then add the sultanas, chilli flakes, cinnamon stick, onion seeds, and ginger. Heat the ingredients gently, stirring occasionally until the sugar has dissolved. Turn the heat up and bring the mixture to the boil.

3 Reduce the heat to a simmer and cook gently on a low heat for about 1 hour, stirring occasionally so it doesn't burn. Stir continuously near the end of the cooking time so it doesn't catch on the base of the pan. The chutney is ready when it is thick and sticky and the vinegar has been absorbed. Remove the cinnamon stick from the pan.

4 Ladle into warm sterilized jars with non-metallic or vinegar-proof lids, making sure there are no air gaps. Cover each pot with a waxed paper disc, seal, and label. Store in a cool, dark place. Allow the flavours to mature for at least 1 month and refrigerate after opening.

quick salted herrings

Whether just cured or also marinated for added richness and flavour, these salted herrings can be served in salads with beetroot, radicchio, and soured cream or horseradish sauce.

🥣 **30 MINS PLUS CURING AND MARINATING**

SPECIAL EQUIPMENT ■ crock or sterilized jar

SERVES 2–4

2 boned, very fresh, herring fillets with heads removed and any excess skin and fins trimmed off

small slivers of lemon peel (optional)

olive oil, to cover

For the cure mix

2 tsp fine sea salt

2 tsp caster sugar

1 tsp brandy

freshly ground black pepper

2 tsp chopped dill

1 Place one fillet, skin-side down, on a clean plate. Mix all the ingredients for the cure mix and spread them evenly over the fillet. Lay the second fillet on top, skin-side up, to make a sandwich. Cover the fillets with cling film, put a heavy weight on top, and leave in the fridge for 24 hours to cure. Turn them after 12 hours (the cure will turn to liquid, which can be drained off) and return to the fridge.

2 The herrings can be eaten at this point, if you wish. Transfer them to a clean dry plate, cover with cling film, and store in the fridge.

3 To marinate the herrings for extra flavour, slice the fillets into slivers, removing any surplus skin (or all the skin, if you prefer). Pack into a small sterilized jar or crock, add the lemon peel (if using), cover completely with oil, and return to the fridge. Leave for 48 hours before eating.

spiced beetroot pickle

This pickle has a lovely deep purple colour, and the fragrance of the star anise and cinnamon blend beautifully with the earthy taste of the beetroot. It is great with Cheddar cheese.

🥣 **15 MINS PLUS MATURING**   🍲 **1–2 HOURS**

SPECIAL EQUIPMENT ■ preserving pan

MAKES 1kg (2¼lb)

1kg (2¼lb) raw beetroots, unpeeled, of similar size

1 litre (1¾ pints) red wine vinegar

225g (8oz) granulated sugar

1 small bay leaf

1 cinnamon stick

1 star anise

4 black peppercorns

1 tsp sea salt

1 Trim off any beet tops, taking care not to cut into the beetroots (or they will "bleed" when cooked) and leaving the roots intact.

2 Put the remaining ingredients in a preserving pan or a large heavy-based, stainless steel pan. Heat gently, stirring until the sugar has dissolved, then bring to the boil.

Add the beetroots, bring back to the boil, reduce the heat, cover tightly, and simmer gently for 1–2 hours, or until the beetroots are really tender when pierced with a skewer. Leave to cool in the liquid.

3 Lift out the beetroots with a slotted spoon. When cool enough to handle, cut off the roots and tops, peel, and dice. Wear rubber gloves to peel the beetroots, or your hands will stain. Pack into warm sterilized jars with non-metallic or vinegar-proof lids.

4 Strain the liquid and return it to the pan. Bring back to the boil and pour over the beetroots to cover them completely. Seal, leave to cool, label, and store in a cool, dark place to allow the flavours to mature for 1 month. Refrigerate after opening.

runner bean and courgette chutney

With its mixture of sweet and tangy flavours, this chutney is perfect served with oily fish, but it is also delicious served with a salad and really perks up bread and cheese.

🥣 **15 MINS PLUS MATURING**   🍲 **1 HR 45 MINS**

SPECIAL EQUIPMENT ■ preserving pan

MAKES 1kg (2¼lb)

600g (1lb 5oz) runner beans, thinly sliced

4 courgettes, thinly sliced

350g (12oz) cooking apples, peeled, cored, and chopped

2 onions, finely chopped

450g (1lb) light soft brown sugar

1 tsp mustard powder

1 tsp turmeric

1 tsp coriander seeds

600ml (1 pint) cider vinegar

1 Put the beans, courgettes, apples, and onions in a preserving pan or a large heavy-based, stainless steel saucepan. Add the sugar, mustard powder, turmeric, and coriander seeds. Pour in the vinegar and stir.

2 Cook over a gentle heat, stirring until all the sugar has dissolved, then bring to a rolling boil and cook, stirring occasionally, for about 10 minutes. Reduce to a simmer and cook for about 1½ hours, stirring from time to time, until the mixture thickens. Stir continuously near the end of the cooking time so the chutney doesn't catch on the base of the pan.

3 Ladle into warm sterilized jars with non-metallic or vinegar-proof lids, making sure there are no air gaps. Cover each pot with a waxed paper disc, seal, and label. Store in a cool, dark place. Allow the flavours to mature for 1 month, then refrigerate after opening.

autumn

at their best

vegetables artichokes ▪ aubergine ▪ beetroot ▪ calabrese broccoli ▪ carrots (maincrop) ▪ celery ▪ chillies ▪ courgettes ▪ cucumbers ▪ fennel ▪ green beans ▪ leeks ▪ marrows ▪ potatoes (maincrop) ▪ pak choi ▪ peppers ▪ pumpkin ▪ romanesco ▪ runner beans ▪ squash ▪ sweet potatoes ▪ sweetcorn ▪ Swiss chard ▪ tomatoes ▪ wild mushrooms

fruit and nuts apples ▪ blackberries ▪ crabapples ▪ currants ▪ damsons ▪ figs ▪ grapes ▪ hazelnuts ▪ loganberries ▪ pears ▪ plums ▪ quinces ▪ rosehips ▪ sloes ▪ walnuts

seafood brown shrimps ▪ brown trout (wild and farmed) ▪ coley ▪ common brown crab ▪ dab ▪ Dover sole ▪ grey mullet ▪ herring ▪ John Dory ▪ langoustines ▪ lemon sole ▪ mackerel ▪ monkfish ▪ North Atlantic lobster ▪ plaice ▪ pollack ▪ rainbow trout (wild and farmed) ▪ razor clams ▪ red gurnard ▪ red mullet ▪ salmon (wild and farmed) ▪ sea bass ▪ sea bream (wild and farmed) ▪ squid ▪ sea trout (wild and farmed) ▪ turbot (wild and farmed)

meat, poultry, game duck (wild and farmed) ▪ goose (wild and farmed) ▪ grouse ▪ hare ▪ lamb ▪ partridge (wild) ▪ pheasant (wild) ▪ rabbit (wild and farmed) ▪ venison (wild and farmed) ▪ wild boar (wild and farmed)

also available

vegetables Brussels sprouts ▪ cabbages ▪ cavolo nero ▪ cauliflower ▪ celeriac ▪ Jerusalem artichokes ▪ horseradish ▪ kale ▪ lettuce ▪ mangetout ▪ mushrooms (cultivated) ▪ onions ▪ parsnips ▪ peas ▪ radishes ▪ shallots ▪ spinach ▪ sugarsnap peas ▪ swede ▪ turnips ▪ watercress **fruit** cranberries ▪ lemons ▪ limes ▪ mangoes ▪ raspberries ▪ strawberries ▪ wild strawberries **seafood** abalone ▪ brill ▪ cod ▪ haddock ▪ hake ▪ halibut ▪ king scallops (farmed) ▪ mussels ▪ native oysters ▪ Pacific or rock oysters ▪ sardines ▪ whiting **meat, poultry, game** beef ▪ chicken ▪ guinea fowl (farmed) ▪ pork ▪ quail (farmed) ▪ turkey ▪ veal

autumn recipe chooser

Ⓥ suitable for vegetarians

Pistou soup p267

Lamb mince and squash with green chillies p294

Vegetables

Acorn squash
Acorn squash and cumin soup p275 Ⓥ
Butter bean and winter squash goulash p317 Ⓥ
Roast squash and blue cheese crostini p260 Ⓥ

Artichoke
Artichoke, green olive, and feta tart p310 Ⓥ
Artichoke risotto p306 Ⓥ
Baby artichokes in oil p349 Ⓥ
Globe artichoke soup p266
Provençal stuffed artichokes p324
Tomato tagliatelle with artichokes p307 Ⓥ
White fish, green beans, and artichoke paella p306

Aubergine
Aubergine massaman curry p289
Chargrilled lamb cutlets and aubergine with red cabbage slaw p290
Chunky ratatouille p305 Ⓥ
Italian-style vegetables p353 Ⓥ
Melanzane alla parmigiana p304 Ⓥ
Paprika rice and aubergine p300 Ⓥ
Smoky aubergine and lamb stew p306
Thai red vegetable curry p318 Ⓥ
Vegetable tempura with chilli dipping sauce p261 Ⓥ

Beetroot
Beef with beetroot and spinach p252
Beetroot and apple soup p254 Ⓥ
Beetroot relish p328 Ⓥ
Beetroot risotto p298 Ⓥ
Beetroot-topped mini rye breads p264 Ⓥ
Borscht p254 Ⓥ
Braised pheasant with beetroot and pears p305
Butterflied mackerel with sweet potato and beetroot pickle p312
Duck breasts with beetroot, blackberries, and spinach p305
Little Gem lettuce with blue cheese and beetroot p252 Ⓥ
Little Gem lettuce with goat's cheese, walnuts, and crispy bacon p252
Pastrami and beetroot on rye p264
Peppered beef with roasted beetroot p305
Spiced beetroot and carrot soup p254 Ⓥ

Broccoli
Broccoli and blue cheese soup p278 Ⓥ
Broccoli and mushroom quiche p318 Ⓥ
Broccoli, tomato, and basil pie p253 Ⓥ
Marinated lamb chops with crushed lemon and chilli broccoli p318

Butternut squash
Brazilian black bean and pumpkin stew p314 Ⓥ
Butternut squash stuffed with beef mince p286
Butternut squash tagine p286 Ⓥ
Lamb cutlets with butternut squash, beans, and mint p280
Lamb mince and squash with green chillies p294
Pasta with butternut squash, cream, and sage p287 Ⓥ
Plum and squash chutney p351 Ⓥ
Pumpkin and ginger soup p275 Ⓥ
Pumpkin stew p282 Ⓥ
Quick pumpkin bread p330 Ⓥ
Squash, thyme, and goat's cheese tart p283 Ⓥ
Sweet and sour pumpkin stew p282 Ⓥ

Cabbage
Borscht p254 Ⓥ
Chargrilled lamb cutlets and aubergine with red cabbage slaw p290
Chicken doner kebab p299
Poussins with plums and cabbage p289

Carrot
Acorn squash and cumin soup p275 Ⓥ
Braised pheasant with vegetables p311
Braised turkey with vegetables p311
French country soup p262 Ⓥ
Genoese minestrone with red pesto p272 Ⓥ
German potato soup p279
Mackerel roasted with carrots, chickpeas, and harissa p302
Piccalilli p348 Ⓥ
Provençal vegetable soup p270 Ⓥ
Spiced beetroot and carrot soup p254 Ⓥ
Spicy, saucy fish p286
Yam pla fu p278

Cauliflower
Piccalilli p348 Ⓥ
Stir-fried Thai vegetables p280

Roast pumpkin, chilli, and ginger dip p264

Celeriac
German potato soup p279 Ⓥ
Pumpkin stew p282 Ⓥ

Celery
Apple, celery, and pecan salad p276 Ⓥ
Beef with celery and mustard p288
Chargrilled lamb cutlets and aubergine with red cabbage slaw p290
Fennel and apple soup p276 Ⓥ
Provençal vegetable soup p270 Ⓥ
Quail's eggs with celery salt p268 Ⓥ
Sausage and chicken gumbo p295
Spicy, saucy fish p286
Stuffed mushrooms with basil and pine nuts p257 Ⓥ
Sweet and sour pumpkin stew p282 Ⓥ
Sweetcorn chowder p279 Ⓥ
Waldorf chicken salad p260

Chilli
Balinese spicy mackerel p324
Beef chilli mole p298
Chargrilled squid salad p262
Chicken doner kebab p299
Chilean pork and beans p314
Duck curry p295
Hot spiced pear pickle p349 Ⓥ
Jamaican corn casserole p320 Ⓥ
Jerk fish p322
Karahi chicken p315
Karahi rabbit p315
Kenyan fish curry p322
Lamb mince and squash with green chillies p294
Paprika rice and aubergine p300 Ⓥ

Aubergine massaman curry p289

Roasted baby leeks with chilli and crispy bacon p326
Roasted monkfish with chilli, tomatoes, anchovies, and capers p281
Roast pumpkin, chilli, and ginger dip p264
Spicy garlic and green vegetable medley p327 Ⓥ
Spicy mixed vegetable medley p327 Ⓥ
Thai dipping sauce p328
Vegetable tempura with chilli dipping sauce p261 Ⓥ

Courgette
Baby courgettes with fish and couscous p316
Butter bean and winter squash goulash p317 Ⓥ
Chunky ratatouille p305 Ⓥ
Crisp sweet potato with courgette and chive mascarpone p261 Ⓥ
Genoese minestrone with red pesto p272 Ⓥ
Italian-style vegetables p353 Ⓥ
Mackerel with courgettes, tomato, and basil p300
Monkfish and white wine stew p303
Piccalilli p348 Ⓥ
Pistou soup p267
Pumpkin stew p282 Ⓥ
Tomato, bean, and courgette stew p317 Ⓥ
Vegetable tempura with chilli dipping sauce p261 Ⓥ
Yellow courgette and tomato chutney p349 Ⓥ

Pumpkin and ginger soup p275

Vegetarian leek and mushroom lasagne p313

Mushroom and ricotta pies with red pepper pesto p256

Tomato tagliatelle with artichokes p307

autumn recipe chooser continued

ⓥ suitable for vegetarians

Baked polenta with wild mushrooms p311

Filo pie with Swiss chard, ricotta cheese, and tomatoes p253

Broccoli and mushroom quiche p318

Sweetcorn
Jamaican corn casserole p320 ⓥ
Spicy mixed vegetable medley p327 ⓥ
Sweetcorn and pepper relish p329 ⓥ
Sweetcorn chowder p279 ⓥ

Sweet potato
African sweet potato soup p278 ⓥ
Butterflied mackerel with sweet potato and beetroot pickle p312
Cajun sweet potato and bean soup p266
Cajun vegetable chips p328 ⓥ
Crisp sweet potato with courgette and chive mascarpone p261 ⓥ
Chilean pork and beans p314
Jamaican corn casserole p320 ⓥ
Peppered beef with roasted beetroot p305
Pheasant and apple soup p254
Pork chops with sweet potatoes, beans, and thyme p280
Spicy minced beef with sweet potato and eggs p294
Sweet potato and butter bean stew p312 ⓥ

Sugarsnap peas
Spicy garlic and green vegetable medley p327 ⓥ
Spicy mixed vegetable medley p327 ⓥ
Sweet and sour stir-fried fish with ginger p317

Swiss chard
Chunky ratatouille p305 ⓥ
Filo pie with Swiss chard, ricotta cheese, and tomatoes p253 ⓥ
Spicy garlic and green vegetable medley p327 ⓥ

Sweet potato and butter bean stew p312 ⓥ

Tomatoes
African sweet potato soup p278 ⓥ
Beef chilli mole p298
Broccoli, tomato, and basil pie p253 ⓥ
Butter bean and winter squash goulash p317 ⓥ
Butternut squash tagine p286 ⓥ
Chicken harira soup p271
Chilean pork and beans p314
Chunky ratatouille p305 ⓥ
Cream of tomato soup p274 ⓥ
Duck curry p295
Filo pie with Swiss chard, ricotta cheese, and tomatoes p253 ⓥ
Greek-style vegetables p329 ⓥ
Grilled sea bream with spice rub p292
Hungarian beef goulash p290
Karahi chicken p315
Karahi rabbit p315
Kenyan fish curry p322
Lamb cutlets with butternut squash, beans, and mint p280
Mackerel with garlic and tomatoes p300
Mackerel with courgettes, tomato, and basil p300
Marrow and tomato gratin p287 ⓥ
Mulligatawny p268
Pistou soup p267
Pork chops with sweet potatoes, beans, and thyme p280
Pumpkin stew p282 ⓥ
Rabbit Provençal p281
Rich fish soup p266

Roasted monkfish with chilli, tomatoes, anchovies, and capers p281
Roasted red pepper, fennel, and tomato soup p273 ⓥ
Sea bream with tomato sauce p292
Smoked mussels in fresh tomato sauce p302
Spicy, saucy fish p286
Squid stew p292
Tomato, bean, and courgette stew p317 ⓥ
Tomato ketchup p326 ⓥ
Yellow courgette and tomato chutney p349 ⓥ

Turnip
Pot roast chicken with turnips and fennel p298
Pumpkin stew p282 ⓥ

Wild mushrooms
Baked polenta with wild mushrooms p311 ⓥ
Dried mushrooms p352 ⓥ
German potato soup p279 ⓥ
Marinated mushroom salad p262 ⓥ
Mixed mushroom and walnut tart p256 ⓥ
Mixed mushroom soup p270 ⓥ
Mushroom and ricotta pies with red pepper pesto p256 ⓥ
Mushroom ketchup p330 ⓥ
Stuffed mushrooms with herbs p257 ⓥ
Stuffed mushrooms with basil and pine nuts p257 ⓥ
Vegetarian leek and mushroom lasagne p313 ⓥ
Venison Wellingtons p282
Viltgryta p314
Warm salad of wild mushrooms p299 ⓥ
Wild mushroom and Gruyère pasta bake p310 ⓥ

Fruit and nuts

Apples
Apple and blackberry brown betty p332 ⓥ
Apple and cinnamon oat cookies p339 ⓥ
Apple and cinnamon strudel p344 ⓥ
Apple and custard tart p337 ⓥ
Apple, celery, and pecan salad p276 ⓥ
Apple jalousie p332 ⓥ

Apple, sultana, and date chutney p350 ⓥ
Apple tart p337 ⓥ
Beetroot and apple soup p254 ⓥ
Blackberry and apple sponge p340 ⓥ
Fennel and apple soup p276 ⓥ
Mulligatawny p268
Pheasant and apple soup p254
Plum and squash chutney p351 ⓥ
Spicy, saucy fish p286
Tarte tatin p336 ⓥ
Toffee apple tray bake p345 ⓥ
Waldorf chicken salad p260

Blackberries
Apple and blackberry brown betty p332 ⓥ
Blackberry and apple sponge p340 ⓥ
Blackberry brioche with mascarpone p340 ⓥ
Blackberry focaccia p333 ⓥ
Duck breasts with beetroot, blackberries, and spinach p252
Pear and blackberry freezer jam p352 ⓥ
Spiced blackberry and pear toasties with mascarpone p340 ⓥ
Trio of sorbets p341 ⓥ

Crab apples
Crab apple jelly p351 ⓥ

Grapes
Grapes marinated in port p346 ⓥ
Grapes marinated in port with goat's cheese croûtes p346 ⓥ
Green grape, spice, and orange cake p346 ⓥ
Red grape and cinnamon cake p346 ⓥ
Schiacciata di uva p346 ⓥ
Simple grape wine p352 ⓥ
Sole veronique p325

Hazelnuts
Chargrilled lamb cutlets and aubergine with red cabbage slaw p290
Green beans with toasted hazelnuts p329 ⓥ
Spicy garlic and green vegetable medley p327 ⓥ
Spicy mixed vegetable medley p327 ⓥ

Figs
Chocolate, fig, and lime roulade p345 ⓥ
Fig and mulled wine tart p339 ⓥ
Fig and vanilla jam p350 ⓥ
Honey-grilled figs with zabaglione p339 ⓥ

Apple and blackberry Brown Betty p332

Fig and vanilla jam p350

Lamb tagine with walnuts and figs p320
Seared halloumi cheese with figs
 p253 (v)
Seared pancetta with figs and crumbled
 feta p253

Pears
Braised pheasant with beetroot and
 pears p305
Chocolate and pear meringue roulade
 p345 (v)
Flaky pear tartlets p336 (v)
Hot spiced pear pickle p349 (v)
Pear and blackberry freezer jam p352 (v)
Pear and cinnamon strudel p344 (v)
Pear and raspberry brown betty p332 (v)
Pear, fennel, and walnut salad p276 (v)
Pear pie with walnut pastry p344 (v)
Pear tarte tatin p336 (v)
Poached pears with chocolate sponge
 p340 (v)
Spiced blackberry and pear toasties with
 mascarpone p340 (v)
Spiced pear pickle p349 (v)
Trio of sorbets p341 (v)

Plums
Chinese-style plum sauce p326 (v)
Cinnamon and plum cobbler p337 (v)
Crispy wild duck with plums p291
Plum and squash chutney p351 (v)
Poussins with plums and cabbage
 p289
Spiced kirsch and plum jam p348 (v)
Spiced port and plum jam p348 (v)

Quinces
Membrillo p351 (v)
Quinces in spiced syrup p353 (v)

Rosehips
Rosehip soup p268 (v)

Walnuts
Cucumber and walnut soup p270 (v)
Lamb tagine with walnuts and figs
 p320
Little Gem lettuce with goat's cheese,
 walnuts, and crispy bacon p252
Mixed mushroom and walnut tart
 p256 (v)
Pear, fennel, and walnut salad p276 (v)
Pear pie with walnut pastry p344 (v)
Red pepper and walnut dip p272 (v)
Stuffed mushrooms with herbs p257 (v)
Tomato tagliatelle with artichokes
 p307 (v)
Waldorf chicken salad p260

Seafood
Cod
Baby courgettes with fish and couscous
 p316
White fish, green beans, and artichoke
 paella p306

Coley
Baby courgettes with fish and couscous
 p316
Fritto misto p273
Quick stir-fried fish with pak choi p291

Grey mullet
Baby courgettes with fish and couscous
 p316
Fritto misto p273
Grey mullet with herb crust p322
Jerk fish p322
Kenyan fish curry p322
Yam pla fu p278

Haddock
Rich fish soup p266
Sweet and sour stir-fried fish with ginger
 p317
White fish, green beans, and artichoke
 paella p306

Halibut
Quick stir-fried fish with pak choi p291
Spicy, saucy fish p286

Herring
Herrings in oatmeal with sweet mustard
 sauce p303

Mackerel
Balinese spicy mackerel p324
Butterflied mackerel with sweet potato
 and beetroot pickle p312
Mackerel roasted with carrots,
 chickpeas, and harissa p302
Mackerel roasted with harissa and
 potatoes p302
Mackerel with courgettes, tomato, and
 basil p300
Mackerel with garlic and tomatoes p300
Pan-fried mackerel in rolled oats p303
Potted fresh mackerel p265
Smoked mackerel pâté p265

Monkfish
Monkfish and white wine stew p303
Monkfish and red wine stew p303
Rich fish soup p266
Roasted monkfish with chilli, tomatoes,
 anchovies, and capers p281
Roast monkfish with peppers p313

Mussels
Grilled pepper-stuffed mussels p265
Mussels in fennel broth p276
Mussels in fennel and pernod broth
 p276
Risotto with mussels p300
Smoked mussels in fresh tomato sauce
 p302

Oysters
Fritto misto p273

Red mullet
Red mullet with Middle Eastern spices
 p302

Salmon
Quick stir-fried fish with pak choi
 p291
Salmon with mushrooms and pak
 choi p291

Sea bass
Sea bass with black bean sauce p325

Sea bream
Grilled sea bream with spice rub p292
Sea bream with tomato sauce p292
Whole stuffed sea bream p281

Sole
Sole veronique p325

Squid
Chargrilled squid salad p262
Fried calamari p273
Fritto misto p273
Marinated squid salad p262
Roasted squid and potato with spiced
 coriander pesto p288
Squid stew p292

Meat
Duck
Crispy duck char sui p291
Crispy wild duck with plums p291
Duck breasts with beetroot, blackberries,
 and spinach p252
Duck curry p295
French-style duck legs p295

Lamb
Chargrilled lamb cutlets and aubergine
 with red cabbage slaw p290
Lamb cutlets with butternut squash,
 beans, and mint p280
Lamb mince and squash with green
 chillies p294
Lamb, spinach, and chickpea hotpot
 p316
Lamb tagine with walnuts and figs p320
Lamb with roasted peppers p304
Marinated lamb chops with crushed
 lemon and chilli broccoli p318
Moroccan harira soup p271
Smoky aubergine and lamb stew p306

Pheasant
Braised pheasant with beetroot and
 pears p305
Braised pheasant with vegetables p311
Pheasant and apple soup p254

Rabbit
Karahi rabbit p315
Rabbit Provençal p281

Venison
Venison Wellingtons p282
Viltgryta p314

Grilled pepper-stuffed mussels p265

Pear and cinnamon strudel p344

Balinese spicy mackerel p324

Poussins with plums and cabbage
p289

Fried calamari p273

beef with beetroot and spinach

The dark, earthy colours and flavours of this dish suit the season. For even stronger shades, try using one of the vividly coloured chards in place of the spinach.

🥣 15 MINS

SERVES 4

350g (12oz) leftover roast beef, sliced

250g (9oz) spinach leaves

450g (1lb) beetroot, cooked, peeled (p255), and quartered

3 tbsp extra virgin olive oil

1 tbsp balsamic vinegar

juice of ½ clementine or satsuma

salt and freshly ground black pepper

handful of thyme, leaves picked

1 In a large bowl, gently toss together the roast beef, spinach, and beetroot. In a small bowl or jug, whisk together the oil, balsamic vinegar, and citrus juice. Season with salt and pepper.

2 When ready to serve, drizzle the dressing over the beef and beetroot salad, and scatter the thyme leaves over the top.

variation

duck breasts with beetroot, blackberries, and spinach

Fry 2 well-seasoned, large duck breasts skin-side down for 5 minutes until well browned and the fat has run. Turn the breasts over and fry the other side for about 5 minutes until tender, but still pink in the middle. Wrap in foil and leave to rest for 10 minutes. Cut in diagonal slices then proceed as in the recipe, but add a handful of ripe blackberries with the spinach and beetroot.

little gem lettuce with blue cheese and beetroot

For a milder flavour, use Dolcelatte rather than Gorgonzola. It is made in a similar way and is sometimes called Dolcelatte Gorgonzola – but note that the fat content is higher.

🥣 15 MINS

SPECIAL EQUIPMENT ▪ food processor

SERVES 4

150g (5½oz) blue cheese, such as Roquefort or Gorgonzola

1 tsp paprika

3 tbsp natural yogurt

1 tbsp chopped mint leaves

salt and freshly ground black pepper

1 Little Gem lettuce

3 beetroots, cooked, peeled (p255), and sliced

1 Put half the cheese, the paprika, yogurt, and mint in a food processor and blitz to a creamy paste. Crumble in the rest of the cheese and season with salt and pepper.

2 Separate the lettuce leaves, creating at least eight "boats". Place a couple of slices of beetroot in each one, then add a heaped teaspoon of the cheese mixture. Serve with fresh crusty bread and chorizo.

variation

little gem lettuce with goat's cheese, walnuts, and crispy bacon

Prepare in the same way, but use 150g (5½oz) soft goat's cheese instead of the blue cheese and simply beat with the paprika and yogurt, then beat in 1 tbsp finely chopped walnuts instead of the mint. Grill or dry-fry 4 smoked streaky bacon rashers until crisp. Drain on kitchen paper, then snip with scissors, or crumble into small pieces. Assemble the dish with the beetroot as before, then sprinkle the crumbled bacon over.

seared halloumi cheese with figs

Halloumi is a traditional Cypriot cheese made from a mixture of goat's and sheep milk. It combines perfectly with figs, which are at their sweetest in the autumn.

🥣 10 MINS 🍲 20 MINS

SERVES 4

300g (10oz) halloumi cheese, cut into 5mm (¼in) slices

8 large ripe figs, cut into quarters lengthways

large handful of mixed salad leaves

60ml (2fl oz) red wine vinegar

small handful of coriander, finely chopped

1 red chilli, deseeded and finely chopped

1 garlic clove, crushed

drizzle of olive oil, to serve

1 Put the halloumi and figs in a large, non-stick frying pan over a medium heat and cook for 2–3 minutes on each side until they start to brown. Once cooked, place on a platter with the salad leaves.

2 Pour the red wine vinegar into the same pan and increase the heat slightly. Add the coriander, chilli, and garlic and simmer over a medium-high heat until the sauce has reduced in volume by three-quarters. Tip sparingly over the figs and cheese. Splash the salad with the oil and serve immediately.

variation

seared pancetta with figs and crumbled feta

Put 12 thin slices of pancetta in a hot frying pan and dry-fry until crisp. Remove from the pan and drain on kitchen paper. Add the figs to the pan and fry for 2–3 minutes as before. Assemble the salad in exactly the same way, then scatter 100g (3½oz) crumbled feta cheese over, instead of the halloumi, before drizzling with olive oil.

filo pie with swiss chard, ricotta cheese, and tomatoes

Swiss chard is a relative of beetroot, but its glossy, crinkled leaves and fleshy stems are eaten rather than its roots.

🥣 15 MINS 🍲 30 MINS

SPECIAL EQUIPMENT ▪ 20cm (8in) round, loose-bottomed cake tin

SERVES 4–6

200g (7oz) ricotta cheese

550g (1¼lb) Swiss chard, chopped

4–6 sun-dried tomatoes in oil, drained and chopped

4 tomatoes, sliced

1 egg

salt and freshly ground black pepper

60g (2oz) butter, melted

8 sheets filo pastry

1 Preheat the oven to 180°C (350°F/Gas 4). In a bowl, mix together the ricotta, Swiss chard, sun-dried and fresh tomatoes, and egg. Season well with salt and pepper.

2 Brush the tin with melted butter. Lay 1 sheet of filo pastry in the tin, letting it hang over the edge on two sides. Lay another sheet at a right angle to the first. Brush with melted butter again. Continue in this way until you have 4 sheets for the base of the pie.

3 Spoon the ricotta mixture into the pie. Fold in the edges of the pastry and top the pie with the remaining 4 sheets of filo pastry, brushing each with a little butter between layers and tucking them in neatly. Brush the top with the remaining butter and bake in the oven for 20–30 minutes until golden and crisp. Serve hot with a salad.

variation

broccoli, tomato, and basil pie

Cook 350g (12oz) broccoli, cut into tiny florets, in boiling salted water for 2–3 minutes until just tender. Drain, rinse in cold water, and drain again. Omit the Swiss chard. Mix with the ricotta and sun-dried and fresh tomatoes as before, then add 2 tbsp chopped basil, 12 halved and stoned green olives, the egg, and seasoning. Make the pie in the same way and bake for 25 minutes.

beetroot and apple soup

Here beetroot soup is given a different twist with plenty of herbs and the sweetness of apples and sugar, set against the sharpness of lemon and soured milk.

🥄 20 MINS   🍲 1 HR   ❄ FREEZABLE

SPECIAL EQUIPMENT ▪ blender or food processor

SERVES 6-8

3 tbsp olive oil

1 onion, grated or finely chopped

2 garlic cloves, grated or finely chopped

salt and freshly ground black pepper

350g (12oz) raw beetroot, peeled (p255) and grated or finely chopped

1 potato, peeled and grated or finely chopped

4 eating apples, peeled, cored, and grated or finely chopped

1.5 litres (2¾ pints) hot vegetable stock or chicken stock

1-2 tbsp dark soft brown sugar

juice of 1 lemon

2 tbsp finely chopped parsley, chives, dill, or coriander, or a mixture

200g (7oz) crème fraîche, soured cream, or thick, creamy yogurt

1 Heat the oil in a large pan over a low heat and add the onion, garlic, and a pinch of salt. Cook gently, stirring once or twice, for 5 minutes until soft but not browned.

2 Add the beetroot, potato, and apples to the pan and stew gently for 10 minutes, stirring occasionally.

Pour in the stock, bring to the boil, then cover with a lid and simmer gently for 45 minutes, or until the beetroot is cooked through.

3 Transfer the mixture to a blender or food processor and blitz in batches until smooth. Season with the sugar, lemon juice, salt, and pepper.

4 Stir the herbs into the cream or yogurt. Ladle the soup into warmed bowls and drop a spoonful of cream into the middle.

variation

spiced beetroot and carrot soup

Make the soup in exactly the same way but substitute 2 large grated or finely chopped carrots for the apples and add 1 star anise, a piece of cinnamon stick, and the finely grated zest and juice of a small orange with the stock. Remove the cinnamon stick and star anise before blitzing the soup.

borscht

During a spell of cold weather, there is little that can be more cheering on the dinner table than a bowl of this startlingly bright, deep pink soup from Eastern Europe.

🥄 50-55 MINS   🍲 1 HR 15 MINS

SERVES 4

3 raw beetroots, trimmed

30g (1oz) butter

1 small carrot, chopped

1 small onion, chopped

½ small white cabbage, cored and shredded

400g can chopped tomatoes

1 litre (1¾ pints) chicken stock or water, plus more if needed

salt and freshly ground black pepper

½ tsp sugar, or to taste

2-3 sprigs of dill, leaves picked and finely chopped

2-3 sprigs of parsley, leaves picked and finely chopped

juice of ½ lemon

1-2 tbsp red wine vinegar

soured cream, to garnish

1 Bring the beetroot to the boil in a pan of salted water. Cook for about 30 minutes until tender.

2 Drain the beetroot. When cool enough to handle, peel off the skin and grate the flesh coarsely.

3 Melt the butter in a large saucepan. Add the carrot and onion and cook, stirring, for 3-5 minutes, until soft but not brown. Add the cabbage, beetroot, tomatoes, stock, salt, pepper, and sugar, and bring to the boil. Simmer for 45-60 minutes. Add more stock if the soup is too thick.

4 Just before serving, stir in the herbs, lemon juice, and vinegar and taste for seasoning. Pour into warmed bowls and top with a spoonful of soured cream.

pheasant and apple soup

This spicy soup is equally delicious made with other game birds, but if they are small, such as pigeon or partridge, use the whole bird including the breasts.

🥄 20 MINS   🍲 1 HR 15 MINS PLUS REHEATING
❄ FREEZABLE

SPECIAL EQUIPMENT ▪ blender or food processor

SERVES 4-6

1 small pheasant

15g (½oz) butter

1 onion, roughly chopped

1 small sweet potato, peeled and roughly chopped

1 small cooking apple, peeled and diced

500ml (16fl oz) medium-sweet cider or apple juice

450ml (15fl oz) chicken stock

5cm (2in) piece of cinnamon stick

1 bay leaf

salt and freshly ground black pepper

150ml (5fl oz) single cream

4 small sprigs of parsley, to garnish

1 Cut the breasts off the pheasant and reserve to cook for a separate dish. Cut the rest of the bird into pieces using a large, sharp knife or poultry shears.

2 Melt the butter in a saucepan. Add the onion and fry gently, stirring, for 2 minutes until softened but not browned. Add the remaining ingredients, except the cream. Bring to the boil, reduce the heat, cover, and simmer gently for 1 hour.

3 Remove the pheasant and leave to cool slightly. Discard the bay leaf and cinnamon, then pour the soup into a blender or food processor and blitz until smooth. Return to the pan and stir in the cream. Taste and adjust the seasoning if necessary.

4 Take the pheasant meat off the bones, discarding the skin, and shred it. Add half to the soup. Reheat the soup but do not boil. Ladle into shallow soup plates, place a small pile of the remaining pheasant in the centre, and garnish with parsley.

Season's best **beetroot**

Beetroots vary in colour, shape, and flavour, but the most common are globe-shaped and red, with an intensely coloured juice. Available from early summer, but best in autumn. They also bring a luscious colour to any dish, like in borscht, a classic Eastern European soup. Their sweetness works well with the aniseed flavours of dill and caraway, with cheeses, nuts, seeds, and carrots.

Beetroot evolved from wild seabeets in India. Their bulb size varies enormously, depending on the fertility of the soil, the time of sowing, and weather conditions.

Burpee's golden beetroot An exceptionally tasty beetroot, this has fine-textured, yellow flesh. It is best when no bigger than a golf ball. Great as a contrast in a red and yellow beetroot salad.

essentials
varieties available

Various varieties of red, golden, and striped beetroots.

buy Glossy and fresh leaves; roots should feel hard, with no mould, cuts, or abrasions.

store For up to 2 weeks in a paper bag in the vegetable drawer of the fridge. Remove leafy tops before storing.

cook Grate or thinly slice raw, bake, roast, or boil.

preserve Pickle, make into chutney or wine.

recipe ideas

Beef with beetroot and spinach p252

Beetroot relish p328

Beetroot risotto p298

Borscht p254

Striped beetroot Grown for looks rather than flavour, this variety is much milder than red beetroot. The colourful striped flesh looks great in salads. When cooked, the stripes fade and the flesh becomes a uniform pink.

how to cook and peel beetroot

Raw, peeled beetroot is delicious grated in salads (particularly when combined with grated carrots). If cooking, do not peel it beforehand or it will "bleed".

1 Cut off the green leaves, leaving short stalks. Don't cut the skin or roots, or the beetroot will bleed when cooked. Wash well.

2 Boil in lightly salted water until tender, for 30 minutes to 1½ hours, depending on size. Drain, cool, then trim and peel off the skin.

Red beetroot The firm, juicy flesh of red beetroot has a uniquely earthy, sweet flavour. Their stalks and leaves can be cooked like spinach, but use fresh as they don't keep as well as the roots.

mushroom and ricotta pies with red pepper pesto

For a slightly sweeter taste and a paler colour, you can use orange or yellow peppers for the pesto.

🥣 25 MINS 🍲 45 MINS ❄ FREEZABLE

SPECIAL EQUIPMENT ▪ blender or food processor

SERVES 4

3 tbsp olive oil

150g (5½oz) button mushrooms, halved

150g (5½oz) mixed wild mushrooms

1 leek, white part only, finely sliced

2 sheets ready-rolled puff pastry

200g (7oz) ricotta cheese

1 egg yolk, lightly beaten

For the red pepper pesto

2 tbsp olive oil

1 onion, sliced

2 red peppers, sliced

2 garlic cloves, crushed

zest and juice of 1 small lemon

salt and freshly ground black pepper

1 Preheat the oven to 200°C (400°F/ Gas 6) and line a baking tray with baking parchment. To make the red pepper pesto, heat the oil in a heavy-based frying pan over a low heat. Add the onion and sweat gently for a few minutes until translucent. Tip in the peppers and sweat for a further 10–15 minutes until soft. Transfer the mixture to a blender or food processor. Add the garlic and lemon zest and juice, and blitz to a chunky purée. Season and set aside.

2 Heat the 3 tbsp oil in a large heavy-based frying pan over a medium heat. Add the mushrooms and leek, and sauté, stirring, for 5 minutes until the mushrooms have browned. Set aside.

3 Cut each pastry sheet into quarters. Using a sharp knife, cut diagonal slashes across the surface of half the pastry squares, taking care not to slice all the way through. Spread the ricotta over the surface of the uncut squares, leaving a 1cm (½in) border of pastry round the edges. Spoon the mushroom and leek mixture evenly over the ricotta, then lay the slit pastry squares evenly over the top of the mushrooms. Pinch and twist together the corners of the pies and brush the tops with the egg yolk.

4 Place the pies on the baking tray and bake in the oven for 25 minutes until golden brown. Serve with the red pepper pesto and a leafy green salad.

mixed mushroom and walnut tart

Autumn is the time when fresh wild mushrooms are in abundance and you will have a choice of varieties such as ceps, field mushrooms, and golden chanterelles.

🥣 15 MINS 🍲 1 HR ❄ FREEZABLE

SPECIAL EQUIPMENT ▪ 12 x 35cm (5 x 14in) rectangular loose-bottomed fluted tart tin ▪ ceramic baking beans

SERVES 6

250g (9oz) ready-made shortcrust pastry

2 eggs, plus 1 lightly beaten

3–4 tbsp olive oil

140g (5oz) mixed wild mushrooms, roughly chopped

200g (7oz) chestnut mushrooms, roughly chopped

3 garlic cloves, grated or finely chopped

50g (1¾oz) walnuts, roughly chopped

salt and freshly ground black pepper

2 handfuls of spinach leaves, roughly chopped

200ml (7fl oz) double cream

1 Preheat the oven to 200°C (400°F/ Gas 6). Roll out the pastry on a floured work surface and use to line the tart tin. Trim away the excess, line the pastry shell with greaseproof paper, and fill with ceramic baking beans. Bake in the oven for 15–20 minutes until the edges are golden. Remove the beans and paper, brush the bottom of the shell with a little of the beaten egg, and return to the oven for 2–3 minutes to crisp. Remove from the oven and set aside. Reduce the oven temperature to 180°C (350°F/Gas 4).

2 Heat the oil in a large, deep frying pan over a low heat. Add the mushrooms, garlic, and walnuts, and season well with salt and pepper. Cook, stirring occasionally, for about 10 minutes until the mushrooms release their juices. Tip in the spinach and cook, stirring, for a further 5 minutes until just wilted. Spoon the mixture into the pastry shell.

3 Mix together the cream and eggs and season well. Carefully pour the cream mixture over the mushroom filling. Sprinkle with a pinch of black pepper and bake in the oven for 15–20 minutes until set. Leave to cool for 10 minutes before releasing from the tin. Serve hot or cold.

stuffed mushrooms with herbs

For those who love the earthy, meaty taste of mushrooms, autumn's bountiful selection is showcased in this recipe. Filled with mixed wild mushrooms and walnuts and perfumed with garlic and plenty of herbs, these stuffed mushrooms are unbeatable.

🥄 25-30 MINS 🍲 15-20 MINS

SPECIAL EQUIPMENT ▪ food processor

SERVES 4

12 large cap mushrooms, total weight about 500g (1lb 2oz)

85g (3oz) mixed wild mushrooms

12-14 sprigs of tarragon, leaves picked and chopped, plus a few sprigs for garnish

10-12 sprigs of chervil, leaves picked and chopped, plus a few sprigs for garnish

7-10 sprigs of thyme, leaves picked and chopped, plus a few sprigs for garnish

3-4 tbsp grated Parmesan cheese

4 tbsp olive oil

3 garlic cloves, finely chopped

juice of ½ lemon

salt and freshly ground black pepper

90ml (3fl oz) double cream

100g (3½oz) walnuts, roughly chopped

1 Pull out the stalks from the large mushrooms, leaving the caps whole for stuffing. Wipe the caps with damp kitchen paper and trim the separated stalks (p259). Wipe the fresh wild mushrooms and trim the stalks. If using dried mushrooms, soak them in hot water for about 30 minutes until plump. Drain and cut into pieces.

2 Finely chop the wild mushrooms and the large mushroom stalks with a sharp knife, or use a food processor, taking care to retain their texture and not to overwork them to a purée. Combine a quarter of the chopped herbs with the Parmesan and set aside.

3 Heat half the oil in a frying pan. Add the chopped mushrooms and garlic with the lemon juice, salt, and pepper. Cook, stirring, for 3–5 minutes, or until all the liquid has

evaporated. Stir in the cream and cook for 1–2 minutes, until slightly thickened. Add the walnuts and the remaining herbs and stir to mix. Remove from the heat and taste for seasoning.

4 Preheat the oven to 180°C (350°F/ Gas 4). Lightly oil a baking dish. Season the mushroom caps and place 1–2 spoonfuls of stuffing in each, mounding it well. Place in the baking dish.

5 Sprinkle about 1 tsp Parmesan and herb topping on each mushroom, along with the remaining oil. Bake for 15–20 minutes, or until the mushrooms are tender when pierced with a knife and the filling is very hot. Serve garnished with the reserved herbs.

variation

stuffed mushrooms with basil and pine nuts

Prepare in exactly the same way, but substitute a handful of fresh basil for the tarragon and chervil, and a small handful of flat-leaf parsley for the thyme. Add 1 finely chopped celery stick and 60g (2oz) toasted pine nuts to the mixture at step 3 instead of the walnuts.

Season's best **wild mushrooms**

Mushrooms add varying levels of earthiness and savoury flavour, as well as texture, to dishes. Foraging for them should be done only with sound knowledge, as there are also some very poisonous varieties. Most wild mushrooms grow in autumn through to early winter, but a few, such as morels, are spring fungi; many are available commercially. They pair well with garlic and herbs and enhance everything from meat to vegetables.

Mushrooms are the fruiting bodies of soil-borne fungi that live off the nutrients they take from living and dead plants. They flourish throughout the world's temperate zones.

Oyster mushroom Young oyster mushrooms are tender and mildly flavoured, with a hint of anise, becoming acrid and tough as they age. Use in stir-fries and Oriental-style soups.

Wood blewit It is a white mushroom with blue-tinged, fat stalk and cap, a faint aniseed smell, and a good flavour. Must eat cooked.

They have delicate flesh that needs gentle handling.

how to clean delicate mushrooms

As delicate mushrooms, such as oyster and chanterelle (and morel), damage easily, always use a soft brush rather than a cloth to clean off the dirt.

Chanterelle (Girolle) Highly prized chanterelles have smooth, tender flesh and a noticeably nutty, fruity flavour that complements egg dishes, chicken, veal, and pork. They are best sautéed.

They have a slight scent of apricots.

1 Clean carefully with a soft pastry brush. Any firmly embedded dirt, leaves, or pine needles can be removed with the point of a small knife.

Cep Also known as Penny Bun, this is one of the most revered of all mushrooms, valued for its smooth, creamy flesh, rich, savoury flavour, and distinguished shape. Delicious sautéed or added to risotto and pasta dishes.

Horse mushroom White with a domed cap and pink gills, or black when flat, this variety is often found in "fairy rings" in meadows. It has an excellent flavour.

Field mushroom Recognizable by its thick, white flesh and pleasant earthy aroma, the field mushroom has pink or brown gills – never white, as you find in the deadly Amanita. Ideal for grilling and frying.

essentials
varieties available

Many varieties of edible fungi, the most common being oyster, cep, chanterelle, horse, field, and wood blewit. Morels are also highly prized in spring.

buy To forage, go with a guide. To purchase, avoid if shrivelled or wet. Choose firm, fresh-looking ones that smell earthy and "mushroomy".

store Fresh mushrooms can be kept in the fridge in a closed paper bag for up to 1 week.

cook Mushrooms suit just about any type of cooking. Fry, bake, grill, barbecue, sauté, or steam. They are also delicious in soups, stews, casseroles, dips, and in pasta and rice dishes.

preserve Preserve in oil; pickle; make into ketchup; dry.

recipe ideas

Dried mushrooms p352

Mixed mushroom and walnut tart p256

Mixed mushroom soup p270

how to clean hardy mushrooms

Carefully clean but do not wash hardy mushrooms, such as ceps, blewits, and field mushrooms, because this makes them waterlogged, reducing their flavour. Most do not need peeling unless large and open, like large field mushrooms.

1 Wipe off any mud or dry earth with a damp cloth or kitchen paper. The pores of old ceps are best removed.

2 Gently scrape or peel, if necessary, the stem with a knife to remove any remaining dirt, and trim the end.

roast pumpkin and ricotta crostini

No vegetable is more closely linked with autumn than pumpkin, with its mellow golden flesh. Here its sweetness is set against the sharper flavour of ricotta cheese.

🥣 20 MINS 🍲 50 MINS

MAKES 16

500g (1lb 2oz) pumpkin, peeled, deseeded, and cut into chunks

2 tbsp olive oil

2 garlic cloves, crushed

grated zest and juice of 1 lemon

2 sprigs of rosemary, leaves picked and chopped

200g (7oz) ricotta cheese

4 sprigs of lemon-scented thyme, leaves picked

For the crostini

2 tbsp olive oil

16 slices of crusty baguette

salt and freshly ground black pepper

1 garlic clove, peeled but left whole

1 Preheat the oven to 200°C (400°F/ Gas 6). To make the crostini, pour the oil over the bottom of a baking tray, then gently press the bread into the oil on both sides. Season with salt and pepper. Bake for 13–15 minutes until golden brown. Remove from the oven and lightly rub each slice with the garlic. Set the crostini aside on a wire rack to cool, but do not turn off the oven.

2 Put the pumpkin on a baking tray and toss with the oil, garlic, lemon zest, and rosemary. Season with salt and pepper, then roast for about 35 minutes until tender and golden. Leave to cool slightly.

3 In a bowl, combine the ricotta, thyme, and a little lemon juice. Spoon a little of the ricotta mixture onto each of the crostini and top with roasted pumpkin, squeezing it a little with your fingers as you go. Arrange on a large serving dish or platter and serve.

variation

roast squash and blue cheese crostini
Prepare in the same way, but use an acorn squash instead of pumpkin and flavour with 6 large chopped sage leaves instead of the rosemary before roasting. At step 3, use 100g (3½oz) each of ricotta and soft blue cheese, instead of all ricotta, and 2 tbsp chopped parsley instead of thyme.

waldorf chicken salad

A contemporary take on a classic, with yogurt in the dressing for lightness. This salad is a great way to use up leftover roast chicken, which saves poaching the chicken breasts.

🥣 25–30 MINS PLUS CHILLING 🍲 25–35 MINS

SERVES 6

4 celery sticks, with leaves if possible

1 onion, quartered

1 carrot, quartered

10–12 black peppercorns

1 bouquet garni, made with 5–6 sprigs of parsley, 2–3 sprigs of thyme, and 1 bay leaf

salt and freshly ground black pepper

4 skinless chicken breasts, total weight about 750g (1lb 10oz)

125g (4½oz) walnuts

500g (1lb 2oz) tart, crisp apples

juice of 1 lemon

175ml (6fl oz) natural yogurt

175ml (6fl oz) mayonnaise

1 Trim the tops from the celery and put the trimmings in a wide pan with the onion, carrot, peppercorns, bouquet garni, and salt. Bring to the boil and simmer for 10–15 minutes. Add the chicken and simmer for 10–12 minutes, turning once, until the juices run clear when the meat is pierced at its thickest point.

2 Remove the pan from the heat and cool the chicken in the poaching liquid for 10–15 minutes, then transfer to kitchen paper to drain. With your fingers, pull the chicken into slivers about 5cm (2in) long – the meat will be juicier this way than it would be if you cut it.

3 Preheat the oven to 180°C (350°F/ Gas 4). Spread the walnut pieces on a baking sheet and bake for 5–8 minutes until crisp, stirring occasionally so that they toast evenly. Meanwhile, slice the celery sticks.

4 Cut the top and bottom ends from the apples. Halve and core them, then dice the flesh. Put in a large bowl, pour the lemon juice over, and toss to coat. Add the chicken, celery, yogurt, mayonnaise, and two-thirds of the walnuts to the apple. Season and stir until combined, then chill for 1 hour.

5 Roughly chop the remaining walnuts. Spoon the salad into individual plates and sprinkle with the chopped nuts.

crisp sweet potato with courgette and chive mascarpone

For this recipe, buy an orange-fleshed variety of sweet potato, both for the attractive colour and because the flesh is moister and creamier than that of the white-fleshed type.

🥄 **15 MINS**   🍲 **25 MINS**

SERVES 4

600g (1lb 5oz) sweet potato, peeled and sliced into 8 even discs

2 tbsp olive oil, plus extra for drizzling

salt and freshly ground black pepper

1 courgette, about 150g (5½oz)

juice of ½ lemon

150g (5½oz) mascarpone

1 tbsp snipped chives, plus extra to garnish

1 Preheat the oven to 200°C (400°F/ Gas 6). Put the sweet potato in a bowl. Add the oil and season with salt and pepper. Toss until the sweet potato is well coated. Transfer to a baking tray and roast for about 25 minutes until golden brown and tender when pierced with a skewer. Set aside to cool.

2 Trim both ends off the courgette, then shave lengthways into thin ribbons using a vegetable peeler or a mandoline. Put in a bowl with the lemon juice and season with salt and pepper. Toss gently to coat thoroughly.

3 Put the mascarpone in a separate bowl, add the snipped chives, and stir through.

4 To serve, put a disc of sweet potato in the centre of each of 4 serving plates. Divide the courgette evenly between each serving, placing it on top of the sweet potato discs. Arrange another disc on the courgette, then spoon on some chive mascarpone. Garnish each serving with 2 chive leaves and drizzle with a little olive oil. Serve immediately.

vegetable tempura with chilli dipping sauce

This dish typifies the clean, fresh flavours of Japanese food. The secret to successful tempura is to make the batter at the last minute and to ensure that the water is really cold.

🥄 **15 MINS**   🍲 **15 MINS**

SERVES 4

2 aubergines, sliced into thin rounds

2-3 courgettes, cut into batons

2 red peppers, deseeded and roughly chopped

500ml (16fl oz) vegetable oil or sunflower oil, for frying

75g (2½oz) plain flour

1 tbsp cornflour

200ml (7fl oz) iced water

For the chilli dipping sauce

2 tbsp rice wine vinegar

2 tbsp light soy sauce

1 tbsp olive oil

1 tbsp caster sugar

1 garlic clove, grated or finely chopped

2 hot red chillies, deseeded and finely chopped

salt and freshly ground black pepper

1 First, make the chilli dipping sauce. Whisk together all the ingredients, seasoning generously with salt and pepper.

2 Once you have all the vegetables prepared, pour the oil into a wok and heat until very hot.

3 Meanwhile, make the batter. Whisk together the flour, cornflour, and iced water. Don't overbeat; it doesn't matter if the batter is a little lumpy.

4 Drop a little of the batter into the oil to test whether it is hot enough – the batter should sizzle straight away and become crisp. Dip the vegetable pieces one by one into the batter and shake away the excess. Carefully add to the oil, a few at a time, and fry for 2–3 minutes until golden and crispy. Remove with a slotted spoon and keep warm on a plate lined with kitchen paper until all the vegetable pieces are cooked. Serve immediately with the chilli dipping sauce.

chargrilled squid salad

For this delicious and quick recipe, make sure you heat the griddle pan until it is searingly hot. The squid is dressed with lemon, garlic, and chilli to give this salad lots of impact.

 15 MINS   2 MINS

SERVES 4

600g (1lb 5oz) small squid, gutted and cleaned (opposite)

4 tbsp olive oil

2 small hot red chillies, deseeded and finely chopped

1 garlic clove, crushed

grated zest and juice of 1 lemon

salt and freshly ground black pepper

For the rocket salad

100g (3½oz) rocket leaves

large handful of flat-leaf parsley, roughly chopped

2 tbsp olive oil

juice of ½ lemon

lemon wedges, to serve

1 Put the tentacles and bodies (tubes and wings attached) in a bowl with the oil, chillies, garlic, and lemon zest and juice. Season with salt and pepper.

2 Heat a ridged griddle pan until hot. Griddle the squid bodies and tentacles over a high heat for 1–2 minutes, turning halfway through cooking, until lightly charred on all sides. Remove to a chopping board. Cut the tentacle clusters in half crossways and put in a bowl. Slice the tubes into 3mm (⅛in) rings, slicing through the wings as you go, and put in the bowl with the tentacles.

3 Add the salad ingredients to the bowl and toss through gently. Serve immediately with lemon wedges.

marinated squid salad

Squid is delicious and tender if cooked very briefly – too long and it becomes leathery. Marinating it in a garlicky dressing enhances its sweet, slightly fishy flavour.

 15 MINS PLUS MARINATING   5 MINS

SERVES 4

300g (10oz) small squid, gutted and cleaned (opposite)

7 tbsp olive oil

salt and freshly ground black pepper

2 tbsp white wine vinegar

3 garlic cloves, crushed

1 tsp paprika

handful of flat-leaf parsley, finely chopped

1 Trim the squid tentacles but leave whole. Cut the bodies into rings. Brush the squid with a little of the oil and season well with salt and pepper.

2 Heat 1 tbsp of the oil in a frying pan, add the squid, and cook over a medium heat, stirring constantly, for 2–3 minutes, or until it is cooked. Remove from the heat and transfer to a serving bowl.

3 Mix the remaining oil with the vinegar, garlic, paprika, and parsley, then season with salt and pepper. Pour over the squid, combine well, and leave to marinate for at least 30 minutes. Serve with fresh crusty bread and a green salad.

variation

marinated mushroom salad
Prepare in the same way, but use 300g (10oz) mixed wild mushrooms, trimmed and cleaned but left whole unless very large, instead of squid. No need to brush with oil, just season, then sauté in 3 tbsp olive oil for 2–3 minutes until tender. Tip the contents of the pan into a salad bowl. Mix the dressing in the same way but use 2 tbsp white balsamic condiment instead of white wine vinegar, 2 crushed garlic cloves instead of 3, and 1 tsp smoked paprika instead of sweet paprika. Add the parsley and seasoning as before and leave to marinate for at least 30 minutes before serving.

french country soup

A mixed vegetable potage (soup) like this is traditional French family fare. It is ladled out of a tureen into wide shallow bowls as a starter all over the country.

15 MINS   45 MINS

SPECIAL EQUIPMENT ▪ blender

SERVES 4

1 tbsp sunflower or groundnut oil

30g (1oz) butter

3 large leeks, cleaned and chopped

1 large floury potato, peeled and roughly cubed

2 large carrots, chopped

750ml (1¼ pints) light vegetable or chicken stock

2 bay leaves

sea salt and freshly ground black pepper

1 Put the oil and half the butter in a large sauté pan over a very moderate heat. Add the leeks, potato, and carrots and cook, stirring frequently, for 5 minutes. Reduce the heat a little, add the stock and bay leaves, then season lightly with sea salt and pepper. Cover and cook gently, stirring occasionally, for 30 minutes, or until the vegetables are very soft.

2 Leave to cool for several minutes, then remove the bay leaves. Transfer the soup to a blender and blitz until smooth. Strain back into the pan through a sieve, using the back of a wooden spoon to push through as much as possible. Pour 100ml (3½fl oz) hot water through the sieve to extract as much as you can from the vegetables.

3 Reheat gently, stirring frequently. Taste and adjust the seasoning, then stir in the remaining butter and serve very hot.

Season's best **squid**

The common squid, nicknamed "ink fish", is the best known. It is particularly good in autumn, though you will find it through summer and into winter. Its size ranges from 2cm (³/₄in) to the much larger 80–90cm (31–35in) and this determines the cooking method. The larger the squid, the more time it will need in the pot. Ideal flavour pairings include chilli, olive oil, lemon juice, garlic, spring onions, and mayonnaise.

essentials
varieties available

Baby squid and larger specimens. Available cleaned and frozen.

buy If buying whole, they should be sweet-smelling and slippery. Sometimes sold neatly cleaned and also sliced in rings.

store Wrap in a sealable plastic bag in the fridge. Eat on the day of purchase.

cook Fry, braise, grill, poach, or casserole whole, cut in rectangles or rings. Whole tubes, flattened out into a sheet and scored, taste excellent barbecued. The tube can also be stuffed with a savoury breadcrumb mix, couscous, quinoa, or rice.

recipe ideas

Chargrilled squid salad p262

Marinated squid salad p262

Roasted squid and potato with spiced coriander pesto p288

Spiced seafood salad p106

Squid stew p292

The mottled skin is best peeled off and reserved for stock, as it toughens and shrinks around the flesh when cooked.

The tough, wing-like fins are best either finely sliced and stir-fried, or reserved to flavour stock.

Common squid The "ink fish" has gained a reputation for being tough and chewy, but is only ever so if it is overcooked. In a hot pan, the meat takes no time at all. At its best, it tastes tender and mellow, with a subtle, distinctive flavour.

how to clean and prepare squid

The edible parts of squid are the tube, tentacles, and wings, and they are eaten all over the world. Over high heat, they cook in a minute or two, becoming translucent; overcooked, they become rubbery.

1 Hold the mantle (body) in one hand and gently pull the tentacles away from it to separate them. The eyes, some viscera, and beak (mouthpiece) will come away with the head.

2 Cut the tentacles with a small knife just below the eyes to separate the viscera. Trim the two long arms level with the remaining tentacles. Discard the head, beak, eyes, and viscera.

3 Locate the hard quill attached to the inside of the mantle and pull it away. Pinch the two fins (wings) together and pull away, with the purple membrane. Pull the membrane from the wings and discard.

roast pumpkin, chilli, and ginger dip

As well as pumpkin, there is a wide variety of squashes at this time of year. Acorn, coquina, and turban squashes would be equally good here.

🥣 **20 MINS**   🍲 **45 MINS**

SPECIAL EQUIPMENT ▪ blender or food processor

SERVES 4

500g (1lb 2oz) pumpkin or butternut squash, peeled and cut into chunks

2 tbsp olive oil

2 garlic cloves, crushed whole with the back of a knife

2 tsp grated or finely chopped fresh root ginger

salt and freshly ground black pepper

½ long red chilli, deseeded and thinly sliced

2 sprigs of flat-leaf parsley, leaves only, plus extra for garnish

grated zest and juice of ½ lemon

75ml (2½fl oz) Greek-style yogurt

drizzle of extra virgin olive oil (optional)

pinch of paprika

slices of grilled sourdough bread, to serve

grilled pancetta or prosciutto, to serve

1 Preheat the oven to 200°C (400°F/ Gas 6). Put the pumpkin on a baking tray and toss with the olive oil, garlic, and ginger. Season with salt and pepper. Roast for about 30 minutes until tender and golden. Set aside.

2 Transfer the cooled pumpkin to a blender or food processor and add the chilli, parsley, and lemon zest and juice. Blitz to a chunky purée and season to taste.

3 Put the pumpkin purée and the yogurt in a bowl and mix thoroughly. Season if needed, then spoon into a serving bowl. Top with a drizzle of extra virgin olive oil (if desired). Garnish with extra parsley and a sprinkle of paprika, and serve on grilled sourdough bread with grilled pancetta or prosciutto laid on top.

beetroot-topped mini rye breads

The combination of dark rye bread and beetroot gives an East European flavour here. Feta or goat's cheese would make good substitutes for the Dolcelatte, if you prefer.

🥣 **15 MINS**

SERVES 8-10

8 thin slices rye bread or pumpernickel

125g (4½oz) Dolcelatte cheese, diced

300g (10oz) beetroot, cooked, peeled (p255), and finely diced

2-3 tbsp creamed horseradish

1 Cut the rye bread into small squares – about 6 squares per slice, depending on how big the slices are.

2 Top each bread square with a fine slice of Dolcelatte cheese, a teaspoonful of diced beetroot, and a tiny amount of creamed horseradish. Arrange on platters and serve.

variation

pastrami and beetroot on rye

Prepare the bread in the same way. Purée the beetroot in a blender or food processor and beat in 100g (3½oz) ricotta cheese. Season and beat in 2 tbsp chopped fresh dill (or 1 tsp dried) and 1 tsp white wine vinegar. Cut 4 slices of pastrami or salt beef into 12 neat pieces. Put a small dollop of the creamed beetroot on each of the bread squares and top with a piece of beef. Add a little blob of horseradish cream and a tiny sprinkling of dill to finish.

smoked mackerel pâté

Sometimes the simplest dishes are among the most delicious. Smoked mackerel pâté belongs in this category – pair it with really good brown bread and you can't go wrong.

🥣 **5 MINS**

SPECIAL EQUIPMENT ▪ blender or food processor ▪ ramekins

SERVES 4

3–4 smoked mackerel fillets, about 300g (10oz) total weight, skinned

300g (10oz) cream cheese

juice of 1–2 lemons, plus 1 lemon, cut into wedges

freshly ground black pepper

1–2 tbsp Greek-style yogurt

thinly sliced and toasted brown bread

1 Using your hands, break up the mackerel into chunks and add to a blender or food processor. Blitz until broken up completely.

2 Spoon in the cream cheese and blitz again until a smooth paste forms. Add the lemon juice a little at a time, pulsing between each addition. Taste as you go, adding more lemon as required. Season with plenty of black pepper and blitz again.

3 Add the yogurt and blitz again until the pâté is completely smooth. Spoon into a serving dish or 4 individual ramekins. Serve with thinly sliced and toasted brown bread and the lemon wedges for squeezing over.

variation

potted fresh mackerel

Grill 4 mackerel fillets, skin-side up, for 5 minutes until cooked. Skin, then flake the fish. Melt 115g (4oz) unsalted butter. Blitz the mackerel with 1 crushed garlic clove, 150g (5½oz) of cream cheese, half the melted butter, and ¼ tsp each of ground mace and cayenne pepper. Flavour with lemon juice and seasoning to taste. Pack in 4 small ramekins or one slightly larger pot and pour the rest of the melted butter over. Chill until firm. Serve as before.

grilled pepper-stuffed mussels

This light dish is perfect for a special romantic meal, but so delicious that you'll want to make it everyday food. To make it even quicker to prepare, use roast peppers from a jar.

🥣 **25–30 MINS**   🍲 **1–2 MINS**

SPECIAL EQUIPMENT ▪ blender or food processor

SERVES 4

small bunch of flat-leaf parsley

1 large red pepper

2 slices of white bread

2 garlic cloves, peeled

2 tbsp olive oil

salt and freshly ground black pepper

250ml (9fl oz) dry white wine

24 large mussels, about 750g (1lb 10oz) total weight, scrubbed and debearded (discard any that do not close when tapped) (364)

lemon wedges, to serve

1 Strip the parsley leaves from the stalks and set them aside separately from each other.

2 Heat the grill. Set the red pepper on a rack about 10cm (4in) from the heat and grill, turning, for 10–12 minutes, until black all over. Seal in a plastic bag and allow to cool, then remove the skin, scrape out the seeds and ribs, and cut the flesh into strips.

3 Trim the crusts from the bread and discard them. Cut the bread into cubes and blitz them in a blender or food processor to form crumbs. Add the parsley leaves, reserving a few for garnishing, and the garlic, oil, and red pepper. Blitz to a purée and season with salt and pepper.

4 Put the wine and parsley stalks into a large saucepan. Bring to the boil and simmer for 2 minutes, then add the mussels.

5 Cover and cook over a high heat, stirring once, for 2–3 minutes until the mussels open. Transfer to a large bowl with a slotted spoon. Discard any that have not opened.

6 Heat the grill. Remove the top shell from each mussel and discard the rubbery ring surrounding the meat.

7 Spoon a little topping onto each mussel. Place the mussels in their bottom shells in a baking dish. Grill for 1–2 minutes until very hot and the topping is heated through. Serve with lemon wedges and a sprinkling of parsley leaves.

rich fish soup

The subtle combinations of meaty monkfish, delicate haddock, aniseed fennel, and the light scent of saffron marry well. You could add some mussels, if you like.

🥄 **15 MINS**   🍲 **1 HR**   ❄ **FREEZABLE**

SPECIAL EQUIPMENT ▪ blender or food processor

SERVES 4–6

1 tbsp olive oil

1 onion, finely chopped

salt and freshly ground black pepper

sprig of thyme

3 garlic cloves, finely chopped

1 fennel bulb, trimmed and finely chopped, the fronds reserved to garnish (optional)

1 red chilli, deseeded and finely chopped

250ml (9fl oz) dry white wine

2 x 400g cans chopped tomatoes

900ml (1½ pints) hot light vegetable stock

pinch of saffron threads

200g (7oz) monkfish, cut into bite-sized pieces

200g (7oz) haddock loin, cut into bite-sized pieces

1 Heat the oil in a large heavy-based pan over a medium heat, add the onion, and cook for 3–4 minutes until soft. Season with salt and pepper and throw in the thyme. Add the garlic and fennel, and cook gently for a further 5 minutes until the fennel begins to soften.

2 Stir through the chilli and cook for 1 minute, then increase the heat, add the wine, let it bubble for a minute, then tip in the canned tomatoes and stock. Add the saffron, bring to the boil, then reduce to a simmer and cook gently, partially covered with a lid, for about 45 minutes. Take care that the sauce doesn't dry out, topping it up with a little hot water if needed.

3 Pour the soup into a blender or food processor and blitz until smooth, then pour into a clean pan. Top up with a little hot water (you will probably need about 300ml/10fl oz in total) and simmer gently. Taste and season as needed, add the fish, put the lid back on, and cook on a low heat for 6–10 minutes, or until the fish is opaque and cooked through. Ladle into warmed bowls and serve with white crusty bread. Garnish with chopped fennel fronds, if desired.

cajun sweet potato and bean soup

This soup makes a substantial meal on its own. It is important to rinse canned beans before cooking with them.

🥄 **10 MINS**   🍲 **1 HR – 1 HR 30 MINS**   ❄ **FREEZABLE**

SPECIAL EQUIPMENT ▪ blender or food processor

SERVES 4–6

1 tbsp olive oil

1 onion, finely chopped

salt and freshly ground black pepper

3 garlic cloves, finely chopped

2 celery sticks, finely chopped

200g (7oz) chorizo, diced

pinch of dried chilli flakes

a few sprigs of thyme

2 sweet potatoes, peeled and diced

2 yellow peppers, deseeded and roughly chopped

2 x 400g cans adzuki beans, drained

400g can kidney beans, drained

900ml (1½ pints) hot vegetable stock

1 Heat the oil in a large heavy-based pan over a medium heat, add the onion, and cook for 3–4 minutes until soft. Season with salt and pepper, stir through the garlic and celery, and cook for a further 10 minutes until the celery is soft. Stir through the chorizo, chilli, and thyme, and cook for 1 minute. Add the sweet potatoes and cook for a few minutes, then add the peppers and let this cook gently for about 5 minutes.

2 Tip in the adzuki and kidney beans, add a little of the stock, increase the heat, and let the mixture simmer. Add the remaining stock, bring to the boil, then reduce to a simmer, partially cover with a lid, and cook for 45–60 minutes. Check occasionally that it's not drying out, topping up with a little hot water if needed.

3 Pour the soup into a blender or food processor and blitz until it is well combined but still retains some texture, then pour back into the pan. Add a ladleful of hot water if it is too thick. Heat through, taste and season as needed, then ladle into warmed bowls and serve with tortilla bread.

globe artichoke soup

Nutmeg and saffron bring out the delicate, nutty taste of the artichoke, while the bacon rashers add a smoky flavour.

🥄 **20 MINS**   🍲 **20 MINS**

SPECIAL EQUIPMENT ▪ blender or food processor

SERVES 4

1 tbsp olive oil

20g (¾oz) butter

½ Spanish onion, finely chopped

1 shallot, finely chopped

1 garlic clove, crushed

¼ tsp grated nutmeg

a few saffron strands

800g (1¾lb) artichoke hearts, chopped

salt and freshly ground black pepper

100ml (3½fl oz) single cream

4 thin smoked streaky bacon rashers

handful of spinach leaves, chopped

1 Heat the oil and butter in a pan over a medium heat, add the onion, shallot, garlic, nutmeg, and saffron, and stir for 3 minutes. Add the artichoke hearts and season. Cook, stirring, for 3 minutes. Pour 1 litre (1¾ pints) hot water into the pan and stir to mix. Bring to a simmer, reduce the heat, cover, and simmer for about 10 minutes, or until the vegetables are tender. Leave to cool.

2 Pour the soup into a blender or food processor and blitz until smooth, then pour back into the pan. Reheat gently. Heat the cream until simmering in a separate pan.

3 Fry the bacon in a pan over a medium heat until crisp, then drain on kitchen paper. Wilt the spinach in the same pan. Stir the cream into the soup, adjust seasoning, then ladle into bowls, stir in the spinach, and float a rasher of bacon in the middle of each bowl. Serve immediately.

pistou soup

Pistou sauce is the Provençal version of Italian pesto but does not contain any pine nuts. It is used in this famous, rustic soup with beans and courgettes, but can also be tossed with pasta or smeared on slices of bread.

🥄 30 MINS 🍲 1 HR 30 MINS

SERVES 4

1 small ham hock, or a thick piece of smoked bacon, about 75g (2½oz)

400g can white haricot beans, such as cannellini, drained and rinsed

150g can borlotti beans, drained and rinsed

125g (4½oz) flat green beans, sliced

1 floury potato, peeled and diced

1 large tomato, skinned, deseeded (p197), and chopped

2 courgettes, chopped

salt and freshly ground black pepper

50g (1¾oz) small macaroni

For the pistou

1 large garlic clove, peeled

coarse sea salt and freshly ground black pepper

small handful of basil leaves

1 small tomato, skinned, deseeded (p197), and chopped

15g (½oz) mimolette cheese or mature Cheddar cheese, grated

1½ tbsp olive oil

1 To make the pistou, pound the garlic in a mortar with a pestle, then add a little sea salt and the basil and pound to a paste. Add the tomato and continue pounding and mixing until you have a thick sauce. Add the pepper, cheese, and oil, mix well, and adjust the seasoning.

2 For the soup, put 2 litres (3½ pints) cold water in a large pan. Add the ham hock. Bring to a simmer, then partly cover with a lid and leave to bubble gently for 30 minutes, skimming occasionally.

3 Add the canned beans and all the vegetables to the ham hock pan. Season lightly. Return to a simmer, then part-cover and let it bubble gently for 1 hour, skimming occasionally.

4 Remove the ham hock and shred the meat. Lift half of the ingredients out of the pan, mash with a fork, then return to the soup with the ham. Add the macaroni and cook until just tender. Stir in the pistou and serve.

quail's eggs with celery salt

This is a classic pairing of ingredients and they are very tasty, too. Quail's eggs have a higher proportion of yolk to white than hen's eggs and are slightly stronger in flavour.

🥣 10 MINS   🍲 15 MINS

SPECIAL EQUIPMENT ▪ food processor

SERVES 4

2 celery sticks, finely chopped

salt

12 fresh quail's eggs or buy ready-prepared ones

1 Preheat the oven to 200°C (400°F/Gas 6). To make the celery salt, spread out the celery over a baking sheet and sprinkle a couple of pinches of salt over it. Stir around a little, then roast in the oven for 5–8 minutes until crisp and dry. Tip the celery into a food processor and blitz until fine.

2 To boil the eggs (if they are not ready-prepared), place them in a pan of gently boiling water, then simmer for 2½ minutes. Drain, then rinse in cold water until cool. Carefully peel away the egg shells. Sit the quail's eggs on a serving plate, and sprinkle with a little salt. Transfer the celery salt to a small bowl or plate and serve alongside the eggs for dipping.

mulligatawny

An Anglo-Indian soup from colonial days, mulligatawny has many variations. For extra heat, pop a split red chilli (with or without its seeds) in the pan when you pour over the stock.

🥣 20 MINS   🍲 45 MINS   ❄ FREEZABLE

SPECIAL EQUIPMENT ▪ blender or food processor

SERVES 4

40g (1¼oz) butter

1 large onion, chopped

5cm (2in) fresh root ginger, peeled and finely chopped

2 garlic cloves, finely chopped

1 Cox apple, unpeeled and diced

1 carrot, sliced

1 celery stick, sliced

1 heaped tbsp mild curry powder

1 tbsp gram flour or plain flour

4 tomatoes, roughly chopped

2 tsp tomato purée

500ml (16fl oz) hot chicken stock

2 bay leaves

salt and freshly ground black pepper

200ml (7fl oz) coconut milk or single cream

175g (6oz) cooked chicken meat, shredded

juice of ½ lime

2 tbsp chopped coriander

1 Melt the butter in a large pan over a low heat, add the onion, ginger, and garlic and cook for 10 minutes until soft but not coloured. Add the apple, carrot, and celery, cover with a lid, and continue cooking for 5 minutes.

2 Stir in the curry powder and fry for 1 minute, stirring all the time. Sprinkle over the gram or plain flour and cook for another 20 seconds.

3 Add the tomatoes and tomato purée, followed by the chicken stock. Add the bay leaves and season with salt and pepper. Bring to the boil, stirring, then reduce the heat and simmer, half-covered, for 20 minutes.

4 Remove the bay leaves, then pour the soup into a blender or food processor and blitz until smooth. Sieve the soup to remove any fibres and skin. Reheat, stir in the coconut milk or cream, and add the shredded chicken. Sharpen with a squeeze of lime and add the chopped coriander.

rosehip soup

Rosehip soup is very popular in Scandinavia where it is served both chilled and hot. Fresh rosehips are best, but you can also make it with pre-soaked dried rosehips.

🥣 30 MINS PLUS CHILLING   🍲 1 HR

SERVES 4

500g (1lb 2oz) ripe rosehips

1 vanilla pod, split lengthways

caster sugar, to taste

100ml (3½fl oz) whipping cream

3 tbsp natural yogurt

2 tbsp lemon juice

50g (1¾oz) slivered almonds, toasted and sprinkled with sugar

amaretti biscuits, to serve (optional)

1 Put the rosehips in a large saucepan and pour over boiling water to cover generously. Add the vanilla pod. Simmer over a low heat for 20–30 minutes until soft. Strain over a bowl, but reserve and set aside the cooking liquid as well as the vanilla pod.

2 Place the sieve with the rosehips over a second bowl. Press out the rosehips to extract a purée and set aside. Tip what's left in the sieve into the saucepan. Add the reserved cooking liquid and the vanilla pod. Return to a simmer and cook for 20 minutes. Strain enough of the mixture into the reserved purée to produce a smooth soup. Stir in sugar to taste. Chill for 1 hour, or until ready to serve.

3 Just before serving, whisk the cream and yogurt together and sweeten to taste. Stir the lemon juice into the chilled soup and pour or spoon into glass bowls. Add a sprinkling of almonds and a dollop of whisked cream, and serve chilled with some amaretti biscuits alongside, if desired.

Season's best **celery**

From a wild, bitter plant grown in marshy areas on the seashore to a widely cultivated mild, sweet, crunchy vegetable, the humble celery has certainly come a long way. At its best in autumn through winter, its texture and distinctive flavour make it a popular choice for many dishes. It pairs brilliantly with all cheeses, nuts, apples, oranges, lentils, seafood, cabbages, and roots.

Celery can be grown in all but extreme climates. It may be green or pale with yellow leaves (if a self-blanching variety, or if it has been earthed up to tenderize the stalks).

essentials
varieties available

Green celery and white, blanched celery; also sold as the trimmed hearts only.

buy The stalks should be stiff, and the leaves fresh looking.

store Celery can be kept for up to 10 days in a perforated plastic bag in the vegetable drawer of the fridge. Wrap in damp kitchen paper, if necessary, to stop it drying out.

cook Enjoy raw, or steam, braise, bake in a gratin, sauté, stir-fry, or add to stuffings.

preserve Add to chutneys, pickles, and relishes; can be preserved in oil.

recipe ideas

Celery and apple salad with blue cheese dressing p471

Celery and celeriac soup p428

Provençal vegetable soup p270

Quail's egg with celery salt p268

Roasted celery with orange and walnuts p470

Green celery A kitchen staple, green celery is delicious both raw and cooked. With a strong flavour, firm, crisp stalks, and a creamy, nutty heart, it is now the most favoured celery.

The stalks are virtually stringless, which makes them particularly palatable.

Giant Pascal This is another popular variety, sold green or blanched. It has noticeably thick, fleshy, succulent stalks with a nutty flavour.

how to prepare celery

When preparing celery sticks for eating raw with cheese at the end of a meal, simply prepare to step 2 and then place in a glass to serve at table. When preparing to cook, they need trimming, strings removing, then either cutting in julienne or chopping.

1 Place the head of celery on a board and cut off the green leaves in one go. Cut off the root end too. Use the leaves for garnish or in stock.

2 Separate into sticks and wash well, then dry. Pare off the strings using a vegetable peeler or a sharp paring knife.

3 Using a chef's knife, cut the sticks into short lengths, then into fine strips (julienne), or chop across the sticks into slices.

provençal vegetable soup

If you have any fresh tomatoes left over early in the autumn use them instead of the canned variety. For added flavour, stir through some basil pesto just before serving.

🥣 15 MINS   🍲 1 HR   ❄ FREEZABLE

SERVES 4-6

1 tbsp olive oil

1 onion, finely chopped

salt and freshly ground black pepper

3 garlic cloves, finely chopped

2 celery sticks, finely chopped

2 carrots, roughly chopped

sprig of tarragon, leaves finely chopped

2 sprigs of rosemary

400g can tomatoes, blended until smooth

900ml (1½ pints) hot vegetable stock

3 potatoes, peeled and chopped into bite-sized pieces

325g (11oz) green dwarf beans or fine green beans, trimmed and chopped into bite-sized pieces

30g (1oz) Parmesan cheese, grated (optional)

1 Heat the oil in a large heavy-based pan over a medium heat, add the onion, and cook for 3–4 minutes until soft. Season with salt and pepper, then stir through the garlic and celery and cook for a further 5 minutes, or until the celery is soft.

2 Stir in the carrots, tarragon, and rosemary and cook for a minute, then tip in the puréed tomatoes and a little stock, and bring to the boil. Add the remaining stock and return to the boil, then reduce to a simmer, partially cover with a lid, and cook gently for about 45 minutes. If more liquid is needed, top up with a little hot water. Add the potatoes for the last 15 minutes of cooking.

3 When the potatoes are soft, add the beans and cook for a further 10 minutes, or until they are cooked but al dente. Taste and season, remove the rosemary, and ladle into warmed large shallow bowls. Sprinkle over the Parmesan, if desired, and serve with some crusty French bread.

mixed mushroom soup

This simple soup recipe with onion, garlic, and parsley brings out the flavour of mixed wild mushrooms beautifully. It is even more delicious when served with soured cream.

🥣 15 MINS   🍲 1 HR   ❄ FREEZABLE

SERVES 4

75g (2½oz) unsalted butter

100g (3½oz) onion, finely chopped

1 garlic clove, finely chopped

15g (½oz) flat-leaf parsley, chopped

225g (8oz) mixed wild mushrooms, diced

4 tbsp milk

salt and freshly ground black pepper

pinch of grated nutmeg

45g (1½oz) flour

1.2 litres (2 pints) hot vegetable or chicken stock

4 tbsp soured cream (optional)

1 Heat half the butter in a heavy-based pan over a medium heat, add the onion, garlic, and parsley, and cook for 3–4 minutes until soft. Add the mushrooms and cook for another 3 minutes. Pour in the milk and season with salt and nutmeg. Cook for a few more minutes and set aside.

2 In another pan, melt the remaining butter. Remove the pan from the heat and beat in the flour. Return the pan to a low heat and cook until the mixture deepens in colour. Remove the pan from the heat once more and add the stock gradually by the ladleful. Stir constantly to avoid lumps forming and return the pan to a low heat.

3 When all the stock has been combined with the flour, add the mushroom mixture and the juices. Bring to the boil and simmer for 15–20 minutes. Season with salt and pepper to taste. Spoon 1 tbsp of soured cream into each bowl, if desired, and serve.

cucumber and walnut soup

This is delicious in the autumn, when it will use up any particularly mature cucumbers, though you may need to remove any hard seeds and bitter skin.

🥣 10-15 MINS PLUS CHILLING

SERVES 4-6

2 cucumbers, about 700g (1lb 9oz) in total

500g (1lb 2oz) Greek-style or thick and creamy yogurt

1 garlic clove

coarse sea salt and freshly ground black pepper

50g (1¾oz) walnuts, plus more chopped walnuts for garnish

handful of mint, leaves finely chopped

2 tbsp fresh lemon juice

extra virgin olive oil, to serve

1 Trim the ends from the cucumbers, peel, cut in half lengthways, scoop out the seeds with a teaspoon, and finely dice the flesh.

2 In a medium bowl, or large measuring jug, mix together the yogurt and 250ml (9fl oz) cold water until combined. Pound the garlic with a large pinch of coarse sea salt in a mortar until smooth. Scrape it into the yogurt. Pound the walnuts in the garlicky mortar to a coarse paste; but do not crush them too fine. Add to the yogurt mixture with the cucumber, mint, lemon juice, and a good grinding of black pepper, and stir well. Taste for seasoning.

3 Cover and chill in the fridge for at least 30 minutes. Pour into bowls and garnish with a drizzle of oil and a few chopped walnuts.

variation

cucumber, almond, and dill soup

Prepare in the same way, but mix the cucumber with the yogurt blended with 250ml (9fl oz) milk instead of water. Substitute 50g (1¾oz) ground almond and a handful of fresh chopped dill (or 2 tsp dried dill) for the walnuts and mint. Continue as before, but garnish with a few toasted flaked almonds.

moroccan harira soup

This is a substantial meal-in-one that is made from lentils and lamb and is full of complex flavours. It's also a dish that tastes better when reheated, so if you have the time, make it a day ahead and reheat to eat.

🥣 25 MINS 🍲 2 HRS ❄ FREEZABLE

SERVES 4-6

1 tbsp olive oil

1 red onion, finely chopped

salt and freshly ground black pepper

3 garlic cloves, finely chopped

1 celery stick, chopped

675g (1½lb) shoulder or shank of lamb, cut into bite-sized pieces

1 tsp ground turmeric

1 tsp ground cinnamon

5cm (2in) piece of fresh root ginger, peeled and finely chopped

1.4 litres (2½ pints) hot vegetable stock

125g (4½oz) green or brown lentils, rinsed well, and picked over for any stones

400g can chickpeas, drained and rinsed

1 tsp harissa paste

a few sprigs of coriander, leaves only, to serve

1 Heat the oil in a large flameproof casserole over a medium heat, add the onion, and cook for 3–4 minutes until soft. Season with salt and pepper, then stir through the garlic and celery, and cook for a further 6–10 minutes until the celery is soft.

2 Add the lamb, turmeric, cinnamon, and ginger. Increase the heat a little, stir until the lamb is coated, and cook for 6–10 minutes until the lamb is no longer pink. Add a ladleful of stock

and bring to the boil. Stir through the lentils and chickpeas, turning them to coat evenly, add the remaining stock, and bring back to the boil.

3 Reduce to a gentle simmer and cook for 1–1½ hours until the lamb is meltingly tender. Check occasionally that it's not drying out, topping up with a little hot water if needed. Stir through the harissa paste and cook for a few more minutes. Ladle into warmed bowls, top with coriander leaves, and serve with lemon wedges on the side.

variation

chicken harira soup

Prepare in the same way, but use 550g (1¼lb) diced skinless chicken thighs instead of lamb. Use red lentils instead of green or brown ones and add 450g (1lb) pumpkin, deseeded, peeled, and diced, and 4 skinned and chopped tomatoes to the mixture at the end of step 2. Up the harissa paste to 1 tbsp.

genoese minestrone with red pesto

A pesto made from fresh tomatoes is a perfect addition here.

🥣 45-50 MINS　　🍲 2 HRS 30 MINS

SPECIAL EQUIPMENT ▪ blender or food processor

SERVES 4

85g (3oz) elbow macaroni

400g can red kidney beans, drained and rinsed

400g can white haricot beans, such as cannellini, drained and rinsed

115g (4oz) fine green beans, trimmed and cut into 1cm (½in) pieces

2 carrots, diced

2 potatoes, peeled and diced

1 small courgette, diced

115g (4oz) shelled fresh peas or defrosted frozen peas

salt and freshly ground black pepper

large bunch of basil

1 large tomato, peeled, deseeded, (p197) and chopped

2 garlic cloves, peeled

120ml (4fl oz) olive oil

85g (3oz) Parmesan cheese, grated

1 Cook the pasta in a pan of boiling salted water for about 12 minutes, or until it is tender but still al dente. Drain, rinse with hot water, and set aside.

2 Put the canned beans in a large saucepan and add the green beans, carrots, potatoes, courgette, peas, and a little salt and pepper. Add 2 litres (3½ pints) water and bring to the boil, then reduce the heat and simmer for 1 hour, until the vegetables are very tender.

3 For the pesto, strip the leaves from the basil stalks, reserving 6 sprigs. Put the basil, tomato, garlic, and some salt and pepper in a blender or food processor and blitz until smooth. With the blades turning, gradually add the oil. Scrape down the sides of the bowl from time to time with a rubber spatula. Taste for seasoning.

4 Add the macaroni to the soup and season to taste. Gently reheat to boiling, but do not cook or the pasta and vegetables will overcook rather than staying firm. Remove from the heat and stir in the tomato pesto. Ladle the soup into warmed bowls, top each serving with basil leaves, and serve the Parmesan separately.

red pepper and walnut dip

While you can buy ready-toasted walnuts, it's easy to do yourself: spread them on a baking sheet and place under a hot grill for 2 minutes. Keep an eye on them; they can burn easily.

🥣 20 MINS　　🍲 30 MINS

SPECIAL EQUIPMENT ▪ blender or food processor

SERVES 8

90ml (3fl oz) olive oil

1 onion, sliced

4 red peppers, deseeded and sliced

2 garlic cloves, crushed

125g (4½oz) toasted walnuts, chopped

grated zest and juice of 1 lemon

1 Heat the oil in a heavy-based pan over a medium heat, add the onion, and cook for 3–4 minutes until soft and translucent. Reduce the heat.

2 Tip in the peppers and cook for about 30 minutes until soft, stirring regularly. Stir through the garlic and cook for a further 30 seconds, or until the garlic has turned white.

3 Transfer the pepper mixture to a blender or food processor. Add the walnuts and lemon zest and juice, and blitz to a chunky purée. Serve with warm pitta breads or crudités, such as carrot or cucumber batons, for dipping.

variation

red pepper and macadamia nut dip

Use macadamia nuts instead of walnuts. You may also like to add about 120ml (4fl oz) Greek-style yogurt and chopped coriander leaves, stirring them through the mixture at the end.

cucumber gratin with toasted olive ciabatta

A clever idea for cooking cucumber to enhance its flavour.

🥣 10 MINS　　🍲 20 MINS

SERVES 4

1 large cucumber, trimmed, peeled, and cut into 1cm (½in) thick slices

1 tbsp chopped thyme

45g (1½oz) butter

300ml (10fl oz) vegetable stock

4 tbsp plain flour

150ml (5fl oz) single cream

115g (4oz) Cheddar cheese, grated

½ tsp English mustard

salt and freshly ground black pepper

For the olive ciabatta

45g (1½oz) butter, softened

2 tbsp finely chopped, pitted black olives

2 tbsp chopped parsley

8 slices ciabatta bread

1 Place the cucumber in a pan with the thyme, 15g (½oz) butter, and the stock. Bring to the boil, reduce the heat, cover, and simmer for 6–8 minutes until tender. Drain thoroughly, reserving the liquid. Place the cucumber in 4 buttered gratin dishes. Melt the remaining butter in the pan, stir in the flour, and cook, stirring, for 1 minute. Remove from the heat and whisk in the reserved cucumber cooking liquid. Bring to the boil and cook for 2 minutes, stirring. Stir in the cream, 85g (3oz) of the cheese, and the mustard. Stir and season to taste.

2 Preheat the grill. Pour the sauce over the cucumber to cover completely. Sprinkle with the remaining cheese. Set aside while you make the olive butter.

3 For the ciabatta, mash the butter with the olives and parsley and season with plenty of pepper. Toast the ciabatta on one side. Place the gratin under the grill and cook for 5 minutes until the cheese melts, bubbles, and turns golden. Cover with foil and place in the base of the grill compartment. Spread the olive butter over the untoasted sides of the ciabatta. Grill until the butter melts and the edges turn brown. Serve slices of the ciabatta hot with the gratin.

fried calamari

This is a popular Mediterranean dish. Avoid overcooking the squid as it will become tough. Serve with a mixed salad and potato wedges for a more filling dish.

🥣 15 MINS 🍲 10 MINS

SERVES 4

2 eggs

2 tbsp cold sparkling water

150g (5½oz) plain flour

1 tsp dried chilli flakes

salt

500g (1lb 2oz) small squid, gutted and cleaned (p263), and cut into 1cm (½in) rings

250ml (9fl oz) vegetable oil or sunflower oil

lemon wedges, to serve

1 Break the eggs into a bowl, add the sparkling water, and beat well with a hand whisk. Put the flour, chilli flakes, and 1 tsp salt on a plate, and mix well. Dip each piece of squid into the egg mixture and then into the flour, making sure they are evenly coated, then set aside.

2 Heat the oil in a deep frying pan over a high heat until hot, then carefully add the squid, one piece at a time. Do not overfill the pan. Cook in batches for 2–3 minutes, or until golden brown. Remove with a slotted spoon and place on kitchen paper to remove any excess oil. Serve with a squeeze of lemon.

variation

fritto misto

Make the batter in the same way, but instead of using all squid, use 200g (7oz) squid, prepared as before, 1 grey mullet fillet, about 175g (6oz), skinned and cut into chunks, and 8 shucked oysters. Dry the fish well before coating. Add ½ tsp coarse, crushed black peppercorns to the flour mixture. Serve the mixed fish just with wedges of lemon and some crusty bread as a starter or, for a main course for 2 people, serve it with a large mixed salad.

roasted red pepper, fennel, and tomato soup

Make this soup early in the autumn when tomatoes and peppers are plentiful. It freezes well and is also a cheering stalwart for winter meals. Serve it with a warm roll.

🥣 25 MINS 🍲 2 HRS ❄ FREEZABLE

SPECIAL EQUIPMENT ▪ blender or food processor

SERVES 4-6

500g (1lb 2oz) tomatoes

1 large fennel bulb, peeled and cut into wedges

1 red onion, cut into wedges

2 red peppers, halved and deseeded

4 garlic cloves, unpeeled

1½ tsp sugar

2 tbsp olive oil

large sprig of rosemary, leaves only

1-2 tbsp vegetable oil

1½ tsp fennel seeds

½ tsp nigella seeds

400ml (14fl oz) passata

1 litre (1¾ pints) hot vegetable stock

1 red chilli, deseeded and chopped

salt and freshly ground black pepper

handful of fennel leaves

1 Preheat the oven to 200°C (400°F/ Gas 6). Slice a cross into the base of each tomato and squeeze the juice and seeds into a bowl. Strain the juice and set aside.

2 Line a roasting tin with baking parchment and add the fennel, onion, peppers, garlic cloves, and squeezed tomatoes. Sprinkle over the sugar, drizzle with the olive oil, and scatter the rosemary on top. Roast the vegetables for about 1 hour, until the tomatoes are soft. Let the vegetables cool before peeling the blackened skin from the peppers. Peel the garlic and discard the skins.

3 Heat the vegetable oil in a large pan and toss in the fennel and nigella seeds, swirling them around for a few seconds. Pour over the passata, the stock, and the reserved tomato juice, and bring to the boil. Add the roasted vegetables and the chilli, and season. Half cover with a lid and simmer for about 45 minutes.

4 Pour the soup into a blender or food processor and blitz until smooth. Strain back into the pan. Reheat, re-season, and sprinkle over fennel leaves. Serve in warmed bowls.

cream of tomato soup

This extra-special version of a classic takes the humble tomato to new heights by using fresh, sun-dried, and roasted varieties.

🥣 30 MINS   🍲 40 MINS

SPECIAL EQUIPMENT ▪ blender or food processor

SERVES 4-6

20 plum tomatoes, about 1.6kg (3½lb)

2 tbsp olive oil

50g (1¾oz) butter

2 onions, finely chopped

2 celery sticks, finely chopped

2 carrots, finely diced

2 garlic cloves, crushed

6 sun-dried tomatoes, finely chopped

1 litre (1¾ pints) hot vegetable stock

2-3 tbsp double cream

salt and freshly ground black pepper

1 To roast the tomatoes, preheat the oven to 200°C (400°F/Gas 6). Sit 12 of the tomatoes in a roasting tin and toss with 1 tbsp of the oil. Roast in the oven for 12–15 minutes until slightly charred. Skin the remaining tomatoes (p197) and finely chop.

2 Heat the butter and remaining oil in a heavy-based pan over a low heat. Add the onions and cook for 8–10 minutes, stirring frequently, until very soft but not coloured. Next, add the celery and carrots, and continue cooking gently for 10 minutes, stirring occasionally. Add the garlic and sauté for another 2 minutes.

3 Mix together the roasted plum tomatoes, skinned tomatoes, and sun-dried tomatoes. Tip into the pan with any juices and cook for 5 minutes, stirring occasionally, to allow the flavours to combine. If the sauce looks too thick or starts catching on the bottom of the pan, add a little of the hot vegetable stock. Pour in the remaining vegetable stock and let the soup simmer for 15–20 minutes.

4 Pour the soup into a blender or food processor and blitz until smooth, then strain into a clean pan. Add the double cream, a teaspoon at a time, until you are happy with the taste and texture. Season with salt and pepper, reheat very gently if needed, and serve.

beef and green bean soup

Choose firm, waxy potatoes that will keep their shape and texture in this deliciously savoury soup.

🥣 20 MINS   🍲 1 HR   ❄ FREEZABLE

SERVES 6

2 tbsp sunflower oil

500g (1lb 2oz) braising beef, cut into 2cm (¾in) cubes

salt and freshly ground black pepper

1 onion, chopped

2-3 sprigs of thyme

1 litre (1¾ pints) hot vegetable stock

1 large potato, peeled and cut into cubes

250g (9oz) green beans, trimmed and cut into small pieces

1-2 tbsp chopped parsley (optional)

1 Heat the oil in a pan over a medium heat, season the meat with salt and pepper, and add half the meat to the hot oil. Brown the meat until golden all over. Remove from the pan and repeat with the rest of the beef. Remove it from the pan, add the onion, and fry until softened.

2 Return the browned meat to the pan, tie the thyme sprigs together with kitchen string, and add them to the pan with the stock. Bring to the boil, cover, and cook over a medium heat for about 40 minutes.

3 Add the potato, bring back to the boil, cover once again, and cook for 10–15 minutes, or until just tender. Add the chopped beans and cook for 4–5 minutes, or until the beans are tender but still al dente.

4 Remove the thyme. Season with salt and pepper, break up the meat pieces slightly, and sprinkle with parsley, if desired, before serving.

black-eyed bean soup

If you can, make this soup in advance and let it stand for a while before reheating – it will taste even better. It's also good made with overgrown runner beans, shelled.

🥣 15 MINS   🍲 40 MINS   ❄ FREEZABLE

SPECIAL EQUIPMENT ▪ blender or food processor

SERVES 4-6

1 tbsp virgin rapeseed oil or sunflower oil

3 leeks, trimmed and sliced

1 small red pepper, deseeded and chopped

1 small yellow pepper, deseeded and chopped

3 garlic cloves

5cm (2in) piece fresh ginger, peeled and grated or roughly chopped

1 small red chilli, deseeded

1 tsp cumin seeds

sea salt and freshly ground black pepper

2 x 400g cans black-eyed beans, drained, rinsed, and drained again

400ml (14fl oz) coconut milk

500ml (16fl oz) hot vegetable stock

1 tsp brown sugar

coriander leaves, to garnish

lime wedges, to serve

1 Heat the oil in a pan over a medium heat, add the leeks and peppers, cover with a lid, and cook, stirring frequently, for 5–7 minutes, or until soft. Meanwhile, put the garlic, ginger, chilli, cumin seeds, and 1 tsp sea salt in a blender or food processor with 4 tbsp water and blitz until completely smooth. Add to the pan, using a little more water to rinse out every last bit. Cook, stirring, for 2–3 minutes, or until most of the liquid has evaporated.

2 Add the beans, coconut milk, stock, sugar, and a good grinding of black pepper and bring to the boil. Reduce the heat and simmer gently for 30 minutes, stirring frequently. Taste for seasoning, then serve each bowlful garnished with fresh coriander and a lime wedge.

pumpkin and ginger soup

This velvety smooth soup can be made using pumpkin or butternut squash, depending on what is in season. The dried chilli flakes and finely chopped ginger give it just the right kick to cut through the richness.

🥣 **15 MINS**   🍲 **1 HR**   ❄️ **FREEZABLE**

SPECIAL EQUIPMENT ▪ blender or food processor

SERVES 4-6

1 tbsp olive oil

1 onion, finely chopped

salt and freshly ground black pepper

3 garlic cloves, finely chopped

5cm (2in) piece of fresh root ginger, peeled and finely chopped

pinch of dried chilli flakes

1 small cinnamon stick

900g (2lb) pumpkin or butternut squash, halved, deseeded, peeled, and cut into cubes

900ml (1½ pints) hot vegetable stock

1 Heat the oil in a large heavy-based pan over a medium heat, add the onion, and cook for 3–4 minutes until soft. Season with salt and pepper, then add the garlic, ginger, chilli flakes, and cinnamon stick. Cook for a few seconds before adding the pumpkin or squash (and a little more oil if needed), stirring to coat.

2 Pour in a little of the stock, increase the heat, and scrape up the bits from the bottom of the pan. Add the remaining stock, boil for 1 minute, then reduce the heat to barely a simmer, cover with a lid, and cook for about 45 minutes until the pumpkin is soft and the flavours have developed. Remove the cinnamon stick.

3 Pour the soup into a blender or food processor and blitz until smooth, then pour back into a clean pan. Add a ladleful of hot water if it is too thick. Heat through, taste, and season as required. Serve with some chunky wholemeal or rye bread.

variation

acorn squash and cumin soup

Prepare in exactly the same way, but add 1 tsp ground cumin instead of the grated ginger, use 675g (1½lb) acorn squash, prepared as the pumpkin, and add 2 large carrots, peeled and roughly chopped at the end of step 1.

pear, fennel, and walnut salad

The Gorgonzola cheese dressing for this salad contrasts well with the sweet pears and aniseed flavour of the fennel.

🥣 30–35 MINS   🍲 5–8 MINS

SERVES 6

60g (2oz) walnuts

1 large fennel bulb

3 ripe pears

1 lemon

For the cheese dressing

125g (4½oz) Gorgonzola cheese

4 tbsp red wine vinegar

salt and freshly ground black pepper

75ml (2½fl oz) olive oil

1 Preheat the oven to 180°C (350°F/Gas 4). Spread the walnuts on a baking sheet and toast them in the heated oven for 5–8 minutes until crisp, stirring occasionally so they toast evenly.

2 To make the cheese dressing, cut the rind from the Gorgonzola and crumble with your fingers or crush with the tines of a fork. Put two-thirds into a bowl, add the red wine vinegar and salt and pepper, and whisk together. Gradually whisk in the oil so the dressing emulsifies and thickens slightly. Stir in the remaining cheese so a few larger pieces are left intact, and taste for seasoning. Cover and put in the fridge to chill.

3 Meanwhile, trim the stalks, root end, and any tough outer pieces from the fennel. Reserve any fronds for decoration. Cut the fennel bulb in half lengthways. Set each fennel half flat-side down on the chopping board and slice it lengthways.

4 Peel the pears, halve lengthways, and remove the core. Set each half cut-side down and cut lengthways into thin slices. Cut the lemon in half and squeeze lemon juice over the pear slices, tossing to coat.

5 On individual plates, arrange the pear and fennel slices and spoon on the cheese dressing. Scatter some toasted walnuts over each serving and decorate with fennel fronds.

variation

apple, celery, and pecan salad
Prepare in exactly the same way, but substitute 60g (2oz) pecan halves instead of walnuts and sprinkle them with 1 tsp mixed spice before toasting. Use 4 crisp eating apples (such as Coxes) instead of the pears and 4 tender celery sticks instead of the fennel bulb.

fennel and apple soup

Fennel will store better in the fridge if you remove the feathery fronds beforehand, but be sure to save a good handful of the fronds for this soup as an attractive garnish.

🥣 10 MINS   🍲 30 MINS

SPECIAL EQUIPMENT ▪ blender or food processor

SERVES 4

2 tbsp virgin rapeseed oil or olive oil

1 onion, chopped

2 garlic cloves, chopped

600g (1lb 5oz) fennel bulbs, trimmed and roughly chopped, the fronds reserved to garnish

1 celery heart with leaves, or 3 celery sticks, chopped

1 cooking apple, peeled, cored, and roughly chopped

sea salt

750ml (1¼ pints) hot vegetable stock

1 Heat the oil in a large pan over a medium heat, add the onion, and cook for 3–4 minutes until soft. Add the garlic and cook for 1–2 minutes until fragrant, then stir in the fennel, celery, and apple with a little sea salt. Stir, cover with a lid, and sweat for 10 minutes, stirring frequently.

2 Pour in the stock and bring to the boil. Simmer for 15 minutes until the fennel is tender. Pour the soup into a blender or food processor and blitz until smooth, then pour back into the pan and season. Serve hot or cold in bowls garnished with torn fennel fronds.

mussels in fennel broth

To clean mussels, scrub them under cold running water with a small stiff brush, then scrape with a knife to remove any barnacles, weeds, or "beards" from each one.

🥣 10 MINS   🍲 20 MINS

SERVES 4

1 tbsp olive oil

1 onion, finely chopped

1 fennel bulb, trimmed and finely chopped

salt and freshly ground black pepper

2 garlic cloves, grated or finely chopped

2 waxy potatoes, peeled and finely diced

300ml (10fl oz) hot vegetable or light fish stock

400ml can coconut milk

1.35kg (3lb) mussels, scrubbed and debearded (discard any that do not close when tapped) (p364)

handful of basil leaves, torn

1 Heat the oil in a large pan over a low heat, add the onion, fennel, and a pinch of salt, and cook for about 5 minutes until softened. Add the garlic and potatoes and cook for a few more minutes, being careful not to allow the mixture to brown.

2 Pour in the stock and bring to the boil. Add the coconut milk, reduce the heat slightly, and simmer gently for about 10 minutes, or until the potatoes are cooked. Bring back to the boil, add the mussels, and put a lid on the pan. Cook for about 5 minutes, until all the mussels are open (discard any that do not).

3 To serve, stir through the basil, taste the broth, and season if needed. Serve immediately.

variation

mussels in fennel and pernod broth
Prepare the mussels as before. Soften the onion with the fennel and 1 finely chopped carrot. Add the garlic but omit the potatoes. Add 150ml (5fl oz) each of water and dry white wine instead of the stock and a good splash of Pernod. Omit the coconut milk. When the mussels are cooked, garnish with a handful of chopped fresh parsley instead of basil.

Season's best **fennel**

Florence fennel looks like a short, fat celery, but is the swollen base of the stem of the fennel plant, best in late summer and autumn. It has a crisp, crunchy texture and sweet, aniseed flavour. It pairs well with seafood, particularly mussels (with a splash of Pernod or other pastis) and is good with cheeses, citrus (roasted with sliced preserved lemons), chicken, lamb, and lentils. The herb fennel and fennel seed do not come from the same plant but taste similar.

Fennel originated in the Mediterranean regions, but is now grown in other mild, temperate climates around the world as well.

Baby fennel More tender than the large bulbs of Florence fennel, these can be eaten whole. They are delicious brushed with oil and grilled on the barbecue.

Use finely chopped fronds to give a subtle aniseed flavour to soups, salads, and fish dishes.

Florence fennel With its sweet, warm, aniseed flavour and crisp texture, fennel makes a tasty salad ingredient. The flavour is subtler when cooked, but the texture remains crunchy.

essentials
varieties available

Varying sizes of mature heads, and baby fennel.

buy Look for clean, freshly cut bulbs with the long stems and fronds attached. Old fennel will look dull with brown patches and the fronds will be limp.

store Bulbs can be kept in a plastic bag in the vegetable drawer of the fridge for a week.

cook Boil or steam whole or in wedges; braise, roast, or sauté; boil thick slices until tender, then chargrill.

preserve Blanch and freeze, make into pickles or relishes, or preserve in oil.

recipe ideas

Beef, fennel, and mushroom hotpot p320

Fennel soup with beans, thyme, and chorizo p279

Pot roast chicken with turnips and fennel p298

how to prepare fennel

This technique shows how to slice fennel for a salad. To prepare fennel for roasting or braising, simply trim as in Step 1, then cut in quarters lengthways or leave baby fennel whole.

1 Trim the stalks, root end, and any tough outer pieces from the fennel. Reserve any fronds for decoration. Cut the fennel bulb in half lengthways.

2 Set each fennel half flat-side down on the chopping board and slice it lengthways into strips and separate the layers.

african sweet potato soup

This recipe is based on a classic African soup that is hot, spicy, and full of flavour. A dollop of peanut butter stirred through lends a rich, satisfying earthiness.

🍲 20 MINS 🍲 20-25 MINS ❄ FREEZABLE

SPECIAL EQUIPMENT ■ blender or food processor

SERVES 4

2 tbsp olive oil

1 onion, chopped

2 garlic cloves, finely chopped

2 tsp grated fresh root ginger

¼ tsp dried crushed chillies

450g (1lb) sweet potatoes, peeled and cut into small chunks

1 red pepper, deseeded and chopped

230g can chopped tomatoes

1 tsp cumin seeds, dry-roasted and crushed

1 tsp coriander seeds, dry-roasted and crushed

900ml (1½ pints) hot vegetable stock

2-3 tbsp smooth or crunchy peanut butter

splash of Tabasco (optional)

drizzle of chilli oil, to serve

1 Heat the olive oil in a large pan, add the onion, and fry for 3 minutes. Stir in the garlic, ginger, and chillies, and fry for 1 minute. Then stir in the sweet potatoes, pepper, tomatoes, and crushed spices, and fry for 2 minutes. Pour in the stock, bring to the boil, then simmer for 12–15 minutes, or until the sweet potatoes are tender.

2 Remove from the heat and blitz in a blender or food processor until smooth. You may need to do this in batches. Pass the soup through a sieve to remove the pepper skin and then return to the pan. Stir in the peanut butter, tasting to decide the amount you like. If you want to add more heat, add some Tabasco. Reheat gently, then drizzle a little chilli oil over each bowl to serve.

yam pla fu

These classic Thai fish balls are best made with well-flavoured fish, such as grey mullet. Great with a squeeze of lime.

🍲 15 MINS 🍲 20-25 MINS

SPECIAL EQUIPMENT ■ food processor

SERVES 4

1 large grey mullet, filleted and scaled

1 tsp oil, plus extra for deep-frying

salt

75g (2½oz) dry-roasted peanuts, to serve

nam prik (hot chilli dipping sauce) or sweet chilli sauce, to serve

For the mango salad

2 green mangoes or papayas, shredded

1 carrot, shredded

2 spring onions, trimmed and finely sliced

½ cucumber, peeled, deseeded, and shredded

60g (2oz) bean sprouts

For the dressing

1 tbsp palm sugar or dark brown sugar

zest and juice of 1 large lime

1 garlic clove, grated or finely chopped

1 tbsp grated fresh root ginger

splash of fish sauce (nam pla), to taste

1-2 bird's eye chillies, finely chopped

large handful of coriander, chopped

large handful of mint, chopped

1 Preheat the oven to 200°C (400°F/Gas 6). Rub the fish with 1 tsp of oil and 2 tbsp salt and arrange on a baking sheet. Roast in the oven for 12–15 minutes until the skin crisps. Cool.

2 Put the fish in a food processor and blitz until finely chopped. Shape into golf balls. Heat the remaining oil to 180°C (350°F/Gas 4) in a large pan. Drop each fish ball into the oil and deep-fry in small batches for about 3 minutes, until brown and crispy. Drain on kitchen paper and keep warm.

4 Toss the salad ingredients in a bowl until evenly mixed. Whisk the dressing ingredients together and toss into the salad with the peanuts. Serve with the fish balls and nam prik.

broccoli and blue cheese soup

Blue cheese and broccoli make a tasty soup, hearty enough for a light meal, but also delicious as a starter.

🍲 15 MINS 🍲 20 MINS

SPECIAL EQUIPMENT ■ blender or food processor

SERVES 4

350g (12oz) broccoli

knob of butter

1 onion, chopped

1 potato, peeled and diced

750ml (1¼ pints) chicken or vegetable stock

1 bay leaf

115g (4oz) blue cheese, diced

4 tbsp double cream, plus extra to garnish

salt and freshly ground black pepper

1 Cut the stalk off the broccoli, peel, then roughly chop. Separate the head into small florets.

2 Melt the butter in a large saucepan. Add the onion and fry gently, stirring for 3 minutes until softened, but not browned. Add the broccoli florets and chopped stalk, potato, stock, and bay leaf. Bring to the boil, reduce the heat, cover, and simmer gently for 20 minutes until the vegetables are really tender. Discard the bay leaf.

3 Purée the soup in a blender or food processor with the cheese. Return to the saucepan, stir in the cream, and season to taste. Reheat, but do not boil. Ladle into warmed soup bowls and garnish each with a small swirl of cream.

fennel soup with beans, thyme, and chorizo

The last-minute addition of paprika-flavoured chorizo gives a spicy flavour to this substantial, filling soup.

🍲 15 MINS PLUS SOAKING   🍲 1 HR

SPECIAL EQUIPMENT ▪ blender or food processor

SERVES 4

250g (9oz) dried haricot beans

1 tbsp sunflower or mild olive oil

1 Spanish onion, finely chopped

2 garlic cloves, crushed

1 fennel bulb, cored and finely chopped

2 tsp dried fennel seeds

1 tbsp finely chopped flat-leaf parsley

2 tsp thyme leaves

salt and freshly ground black pepper

100g (3½oz) chorizo, diced

1 Soak the beans overnight in cold water, then drain and rinse. Heat the oil in a heavy pan over a medium heat, add the onion, and stir for 2 minutes. Add the garlic, fennel and seeds, parsley, and half the thyme, and cook for 3–5 minutes until softened. Tip in the beans. Stir in 2 litres (3½ pints) water and season lightly.

2 Simmer for 40 minutes, or until the beans are tender, skimming from time to time. Cool a little, then pour into a blender or food processor and pulse briefly. Return to the pan, taste, and adjust the seasoning if necessary.

3 Gently reheat the soup. Meanwhile, place a non-stick pan over a medium-high heat and fry the chorizo for 2–3 minutes until crisp, stirring frequently. Drain on kitchen paper. Ladle the soup into bowls, add a little chorizo to each, and finish with a scattering of thyme. Serve immediately.

german potato soup

If you can't obtain fresh chanterelle mushrooms for this, they are also sold in jars or cans. Drain and rinse them before frying.

🍲 25 MINS   🍲 45 MINS

SPECIAL EQUIPMENT ▪ blender or food processor

SERVES 6

75g (2½oz) butter

¼ celeriac, diced

250g (9oz) carrots, diced

675g (1½lb) floury potatoes, peeled and diced

1 onion, studded with a bay leaf and a clove

1.5 litres (2¾ pints) hot vegetable stock

200g (7oz) leeks, sliced

1 onion, diced

200g (7oz) chanterelles, large ones halved

120ml (4fl oz) whipping cream, or 150g (5½oz) crème fraîche

salt and freshly ground black pepper

pinch of dried marjoram

pinch of grated nutmeg

2 tbsp chopped flat-leaf parsley, chervil, or chives

1 Melt two-thirds of the butter in a large pan, add the celeriac and carrots, and cook, stirring frequently, for 6–8 minutes or until light brown. Add the potatoes, clove-studded onion, and stock, and bring to the boil. Lower the heat, cover, and simmer for 20 minutes, or until tender. Add the leeks, cover again, and cook for 10 more minutes.

2 Meanwhile, melt the remaining butter in a pan, add the diced onion, and fry, stirring, for 4–5 minutes, until soft but not brown. Add the chanterelles and fry, stirring, for 5 minutes.

3 Remove the clove-studded onion from the soup and discard. Pour about one-third of the soup into a blender or food processor and blitz until smooth. Stir in the cream and return to the pan. Season, then add the marjoram, nutmeg, fried onion, and chanterelles, and reheat gently. Serve sprinkled with the herbs.

sweetcorn chowder

If you have grown your own sweetcorn, wait until the very last minute to harvest it – the quicker you get it from the plot to the pan, the sweeter it will be.

🍲 10 MINS   🍲 30 MINS

SPECIAL EQUIPMENT ▪ blender or food processor

SERVES 4–6

4 sweetcorn cobs (about 450g/1lb kernels)

salt and freshly ground black pepper

2 bay leaves

2 tbsp olive oil

1 large onion, chopped

4 fresh sage leaves, chopped, or ½ tsp dried sage, crushed

1 tsp fresh thyme leaves, or ½ tsp dried thyme

1 carrot, chopped

2 celery sticks, chopped

1 large potato, peeled and chopped

200g (7oz) cream cheese

120ml (4fl oz) milk

single cream, to serve

pinch of paprika, to serve

1 Stand each corn cob upright in a large bowl and strip the kernels by cutting downward with a sharp knife. Set the kernels aside. Place the cobs in a large saucepan and add 500ml (16fl oz) water, a generous dose of salt, and bay leaves. Bring to the boil and simmer, covered, for 15 minutes. Remove and discard the cobs and bay leaves.

2 Heat the oil in a saucepan and cook the onions until translucent. Add the herbs and remaining vegetables, except the corn kernels. Cook for about 5 minutes until softened. Add the corn cob stock and simmer until the potato is collapsing. Meanwhile, place the kernels in a pan and barely cover with cold water. Bring to the boil and cook for 2 minutes. Set aside.

3 Add the cheese and milk to the soup and purée until smooth. Stir in the corn kernels with their cooking liquid. Give the chowder one more blitz if desired, to break up the corn kernels slightly. Reheat, adjust the seasoning and ladle into bowls. Drizzle with single cream and dust with paprika.

stir-fried thai vegetables

Almost any crisp vegetable is excellent stir-fried.

30–35 MINS **15–20 MINS**

SERVES 4

300g (10oz) long-grain rice

salt

30g (1oz) dried Oriental mushrooms, or other dried wild mushrooms

60g (2oz) skinned unsalted peanuts

3 tbsp fish sauce (nam pla)

2 tbsp oyster sauce

1 tsp cornflour

1 tsp sugar

1 lemongrass stalk, trimmed, sliced in half lengthways, and chopped

3 tbsp vegetable oil

2 garlic cloves, finely chopped

2 dried red chillies, left whole

1 cauliflower, cut into florets

1 red pepper, deseeded and cut into strips

175g (6oz) bean sprouts, rinsed

500g (1lb 2oz) pak choi, trimmed and shredded

175g (6oz) mangetout, trimmed

3–5 sprigs of basil, leaves picked

1 Cook the rice in boiling salted water for 10–12 minutes, until barely tender. Drain, rinse in cold water, drain again, and set aside.

2 Preheat the oven to 190°C (375°F/ Gas 5). Butter a baking dish and enough foil to cover the dish. Put the mushrooms in a bowl, pour over warm water to cover, set aside for 30 minutes to soften, then drain and slice. Meanwhile, scatter the peanuts on a baking sheet and toast in the oven until brown, 5–7 minutes, then chop coarsely. Then turn the oven to its lowest setting. Spread the rice in the baking dish, gently fluff up the grains with a fork, cover with the buttered foil, and put in the oven.

3 Put the fish sauce, oyster sauce, cornflour, sugar, and lemongrass in a small bowl and whisk together. Heat the oil in a wok. Add the garlic and chillies, stir-fry for 30 seconds, then add the cauliflower, red pepper, bean sprouts, and pak choi and cook for 3 minutes, stirring constantly. Tip in the mushrooms and mangetout and stir-fry for 3 minutes more. Add the basil leaves and fish sauce mix to the wok and stir-fry for 2 minutes more. Remove the chillies and discard. Pile the rice on warmed plates. Spoon the vegetables and sauce over it, sprinkle with peanuts, and serve.

lamb cutlets with butternut squash, beans, and mint

The sweet, dense orange flesh of butternut squash marries well with tender lamb in this easy autumnal dish. The bigger the butternut squash, the more developed its flavour will be.

15 MINS **30 MINS**

SERVES 4

2 tbsp olive oil

pinch of five-spice powder

pinch of cayenne pepper

salt and freshly ground black pepper

8 lamb cutlets

1 butternut squash, halved, deseeded, peeled, and roughly chopped

10 cherry tomatoes

125g (4½oz) fine green beans, trimmed

handful of mint leaves, roughly chopped

1 Preheat the oven to 200°C (400°F/ Gas 6). Put half the oil with the five-spice powder and cayenne pepper in a small bowl, season with some salt and pepper, and mix together well. Brush half of it over the lamb cutlets and place them in a roasting tin. Mix the remainder with the squash and add to the tin. Cook in the oven for 20–30 minutes, or until the lamb is cooked to your liking and the squash is golden.

2 Meanwhile, put the tomatoes and green beans in a bowl and toss with the remaining oil. Add to the roasting tin for the last 10 minutes of cooking so they just char slightly. Sprinkle with the chopped mint leaves and serve.

variation

pork chops with sweet potatoes, beans, and thyme

Prepare as before, but use 4 lean pork chops instead of the 8 lamb cutlets and use 1 tsp Cajun spices instead of the five-spice powder and cayenne pepper. Substitute 1 fairly large sweet potato, peeled and cut into chunks instead of the butternut squash. Cook for 30–40 minutes until tender, adding the cherry tomatoes and beans for the last 10 minutes of cooking, as before. Sprinkle with a handful of thyme leaves instead of chopped mint.

rabbit provençal

A wonderful dish of rabbit and dried herbes de Provence with semi-dried tomatoes that are first baked slowly in the oven.

🥣 35–40 MINS PLUS MARINATING   🍲 3 HRS – 3 HRS 30 MINS

SERVES 4

1 rabbit, about 1.35kg (3lb) total weight, cut into 8 pieces

2 shallots, chopped

250ml (9fl oz) dry white wine

4 tbsp olive oil

2 tbsp herbes de Provence

1 tbsp plain flour

250ml (9fl oz) chicken stock

5–7 sprigs of thyme

For the tomatoes

6 plum tomatoes, about 500g (1lb 2oz) total weight

1 tbsp olive oil

salt and freshly ground black pepper

1 Combine the rabbit, shallots, white wine, half the oil, and the herbes de Provence in a shallow, non-metallic dish that is wide enough to hold the rabbit pieces in a single layer. Turn each of the rabbit pieces until completely coated in the other ingredients. Then cover and chill in the fridge for 2–3 hours to marinate.

2 Preheat the oven to 130°C (250°F/ Gas ½). Brush a grill rack with oil. Core the tomatoes and cut each lengthways into 3 slices. Put them in a bowl with the oil, salt, and pepper, and toss to coat. Arrange the tomato slices on the grill rack and bake for 2–2½ hours, until slightly shrivelled. Transfer to a plate and increase the oven temperature to 190°C (375°F/Gas 5).

3 Remove the rabbit from the marinade and reserve the marinade. Season the rabbit with salt and pepper. Heat half the remaining oil in a casserole. Add half the rabbit pieces and cook for 5 minutes, until browned. Transfer to a plate, add the remaining oil, and brown the remaining pieces of rabbit.

4 Return all the rabbit pieces to the casserole and sprinkle in the flour. Cook for 2–3 minutes, then stir in the marinade and stock. Cover and bake in the oven for 50–55 minutes, stirring occasionally, until very tender. Return the tomatoes to the oven for the last 10 minutes to heat through. Strip the thyme leaves from the stems. Serve the rabbit and tomatoes sprinkled with the thyme.

roasted monkfish with chilli, tomatoes, anchovies, and capers

Monkfish is a firm-textured fish that is succulent and meaty enough to take on the robust flavours of a chilli, anchovy, and caper paste, which is applied just before the fish is roasted.

🥣 20 MINS   🍲 30 MINS

SERVES 4

1kg (2¼lb) monkfish tail fillets

drizzle of olive oil

salt and freshly ground black pepper

2 red chillies, deseeded and finely chopped

6–8 salted anchovies, finely chopped

2–3 tsp capers, rinsed, gently squeezed dry, and chopped

12 cherry tomatoes

1 Preheat the oven to 200°C (400°F/ Gas 6). Sit the monkfish fillets in a roasting tin and drizzle over a little oil. Season well with salt and pepper and set aside.

2 Using a mortar and pestle, pound together the chillies, anchovies, and capers until they become a paste. Alternatively, squash into a paste with a fork. Then, using your hands, smother the monkfish with the paste.

3 Put the fish back into the roasting tin and cook in the oven for about 10 minutes. Throw in the tomatoes and roast for a further 5–10 minutes until the fish is cooked through.

4 Leave to rest for 5 minutes, then serve immediately with a green salad or baby roast potatoes.

variation

whole stuffed sea bream

Make the paste in the same way. Use it to stuff 4 small, boned sea bream (about 400g/14oz each) instead of the monkfish. Place side by side in a large, oiled roasting tin and drizzle with olive oil. Bake as before.

pumpkin stew

This stew is delicious with Cheddar cheese grated on top.

🥣 **25 MINS**　　🍲 **1 HR 10 MINS**

SPECIAL EQUIPMENT ▪ food processor

SERVES 4

- 1 small celeriac, peeled and diced into 2.5cm (1in) pieces
- 1 tsp lemon juice
- 1 small pumpkin, halved, deseeded, peeled and diced into 2.5cm (1in) pieces
- 2 ripe tomatoes
- 60g (2oz) butter
- 2 small leeks, cut into 2.5cm (1in) slices
- 1 garlic clove, finely chopped
- 2 tbsp plain flour
- 250ml (9fl oz) vegetable or chicken stock, plus more if needed
- salt and freshly ground black pepper
- cayenne pepper
- 1 celery stick, cut into 1cm (½in) slices
- 1 large turnip, peeled and cut into 2.5cm (1in) dice
- 1 small butternut squash, halved, deseeded, peeled, and diced into 2.5cm (1in) pieces
- 1 courgette, diced into 2.5cm (1in) pieces
- 2-3 sprigs of thyme, leaves picked

1 Put the cubes of celeriac in a large bowl of water along with the lemon juice, to prevent discolouration. Cook the pumpkin in a pan of boiling water for about 10 minutes until tender. Drain, then blitz to a purée in a food processor. Cut the cores from the tomatoes and score an "x" on the base of each. Immerse them in a bowl of boiling water until the skin starts to split, then plunge into a bowl of cold water. Peel off the skin. Cut in half and squeeze out the seeds, then cut each half into quarters.

2 Heat the butter in a casserole, add the leeks and garlic, and soften over low heat, stirring occasionally, for 3–5 minutes. Add the flour and cook, stirring, for 1–2 minutes, until foaming, then stir in the stock and pumpkin purée. Drain the celeriac and add it to the pot along with some salt, pepper, and cayenne to taste. Bring to the boil and simmer gently for 20 minutes. Add the celery and turnip and simmer for 20 minutes more, until the vegetables are beginning to soften.

3 Add the butternut squash, courgette, tomatoes, and thyme leaves and simmer for 10 minutes longer. Taste and season, if needed. Ladle into warmed bowls and serve.

sweet and sour pumpkin stew

Puy lentils add texture to this dish, as they hold their shape well when cooked. Add a little chilli for heat, if you wish.

🥣 **15 MINS**　　🍲 **1 HR**　　❄ **FREEZABLE**

SERVES 4

- 2 tbsp olive oil
- 1 onion, finely chopped
- salt and freshly ground black pepper
- 3 garlic cloves, finely chopped
- 1 carrot, finely diced
- 2 celery sticks, finely diced
- 2 bay leaves
- 4 tbsp red wine vinegar
- pinch of demerara sugar
- 1 pumpkin or large butternut squash, peeled and chopped into chunky pieces (about 500g/1lb 2oz prepared weight)
- 900ml (1½ pints) hot vegetable stock
- 150g (5½oz) Puy lentils, rinsed and picked over for any stones
- bunch of mint leaves, roughly chopped
- pumpkin seeds, to serve

1 Heat the oil in a large flameproof casserole over a medium heat, add the onion, and cook for 3–4 minutes until soft. Season well with salt and pepper, add the garlic, carrot, celery, and bay leaves, and cook for a further 5 minutes until soft. Increase the heat, add the vinegar, let it simmer for a minute, then stir in the sugar and pumpkin. Turn to coat well, add a little stock, and cook on high for a minute. Stir through the lentils, add the remaining stock, and bring to the boil.

2 Partially cover with the lid, reduce the heat, and simmer for 45 minutes, or until the lentils are soft. Top up with water if the stew becomes too dry. Taste and season, and remove the bay leaves. Stir through the mint, then serve on a bed of rice with some pumpkin seeds scattered over.

venison wellingtons

Wild mushrooms and venison in pastry make a special meal.

🥣 **40 MINS**　　🍲 **45 MINS**

SERVES 4

- 2 tbsp olive oil
- sea salt and freshly ground black pepper
- 4 venison loin steaks, each 120-150g (4¼-5½oz)
- 30g (1oz) unsalted butter
- 2 shallots, finely chopped
- 1 garlic clove, finely chopped
- 200g (7oz) mixed mushrooms, including wild mushrooms, chopped
- 1 tbsp chopped thyme leaves
- 1 tbsp brandy or Madeira
- 10g (¼oz) dried wild mushrooms (optional), rehydrated (see packet)
- 500g (1lb 2oz) ready-made puff pastry
- 1 egg, beaten, for glazing

1 Preheat the oven to 200°C (400°F/ Gas 6). Heat the oil in a frying pan. Season the venison and fry them, two at a time, for 2 minutes each side, until browned all over. Remove from the pan and set aside to cool. Melt the butter in the pan over a medium heat, add the shallots, and cook for 5 minutes until soft. Add the garlic, cook for 1–2 minutes, then add the mushrooms and thyme and cook for 5 minutes until soft and any juices evaporate. Add the brandy and cook over a high heat for 1 minute. Remove from the heat and let cool. If using dried mushrooms, drain, chop, and add to the mushroom mixture.

2 Cut the pastry into 4 equal pieces and roll out rectangles 5mm (¼in) thick and large enough to wrap around each steak. Pat each steak dry with kitchen paper. Place a quarter of the mushroom filling at one end of the pastry rectangle, leaving an edge of 2cm (¾in). Place a steak on top, brush the edges of the pastry with beaten egg, fold the pastry over, press the edges down, and crimp them in. Repeat with the remaining steaks and pastry. Cut small slits in the tops of the pastry wellingtons and brush with more beaten egg. Place on a heavy baking tray, bake for 20–25 minutes, or until puffed and golden, remove from the oven, allow to cool for 5 minutes, and then serve.

squash, thyme, and goat's cheese tart

If you are planning a relaxed weekend lunch with friends, or want a dish to last for a couple of meals, try this tart, which relies on the creamy, buttery flavours of autumnal squash to balance the tang of soft goat's cheese.

🥣 15 MINS   🍲 1 HR 15 MINS   ❄ FREEZABLE

SPECIAL EQUIPMENT ▪ 20cm (8in) round loose-bottomed fluted tart tin ▪ ceramic baking beans

SERVES 4-6

300g (10oz) ready-made shortcrust pastry

2 eggs, lightly beaten

1-2 tbsp olive oil

1 onion, finely chopped

salt and freshly ground black pepper

2 garlic cloves, grated or finely chopped

1kg (2¼lb) butternut squash, peeled, deseeded, and chopped into small cubes

a few sprigs of thyme, leaves picked

125g (4½oz) soft goat's cheese

200ml (7fl oz) double cream

1 Preheat the oven to 200°C (400°F/ Gas 6). Roll out the pastry on a floured work surface to a large circle about 3mm (⅛in) thick and use to line the tart tin, pressing it into the corners. Trim away the excess and prick the bottom all over with a fork. Line the pastry shell with greaseproof paper and fill the base with ceramic baking beans. Bake the pastry shell in the oven for about 15–20 minutes until the edges of the pastry are golden. Remove the tart tin from the oven, remove the beans and paper, brush the bottom of the pastry shell with a little of the beaten egg, and return to the oven for 2–3 minutes to crisp. Remove from the oven once again and set aside. Reduce the oven temperature to 180°C (350°F/Gas 4).

2 Meanwhile, heat 1 tbsp of the oil in a large frying pan over a low heat. Add the onion and a little salt, and cook gently for about 5 minutes until soft and translucent. Add the garlic, squash, and half of the thyme leaves, and continue cooking over a low heat for 10–15 minutes until the squash softens and begins to turn golden. You may have to add a little more oil.

3 Spoon the squash and onion mixture into the pastry shell, then crumble over the goat's cheese. Mix the cream with the remaining beaten egg and season well with salt and pepper. Pour the cream mixture over the tart filling, then sprinkle with the remaining thyme leaves. Bake in the oven for 20–25 minutes until the tart is puffed and set. Leave to cool for at least 10 minutes before releasing it from the tin. Serve the tart while still warm with a rocket salad.

Season's best **winter squashes**

Winter squashes have a hard skin, large seeds, and can have a rich, robust sweetness that intensifies as they ripen. They are at their best when harvested, but can be stored, too. They have denser flesh than the summer varieties and add depth of flavour to many dishes. They taste great with cheeses, particularly blue ones, and are complemented by garlic, spices, tomatoes, nuts, and seeds.

Native to Mexico and Central America, squashes are now grown in tropical and warm, temperate regions around the world. They come in many different colours, shapes, and sizes.

Pumpkin Pumpkins are usually more fibrous and watery than other squash. If sold in pieces, use within a few days as the flesh is more perishable once cut.

You can distinguish this from marrow by its creamy-yellow stripy skin.

Delicata Also known as sweet potato squash, this variety is renowned for its exceptionally smooth, moist, honey-flavoured flesh. Ideal for pumpkin pie and cakes.

how to peel butternut squash

All winter squashes must be halved (except for vegetable marrow, which is usually thickly sliced) and deseeded. Unless stuffing, the hard skin is usually removed. The flesh can then be cut into chunks before cooking.

1 Holding the squash firmly on a board, use a chef's knife to halve lengthways, working from the stalk end to the core end. For vegetable marrow, cut in thick slices.

2 Using a spoon, firmly scrape out the seeds and fibres from each half and discard (or keep the seeds to roast, then use for salads or snacks).

3 If stuffing, there is no need to peel; otherwise use a vegetable peeler or small sharp knife to cut off the skin. Cut into pieces or chunks to cook.

Butternut squash One of the more common varieties of winter squash, butternut has smooth, dense flesh that becomes sweet and nutty when baked or steamed. The cavity can be stuffed.

Harlequin squash Cream and green, this dumpling-shaped variety has high sugar content. It is excellent when roasted.

The seeds can be washed, dried, tossed in oil, and roasted in the oven, then tossed in salt and kept in an airtight jar.

Spaghetti marrow A mellow-tasting squash, this has flesh that separates into long spaghetti-like strands as it cooks. Use as spaghetti, with or without sauce, or in salads, soups, and casseroles.

Turban squash Also known as Turk's turban, this is a distinctively shaped variety with bland, slightly dry, yellow-orange flesh. The internal cavity is larger than most winter squashes, so there is correspondingly less flesh.

The bottom half can be cut off and hollowed out for stuffing, or used as a striking bowl for soup.

essentials
varieties available

Types include butternut, acorn, turban, harlequin, crown prince, and onion squashes, marrow, spaghetti marrow, and pumpkin.

buy Avoid any with damaged skin. Young marrows may be tender-skinned but for others, if ripe, your nail should not be able to pierce it.

store Whole ones can be kept for several weeks in a cool dark place on newspapers; keep cut ones in the fridge for a few days.

cook Steam, boil, fry, bake, roast, stew, or purée for soups and desserts.

preserve Make jam and chutney; roast and salt the seeds; candy pumpkin as a sweetmeat.

recipe ideas

Butternut squash stuffed with beef mince p286

Butternut squash tagine p286

Pumpkin pie p345

Roast pumpkin, chilli, and ginger dip p264

Squash, thyme, and goat's cheese tart p283

butternut squash tagine

Most squashes ripen as summer draws to a close and thoughts turn towards autumnal fare. A spicy tagine with flavoursome butternut squash suits this transition perfectly.

🥣 20 MINS   🍲 1 HR

SERVES 4

4 tbsp light olive oil

2 red onions, finely chopped

1 large red pepper, deseeded and diced

4 garlic cloves, chopped

1 thumb-sized piece fresh root ginger, finely chopped

1 tsp chilli powder

1 tsp cinnamon

2 tsp smoked paprika

2 tsp ground coriander

1 tbsp ground cumin

2 x 400g cans chopped tomatoes

600ml (1 pint) vegetable stock

2 tbsp clear honey

sea salt and freshly ground black pepper

400g (14oz) butternut squash, halved, deseeded, peeled, and diced

200g (7oz) cooked chickpeas

100g (3½oz) dried apricots, chopped

bunch of coriander leaves, chopped

1 Pour the oil into a large saucepan. Add the onions, red pepper, garlic, and ginger, and fry over a low heat for 2 minutes until they are softened, but not browned.

2 Add the chilli, cinnamon, smoked paprika, ground coriander, and cumin, and continue to cook for a further 2 minutes over a low heat to release the flavour of the spices. Add the tomatoes, stock, and honey and season well. Bring the sauce to the boil, then turn down the heat. Simmer slowly, uncovered, for 30 minutes.

3 Add the butternut squash, chickpeas, and chopped dried apricots, and continue to cook for 10–15 minutes until the squash is soft, but not falling apart. Add more water if it is beginning to look a little dry. Season to taste and stir in the chopped coriander before serving with some herby couscous.

spicy, saucy fish

Serve this halibut with poppadums and aromatic basmati rice.

🥣 30-35 MINS   🍲 30-35 MINS

SPECIAL EQUIPMENT ▪ blender

SERVES 6

30g (1oz) butter

1 apple, peeled, cored, and diced into 1cm (½in) pieces

3 onions, 1 finely chopped and 2 thinly sliced

1 tsp ground cumin

1 tsp ground coriander

½ tsp ground ginger

½ tsp ground cloves

¼ tsp cayenne pepper, or ½ tsp crushed chillies

1½ tbsp cornflour

200ml (7fl oz) coconut milk

450ml (15fl oz) fish stock

salt and freshly ground black pepper

1kg (2¼lb) halibut fillets, skinned

4 tbsp vegetable oil

2 tbsp paprika

2 x 400g cans chopped tomatoes

6 garlic cloves, finely chopped

4 bay leaves

2 celery sticks, peeled and thinly sliced

2 carrots, thinly sliced

1 To make the spicy sauce, melt the butter in a saucepan. Add the apple and chopped onion and cook for 3–5 minutes until soft. Add the cumin, coriander, ginger, cloves, and cayenne. Stir over a low heat for 2–3 minutes. Put the cornflour and 2–3 tbsp of the coconut milk in a small bowl and blend to a smooth paste. Add the remaining coconut milk and 150ml (5fl oz) of stock to the saucepan and bring to the boil. Stir in the cornflour paste; the sauce will thicken at once. Remove from the heat, season to taste, and set aside.

2 Rinse the fish, pat dry with kitchen paper, and cut into 2.5cm (1in) cubes. Heat the oil in a casserole. Add the sliced onions and cook for 3–5 minutes until soft. Add the paprika and cook for about 1 minute, stirring to combine it evenly with the onions. Add the remaining stock, tomatoes, garlic, bay leaves, celery, and carrots. Season and bring to the boil. Reduce the heat and simmer until the liquid is reduced by a third; it should take 15–20 minutes.

3 Add the spicy sauce, stir well, and bring back to the boil. Add the fish, cover with a lid, and simmer, stirring occasionally, for 12–15 minutes, until the fish flakes easily. Discard the bay leaves and taste for seasoning, then serve in warmed bowls.

butternut squash stuffed with beef mince

A simple all-in-one dish that uses a halved squash as "bowls".

🥣 15 MINS   🍲 1 HR

SERVES 4

1 butternut squash, halved and deseeded

2 tbsp olive oil

1 onion, finely chopped

675g (1½lb) minced beef

salt and freshly ground black pepper

handful of flat-leaf parsley, finely chopped

Gruyère cheese, grated, to serve

1 Preheat the oven to 200°C (400°F/ Gas 6). Put the squash halves in a roasting tin, drizzle over half the oil, and roast in the oven for about 10–15 minutes until softened.

2 Meanwhile, heat the remaining oil in a frying pan over a medium heat, add the chopped onion, and cook for 3–4 minutes until soft. Add the beef and cook, stirring frequently, for about 5 minutes until the meat starts to colour. Season with salt and pepper, and stir through the parsley.

3 Remove the squash from the oven and spoon the mince into the hollows. Cover with foil and roast for 30 minutes. Then remove the foil, sprinkle over the Gruyère cheese, and return to the oven for about 5 minutes, or until the Gruyère cheese has melted.

marrow and tomato gratin

Although less sweet than courgettes, marrow becomes more concentrated in flavour when baked and makes a good base for other ingredients. This gratin tastes great with chicken.

🥣 20 MINS   🍲 50 MINS

SERVES 4

2 tbsp olive oil

1 onion, finely chopped

900g (2lb) marrow, halved, deseeded, peeled, and cut into cubes

450g (1lb) tomatoes, finely chopped

3 garlic cloves, grated or finely chopped

handful of flat-leaf parsley, finely chopped

salt and freshly ground black pepper

3 tbsp fresh breadcrumbs

50g (1¾oz) Parmesan cheese, grated

1 Preheat the oven to 200°C (400°F/ Gas 6). Heat the oil in a large pan, add the onion, and cook over a low heat for 5 minutes, or until soft and translucent. Add the marrow and cook for a further 5 minutes, then add the tomatoes and garlic and cook over a low heat for 10 minutes, or until the tomatoes start to break down. Stir through the parsley and season well with salt and pepper.

2 Spoon the mixture into one large gratin dish or four small ones. Sprinkle over the breadcrumbs and Parmesan cheese and bake in the oven for 20–30 minutes, or until the top is crisp and golden, then serve.

pasta with butternut squash, cream, and sage

This filling dish is so easy to make – the butternut squash needs just a little initial cooking in the oven. This meal is hard to beat as the nights draw in and the weather turns colder.

🥣 15 MINS   🍲 20 MINS

SERVES 4

1 butternut squash, halved, deseeded, peeled, and cubed

pinch of chilli flakes

2 tbsp olive oil

1 red onion, finely chopped

2 garlic cloves, grated or finely chopped

6 sage leaves, roughly chopped

150ml (5fl oz) double cream

salt and freshly ground black pepper

350g (12oz) conchiglie

Parmesan cheese, grated, to serve

1 Preheat the oven to 200°C (400°F/ Gas 6). Place the squash in a large roasting tin, sprinkle with chilli flakes, and drizzle with 1 tbsp of the oil. Combine well and roast in the oven for 10–15 minutes, or until the squash starts to soften.

2 Heat the remaining oil in a large frying pan, add the onion, and cook over a low heat for 5 minutes, or until soft and translucent. Add the almost-cooked squash, garlic, and sage leaves, and stir together. Pour in the cream and simmer gently for 5 minutes. Season well with salt and lots of pepper.

3 Meanwhile, cook the pasta in a large pan of boiling salted water for 10 minutes, or until it is tender but still al dente. Drain, keeping back a tiny amount of the cooking water. Return the pasta to the pan and toss it with the reserved cooking water. Then toss the pasta with the sauce, sprinkle with Parmesan, and serve.

roasted squid and potato with spiced coriander pesto

Squid is sweet and tender when cooked quickly (or very slowly). Choose baby squid for the most succulent option.

🥣 10 MINS 🍲 20 MINS

SPECIAL EQUIPMENT ▪ food processor

SERVES 4

large handful of coriander

large handful of basil leaves

2 garlic cloves, chopped

large handful of pine nuts

pinch of chilli flakes, plus extra (optional)

60g (2oz) Parmesan cheese, grated

150ml (5fl oz) extra virgin olive oil (use more or less as required)

salt and freshly ground black pepper

1.1kg (2½lb) waxy potatoes, peeled and cubed

2 tbsp olive oil

350g (12oz) squid, gutted, cleaned, and scored (p263, or you can ask your fishmonger to do this)

1 Preheat the oven to 200°C (400°F/Gas 6). To make the pesto, put the coriander, basil, garlic, and pine nuts in a food processor and blitz until the nuts are ground. Add the chilli flakes and most of the Parmesan cheese and blitz again. Now slowly add the extra virgin olive oil in a gradual stream and pulse until the pesto forms a smooth paste and reaches the right consistency. Stir through the remaining Parmesan, taste, and season with salt and pepper if it needs it. Set aside.

2 Put the potatoes in a roasting tin. Drizzle over 1 tbsp of the olive oil and toss through. Season with salt and pepper. Roast in the oven for 15–20 minutes until golden.

3 Meanwhile, mix the squid with the chilli flakes (if using) and remaining olive oil in a bowl. Add to the potatoes for the last 10 minutes or so of cooking and cook until the squid is slightly charred. Toss everything together, then serve hot with the coriander pesto.

pork with fennel and mustard

Bulbous fennel has a light, aromatic aniseed taste. Eaten raw it is distinctive, crisp, and refreshing, but once cooked its flavours soften and sweeten, and marry well with pork.

🥣 20 MINS 🍲 45 MINS ❄ FREEZABLE

SERVES 4

3 tbsp olive oil

1 large onion, sliced

2 small fennel bulbs, sliced

550g (1¼lb) lean pork, cut into bite-sized pieces

4 garlic cloves, finely chopped

5 tbsp dry white wine

1 tbsp wholegrain mustard

½ tsp paprika

small handful of flat-leaf parsley, chopped

½ tbsp chopped sage leaves

½ tbsp chopped rosemary leaves

1 tbsp plain flour

450ml (15fl oz) milk

salt and freshly ground black pepper

1 Preheat the oven to 180°C (350°F/Gas 4). Heat the oil in a large heavy-based pan, add the onion and fennel, and cook for 5 minutes, or until the vegetables begin to soften. Add the pork and cook, stirring occasionally, for 5 minutes, or until it is no longer pink. Add the garlic and cook for 1 minute, then stir in the wine and mustard, raise the heat, and allow to boil for 3 minutes while the alcohol evaporates. Stir in the paprika, parsley, sage, and rosemary, then add the flour and mix well. Add a little of the milk, mix to a smooth paste, then stir in the rest of the milk. Season well with salt and pepper and cook for 5 minutes, adding a little more milk if the mixture looks dry.

2 Transfer to a casserole dish, cover, cook in the oven for 25 minutes or until piping hot, and serve.

variation

beef with celery and mustard
Prepare in exactly the same way, but use 2 celery hearts, sliced, instead of the fennel and 500g (1lb 2oz) beef frying steak, cut in thin strips, instead of the pork. Substitute 2 tsp chopped fresh thyme instead of the sage.

aubergine massaman curry

This is a spicy Thai curry with the distinctively sweet flavours of cinnamon and cardamom. The peanuts add a contrasting texture to the potatoes and aubergine.

🥣 15 MINS   🍲 1 HR

SPECIAL EQUIPMENT ▪ food processor

SERVES 4-6

2 red chillies, deseeded

1 lemongrass stalk, tough outer leaves removed

5cm (2in) piece of fresh root ginger, peeled and roughly chopped

5 cardamom pods, crushed

1 tbsp sunflower oil

1 onion, finely chopped

salt and freshly ground black pepper

600ml (1 pint) hot vegetable stock

400ml can coconut milk

1 cinnamon stick, broken

splash of dark soy sauce

splash of fish sauce (nam pla)

4 potatoes, peeled and chopped into bite-sized pieces

6 baby aubergines, halved lengthways, or use 2 large ones, roughly chopped

85g (3oz) roasted unsalted peanuts, roughly chopped

1 tbsp palm sugar or demerara sugar (optional)

1 Put the chillies, lemongrass, ginger, and cardamom in a food processor and blitz with a drop of the oil to make a paste.

2 Heat the remaining oil in a large heavy-based pan over a medium heat, add the onion, and cook for 3–4 minutes until soft. Then add the paste and some seasoning and cook for a few minutes more. Stir in the stock and coconut milk, bring to the boil, then add the cinnamon stick, soy sauce, and fish sauce, and cook on a low heat for about 20 minutes. Stir in the potatoes and aubergines and cook the curry for a further 20 minutes.

3 Stir in half the peanuts, taste, and adjust the flavour by adding the sugar, if desired, and more salt or fish sauce, as needed. Ladle into warmed bowls and sprinkle with the remaining peanuts. Serve with rice and lime wedges.

poussins with plums and cabbage

If you prefer, this recipe is equally good made with a chicken. Much of this dish can be made ahead and kept, covered, in the fridge; simply reheat and make the plum sauce before serving.

🥣 15 MINS   🍲 1 HR 45 MINS

SERVES 4

2-3 poussins, each about 500g (1lb 2oz) in weight, trussed with string

salt and freshly ground black pepper

½ Savoy cabbage, cored and coarsely shredded

2 tbsp vegetable oil

250g (9oz) streaky bacon rashers, sliced

400g (14oz) purple plums, halved and stoned

1 onion, peeled and studded with 1 clove

1 bouquet garni

250ml (9fl oz) dry white wine

500ml (16fl oz) hot chicken stock

1 Preheat the oven to 180°C (350°F/ Gas 4). Season the poussins and set aside. Cook the cabbage in a pan of salted boiling water for 2 minutes until it begins to soften. Drain and set aside. Heat the oil in a large flameproof casserole, add the birds, one or two at a time, and cook for 5–10 minutes until browned all over.

Remove and set aside. Reduce the heat and cook the bacon, stirring, for 3–5 minutes until the fat has rendered. Spoon off all but 2 tbsp of fat and spread half the cabbage across the base of the casserole. Add the poussins, two-thirds of the plums, the onion, and bouquet garni. Cover with the remaining cabbage and pour over the wine and stock. Cover and cook in the oven for 45–55 minutes, until the birds are cooked and the juices run clear if the thighs are pierced with a sharp knife.

2 Discard the onion and bouquet garni. Transfer the cabbage to a serving dish. Set the birds on top (with strings removed), cover with foil, and keep warm. Add the last of the plums to the cooking liquid and simmer for 5–8 minutes until tender, then remove and transfer to the serving dish. Boil the plum sauce for 10–15 minutes until reduced by about half, season if needed, then serve with the poussins and cabbage.

chargrilled lamb cutlets and aubergine with red cabbage slaw

Red cabbage coleslaw gives this dish of lamb and grilled aubergine a refreshingly different twist.

🥣 25 MINS   🍲 10 MINS

SERVES 4

12 lamb cutlets, trimmed of any fat

2 tbsp olive oil

salt and freshly ground black pepper

1 aubergine, about 300g (10oz), thinly sliced lengthways

½ small red cabbage

100g (3½oz) fine green beans, trimmed, blanched, and thinly sliced diagonally

1 small cucumber, thinly sliced or shaved lengthways

1 small red onion, thinly sliced in rounds

2 celery sticks, peeled and thinly sliced diagonally

60g (2oz) hazelnuts, chopped

small handful of chives, snipped

2 tbsp extra virgin olive oil

1 tsp balsamic vinegar

1 Heat the grill to medium. Brush the lamb cutlets with olive oil and season with salt and pepper. Grill the lamb under a medium heat for 3–5 minutes on each side until cooked to your liking. Remove the lamb to a plate and set aside to rest in a warm place. Turn the grill to high and brush the aubergine slices with a little olive oil and season with black pepper. Grill the aubergine under a high heat for about 3 minutes on each side until golden. Remove the aubergine and transfer to the plate of lamb.

2 Finely slice or shred the red cabbage and place in a mixing bowl. Add the remaining ingredients, season with salt and pepper, toss gently, and serve with the lamb cutlets and aubergine slices.

hungarian beef goulash

Make the most of the season's glossy peppers and tomatoes with this traditional beef stew.

🥣 25–30 MINS   🍲 2 HRS 45 MINS

SERVES 4

1 tbsp vegetable oil

60g (2oz) smoked bacon, diced

6 onions, about 750g (1lb 10oz) total weight, chopped

2 tbsp paprika

750g (1lb 10oz) braising steak, cut into 4cm (1½in) cubes

2 garlic cloves, finely chopped

½ tsp caraway seeds

2 tomatoes, deseeded, and chopped

2 green peppers, sliced

salt and freshly ground black pepper

1 egg

45g (1½oz) plain flour

120ml (4fl oz) soured cream (optional)

1 Heat the oil in a casserole, add the bacon, and stir for 3–5 minutes until it is lightly browned and the fat has rendered. Stir in the onions. Cut a piece of foil to fit the casserole, then cover the mixture and put on the lid. Cook over a low heat, stirring occasionally, for 20–25 minutes until the onions are soft and translucent.

2 Preheat the oven to 180°C (350°F/Gas 4). Stir the paprika into the onions and bacon and cook for 2 minutes; don't let the paprika scorch. Add the steak, garlic, caraway seeds, and 500ml (16fl oz) water and stir. Bring to the boil, stirring, then cover and cook in the oven for 1–1½ hours until the beef is almost tender.

3 Stir the tomatoes and peppers into the goulash. Season to taste. Cover and cook for 30–45 minutes more until the meat is very soft and the stew rich and thick. Taste for seasoning.

4 Lightly beat the egg in a small bowl. Put the flour and a little salt in another bowl, then stir in the egg. Transfer the goulash to the top of the stove and heat to boiling. Using 2 teaspoons, drop spoonfuls of the dumpling mix into the goulash and simmer for 5–7 minutes until cooked.

5 Ladle the goulash and dumplings into warmed soup bowls. Top each serving with a spoon of soured cream, if desired.

crispy duck char sui

Char sui is a Chinese barbecue sauce traditionally used with pork, chicken, or duck. It has a lovely spicy sweet-sour flavour that cuts through the richness of the duck meat.

🥣 15 MINS   🍲 45 MINS

SERVES 4

4 duck thigh and leg joints, with small incisions made all over with a knife

3 garlic cloves, grated or finely chopped

3 tbsp light soy sauce

3 tbsp rice wine

1 tbsp hoisin sauce

2 tbsp clear honey

2 tsp five-spice powder

salt and freshly ground black pepper

1 Preheat the oven to 200°C (400°F/Gas 6). Put all the ingredients in a large bowl and season with salt and pepper. Mix everything together so that the duck is well coated. Wrap the coated duck pieces in foil and roast in the oven for 30 minutes.

2 Preheat the grill until hot. Carefully unwrap the foil and sit the duck on the hot grill, skin-side up. Grill under a high heat, turning frequently, for 10–15 minutes until the skin is golden and crisp. Remove to a plate and leave to rest in a warm place for about 10 minutes. Then cut the crispy duck into slices and serve with a crisp green salad.

variation

crispy wild duck with plums

Prepare in the same way but use 2 small wild ducks, halved, instead of the leg portions. Roast in the oven for 30–40 minutes. Brush 8 halved and stoned just-ripe plums with a mixture of 2 tbsp clear honey and 4 tbsp soy sauce in a shallow, flameproof dish. Grill alongside the duck or, pan-fry in 1 tbsp sunflower oil for 1–2 minutes each side until softening but still holding their shape. Serve with the duck and salad.

salmon with mushrooms and pak choi

Chestnut mushrooms have a lovely meaty taste and give depth to the mild flavours of salmon and pak choi in this dish.

🥣 15 MINS   🍲 25 MINS

SERVES 4

1 tbsp olive oil

1 tbsp dark soy sauce

½ tbsp mirin

5cm (2in) piece of fresh root ginger, peeled and finely chopped

2 garlic cloves, grated or finely chopped

salt and freshly ground black pepper

4 salmon fillets, approx 150g (5½oz) in weight

2 heads of pak choi, quartered lengthways

200g (7oz) chestnut mushrooms, large ones halved

1 Preheat the oven to 200°C (400°F/Gas 6). Put the oil, soy sauce, mirin, ginger, and garlic in a bowl and mix together well. Season with salt and pepper.

2 Put the salmon fillets, pak choi, and mushrooms in a roasting tin, then drizzle over the oil mixture and combine well. Put into the oven to roast for 20–25 minutes, or until the salmon is cooked through, and serve with plain rice.

variation

quick stir-fried fish with pak choi

Dice 600g (1lb 5oz) salmon steak or chunky white fish, such as coley or halibut. Slice the 200g (7oz) mushrooms and thickly shred the 2 heads of pak choi. Heat 1 tbsp olive oil or sunflower oil in a wok or large saucepan over a medium heat. Stir-fry the fish and mushrooms for 2 minutes. Add the pak choi and stir-fry for a further 1–2 minutes until slightly wilted. Add the flavourings as in the original recipe but add ½ tsp Chinese five-spice powder as well. Stir-fry briefly to combine. Moisten with a splash of water or chicken stock, then serve spooned onto egg noodles or rice.

grilled sea bream with spice rub

The firm flesh of bream is wonderful with the strong flavours in this recipe. Make the spice rub up to 6 hours ahead and store in an airtight container at room temperature.

🥄 15 MINS   🍲 6–8 MINS   ❄ FREEZABLE

SERVES 4

4 sea bream fillets, about 150g (5½oz) each, scaled and pinboned

1 tbsp walnuts

4 plum tomatoes, chopped

1 tbsp chopped coriander leaves

1½ tsp walnut or olive oil

sea salt and freshly ground black pepper

lemon wedges, to serve

For the spice rub

3 tbsp walnut or olive oil

4 tbsp chopped coriander leaves

2 garlic cloves, crushed

1 tsp crushed coriander seeds

1 tsp lemon juice

1 small green chilli, deseeded and finely chopped

salt

1 Mix all the ingredients for the spice rub together in a bowl and season with salt. Preheat the grill to its highest setting.

2 Line a baking sheet with foil and place the fish fillets on it, skin-side down. Brush the spice rub over the fish. Place under the grill for 6–8 minutes, until cooked through and lightly golden. Remove from the heat and keep warm.

3 Meanwhile, for the tomato salad, toast the walnuts by stirring them in a dry frying pan over a medium heat for 2–3 minutes, then remove and lightly crush. Mix with the tomatoes, coriander, and walnut or olive oil, and season with sea salt and pepper. Serve the fish with the salad and lemon wedges on the side.

sea bream with tomato sauce

Make sure you use well-flavoured tomatoes, as they make all the difference to the finished dish. You can make the tomato sauce 2–3 days in advance, cover, and store in the fridge.

🥄 10 MINS   🍲 25 MINS

SERVES 4

4 small sea bream, about 350g (12oz) in total, scaled, gutted, and trimmed

1 tbsp plain flour

salt and freshly ground black pepper

5 tbsp extra virgin olive oil

1 onion, finely chopped

2 celery sticks, finely sliced

2 garlic cloves, chopped

8 plum tomatoes, roughly chopped

5 tbsp dry white wine

pinch of sugar

2 tbsp chopped flat-leaf parsley

1 Preheat the oven to 190°C (375°F/ Gas 5). Slash the sea bream 3–4 times on each side with a sharp knife. Mix the flour with some salt and pepper and dust it over the fish. Arrange in a baking tray.

2 Heat the oil in a pan over a low heat, add the onion, celery, and garlic, and cook for 2–3 minutes, until the vegetables soften. Add the tomatoes and wine, and cook for 3–4 minutes, until the juices run. Season with salt and pepper and add the sugar.

3 Spoon the tomato sauce over the fish and bake in the oven for 15–20 minutes, or until cooked. The flesh will be white and opaque.

4 Slide the fish onto a large, warmed serving dish, sprinkle with parsley, and serve immediately.

squid stew

Squid transforms when it is cooked slowly. It defies all rubbery associations and becomes wonderfully tender.

🥄 30 MINS   🍲 1 HR 15 MINS – 1 HR 45 MINS   ❄ FREEZABLE

SERVES 4–6

1 tbsp olive oil

1 onion, finely chopped

salt and freshly ground black pepper

1 bay leaf

a few sprigs of thyme

3 garlic cloves, sliced

2 red chillies, deseeded and sliced into thin strips

200g (7oz) chorizo, sliced

1.1kg (2½lb) squid, gutted, cleaned and cut into rings (and tentacles, if you wish) (p263)

250ml (9fl oz) red wine

400g can chopped tomatoes

650ml (1 pint 2fl oz) vegetable stock

400g can butter beans, drained

handful of curly parsley, finely chopped

1 Preheat the oven to 170°C (325°F/ Gas 3). Heat the oil in a large flameproof casserole over a medium heat, add the onion, and season with salt and pepper. Add the bay leaf and thyme, and cook gently for about 6 minutes until the onions are soft.

2 Stir in the garlic, chillies, and chorizo, and cook for a few minutes. Then add the squid (in batches, if necessary) and cook for a few more minutes, until the squid starts to colour slightly. Increase the heat and pour in the wine. Let it simmer for 1–2 minutes, then add the tomatoes and stock, and bring to the boil.

3 Tip in the butter beans and stir, then add some seasoning, cover with a lid, and put in the oven for 1–1½ hours. Check occasionally that it is not drying out and top up with a little hot water if required. Taste and season if needed, remove the bay leaf and thyme, and stir through the parsley. Ladle into warmed bowls and serve with crusty bread.

Season's best **sea bream**

There are several species of sea bream, best from late summer to autumn, but farmed all year. All have a round, flattish body with a long, single, spiny dorsal fin. They have a good flavour with firm, dense flesh. Sea bream is excellent cooked simply with a few herbs, some butter, and garlic, but can be served in numerous dishes. They go particularly well with sweet spices and chilli, tomatoes, celeriac, and olives.

Sea bream fillet The white, well-textured flesh tastes its best when simply pan-fried.

It is easily recognized by its long, spiny dorsal fin and large scales.

Sea bream This is a well-flavoured fish. It is one of the most versatile, and one many people haven't heard of or tried.

essentials
varieties available

Whole or fillets, farmed and wild black bream, white bream, and red bream.

buy Choose line- or net-caught fish with firm bodies, bright eyes, and red gills. Fillets should smell fresh and be moist.

store Best eaten on the day of purchase.

cook Pan-fry, grill, stuff and bake.

recipe ideas

Grilled sea bream with spice rub p292

Sea bream with tomato sauce p292

Whole stuffed sea bream p281

how to cook sea bream en papillote

Cooking any small whole fish in a parcel retains all its flavour and natural juices. Open the parcel at the table for maximum mouthwatering aroma.

1 Lay the prepared fish on a sheet of baking parchment placed on a baking sheet. Top with lemon slices, fresh herbs, seasoning, and a knob of butter.

2 Fold the paper over the fish and envelop it completely, leaving enough paper to seal.

3 Twist and fold the edge all round to seal the fish. Bake at 190°C (375°F/Gas 5) for about 20 minutes.

lamb mince and squash with green chillies

Lamb with sweet squash is the perfect combination and the minced meat benefits from long, slow cooking. Stirring mint and oregano leaves into the dish adds a distinct freshness.

🥣 25 MINS　🍲 1 HR 30 MINS – 2 HRS　❄ FREEZABLE

SERVES 4–6

2 tbsp olive oil

1 butternut squash, peeled, deseeded, and chopped into bite-sized pieces

salt and freshly ground black pepper

1 onion, finely chopped

handful of fresh oregano, leaves only, or 1 tsp dried oregano

handful of thyme, leaves only

3 garlic cloves, finely chopped

1 green chilli, deseeded and finely chopped

450g (1lb) lamb mince

900ml (1½ pints) hot vegetable stock

400g can chopped tomatoes

60g (2oz) sultanas

bunch of mint leaves, finely chopped

1–2 tsp harissa paste

1 Preheat the oven to 180°C (350°F/ Gas 4). Heat half the oil in a large flameproof casserole over a medium heat and add the squash. Season with salt and pepper, and cook for 5–8 minutes, stirring, until it starts to turn golden. Remove the squash from the casserole and set aside.

2 Heat the remaining oil in the casserole, add the onion, and cook for 3–4 minutes until soft. Stir in the oregano, thyme, garlic, and chilli, and cook for a few more minutes. Add the mince, increase the heat a little, and cook, stirring, for 5–8 minutes until it is no longer pink. Reduce the heat, return the squash to the casserole, add the stock and tomatoes, and bring to the boil. Reduce to a simmer,

stir in the sultanas, cover with the lid, and put in the oven for 1–1½ hours. Check occasionally that it is not drying out, topping up with a little hot water if needed.

3 Taste and season, if necessary, then stir in the mint and harissa paste to taste. Serve with rice or warmed pitta bread and a lightly dressed, crisp green salad.

variation

spicy minced beef with sweet potato and eggs
Prepare as for the lamb mince, but use a fairly large sweet potato instead of the butternut squash and add a diced green pepper. Use 450g (1lb) extra-lean minced beef instead of the lamb mince. Add 1 tbsp sambal olek instead of the harissa paste to add extra fire and flavour. Spoon onto 4 plates and top each with a fried egg. Serve with rolled-up flour tortillas instead of pitta breads or rice.

french-style duck legs

In this simplified version of duck confit, duck legs are steeped in a fragrant marinade and served with the traditional lentils.

🥣 15 MINS PLUS MARINATING   🍲 3 HRS 45 MINS

SERVES 4

4 duck legs

500g (1lb 2oz) duck or goose fat

a few sprigs of rosemary

1 tbsp olive oil

1 onion, finely chopped

salt and freshly ground black pepper

2 garlic cloves, finely chopped

a few sprigs of thyme, leaves only

2 carrots, finely diced

1 bay leaf

1 tbsp dry sherry

250g (9oz) Puy lentils, rinsed and picked over for any stones

450ml (15fl oz) hot chicken stock

For the marinade

3 tbsp brandy

1 tbsp black peppercorns, crushed

3 garlic cloves, finely chopped

pinch of ground cinnamon

a few sprigs of thyme

1 tbsp sea salt

1 Put the duck legs in a dish and add the marinade ingredients. Cover with cling film, sit a weight on top, and refrigerate overnight. Preheat the oven to 150°C (300°F/Gas 2) and melt the duck fat in a large flameproof casserole. Add the legs (discard the liquid), ensuring they are covered in the fat. Add the rosemary, cover, and put in the oven for 3 hours, or until the meat is fork tender and the skin crispy. Let the casserole cool, remove the legs, and drain off the excess fat.

2 Meanwhile, heat the oil in a pan over a medium heat, add the onion, and cook for 3–4 minutes until soft. Season, then stir in the garlic, thyme, carrots, and bay leaf. Stir over a low heat for 6–10 minutes, then increase the heat, add the sherry, and cook for 2 minutes. Stir in the lentils and then the stock. Bring to the boil, reduce to a simmer, and cook for 40 minutes, or until the lentils are tender. Add hot water if they start to dry out. Adjust the seasoning, remove the bay leaf and thyme, and serve with the duck.

duck curry

Duck curry is extremely rich and has a great depth of flavour. If you like your curry hot, use two red chillies rather than the one specified and leave the seeds in for an even greater kick.

🥣 15 MINS   🍲 2 HRS

SERVES 4

2 duck breasts

1 tbsp sunflower oil

1 onion, finely chopped

2 celery sticks, finely chopped

salt and freshly ground black pepper

3 garlic cloves, finely chopped

1 red chilli, deseeded and finely chopped

5cm (2in) piece of fresh root ginger, peeled and finely chopped

2 carrots, finely chopped

1 tbsp garam masala

1 tsp ground turmeric

1 tsp paprika

1 tbsp tomato purée

2 x 400g cans chopped tomatoes

900ml (1½ pints) hot vegetable stock

1 Preheat the oven to 180°C (350°F/Gas 4). Heat a large flameproof casserole over a medium-high heat and add the duck breasts, skin-side down. Cook each side for 3–6 minutes, or until golden. Remove and set aside.

Heat the oil in the casserole over a medium heat, add the onion and celery, and cook for 5 minutes until soft. Season with salt and pepper, stir in the garlic, chilli, and ginger, and cook for 2 more minutes.

2 Add the carrots, turn to coat, and cook for 5 minutes, stirring from time to time. Stir in the spices and tomato purée and cook for 1–2 minutes, then tip in the tomatoes and stock. Bring to the boil, reduce to a simmer, and return the duck breasts to the casserole. Cover with the lid and put in the oven for 1½ hours. Check occasionally that it is not drying out, topping up with hot water if needed.

3 Remove from the oven and spoon out the duck breasts. Peel off the skin and shred the meat. Put the meat back into the casserole and return to the oven for another 30 minutes, uncovered if the sauce is too thin. Adjust the seasoning if necessary. Serve with rice and chapatis.

sausage and chicken gumbo

Cajun gumbo is related to paella and often contains seafood. If you wish to add some, do it at the end of the cooking time.

🥣 20 MINS   🍲 2 HRS

SERVES 4-6

1 tbsp olive oil

1 onion, finely chopped

salt and freshly ground black pepper

3 celery sticks, finely diced

2 red peppers, deseeded and finely chopped

2 garlic cloves, finely chopped

400g (14oz) pork sausages, each sliced into 3 pieces

2 tbsp plain flour

2-3 tsp Cajun seasoning

400g (14oz) chicken breast, cut into bite-sized pieces

900ml (1½ pints) hot chicken stock

1 Preheat the oven to 170°C (325°F/Gas 3). Heat the oil in a large flameproof casserole over a medium heat, add the onion, and cook for 3–4 minutes

until soft. Season, stir in the celery, peppers, and garlic, and cook for a further 5–8 minutes until very soft. Add the sausages to the casserole and cook for 5–8 minutes until they are no longer pink.

2 Mix the flour and Cajun seasoning on a plate and toss the chicken in it. Add to the casserole and cook, stirring, for 5–8 minutes, then add a little stock and bring it to the boil. Pour in the remaining stock and continue boiling for a minute. Reduce to a simmer and check the seasoning.

3 Cover the casserole with the lid and put in the oven for 1½ hours. Check occasionally that it is not drying out and top up with a little hot water, if needed. Taste and season, then ladle out over warmed bowls of rice.

Season's best **duck**

Versatile and easy to cook, ducks are delicious and fairly rich. Those bred from the wild mallard have dark, rich meat with a thick layer of fat under the skin, while the ones from the Muscovy duck are larger and leaner. Wild ducks are leaner with a more gamey flavour. Farmed ducks are available all year; wild ones, in autumn and early winter. They taste phenomenal with the sharp and fruity flavours of garlic, spring onions, ginger, apples, cherries, plums, oranges, olives, and wine.

Duck The ratio of meat to bone is low in a duck, but since it is rich, portions can be small. An average duck will serve 4 people. After roasting, store the drained-off duck fat in the fridge and use for roasting potatoes.

The breast meat remains succulent under the layer of fat.

Put an onion or herbs inside for flavour when roasting.

Leg Duck legs have superb flavour. They take longer to cook than breast meat and have a little more sinew, but can be grilled, roasted, or used to make confit. Prick or slash the skin and fat layer beneath before cooking.

Breast Duck breasts have dense, rich meat. If cooking whole, score or prick through the skin and fat, then fry skin-side down, or grill skin-side up, to melt and release excess fat. Or remove all skin and fat, before cooking whole or in pieces.

The small inner fillets are sometimes sold separately as aiguillettes.

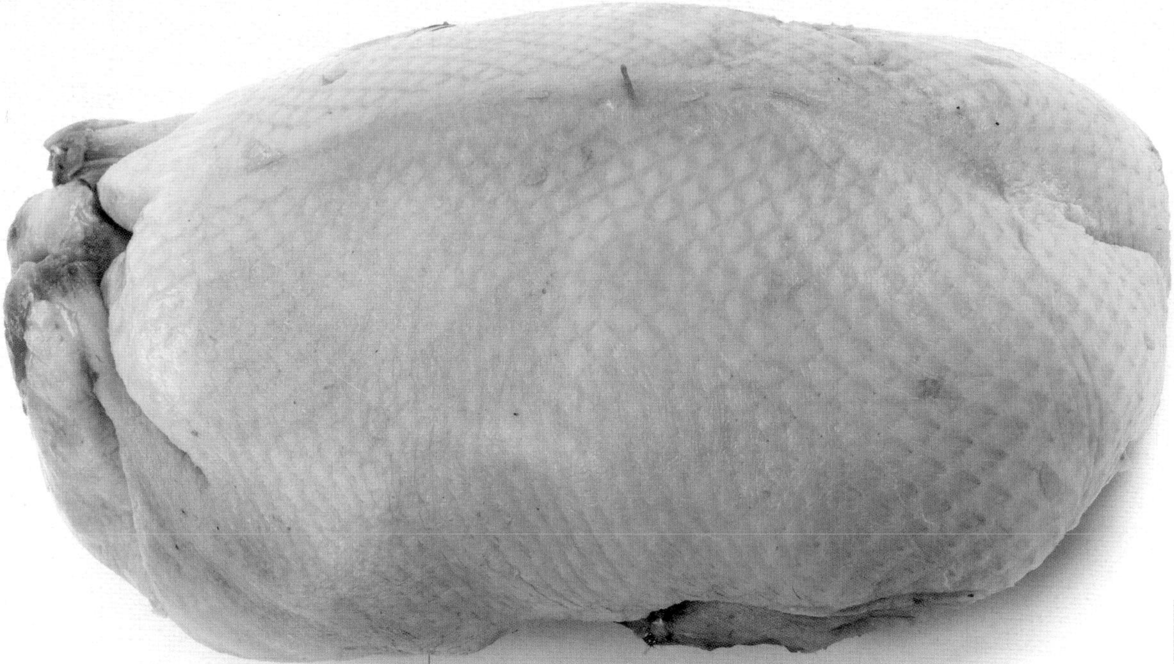

Mallard Many mallard are lured into ponds with grain, and eating this can make their fat quite yellow. Whiter fat usually indicates a more varied diet.

If the skin has no fat or is of poor quality, remove it before cooking.

how to joint a duck

For braising or casseroling, cut the bird into pieces. To roast, leave the bird whole. This technique gives you eight small portions, which is ample for four people. Use the cut-away rib bones and backbone for stock to braise or casserole the duck in, or for soup.

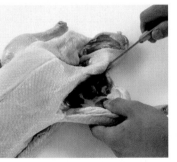

1 Trim the excess fat and skin. Using a sharp knife, cut down between a leg and the body. Twist to break the joint. Cut the whole leg. Repeat with the other.

2 Cut each leg in half at the joint between the thigh and the drumstick, using the line of white fat on the underside as a guide.

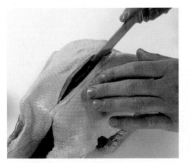

3 Slit closely along both sides of the breastbone to loosen the skin and meat from the bone. With poultry shears or a sharp knife, cut along the breastbone, to split it lengthways in half.

4 Turn the bird over. Cut away the rib bones and backbone. Leave the breast pieces with the wing joints attached. Cut each breast piece diagonally in half. Remove any sharp bones.

essentials
varieties available

Several popular breeds including wild mallard, Aylesbury, Pekin, and Muscovy (Barbary).

buy Look for birds with plump breasts and firm skin. Rich duck meat is filling, so a large breast will stretch for 2 people if cut in pieces. Allow at least 500g (1lb 2oz) per person with whole birds.

store Keep whole birds and pieces well wrapped, at the bottom of the fridge, for up to 3 days.

cook Roast whole duck. Grill, fry, or barbecue duck breasts to serve pink; score or prick skin to release the fat and start cooking them fat-side to the heat. Or slice the flesh into strips for stir-fry. Grill or barbecue legs, or use them for stews and confit.

preserve Freeze, with giblets separate. Duck can be smoked or the legs confited (salted, then slowly cooked in oil, and stored in it).

recipe ideas

Chinese roast duck p369

Duck curry p295

Duck in orange sauce p450

French-style duck legs p295

beetroot risotto

This colourful risotto is best when cooked with freshly harvested beetroots. The earthy flavour of the beetroot and the sharp tang of goat's cheese combine beautifully.

🥣 30 MINS   🍲 1 HR

SPECIAL EQUIPMENT ▪ food processor

SERVES 4

500g (1lb 2oz) raw beetroot, peeled and diced

2 tbsp extra virgin olive oil, plus extra for tossing

sea salt and freshly ground black pepper

6 tbsp sunflower oil

20 sage leaves

2 onions, finely diced

2 garlic cloves, crushed

350g (12oz) risotto rice

1 litre (1¾ pints) hot vegetable or chicken stock

60g (2oz) Parmesan cheese, grated

200g (7oz) firm goat's cheese, diced into 1cm (½in) pieces

1 Preheat the oven to 200°C (400°F/ Gas 6). Toss the beetroot in a little olive oil, sea salt, and pepper. Wrap in foil and cook in the oven for 30–40 minutes until soft.

2 In a small pan, heat the sunflower oil over a high heat until smoking. Drop in most of the sage leaves, a few at a time, and deep-fry for 5 seconds, or until they stop fizzing. Remove and drain.

3 Remove the beetroot from the oven and purée in a food processor with 4 tbsp water, the remaining sage leaves, and some sea salt and pepper. Set aside.

4 Fry the onions in the olive oil over a moderate heat for 3 minutes, until soft. Add the garlic and cook for 1 minute. Pour in the rice and stir, so that the grains are coated in oil.

5 Keeping the stock on a low simmer, add a ladleful at a time to the rice, stirring continuously until each ladleful is absorbed, for about 15 minutes, until the rice is almost cooked. Add the beetroot purée to the risotto and cook, stirring, for another 5–10 minutes until the rice is al dente and creamy.

6 Remove the rice from the heat, season, then stir in two-thirds of the Parmesan and fold in the goat's cheese. Garnish with the fried sage leaves and remaining Parmesan.

pot roast chicken with turnips and fennel

This slow-cooked whole chicken is simplicity itself and yields meltingly tender results. Use the bones for stock afterwards.

🥣 15 MINS   🍲 2 HRS – 2 HRS 30 MINS

SERVES 4–6

2 tbsp olive oil

1 whole chicken, weighing about 1.35kg (3lb)

salt and freshly ground black pepper

6 pork sausages, roughly chopped

1 fennel bulb, roughly chopped

1 bay leaf

2 sprigs of rosemary

250ml (9fl oz) white wine

250g (9oz) turnips, peeled and roughly chopped

900ml (1½ pints) hot chicken stock

1 Preheat the oven to 180°C (350°F/ Gas 4). Heat half the oil in a large flameproof casserole, season the chicken with salt and pepper, then add it to the casserole, breast-side down. Cook for about 10 minutes, then turn and cook the other side for about the same time. Remove and set aside.

2 Heat the remaining oil in the casserole on a high heat, add the sausages, and cook for 6–8 minutes until browned. Then reduce the heat, add the fennel, bay leaf, and rosemary, and cook for a further 5 minutes. Increase the heat, add the wine, and let it bubble for a minute, then add the turnips.

3 Return the chicken to the casserole, breast-side down, and arrange the vegetables around it. Add the stock, bring to the boil, then cover and put in the oven for 1½–2 hours. Check occasionally that it is not drying out and top up with a little hot water, if needed. Carefully remove the chicken from the casserole, together with the bay leaf and rosemary, peel off the skin, and shred the meat back into the casserole. Serve immediately with steamed Savoy cabbage.

beef chilli mole

This is a Mexican-inspired dish with lots of chilli heat.

🥣 15 MINS   🍲 2 HRS 30 MINS   ❄ FREEZABLE

SPECIAL EQUIPMENT ▪ food processor

SERVES 4

700g (1lb 8oz) stewing beef, cut into bite-sized pieces

1 tbsp chipotle sauce or salsa

3 tbsp olive oil

30g (1oz) sesame seeds, toasted

60g (2oz) almonds, skin on, toasted

1 red pepper, deseeded and roughly chopped

4 tomatoes, roughly chopped

2 flour tortillas, roughly torn

600ml (1 pint) hot vegetable stock

3 garlic cloves, finely chopped

1 red chilli, deseeded and finely chopped

1 green chilli, deseeded and finely chopped

salt and freshly ground black pepper

small bunch of coriander, leaves chopped

1 red onion, finely chopped

1 Preheat the oven to 160°C (325°F/ Gas 3). Toss the beef in the sauce. Heat 1 tbsp of the oil in a flameproof casserole and cook the beef for 5–8 minutes until browned. Remove and set aside.

2 Grind the sesame and almonds in a food processor, then leave them in it. Heat 1 tbsp of the oil in the casserole, add the pepper and tomatoes, and cook for 2–3 minutes until soft. Add to the food processor and blitz to a paste. Add the tortillas and 2 ladles of stock, and blitz to a sauce consistency.

3 In the remaining oil, cook the garlic and chillies for 1 minute. Add the sauce, the remaining stock, and seasoning. Bring to the boil, reduce to a simmer, and add the beef. Cover and put in the oven for 2 hours. Top up occasionally with hot water if needed. Stir in the coriander and serve scattered with the onion.

chicken doner kebab

While doner kebab is often associated with too many calories, this fresh-tasting version with zingy flavours is a healthy and delicious take on a traditional favourite.

🥣 15 MINS PLUS MARINATING   🍲 15 MINS

SERVES 4

1 tsp cayenne pepper

1 tbsp olive oil

juice of 1 lemon

4 skinless chicken breasts, cut into fine strips

4 pitta breads

1 crispy lettuce, such as cos or Little Gem, shredded

2 onions, sliced

¼ red cabbage, shredded

hot chilli sauce, to taste

garlic mayonnaise, to taste

1 ripe tomato, sliced

¼ cucumber, sliced

4 whole pickled green chillies

1 In a bowl, mix together the cayenne pepper, oil, and a quarter of the lemon juice. Add the chicken strips and leave to marinate in the fridge for 1 hour.

2 Heat the grill until hot. Arrange the chicken strips in a shallow baking tin and cook under the hot grill for about 10 minutes, turning occasionally.

3 Lightly toast the pitta breads and cut open along one edge to form a pocket.

4 Stuff each pitta pocket with a handful of lettuce, onion, and red cabbage, then the chicken pieces. Dress with the remaining lemon juice and some chilli sauce and garlic mayonnaise to taste. Garnish with the tomato slices, cucumber, and a pickled chilli. Serve immediately.

variation

chicken shish kebabs

Cut the chicken breasts into bite-sized pieces. Mix with the cayenne, olive oil, and lemon juice, but add 1 tsp dried oregano and a crushed garlic clove to the marinade. When ready to cook, thread alternately on 8 soaked wooden skewers with cubes of red and green pepper. Grill for 8–10 minutes, turning occasionally, until cooked through.

warm salad of wild mushrooms

To make expensive wild mushrooms go further, you can replace half the amount with field mushrooms for this salad.

🥣 25-30 MINS   🍲 8-10 MINS

SERVES 4

375g (13oz) mixed wild mushrooms, such as chanterelles, oyster mushrooms, and ceps

30-45g (1-1½oz) butter

2 shallots, finely diced

1 small bunch of parsley, leaves picked and chopped

1 small head of frisée, leaves picked

1 small head of radicchio, leaves picked

75g (2½oz) rocket leaves

For the vinaigrette

2 tbsp red wine vinegar

½ tsp Dijon mustard

salt and freshly ground black pepper

3 tbsp vegetable oil

3 tbsp walnut oil

1 First make the vinaigrette. In a bowl, whisk together the vinegar, mustard, salt, and pepper. Gradually whisk in the vegetable and walnut oils, so that the vinaigrette emulsifies and thickens slightly. Taste for seasoning.

2 Wipe the mushrooms with damp kitchen paper. Trim the stalks and remove any woody portions. Place the mushrooms on a chopping board and cut them into medium-sized pieces.

3 Heat the butter in a frying pan until foaming. Add the shallots and cook, stirring occasionally, for 2–3 minutes, until soft. Add the mushrooms, salt, and pepper. Cook, stirring, for 5–7 minutes, until the mushrooms are tender and all the liquid has evaporated. Stir in the parsley and taste for seasoning, adjusting if necessary.

4 Briskly whisk the vinaigrette to re-emulsify it, then pour it over the salad leaves in a bowl and toss them well until all are coated. Taste for seasoning. Divide the salad leaves between 4 plates and spoon over the mushrooms from the pan. Serve at once while the salad remains crisp and the mushrooms are still warm from the stove.

mackerel with garlic and tomatoes

When buying fresh mackerel, they should feel firm and rigid, and their bodies shiny and eyes bright. They are best eaten on the day of purchase or within 24 hours if kept chilled.

🥣 **10 MINS**   🍲 **25 MINS**

SERVES 4

24 cherry tomatoes on the vine, snipped with a little of the stem left

4 garlic cloves, peeled

a few sprigs of thyme

grated zest of 1 lemon

pinch of dried chilli flakes

1-2 tbsp olive oil

salt and freshly ground black pepper

4 mackerel fillets, each 115-150g (4-5½oz)

1 Preheat the oven to 200°C (400°F/Gas 6). Put the tomatoes, garlic, and thyme sprigs in a roasting tin. Sprinkle over the lemon zest and chilli flakes. Drizzle with the oil and season with salt and pepper. Roast in the oven for about 10 minutes until the tomatoes begin to soften.

2 Remove from the oven, sit the mackerel on top of the tomatoes, then cover the roasting tin with foil. Return to the oven and cook for a further 10–15 minutes, until the fish is cooked through. Remove the sprigs of thyme and discard. Serve hot with salad and fresh crusty bread.

variation

mackerel with courgettes, tomato, and basil

Prepare in the same way, but add 2 large sliced courgettes to the roasting tin with the tomatoes. Add a small handful of chopped basil instead of the thyme. Drizzle the fish with a little chilli oil before cooking in the oven and garnish when cooked, with torn basil leaves.

risotto with mussels

Mussels make a lovely, rich risotto, with the fennel adding a subtle aniseed flavour to the creamy rice.

🥣 **20 MINS**   🍲 **45-55 MINS**

SERVES 4-6

1 tbsp olive oil

25g (scant 1oz) butter

1 onion, finely chopped

salt and freshly ground black pepper

3 garlic cloves, finely chopped

pinch of dried chilli flakes

1 fennel bulb, trimmed and finely chopped

300g (10oz) arborio rice or carnaroli rice

120ml (4fl oz) white wine

900ml (1½ pints) hot vegetable stock

900g (2lb) mussels, scrubbed and debearded (discard any that do not close when tapped) (p364)

bunch of flat-leaf parsley, finely chopped

a few sprigs of dill, finely chopped

juice of 1 lemon, to serve (optional)

1 Heat the oil and butter in a heavy-based pan over a medium heat, add the onion, and cook for 3–4 minutes until soft. Season with salt and pepper, stir in the garlic and chilli flakes, and cook for 1 minute.

2 Add the fennel and cook for about 5 minutes until soft, then stir through the rice. Increase the heat, add the wine, and let it simmer for 1–2 minutes until it has been absorbed. In a separate saucepan, simmer the stock. Add a ladleful to the rice and stir, until it has been absorbed. Continue doing this for 30–40 minutes, or until the rice is cooked al dente and is creamy. You may not need all the stock or you may need a little more.

3 Stir in the mussels, cover, and leave for a few minutes until the mussels have opened (discard any that do not open). Stir through the parsley and dill, and add a squeeze of lemon juice, if using. Taste and season with some pepper if needed. Serve immediately.

paprika rice and aubergine

Aubergine and paprika work together really well, as the aubergine absorbs the flavour of this pungent spice. The chickpeas make this a substantial supper dish.

🥣 **20 MINS**   🍲 **45-55 MINS**

SERVES 4-6

3-4 tbsp olive oil

2 aubergines, chopped into bite-sized pieces

1 tbsp paprika

1 onion, finely chopped

1 tsp dried mint

salt and freshly ground black pepper

3 garlic cloves, finely chopped

2 green chillies, deseeded and finely chopped

grated zest of 1 lemon and juice of 2 lemons

350g (12oz) easy-cook basmati rice

400g can chickpeas, drained and rinsed

900ml (1½ pints) hot vegetable stock

small bunch of coriander leaves, roughly chopped

small bunch of flat-leaf parsley, roughly chopped

1 Heat half the oil in a heavy-based pan over a medium heat. Toss the aubergines in the paprika, add to the pan, and cook for 6–8 minutes, adding more oil if needed. Remove and set aside. Heat the remaining oil, if necessary, and reduce the heat to low. Add the onion and mint, season, and cook for 3–4 minutes until soft. Stir through the garlic, chillies, and lemon zest and cook for 2 minutes.

2 Stir through the rice. Add the lemon juice and chickpeas and return the aubergines to the pan. Pour in the stock and season again. Partially cover with a lid and cook for 30–40 minutes, topping up with a little hot water if needed, and stirring occasionally. Stir through the herbs. Serve with a lightly dressed leaf and tomato salad and some lamb cutlets.

Season's best **mackerel**

Mackerel is inexpensive and versatile and, being an oily fish, is great for your heart. It is in season from late summer through winter but is superb in autumn. All species (including bonito, chub, and king) have moist, brownish grey flesh and rich flavour. They are great grilled or fried whole, but can be boned and stuffed or filleted. They pair well with sharp fruits, such as rhubarb, citrus, or cranberry and are excellent with mustard, horseradish, chilli, and tomatoes.

Atlantic mackerel This commercially important pelagic species is the most northerly member of the family. It is found extensively in the North Atlantic, with smaller pockets in the Mediterranean. It can grow up to 60cm (2ft) long. Grilling, barbecuing, and roasting make the most of the creamy-textured flakes.

The Atlantic mackerel is easily recognized by the bar or scribble markings along its back.

The skin should be shiny and slippery.

how to remove the gills

Remove the gills as soon as possible, as they contain bacteria, which cause the fish to decompose. However, the bones, head, and tail may be removed once the fish is cooked, if you prefer.

1 Firmly lift the gill flap with your thumb and forefinger and cut the throat with the tip of a sharp filleting knife. Lifting the gill makes it easier to get a clean cut through the fish.

2 Insert a thumb and index finger around the gills, and pull. They should come out fairly easily. If not, cut through the gills where they attach to the head, then pull them out.

how to gut through the stomach

Remove the guts (the internal organs) of the fish, as they quickly decompose. Once you have removed the guts, loosen and extract the dark bloodline running along the spine near the head and thoroughly rinse the belly cavity to remove any remaining traces of blood or viscera.

1 Insert a slim filleting knife into the vent (you will see a small hole), and with a single stroke cut along the belly to the chin.

2 With the back of the knife, release the bloodline, then scrape it away with the guts. Rinse, then firmly wipe the belly cavity clean.

essentials

varieties available

Atlantic mackerel, also available smoked, canned, dried, salted, and as frozen fillets.

buy Look for line-caught mackerel that are still stiff with rigor mortis.

store Wrap well and store in the coldest part of the fridge, as it doesn't keep well. Best eaten within 24 hours of purchase.

cook Grill, bake, barbecue, and roast. Also, cured and used in sushi and sashimi.

preserve Smoke, freeze.

recipe ideas

Butterflied mackerel with sweet potato and beetroot pickle p312

Mackerel roasted with harissa and potatoes p302

Mackerel with garlic and tomatoes p300

mackerel roasted with harissa and potatoes

Ask your fishmonger to gut the fish if you would rather not do it yourself. To check if the mackerel is cooked, slit the fish at the thickest part; the flesh should appear just opaque.

10 MINS **30 MINS**

SERVES 4

4 (or 8, if small) mackerel, gutted (p301) and washed

3–4 tsp harissa paste

1½ tbsp olive oil

2 limes, quartered

1.1kg (2½lb) small potatoes, scrubbed and halved

handful of coriander, finely chopped

1 Preheat the oven to 200°C (400°F/ Gas 6). Lay the mackerel in a roasting tin, then mix the harissa paste and half the oil together. Drizzle the harissa mixture over the fish, making sure they are covered inside and out. Add the limes to the tin, then toss the potatoes with the remaining oil and add them to the tin, too.

2 Roast in the oven for 20–30 minutes, or until the potatoes are cooked through – the fish will be cooked by then as well. Scatter with the coriander leaves and serve with a crisp green salad.

variation

mackerel roasted with carrots, chickpeas, and harissa

Use 500g (1lb 2oz) baby chantenay carrots, topped and tailed, instead of the potatoes. Blanch them in lightly salted water for 3 minutes. Drain. Place in the roasting tin, toss in 2 tbsp olive oil, cover with foil, and roast for 45 minutes. Add a drained 400g can of chickpeas and sprinkle with 1 tbsp chopped fresh thyme and 1 tbsp black mustard seeds. Lay the fish on top. Smear with the harissa mix as before and add the limes. Roast, uncovered, as before.

smoked mussels in fresh tomato sauce

This is a great starter or sauce for pasta. When smoking the mussels, turn on the extractor fan and open a window.

20 MINS **25 MINS**

SPECIAL EQUIPMENT ▪ wok with a lid and rack

SERVES 4

1 level tbsp beech or alder wood chips

750g (1lb 10oz) mussels, scrubbed and debearded (discard any that do not close when tapped) (p364)

1–2 tbsp olive oil

2 large shallots, finely diced

2 garlic cloves, finely diced

400g can chopped tomatoes or passata

6 ripe tomatoes (about 450g/1lb), skinned (p197), deseeded, and cut into bite-sized pieces

salt and freshly ground black pepper

a few sprigs of parsley, chopped

1 Wrap the wood chips in kitchen foil to form a flat parcel. Pierce several holes in the top of the parcel to allow the smoke to escape. Place in the bottom of the wok, then insert the wire rack. Spread the mussels out evenly on the rack, put the lid on tightly, and seal the join with a strip of kitchen foil. If there are too many mussels to fit in 1 layer on the rack, cook them in 2 batches.

2 Smoke over a high heat for 5 minutes until the mussels have opened. Turn off the heat, wait for the smoke to subside, and remove the mussels, setting them aside (discard and throw away any that haven't opened). Remove the parcel of wood chips and reserve any juices.

3 Wash and dry the wok. Set it over a low heat, add the oil, and fry the shallots and garlic for about 5 minutes, until soft. Add the mussels and toss for 2–3 minutes, then add the canned tomatoes, bring to the boil, and simmer for 5–10 minutes. Add the fresh tomatoes and the reserved juices, to taste. Toss, season, and serve with the parsley.

red mullet with middle eastern spices

A sprinkling of the pretty purple spice that is sumac adds a tangy, lemony flavour to this fish dish.

20 MINS **1 HR 20 MINS**

SERVES 4–6

1 tbsp olive oil

6 shallots, finely chopped

1 fennel bulb, trimmed and finely chopped

1 carrot, finely chopped

½ tsp ground cumin

1 tsp sumac or use a preserved lemon, flesh discarded and rind finely chopped (optional)

900ml (1½ pints) hot vegetable stock

4 plum tomatoes, roughly chopped

salt and freshly ground black pepper

8 black olives, stoned

about 1.6kg (3½lb) red mullet, filleted and cut into chunky pieces

handful of coriander, finely chopped

handful of mint, finely chopped

1 Heat the oil in a heavy-based pan or tagine, add the shallots, fennel, and carrot, and cook for 5 minutes until soft. Stir through the cumin and sumac or preserved lemon, and cook for a further minute. Add the stock, tomatoes, and seasoning, and bring to the boil, then reduce to a simmer.

2 Add the olives, partially cover with a lid, and simmer for about 1 hour, stirring and topping up with hot water, if needed. Sit the fish on top of the tomato mixture, cover with the lid, and cook for a further 10 minutes, or until the fish is cooked through.

3 Stir through most of the coriander and mint, and add seasoning, if needed. Serve with couscous and scatter over the remaining fresh herbs.

pan-fried mackerel in rolled oats

A traditional Scottish recipe. For true authenticity (and lots of added flavour), use lard or bacon drippings instead of oil.

🍴 15–20 MINS   🍲 8–12 MINS

SERVES 6

2 eggs

30g (1oz) plain flour, plus 2 tbsp

175g (6oz) rolled oats

salt and freshly ground black pepper

6 large mackerel fillets

60g (2oz) butter

juice of ½ lemon

1 tbsp Dijon mustard, or to taste

75ml (2½fl oz) vegetable oil, plus more if needed, for frying

lemon wedges, to serve

a few sprigs of watercress, to serve

1 Beat the eggs in a dish. Sift 30g (1oz) flour onto a sheet of baking parchment. With your fingers, combine the rolled oats and some salt and pepper on a second sheet of baking parchment. Turn each mackerel fillet in the flour to coat evenly. Then dip the mackerel in the egg and finally coat in the seasoned oats. Set aside on a plate.

2 Melt a third of the butter. Add 2 tbsp flour and whisk to a paste until foaming. Remove from the heat. Whisk in 300ml (10fl oz) boiling water. The sauce will thicken. Return to the heat and whisk for 1 minute. Remove from the heat, add the remaining butter, and whisk. Add the lemon juice and mustard and season.

3 Line a baking sheet with kitchen paper. Heat the oil in a large frying pan. Add half the fish and cook for 2–3 minutes on each side, until crisp and golden. Transfer to the baking sheet and keep warm while you cook the remaining fish. Drain off any water and add extra oil between batches when frying, if necessary. Serve with lemon wedges, watercress, and the sauce.

variation

herrings in oatmeal with sweet mustard sauce

Prepare in exactly the same way but use 6 large herring fillets (pin-boned thoroughly) instead of mackerel and use 175g (6oz) medium oatmeal instead of the rolled oats. For the mustard sauce, use English mustard instead of Dijon, sweeten with 1 tbsp demerara sugar, and sharpen with a dash of white wine vinegar.

monkfish and white wine stew

The delicate flavour of monkfish here is highlighted by white wine. If you can find small field or horse mushrooms, they taste wonderful with the monkfish and courgettes.

🍴 45–50 MINS   🍲 25–30 MINS

SERVES 6

75g (2½oz) butter

2 shallots, diced

2 garlic cloves, finely chopped

2 leeks, trimmed and cut diagonally

500g (1lb 2oz) small courgettes, cut into bite-sized pieces

salt and freshly ground black pepper

250g (9oz) mushrooms, trimmed

3–5 sprigs of thyme, leaves picked

1 bay leaf

250ml (9fl oz) dry white wine

500ml (16fl oz) hot fish stock

750g (1lb 10oz) monkfish fillets, skinned and cut into 1cm (½in) slices

3 tbsp plain flour

small bunch of parsley, leaves chopped

1 Melt 30g (1oz) of the butter in a large pan over a medium heat, add the shallots, garlic, leeks, and courgettes, and cook for 3–5 minutes, until soft. Season, then add the mushrooms, thyme, bay leaf, wine, and stock, cover, and simmer gently for 25–30 minutes.

2 Add the monkfish and stir very gently to combine. Do not stir too vigorously or the fish may fall apart. Cover the pan, bring back to the boil, and simmer for 3–5 minutes until the fish is opaque and cooked through.

3 Fork together the remaining butter with the flour to a paste. Add to the pan and simmer for 2 minutes. Discard the bay leaf, stir in half the parsley, and add seasoning, if needed. Serve sprinkled with the remaining parsley.

variation

monkfish and red wine stew

Cook the shallots in butter for 1 minute. Add 500ml (16fl oz) red wine and reduce by half. Peel 250g (9oz) pickling onions. Melt 30g (1oz) butter in a pan, add the onions, and cook for 5–8 minutes until golden. Add the mushrooms and cook for 3–5 minutes, until the liquid evaporates. Add the stock and monkfish to the wine, cover, and simmer for 3–5 minutes. Stir in the onions and mushrooms, and thicken as directed.

melanzane alla parmigiana

This is a classic Italian recipe that makes perfect use of aubergines baked in a tomato sauce layered with Parmesan.

20 MINS　20 MINS　❄ FREEZABLE

SERVES 4

3 tbsp olive oil

4 garlic cloves, finely sliced

2 x 400g cans chopped tomatoes

1 tbsp tomato purée

1 tsp dried oregano

1 tsp thyme leaves

salt and freshly ground black pepper

2 aubergines, cut into 1cm (½in) slices

150g (5½oz) Parmesan cheese, grated

200g (7oz) mozzarella, torn into pieces

1 Preheat the oven to 180°C (350°F/ Gas 4). Heat 2 tbsp of the oil in a large heavy-based pan over a low heat, add the garlic, and cook for 30 seconds. Add the chopped tomatoes, tomato purée, oregano, and thyme and bring to the boil. Season with salt and pepper, then remove the pan from the heat.

2 Put the aubergine slices in a bowl and brush with the rest of the oil. Heat a non-stick frying pan over a medium heat, add the aubergines (in batches, if necessary) and cook on each side for 3 minutes, or until golden brown. When each piece is done, remove with a slotted spoon and place on a plate.

3 Pour a 1cm (½in) layer of tomato sauce in the bottom of an ovenproof dish and cover with aubergine slices. Sprinkle with a handful of Parmesan cheese, then repeat the process until all of the ingredients are used up (you should get 3–4 layers), making sure there is a 1cm (½in) layer of tomato sauce at the top. Cover with the mozzarella and cook for 25–30 minutes until browned on top and piping hot. Serve with a green salad.

lamb with roasted peppers

Such a great way to use up a glut of peppers, which are so abundant at this time of year. Don't feel that you have to limit yourself to red and green ones – yellow is just as good.

15 MINS　30 MINS

SERVES 4

4 large lamb chump chops, or 8 small lamb chump chops

2 red peppers, deseeded and roughly chopped

2 green peppers, deseeded and roughly chopped

1 tbsp olive oil

salt and freshly ground black pepper

knob of butter

1 onion, finely chopped

125g (4½oz) chestnut mushrooms, finely chopped

small handful of flat-leaf parsley, finely chopped

1 Preheat the oven to 200°C (400°F/Gas 6). Sit the chops in a roasting tin and cut a pocket in each one. Toss the peppers with the oil, season well with salt and pepper, then add to the tin.

2 Melt the butter in a pan over a medium heat, add the onion, and cook for 3–4 minutes, or until soft and translucent. Add the mushrooms and cook for a further 5 minutes, or until the mushrooms have broken down. Stir through the parsley, season with salt and pepper, then spoon the mixture into the pocket of each lamb chop. If there's some left over, scatter it over the top.

3 Put the roasting tin in the oven to cook for 20–30 minutes, or longer if you like your meat well done. Toss with the peppers and serve with small cubed roasted potatoes and a spoonful of chilli or mint jelly.

chunky ratatouille

Ratatouille is a vegetarian evergreen; aubergines mixed with courgettes and tomatoes result in a juicy and flavourful dish.

🥣 15 MINS 🍲 30 MINS

SERVES 4

1 tbsp olive oil

1 onion, finely chopped

salt and freshly ground black pepper

1 bay leaf

2 garlic cloves, thinly sliced

1–2 tsp dried oregano

pinch of fennel seeds

1 aubergine, cut into chunky pieces

1 small glass of red wine

150ml (5fl oz) tomato juice

2 small courgettes, cut into chunky pieces

3 tomatoes, roughly chopped

large handful of Swiss chard leaves

chopped flat-leaf parsley, to garnish

1 Heat the oil in a large pan over a medium heat, add the onion, a pinch of salt, and the bay leaf, and cook for 3–4 minutes until the onion is soft and translucent.

2 Add the garlic, oregano, fennel seeds, aubergine, and wine. Let it simmer for a minute, then add the tomato juice. Cook for about 10 minutes, until the aubergine is soft.

3 Add the courgettes and tomatoes, and cook for a further 5–10 minutes. Stir through the Swiss chard, and cook for a further 1–2 minutes until all the vegetables are tender. Taste, and season if needed. Garnish with the chopped parsley, and serve hot with fluffy rice or some fresh crusty bread.

braised pheasant with beetroot and pears

The rich gamey flavour of pheasant goes really well with the sweet earthiness of beetroot and the muted fragrance of pears. Braising upside-down keeps the flesh of the bird moist.

🥣 25 MINS 🍲 1 HR

SERVES 4

15g (½oz) butter

12 pickling onions, peeled and left whole

75g (2½oz) pancetta, diced

2 slightly underripe pears, quartered and cored

1 cock pheasant, quartered (or 2 small hens, halved)

4 beetroot, cooked, peeled (p255), and cut into chunks

300ml (10fl oz) medium-sweet cider

300ml (10fl oz) chicken stock

salt and freshly ground black pepper

a good pinch of caster sugar

1 bay leaf

chopped parsley, to garnish

1 Preheat the oven to 180°C (350°F/ Gas 4). Heat the butter in a large flameproof casserole. Add the onions, pancetta, and pear quarters and cook, stirring, for 5 minutes, or until lightly golden. Remove from the pan with a slotted spoon.

2 Add the pheasant and brown all over. Remove from the casserole. Return the onions, pancetta, and pears to the casserole. Place the pheasant on top, flesh-side down. Put the beetroot around the edge. Blend the cider and stock together and pour into the casserole. Bring to the boil, season well with salt and pepper, and tuck in the bay leaf. Cover with a lid and cook in the oven for 50–60 minutes until tender.

3 Discard the bay leaf. Taste and season again, if necessary. Remove the pheasant, vegetables, and pears with a slotted spoon and keep warm. Boil the liquid rapidly for a few minutes until reduced and thickened slightly. Put the pheasant and vegetables on warmed plates. Spoon the sauce over and sprinkle with a little chopped parsley. Serve hot with jacket potatoes and green beans.

peppered beef with roasted beetroot

Beetroot is a wonder vegetable that can be cooked in many ways. Wear kitchen gloves when peeling it, though, to avoid staining your hands with the vivid juice.

🥣 15 MINS 🍲 1 HR

SERVES 4

1.1kg (2½lb) beef fillet

1–2 tbsp cracked black pepper

2–3 tbsp olive oil

500g (1lb 2oz) beetroot, cooked and peeled (p255)

1 tbsp balsamic vinegar

6 sweet potatoes, peeled and quartered

salt

handful of thyme sprigs

creamed horseradish, to serve

1 Preheat the oven to 190°C (375°F/ Gas 5). Roll the beef in the black pepper, covering it all over. Put 1 tbsp of the oil in a roasting tin and set the tin over a high heat. When very hot, add the beef and cook for 5–6 minutes, or until lightly browned on all sides.

2 Toss the beetroot with the balsamic vinegar and add to the tin. Toss the sweet potatoes with the remaining oil and add to the tin. Season with a pinch of salt, sprinkle with the thyme, and put in the oven to cook for about 20 minutes if you like your beef rare; 40 minutes, for medium; and 50 minutes, for well done.

3 Remove the beef and keep it warm while it rests. If the sweet potatoes are not ready, continue cooking until they are golden and beginning to char around the edges. Slice the beef and serve with the beetroot, sweet potatoes, and a little creamed horseradish on the side.

white fish, green beans, and artichoke paella

Haddock or cod are the best fish to use in this dish because they won't break up too easily, nor will their robust flavour be overwhelmed by the rest of the ingredients.

🥄 15 MINS   🍲 30 MINS

SERVES 4-6

1 tbsp olive oil

1 onion, finely chopped

salt and freshly ground black pepper

pinch of ground turmeric

2 garlic cloves, grated or finely chopped

200g (7oz) green beans, trimmed

3 cooked artichoke hearts (p309), quartered

4 tomatoes, skinned (p197) and chopped

pinch of hot or regular paprika

400g (14oz) basmati rice

1.4 litres (2½ pints) hot vegetable stock

675g (1½lb) white fish, such as haddock or sustainable cod, skinned and cut into chunky pieces

handful of dill or flat-leaf parsley, finely chopped

juice of 1 lemon

1 Heat the oil in a large heavy-based pan over a medium heat, add the onion and a pinch of salt, and cook for 3–4 minutes until soft and translucent. Stir through the turmeric, then add the garlic, beans, and artichokes. Cook gently for about 5 minutes until the beans begin to wilt, adding a little more oil if needed.

2 Add the tomatoes and paprika, and cook for 5 minutes. Tip in the rice and stir through. Pour in half of the hot stock. Bring to the boil, then reduce the heat slightly and simmer for about 15 minutes. Add the remaining stock and the fish, cover, and cook over a low heat until the rice and fish are cooked through.

3 Keep the lid on the pan until ready to serve, then stir through the herbs and lemon juice. Season with salt and pepper and serve immediately.

artichoke risotto

This is a perfect light supper for vegetarians, although you could stir through pancetta to add a salty twist.

🥄 20 MINS   🍲 45-50 MINS

SERVES 4

1 tbsp olive oil

50g (1¾oz) butter

1 onion, finely chopped

salt and freshly ground black pepper

3 garlic cloves, finely chopped

300g (10oz) arborio rice or carnaroli rice

250ml (9fl oz) white wine

about 1 litre (1¾ pints) hot vegetable stock or chicken stock

6 cooked artichoke hearts (p309), halved

25g (scant 1oz) Parmesan cheese, grated, plus extra to serve

1 Heat the oil and half the butter in a large heavy-based pan over a medium heat, add the onion, and cook for 3–4 minutes until soft. Season with salt and pepper, stir through the garlic, and cook for about 1 minute.

2 Stir through the rice and turn it in the oily butter so all the grains are coated, and cook for a few seconds. Increase the heat, add the wine, and let it bubble for 1–2 minutes, or until it has been absorbed. In a separate saucepan, simmer the stock. Add a ladleful to the rice and stir, until it has been absorbed. Continue doing this for 30–35 minutes until the rice is cooked al dente and is creamy. You may not need all the stock or you may need a little more.

3 Add the artichokes to the risotto for the last 10 minutes of cooking and carefully stir them through. Dot with the remaining butter and stir it in together with the Parmesan cheese. Taste and season, if needed. Serve with more Parmesan and some lightly dressed wild rocket and tomato salad on the side.

smoky aubergine and lamb stew

Aubergine and lamb are a classic combination from the Middle East, and the paprika adds a fine smoky flavour.

🥄 15 MINS   🍲 1 HR 45 MINS

SERVES 4

2 tbsp olive oil

1 large aubergine, cubed

1 tsp smoked paprika

500g (1lb 2oz) middle neck of lamb, chopped into large chunks

1 small onion, roughly chopped

140g (5oz) chorizo, diced

2 tsp sherry vinegar

2 garlic cloves, finely chopped

pinch of ground cumin

280g canned chickpeas, drained and rinsed

a few sprigs of thyme, leaves picked

600ml (1 pint) hot vegetable stock

1 Heat 1 tbsp of the oil in a flameproof casserole over a medium heat, add the aubergine and smoked paprika, and toss to coat. Cook, stirring and adding more oil as needed, for 6–8 minutes until the aubergine begins to colour. Remove with a slotted spoon and set aside.

2 Add a drizzle of oil and cook the lamb (in batches, if necessary) for 4–6 minutes until brown on all sides. Remove and set aside. Add the onion and chorizo (again, with a little oil, if needed), and cook for 2 minutes, then add the vinegar. Increase the heat and cook for 2 minutes until it has evaporated. Stir to scrape up the bits from the bottom of the casserole, then add the garlic and cumin.

3 Return the lamb, add the chickpeas and thyme, and pour in the stock. Bring to the boil, then partially cover and cook for 1 hour, checking the liquid level and topping up with hot water if needed. Add the aubergine and cook for 30 minutes more. Serve with couscous.

tomato tagliatelle with artichokes

This flavourful pasta can be made, dried, and stored, loosely wrapped, in the refrigerator for up to 48 hours. Use a good extra virgin olive oil so the flavour of the finished dish is intense. Walnuts complement the artichokes in the sauce perfectly.

🥣 **50-60 MINS PLUS DRYING**   🍲 **3-4 MINS**

SPECIAL EQUIPMENT ▪ pasta machine

SERVES 4-6

5 tbsp extra virgin olive oil

2 shallots, finely chopped

4 garlic cloves, finely chopped

6 large cooked artichoke hearts (p309), thickly sliced

3 tbsp dry white wine

salt and freshly ground black pepper

small bunch of parsley, leaves chopped

45g (1½oz) walnuts, roughly chopped

30g (1oz) Parmesan cheese, grated

For the tagliatelle

300g (10oz) strong plain flour, plus more if needed

3 eggs

1 tbsp vegetable oil

salt

2½ tbsp tomato purée

1 To make the tagliatelle, sift the flour onto a work surface. With your fingers, make a well in the centre. Add the eggs, oil, 1 tsp salt, and the tomato purée. Gradually mix in the flour to make a firm dough and press into a ball. Knead for 5-10 minutes, until elastic.

2 Cut the dough into 3 or 4 pieces and roll through a pasta machine, ending at the second narrowest setting and the wider of the machine's cutters. Toss the tagliatelle gently in a little flour, coil in bundles and leave for 1-2 hours on a floured tea towel.

3 Heat the oil in a pan over a low heat, add the shallots and garlic, and cook for 1-2 minutes, until soft but not brown. Add the artichokes and white wine and simmer for 2-3 minutes. Season to taste with salt and pepper. Stir only very gently, to avoid breaking up the artichokes.

4 Fill a large pan with water, bring to the boil, and add 1 tbsp salt. Add the tagliatelle and simmer for 2-3 minutes, or until it is tender but still al dente, stirring to prevent sticking. Drain and add the tagliatelle to the pan of artichoke mixture and toss over a medium heat until the pasta is hot and evenly coated with olive oil.

5 Pile the pasta onto a warmed serving dish and sprinkle evenly with the parsley and walnuts. Finish by sprinkling with most of the Parmesan cheese, offering the remainder on the side.

Season's best **globe artichokes**

A globe artichoke resembles an unopened flower bud and has an earthy, nutty flavour with slight astringency. It is available from early summer, but peaks again in autumn. It is delicious simply served with melted butter or vinaigrette, stuffed whole, or the hearts only, served in a variety of dishes such as pasta, pies, and salads. Good flavour pairings include sausages, prosciutto, pancetta, anchovies, tomatoes, Parmesan cheese, and white wine.

Ranging in size from tiny buds to huge purple or green heads, globe artichokes need plenty of space and water. They are grown across Europe, Africa, and in North America, mainly coastal California.

Baby purple artichokes These are fully mature, but picked from the lower part of the plant where they don't develop as much. They taste similar to the large ones, but with a mildly smoky flavour.

Trim the stalks and about 1cm (½in) off the tops before eating whole, or in halves or quarters, raw or cooked.

how to prepare artichokes to serve whole

This is an elegant way to serve artichokes, and is also necessary if you are stuffing them. When not needing to impress, you can trim the stalk and boil whole. The hairy choke inside is inedible, so either remove it or leave for your diners to discard when eating.

1 Holding the stalk to steady the artichoke, cut the tough tips off the leaves with strong kitchen scissors.

2 Use a chef's knife to cut the stalk from the base as close as possible to the leaves, so the heads will sit upright when served on a plate.

3 Cut off the pointed tip, pull away the small inner leaves, scrape out the hairy choke, and brush with lemon.

how to prepare artichoke hearts

If you are planning to serve just the hearts, you will need to remove all the leaves and the choke. Rub all cut surfaces of the artichoke with lemon as soon as it is prepared, or drop it into water acidulated with lemon juice until ready to cook. This is important as the artichoke flesh discolours quickly when exposed to air. Wash your hands well, as the juice is very bitter (like dandelions).

1 Cut or pull away all the leaves from the artichoke, then cut the stalk from the base.

2 With a sharp knife, cut off the soft middle cone of leaves just above the hairy choke, or pull them away firmly with the hands.

3 Trim away the bottom leaves with a paring knife. Rub the exposed flesh with lemon juice to reduce browning.

4 Scoop out the hairy choke with a teaspoon and discard. Rub the heart with lemon juice, or put in a bowl of acidulated water until ready to cook.

essentials
varieties available
Green globe, baby purple and green artichokes.

buy Choose firm tight heads that feel heavy.

store Best eaten fresh, or store in the vegetable box in the fridge for up to 5 days.

cook Steam or boil large globes; steam, boil, braise, or roast hearts; halve or quarter baby ones and grill or eat raw.

preserve Freeze hearts and baby ones, or preserve them in oil.

recipe ideas

Artichoke, green olive, and feta tart p310

Artichoke risotto p306

Baby artichokes in oil p349

Globe artichoke soup p266

Provençal stuffed artichokes p324

Green globe Widely available, this popular large-headed variety has succulent fleshy leaves with an earthy flavour.

The large leaves are pulled off and the fleshy bases eaten before enjoying the prize – the creamy-textured heart.

Draw the leaves through your teeth to eat their juicy flesh.

artichoke, green olive, and feta tart

There is a nice Mediterranean touch to this tart with salty olives and feta cheese counterbalancing the sweet artichoke.

🥄 15 MINS　　🍲 1 HR

SPECIAL EQUIPMENT ▪ 35 x 12cm (14 x 5in) loose-bottomed fluted tart tin
▪ ceramic baking beans

SERVES 6

250g (9oz) ready-made shortcrust pastry

3 eggs, 1 lightly beaten, for egg wash

1 tbsp olive oil

1 onion, finely chopped

2 garlic cloves, grated or finely chopped

5 large cooked artichoke hearts (p309)

12 green olives, pitted

175g (6oz) feta cheese, cubed

a few sprigs of thyme, leaves picked

200ml (7fl oz) double cream

salt and freshly ground black pepper

1 Preheat the oven to 200°C (400°F/Gas 6). Roll out the pastry on a floured work surface and use it to line the tart tin. Trim away the excess, then line the pastry shell with greaseproof paper and fill with ceramic baking beans. Bake in the oven for 15–20 minutes until the edges are golden. Remove the beans and paper, brush the bottom of the shell with a little of the egg wash, and return to the oven for 2–3 minutes to crisp. Remove from the oven and set aside. Reduce the oven temperature to 180°C (350°F/Gas 4).

2 Heat the oil in a pan over a low heat, add the onion, and cook for about 5 minutes until soft. Add the garlic and cook for a few more seconds. Spoon the onion mixture evenly over the bottom of the tart shell. Arrange the artichokes and olives over the top and sprinkle with the feta and thyme leaves.

3 Mix together the cream, 2 eggs, and seasoning. Pour over the tart filling. Bake in the oven for 25–35 minutes until set, puffed, and golden. Leave to cool for about 10 minutes before releasing from the tin. Serve warm, or at room temperature, with a rocket and tomato salad.

wild mushroom and gruyère pasta bake

The wild and domestic mushrooms make this a sophisticated take on an old favourite. Serve with a tomato salad.

🥄 30-35 MINS　　🍲 25-30 MINS

SPECIAL EQUIPMENT ▪ 2-litre (3½-pint) baking dish

SERVES 6

45g (1½oz) butter

3 shallots, finely chopped

3 garlic cloves, finely chopped

125g (4½oz) mixed wild mushrooms, sliced

125g (4½oz) button mushrooms, sliced

salt and freshly ground black pepper

2 tbsp white breadcrumbs

small bunch of chives, snipped

30g (1oz) Parmesan cheese, grated

1 litre (1¾ pints) milk

1 slice of onion

6 black peppercorns

1 bay leaf

2 tbsp plain flour

pinch of grated nutmeg

225g (8oz) Gruyère cheese, grated

375g (13oz) penne pasta

1 Preheat the oven to 180°C (350°F/Gas 4) and butter the baking dish. Melt 15g (½oz) butter in a pan over a low heat, add the shallots, and cook for about 1 minute until soft. Add the garlic, mushrooms, and seasoning. Cook, stirring, for 3–5 minutes, until the liquid has evaporated. For the topping, combine the breadcrumbs in a bowl with a quarter of the chives and the Parmesan cheese. Set aside.

2 Scald the milk in a pan with the onion, peppercorns, and bay leaf. Remove from the heat. Melt the remaining butter in another pan and whisk in the flour. Remove from the heat and strain in two-thirds of the milk. Return to the heat and whisk until it boils. Add the nutmeg and seasoning and simmer for 2 minutes. Remove from the heat, add the Gruyère, and whisk in the remaining milk.

3 Cook the pasta in a pan of boiling water for about 12 minutes, or until it is tender but still al dente. Drain and mix with the mushrooms, sauce, and remaining chives. Spoon into the dish and sprinkle over the topping. Bake for 25–30 minutes, or until golden.

braised turkey with vegetables

The beauty of this dish is that you can cook it in just the one pot. Saves on washing up and the end result is succulent, too. Serve the casserole with baked or mashed potatoes.

🥄 20 MINS   🍲 50 MINS   ❄ FREEZABLE

SERVES 4

1 tbsp olive oil

knob of butter

2 skinless turkey breasts

salt and freshly ground black pepper

1 onion, sliced

1 carrot, sliced

½ fennel bulb, sliced

a few tarragon leaves, roughly chopped

300ml (10fl oz) hot chicken stock

small handful of flat-leaf parsley, finely chopped, to serve

grated zest of 1 lemon, to serve

1 Preheat the oven to 180°C (350°F/Gas 4). Heat the oil and butter in a flameproof casserole, season the turkey well with salt and pepper, then cook over a medium heat, stirring occasionally, for 10 minutes, or until lightly golden all over.

2 Add the vegetables and tarragon and season well with salt and pepper. Pour in enough stock so that it comes almost to the top of the dish but doesn't cover the ingredients. Cover with a lid and cook in the oven for 40 minutes, or until the turkey and vegetables are tender.

3 Leave to cool slightly, then remove the turkey with a slotted spoon, discard the skin, and slice the meat. Return the meat to the casserole and re-heat gently until piping hot. Top with the parsley and lemon zest, and serve with a pinch of black pepper.

variation

braised pheasant with vegetables

Prepare in the same way, but use 1 cock pheasant, cut in quarters, instead of the turkey breasts. Fry 60g (2oz) smoked lardons in the oil and remove before browning the pheasant. Add to the casserole with the vegetables and 1 tbsp brandy with the stock. Roast for 1 hour, not 40 minutes.

baked polenta with wild mushrooms

This is a hugely comforting dish, with its sweet polenta and meltingly unctuous cheese and mushrooms.

🥄 40–45 MINS PLUS CHILLING   🍲 20–25 MINS

SPECIAL EQUIPMENT ▪ 23 x 33cm (9 x 13in) baking dish

SERVES 6

375g (13oz) fine polenta

250g (9oz) mixed wild mushrooms

375g (13oz) button mushrooms

3 tbsp olive oil

3 garlic cloves, finely chopped

5-7 sprigs of thyme or rosemary, leaves picked

120ml (4fl oz) dry white wine

250ml (9fl oz) hot vegetable stock or water

4 tbsp double cream

salt and freshly ground black pepper

250g (9oz) fontina cheese, sliced

1 Sprinkle 2 baking sheets with water. Bring 1.5 litres (2¾ pints) water to the boil in a pan and add 1 tbsp salt. Over a medium heat, slowly whisk in the polenta in a thin, steady stream. Cook, stirring, for 10–15 minutes, until thick enough to pull away from the pan, yet soft and smooth. Spread on the baking sheets in a layer about 30cm (12in) square. Cool, then chill for 1 hour until firm.

2 Trim all the mushroom stalks. Cut the wild mushrooms into slices and the button mushrooms into halves, or quarters if large. Heat the oil in the frying pan. Add all the mushrooms, the garlic, and thyme or rosemary and cook, stirring, for 5–7 minutes, until the mushrooms are tender and the liquid has evaporated. Add the wine, simmer for 2–3 minutes, then add the stock and cook until reduced by half. Pour in the cream, cook until the liquid thickens, and season.

3 Preheat the oven to 220°C (425°F/Gas 7). Brush the baking dish with oil. Cut the chilled polenta into 6 x 10cm (4in) squares; reserve the trimmings. Arrange half the squares in the dish in a single layer.

4 Spoon half the mushroom stew over, then half the fontina. Repeat with another layer of polenta and mushrooms. Top with the remaining fontina. Bake for 20–25 minutes, until the cheese has melted, and serve very hot.

butterflied mackerel with sweet potato and beetroot pickle

To butterfly a fish means to remove its head, open the body and debone it. It takes a bit of time, but it's well worth it for the delicate pieces of fish that you are left with.

🥣 15 MINS 🍲 15 MINS

SERVES 4

2 sweet potatoes, peeled and diced

4 mackerel, about 100g (3½oz) each, butterflied

4 medium-to-large beetroots, cooked, peeled (p255), and diced

1 small onion, finely chopped

1–2 tsp onion seeds

juice of 1 orange

1 Cook the sweet potato in a pan of boiling salted water for 3–5 minutes until just beginning to soften; do not overcook. Drain and allow to cool.

2 Preheat the grill to high. Sit the mackerel on an oiled baking tray and grill for 3–4 minutes on each side until cooked through.

3 Meanwhile, to make the pickle, gently mix together the sweet potato and beetroot, then stir through the onion and onion seeds. Pour over the orange juice and stir until everything is coated.

4 Serve the mackerel hot, with a little of the sweet potato and beetroot pickle, or serve the pickle separately in a dish for diners to help themselves. Accompany with sautéed potatoes or a crisp, green salad.

sweet potato and butter bean stew

Gently spiced and flavoured with maple syrup, this is a pleasingly chunky stew with a silky texture from the sweet potatoes. Wilt the chard or spinach only slightly to retain its bite.

🥣 10 MINS 🍲 30 MINS

SERVES 4

450g (1lb) sweet potatoes, peeled and cut into thick slices

2 tbsp maple syrup

1 tbsp olive oil

1 red onion, finely chopped

1 tsp cumin seeds

salt and freshly ground black pepper

400g can whole plum tomatoes, chopped

splash of balsamic vinegar

400g can butter beans, drained and rinsed

handful of Swiss chard or spinach leaves

150ml (5fl oz) Greek-style yogurt

handful of mint leaves, to garnish

1 Cook the sweet potatoes and maple syrup in a large wide pan of boiling salted water for 10 minutes until tender, but not too soft. Drain well and set aside to keep warm.

2 Meanwhile, heat the oil in a large heavy-based pan over a low heat, add the onion, cumin seeds, and a pinch of salt and cook for about 5 minutes until the onion is soft and translucent. Tip in the tomatoes, including any juices, add the balsamic vinegar, and cook for about 10 minutes. Taste and season with salt and pepper.

3 Add the butter beans and simmer for a further 5 minutes, then stir through the Swiss chard or spinach. Cook for a couple of minutes more until the leaves just wilt. Remove from the heat and top with the sweet potatoes.

4 Preheat the grill to hot. Transfer vegetables to an ovenproof dish, top with yogurt, and grill until golden. Garnish with mint leaves.

roast monkfish with peppers

Monkfish is a firm, meaty white fish and, as such, is great teamed with the robust flavour of bacon or pancetta. Sweet red peppers counterbalance the salty bacon.

🥣 **15 MINS**   🍲 **30 MINS**

SERVES 4

675g (1½lb) monkfish (one or two pieces), membrane removed

4 red peppers, deseeded and cut into strips

1 tbsp olive oil

½ tsp mild paprika

12 streaky bacon or pancetta rashers

rocket leaves, to serve

1 Preheat the oven to 200°C (400°F/Gas 6). Toss the monkfish and peppers with the olive oil, then sprinkle over the paprika. Wrap the fish with the bacon or pancetta until entirely covered, then place in a roasting tin with the peppers.

2 Cook for 20–30 minutes, or until the bacon is crispy and the fish is opaque and cooked through. Remove from the oven and keep warm while the fish rests for 10 minutes. Slice the fish and serve with the peppers and a rocket salad.

vegetarian leek and mushroom lasagne

A lasagne doesn't have to be made with minced beef; a meat-free version is just as tasty, filling, and satisfying.

🥣 **25 MINS**   🍲 **45–50 MINS**   ❄ **FREEZABLE**

SERVES 4

3 tbsp olive oil

2 large leeks, trimmed and sliced

200g (7oz) chestnut mushrooms, sliced

200g (7oz) mixed wild mushrooms, chopped

1 large red chilli, deseeded and finely chopped

3 garlic cloves, chopped

75ml (2½fl oz) dry white wine

small handful of thyme leaves

1 tbsp plain flour

450ml (15fl oz) milk

175g (6oz) Cheddar cheese, grated

4 tomatoes, 3 roughly chopped and the remaining 1 sliced, to serve

salt and freshly ground black pepper

225g (8oz) lasagne sheets

1 Preheat the oven to 180°C (350°F/Gas 4). Heat the oil in a large pan over a low heat, add the leeks, and cook, stirring frequently, for 5 minutes, or until starting to soften. Add the mushrooms and cook for 5 minutes, then add the chillies and garlic, and cook for 1 minute. Pour in the wine, raise the heat, and boil for 3 minutes while the alcohol evaporates. Stir in the thyme.

2 Add the flour and mix well. Add a little of the milk, mix, then add the rest of the milk and cook for 5 minutes, stirring frequently. Add almost all the cheese, remove from the heat, and combine well. Stir in the chopped tomatoes and season well.

3 Put a 1cm (½in) layer of the mixture in the bottom of an ovenproof dish, then cover with a layer of the lasagne sheets. Pour in another layer of sauce and cover with lasagne. Repeat until all the sauce is used up, finishing with a layer of sauce. Top with the remaining cheese and the sliced tomatoes. Cook in the oven for 25–30 minutes until brown on top and piping hot.

brazilian black bean and pumpkin stew

If you prefer a meaty meal, you could add some spicy sausage or chorizo to this colourful and gutsy dish. Black beans are also called turtle beans and need soaking overnight.

🥄 **25 MINS PLUS SOAKING**   🍲 **2 HRS 30 MINS – 3 HRS**

❄ **FREEZABLE**

SERVES 4–6

325g (11oz) dried black beans, soaked in cold water overnight and drained

1 tbsp olive oil

1 onion, finely chopped

salt and freshly ground black pepper

3 garlic cloves, finely chopped

1 small pumpkin or butternut squash, peeled, deseeded, and diced

2 red peppers, deseeded and diced

2 x 400g cans chopped tomatoes

1 small green chilli, deseeded and diced

900ml (1½ pints) hot vegetable stock

1 mango, peeled, stone removed, and diced

bunch of coriander, chopped

1 Preheat the oven to 170°C (325°F/Gas 3). Put the beans in a large heavy-based pan and cover with water. Bring to the boil, then reduce to a simmer, partially cover with the lid, and cook on a low heat for 1 hour. Drain and set aside.

2 Heat the oil in a large heavy-based pan over a medium heat, add the onion, and cook for 3–4 minutes until soft. Season with salt and pepper, stir in the garlic, and cook for 1–2 minutes until soft. Stir in the pumpkin or butternut squash, red peppers, tomatoes, and chilli.

3 Add the beans, pour in the stock, and bring to the boil. Then reduce to a simmer, cover with the lid, and put in the oven for 1½–2 hours. Taste and adjust the seasoning, if necessary, then stir in the mango and coriander. Serve with some soured cream and rice on the side.

viltgryta

This venison stew with chanterelles is a Swedish favourite. Serve with boiled potatoes and lingonberry jelly.

🥄 **10 MINS PLUS MARINATING**   🍲 **2 HRS 15 MINS – 2 HRS 30 MINS**

SERVES 6

1kg (2¼lb) boned venison haunch, diced

oil or butter, for frying

300ml (10fl oz) venison or beef stock

2 onions, chopped

350g (12oz) chanterelle mushrooms

1 tbsp wine vinegar

2 tsp sugar

salt and freshly ground black pepper

150ml (5fl oz) double cream

2 tbsp plain flour

For the marinade

300ml (10fl oz) red wine

2 tbsp olive oil

¼ tsp cracked black pepper

¼ tsp ground cloves

2 tsp juniper berries, crushed

½ tsp dried thyme

2 bay leaves

1 Mix together all the marinade ingredients in a deep bowl. Add the venison, cover, and leave to marinate for 24 hours, turning once or twice.

2 Strain the marinade and reserve. Pat the meat dry. Heat the oil or butter in a large pan over a medium heat and cook the meat until browned on all sides. Add the marinade and enough stock to cover the meat. Bring to the boil, then cover and simmer for 1½ hours.

3 In another pan, heat more butter and cook the onions until soft. Add the chanterelles and fry until the moisture is driven off. Stir in the vinegar and sugar, then add this mixture to the stew.

4 Simmer for a further 30–45 minutes, or until the meat is almost cooked. Season with salt and pepper. Whisk the cream and flour together and mix into the stew. Simmer for 20 more minutes, adding more stock or water if too thick.

chilean pork and beans

Swap the sweet potatoes for squash in this recipe, if you wish. Serve with rice or flour tortillas.

🥄 **20 MINS PLUS SOAKING**   🍲 **3 HRS – 3 HRS 30 MINS**

SERVES 6

200g (7oz) dried red kidney beans, soaked in cold water overnight, drained, and rinsed

2 tbsp olive oil

900g (2lb) boned loin of pork, cut into bite-sized pieces

1 large onion, finely sliced

2 garlic cloves, finely chopped

salt and freshly ground black pepper

400g can chopped tomatoes

1 tbsp tomato purée

a few sprigs each of parsley, coriander, and oregano, leaves picked and chopped

1 green chilli, deseeded and diced

2 green peppers, deseeded and diced

500g (1lb 2oz) sweet potatoes, peeled and cut into 2.5cm (1in) cubes

2 tbsp red wine vinegar

1 Boil the beans in fresh water for 10 minutes. Cover the pan and simmer for 1 hour until almost tender. Drain.

2 Preheat the oven to 180°C (350°F/Gas 4). Heat the oil in a casserole over a medium heat and cook the pork for about 10 minutes until browned. Remove and set aside. Add the onion, garlic, and seasoning, and cook gently, covered, for 15 minutes until the onion is soft and brown. Add the pork, tomatoes, tomato purée, herbs, and 500ml (16fl oz) hot water. Cover with a lid and cook in the oven for 1¼–1½ hours until the pork is just tender.

3 Add the beans and vegetables and water to cover. Return to the oven and cook for 45–60 minutes, then transfer to the hob. Stir in the vinegar and simmer, uncovered, for 5 minutes. Check the seasoning and serve.

karahi chicken

Ripe, late-season tomatoes are the stars in this simple recipe. This is a relatively dry curry, although if you prefer more sauce, you can top up the stock during cooking. Fresh ginger and bird's eye chillies make the dish more fragrant.

🥘 15 MINS   🍲 1 HR

SPECIAL EQUIPMENT ▪ blender or food processor

SERVES 4

1 tsp coriander seeds

2 green chillies, deseeded

3 garlic cloves

1 tsp ground turmeric

2 tbsp sunflower oil

8 chicken thighs, with skin on, slashed a few times across each thigh

salt and freshly ground black pepper

1 onion, roughly chopped

6 tomatoes, roughly chopped

900ml (1½ pints) hot vegetable stock

5cm (2in) piece of fresh root ginger, peeled and finely chopped

3–4 green bird's eye chillies, left whole

bunch of coriander, finely chopped

1 Put the coriander seeds, green chillies, garlic, turmeric, and half the oil into a blender or food processor and blitz to a paste. Season the chicken with salt and pepper and smother with the paste, using your hands and pushing it into all the cuts. Heat half the remaining oil in a large flameproof casserole over a medium-high heat and add the chicken pieces. Cook for 5–6 minutes on each side or until beginning to colour, then remove and set aside.

2 Heat the remaining oil in the casserole over a medium heat, add the onion, and cook for 3–4 minutes until soft. Then add the tomatoes

and cook for a further 5–10 minutes until they too are soft. Pour in the stock and bring to the boil. Reduce to a simmer, stir in the ginger and bird's eye chillies, and return the chicken to the casserole. Cover with the lid and cook gently for 30–40 minutes, keeping an eye on the sauce. You want it to be fairly dry, but if it is sticking, add a little hot water.

3 Remove the bird's eye chillies, then taste and season, as necessary, stirring through the coriander. Serve with rice, chapatis, and some minted yogurt on the side.

variation

karahi rabbit

Prepare in the same way, but use a rabbit, jointed into 8 pieces instead of the chicken thighs. For the spice paste, toast 1 tsp cumin seeds in a dry frying pan for 30 seconds and add with ¼ tsp ground cloves to the other spices in the food processor. Add 2 diced red peppers with the tomatoes at step 2, then continue as before.

lamb, spinach, and chickpea hotpot

This hearty and nutritious hotpot will be equally good served with potatoes, rice, couscous, or quinoa. If you prefer to use fresh chickpeas, soak them overnight before cooking.

🥄 25 MINS   🍲 20 MINS   ❄ FREEZABLE

SERVES 4

350g (12oz) lean lamb, diced into 2cm (¾in) pieces

1 tbsp plain flour

½ tsp paprika

3 tbsp olive oil

1 large red onion, diced

3 garlic cloves, chopped

400g can chickpeas, drained and rinsed

½ small glass of dry white wine

400g can chopped tomatoes

salt and freshly ground black pepper

300g (10oz) baby leaf spinach

1 Put the lamb, flour, and paprika in a mixing bowl and combine well. Heat the oil in a large heavy-based pan over a medium heat, add the onion, and cook, stirring frequently, for 5 minutes, or until softened and translucent.

2 Add the diced lamb and cook, stirring occasionally, for 5 minutes, or until it is evenly browned. Stir in the garlic and chickpeas, and cook for 1 minute.

3 Pour in the wine and allow to boil for 3 minutes while the alcohol evaporates. Add the tomatoes, bring to the boil, then reduce the heat and simmer for 15 minutes. Season well with salt and pepper, stir in the spinach, and cook for 3 minutes. Serve piping hot.

baby courgettes with fish and couscous

While couscous can be made from a variety of grains, including barley, it is usually manufactured from durum wheat semolina. It is available as both wholemeal and fine.

🥄 20 MINS   🍲 25 MINS

SERVES 4

4 tbsp olive oil

300g (10oz) baby courgettes, halved lengthways

zest and juice of 1 lime

1½ tbsp tomato purée

½ tsp five-spice powder

½ tsp cayenne pepper

1 tsp paprika

½ tsp freshly ground black pepper

handful of flat-leaf parsley, finely chopped

2 garlic cloves, grated or finely chopped

300g (10oz) white fish, such as grey mullet, coley, or cod, skinned and cut into chunky bite-sized pieces

220ml (7½fl oz) hot vegetable stock

225g (8oz) couscous

1 Preheat the oven to 150°C (300°F/ Gas 2). Put 1 tbsp of the oil in a bowl, add the courgettes, and mix well until evenly coated. Fry in a hot grill pan for 2 minutes on each side, then set aside. You may need to do this in batches.

2 Add the rest of the oil to the bowl, together with the lime juice and zest, tomato purée, five-spice powder, cayenne, paprika, black pepper, parsley, and garlic. Mix well, then add the fish, stock, couscous, and courgettes and combine carefully.

3 Transfer to a flameproof dish and cover with foil. Cook in the oven for 20 minutes, then stir well and serve.

tomato, bean, and courgette stew

A colourful stew that delivers on flavour, whilst also being hearty and nutritious. The beans add bite, and the tomato sauce makes it a perfect, warming meal.

 10 MINS 🍲 20 MINS

SERVES 4

3 tbsp olive oil

1 large onion, finely chopped

2 courgettes, chopped into chunky pieces

3 garlic cloves, finely sliced

400g can borlotti beans, drained and rinsed

3 tomatoes, diced

1 tsp paprika

1 tsp dried oregano

salt and freshly ground black pepper

drizzle of chilli oil, to serve (optional)

1 Heat the oil in a deep frying pan, add the onion, and cook over a medium heat for 3 minutes. Add the courgettes and cook for a further 5 minutes, stirring constantly.

2 Add the garlic and beans, cook for 1 minute, then add the tomatoes, paprika, and oregano. Cook for 10 minutes, stirring occasionally, then season with salt and pepper. Drizzle with chilli oil (if using) and serve with some fresh crusty bread.

variation

butter bean and winter squash goulash

Prepare in the same way but add a small diced acorn squash with the courgettes. Stir in 1 tbsp sweet paprika instead of 1 tsp, and add 1 tsp smoked paprika, too. Use 1 or 2 drained 400g cans of butter beans instead of borlotti beans (depending on appetites) and a pinch of caster sugar. When cooked, serve each bowl topped with a dollop of soured cream, sprinkled with a few caraway seeds.

sweet and sour stir-fried fish with ginger

You can use any white fish to make this Oriental-style dish as long as it is firm-fleshed enough to withstand stir-frying.

🥣 10 MINS 🍲 20 MINS

SERVES 4

1-2 tbsp cornflour

salt and freshly ground black pepper

675g (1½lb) thick white fish fillets, such as haddock, cut into strips

1-2 tbsp vegetable oil or sunflower oil

1 onion, roughly chopped

2 garlic cloves, grated or finely chopped

2.5cm (1in) piece of fresh root ginger, peeled and finely sliced

large handful of mangetout or sugarsnap peas, sliced into strips

For the sauce

1 tbsp white wine vinegar

1 tbsp tomato purée

1 tbsp sugar

1 tsp cornflour

2 tsp light soy sauce

2 tbsp pineapple juice

1 First, make the sauce. Mix together the vinegar, tomato purée, sugar, cornflour, soy sauce, and pineapple juice in a jug, and set aside.

2 To prepare the fish, put the cornflour on a plate and season with salt and pepper. Toss the fish in the seasoned flour to coat.

3 In a wok, heat about half of the oil until hot, then add the fish. Stir-fry for about 5 minutes until golden. Remove the fish with a slotted spoon and set aside to keep warm.

4 Carefully wipe out the wok with kitchen paper and add a little more oil. When hot, add the onion and stir-fry until it begins to soften, then add the garlic and ginger and stir-fry for a few more minutes.

5 Pour the sweet and sour sauce into the wok and allow it to boil for a few minutes, stirring constantly. Reduce the heat to medium, add the mangetout or sugarsnap peas, and stir-fry for 1 minute. Return the fish to the wok, quickly toss together to combine, and serve hot with sticky or steamed rice.

broccoli and mushroom quiche

Both broccoli stalks and florets earn a starring role in this lovely autumnal quiche flavoured with garlic, Parmesan, and nutmeg.

🥣 20 MINS　🍲 30-35 MINS

SPECIAL EQUIPMENT ▪ 25cm (10in) round loose-bottomed fluted flan tin ▪ ceramic baking beans

SERVES 6-8

300g (10oz) ready-made shortcrust pastry

1-2 heads of broccoli, total weight about 500g (1lb 2oz)

salt and freshly ground black pepper

30g (1oz) butter

175g (6oz) mushrooms, sliced

2 garlic cloves, finely chopped

3 eggs, plus 2 egg yolks

375ml (13fl oz) milk

250ml (9fl oz) double cream

60g (2oz) Parmesan cheese, grated

grated nutmeg

1 Preheat the oven to 220°C (425°F/Gas 7). Lightly flour a work surface and roll out the pastry to a 30cm (12in) round. Use to line the tin, pressing it into the corners. Trim away the excess and prick the bottom all over with a fork. Line the pastry shell with greaseproof paper and fill with ceramic baking beans. Bake in the oven for 12-15 minutes until the edges are golden. Remove the beans and paper and return to the oven for 2-3 minutes to crisp. Remove from the oven and set aside. Reduce the oven temperature to 190°C (375°F/Gas 5).

2 Cut the florets from the broccoli stalk, then slice the stalk lengthways into sticks. Half-fill a saucepan with water and bring to the boil. Add salt, then the broccoli. Cook until just tender; it should take only about 3-5 minutes. Drain and set aside.

3 Melt the butter in a frying pan, add the mushrooms and garlic, and sauté until the mushrooms have first given out all their liquid, and then all that liquid has evaporated.

4 Whisk together the eggs, egg yolks, milk, cream, grated cheese, salt, pepper, and a pinch of nutmeg. Spread the mushrooms in the pastry shell. Arrange the broccoli on top. Ladle the cheese custard over to fill almost to the rim. Bake for 30-35 minutes, until browned and the custard has a slight wobble in the centre when shaken. Serve hot or at room temperature.

thai red vegetable curry

This versatile curry can be easily adapted to embrace the best seasonal produce. Aubergine and peppers are featured here but squashes would also be delicious.

🥣 15 MINS　🍲 20 MINS

SERVES 4

1-2 tbsp Thai red curry paste

400ml can coconut milk

2 aubergines, cut into chunks

6 kaffir lime leaves, torn in half lengthways

300ml (10fl oz) hot vegetable stock

1 tbsp palm sugar or demerara sugar

splash of dark soy sauce

pinch of salt

1 red pepper, deseeded and cut into strips

1 green pepper, deseeded and cut into strips

juice of 1 lime

handful of coriander

1 Heat the curry paste in a large frying pan or wok over a medium-high heat for a few seconds, stirring around the pan. Shake the can of coconut milk, then pour into the pan or wok. Bring to a gentle boil, stirring occasionally, and cook for 2-3 minutes until the sauce releases its aroma.

2 Add the aubergine, lime leaves, stock, sugar, and soy sauce. Season with salt and bring to the boil again. Reduce the heat slightly and simmer gently for about 15 minutes until the aubergines are soft.

3 Now add the peppers and lime juice and stir well. Taste and adjust the seasoning accordingly, adding more sugar (sweetness), lime juice (sourness), or salt as needed. Stir in the coriander and serve immediately with some jasmine or sticky rice.

marinated lamb chops with crushed lemon and chilli broccoli

This traditional Western dish is given an international twist with the addition of some chilli flakes and soy sauce.

🥣 5 MINS PLUS MARINATING　🍲 30 MINS

SERVES 4

2 tbsp sherry vinegar, cider vinegar, or white wine vinegar

pinch of sugar

splash of dark soy sauce

4 lean lamb loin chops, fat removed

salt and freshly ground black pepper

handful of rosemary sprigs

1 head or about 300g (10oz) broccoli, florets and stalks chopped fairly small

juice of 1 lemon

pinch of chilli flakes

mint jelly, to serve

1 Preheat the oven to 200°C (400°F/Gas 6). First, prepare the marinade. Mix together the vinegar, sugar, and soy sauce, then pour it over the lamb. Leave to marinate for 5 minutes, or longer if time permits.

2 Sit the lamb chops in a roasting tin, season well with salt and pepper, and throw in the rosemary sprigs. Roast in the oven for 20-30 minutes until cooked to your liking.

3 While the lamb is cooking, put the broccoli in a pan of boiling salted water and cook for about 10 minutes until just soft. Drain, keeping the broccoli in the pan, then mash very gently with a fork. Squeeze the lemon juice over and add the chilli, a pinch of salt, and some pepper. Put a lid on the pan and give it a shake. Serve immediately with the roasted lamb chops and a dollop of mint jelly.

Season's best **broccoli**

Broccoli is made up of the unopened flower heads of the plant, much like cauliflower. The popular calabrese variety has a fine texture and a light, sweet, cabbage-like flavour. Available spring through early winter, it works best with bacon, cheese, pesto, Hollandaise sauce, lemon, garlic, pine nuts, and olive oil. Other varieties such as sprouting broccoli and broccoli rabe (rapini) are available in late winter and spring, but may be used in the same way.

Calabrese (Italian sprouting broccoli) is widely grown in temperate climates, particularly in the cooler regions around the world. The buds are tightly packed in large, pebbly heads on thick stalks.

Dark green, closed buds are a sign of freshness.

The stalk can be peeled and cooked too.

Broccoli (Calabrese) The most common variety of broccoli, this is a rich green colour with a meaty flavour and, if not overcooked, a crunchy texture. It is packed with nutrients that are best retained by steaming.

essentials

varieties available

Several popular varieties, all with the characteristic tight, dark green heads.

buy Select dark green, firm heads, with stalks that can be snapped off. Avoid if pliable or if even one tiny yellow flower is showing: it is past its best.

store Keeps well in a plastic bag in the vegetable drawer of the fridge for 3–4 days.

preserve Blanch the florets and freeze in sealable bags.

recipe ideas

Broccoli and mushroom quiche p318

Marinated lamb chops with crushed lemon and chilli broccoli p318

Spaghetti with chilli, broccoli, and spring onion p50

how to prepare broccoli

Broccoli is trimmed and separated into florets before using raw, blanched, or cooked. When cut off, the thick stalk can be peeled, cut in matchsticks, and cooked with the florets.

1 Lay the broccoli stalk flat on a clean cutting board and cut off the thick portion of the stalk.

2 To remove the florets, slide the knife between the smaller stalks through the head and cut down the stalk. Cut into smaller florets, if required.

jamaican corn casserole

There is plenty of vibrant colour and a lot of heat in this vegetable dish. Look for corn cobs with tightly packed, plump kernels and glossy, firm peppers for the best flavour.

🥣 20 MINS   🍲 1 HR 30 MINS - 2 HRS

SERVES 4–6

2 tbsp olive oil

2 onions, finely chopped

salt and freshly ground black pepper

3 garlic cloves, finely chopped

1 tsp cayenne pepper

3 sweetcorn cobs, cut into slices about 1cm (½in) thick

2 red peppers, deseeded and roughly chopped

3 sweet potatoes, peeled and diced

175g (6oz) yellow split peas

300ml (10fl oz) hot vegetable stock

400ml can coconut milk

small handful of thyme

1 Scotch bonnet chilli, left whole

lime wedges, to serve (optional)

1 Preheat the oven to 170°C (325°F/ Gas 3). Heat the oil in a large flameproof casserole over a medium heat, add the onions, and cook for 3–4 minutes until soft. Season with salt and pepper, then stir in the garlic and cayenne pepper and cook for 1 minute. Add the sweetcorn, peppers, and sweet potatoes and turn them so they are all evenly coated. Then stir through the split peas and a little of the stock.

2 Bring to the boil, then add the remaining stock and coconut milk. Bring back to the boil, reduce to a simmer, season, and add the thyme and the Scotch bonnet. Cover with a lid and put in the oven to cook for 1½–2 hours. Check occasionally that it is not drying out, topping up with a little hot water if needed.

3 Remove the Scotch bonnet, taste, and season again if necessary. Ladle into warmed bowls and serve with the lime wedges, if using, and some plain rice.

beef, fennel, and mushroom hotpot

Fennel and mushrooms gently infuse this warming dish.

🥣 40 MINS   🍲 1 HR 45 MINS   ❄ FREEZABLE

SERVES 4

550g (1¼lb) stewing beef, cut into bite-sized pieces

salt and freshly ground black pepper

½ tbsp plain flour

1 tsp mild paprika

1½ tbsp olive oil

1 onion, finely sliced

1 large fennel bulb, trimmed and cut into eighths

5 tbsp dry white wine

600ml (1 pint) hot beef stock or vegetable stock

knob of butter

225g (8oz) chestnut mushrooms, quartered

pinch of dried oregano

1 Preheat the oven to 180°C (350°F/ Gas 4). Season the meat well, then place the pieces in a mixing bowl and toss with the flour and paprika until the pieces are all evenly coated.

2 Heat half the oil in a cast-iron pan, add the meat, and cook over a medium heat, stirring frequently, for 8–10 minutes or until evenly browned. Remove with a slotted spoon and set aside.

3 Add the remaining oil, add the onion, and cook for 6–8 minutes or until soft. Season well, then add the fennel and cook, stirring occasionally, for 6 minutes, or until beginning to soften slightly. Add the wine, raise the heat, and simmer for 1–2 minutes until the alcohol evaporates. Return the meat to the pan, pour in the stock, and bring to the boil. Cover with the lid and cook in the oven for 1 hour.

4 Melt the butter in a frying pan, add the mushrooms and oregano, and cook, stirring occasionally, for 5 minutes or until soft. Stir into the beef and fennel, cook for a further 30 minutes, then serve.

lamb tagine with walnuts and figs

Fig adds a sweet stickiness to this tagine and works well with lamb. You could use dried figs for a sweeter finish.

🥣 20 MINS   🍲 1 HRS 45 MINS - 2 HRS 15 MINS

SERVES 4–6

1–2 tbsp olive oil

900g (2lb) lean lamb, cut into cubes

salt and freshly ground black pepper

2 onions, sliced

3 garlic cloves, finely chopped

grated zest and juice of 1 lemon

1 tsp ground cinnamon

½ tsp ground coriander

½ tsp ground ginger

2 tsp paprika

1 tbsp tomato purée

2 tbsp clear honey

2 x 400g cans chickpeas, drained

900ml (1½ pints) hot vegetable stock

75g (2½oz) walnuts, chopped

large handful of flat-leaf parsley, roughly chopped

4 figs, quartered

1 Preheat the oven to 150°C (300°F/ Gas 2). Heat 1 tbsp of the oil in a large flameproof casserole or tagine over a medium-high heat, season the lamb, and cook (in batches, if needed) for 6–8 minutes until browned all over. Remove and set aside.

2 Cook the onions, garlic, and lemon zest and juice in the casserole over a medium heat for 2 minutes. Add seasoning, then stir though the spices and tomato purée.

3 Add the honey, chickpeas, and stock. Bring to the boil, then reduce the heat to a simmer, return the meat, and add the walnuts and half the parsley. Cover with the lid and cook in the oven for 1½ hours. Top up with hot water if it starts to dry out. Stir in the figs, re-cover, and cook in the oven for a further 30 minutes. Garnish with the remaining parsley.

middle eastern lentils and peppers

Late-season red peppers are teamed with typical Middle Eastern ingredients, such as lentils and chickpeas in this lightly spiced rice dish. It is traditionally cooked in a tagine, a special earthenware pot with a conical lid, but any heavy-based pan will do.

15 MINS   45 MINS

SERVES 4-6

100g (3½oz) brown or green lentils, rinsed

salt and freshly ground black pepper

1 tbsp olive oil

1 onion, finely chopped

3 garlic cloves, finely chopped

pinch of dried oregano

grated zest and juice of 1 lemon

½ tsp ground allspice

pinch of grated nutmeg

½ tsp ground cumin

2 red peppers, deseeded and sliced into strips

200g (7oz) rice

900ml (1½ pints) hot vegetable stock

400g can chickpeas, drained and rinsed

bunch of parsley, finely chopped

1 Put the lentils in a large heavy-based pan or tagine, season with salt and pepper, and cover with water. Bring to the boil, then simmer for about 30 minutes until the lentils are beginning to soften, but don't let them turn mushy. Drain and set aside.

2 Meanwhile, heat the oil in another heavy-based pan over a medium heat, add the onion, and cook for 3–4 minutes until soft. Season, then stir through the garlic, oregano, lemon zest, allspice, nutmeg, and cumin and cook for a minute.

3 Add the peppers and cook for about 5 minutes, stirring to coat with spices. Cook for 2–3 minutes until soft, then stir in the rice and a little stock. Bring to the boil, add most of the stock, and boil for 1 minute.

Reduce to a simmer, add the canned chickpeas, and cook on a very low heat for 15–20 minutes. Check occasionally that it is not drying out, topping up with a little hot stock if needed. Then stir through the cooked lentils, taste and season, and add the parsley and lemon juice. Serve with yogurt and pitta bread.

grey mullet with herb crust

This recipe works well with fish that have a slightly earthy taste, such as grey mullet. Soaking the grey mullet in a little acidulated water before cooking improves its flavour.

🥣 15 MINS   🍲 12-15 MINS

SERVES 4

4 grey mullet fillets, about 175g (6oz) each, skinned

45g (1½oz) butter

1 tbsp chopped flat-leaf parsley

juice of ½ lemon

salt and freshly ground black pepper

a few sprigs of sage, to garnish

lemon wedges, to garnish

For the crust

8 tbsp fresh breadcrumbs

2 tbsp melted butter

1 tbsp chopped sage

1 tbsp snipped chives

grated zest of ½ lemon

1 Preheat the oven to 200°C (400°F/ Gas 6). Arrange the fish on a baking sheet. Mix the butter, parsley, and lemon juice, and season with salt and plenty of pepper. Spread a thin layer of butter over each fish.

2 To make the crust, mix together the breadcrumbs, melted butter, sage, chives, and lemon zest. Season lightly and sprinkle over the fish, pressing to stick to the butter.

3 Roast in the oven for 12–15 minutes, or until the fish is cooked – it will be firm, white, and opaque.

4 Transfer to a warmed serving dish, garnish with the sage and lemon wedges, and serve with green beans.

jerk fish

This style of cooking comes from the Caribbean, where jerk seasoning is used to flavour and tenderize meat and fish.

🥣 10 MINS PLUS MARINATING   🍲 5 MINS

SPECIAL EQUIPMENT ▪ blender or food processor

SERVES 4

675g (1½lb) grey mullet fillets

lime wedges, to serve

For the jerk seasoning

6 garlic cloves

4 fresh Scotch Bonnet chillies

2 small onions, quartered

2 tbsp fresh thyme leaves

3 tbsp muscovado sugar

2 tsp ground allspice

1 tsp ground cinnamon

½ tsp grated nutmeg

1 tsp freshly ground black pepper

½ tsp salt

1 Blitz all the ingredients for the jerk seasoning to a smooth, wet paste. Put the fish in a plastic freezer bag, tip in the jerk seasoning, coating the fish well, and seal. Marinate in the fridge for at least 2 hours, or preferably overnight.

2 Heat the grill until hot. Grill the fish for 3–5 minutes on each side until nicely browned and just cooked through; be careful not to overcook.

3 Cut the fish fillets into chunky slices and serve immediately with lime wedges for squeezing over, fresh crusty bread, and a crunchy salad. Alternatively, serve with rice and some West Indian hot pepper sauce on the side.

kenyan fish curry

Fiery, broth-like curries, enriched with coconut milk, are typical of the dishes from East Africa.

🥣 20 MINS   🍲 45 MINS

SPECIAL EQUIPMENT ▪ coffee grinder

SERVES 4-6

juice of 1 lime

1 tsp black peppercorns, crushed

600g (1lb 5oz) grey mullet fillets, skinned and cut into 5cm (2in) pieces

6 tbsp vegetable oil

1 red onion, finely chopped

1 red pepper, deseeded and finely chopped

1 red chilli, finely chopped

4 garlic cloves, finely chopped

250g (9oz) plum tomatoes, skinned (p197) and finely chopped

200ml (7fl oz) coconut milk

1 tbsp tamarind paste

For the spice mixture

2 dried chillies

¾ tsp coriander seeds

¾ tsp cumin seeds

1 tsp mustard seeds

¼ tsp ground turmeric

1 To make the spice mixture, dry-roast the chillies and seeds, then grind to a powder using a mortar and pestle or coffee grinder. Combine with the turmeric and set aside.

2 Combine the lime juice with the peppercorns and pour over the fish. Heat the oil in a heavy pan over a medium heat. Cook the fish for 1 minute on each side until lightly coloured, but not quite cooked through. Remove and set aside.

3 Add the onion to the pan, cover, and cook for 5 minutes until soft. Tip in the red pepper, chilli, and garlic, and cook, uncovered, for 10 minutes. Stir in the spice mixture and fry briskly for 1 minute, then stir in the tomatoes, and bring to the boil. Pour in 200ml (7fl oz) water and simmer for 20 minutes until thickened. Stir in the coconut milk and tamarind paste and simmer for a further 15 minutes. Add the fish and simmer for 5–10 minutes. Serve hot with rice.

Season's best **grey mullet**

The dashingly sleek silver-grey mullet is similar to sea bass, but with larger scales and a delicious, moist flesh – particularly if caught out at sea. Those caught near land taste a little muddy. At its best in autumn, its unique flavour can take on robust spices, fragrant herbs, and other strong flavourings, such as anchovy, tomatoes, citrus, and garlic.

Common grey mullet Its numerous names include black true, flathead, or striped mullet; it is not related to the red mullet. Long-living and slow-growing, grey mullet stocks are not subject to quota restrictions.

The grey mullet's olive-green back has silver shading at the sides.

The flesh is pink in colour, cooking to an off-white, and it is firm and meaty.

Grey mullet fillet Mullet fillet is tender and slightly oily with a firm, meaty flesh. The flesh is pink in colour, cooking to an off-white. The fillet does have a few fine bones, though, so needs careful pin-boning before cooking.

essentials
cuts available

Common grey mullet. Sold whole or in fillets; also available dried and salted. The roe is available fresh, dried, or salted.

buy Line-caught. Whole fish should be firm with bright eyes. Fillets should smell fresh and be moist.

store Best eaten on the day of purchase, or keep wrapped, in the coldest part of the fridge, for up to 24 hours.

cook Pan-fry, roast, steam, or bake. The salted roe is used to make taramasalata.

recipe ideas

Baby courgettes with fish and couscous p316

Grey mullet with herb crust p322

Yam pla fu p278

how to descale a grey mullet

Visible scales on all fish from sardines to grey mullet need removing before cooking as they are inedible. Work in a clear space and lay down newspaper or greaseproof paper, as the scales can fly about.

1 Dip your fingers in salt to grip the tail without it slipping. Place the fish on paper to catch the scales. Hold the fish firmly by the tail.

2 Scrape away the scales with the back of a knife working from tail to head end. Rinse the fish under cold water and pat dry.

balinese spicy mackerel

Typical of the cuisine of Indonesia, this recipe uses kecap menis, soy sauce, and molasses. Lime wedges and fresh coriander make an attractive garnish.

🥣 **10 MINS PLUS CHILLING** 🍲 **15 MINS**

SPECIAL EQUIPMENT ▪ blender or food processor

SERVES 4

4 small mackerel, skin on, filleted, pinboned, and cut in half lengthways

juice of 2 limes

½ tsp ground turmeric or 2 tsp freshly grated turmeric

salt

3 tbsp vegetable oil

1 lemongrass stalk, split into 4

3 tbsp kecap manis

For the chilli paste

3 red chillies, deseeded (optional) and finely chopped

6 shallots, chopped

2 garlic cloves, crushed

5 roasted candlenuts or macadamia nuts

1 tbsp grated fresh root ginger

1 tbsp tamarind paste

½ tsp caster sugar

salt and freshly ground black pepper

1 Sprinkle the mackerel with the lime juice, turmeric, and ½ tsp salt. Cover and refrigerate for 15–30 minutes.

2 Put the chillies, shallots, garlic, nuts, ginger, tamarind paste, and sugar into a blender or food processor and blitz to chop very finely. Season lightly.

3 Pat the mackerel dry with kitchen paper. Heat the oil in a large frying pan or wok. Fry the mackerel skin-side down, a few pieces at a time, until firm, opaque, and brown. Avoid stirring to prevent the fish from breaking up. Remove from the pan.

4 Add the chilli paste to the pan and fry over a medium heat until fragrant. Add 150ml (5fl oz) water and the lemongrass, bring to the boil, and simmer for 2–3 minutes. Return the fish, add the kecap manis, and stir over a gentle heat until the ingredients are combined and the sauce reduced and bubbling. Serve with rice.

provençal stuffed artichokes

Artichokes braised in wine, served with rich red pepper sauce.

🥣 **50–55 MINS** 🍲 **40–45 MINS**

SPECIAL EQUIPMENT ▪ food processor

SERVES 4

4 globe artichokes, total weight about 1.35kg (3lb), prepared to serve whole with choke removed (p308)

½ lemon

salt and freshly ground black pepper

45g (1½oz) butter

3 small onions, finely chopped

6 garlic cloves, finely chopped

250g (9oz) mushrooms, finely chopped

250g (9oz) Parma ham, cut into strips

2 anchovy fillets, finely chopped

175g (6oz) pitted black olives, finely chopped

4 slices of white bread, made into crumbs

2–3 sprigs of thyme, leaves picked

large pinch of ground allspice

250ml (9fl oz) white wine

2 tbsp olive oil

750g (1lb 10oz) red peppers, roasted, peeled (p171), and chopped

400g can chopped tomatoes

1 garlic clove, chopped

2 spring onions, trimmed and chopped

bunch of basil, leaves chopped

1 Rub all cut surfaces of the prepared artichokes with the lemon half to prevent discolouration. Boil in salted water for 25–30 minutes until almost tender and a leaf can be pulled out with a slight tug. Remove with a slotted spoon and set them upside-down on a wire rack to drain.

2 Melt the butter in a frying pan, add the onions and garlic, and cook, stirring, until soft but not brown. Stir in the mushrooms, Parma ham, anchovies, and olives, then remove from the heat. Add the breadcrumbs, thyme leaves, and allspice and mix thoroughly. Season with pepper.

3 Preheat the oven to 180°C (350°F/Gas 4). Fill the artichokes with the stuffing and tie with string to hold the leaves together. Put the artichokes in a flameproof casserole. Add the wine and boil for 5 minutes, or until reduced by half. Half-cover the artichokes with water; season. Bring back to the boil and cover.

4 Bake in the oven for 40–50 minutes, basting occasionally with the wine and juices, until tender and a central leaf can be pulled out easily.

5 Heat the olive oil in a frying pan. Add the remaining ingredients and cook, stirring occasionally, for 15–20 minutes, until thickened. Blitz to a coarse purée in a food processor. Season to taste. Discard the strings from the artichokes. Serve on plates with the sauce spooned around the bases. Pass extra sauce separately.

beef and leek couscous

Subtle, sweet leeks and paprika enhance this tasty beef dish.

🥣 **25 MINS** 🍲 **30 MINS**

SERVES 4

4 tbsp olive oil

3 leeks, finely sliced

350g (12oz) lean minced beef

1 red chilli, deseeded and finely chopped

1 tsp sweet paprika

3 garlic cloves, sliced

5 tbsp dry white wine

240ml (8fl oz) hot beef stock

small handful of flat-leaf parsley, finely chopped

225g (8oz) couscous

1 Preheat the oven to 150°C (300°F/Gas 2). Heat the oil in a heavy-based pan, add the leeks, and cook over a medium heat for 5 minutes. Add the mince and cook, stirring, for 10 minutes, or until it is no longer pink.

2 Stir in the chillies, paprika, and garlic and cook for 2 minutes. Pour in the wine and cook for 3 minutes until the alcohol evaporates, then add the stock and parsley and combine well. Stir in the couscous, cover with a lid, and cook in the oven for just 15 minutes. Then remove from the oven, stir well, and serve.

sole veronique

This dish of sole poached with white grapes is part of the classic French repertoire. You can use other flatfish in season, such as flounder.

🥣 30 MINS 🍲 20 MINS

SERVES 4

4 lemon sole, skinned and filleted

½ onion, thinly sliced

6 black peppercorns

1 bay leaf

100ml (3½fl oz) dry white wine

175g (6oz) seedless white grapes, peeled

For the sauce

45g (1½oz) butter

1 heaped tbsp plain flour

5 tbsp warm milk

5 tbsp double cream

salt and freshly ground white pepper

1 Preheat the oven to 180°C (350°/Gas 4). Fold the sole fillets into 3, skin-side in. Arrange them in an ovenproof dish and scatter the onion, peppercorns, and bay leaf around them. Mix the wine with 100ml (3½fl oz) water, pour it over the fish and onion, and cover with buttered greaseproof paper.

2 Poach the fish in the oven for 10–12 minutes or until it is cooked; it will be white and opaque. Remove the fish and keep warm. Strain the cooking liquor into a saucepan and boil rapidly to reduce to 150ml (5fl oz).

3 For the sauce, in another saucepan, melt half the butter, remove from the heat, and stir in the flour. Cook over a low to medium heat for 30 seconds. Remove from the heat and blend in the milk, then the fish liquor. Return to a low heat and bring to the boil, stirring. Stir in the cream, remove from the heat, and whisk in the remaining butter. Season, add the grapes, and heat through.

4 Lift the fish carefully onto warmed plates. Spoon the sauce over the fish to serve.

sea bass with black bean sauce

This is a wonderful combination – the well-flavoured sea bass works beautifully with the saltiness of the sauce.

🥣 25 MINS 🍲 30 MINS

SPECIAL EQUIPMENT ▪ bamboo steamer

SERVES 4

3 tbsp fermented black beans (available at Oriental supermarkets)

2 tbsp sunflower oil

2 spring onions, trimmed and chopped

5cm (2in) piece of fresh root ginger, cut into matchsticks

1 garlic clove, very finely sliced

3 tbsp dark soy sauce

2 tbsp Chinese rice wine or dry sherry

1 tsp caster sugar

300ml (10fl oz) fish stock

1 tsp cornflour

4 sea bass fillets, about 175g (6oz) each, scaled and pinboned

a few sprigs of coriander, to garnish

drizzle of sesame oil

1 Rinse the black beans very thoroughly under cold running water. Heat the sunflower oil in a large frying pan over a low heat. Add the spring onions and ginger and fry until aromatic. Add the garlic and stir-fry for another minute.

2 Remove the pan from the heat and add the soy sauce, rice wine, sugar, and three-quarters of the stock. Return to the heat, bring to the boil, and simmer for a couple of minutes. Mix the cornflour with the remaining stock in a small bowl.

3 Arrange the fish on a bamboo steamer and cook for 7–8 minutes, covered, over a large saucepan of simmering water.

4 Meanwhile, stir the cornflour mixture into the hot stock with the beans, bring to the boil, then reduce the heat and simmer for 2–3 minutes until thickened slightly.

5 Arrange the fish on a platter with the coriander. Spoon the sauce over and drizzle with sesame oil. Serve with rice.

roasted baby leeks with tomato dressing

Leeks are rarely used as a main ingredient, but they sometimes deserve to be given a starring role. Served like this, baby leeks make a delicious starter or side dish.

 10 MINS 12 MINS

SERVES 4

1 tbsp finely chopped sun-dried tomatoes in oil

3 tbsp extra virgin olive oil, plus extra for tossing

1 tbsp red wine vinegar

1 tbsp very finely chopped black and green olives

1 tbsp finely chopped basil

sea salt and freshly ground black pepper

8 baby leeks, washed and trimmed

1 Preheat the oven to 200°C (400°F/ Gas 6). Put the tomatoes with a little of their oil, the olive oil, vinegar, olives, and basil in a mixing bowl and combine. Season with sea salt and pepper to taste.

2 Put the leeks in a pan of boiling water and cook over a high heat for 2 minutes. Then drain well.

3 Toss a little olive oil in a roasting tin and place the leeks in the tin. Roast in the oven for 10 minutes until golden and tender. Spoon the dressing over to serve.

variation

roasted baby leeks with chilli and crispy bacon
Blanch 8–12 baby leeks as in step 2. Place in the roasting tin and toss with the 3 tbsp olive oil, 1 tbsp white balsamic condiment, and plenty of freshly ground black pepper. Scatter 1 red chilli, deseeded and finely chopped, and 1 tbsp fresh thyme leaves over. Roast as before. Transfer to a warm serving dish. Meanwhile dry-fry 60g (2oz) diced pancetta until crisp. Scatter over the leeks before serving.

chinese-style plum sauce

Use this authentic-tasting plum sauce as a dip, as a baste for grilled or roasted duck, chicken, or pork, or to replace hoi-sin sauce to smear on Chinese pancakes with crispy duck.

 20 MINS 45–50 MINS

SPECIAL EQUIPMENT ▪ blender or food processor

MAKES APPROX 600ml (1 PINT)

½ tsp wasabi paste or English mustard

150ml (5fl oz) rice (or white) wine vinegar

500g (1lb 2oz) ripe dark red or blue plums, halved and stoned

1 onion, chopped

1 garlic clove, crushed

60g (2oz) dark soft brown sugar

5 tbsp clear honey

2 tbsp dark soy sauce

1 tsp Chinese five-spice powder

2 tbsp sake or dry sherry

1 Mix the wasabi paste or mustard and vinegar in a large saucepan until blended. Add the plums, onion, and garlic. Bring to the boil, reduce the heat, partly cover the pan with the lid, and simmer gently for 10–15 minutes until the plums are pulpy.

2 Put the mixture in a blender or food processor and blitz to a purée. Return the purée to the pan and stir in the remaining ingredients. Bring back to the boil, stirring continuously, then reduce the heat and simmer, uncovered, for 25 minutes, stirring occasionally, until thick and rich.

3 Spoon into warm sterilized jars, top with waxed paper discs, allow to cool, seal, and label. Store in a cool, dark place for up to 3 months. Once opened, store in the fridge and use within 2 weeks.

tomato ketchup

Home-made tomato ketchup is full of goodness and free from chemical additives. This authentic-tasting recipe has the right balance of sweetness, acidity, and spice.

 15 MINS 45 MINS – 1 HOUR 5 MINS

SPECIAL EQUIPMENT ▪ blender or food processor
▪ preserving pan ▪ nylon sieve

MAKES APPROX 750ml (1¼ PINTS)

1kg (2¼lb) ripe tomatoes, roughly chopped

1 carrot, chopped

1 small onion, chopped

1 celery stick, chopped

good pinch of ground cloves

1 large bay leaf

2 mace blades

1 tsp sea salt

150ml (5fl oz) red wine vinegar

60g (2oz) light soft brown sugar

1 Put all the ingredients except the brown sugar in a preserving pan or a large heavy-based, stainless steel saucepan. Bring to the boil, reduce the heat, cover with a lid, and simmer for 30 minutes. Then remove the lid and cook for a further 15 minutes, stirring occasionally.

2 Discard the mace and bay leaf. Put the mixture in a blender or food processor, blitz to a purée, then rub it through a nylon sieve back into the rinsed-out pan.

3 Stir in the sugar over a low heat, then bring back to the boil. Continue boiling, stirring all the time, for 5 minutes until the sauce becomes the consistency of thick cream.

4 Pour into warm sterilized screw-topped jars with non-metallic or vinegar-proof lids. Cover with waxed paper discs, cool, seal, and label. Store in a cool, dark place for up to 3 months. Once opened, store in the fridge and use within 2 weeks. Shake before use.

spicy garlic and green vegetable medley

Vibrant autumn leafy greens, such as spinach and Swiss chard, and pak choi with its soft leaves and fleshy ends are all best served lightly stir-fried to retain their mild yet distinctive flavours.

15 MINS   15 MINS

SERVES 4

handful of hazelnuts

1 tbsp sesame oil or vegetable oil

2 green chillies, deseeded and finely chopped

3 garlic cloves, thinly sliced

1 tbsp dark soy sauce

1 tbsp Chinese rice wine

1–2 heads of pak choi, quartered lengthways

handful of spinach or Swiss chard

2 handfuls of sugarsnap peas or mangetout, sliced into strips

salt and freshly ground black pepper

1 Spread the hazelnuts over a baking tray and toast under a hot grill until golden brown, turning them frequently. While the hazelnuts are still hot, put them in a clean tea towel and rub off the skins. Then roughly chop and set aside.

2 Heat the oil in a wok over a medium-high heat and swirl it around to coat the surface. Add the chillies and garlic and cook for 10 seconds, then add the soy sauce and Chinese rice wine, and cook for a few more seconds.

3 Throw in the pak choi and spinach or Swiss chard and stir-fry for a minute. Add the sugarsnap peas or mangetout and stir-fry for a minute more. Toss, then season with salt and pepper. Serve immediately with the hazelnuts scattered over the top and some fluffy rice.

variation

spicy mixed vegetable medley

Prepare in the same way but omit the spinach or Swiss chard and add 100g (3½oz) baby corn cobs, cut in thick diagonal slices, a handful of oyster mushrooms, cut in pieces if large, and red or yellow peppers, deseeded and cut in strips at step 3. Add a splash more of rice wine and soy sauce to taste.

chunky potato wedges

Potatoes are incredibly versatile, but it is often the most basic of preparation and cooking methods that brings out their true flavour. This dish couldn't be simpler and tastes delicious.

🥣 10 MINS   🍲 40 MINS

SERVES 4–6

900g (2lb) all-purpose potatoes, such as Maris Piper, skins on, washed, quartered lengthways, and if large, sliced again lengthways

2 tbsp olive oil

sea salt

1 Preheat the oven to 200°C (400°F/ Gas 6). Put the potatoes in a large roasting tin, add the oil, and combine well with your hands.

2 Sprinkle with plenty of sea salt and put in the oven to roast for 40 minutes, or until the wedges are crispy and golden.

variation

cajun vegetable chips

Use 1 small sweet potato and 1 large potato, both scrubbed but not peeled, and cut into thick chips, and 1 wedge of pumpkin, peeled, deseeded, and cut into thick chips. Place them all in a large roasting tin and toss with 2–3 tbsp olive oil. Sprinkle with 1 tbsp Cajun spice mix instead of the sea salt and toss again. Bake as before, then sprinkle with a few grains of coarse sea salt before serving.

beetroot relish

This is a sweet relish with a hint of spice – perfect to serve with cheeses or beef. If you want to save time making the relish, pre-cook the beetroots the night before.

🥣 10 MINS   🍲 2 HOURS 5 MINS

SPECIAL EQUIPMENT ■ muslin ■ preserving pan

MAKES APPROX 1kg (2¼lb)

1.35kg (3lb) raw beetroots

1 tsp caster sugar

450g (1lb) shallots, finely chopped

600ml (1 pint) cider or white wine vinegar

1 tbsp pickling spices, placed in muslin with the ends brought together and tied firmly to make a spice bag

450g (1lb) granulated sugar

1 Put the beetroots in a preserving pan or a large heavy-based, stainless steel saucepan, pour over enough water to cover them, and add the caster sugar. Bring to the boil and simmer for 1 hour, or until the beetroot is soft and cooked. Drain and leave to cool. When cool enough to handle, peel and dice each into small, neat pieces.

2 Put the shallots and vinegar in the rinsed-out preserving pan or saucepan and cook for 10 minutes on a low heat. Add the chopped beetroots and the muslin bag of pickling spices. Give the mixture a stir, add the granulated sugar, and heat gently until the sugar has all dissolved. Bring to the boil and cook at a rolling boil for 5 minutes, then reduce the heat to a simmer and cook the relish for about 40 minutes, or until the mixture thickens.

3 Remove the spice bag and ladle into warm sterilized jars with non-metallic or vinegar-proof lids, making sure there are no air gaps. Seal, label, and store in a cool, dark place. Allow to mature for 1 month and refrigerate after opening.

thai dipping sauce

A staple in Thailand, this hot sauce is good served with most things. It will improve in flavour after standing for a few days.

🥣 10 MINS

SPECIAL EQUIPMENT ■ food processor

SERVES 4

1 tsp palm sugar or demerara sugar, plus extra if needed

3 garlic cloves, crushed

3–4 red chillies, deseeded and finely chopped (leave in the seeds if you want a fiery-hot sauce)

2 tbsp fish sauce (nam pla)

1 tbsp light soy sauce

juice of 1 lime, plus extra if needed

2 tbsp chopped coriander

salt

1 This can be made with a pestle and mortar, or in a small food processor. If using a pestle and mortar, pound the sugar, garlic, and chillies to a smooth paste, then stir in the rest of the ingredients. Check the seasoning and add a little salt to taste, adding more sugar or lime juice, if needed. If using a processor, blitz together all the ingredients except the lime juice, coriander, and salt. Add the lime juice and salt to taste, then stir in the chopped coriander.

2 Allow the sauce to sit for a few minutes to enable the flavours to mingle, then taste again and add more lime juice, salt, or sugar as needed. Spoon into a jar, seal, keep in the fridge, and use within a week.

green beans with toasted hazelnuts

Let the flavour of in-season green beans shine with this simple recipe – all that's needed are nuts to add crunch.

🥣 **5 MINS** 🍲 **5 MINS**

SERVES 4

250g (9oz) fine green beans, trimmed

pinch of salt

25g (scant 1oz) butter

75g (2½oz) hazelnuts, roughly chopped and toasted

1 Put the beans in a pan of salted water and boil for 5–6 minutes, or until they are cooked but still have a bit of bite to them. Drain, then refresh under cold water so they stop cooking and retain their colour.

2 Transfer to a serving dish, top with the butter and toasted hazelnuts, and serve with roast chicken or lamb.

greek-style vegetables

This piquant dish is great on the side of a rich main course, or as an appetizer. You can make it up to two days in advance and allow the flavours to mellow while it chills in the fridge.

🥣 **25-30 MINS** 🍲 **25-30 MINS**

SPECIAL EQUIPMENT ▪ muslin ▪ food processor

SERVES 4

10g (¼oz) coriander seeds

½ tbsp black peppercorns

2 bay leaves

2-3 sprigs of thyme

1-2 sprigs of parsley

1 tbsp tomato purée

375ml (13fl oz) vegetable stock or water, plus more if needed

juice of ½ lemon

2 tbsp dry white wine

12 baby onions

2 tbsp vegetable oil

2 tbsp olive oil

250g (9oz) button mushrooms, trimmed

200g (7oz) can chopped tomatoes

salt and freshly ground black pepper

250g (9oz) fennel bulbs, sliced

20g (¾oz) raisins

1 Combine the coriander seeds, black peppercorns, bay leaves, and thyme and parsley sprigs in a small bowl. Place the mixture on a small piece of muslin, bring the ends together, and tie firmly with string to make a bag.

2 To make the cooking liquid, whisk the tomato purée, half the vegetable stock or water, the lemon juice, and white wine in a bowl.

3 Put the baby onions in a bowl, cover with hot water, and let stand for 2 minutes. Drain and peel, leaving a little of the root attached.

4 Heat the vegetable oil and olive oil in a sauté pan. Add the baby onions and sauté for 3 minutes or so until lightly browned. Add the mushrooms, spice bag, and tomatoes. Pour in the cooking liquid so it just covers the vegetables, add some salt and the fennel, and bring to a fast boil over a high heat. Add the raisins and stir occasionally, adding a little stock or water as the liquid evaporates. Cook the vegetables for 25–30 minutes until tender to the tip of a knife. Then remove the spice bag, taste for seasoning, and serve.

sweetcorn and pepper relish

As its name implies, this diced sweetcorn and pepper relish packs a tangy punch of flavour. It is part pickle, part chutney, but cooked for a shorter time than a chutney.

🥣 **10 MINS** 🍲 **25-30 MINS**

MAKES APPROX 1kg (2¼lb)

4 sweetcorn cobs, kernels removed (about 450g/1lb kernels, p155)

2 red peppers, or 1 green and 1 red pepper, deseeded and finely diced

2 celery sticks, finely sliced

1 red chilli, deseeded and finely sliced (optional)

1 onion, peeled and finely sliced

450ml (15fl oz) white wine vinegar

225g (8oz) sugar

2 tsp sea salt

2 tsp mustard powder

½ tsp ground turmeric

1 Blanch the kernels in a saucepan of boiling water for 2 minutes, then drain well. Put the sweetcorn and the other ingredients in a large saucepan and cook over a medium heat, stirring until the sugar has dissolved. Then bring to the boil. Turn the heat down and simmer gently, stirring frequently, for 15–20 minutes or until the mixture has thickened slightly and has only a little liquid left in the bottom of the pan when you draw a wooden spoon across it. The relish should be a spoonable consistency and wetter than a chutney.

3 Check the seasoning is right, then pot into warm sterilized jars. Seal with non-metallic or vinegar-proof lids, leave to cool, and label. Store in a cool, dark place. Like all relishes, this can be eaten immediately or stored. Once opened, store in the fridge.

quick pumpkin bread

The grated pumpkin in this quick bread ensures that it keeps moist for days. It's a perfect accompaniment for soup.

🥣 **20 MINS**   🍲 **50 MINS**   ❄️ **FREEZABLE**

MAKES 1

300g (10oz) plain flour

100g (3½oz) wholemeal self-raising flour

1 tsp bicarbonate of soda

½ tsp fine salt

120g (4¼oz) pumpkin or butternut squash, halved, deseeded, peeled, and roughly grated

30g (1oz) pumpkin seeds

300ml (10fl oz) buttermilk

1 Preheat the oven to 220°C (425°F/Gas 7). Put the flours, bicarbonate of soda, and salt in a mixing bowl and mix well. Add the grated pumpkin and seeds, and stir the ingredients well to combine so that no clumps remain. Make a well in the centre and pour in the buttermilk. Stir together to form a dough.

2 Using your hands, bring the mixture together into a ball, then turn it out onto a floured work surface. Knead the dough for 2 minutes until it forms a smooth mass. You may need to add a little more flour if it feels too sticky.

3 Shape the dough into a round 15cm (6in) in diameter and place on a lined baking sheet. Use a sharp knife to slash a cross into the top to help the bread to rise when baking.

4 Cook for 30 minutes in the centre of the oven until risen. Then reduce the oven to 200°C (400°F/Gas 6) and cook for 20 minutes more until the base sounds hollow when tapped.

5 Transfer the bread to a wire rack and allow it to cool for at least 20 minutes before serving.

mushroom ketchup

Thin ketchups such as this can be used as a concentrated flavouring in soups, sauces, gravies, and savoury dishes.

🥣 **1 HR 30 MINS PLUS STANDING**   🍲 **1 HR**

SPECIAL EQUIPMENT ▪ fine nylon sieve ▪ muslin

MAKES APPROX 300ml (10fl oz)

2kg (4½lb) field or large open cultivated mushrooms, wiped and finely chopped

30g (1oz) sea salt

1 tsp black peppercorns

1 tsp allspice berries

½ tsp cloves

½ cinnamon stick

1 small shallot

300ml (10fl oz) red or white wine vinegar

a few pieces of dried cep

6 salted anchovies, rinsed (or 2 tbsp dark soy sauce)

2 mace blades

2 tsp brandy (optional)

1 Put the chopped mushrooms in a large bowl. Sprinkle over the sea salt, toss together with your hands to mix well, cover, and set aside for 24 hours, squashing the mushrooms down occasionally.

2 Grind the peppercorns, allspice, cloves, and cinnamon in a pestle and mortar. Peel and finely chop the shallot, measure the vinegar, and select a few dried ceps. Check the chopped mushrooms; they should have now reduced to a third of their original volume.

3 Put the mushrooms, their juice, the ground spices, and the shallot in a saucepan with the vinegar, dried ceps, anchovies, and mace. Bring to the boil, cover with a lid, and simmer very gently for 1 hour.

4 Strain the cooked ingredients through a fine nylon sieve set over a clean bowl. Press the mixture hard against the sides of the sieve to extract as much liquor as possible.

5 Tip the contents of the sieve onto a square of muslin, gather up the corners, and squeeze the muslin ball tightly to extract the last of the liquor. Check the quantity of the liquor; if it is more than 300–400ml (10–14fl oz), return to the pan and cook until its volume reduces to about 300ml (10fl oz). Pour the liquor into a warm sterilized bottle, add the brandy (if using), seal, and store in a cool, dark place. Once opened, keep refrigerated for 4–6 months.

fennel gratin

The rich, creamy gratin topping on this Italian dish works perfectly with the subtle aniseed flavour of fennel.

🥣 **5 MINS**   🍲 **40 MINS**

SERVES 4

2 fennel bulbs, trimmed and cut lengthways into 6 slices or wedges

salt and freshly ground black pepper

a small sprig of rosemary, leaves picked and finely chopped (optional)

150ml (5fl oz) double cream

25g (scant 1oz) Parmesan cheese, grated

1 Preheat the oven to 180°C (350°F/Gas 4). Add the fennel to a pan of boiling salted water and simmer gently for about 5 minutes, or until starting to soften. Drain well.

2 Arrange the fennel in a shallow baking dish. Sprinkle over the rosemary, if using, and season with salt and pepper. Pour over the cream and sprinkle with half the Parmesan cheese. Cover the dish with foil and bake in the oven for 30 minutes.

3 Remove the foil. Sprinkle over the remaining Parmesan and put back into the oven, uncovered, to bake for a further 5 minutes, or until the top turns lightly golden. Serve hot.

black olive and pepper ciabatta

A good ciabatta should be well risen and crusty, with large air pockets. Using black olives and roasted red peppers in this easy-to-master recipe makes for an unusual, tasty loaf studded with black and red.

40 MINS PLUS RISING AND PROVING   **30 MINS**   **FREEZABLE**

MAKES 2

2 tsp dried yeast

2 tbsp olive oil

450g (1lb) strong white bread flour

1 tsp sea salt

50g (1¾oz) stoned black olives, drained, roughly chopped, and dried with kitchen paper

1 red pepper, roasted, peeled (p171), and roughly chopped

1 Dissolve the yeast with 350ml (12fl oz) warm water in a bowl, then add the oil. Put the flour and salt in a separate mixing bowl. Make a well in the centre of the flour, pour in the yeast mixture, and stir together to form a soft dough.

2 Knead the dough for 10 minutes on a floured work surface, then stretch it out thinly and scatter over the olives and pepper. Bring the sides of the dough together to cover the olives and pepper. Knead the dough briefly until the olives and pepper are fully incorporated. Put the dough in an oiled bowl, cover loosely with cling film, and leave to rise in a warm place for up to 2 hours until doubled in size.

3 Turn the dough out onto a floured work surface and knock it back. Divide it into 2 pieces, then knead and mould each piece into a 30 x 10cm (12 x 4in) traditional slipper shape. Place the loaves on a lined baking sheet, cover with cling film and a tea towel, and leave for 1 hour until they have doubled in size.

4 Preheat the oven to 230°C (450°F/ Gas 8). Spray the loaves with a mist of water and bake in the centre of the oven for 30 minutes until golden brown; spray the loaves with water every 10 minutes. The bread is cooked when the base sounds hollow when tapped. Cool for 30 minutes before cutting.

apple and blackberry brown betty

This classic combination of tart apples and juicy blackberries is topped by a layer of zesty lemon breadcrumbs.

🥣 15 MINS 🍲 40 MINS ❄ FREEZABLE

SPECIAL EQUIPMENT ▪ 1.2-litre (2-pint) ovenproof dish

SERVES 4

100g (3½oz) fine white breadcrumbs

generous knob of butter, softened

zest of 1 lemon

3 Bramley apples, peeled, cored, and sliced

150g (5½oz) blackberries

150ml (5½fl oz) fresh orange juice

2–3 tbsp caster sugar (depending on the tartness of the fruit)

1 Preheat the oven to 190°C (375°F/ Gas 5). Put the breadcrumbs, butter, and lemon zest in a mixing bowl, combine well, and set aside.

2 Place the apples in a greased ovenproof dish, then stir in the blackberries, orange juice, and enough of the caster sugar to sweeten. Sprinkle the breadcrumbs on top and bake for 35–40 minutes or until golden and piping hot. Serve while hot with cream or ice cream.

variation

pear and raspberry brown betty

Prepare in exactly the same way but use wholemeal breadcrumbs instead of white ones. Substitute 4 ripe pears for 2 of the cooking apples. Use 150g (5½oz) raspberries instead of blackberries and 150ml (5fl oz) apple juice instead of orange juice. 1–2 tbsp sugar will be sufficient to sweeten. Serve with scoops of vanilla ice cream.

apple jalousie

In this pastry, the top layer of dough is slashed before baking to look like a *jalousie*, French for louvred shutter.

🥣 1 HR 15 MINS – 1 HR 30 MINS PLUS CHILLING 🍲 30–40 MINS

SERVES 6–8

15g (½oz) unsalted butter

1kg (2¼lb) tart eating apples, peeled, cored, and diced

2.5cm (1in) piece of fresh root ginger, peeled and finely chopped

100g (3½oz) caster sugar

500g (1lb 2oz) ready-made puff pastry

1 egg white

1 Melt the butter in a large frying pan. Add the apples, ginger, and all but 2 tbsp of the sugar. Sauté briskly, stirring often, for 15–20 minutes until the apples are tender and caramelized. Taste, adding more sugar if needed. Set aside to cool.

2 Sprinkle a baking sheet evenly with cold water. Roll out the puff pastry on a floured work surface and trim into a 28 x 32cm (11 x 12½in) rectangle. Cut in half lengthways. Then fold one of the halves in half lengthways and cut across the fold at 5mm (¼in) intervals to form the shutter effect, leaving an uncut border at the edges. Use a very sharp knife so you don't press down hard, or the pastry will be hard to unfold. Transfer the uncut rectangle to the baking sheet and press it down lightly. Spoon the apple filling down the centre, leaving a 2cm (¾in) border. Moisten the border with cold water using a pastry brush. Top with the slashed dough rectangle, then press the edges together with your fingertips and trim the edges. Scallop the edges at close intervals with the back of a small knife. Leave to chill in the fridge for 15 minutes. Preheat the oven to 220°C (425°F/ Gas 7).

3 Bake for 20–25 minutes until puffed and light brown. Meanwhile, whisk the egg white just until frothy. Brush the hot jalousie with the egg white and sprinkle the remaining sugar on top. Return to the oven and continue baking for 10–15 minutes until the sugar glaze is crisp and the pastry is deep golden. Transfer to a wire rack and let cool. Then cut the jalousie across into 6–8 slices and serve warm or at room temperature.

blackberry focaccia

The addition of blackberries turns this classic bread into a lovely sweet dessert, tea-time treat, or as part of a meal on the go.

🥣 30-35 MINS PLUS RISING AND PROVING   🍲 15-20 MINS

SPECIAL EQUIPMENT ▪ 38 x 23cm (15 x 9in) Swiss roll tin

SERVES 6-8

1 tbsp dried yeast

425g (15oz) strong white bread flour, plus extra for dusting

1 tsp salt

3 tbsp caster sugar

90ml (3fl oz) extra virgin olive oil

300g (10oz) blackberries

1 Sprinkle the yeast over 4 tbsp lukewarm water in a small bowl. Leave to stand for 5 minutes until dissolved, stirring once.

2 Put the flour, salt, and 2 tbsp of the sugar in a mixing bowl and mix together. Make a well in the centre of the mix and add the dissolved yeast, 4 tbsp of the oil, and 240ml (8fl oz) lukewarm water. Draw in the flour and mix to form a smooth dough. The dough should be soft and sticky; avoid adding more flour to dry it out.

3 Flour your hands and the dough, and turn it out onto a floured surface. Knead for 5–7 minutes until smooth and elastic. Transfer to an oiled bowl and cover with a damp tea towel. Leave to rise in a warm place for about 1–1½ hours until doubled in bulk.

4 Generously brush the tin with oil. Turn out the dough and knock out the air. Cover with a dry tea towel and leave to rest for 5 minutes. Transfer to the tin, flattening it with your hands so it fills the tin. Scatter

the blackberries over the surface of the dough, cover with the tea towel, and leave to prove in a warm place for 35–45 minutes until puffed.

5 Preheat the oven to 200°C (400°F/ Gas 6). Brush the dough with the remaining oil and sprinkle over the rest of the sugar. Bake at the top of the oven for 15–20 minutes, until lightly browned. Cool slightly on a wire rack, then serve warm.

Season's best **apples**

In green, red, yellow, or russet; tasting sour, sharp, or sweet; some crisp, some soft, apples ripen in late summer or autumn and many can be stored over the winter. Most, except sour cooking apples or the bland red ones, can be eaten raw or cooked. Apples pair well with cheeses, rich meats such as pork, gammon, duck, and game, and with nuts, other fruits, sweet spices, and chocolate.

Apples grown in cooler climates have the best flavour. There are numerous eating and cooking apple varieties, but only the bright, round, perfect ones are commercially cultivated.

Cox's Orange Pippin This scented, mottled yellow-green apple with an orange-red flush has a crisp and juicy flesh. Its superb flavour has made it one of the favourite dessert apples.

Fiesta Also known as Red Pippin, this variety is a Cox's offspring. It has a sweet flavour with slight acidity, and is greatly preferred for juicing.

Pink Lady (Cripps Pink) One of the best-looking apple varieties available, this eating apple has a strong pink blush, tender skin, crisp and firm flesh, and a well-balanced flavour.

how to core, peel, and chop apples

Apples can be cored, then stuffed and baked with their skin on; or peeled and cut into rings or slices; or after coring and peeling, chopped into neat pieces, depending on the recipe.

1 To core, push a corer straight into the stalk of the apple and through to the bottom. Twist and loosen the core, then pull it out with the corer.

2 Using a peeler or a sharp paring knife, gently remove the skin of the apple by making a circular path around the body from top to bottom.

3 Place the cored apple on its side and slice down to make rings. To chop, stack the rings. Slice through at regular intervals to cut into small, even pieces.

Granny Smith Originally Australian, this largish apple has glossy, luminous green skin (that turns yellow in some climates) and firm, crunchy flesh. Its intensely sharp flavour adds interest to fruit salads.

Royal Gala This variety is a cross between Golden Delicious and Cox's Orange Pippin. It is a medium-sized fruit with a crisp, sweet, and juicy flesh.

Edward VII A well-known variety of cooking apple, this is green-skinned with a delicate taste, which works well with added flavourings such as blackberries or sweet spices.

▼ **Golden Delicious** A popular supermarket variety, the thin-skinned fruit is crisp, sugary, and mild. They are best kept chilled for eating fresh, but are also good baked.

◄ **Egremont Russet** This golden, classic russet apple has a dry, but excellent, sweet-sharp flesh. Used in savoury salads, it is a perfect partner for cheese.

The colour of Golden Delicious ranges from pale green to yellow-gold.

◄ **Bramley's Seedling** This variety is a classic cooking apple. It is a large, green-skinned apple with an acidic, fragrant flesh.

essentials
varieties available
Numerous sweet eating varieties including all the pippins, russets, red-skinned and green-skinned ones plus several popular sour cooking apples.

buy Choose unblemished fruit with firm, unwrinkled skin and a faint aroma around the stem.

store Can be kept in open bags at the bottom of the fridge for several weeks; transfer to the fruit bowl as needed.

cook Slice or chop for tarts, pies, or fritters; or poach and purée for sauces. Core and bake whole.

preserve Bottle in syrup; make into chutney or apple butter; dry in rings, or freeze.

recipe ideas
Apple and blackberry Brown Betty p332

Apple and cinnamon oat cookies p339

Apple jalousie p332

Beetroot and apple soup p254

Tarte tatin p336

Toffee apple tray bake p345

flaky pear tartlets

These are a party favourite, a spectacular contrast of hot and cold, and need very little last-minute preparation.

🥣 35–40 MINS PLUS CHILLING   🍲 30–40 MINS

SERVES 8

450g (1lb) ready-made all-butter puff pastry

1 egg beaten with ½ tsp salt, to glaze

200g (7oz) caster sugar

120ml (4fl oz) double cream

4 pears

juice of 1 lemon

For the Chantilly cream

120ml (4fl oz) double cream

1–2 tsp icing sugar

½ tsp vanilla extract

1 Sprinkle 2 baking sheets with cold water. Roll out the puff pastry dough, cut in half lengthways, then cut diagonally at 10cm (4in) intervals along the length of each piece, to make 8 diamond shapes. Transfer to the baking sheets and brush with the glaze. With the tip of a knife, score a border around each. Chill for 15 minutes.

2 Preheat the oven to 220°C (425°F/Gas 7). Bake the cases for about 15 minutes, until they start to brown, then reduce the temperature to 190°C (375°F/Gas 5) and bake for 20–25

minutes more, until golden and crisp. Transfer to wire racks to cool, then cut out the lid from each case and scoop out any under-cooked pastry from inside.

3 Put 120ml (4fl oz) water in a saucepan and dissolve 150g (5½oz) of the sugar. Boil, without stirring, until golden. Reduce the heat. Remove from the heat, stand back, and add the cream. Heat gently until the caramel dissolves. Cool.

4 Whip the cream for the Chantilly cream until soft peaks form. Add the icing sugar and vanilla, and continue whipping until stiff peaks form. Chill.

5 Butter a baking sheet. Heat the grill. Peel and core the pears. Thinly slice lengthways, keeping attached at the stalk end. Flatten with your fingers, transfer to the sheet, brush with lemon, and sprinkle with the remaining sugar. Grill until caramelized.

6 Transfer the pastry cases to plates and place Chantilly cream and a pear fan in each. Pour a little cold caramel sauce over each fan and partially cover with the pastry lids.

tarte tatin

The special deliciousness of this upside-down tart comes from cooking the apples in the caramel itself.

🥣 45–50 MINS PLUS CHILLING   🍲 20–25 MINS

SERVES 8

14–16 apples, about 2.4kg (5lb 6oz)

1 lemon, halved

125g (4½oz) unsalted butter

200g (7oz) caster sugar

250g (9oz) ready-made sweet shortcrust pastry

crème fraîche, to serve

1 With a vegetable peeler, carefully peel the apples, then halve and core them. Rub the apples all over with the cut lemon to prevent discoloration.

2 Melt the butter in a heavy, ovenproof frying pan. Add the sugar. Cook over a medium heat, stirring occasionally, for 3–5 minutes, until caramelized to a deep golden brown. Remove from the heat and allow to cool to tepid. Arrange the apple halves over in concentric circles to fill the pan, packing them tightly.

3 Cook the apples over a high heat for 15–25 minutes, until caramelized. Turn once to caramelize on both sides. Remove from the heat and leave to cool for 10–15 minutes.

4 Meanwhile, preheat the oven to 190°C (375°F/Gas 5). Roll out the pastry to a circle about 2.5cm (1in) larger than the pan. Roll up the dough around the rolling pin, then drape it over the pan. Tuck the edges around the apples. Bake for 20–25 minutes, until golden brown. Let cool, then set a plate on top, hold firmly together, and invert. If any apples stick to the pan, replace on the tart. Spoon some caramel over the apples. Serve with crème fraîche.

variation

pear tarte tatin

Substitute the apples for 12–14 well-flavoured, firm pears (about 2.4kg/5lb 6oz total weight). Peel, halve, and core the pears and rub them with lemon. Caramelize the pears as directed in the main recipe, arranging them with the tapered ends pointing inwards. Cook until the liquid completely evaporates; this may take longer than the apples. Top with the pastry and bake as before.

apple tart

When Bramley apples are in season, it is the classic apple tart that comes to mind. Slice the apples thinly for a pretty effect.

🥄 10 MINS   🍲 25 MINS   ❄️ FREEZABLE

SPECIAL EQUIPMENT ▪ 20cm (8in) round fluted tart tin ▪ ceramic baking beans

SERVES 6

225g (8oz) ready-made sweet shortcrust pastry

1 egg, beaten

4 Bramley apples, peeled, cored, and thinly sliced

2-3 tbsp golden caster sugar

knob of butter

1 Preheat the oven to 220°C (425°F/ Gas 7). On a lightly floured surface, roll the pastry out as thinly as you can. Use to line the tart tin, pressing it into the corners. Trim away the excess and prick the bottom all over with a fork. Line the pastry shell with greaseproof paper and fill with ceramic baking beans. Bake in the oven for 10 minutes, or until the edges are golden. Remove the beans and paper, brush the bottom of the shell with a little of the egg wash, and return to the oven for 2–3 minutes to crisp. Remove from the oven and set aside. Allow the tart case to cool, but leave the oven on.

2 Arrange the apple slices in the tart case in a neat, overlapping design. Sprinkle with the sugar and dot with the butter. Bake in the oven for 10–15 minutes, or until the apples begin to caramelize and the pastry is golden. Leave to cool. Remove from the tin and place on a plate to serve.

variation

apple and custard tart

Make and bake the pastry case as before. Make a custard by whisking 1½ tbsp each of plain flour and cornflour with 3 tbsp caster sugar, 200ml (7fl oz) milk, and 1 large egg together in a saucepan until smooth. Bring to the boil, whisking, and cook for 2 minutes. Add a few drops of vanilla extract. Transfer to the pastry case and spread evenly. Top with the sliced cooking apples, then glaze and bake as before.

cinnamon and plum cobbler

Use really ripe plums for this recipe. The brown sugar and cinnamon will add a sweet, dark, spicy flavour to them.

🥄 20 MINS   🍲 30 MINS

SPECIAL EQUIPMENT ▪ 1.7-litre (3-pint) ovenproof dish

SERVES 6-8

1kg (2¼lb) plums, stoned and halved

50g (1¾oz) light soft brown sugar

1 tsp cinnamon

25g (scant 1oz) unsalted butter, chilled and diced

For the cobbler

225g (8oz) self-raising flour

2 tsp baking powder

75g (2½oz) caster sugar

½–¾ tsp ground cinnamon, to taste

salt

75g (2½oz) unsalted butter

1 egg

100ml (3½fl oz) buttermilk

1 tbsp light soft brown sugar

ice cream, custard, or cream, to serve (optional)

1 Preheat the oven to 190°C (375°F/ Gas 5). Toss the plum halves with the sugar and cinnamon. Put them in the dish and dot with the butter.

2 To make the cobbler, sift the flour, baking powder, sugar, cinnamon, and a pinch of salt into a bowl. Rub in the butter until the mixture resembles fine crumbs. Whisk together the egg and the buttermilk. Add the liquid to the dry ingredients and bring together to form a soft, sticky dough.

3 Drop heaped tablespoonfuls of the dough over the surface of the fruit, leaving a little space between them. Sprinkle with the soft light brown sugar.

4 Bake in the centre of the preheated oven for 30 minutes, or until golden and bubbling. The cobbler is ready when a skewer inserted into the centre of the topping comes out clean. Leave to cool for at least 5 minutes before serving with ice cream, custard, or cream.

Season's best **figs**

These delicate, almost sensual fruits are known for their honeyed, succulent flesh and tiny, crunchy seeds, which bring a unique taste and texture to many dishes. They ripen late summer through autumn and taste phenomenal with cheeses, cream, fruits, and nuts, poached in wine or syrup, or served with rich meats such as game, duck, proscuitto, or liver pâtés.

Native to the Middle East, figs grow widely on deciduous trees or large shrubs in Mediterranean climates, but also thrive in sunny, sheltered positions in cooler regions.

White fig "White" figs cover a range of varieties, but they are in fact typically light green in colour with strawberry-pink flesh that makes them perfect for both eating fresh and preserving.

When ripe, white figs look plump and pale green.

The flesh is loaded with tiny, edible seeds.

Purple fig Brown Turkey and Black Mission are two popular varieties of this type. They are sweet, fragrant, and delicate when ripe, and usually have dark pink or red flesh.

When ripe, fig skin has a delicate white bloom.

Yellow fig This includes a range of yellow-green varieties with flesh that ranges from pale amber to green-yellow and deep red. The pulp is full of seeds that are actually tiny individual fruits.

essentials
varieties available

Numerous varieties of white, yellow, or purple-skinned figs, which range in colour inside from gold to deep red.

buy Ripe figs damage easily. They should be unblemished, feel heavy in the hand, and just yield with a little pressure. A few beads of sugar juice around the stem is a good indication of ripeness.

store Eat as soon as possible, but they can be stored in the fridge for a day; serve at room temperature. Keep underripe figs at room temperature until the skin softens.

cook Enjoy fresh; poach in syrup; bake or stew for sauces and sweet or savoury dishes.

preserve Bottle or make into jam; dry.

recipe ideas

Fig and mulled wine tart p339

Fig and vanilla jam p350

Fresh figs in honey syrup p244

Figs with cassis mascarpone p220

Lamb tagine with walnuts and figs p320

Seared halloumi cheese with figs p253

honey-grilled figs with zabaglione

The figs in this dish are lightly caramelized when grilled, smothered in lime-scented honey, and are then set on a sweet sherry foam for a truly decadent dessert.

🥣 **10 MINS**   🍲 **5 MINS**

SPECIAL EQUIPMENT ▪ electric hand whisk

SERVES 4

4 large figs

grated zest and juice of 1 lime

2 tbsp clear honey

2 eggs

30g (1oz) caster sugar

3 tbsp sweet sherry

1 Cut the figs in half not quite right through so they are "butterflied". Place in a shallow bowl, add the lime juice, and gently toss.

2 Half-fill a pan with water and set over a medium heat to bring to a simmer. Preheat the grill. Warm the honey in a small heatproof bowl (under the grill or in the pan of heating water) and mix with the grated lime zest. Place the figs on oiled foil in a shallow flameproof dish. Drizzle all over with the honey. Grill for 4–5 minutes until caramelized at the edges.

3 Meanwhile, put the eggs, sugar, and sherry in a heatproof bowl over the pan of simmering water. Whisk with an electric hand whisk until voluminous, pale, thick, and foamy.

4 Spoon the zabaglione into shallow glass serving dishes and carefully place a caramelized fig in the centre of each. Drizzle the honey juices from the foil around each fig and serve immediately.

apple and cinnamon oat cookies

Adding grated apple to the biscuit dough makes these cookies deliciously soft and chewy.

🥣 **20 MINS**   🍲 **10-15 MINS**   ❄ **FREEZABLE**

SPECIAL EQUIPMENT ▪ electric hand whisk

MAKES 24

100g (3½oz) unsalted butter, softened

200g (7oz) light soft brown sugar

1 egg

1 tsp vanilla extract

1 tbsp runny honey

125g (4½oz) self-raising flour, sifted

125g (4½oz) oats

2 tsp cinnamon

salt

2 apples, peeled, cored, and finely grated

a little milk, if needed

1 Preheat the oven to 190°C (375°F/ Gas 5). Line 2 or 3 baking sheets with baking parchment. Put the butter and sugar in a bowl and cream together with an electric hand whisk until pale and creamy. Add the egg, vanilla extract, and honey, and beat well until smooth.

2 With a wooden spoon, stir the flour, oats, and cinnamon, together with a pinch of salt, into the creamed mixture to combine. Mix in the apples. If the mixture seems too stiff, add a little milk. Take walnut-sized pieces of dough and roll them into a ball between your palms. Place on the prepared baking sheets and flatten slightly, leaving space for the biscuits to spread.

3 Bake for 10–15 minutes until golden brown. Leave to cool slightly and then transfer to a wire rack to cool completely.

fig and mulled wine tart

With their delicate flavour, figs call for the simplest treatment.

🥣 **25-30 MINS PLUS CHILLING**   🍲 **15-20 MINS**

SPECIAL EQUIPMENT ▪ 25cm (10in) round loose-bottomed fluted tart tin

SERVES 6-8

375g (13oz) ready-made sweet shortcrust pastry

250ml (9fl oz) milk

½ vanilla pod, split lengthways

3 egg yolks

3 tbsp caster sugar

2 tbsp flour

10g (¼oz) unsalted butter

90ml (3fl oz) double cream, whipped

pared zest of 1 orange

pared zest of 1 lemon

1 nutmeg, crushed

100g (3½oz) caster sugar

5cm (2in) piece of cinnamon stick

2 whole cloves

500ml (16fl oz) dry red wine

500g (1lb 2oz) figs, skins pricked

1 Preheat the oven to 190°C (375°F/ Gas 5). Butter the tart tin. Roll out the pastry on a floured surface and use to line the tin. Chill for 15 minutes, then bake for 15–20 minutes until golden. Put on a wire rack, loosen the tin, and let the pastry cool.

2 For the pastry cream, bring the milk and vanilla to the boil in a pan. Remove from the heat. In a bowl, whisk the egg yolks and sugar until thick. Stir in the flour and then the hot milk. Return to the pan. Bring to the boil, whisking, until thickened. Reduce the heat and cook, whisking, for about 2 minutes, until it softens. Remove from the heat, discard the vanilla pod, and transfer to a bowl. Rub the butter over and chill for 30 minutes. Fold in the whipped cream.

3 Put the zest and nutmeg into a pan with the sugar, spices, and wine. Heat, stirring, to dissolve the sugar. Bring to the boil, then add the figs. Poach for 3–5 minutes, until the figs are tender. Remove the figs and set aside. Simmer the syrup until reduced to about 120ml (4fl oz). Strain and cool. Halve the figs, then cut them nearly through into quarters. Spread the pastry cream over the chilled pastry shell and arrange the figs on top. Spoon 1–2 tbsp syrup over the figs. Just before serving, spoon over the rest.

blackberry brioche with mascarpone

This is the ultimate in fast desserts, yet it looks impressive and is incredibly tasty. It is pleasing to think that an afternoon's blackberry picking can give such rewarding results.

🥣 5 MINS   🍲 10 MINS

SERVES 4

50g (1¾oz) butter

50g (1¾oz) caster sugar

400g (14oz) blackberries

4–8 slices of brioche

200g (7oz) mascarpone cheese

1 Melt the butter in a frying pan. Add the sugar and allow it to melt and start to turn golden brown, shaking the pan to dissolve the sugar.

2 Add the blackberries to the pan and allow them to cook over a high heat for 2–3 minutes, until they are heated through and softened, but have not broken up. Leave the berries to cool slightly while you toast the slices of brioche.

3 Thickly spread the mascarpone cheese over the slices of toasted brioche and top with the sugary, fried berries. Spoon over any excess juice that is left in the pan and serve.

variation

spiced blackberry and pear toasties with mascarpone

Prepare in the same way, but use 200g (7oz) blackberries and 2 ripe pears, peeled, cored, and diced, and add to the pan at step 2 with ½ tsp mixed spice. Toast 8 slices of fruit bread instead of the brioche, and spread with the mascarpone in the same way as before. For a low-fat alternative, use quark instead of mascarpone.

blackberry and apple sponge

There are many different ways to use blackberries and with the onset of shorter, cooler days, combining them with apples beneath a steaming layer of sponge is truly comforting.

🥣 20 MINS   🍲 50 MINS   ❄ FREEZABLE

SPECIAL EQUIPMENT ▪ electric hand whisk ▪ 1.2-litre (2-pint) ovenproof dish

SERVES 6

125g (4½oz) butter, softened

125g (4½oz) caster sugar

2 large eggs

175g (6oz) self-raising flour, sifted

2 Bramley apples, peeled, cored, and roughly chopped

250g (9oz) blackberries

2 tbsp caster sugar

icing sugar, to dust (optional)

1 Preheat the oven to 180°C (350°F/Gas 4). Put the butter and sugar in a bowl and cream together with an electric hand whisk until pale and creamy. Beat in the eggs, one at a time, adding 1 tbsp of the flour after each egg. Mix in the remaining flour and set aside. Put the apples and blackberries in the ovenproof dish, then stir in the caster sugar along with 2 tbsp cold water. Spoon the sponge mixture over the top and smooth the surface.

2 Bake for 50 minutes, or until golden brown and firm to the touch; a skewer should come out clean when inserted in the centre. Dust with icing sugar, if using, and serve while steaming hot.

variation

poached pears with chocolate sponge

Poach 4 peeled, cored, and halved pears in light syrup. Drain and place in the ovenproof dish. Add 2 tbsp of the syrup. Make the sponge in the same way, but replace 25g (scant 1oz) of the plain flour with cocoa powder. Spoon over and bake as before. Serve the pear syrup separately.

trio of sorbets

What better way to enjoy the essence of fresh fruit? This trio of blackberry, pear, and mango sorbets makes a pretty picture in a bowl. If you prefer, choose your favourite fruit and increase the quantities to make just one of the sorbets.

🥣 40–50 MINS PLUS FREEZING   🍲 15–20 MINS   ❄️ FREEZABLE

SPECIAL EQUIPMENT ▪ food processor ▪ ice cream maker

SERVES 8

300g (10oz) sugar, plus more if needed

400g (14oz) blackberries, plus more if needed

3 lemons, plus more if needed

750g (1lb 10oz) ripe pears

about 2 tbsp Poire Williams liqueur

625g (1lb 6oz) ripe mangoes, peeled, stone removed, and roughly chopped

1 Put the sugar and 375ml (13fl oz) water in a pan and heat until the sugar has dissolved. Bring to the boil and cook without stirring for 2–3 minutes, until the syrup is clear. Pour into a measuring jug and let it cool.

2 Put the blackberries in a food processor and blitz to a purée. Work it through a sieve held over a bowl, to remove the seeds. There should be 175ml (6fl oz) purée. If necessary, purée a few more berries.

3 Squeeze the lemons; there should be just over 120ml (4fl oz) juice. Keep the lemon halves. Add 4 tbsp water, 2 tbsp of the lemon juice, and one-third of the sugar syrup to the blackberry purée. Taste and stir in more lemon or sugar if needed. Chill, then taste again. Pour the mixture into an ice cream maker and churn until firm. Meanwhile, chill a bowl in the freezer. Transfer the sorbet to

the chilled bowl. Cover and freeze for at least 4 hours, to allow the flavour to mellow. Wash the food processor.

4 For the pear sorbet, pour half the remaining syrup into a small pan. Add 2 tbsp of the lemon juice. Peel, core, and quarter the pears, and rub with the reserved lemon halves. Cut the pear into chunks and drop them into the pan of syrup. Bring to the boil, then reduce the heat and simmer the pears for 5–10 minutes, until soft and translucent. Purée with their syrup in the food processor. Work through a sieve held over a bowl. There should be nearly 500ml (16fl oz) pear purée. Stir in the liqueur and taste, adding

more liqueur, lemon juice, or sugar if needed. Freeze the sorbet, as for the blackberry sorbet.

5 For the mango sorbet, clean the food processor once again and put the mango flesh into it. Add the remaining sugar syrup and lemon juice. Purée until smooth. There should be nearly 500ml (16fl oz) purée. Taste and add more lemon juice or sugar, if needed. Freeze as for the blackberry sorbet.

6 Soften all the sorbets in the fridge for 30 minutes before serving, so the true flavours emerge. Scoop the sorbets into bowls, and serve with fresh fruit, if desired.

Season's best **pears**

These delectable fruits are harvested in autumn and stored for the winter. Their fine, granular, white flesh is soft, juicy, and perfumed. Pears ripen from the inside out and pass from rock-hard to woolly very quickly, so they should be eaten as soon as possible, once ripe. They are great with cheeses, pork, game and cured meats, walnuts, sweet spices, such as star anise, ginger, cinnamon, and cloves. Their marriage partner is chocolate.

Pears are often picked when not quite ripe, to prevent them from deteriorating too quickly. They are related to the apple but, generally, have a shorter season.

Concorde This variety looks like a more regular, pear-shaped Conference pear, pictured right. It has an exceptionally good flavour.

Beurré Bosc Recognized by its long, tapered neck, lengthy stalk, and dark green-yellow russeted skin, this variety has an aromatic, crisp, and sweetly spicy flesh. It holds its shape well when poached or baked.

Doyenné du Comice Considered to be the best-flavoured dessert pear, the creamy-pink flesh of this variety is juicy, with a melting texture and spicy flavour. Serve fresh as a special dessert.

how to core and peel pears for poaching

Peeled fruit can absorb the poaching flavours better. It is more pleasant not to have to fiddle with the core when eating the poached fruit, though removing the core first is not essential.

1 Use a melon baller or a small spoon to scoop out the small core through the base of the pear.

2 Use a vegetable peeler or a small, sharp knife to pare off the skin thinly and evenly, leaving the stalk in place.

Conference You can identify this pear by its long, thin shape and russeting on the skin, that turns from green to yellow as the fruit ripens. Sweet, creamy, and juicy, it is perfect for fruit salads as well as poaching, baking, or bottling.

It is often irregular in shape, even bent, but that doesn't alter its excellent flavour.

It is golden-skinned with a deep flavour and good, juicy flesh.

Williams Bon Chrétien Also known as Bartlett, this aromatic pear is traditionally pear-shaped with a rounded bell on the bottom half of the fruit, and a definitive shoulder with a smaller neck.

Red Williams A dual-purpose pear that ripens in late summer or early autumn. It is juicy with a smooth texture and red skin.

essentials
varieties available
Several varieties with green, yellow, or red skin that is sometimes russeted.

buy When ripe, the stalk end should yield gently if pressed. Never buy pears that are too soft or bruised, and always handle with care as they damage easily. Brown russeting is normal.

store Ripen hard fruit in a paper bag at room temperature. Once ripe, keep in open bags at the bottom of the fridge, but serve at room temperature.

cook Eat raw when ripe, or poach or bake. Can be stuffed.

preserve Use in pickles and chutneys; bottle in syrup or alcohol; make fruit butter.

recipe ideas

Chocolate and pear meringue roulade p345

Pear and blackberry freezer jam p352

Pear and cinnamon strudel p344

Pear, fennel, and walnut salad p276

Pear pie with walnut pastry p344

Pears poached in red wine and thyme p414

pear pie with walnut pastry

In this speciality from central France, wedges of pear are sandwiched between a double crust of walnut pastry. Serve the pie warm, with crème fraîche or whipped cream.

🥣 35–40 MINS PLUS CHILLING   🍲 35–40 MINS

SPECIAL EQUIPMENT ▪ 23cm (9in) round loose-bottomed fluted tart tin

SERVES 6-8

75g (2½oz) walnuts, very finely chopped

500g (1lb 2oz) ready-made sweet shortcrust pastry

875g (1lb 15oz) pears

½ tsp freshly ground black pepper

juice of 1 lemon

1 tbsp caster sugar

1 Preheat the oven to 190°C (375°F/Gas 5) and brush the tart tin with melted butter. Lightly flour the work surface and knead the walnuts into the pastry. Roll out two-thirds of the dough into a 28cm (11in) round and line the tin, trimming the edges. Rewrap all excess dough and return to the fridge. Chill the pastry shell for about 1 hour, until very firm.

2 Peel, core, and quarter the pears, then put in a bowl and toss with the pepper and lemon juice. Arrange the pear wedges in a cartwheel pattern on the bottom of the pastry shell. Roll out the remaining dough into a 25cm (10in) round; stamp out a 5cm (2in) round from the centre. Place the 25cm (10in) round over the pears, trim, and press the edges together firmly to seal.

3 Brush the top of the pie with water and sprinkle with the sugar. Chill the pie for about 15 minutes until firm. Meanwhile, heat a baking sheet in the oven. Put the pie on the baking sheet so the heat starts to cook the pastry base immediately, and bake the pie for 35–40 minutes until the pastry is browned and the pears are tender when pierced with a metal skewer. If the top crust threatens to scorch before the pie is ready, cover it loosely with foil and continue to bake until the fruit is tender.

pear and cinnamon strudel

Here you have a favourite dessert from Austria, but filled with a variation on the usual: in place of tart apples, there are sweet pears, which complement cinnamon just as happily.

🥣 10 MINS   🍲 35–40 MINS   ❄ FREEZABLE

SERVES 6

4 ripe pears, peeled, cored, and diced

2 tsp ground cinnamon

handful of raisins

1-2 tbsp golden caster sugar

4 sheets of filo pastry

50g (1¾oz) butter, melted

icing sugar, for dusting

1 Preheat the oven to 200°C (400°F/Gas 6). For the filling, place the pear, cinnamon, raisins, and sugar in a bowl and mix well. Set aside.

2 Lay a sheet of filo pastry on a large piece of baking parchment. Brush the filo sheet with some of the melted butter and lay a second sheet on top. Repeat to form 4 layers of filo. Spoon the pear filling down the middle of the layered filo sheets leaving a 5cm (2in) gap at each end.

3 Using the baking parchment, carefully lift one side of the filo over the filling. Brush this edge with melted butter (to help the second side stick).

Again, use the baking paper to help lift the second side of the filo over the filling, overlapping the filo and enveloping the filling. Lightly seal. Seal the ends with melted butter and trim any excess pastry from the ends.

4 Line a large baking tray with baking parchment. Lift the strudel onto the tray and, using the paper to help, roll the strudel over so the seam is on the bottom. Brush the strudel all over with melted butter and bake in the oven for 35–40 minutes, or until golden brown on top. Dust with icing sugar and serve with ice cream or a dollop of crème fraîche.

variation

apple and cinnamon strudel

For a more classic strudel, use the same quantity of apples in place of the pears. Make the dessert in exactly the same way.

pumpkin pie

This delicate version of the classic American dessert has seasonally warm tones of cinnamon and mixed spice. Serve it with thick cream or vanilla ice cream, if you like.

🥄 **30 MINS**   🍲 **1 HR – 1 HR 15 MINS**

SPECIAL EQUIPMENT ▪ 22cm (9in) round loose-bottomed tart tin ▪ food processor ▪ ceramic baking beans

SERVES 6–8

325g (11oz) ready-made sweet shortcrust pastry

3 eggs

100g (3½oz) light soft brown sugar

1 tsp ground cinnamon

1 tsp mixed spice

200ml (7fl oz) double cream

400g (14oz) roasted and puréed pumpkin, or 425g can processed pumpkin

1 Preheat the oven to 180°C (350°F/ Gas 4). Roll out the pastry on a floured surface to a thickness of 3mm (⅛in) and line the tin, leaving an overlapping edge of at least 2cm (¾in). Prick the base all over with a fork. Line the pastry case with baking parchment and weigh it down with ceramic baking beans. Place the case on a baking sheet and blind bake for 20 minutes. Remove the beans and the paper and return to the oven for 5 minutes if the centre is uncooked.

2 In a large bowl, whisk together the eggs, sugar, spices, and cream. Then beat in the pumpkin until smooth. Partially pull out an oven rack from the oven and place the pastry case on it. Pour the filling into the case and slide the rack back into the oven.

3 Bake for 45–50 minutes until the filling is quite set, but before it begins to bubble up at the edges. Trim the pastry edge while still warm, then leave the pie to cool in its tin for at least 15 minutes before turning out.

toffee apple tray bake

Smothered in toffee sauce, this apple sponge cake is sure to please. Serve warm or cold with a spoonful of crème fraîche.

🥄 **20 MINS**   🍲 **45 MINS**

SPECIAL EQUIPMENT ▪ electric hand whisk ▪ 22 x 30cm (8¾ x 12in) baking tin

MAKES 18

350g (12oz) Bramley apples, peeled, cored, and thinly sliced

squeeze of lemon juice

350g (12oz) self-raising flour

2 tsp baking powder

350g (12oz) light soft brown sugar

4 large eggs, lightly beaten

225g (8oz) butter, melted

1 tbsp caster sugar

For the toffee sauce

100g (3½oz) butter

100g (3½oz) light soft brown sugar

1 tbsp lemon juice

salt

1 Preheat the oven to 180°C (350°F/ Gas 4). Line the base and sides of the tin with baking parchment. Toss the apple slices in a bowl with the lemon juice to prevent discolouration.

2 Sift the flour into a large mixing bowl, add the baking powder and brown sugar, and stir well. Mix in the eggs and melted butter to make a smooth batter. Pour into the tin and smooth the top. Arrange the apple slices in three or four long lines along the top of the mixture and sprinkle with the caster sugar. Bake for 45 minutes, or until the cake is firm to the touch and a skewer comes out clean when inserted in the centre.

3 Meanwhile, make the sauce by melting the butter, sugar, and lemon juice in a pan with a pinch of salt, whisking with an electric hand whisk until the mixture is thick and smooth. Leave to cool slightly. Pour the sauce over the cake while it is still in the tin, brushing the sauce over the top. Cut into squares and serve.

chocolate and pear meringue roulade

To help you roll the meringue into the roulade, use the baking parchment, pulling it back from the meringue as you roll.

🥄 **25 MINS**   🍲 **15 MINS**   ❄️ **FREEZABLE**

SPECIAL EQUIPMENT ▪ electric hand whisk ▪ 25 x 35cm (10 x 14in) Swiss roll tin

SERVES 8

5 egg whites, at room temperature

225g (8oz) caster sugar

½ tsp white wine vinegar

1 tsp cornflour

½ tsp vanilla extract

30g (1oz) cocoa powder, sifted

icing sugar, for dusting

250ml (9fl oz) double cream, whipped

3 small pears, peeled, cored, and diced

1 Preheat the oven to 180°C (350°F/ Gas 4) and line the tin with baking parchment. Beat the egg whites with an electric hand whisk until stiff peaks form. Continuing to whisk, add the caster sugar, a little at a time. Gently fold in the vinegar, cornflour, vanilla extract, and cocoa powder. Pour the mixture into the tin, smooth the surface, and bake in the centre of the oven for 15 minutes. Remove from the oven and let it cool.

2 Carefully turn the meringue out of the tin onto another piece of baking parchment dusted with icing sugar. Spread the cream over the underside of the roulade with a palette knife. Sprinkle the pears over it. Roll the meringue up around the cream filling. Place seam-side down on a serving plate, cover, and chill. Sift over icing sugar to serve.

variation

chocolate, fig, and lime roulade

Prepare the roulade in the same way. For the filling, poach 6 ripe figs in syrup (115g/4oz sugar and 300ml/10fl oz water) with the juice of 1 lime for 10 minutes. Cool, drain, chop, discarding the stalks, and mix with the finely grated zest of the lime. Use instead of the pears in the filling.

red grape and cinnamon cake

Eat this delightful cake warm as a dessert with cream, yogurt, or custard, or cold with a cup of coffee. The grapes turn into a layer of sticky fruit on top of the cake and keep it moist.

🥣 **30 MINS**   🍲 **50 MINS**

SPECIAL EQUIPMENT ▪ 20cm (8in) round springform cake tin ▪ blender or food processor

SERVES 6–8

300g (10oz) red grapes, halved lengthways

2 tbsp light soft brown sugar

150g (5½oz) caster sugar

150g (5½oz) butter, softened

3 eggs

½ tsp vanilla extract

150g (5½oz) self-raising flour

1 tsp ground cinnamon

1 heaped tsp baking powder

1 Preheat the oven to 180°C (350°F/Gas 4). Line the cake tin with greaseproof paper. Spread the grapes evenly, skin-side down, on the bottom of the cake tin and scatter the brown sugar over the top.

2 Put the caster sugar and butter in a blender or food processor and blitz. When the mixture is smooth, add the eggs and vanilla extract and pulse to mix well. Add the flour, cinnamon, and baking powder and pulse the mixture again briefly until it is blended.

3 Spread the sponge mixture over the grapes. Place the cake tin on a baking tray and bake in the centre of the oven for approximately 50 minutes until risen and golden brown and a skewer through the middle comes out clean. Turn the cake out onto a serving plate, carefully peeling off the greaseproof paper to reveal the grape topping. Serve warm or cold.

variation

green grape, spice, and orange cake

Prepare in the same way, but use 300g (10½oz) green grapes instead of red. Flavour the sponge with the finely grated zest of 1 orange and 1 tsp mixed spice, instead of the cinnamon.

schiacciata di uva

This sweet Italian "squashed" bread is similar to a sweetened focaccia, and can be served either warm or cold.

🥣 **25 MINS PLUS RISING AND PROVING**   🍲 **20–25 MINS**

SPECIAL EQUIPMENT ▪ 20 x 30cm (8 x 12in) Swiss roll tin

MAKES 1

700g (1lb 9oz) strong white bread flour

1 tsp fine salt

2 tbsp caster sugar

1½ tsp dried yeast

1 tbsp olive oil

500g (1lb 2oz) small red seedless grapes, washed

3 tbsp caster sugar

1 tbsp finely chopped rosemary (optional)

1 Put the flour, salt, and sugar into a large bowl. Dissolve the yeast in 450ml (15fl oz) warm water, then add the oil. Gradually pour the yeast mixture into the flour mixture, stirring to form a soft dough. Knead for 10 minutes on a floured work surface until smooth, glossy, and elastic. The dough should remain soft. Put the dough in a lightly oiled bowl and cover it loosely with cling film. Leave to rise in a warm place for up to 2 hours until doubled in size.

2 Turn the dough out onto a floured work surface and gently knock it back. Knead it briefly and divide it into 2 portions, with roughly one-third of the dough in one and two-thirds in the other. Lightly oil the Swiss roll tin.

3 Take the largest piece of dough and roll it out roughly to the size of the tin. Place it in the tin and stretch it out to fill the tin, using your fingers to mould it to the sides. Scatter two-thirds of the grapes over the surface and sprinkle with 2 tbsp caster sugar.

4 Roll out the smaller piece of dough to fit on top of the grapes, stretching it out with your hands if necessary. Scatter the remaining grapes, and the chopped rosemary (if using) on the surface. Place the dough on a large baking tray and cover it loosely with lightly oiled cling film and a clean tea towel. Leave it to prove in a warm place for up to 1 hour until well risen and almost doubled in size. Preheat the oven to 200°C (400°F/Gas 6).

5 Scatter the remaining tbsp of caster sugar on top of the risen dough. Bake for 20–25 minutes until well risen and golden brown. Remove from the oven and allow to cool for at least 10 minutes before serving.

grapes marinated in port

Juicy grapes steeped in port – a sweet dessert wine made of red grapes – have a lovely deep flavour, and are a clever twist on grapes and cheese at the end of a meal.

🥣 **10 MINS PLUS MARINATING**

SERVES 4

bunch of seedless red grapes

bunch of seedless green grapes

drizzle of port

vanilla ice cream, to serve

1 Prick the grapes with a knife, then place them in a large shallow serving dish and drizzle with port. Leave to marinate in the fridge for several hours or overnight.

2 To serve, bring the grapes back to room temperature, then spoon into glass dishes and top with a scoop of vanilla ice cream.

variation

grapes marinated in port with goat's cheese croûtes

Cut each bunch of grapes into 4 small bunches. Prick and marinate as before, turning a few times. Toast 4 diagonal slices of baguette. Top each with slices of goat's cheese and grill until just melted. Serve each croûte with a bunch each of red and green grapes on the side, with the port juices spooned over them.

Season's best **grapes**

These sun-loving fruit are harvested in autumn after the long days of summer. Seeded and seedless varieties in green, red, or black are produced – some for eating, some for wine. Grapes are popularly used in savoury and fruit salads, sauces, poultry stuffings, tarts, and puddings. Good flavour pairings include chicken, fish, cheeses, and nuts. The leaves from the grapevines are also used in the kitchen, and are delicious stuffed.

All grapes need sunshine to ripen but many varieties thrive in temperate climates as well as the hotter countries, which are more famous for wine-making.

Italia This well-known seeded variety of the muscat type of grape has a delicious flowery flavour, juicy flesh, and thin skin. Halve and seed for fruit salads.

Muscat Rosada Also called Moscatel Rosada and Muscat Rosa, this is a gourmet grape with a rich, musky flavour. It has crisp skin and juicy flesh that contains seeds. Reserve for a special fruit dessert or to eat fresh.

Grapes that have been carefully transported retain their dusty "bloom".

Concord The oldest North American grape variety, this has medium to large, blue-black fruit. Eat fresh or use for making deeply coloured jam, jelly, and juice, as well as wine.

Ribier A popular large, seeded variety, this has crisp, jet-black skin and juicy flesh with a mild flavour. A bunch of these is a perfect complement to a cheeseboard.

Choose triangular bunches laden with plump grapes of equal size.

essentials
varieties available

Numerous varieties: green (white), red, or black, seeded or seedless. Also available dried as currants, sultanas, and raisins; wine and juice.

buy Avoid wrinkled grapes or those with brown spots.

store Store unwashed bunches carefully on several layers of kitchen paper or in an open paper bag in the fridge for up to 5 days.

cook Peel or seed, if necessary; sauté for cream and wine sauces; add to poultry stuffings; use in tarts and puddings.

preserve Make into juice or wine.

recipe ideas

Grapes marinated in port p346

Red grape and cinnamon cake p346

Simple grape wine p352

spiced port and plum jam

The addition of some port and cinnamon turns this into a rather special plum jam. Enjoy it dolloped onto hot steamed puddings, or spread onto dark fruit tea breads.

🥣 10 MINS   🍲 30–35 MINS

SPECIAL EQUIPMENT ▪ preserving pan ▪ sugar thermometer

MAKES APPROX 2kg (4½lb)

1.8kg (4lb) dark plums, halved and stoned

1 cinnamon stick, snapped in half

juice of 1 lime

1.35kg (3lb) sugar

2–3 tbsp port (depending on your taste preference)

1 Put the plums, cinnamon stick, and lime juice into a preserving pan or a large heavy-based saucepan, then pour over 600ml (1 pint) water.

2 Simmer gently on a low heat for 15–20 minutes, or until the plums begin to break down and soften.

3 Add the sugar, stir until it has all dissolved, then bring to the boil and keep at a rolling boil for 5–8 minutes, or until the jam begins to thicken and reaches the setting point. Remove the pan from the heat and test for a set with a sugar thermometer or

a wrinkle test (chill a saucer in the fridge before cooking). If you use a thermometer, the temperature must reach 105°C (220°F); the mixture will also thicken around the sides of the pan, boil sluggishly, and the bubbles "plop" rather than froth. Or put 1 tsp jam on the chilled saucer, allow to cool for a moment, then push it with a finger. If it leaves a trail and wrinkles slightly, the jam is set.

4 Lift out the cinnamon stick and discard, stir in the port, then ladle into warm sterilized jars, cover with waxed paper discs, seal, and label. Store in a cool, dark place and refrigerate after opening.

variation

spiced kirsch and plum jam
Make in exactly the same way but flavour the jam with 2 star anise instead of the cinnamon stick and add 2–3 tbsp kirsch instead of the port.

piccalilli

Originally known as "Indian pickle", this classic recipe contains cauliflower, courgettes, beans, and carrots. Its characteristic yellow colour and flavour is due to a turmeric and mustard mix.

🥣 15 MINS PLUS STANDING AND MATURING   🍲 20 MINS

SPECIAL EQUIPMENT ▪ preserving jar

MAKES 2.25kg (5lb)

1 large cauliflower, cut into florets

2 large onions, peeled, quartered, and sliced finely, or use pickling onions

900g (2lb) mixed vegetables such as courgettes, runner beans, carrots, and green beans, cut into bite-sized pieces

60g (2oz) sea salt

2 tbsp plain flour

225g (8oz) granulated sugar (increase this quantity slightly if you don't like the pickle too sharp)

1 tbsp turmeric

60g (2oz) English mustard powder

900ml (1½ pints) ready-spiced pickling vinegar

1 Put all the vegetables in a large non-metallic bowl. Dissolve the sea salt in 1.2 litres (2 pints) of water and pour the brine over the vegetables. Put a plate on top of the vegetables to keep them submerged in the brine and leave for 24 hours.

2 Drain the vegetables and rinse in cold water. Bring a large pan of water to the boil, add the vegetables, and blanch for 2 minutes. Do not overcook – they should remain crunchy. Drain and refresh in cold water.

3 Put the flour, sugar, turmeric, and mustard powder in a small bowl and mix in a little of the vinegar to make a paste. Put the paste in a large stainless steel saucepan along with the remaining vinegar, bring to the boil, and stir continuously so no lumps appear. Reduce the heat and simmer for about 15 minutes

4 Add the vegetables to the sauce and stir well so they are all coated. Ladle into warm sterilized jars with non-metallic or vinegar-proof lids, making sure there are no air gaps, seal, and label. Store in a cool, dark place to allow the flavours to mature for at least 1 month and refrigerate after opening.

baby artichokes in oil

Baby artichokes are a delicacy, and the whole inner choke can be used. Serve as an antipasti or add to fresh pasta.

🥣 **10 MINS PLUS MARINATING**   🍲 **10 MINS**

SPECIAL EQUIPMENT ▪ preserving pan

MAKES APPROX 500g (1lb 2oz)

10 baby artichokes

300ml (10fl oz) white wine vinegar

1 tbsp salt

450ml (15fl oz) extra virgin olive oil

75ml (2½fl oz) white wine vinegar

handful of black peppercorns

1 Trim the artichoke stalks and snap off the hard outside leaves (about 5–6 layers) until you reach the paler, more tender leaves. Cut off about 2.5cm (1in) from the top of each artichoke and discard. Leave whole or cut in half.

2 Put the vinegar, salt, and 300ml (10fl oz) water in a preserving pan or heavy-based, stainless steel saucepan and bring to the boil. Add the prepared artichokes and blanch for 3–5 minutes in the simmering vinegar mix; they should still retain plenty of bite. Drain and leave to cool, then cut lengthways into quarters.

3 For the oil marinade, put the oil, vinegar, and peppercorns into a saucepan and bring to the boil. Add the artichokes and bring back to the boil, then turn the heat off and leave it to cool with the artichokes still sitting in the marinade.

4 Using a slotted spoon, remove the cooled artichokes and put them into a sterilized jar with a non-metallic or vinegar-proof lid. Pour the marinade over the top until the artichokes are completely covered (or you can strain the oil mixture first if you prefer). Seal, label, and store in the fridge. Once opened, keep refrigerated, top up with oil if necessary so the artichokes are always covered, and use within 2 months.

yellow courgette and tomato chutney

Colourful and creamy textured, yellow courgettes are ideal for this chutney – or use any other squash.

🥣 **10 MINS PLUS MATURING**   🍲 **2 HRS 35 MINS**

SPECIAL EQUIPMENT ▪ preserving pan

MAKES APPROX 1kg (2¼lb)

450g (1lb) yellow courgettes, trimmed and diced

250g (9oz) onions, roughly chopped

350g (12oz) ripe tomatoes, roughly chopped

350g (12oz) granulated sugar

300ml (10fl oz) white wine vinegar

1 garlic clove, finely chopped

1cm (½in) piece of fresh root ginger, peeled and finely chopped

¼ tsp dried chilli flakes

large pinch of sweet paprika

large pinch of ground white pepper

½ tsp sea salt

1 Put all the ingredients in a preserving pan or a large heavy-based, stainless steel saucepan.

2 Bring slowly to the boil, stirring to dissolve the sugar. Reduce the heat and simmer for 2½ hours until a wooden spoon drawn across the base of the pan leaves a trail. Stir frequently towards the end so the chutney doesn't catch and burn on the base of the pan. If necessary, turn up the heat towards the end of cooking and boil rapidly until it is thick and glossy.

3 Ladle into warm sterilized jars with non-metallic or vinegar-proof lids, making sure there are no air gaps. Cover each pot with a waxed paper disc, seal, and label. Store in a cool, dark place. Allow the flavours to mature for at least 1 month and refrigerate after opening.

spiced pear pickle

Serve this hot-pickled, sweet-sour pear condiment with cold meats, hamburgers, and cheese, or with rice or spiced dishes.

🥣 **10 MINS PLUS MATURING**   🍲 **25–30 MINS**

SPECIAL EQUIPMENT ▪ preserving pan

MAKES APPROX 900ml (1½ PINTS)

1kg (2¼lb) firm, shapely pears such as Williams or Conference, peeled, cored, and cut into quarters

For the syrup

350g (12oz) granulated sugar

175ml (6fl oz) cider vinegar

zest of ½ lemon

2.5cm (1in) piece of fresh root ginger, peeled and chopped

seeds from 6 cardamom pods

1 For the syrup, put all the syrup ingredients into a preserving pan or a large heavy-based, stainless steel saucepan and bring gently to the boil, stirring to dissolve the sugar. Simmer for 5 minutes, then remove from the heat.

2 Put the quartered pears into the syrup so they are completely covered, and poach gently for about 5–10 minutes until just soft. They are ready when a skewer can be inserted into the flesh. Remove each pear with a slotted spoon as soon as it is ready.

3 Pack the pears into warm sterilized jars. Return the pan of syrup and spices to the heat, bring back to the boil, and cook for 5 more minutes or so. When the boiling syrup has reduced by about a third, pour it over the pears, filling the jars to the brim so it completely covers the pears.

4 To keep the pears submerged, cover with a waxed paper disc. Seal with vinegar-proof lids, label, and store in a cool, dark place for 1 month before using. Refrigerate after opening.

variation

hot spiced pear pickle

Prepare in the same way, but add 2 dried chipotle chillies and 2 small bay leaves to the spice syrup. Tuck them into the jars with the syrup if you like a stronger flavour.

fig and vanilla jam

This rich, densely fruity jam goes well with both sweet and savoury foods – it's delicious with cold ham or cheese. Add a splash of ginger wine at the end for a hint of spice, if you like.

🥣 5 MINS 🥘 45–50 MINS

SPECIAL EQUIPMENT ▪ preserving pan ▪ sugar thermometer

MAKES APPROX 1.1kg (2½lb)

675g (1½lb) ripe figs with soft skins, topped, tailed, and cut into quarters

zest and juice of 1 lemon

1 small cooking apple, peeled, cored, and coarsely chopped

1 vanilla pod, sliced lengthwise

675g (1½lb) granulated sugar

1 Put the figs in a preserving pan or a large heavy-based saucepan with the lemon zest and juice, chopped apple, and vanilla pod. Cook on a low heat for about 20 minutes or so, stirring occasionally, until the figs have softened and broken down.

2 Add the sugar and cook on a low heat, stirring continuously, until the sugar has all dissolved. Then bring to the boil and cook at a rolling boil, stirring occasionally, for about 15–20 minutes or until it reaches the setting point. Skim away any scum as it cooks. Remove the pan from the heat and test for a set with a sugar thermometer or a wrinkle test (chill a saucer in the fridge before cooking). If you use a thermometer, the temperature must reach 105°C (220°F); the mixture will also thicken around the sides of the pan, boil sluggishly, and the bubbles "plop" rather than froth. Or put 1 tsp jam on the chilled saucer, allow to cool for a moment, then push it with a finger. If it leaves a trail and wrinkles slightly, the jam is set.

3 Carefully remove the vanilla pod, then ladle into warm sterilized jars, cover with discs of waxed paper, seal, and label. Store in a cool, dark place and refrigerate after opening.

apple, sultana, and date chutney

This substantial, adaptable chutney gets better with age. Dried cranberries, figs, or dried apricots also complement apples well and can be used instead of the dried dates.

🥣 30 MINS PLUS MATURING 🥘 1 HR 45 MINS

SPECIAL EQUIPMENT ▪ preserving pan

MAKES APPROX 1.8kg

2kg (4½lb) cooking apples (approx 8–10), peeled, cored, and chopped

3 onions, peeled and finely chopped

2.5cm (1in) piece of fresh root ginger, peeled and finely chopped

115g (4oz) sultanas

125g (4½oz) ready-to-eat stoned dates, chopped

1 tsp mustard seeds

1 litre (1¾ pints) cider vinegar

500g (1lb 2oz) granulated sugar

1 Put the apples, onions, ginger, sultanas, dates, and mustard seeds in a preserving pan or a large heavy-based saucepan. Stir everything together, then pour in the cider vinegar and add the sugar.

2 Cook on a low heat, stirring until the sugar has dissolved, then bring to the boil, reduce the heat, and cook gently for about 1½ hours. The mixture is ready when it is thick and sticky, and a wooden spoon drawn across the base of the pan leaves a trail. Stir continuously near the end of the cooking time so that the chutney doesn't catch and burn on the base of the pan.

3 Ladle into warm sterilized jars with non-metallic or vinegar-proof lids, making sure there are no air gaps. Cover with waxed paper discs, seal, and label. Store in a cool, dark place to allow the flavours to mature for 1 month. Refrigerate after opening.

crab apple jelly

Make this jelly while autumn crab apples are in abundance.

🥣 15 MINS PLUS STRAINING   🍲 45 MINS

SPECIAL EQUIPMENT ▪ preserving pan ▪ nylon sieve or jelly bag ▪ sugar thermometer

MAKES APPROX 1.35kg (3lb)

1.1kg (2½lb) crab apples, washed and roughly chopped with the pips and stalks left intact

zest of 1 lemon, thinly pared

about 900g-1.1kg (2-2½lb) granulated sugar (see method)

1 Put the crab apples in a preserving pan or a large heavy-based pan, pour over 1.4 litres (2½ pints) water, and add the lemon zest. Cook gently for 30 minutes, or until the apples become pulpy. Tip the pulp into a nylon sieve or jelly bag set over a large clean bowl and strain overnight.

2 Measure the juice and calculate 450g (1lb) of sugar for every 600ml (1 pint) of juice. Pour the juice back into the cleaned pan and bring to a simmer over a moderate heat. Add the sugar and stir until it has all

dissolved. Bring to the boil and cook at a rolling boil for 10 minutes, or until the setting point is reached. Remove the pan from the heat and test for a set with a sugar thermometer or a wrinkle test (chill a saucer in the fridge before cooking). If you use a thermometer, the temperature must reach 105°C (220°F); the mixture will also thicken around the sides of the pan, boil sluggishly, and the bubbles "plop" rather than froth. Or put 1 tsp jelly on the chilled saucer, allow to cool for a moment, then push it with a finger. If it leaves a trail and wrinkles slightly, the jelly is set.

3 Skim off any surface scum, ladle into warm sterilized jars, cover with waxed paper discs, seal, and label. Store in a cool, dark place and refrigerate after opening.

plum and squash chutney

This is a true autumnal chutney: an inspired combination of plums, apples, and squashes that harmonize beautifully.

🥣 30 MINS PLUS MATURING   🍲 2 HRS 15 MINS - 2 HRS 45 MINS

SPECIAL EQUIPMENT ▪ preserving pan ▪ muslin

MAKES APPROX 1.5kg (3lb 3oz)

500g (1lb 2oz) squash, peeled and cut into cubes

500g (1lb 2oz) plums, stoned and roughly chopped

500g (1lb 2oz) cooking apples, peeled, cored, and diced

250g (9oz) onions, diced

250g (9oz) raisins or sultanas

250g (9oz) light soft brown sugar

400ml (14fl oz) cider or white wine vinegar

1½ tsp dried chilli flakes

½ tsp sea salt

For the spice bag

2 mace blades

1 heaped tsp coriander seeds

12 black peppercorns

12 cloves

2cm (¾in) piece of fresh root ginger, peeled and cut into cubes

1 Tie the spices in a piece of muslin and put the spice bag in a preserving pan or large heavy-based saucepan. Add the other ingredients and heat gently, stirring occasionally, until all the sugar has dissolved.

2 Bring to the boil, turn the heat down, and simmer for 2-2½ hours, stirring occasionally until the mixture thickens and becomes sticky, and a wooden spoon drawn across the base of the pan leaves a trail. Stir frequently near the end of cooking.

3 Ladle into warm sterilized jars with non-metallic or vinegar-proof lids, cover with waxed paper discs, seal, and label. Store in a cool, dark place to mature for 1-2 months and refrigerate after opening.

membrillo

Made from puréed quinces, membrillo is an intensely flavoured fruit cheese that is solid enough to slice. It keeps for 12 months or longer and is excellent with cheeses.

🥣 10 MINS PLUS COOLING AND MATURING   🍲 1 HR 20 MINS

SPECIAL EQUIPMENT ▪ preserving pan ▪ mouli food mill ▪ ramekins

MAKES 750g-1kg (1lb 10oz-2¼lb)

1kg (2¼lb) quinces, scrubbed and roughly chopped

juice of ½ lemon

about 450g (1lb) granulated sugar (see method)

1 Put the quinces in a preserving pan or a large heavy-based saucepan with 600ml (1 pint) water. Add the lemon juice, bring to the boil, and simmer for 30 minutes or so. Once the fruit is soft enough, crush it with a potato masher or fork until it becomes a soft, syrupy pulp. Set the cooked pulp aside to cool.

2 Sieve the pulp in batches over a large, clean bowl, pressing the pulp hard against the sieve with a wooden spoon to extract as much of the purée as possible (or use a mouli food mill). Measure the purée: for every 450ml (15fl oz) of purée, calculate 450g (1lb) of sugar.

3 Put the purée and sugar back in the pan and stir over a low heat to dissolve the sugar. Then bring to

the boil and simmer gently for 45-60 minutes or longer until the purée reduces down to a dark, very thick, glossy paste. It is ready when it makes a "plopping" noise, sticks to the wooden spoon, and leaves a trail if the spoon is scraped across the bottom of the pan. Stir frequently near the end of cooking so the paste doesn't catch and burn on the base of the pan.

4 Lightly grease some warm sterilized ramekin dishes or moulds with a little oil. Spoon in the paste and level the top. Seal with waxed paper discs and cellophane if leaving in the ramekin dishes, otherwise leave to cool. If you are turning the membrillos out of their ramekin dishes, loosen each with a palette knife, turn it out, wrap in waxed paper, and tie with string. Leave to mature in a cool, dark place for 4-6 weeks. Serve thinly sliced with a cheeseboard or platter of cold meats, or as an after-dinner sweetmeat.

simple grape wine

Grapes contain the right amounts of sugar and acids to make wine. Use sterilized equipment to avoid problems like mould.

🍲 **2 HOURS PLUS FERMENTING AND STORING**

SPECIAL EQUIPMENT ▪ hydrometer ▪ litmus paper ▪ muslin ▪ sterilized demijohn ▪ sterilized airlock ▪ sterilized siphon

MAKES 4.5 LITRES (1 GALLON)

5kg (11lb) ripe white grapes, washed, with stalks removed

1 Campden tablet

1 tsp pectolase

up to 1kg (2¼lb) unrefined cane sugar

1 tsp tartaric acid or
   1 tsp potassium carbonate

1 sachet hock wine yeast

1 Put the grapes in a sterilized bucket or container. Using a sterilized plastic potato masher, mash the grapes well. Add the Campden tablet and pectolase and leave for 24 hours.

2 Dissolve 100g (3½oz) of the sugar in 50ml (2fl oz) hot water, allow to cool, and add to the grapes. Repeat the process until a gravity of 1,090 can be read on your hydrometer. Use a litmus paper to test the acid level (the ideal level is 3–3.4 pH). If it is not acidic enough, add the tartaric acid; if it is too acidic, add the potassium carbonate instead. Pour some of the grape mixture into a muslin cloth suspended over a sterilized bowl. Strain the grape mixture in batches to collect all the juice.

3 Pour the collected juice into a demijohn using a sterilized funnel. Add the yeast and attach the airlock. Leave to ferment at 21–24°C (70–75°F) for 3–4 months. Fermentation is complete when the bubbles have stopped and the water in the airlock is level. (To ensure fermentation is finished, move to a warm place for 24 hours to see if the bubbling has truly ceased.)

4 Being careful not to disturb the sediment (which spoils the flavour), draw off the clear liquid using a siphon, bottle into sterilized bottles, leaving 2cm (¾in) of space at the top, and seal. Store in a cool, dark place, ideally a cellar. The wine can be drunk immediately, but is better left for 6 months. Like commercial wine, its keeping qualities will vary, but it can last years.

dried mushrooms

The sweet earthy flavour of mushrooms intensifies when dried and makes them an essential storecupboard ingredient. If dried properly, they will keep for 9–12 months.

🍲 **15 MINS PLUS DRYING**   🍲 **4–6 HOURS**   ❄ **FREEZABLE**

SPECIAL EQUIPMENT ▪ wood-burning stove radiator, boiler, Aga, night storage heater, or warm airing cupboard

MAKES APPROX 60g (2oz)

450g (1lb) brown chestnut, shitaki, and buna-shimeji mushrooms, or freshly picked wild mushrooms

1 Leave any small mushrooms whole and slice the large mushrooms into 5mm–1cm (¼–½in) thick slices. Arrange on trays lined with kitchen paper or wire racks, making sure they don't overlap. Place the trays in the oven on the lowest setting (50–60°C/120–140°F/Gas ¼) for 4–6 hours. If you have an electric oven, leave the door slightly ajar using a skewer. To air-dry the mushrooms, leave the racks or trays 5–10cm (2–4in) above a wood-burning stove radiator, boiler, Aga, night storage heater, or warm airing cupboard, overnight.

2 The mushrooms are ready when they have shrunk to at least half their original size, but are still pliable. Remove the trays from the oven and set aside until the mushrooms are completely cold.

3 Put in glass containers. Add a few grains of rice, if you like, as an extra precaution to help keep the mushrooms dry. Store in a cool, dark place until needed.

pear and blackberry freezer jam

Freezing ripe pears and blackberries as a puréed autumn "jam" is a great way to preserve their fresh flavours and nutrients.

🍲 **10–12 MINS**   🍲 **5–8 MINS**   ❄ **FREEZABLE**

MAKES APPROX 750g (1lb 10oz)

2 ripe pears, peeled, cored, and roughly chopped

225g (8oz) ripe blackberries

2 tbsp lemon juice

1 tsp mixed spice

1 tbsp agar flakes or 1 tsp agar powder

140g (5oz) caster sugar

1 Ensure the fruit is at room temperature, then put in a bowl with the lemon juice and spice. Roughly crush with a potato masher or fork (don't reduce to a smooth pulp).

2 Put 200ml (7fl oz) water in a small saucepan, sprinkle the agar flakes or powder over it, and set aside to soften for 2–3 minutes. Give the pan a gentle swirl, then bring the water slowly to the boil over a low heat without stirring. Simmer gently for 3–5 minutes, stirring occasionally, until the agar has dissolved. Add the sugar and stir over a low heat until it has dissolved for 2–3 minutes. Remove from the heat and pour over the fruit, stirring the fruit gently until the ingredients are well mixed.

3 Pour into clean freezer pots, leaving 1cm (½in) of space at the top. Set aside to cool, then seal and label. Leave overnight in the fridge to thicken, then freeze. To use, thaw in the fridge, then keep refrigerated and use within 2 weeks.

marrow and orange jam

A traditional preserve using young fresh marrows.

🥣 **5 MINS PLUS STANDING**　🍲 **35–40 MINS**

SPECIAL EQUIPMENT ▪ preserving pan ▪ sugar thermometer

MAKES 1.5kg (3lb 3oz)

1 large marrow (approx 900g/2lb), peeled and cut into 1cm (½in) pieces

juice of 2 lemons

900g (2lb) jam sugar

juice of 1 orange and zest of 2 large oranges

1 Put the marrow pieces and lemon juice in a preserving pan or a large heavy-based saucepan. Bring to the boil and simmer for 15 minutes, or until the marrow starts to soften. Add a little water if it starts to dry out and be careful it doesn't burn. This will all depend on the water content of your marrow.

2 Add the sugar and orange juice and zest and heat gently, stirring until all the sugar has dissolved. Turn up the heat and bring to the boil. When the jam reaches a rolling boil, cook for

about 20 minutes, or until it reaches the setting point. Remove the pan from the heat while you test for a set with a sugar thermometer or using a wrinkle test (chill a saucer in the fridge before cooking). If you use a thermometer, the temperature must reach 105°C (220°F); the mixture will also thicken around the sides of the pan, boil sluggishly, and the bubbles "plop" rather than froth. Or put 1 tsp jam on the chilled saucer, allow to cool for a moment, then push it with a finger. If it leaves a trail and wrinkles slightly, it is set.

3 Leave the jam for 5–10 minutes so the marrow pieces are evenly distributed, then ladle into warm sterilized jars, cover with discs of waxed paper, seal, and label. Store the jam in a cool, dark place and refrigerate after opening.

italian-style vegetables

These vegetables are cooked first in vinegar before being stored in oil and refrigerated. Serve with a drizzle of fresh oil, torn basil leaves or chopped parsley, and good bread.

🥣 **20 MINS PLUS MATURING**　🍲 **10 MINS**

MAKES APPROX 675g (1½lb)

600g (1lb 5oz) mixed vegetables (e.g. aubergines, fennel, romanesco florets, courgettes, small shallots, celery, carrots, peppers, button mushrooms)

about 500ml (16fl oz) white wine vinegar

2 tsp granulated sugar

2 tsp sea salt

about 150ml (5fl oz) extra virgin olive oil

seasonings - choose from

1 tsp fennel seeds

1 tsp dried oregano

1 fresh or dried bay leaf

1 sprig of rosemary

1 sprig of lemon thyme

pinch of chilli flakes

1 Wash, peel as necessary, and dice or slice each vegetable into evenly sized pieces about 1cm (½in) thick.

Leave small shallots and mushrooms whole. Put a batch of vegetables in a stainless steel saucepan and add enough vinegar to just cover them. Add the sugar and salt and bring to the boil. Boil the soft vegetables for 2–3 minutes and firmer vegetables for 5–10 minutes until al dente. Then remove from the pan, pat dry with kitchen paper, and allow to cool.

2 Loosely pack the vegetables into sterilized jars and add the seasonings. Cover with olive oil and press the vegetables down lightly to remove any air pockets. Top up with oil, then seal and store in the fridge. Leave for at least 1 week before opening. Top up with extra oil once opened so the vegetables are always covered with 1cm (½in) of oil. They will keep for 1–2 months in the fridge.

quinces in spiced syrup

Try these bottled quinces with ice cream or cream, or chopped or puréed and served with game, pork, or duck.

🥣 **5 MINS**　🍲 **25 MINS PLUS HEAT-PROCESSING**

SPECIAL EQUIPMENT ▪ sterilized screw-band jars or kilner jars

MAKES 1 LITRE (1¾ PINTS)

900g (2lb) quinces, scrubbed

1 tbsp lemon juice

275g (9½oz) caster sugar

2 star anise, 1 cinnamon stick, or 2 cloves

1 Put the quinces in a large pan, add 600ml (1 pint) water, bring to the boil, and cook for 2 minutes. Remove and plunge into cold water. Reserve the pan of water. Peel, core, and quarter the quinces and put in a bowl of cold water with the lemon juice.

2 Add the sugar to the pan of water. Heat gently until it dissolves, then stir well. Drain the quinces and add them and the star anise to the pan. Bring to the boil, reduce the heat, cover, and poach the quinces for 12–15 minutes, or until just tender.

3 Pack the quinces tightly into the warm sterilized jars, leaving 1cm (½in)

of space at the top. Bring the syrup back to the boil and pour over the fruit to cover it completely. Tap the jar gently on a wooden board to remove air bubbles. Fit the rubber band or metal lid seal and clamp on the lid. If using screw-band jars, loosen by a quarter turn. Place the filled jars in a deep roasting tray lined with newspaper to soak up spills.

4 Put the tray in the centre of the oven for 40–50 minutes to heat-process (remove the remaining air in the jars). Remove from the oven and tighten the clips or lids (or screw on plastic screw-band lids). Leave for 24 hours, then unscrew or unclip and test the lids are firmly sealed before refastening and storing. (If using kilner jars with metal lids, you will know if you have a seal as the lid becomes slightly concave and is firm once pressed.) Store the jars in a cool, dark place and refrigerate once open.

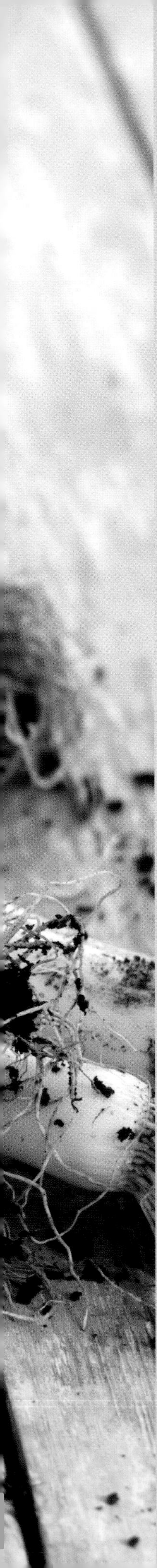

early winter

at their best

vegetables beetroot ▪ Brussels sprouts ▪ cabbages ▪ cardoons ▪ carrots (maincrop) ▪ cauliflower ▪ cavolo nero ▪ celeriac ▪ celery ▪ chicory ▪ horseradish ▪ Jerusalem artichokes ▪ kale ▪ leeks ▪ pak choi ▪ parsnips ▪ potatoes (maincrop) ▪ pumpkin ▪ radicchio ▪ romanesco ▪ salsify ▪ shallots ▪ squash ▪ sweet potatoes ▪ swede ▪ turnips

fruit and nuts apples ▪ chestnuts ▪ clementines ▪ cranberries ▪ dates ▪ forced rhubarb ▪ grapefruit ▪ kiwi fruit ▪ lemons ▪ limes ▪ oranges ▪ pears ▪ pomegranate ▪ quinces ▪ satsumas ▪ tangerines

seafood brill ▪ cod ▪ cold water prawns ▪ coley ▪ common brown crab ▪ crayfish (farmed) ▪ dab ▪ Dover sole ▪ haddock ▪ hake ▪ halibut ▪ lemon sole ▪ mussels ▪ native oysters ▪ Pacific or rock oysters ▪ pollack ▪ plaice ▪ razor clams ▪ red gurnard ▪ sea bass ▪ turbot (wild and farmed)

meat, poultry, game duck (wild and farmed) ▪ goose (wild and farmed) ▪ grouse ▪ hare ▪ partridge (wild) ▪ pheasant (wild) ▪ rabbit (wild and farmed) ▪ turkey ▪ venison (wild and farmed)

also available

vegetables calabrese broccoli ▪ mushrooms (cultivated and wild) ▪ onions ▪ spinach ▪ spring greens ▪ Swiss chard ▪ watercress **fruit** avocados ▪ crabapples ▪ sloes ▪ rosehips **seafood** abalone ▪ brown trout (farmed) ▪ grey mullet ▪ herring ▪ John Dory ▪ king scallops (farmed) ▪ langoustines ▪ monkfish ▪ North Atlantic lobster ▪ rainbow trout (farmed) ▪ red mullet ▪ salmon (farmed) ▪ sardines ▪ sea bream (farmed) ▪ sea trout (farmed) ▪ squid ▪ whiting **meat, poultry, game** beef ▪ chicken ▪ guinea fowl (farmed) ▪ lamb ▪ pork ▪ quail (farmed) ▪ veal ▪ wild boar (farmed)

early winter recipe chooser

Butternut squash pasta in chilli and Parmesan sauce p393

Roast sweet potato and chilli tortilla p390

Pears poached in red wine and thyme p414

Vegetables

Baby onions
Beef and anchovy casserole p392
Pork chops with apple and baby onions p371

Beetroot
Carrot and beetroot salad with balsamic vinaigrette p404 ⓥ
Goat's cheese, pear, and beetroot salad p358 ⓥ
Smoked trout with beetroot, apple, and dill relish p358

Brussels sprouts
Brussels sprouts with chestnuts and pancetta p395
Brussels sprouts with whole chestnuts and sausages p395
Potato, celeriac, and sprouts sauté p403

Butternut squash
Belly pork and squash p374
Butternut squash pasta in chilli and Parmesan sauce p393 ⓥ
Kichidi p384 ⓥ
Roasted squash with sage and onion p407 ⓥ
Spiced butternut squash soup p359 ⓥ
Squash, sage, and blue cheese risotto p384 ⓥ
Squash, spinach, and horseradish bake p370 ⓥ
Squash with chestnuts and cranberries p407 ⓥ

Cabbage
Cabbage stuffed with chestnut and pork p367
Carrot and shredded cabbage with peanuts p404
Creamy coleslaw p399 ⓥ
Garbure p384
Ham hock with red cabbage p375
Ham hock with white cabbage and celery p375
Hot and spicy white cabbage p398 ⓥ

Portuguese haddock soup p363
Red cabbage and bacon salad p398
Red cabbage pickle p421 ⓥ
Sauerkraut p421 ⓥ
Slow-cooked Swedish red cabbage p394 ⓥ
Spicy pork with caraway seeds and cabbage p390
Sweet and sour cabbage p398 ⓥ
Winter braised white cabbage and celery p394 ⓥ

Cardoons
Baked cardoons with cheese p365 ⓥ

Carrot
Beef and carrot casserole p387
Beef and parsnip casserole p388
Braised oxtail p368
Caramelized carrots p406 ⓥ
Carrot and beetroot salad with balsamic vinaigrette p404 ⓥ
Carrot and coriander relish p420 ⓥ
Carrot and noodle salad p404
Carrot and shredded cabbage with peanuts p404
Celeriac rémoulade with carrot salad p406 ⓥ
Chicken salad with carrot and apple relish p391
Corned beef hash with horseradish p374
Cream of vegetable soup p362 ⓥ
Creamy coleslaw p399 ⓥ
Fragrant honeyed mixed roots p406 ⓥ
Japanese-style fish broth p362
Mixed vegetable purée p395 ⓥ
Ribollita p358 ⓥ
Shepherd's pie p370
Turkey broth p362
Turkey, ham, and white bean soup p362

Cauliflower
Cauliflower curry p392 ⓥ

Cavolo nero
Portuguese haddock soup p363
Ribollita p358 ⓥ

Celeriac
Beef and celeriac casserole with stout and anchovies p387
Belly pork and prunes p392
Celeriac rémoulade with carrot salad p406 ⓥ
Celeriac soufflé pie p374
Chicken with garlic and spiced celeriac p387
Fragrant honeyed mixed roots p406 ⓥ
Griddled sweet potato and celeriac p395 ⓥ
Mixed vegetable purée p395 ⓥ
Potato, celeriac, and sprouts sauté p403 ⓥ
Roast celeriac and leek tortilla p390 ⓥ
Roasted sweet potato and celeriac with garlic and herbs p407 ⓥ
Turkey salad with celeriac and orange relish p391

Celery
Baked turkey rolls with celery, chestnuts, and chanterelles p383
Braised oxtail p368
Chestnut and celery stuffing p402 ⓥ
Cream of vegetable soup p362 ⓥ
Ham hock with white cabbage and celery p375
Potato, celery, and parsnip bake p400 ⓥ
Roast pork with bacon and celery hearts p371
Smoked haddock, celery, and cheese chowder p363
Turkey broth p362
Winter braised white cabbage and celery p394 ⓥ

Chicory
Roast pork with bacon and chicory p371
Smoked trout with beetroot, apple, and dill relish p358

Horseradish
Corned beef hash with horseradish p374
Horseradish sauce p404 ⓥ
Potato and horseradish mash p403
Salmon, horseradish, and kale bake p368
Squash, spinach, and horseradish bake p370 ⓥ

Jerusalem artichoke
Venison and artichoke casserole p388

Kale
Portuguese haddock soup p363
Potato and horseradish mash p403
Ribollita p358 ⓥ
Salmon, horseradish, and kale bake p368

Leek
Beef and anchovy casserole p392
Cheesy leeks on toast p360 ⓥ
Cream of vegetable soup p362 ⓥ
Leek and potato soup p360 ⓥ
Leeks hollandaise p399 ⓥ
Leeks vinaigrette p399 ⓥ
Potato and leek croquettes p360 ⓥ
Potato and leek gratin p402 ⓥ
Roast celeriac and leek tortilla p390 ⓥ
Turkey broth p362
Turkey, ham, and white bean soup p362

Parsnip
Beef and parsnip casserole p388
Braised oxtail p368
Cream of vegetable soup p362 ⓥ
Fragrant honeyed mixed roots p406 ⓥ
Mustard chicken casserole p378
Parsnip and Parmesan bread p400 ⓥ
Potato, celery, and parsnip bake p400 ⓥ
Pumpkin and parsnip cassoulet p366 ⓥ
Turkey broth p362

Potato
Beef and celeriac casserole with stout and anchovies p387
Beef and herb potato pie p391
Cauliflower curry p392 ⓥ
Chicken with garlic and spiced celeriac p387
Corned beef hash with horseradish p374
Cream of vegetable soup p362 ⓥ
Dauphinoise potatoes p402 ⓥ
Leek and potato soup p360 ⓥ
Patatas bravas p400 ⓥ
Pork with potatoes and mushrooms in wine p389
Portuguese haddock soup p363
Potato and horseradish mash p403
Potato and leek croquettes p360 ⓥ
Potato and leek gratin p402 ⓥ
Potato, celeriac, and sprouts sauté p403
Potato, celery, and parsnip bake p400 ⓥ
Ribollita p358 ⓥ
Shepherd's pie p370

Pumpkin
Chicken with garlic, preserved lemons, and pumpkin p387
Pumpkin and orange spiced jam p417 ⓥ
Pumpkin and parsnip cassoulet p366 ⓥ
Pumpkin farfalle with blue cheese sauce p393 ⓥ
Swiss chard and pumpkin bake p370 ⓥ

Salsify
Salsify fritters p402 Ⓥ

Shallots
Moroccan roasted sweet potato soup
p363 Ⓥ

Roast pork with bacon and chicory
p371

Venison, shallot, and chestnut hotpot
p388

Spinach
Chicken salad with carrot and apple
relish p391

Clear soup with sea bass p368

Squash, spinach, and horseradish bake
p370 Ⓥ

Swede
Braised oxtail p368

Mixed vegetable purée p395 Ⓥ

Turkey, ham, and white bean soup p362

Sweet potato
Curried sweet potato croquettes p360 Ⓥ

Griddled sweet potato and celeriac
p395 Ⓥ

Jamaican-style fish with sweet potatoes
p376

Mixed vegetable purée p395 Ⓥ

Moroccan roasted sweet potato soup
p363 Ⓥ

Roast sweet potato and chilli tortilla
p390 Ⓥ

Roasted sweet potato and celeriac with
garlic and herbs p407 Ⓥ

Soy and sesame-glazed sweet potatoes
p394 Ⓥ

Sweet potato and rosemary rolls
p401 Ⓥ

Sweet potato paratha p403 Ⓥ

Swiss chard
Cheesy Swiss chard crêpes p377 Ⓥ

Gratin of Swiss chard with haricots and
pancetta p401

Swiss chard and pumpkin bake p370 Ⓥ

Turnip
Cream of vegetable soup p362 Ⓥ

Duck with turnips and apricots p389

Mixed vegetable purée p395 Ⓥ

Turkey broth p362

Fruit and nuts

Apples
Apple butter p416 Ⓥ

Apple, sultana, and pecan cake p410 Ⓥ

Carrot and shredded cabbage with
peanuts p404

Chicken salad with carrot and apple
relish p391

Cider p420 Ⓥ

Classic apple crumble p411 Ⓥ

Cranberry and apricot chutney p418 Ⓥ

Curried apple, peach, and walnut chutney
p421 Ⓥ

Dried apples p416 Ⓥ

Pork chops with apple and baby onions
p371

Slow-cooked Swedish red cabbage
p394 Ⓥ

Smoked trout with beetroot, apple, and
dill relish p358

Sweet and sour cabbage p398 Ⓥ

Winter braised white cabbage and celery
p394 Ⓥ

Chestnuts
Baked turkey rolls filled with chestnuts
and mushrooms p383

Baked turkey rolls with celery, chestnuts,
and chanterelles p383

Brussels sprouts with chestnuts and
pancetta p395

Brussels sprouts with whole chestnuts
and sausages p395

Cabbage stuffed with chestnut and pork
p367

Chestnut and celery stuffing p402 Ⓥ

Partridge soup p365

Pork escalopes with tangerine, prunes,
and chestnuts p383

Sausage and chestnut stuffing p402

Slow-cooked lamb with orange and
chestnuts p366

Squash with chestnuts and cranberries
p407 Ⓥ

Venison, shallot, and chestnut hotpot
p388

Dates
Middle Eastern date cakes with
pomegranate drizzle p414 Ⓥ

Cranberries
Cranberry and apricot chutney
p418 Ⓥ

Cranberry and orange butter p418 Ⓥ

Cranberry jelly p416 Ⓥ

Cranberry sauce with orange p418 Ⓥ

Cranberry sauce with port p418 Ⓥ

Festive wild rice salad p379

Squash with chestnuts and cranberries
p407 Ⓥ

Turkey and cranberry casserole p378

Winter braised white cabbage and celery
p394 Ⓥ

Grapefruit
Beef with soy, lime, and a grapefruit and
ginger salsa p377

Grapefruit granita with almond biscuits
p413 Ⓥ

Kiwi fruit
Prosciutto with kiwi on herb croûtes
p359

Lemons
Cold lemon soufflé p413

Lemon sorbet p412 Ⓥ

Lemon tart p412 Ⓥ

Oranges and tangerines
Chicken and orange tagine p373

Chocolate orange truffle cake p409 Ⓥ

Cranberry and orange butter p418 Ⓥ

Cranberry sauce with orange p418 Ⓥ

Hazelnut, chocolate, and orange tart
p415 Ⓥ

Orange and chocolate tiramisu p408 Ⓥ

Orange and pistachio Swiss roll p408 Ⓥ

Orange marmalade p417 Ⓥ

Pears poached in red wine and thyme
p414 Ⓥ

Pistachio and orange biscotti p411 Ⓥ

Pork escalopes with tangerine, prunes,
and chestnuts p383

Roast leg of pork with orange p376

Slow-cooked lamb with orange and
chestnuts p366

Tangerine and almond biscotti p411 Ⓥ

Turkey salad with celeriac and orange
relish p391

Pears
Chocolate mousse with cinnamon pears
p414 Ⓥ

Goat's cheese, pear, and beetroot salad
p358 Ⓥ

Ham with pears p359

Hot and spicy white cabbage p398 Ⓥ

Mulled pears p420 Ⓥ

Normandy pear tart p410 Ⓥ

Pear cake p408 Ⓥ

Pear, coffee, and walnut tiramisu p408 Ⓥ

Pears poached in red wine and thyme
p414 Ⓥ

Pomegranates
Middle Eastern date cakes with
pomegranate drizzle p414 Ⓥ

Shredded turkey, mint, and pomegranate
salad p373

Turkish lamb and pomegranate pilaf p373

Quinces
Spiced quince dulce de leche pie
p412 Ⓥ

Seafood

Cod
Jamaican-style fish with sweet potatoes
p376

Japanese-style fish broth p362

Haddock
Jamaican-style fish with sweet potatoes
p376

Portuguese haddock soup p363

Smoked haddock, celery, and cheese
chowder p363

Mussels
Mussels in a coconut and lemongrass
broth p363

Pasta and mussel salad p385

Red curry mussels p363

Steamed mussels with saffron-cream
sauce p365

Sea bass
Clear soup with sea bass p368

Meat

Duck
Chinese roast duck p369

Duck with turnips and apricots p389

Garbure p384

Goose
Stuffed roast goose p378

Partridge
Partridge soup p365

Turkey
Baked turkey rolls filled with chestnuts
and mushrooms p383

Baked turkey rolls with celery, chestnuts,
and chanterelles p383

Festive wild rice salad p379

Roast turkey with parsley and onion
stuffing p382

Roast turkey with sage and bacon stuffing
p382

Shredded turkey, mint, and pomegranate
salad p373

Turkey and cranberry casserole p378

Turkey broth p362

Turkey escalopes stuffed with prunes and
pecans p383

Turkey, ham, and white bean soup p362

Turkey salad with celeriac and orange
relish p391

Warm turkey and chickpea salad p382

Warm white bean and turkey salad p382

Venison
Venison and artichoke casserole p388

Venison, shallot, and chestnut hotpot p388

Ham hock with red cabbage p375

smoked trout with beetroot, apple, and dill relish

This is a wonderfully colourful and tasty light meal – dill and trout complement each other perfectly and the apples bring a sweet flavour to balance the bitterness of the chicory.

🥣 **15 MINS**

SERVES 4

3–4 tsp creamed horseradish

½ red onion, finely diced

1–2 heads of chicory, leaves separated and rinsed

2 large cold-smoked trout fillets, about 225g (8oz) each, flaked

drizzle of olive oil

juice of ½ lemon

salt and freshly ground black pepper

2–3 eating apples

2 beetroots, cooked, peeled (p255), and diced

handful of dill, finely chopped

1 In a small bowl, mix together the horseradish and half of the red onion. Set aside.

2 Arrange the chicory and flaked trout on a serving plate and drizzle the oil and lemon juice over. Sprinkle over a pinch of salt and some pepper.

3 Peel, core, and chop the apple into bite-sized pieces. Put in a separate bowl with the beetroot and dill, and mix together to make the relish.

4 To serve, spoon the relish over the chicory and fish. Sprinkle over the remaining red onion and serve with the creamed horseradish on the side.

variation

goat's cheese, pear, and beetroot salad

Omit the horseradish. Arrange the leaves from 1–2 heads red chicory on serving plates with 200g (7oz) diced goat's cheese instead of the trout. Mix ½ small finely diced red onion with 2 peeled, cored, and chopped pears instead of apple, the 2 diced beetroot, and a handful of fresh thyme, leaves only, instead of dill. Dress as before.

ribollita

This hearty soup from Italy features the unusual combination of potatoes and bread: good and filling for the winter months.

🥣 **20 MINS** 🍲 **50 MINS** ❄ **FREEZABLE**

SERVES 4

1 tbsp olive oil, plus extra to serve

1 onion, finely chopped

salt and freshly ground black pepper

2 garlic cloves, grated or finely chopped

2 carrots, finely chopped

200g can chopped tomatoes

400g can cannellini beans, drained and rinsed

225g (8oz) potatoes, peeled and cut into bite-sized pieces

175g (6oz) cavolo nero or curly kale, chopped

750ml (1¼ pints) hot vegetable stock

2 tsp finely chopped rosemary leaves

¼ ciabatta, cut into cubes, to serve

Parmesan cheese, grated, to serve

1 Heat the oil in a pan over a low heat, add the onion, and cook for 6–8 minutes, or until soft and translucent. Season with salt and pepper, then add the garlic and carrots, and cook for 5 minutes.

2 Stir through the tomatoes, beans, potatoes, and cavolo nero or curly kale and cook for 5 minutes. Pour in the stock, add the rosemary, and leave to simmer on a low heat for 15–20 minutes, or until the potatoes are soft.

3 Meanwhile, preheat the oven to 200°C (400°F/Gas 6). Place the ciabatta cubes on a baking tray, drizzle with oil, and bake in the oven for 10 minutes, or until golden. Taste the soup and season, if necessary. Serve topped with the ciabatta, a drizzle of oil, and a sprinkling of Parmesan cheese.

spiced butternut squash soup

Butternut squash is a type of winter squash and has a deliciously sweet, dense, and buttery flavour. It is also very versatile, so makes a fine storecupboard ingredient.

🥣 20 MINS 🍲 40 MINS ❄ FREEZABLE

SPECIAL EQUIPMENT ▪ blender or food processor

SERVES 4

1 tbsp olive oil

1 onion, finely chopped

salt and freshly ground black pepper

2 garlic cloves, grated or finely chopped

2 sage leaves, finely chopped

1 red chilli, deseeded and finely chopped

pinch of grated nutmeg

1 butternut squash, halved, deseeded, peeled, and chopped into small pieces

1 potato, peeled and diced

750ml (1¼ pints) hot vegetable stock

chilli oil, to serve

Gruyère cheese, grated, to serve

1 Heat the oil in a pan over a low heat, add the onion, and cook for 6–8 minutes, or until soft and translucent. Season, then stir through the garlic, sage, chilli, and nutmeg, and cook for a few seconds.

2 Stir in the squash, add the potato and stock, and bring to the boil. Reduce to a simmer and cook for 20–30 minutes, or until the squash and potatoes are soft. Pour the soup into a blender or food processor and blitz until smooth. Season again with salt and pepper. Pour the soup into a bowl and serve drizzled with chilli oil and a sprinkling of Gruyère cheese.

ham with pears

Thin slices of cured ham wrapped around fruit make tasty morsels at a party. The firm texture of Conference pears makes them particularly good for this recipe.

🥣 10 MINS PLUS COOLING 🍲 15 MINS

SERVES 4

100ml (3½fl oz) dry sherry

100g (3½oz) caster sugar

3 ripe pears, peeled and cut into quarters

150g (5½oz) thinly sliced Serrano or Parma ham

chilli oil or mint yogurt, to serve

1 Put the sherry and sugar in a pan, add 250ml (9fl oz) water, and bring to the boil. Add the pears, return to the boil, and simmer gently for 15 minutes, or until they begin to soften. Turn off the heat and allow to cool for 30 minutes.

2 Wrap each quarter of pear in a piece of ham. Arrange on a serving plate and serve drizzled with chilli oil or mint yogurt.

variation

prosciutto with kiwi on herb croûtes

Peel and quarter 2 kiwi fruit (no need to poach). Wrap each quarter in half a slice of raw cured ham. Mash 30g (1oz) butter with ½ tsp dried mixed herbs, 1 crushed garlic clove, and a good grinding of black pepper. Toast 8 slices of ciabatta bread under a preheated grill. Turn off the grill. Spread each with a little of the herb butter and return to the cooling grill until melted into the toast. Top each with a kiwi and ham roll.

leek and potato soup

An enduring classic, this warming soup can be blended to a smooth purée or left with a chunky texture. Either way, it is always satisfying, especially served with rustic bread.

🥣 15 MINS   🍲 40 MINS

SPECIAL EQUIPMENT ▪ blender or food processor

SERVES 4

1 tbsp olive oil

1 onion, finely chopped

salt and freshly ground black pepper

2 garlic cloves, grated or finely chopped

3 sage leaves, finely chopped

450g (1lb) leeks, trimmed and finely sliced

1.2 litres (2 pints) hot vegetable stock

450g (1lb) potatoes, peeled and roughly chopped

75ml (2½fl oz) double cream, to serve

1 Heat the oil in a pan, add the onion, and cook over a low heat for 6–8 minutes, or until soft and translucent. Season with salt and pepper, then stir in the garlic and sage. Add the leeks and stir well, then cook over a low heat for 8–10 minutes until soft.

2 Pour in the stock, bring to the boil, then add the potatoes and simmer for about 20 minutes until soft. Pour the soup into a blender or food processor and blitz until smooth, then pour it back into the pan. Taste, and season if needed. Stir in the cream and heat until piping hot. Serve immediately in warmed bowls.

potato and leek croquettes

These easy-to-make bites filled with savoury flavour are the perfect appetizer for winter stews and roasts.

🥣 20 MINS PLUS CHILLING   🍲 30 MINS   ❄ FREEZABLE

SERVES 4

1 tbsp olive oil

1 leek, white part, trimmed and finely chopped

1 garlic clove, grated or finely chopped

500g (1lb 2oz) floury potatoes, such as Maris Piper or King Edward, peeled and cut into chunks

3 eggs

60g (2oz) Parmesan cheese, grated

2 tbsp chopped flat-leaf parsley

salt and freshly ground black pepper

60g (2oz) plain flour

150g (5½oz) fine breadcrumbs

light olive oil, for deep-frying

1 Heat the olive oil in a frying pan over a low heat, add the leek, and sweat for 8–10 minutes until soft. Add the garlic and cook for 30 more seconds without colouring. Set aside to cool.

2 Cook the potatoes in a pan of boiling salted water for 15–20 minutes until tender. Drain, return to the pan, and mash until very smooth. Add the leek and garlic mixture, 1 of the eggs, Parmesan, and parsley. Season. Stir thoroughly and then chill for at least 1 hour to firm.

3 Spread the flour over a flat tray, and lightly beat the remaining 2 eggs in a shallow bowl. Put the breadcrumbs on a separate plate. Using wet hands, roll the chilled mixture into 12 balls, each about the size of a golf ball, then form into oblong shapes. Gently roll the croquettes in the flour until well coated, then dip each one in the beaten egg, and lastly coat in the breadcrumbs.

4 Heat enough oil for deep-frying in a deep frying pan over a medium-high heat. Cooking in batches, deep-fry the croquettes for 10–15 minutes until golden brown. Serve hot.

variation

curried sweet potato croquettes

Prepare in the same way but sweat a small chopped onion instead of the leek and stir in 1 tbsp medium curry powder. Use 1 large potato and 1 large sweet potato instead of floury potatoes, then continue at step 2. Flavour with 2 tbsp fresh chopped coriander instead of parsley.

cheesy leeks on toast

The leek is a versatile vegetable indeed. Here it is steamed to soften and then mixed with a cheese sauce. Spread over toast and grilled, the end result is perfect for a light lunch.

🥣 10 MINS   🍲 10 MINS

SERVES 4

1 tbsp olive oil

1 leek, trimmed and chopped

25g (scant 1oz) butter

150ml (5fl oz) brown ale

175g (6oz) mature Cheddar cheese, grated

1 tbsp plain flour

2 tsp English mustard

splash of Worcestershire sauce

salt and freshly ground black pepper

2 egg yolks

4 slices of bread

1 Heat the oil in a pan over a low heat. Add the leek and sweat gently until soft. Remove from the pan with a slotted spoon and set aside.

2 Put the butter, brown ale, and cheese in the same pan and cook gently, stirring, until melted and smooth. Remove from the heat and stir in the flour until smooth. Return to the heat, stirring continuously, for 1–2 minutes.

3 Remove the pan from the heat once again and stir in the mustard, Worcestershire sauce, and the reserved leeks. Season with salt and pepper, then leave to cool and stir in the egg yolks until combined.

4 Preheat the grill to hot. Toast the slices of bread on one side, then turn them over and smother with the cheesy leeks. Cook until the topping is simmering and golden, and then serve immediately.

Season's best **leeks**

Leeks are believed to be descendents of the wild onion found across Europe. They have long, cylindrical stems, with many layers of tightly wrapped leaves that are white where they have been earthed and green where exposed to light. When cooked, they have a mild flavour, but are pungent when raw. Although in season from autumn to late winter, they are at their best in early winter. They pair well with fish, cream, cheese, potatoes, lemon, and olive oil.

Cultivated in temperate zones, leeks can tolerate cold, making them a staple winter vegetable. The white part that grows underground stays tender, while the exposed green tops become coarse.

essentials

varieties available

Baby leeks to eat whole or thinly sliced, and large maincrop ones to slice or chop.

buy Choose those with a long run of white that "gives" slightly when bent. Avoid stiff leeks.

store Store unwashed and wrapped in a sealed plastic bag in the vegetable drawer for up to a week.

cook Boil, steam, sauté, or stir-fry slices; braise or grill whole or split. Use in soups, stews, and savoury pie fillings.

preserve Blanch and freeze.

recipe ideas

Fish and leek pie p461

Leek and potato soup p360

Leeks vinaigrette p399

Potato and leek croquettes p360

Baby leek These are tender enough to eat thinly sliced in a salad. They also make a tasty topping for pizzas and savoury tarts, and are good grilled or roasted whole.

The coarse outer leaves need not be wasted. Chop them roughly and add to the stockpot.

how to wash and cut leeks julienne

Leeks need thorough washing as dirt gets trapped between the layers. Cut them into julienne strips to cook or to use raw for salads or garnish. For use in purées, stews, and casseroles, simply slice or chop after washing.

1 Trim both ends of the leek. Cut in half lengthways and gently spread the layers. Rinse under cold running water and shake off excess.

2 For julienne, cut off all the green part, then cut the white in desired lengths. Slice, cut-side down, into 3mm (¹⁄₈in) wide strips.

Leek Ranging in size from pencil thin to fat-shanked giants, leeks add texture and flavour to all kinds of dishes. Leeks should bend; if stiff, they will be tough and "woody" inside.

turkey broth

Make thrifty use of leftover turkey by creating your own stock, simmering the carcass after a roast dinner. This broth, however, is every bit as appealing when made with chicken.

🥣 20 MINS   🍲 25 MINS

SERVES 6

1 litre (1¾ pints) turkey stock or chicken stock

120ml (4fl oz) dry white wine

1 carrot, finely diced

1 parsnip, finely diced

2 celery sticks, finely diced

1 leek, white part, trimmed and finely diced

1 small turnip, finely diced

salt and freshly ground black pepper

225g (8oz) cooked turkey meat, finely diced

100ml (3½fl oz) single cream

2 tbsp chopped flat-leaf parsley

1 Bring the stock and wine to the boil in a large pan, then stir in the carrot, parsnip, celery, leek, and turnip. Season, partially cover with a lid, and simmer for 20 minutes.

2 Stir in the cooked turkey, cream, and chopped parsley, and reheat gently. Serve the soup with plenty of crusty bread.

variation

turkey, ham, and white bean soup

Prepare in the same way but use 1 whole finely chopped leek (not just the white part), 2 finely diced carrots, and ¼ finely diced swede instead of the original vegetables. Add a drained 400g can of haricot beans and a mixture of 115g (4oz) finely diced ham and 115g (4oz) finely diced turkey instead of all turkey. Add 2 tbsp chopped thyme leaves instead of parsley.

japanese-style fish broth

The hot and fragrant broth in this recipe is a perfect foil for the delicate white fish. You could add some noodles to the soup, if you wish, or some soya beans for a little more bulk.

🥣 15 MINS   🍲 1 HR

SERVES 4–6

25g (scant 1oz) dried shiitake mushrooms

3 carrots, finely sliced on the diagonal

1 tbsp dark soy sauce, plus extra to taste

5cm (2in) piece of fresh root ginger, peeled and finely sliced

small bunch of coriander

1 leek, trimmed and finely sliced on the diagonal

250g (9oz) white fish, such as cod, coley, or pollack, skinned (p75)

For the broth

2 sheets of kombu (dried kelp), wiped clean and soaked for 30 minutes (optional)

25g (scant 1oz) dried bonito flakes (optional)

OR

1.5 litres (2¾ pints) hot light vegetable stock

1 tsp fish sauce (nam pla)

1 tbsp rice vinegar

1 To make the broth, put 1.2 litres (2 pints) water in a large heavy-based pan and add the kombu and bonito flakes, if using. Almost bring to the boil, drain through a sieve, and return the water to the pan (reserve the kombu and bonito flakes for another use). If not using kombu and bonito, put the vegetable stock into a heavy-based pan, add the fish sauce and rice vinegar, and simmer very gently for 20 minutes.

2 Meanwhile, soak the shiitake mushrooms in warm water for 20 minutes. Drain and add to the broth along with the carrots, soy sauce, ginger, and coriander. Partially cover with a lid and simmer gently for 20 minutes, or until the carrots are cooked, then stir through the leek and cook for a further 10 minutes. Add the fish, cover with the lid, and cook for a few minutes until the fish is opaque and cooked through. Adjust the flavour with soy sauce and serve.

cream of vegetable soup

Soup is always a brilliant way to use up vegetables. Here, parsnips, leeks, and turnips combine into one delicious whole.

🥣 15 MINS   🍲 40–55 MINS

SPECIAL EQUIPMENT ▪ blender or food processor

SERVES 6

45g (1½oz) butter

2 carrots, sliced

1 leek, white part, trimmed and finely sliced

2 parsnips, sliced

1 onion, sliced

1 small turnip, sliced

3 celery sticks, sliced

1 potato, peeled and sliced

1.2 litres (2 pints) hot vegetable stock

2 tsp thyme leaves

1 bay leaf

pinch of grated nutmeg

salt and freshly ground black pepper

3 tbsp single cream

3 tbsp milk

bunch of chives, snipped, to garnish

1 Melt the butter in a large pan, add the carrots, leek, parsnips, onion, turnip, celery, and potato, and stir to coat well. Cover the pan with a lid and cook for 10–15 minutes, or until the vegetables have softened.

2 Add the stock, thyme, bay leaf, and nutmeg, then season. Bring to the boil and simmer uncovered for 30–40 minutes, or until the vegetables are meltingly soft. Scoop out the bay leaf and discard.

3 Pour the soup into a blender or food processor and process until smooth, then pour or strain back into the pan. Stir in the cream and milk, adding more milk if the consistency is still too thick. Season, then reheat gently. Garnish with the chives and serve.

moroccan roasted sweet potato soup

The vegetables for this soup are cooked in the oven, which brings out their naturally sweet flavour. This north African soup is made even more filling served with warm pitta bread.

🥣 20 MINS　　🍲 50 MINS

SPECIAL EQUIPMENT ▪ blender or food processor

SERVES 4

675g (1½lb) sweet potatoes, peeled and cut into large chunks

6 large shallots, quartered

3 large garlic cloves, unpeeled

1 carrot, cut into large chunks

1 tbsp harissa paste, plus extra to serve

2 tbsp olive oil

salt and freshly ground black pepper

900ml (1½ pints) hot vegetable stock

1 tsp runny honey

generous squeeze of lemon juice

natural yogurt, to serve

warm pitta bread, to serve

1 Preheat the oven to 200°C (400°F/ Gas 6). Put the sweet potatoes, shallots, garlic, and carrot in a roasting tin. Mix the harissa paste with the oil, then pour over the vegetables and mix so they are well coated. Season with black pepper, then roast, turning occasionally, for 40 minutes, or until tender and turning golden. Remove from the oven.

2 Squeeze the garlic cloves out of their skins into the roasting tin. Stir in the stock and honey, then scrape up all the bits from the bottom of the tin. Pour the soup into a blender or food processor and blitz until smooth, then pour back into the pan and reheat gently.

3 Add the lemon juice and season. Swirl the yogurt with a little harissa paste and top each bowl with a spoonful. Serve with warm pitta bread.

portuguese haddock soup

The strong flavours of cavolo nero (or Savoy cabbage if you can't get hold of cavolo nero) and smoked haddock develop in minutes, making this soup very satisfying.

🥣 20 MINS　　🍲 20 MINS

SERVES 4

300g (10oz) leaves of cavolo nero, kale, or Savoy cabbage

2 tbsp olive oil

1 Spanish onion, finely chopped

3 garlic cloves, crushed

1 large waxy potato, peeled and diced

250ml (9fl oz) whole or semi-skimmed milk

salt and freshly ground black pepper

300g (10oz) smoked haddock fillet, skinned and flaked

1 Rinse the greens, cut out the large ribs and discard, then finely shred the leaves. Heat the oil in a pan over a medium heat, add the onion and garlic, and cook for 4–5 minutes until the onion and garlic are soft.

2 Add the potato and milk, then pour in enough water to cover everything by 2–3cm (¾–1¼ in). Season generously, bring to a simmer, and cook for 5 minutes. Add the greens and continue cooking for 10–15 minutes until the vegetables are tender.

3 Stir in the haddock and simmer for a minute, then remove from the heat and cover. Leave to stand for 5 minutes before serving.

variation

smoked haddock, celery, and cheese chowder

Omit the cavolo nero. Cook in the same way, but add 2 finely chopped celery sticks with the onion and omit the garlic. Cook for 15–20 minutes, then add the smoked haddock and simmer for a minute. Remove from the heat and stir in 60g (2oz) strong Cheddar cheese, cover, and leave to stand as before.

mussels in a coconut and lemongrass broth

These succulent mussels in their moat of gingery juices are terrific served with a mound of fluffy rice on the side, but crusty bread mops up the broth just as successfully.

🥣 20 MINS　　🍲 30-35 MINS

SERVES 4

100g (3½oz) butter

2 onions, finely chopped

2 red chillies, finely chopped

5cm (2in) piece of fresh root ginger, peeled and finely grated

5 large garlic cloves, finely chopped

2 lemongrass stalks, split lengthways and lightly bruised

120ml (4fl oz) ginger wine

400ml (14fl oz) hot fish stock

1.5kg (3lb 3oz) mussels, scrubbed and debearded (discard any that do not close when tapped) (p364)

150ml (5fl oz) coconut milk

3 tbsp coconut cream

salt and freshly ground black pepper

juice of 1–2 limes, to taste

3 tbsp chopped coriander leaves

1 Melt the butter in a large pan over a low heat and gently cook the onions, chillies, ginger, garlic, and lemongrass for 10 minutes until soft but not coloured.

2 Increase the heat to high and add the ginger wine followed by the stock. Bring to the boil before tipping in the mussels. Cover the pan and cook for 5–7 minutes, until the mussel shells have opened. Discard the lemongrass along with any mussels that remain closed.

3 Pour in the coconut milk and cream, and bring to the boil. Season with salt and pepper, sharpen with lime juice, and stir in the coriander leaves before serving.

variation

red curry mussels

Scrub and debeard the mussels. Cook the onions and 2 finely chopped celery sticks in 3 tbsp sunflower oil instead of butter, and omit the other flavourings. Stir in 4 tbsp Thai red curry paste, then a 400g can of coconut milk and 1 tbsp fish sauce (nam pla) instead of the ginger wine, stock, coconut cream, and milk. Cook the mussels as in step 2. Sharpen with lime juice to taste and add the coriander before serving.

Season's best **mussels**

Common mussels live in cool waters all over the world, unlike the larger, green-lipped mussel imported from New Zealand alone. At their best in winter, they are harvested from the wild by dredging and hand-gathering, but are also farmed, rope grown. One of the most sustainable seafoods, they taste great when cooked in wine, cider, or vermouth with shallots and garlic, and also with the aniseed flavours of pastis and fennel. Try, too, with chorizo, chilli, and saffron.

Marine blue mussels grow in abundance in temperate and polar waters worldwide. Freshwater ones live in cool, clean lakes and rivers.

Common mussels Also known as the blue mussel, their shell varies from brown to a bluish-purple. The mussels attach themselves to rocks, or when farmed, to rope, by a strong thread called the byssus thread (or beard), a protein they secrete. They taste slightly salty, with an intense flavour of the sea.

Rope-grown mussels have little barnacle growth on the shell and are glossy. They require minimal preparation.

essentials
varieties available

The native variety is the blue mussel. Large green-lipped mussels are imported. Also available frozen, canned in brine or vinegar, smoked; often included in frozen seafood mix.

buy Shells should not be damaged and should shut or close quickly when tapped sharply. They should smell pleasantly of the sea.

store Eat on day of purchase.

cook Steam, usually in a pan with some stock, wine, or water with other flavourings. Cream may be added. Eat with the cooking liquid or add to rice, pasta, or fish sauces.

recipe ideas

Cod and mussel chowder p460

Mussels in a coconut and lemongrass broth p363

Pasta and mussel salad p385

Risotto with mussels p300

Steamed mussels with saffron-cream sauce p365

how to prepare mussels

Mussels must be scrubbed and de-bearded before use. Before doing this, if there is time, place the mussels in a large bowl of cold water, sprinkle with oats, and leave for 2 hours to help them self-clean inside.

1 In the sink, scrub the mussels under cold, running water. Rinse away grit or sand and remove any barnacles with a small, sharp knife. Discard any mussels that are open.

2 To remove the "beard", pinch the dark stringy piece between your fingers, pull it away from the mussel, and discard.

baked cardoons with cheese

The delicate flavour of cardoons is particularly well enhanced when they are baked and topped with a delicious cheese sauce in this Italian classic.

🥣 15 MINS   🍲 50 MINS - 1 HR 10 MINS

SERVES 4

1kg (2¼1b) cardoons, tough outer stalks discarded

salt and freshly ground black pepper

juice of 1 lemon

25g (scant 1oz) butter

1 heaped tbsp plain flour

300ml (10fl oz) milk

60g (2oz) Parmesan cheese, grated

1 Trim the cardoons and remove any strings, then cut across into 7.5cm (3in) pieces. Put the cardoons into a pan of salted water and add the lemon juice. Bring to the boil, then reduce the heat and simmer for 30–45 minutes, or until softened. Drain well and arrange in a baking dish.

2 Preheat the oven to 180°C (350°F/Gas 4). Melt the butter in a small pan, then remove from the heat and stir in the flour. Gradually stir in the milk. Return to the heat and cook, stirring, until smooth and thickened. Remove from the heat, season with salt and pepper, and stir in half the Parmesan cheese. Pour evenly over the cardoons and sprinkle with the remaining Parmesan.

3 Bake for 20–25 minutes, or until golden and bubbling. Serve hot with some crusty bread.

partridge soup

This is a substantial soup that is a great way to make one partridge suffice for four people. You could use any other small game bird, such as quail, in exactly the same way.

🥣 20 MINS   🍲 1 HR 20 MINS

SERVES 4

1 tbsp sunflower oil

1 partridge, quartered

1 onion, unpeeled and quartered

900ml (1½ pints) hot chicken stock

1 bouquet garni

salt and freshly ground black pepper

1 potato, peeled and diced

1 carrot, diced

1 small turnip, diced

2 tbsp plain flour

200g (7oz) ready-cooked chestnuts, peeled and quartered

2 tbsp amontillado sherry

dash of soy sauce

a little chopped flat-leaf parsley, to garnish

1 Heat the oil in a saucepan over a medium heat, add the partridge pieces, and cook until they are browned all over. Add the onion, stock, bouquet garni, and a little salt and pepper. Bring to the boil, reduce the heat, cover with a lid, and simmer gently for 1 hour.

2 Strain the stock and return to the pan. Add the potato, carrot, and turnip. Bring back to the boil, partially cover, and simmer gently for about 20 minutes until the vegetables are really tender. Meanwhile, take all the meat off the partridge, discarding the skin, and shred the meat.

3 Remove the bouquet garni from the soup and discard. Mix the flour with 4 tbsp water and add to the soup. Bring to the boil, stirring, until lightly thickened and simmer for 2 minutes.

4 Add the shredded meat, chestnuts, and sherry to the soup and simmer for 2 minutes. Add the soy sauce to taste. Ladle into warmed bowls, garnish with a little chopped parsley, and serve immediately.

steamed mussels with saffron-cream sauce

From the shores of Brittany comes this delectable dish. Just steam the mussels briefly so they are juicy and sumptuous.

🥣 25-30 MINS   🍲 10-12 MINS

SERVES 4-6

3 shallots, very finely chopped

250ml (9fl oz) dry white wine

1 bouquet garni, made with 5-6 sprigs of parsley, 2-3 sprigs of thyme, and 1 bay leaf

large pinch of saffron threads

salt and freshly ground black pepper

3kg (6½lb) mussels, scrubbed and debearded (discard any that do not close when tapped) (p364)

120ml (4fl oz) double cream

5-7 sprigs of flat-leaf parsley, leaves picked and finely chopped

1 Put the shallots, wine, bouquet garni, saffron, and plenty of pepper in a casserole with a lid. Bring to the boil and simmer for 2 minutes. Add the mussels, cover, and cook over a high heat, stirring occasionally, for 5-7 minutes. Discard any mussels that have not opened. With a slotted spoon, transfer the mussels to a large, warmed bowl.

2 Cover the mussels tightly with foil and keep in a warm place while making the sauce. You must work quickly now so they remain as plump and moist as possible and lose none of their fresh-cooked savour.

3 Discard the bouquet garni and bring the cooking liquid to the boil. Simmer until reduced by half. Pour in the cream, stirring, and bring back to the boil. Simmer for about 2-3 minutes, stirring, until slightly thickened. Lift out the spoon and run your finger across; it should leave a clear trail. Stir in the parsley and season to taste. Remove the foil, spoon the saffron-cream sauce over the mussels, and serve immediately.

slow-cooked lamb with orange and chestnuts

Hearty chestnuts give substance to this classic combination of lamb and orange. The tagine tastes even better reheated the next day as the flavours will have melded together.

🥣 15 MINS   🍲 2 HRS 15 MINS   ❄ FREEZABLE

SERVES 4–6

½ tsp ground cinnamon

½ tsp ground cumin

½ tsp ground coriander

salt and freshly ground black pepper

900g (2lb) lean leg of lamb, diced

2–3 tbsp olive oil

1 onion, chopped

1 cinnamon stick

175g (6oz) ready-cooked chestnuts

150ml (5fl oz) fresh orange juice

900ml (1½ pints) hot lamb stock

2 oranges, peeled and cut into thick slices

bunch of coriander, roughly chopped

1 Preheat the oven to 160°C (325°F/Gas 3). In a large bowl, mix together the ground spices and season with salt and pepper. Toss the meat in the mixture. Heat half the oil in a large flameproof casserole or tagine over a medium-high heat, add the lamb in batches (with extra oil if necessary),

and cook for 6–8 minutes, or until the lamb is browned on all sides. Remove and set aside.

2 Heat the remaining oil in the casserole over a medium heat. Add the onion and cinnamon stick and stir so the onion is coated in any residual lamb juices. Cook for 3–4 minutes until the onion is soft. Stir in the chestnuts and pour in the orange juice. Increase the heat and let it simmer for a minute, stirring. Reduce the heat and return the lamb to the casserole along with any juices from the lamb.

3 Pour in the stock, bring to the boil, then reduce to a simmer, cover with the lid, and put in the oven for 2 hours. Check occasionally that it's not drying out, and top up with a little hot water, if needed. Add the orange slices for the last 30 minutes of cooking. Check for seasoning, stir through the coriander, and serve with couscous.

pumpkin and parsnip cassoulet

This light, vegetarian version of the traditional meaty cassoulet features creamy haricot beans with a crispy topping.

🥣 15 MINS   🍲 1 HR 45 MINS   ❄ FREEZABLE

SERVES 4–6

2 tbsp olive oil

1 onion, finely chopped

salt and freshly ground black pepper

3 garlic cloves, finely chopped

1 tsp ground cloves

2 carrots, finely chopped

2 celery sticks, finely chopped

1 bay leaf

450g (1lb) pumpkin (prepared weight), chopped into bite-sized pieces

450g (1lb) small parsnips, sliced into rounds

250ml (9fl oz) white wine

a few sprigs of thyme

400g can tomatoes

400g can haricot beans, rinsed and drained

900ml (1½ pints) hot vegetable stock

For the topping

125g (4½oz) breadcrumbs, lightly toasted

30g (1oz) Parmesan cheese, grated

1 tbsp chopped flat-leaf parsley

1 Preheat the oven to 180°C (350°F/Gas 4). Heat the oil in a large flameproof casserole over a medium heat, add the onion, and cook for 3–4 minutes until soft. Season, add the garlic, cloves, carrots, celery, and bay leaf, and cook, stirring occasionally, on a very low heat for 8–10 minutes until it is all soft. Stir through the pumpkin and parsnips and cook for a few minutes more, then pour in the wine. Increase the heat, stir, and let it bubble for a minute or two. Then add the thyme, tomatoes, beans, and stock, and bring to the boil. Reduce to a simmer, season, cover with the lid, and put in the oven for 40 minutes.

2 Mix the topping ingredients together in a bowl, sprinkle it over the cassoulet, and put back in the oven for 30 minutes. Then remove the lid and cook for about 10 minutes until the topping is golden. Ladle into warmed bowls and serve with crusty bread.

cabbage stuffed with chestnut and pork

An old favourite, ideal for a cold day, and easier than you might imagine to assemble. Everyone loves the rich, healthy stuffing.

🥣 **35-40 MINS**   🍲 **1 HR 30 MINS**

SPECIAL EQUIPMENT ▪ food processor

SERVES 6

1.35kg (3lb) head of Savoy cabbage

salt and freshly ground black pepper

125g (4½oz) lean, boneless pork

2 onions, finely chopped

2 slices of white bread, crusts removed

60g (2oz) butter

2 celery sticks, peeled and thinly sliced

500g (1lb 2oz) cooked, peeled chestnuts (approx 675g/1½lb unshelled weight), chopped

10 sprigs of parsley, leaves picked and chopped

10-12 sage leaves, finely chopped

grated zest of 1 lemon

2 eggs, lightly beaten

2 tbsp vegetable oil

500g can chopped tomatoes

1 tbsp tomato purée

1 garlic clove, finely chopped

1 bouquet garni

pinch of granulated sugar

125g (4½oz) mushrooms, sliced

1 Cut the outside leaf from the base of the cabbage stalk and peel off the leaf without tearing it. Repeat, removing 9 more cabbage leaves, and wash them all well in cold water to remove any dirt. Bring a large saucepan of water to the boil, add a little salt, and blanch the leaves for 1 minute. Transfer to a bowl of cold water. Trim and discard the stalk from the cabbage. Cook the cabbage head in the boiling water for 3–4 minutes. Transfer to a bowl of cold water, and when cool, drain, stalk-end down. Drain and pat dry the individual leaves with kitchen paper. Remove and discard the rib at the centre of each leaf. Slice the cabbage head in half. Remove the core and discard, then shred the head reasonably fine.

2 Blitz the pork in a food processor with one of the onions, and set aside. Put the bread slices in the food processor and pulse to crumbs.

3 Melt the butter in a frying pan, add the shredded cabbage, and cook, stirring, for 7–10 minutes until tender. Transfer to a large bowl. Put the pork and onion mixture into the frying pan with the celery. Cook, stirring, until the pork is crumbled and brown; it should take 5–7 minutes. Add the breadcrumbs, chestnuts, herbs, zest, salt, pepper, and pork to the bowl of cabbage, stirring well. Stir the eggs into the stuffing.

4 Line another bowl with a damp tea towel. Arrange 9 cabbage leaves in a layer around the inside. Allow 5cm (2in) of the leaves to extend above the rim. Set the last leaf in the bottom of the bowl. Spoon in the stuffing, then fold the ends of the cabbage leaves over to enclose the stuffing completely. Gather the ends of the cloth together over the top and tie tightly with string. Bring a large pan of water to the boil. Lift

up the tied ends of the tea towel and transfer the stuffed cabbage to the pan, immersing it in the water. Set a heatproof plate on top to weigh it down and simmer for 50–60 minutes.

5 Heat half of the oil in a frying pan. Add the remaining onion and cook until soft. Stir in the tomatoes, tomato purée, garlic, bouquet garni, and sugar, and cook, stirring occasionally, for 8–10 minutes until fairly thick. Remove from the heat and sieve the tomato sauce into a bowl. Heat the remaining oil in the frying pan and sauté the mushrooms until tender. Stir in the tomato sauce and season well.

6 Lift the cabbage from the pan, drain, and allow to cool slightly. Unwrap the tea towel and set the stuffed cabbage, stalk down, on a warmed serving plate. Serve the sauce separately.

clear soup with sea bass

White radish or daikon adds some hot flavour to this broth.

🥣 30-35 MINS   🍲 25 MINS

SPECIAL EQUIPMENT ▪ muslin

SERVES 4

10cm (4in) sheet of kombu (dried kelp)

10g (¼oz) dried bonito flakes

½ small carrot, sliced

salt

2.5cm (1in) piece of daikon, cut into 8 wedges

1 sea bass (about 375g/13oz), cleaned and cut into 4 steaks, head and tail discarded

1 tbsp Japanese rice wine

1 tbsp cornflour

1 lemon

125g (4½oz) spinach leaves

1 tsp Japanese soy sauce, or to taste

1 Put 1 litre (1¾ pints) cold water in a large saucepan and add the kombu. Bring to the boil over a high heat, then immediately remove from the heat and discard the kombu. Sprinkle the dried bonito flakes evenly over the surface of the water. Let the stock stand for 3–5 minutes until the flakes settle to the bottom. Line a sieve with damp muslin, then strain the stock through the muslin.

2 Half-fill a saucepan with water and bring to the boil. Add the carrot and a pinch of salt, and simmer for 3–5 minutes until tender. Drain and set aside. Repeat with the daikon wedges, simmering for 8–10 minutes until just tender. Drain and set aside.

3 Toss the fish with the rice wine. Put the cornflour on a plate and press both sides of each sea bass steak into it, shaking off any excess. Bring a saucepan of water to the boil, add the steaks, and bring back to a gentle simmer. Cook for 2–3 minutes, until just firm, then drain and set aside.

4 With a vegetable peeler, pare 2–3 strips of zest from the lemon, being sure to leave behind any white pith. Cut the zest into 12 very thin strips. Trim and discard any tough stalks from the spinach. Bring a pan of water to the boil, add the spinach, and simmer for 3 minutes or until tender. Drain, rinse with cold water, then gently squeeze. Chop, divide into 4 small piles, and keep warm.

5 Bring the soup stock to a very gentle boil with the soy sauce. Taste, adding more soy sauce if you like. Arrange the fish, carrot, and daikon in 4 warmed bowls. Ladle in the soup and garnish each bowl with 3 strips of lemon zest and a bundle of spinach. Serve immediately.

salmon, horseradish, and kale bake

This recipe is perfect for a mid-week meal with family or friends, as you can put all the ingredients together in next to no time and then put it in the oven to finish.

🥣 10 MINS   🍲 35 MINS

SERVES 4

4 salmon fillets, above 150g (5½oz) each, skinned (p75)

1.2 litres (2 pints) milk, plus enough to cover the fish

150g (5½oz) butter

2 tbsp plain flour

150g (5½oz) mature Cheddar cheese, grated

2 tsp Dijon mustard

salt and freshly ground black pepper

2 handfuls of kale

1-2 tbsp creamed horseradish

1 Preheat the oven to 200°C (400°F/ Gas 6). Sit the salmon fillets in a frying pan and pour over enough milk to cover (leaving the 1.2 litres/2 pints for the cheese sauce). Poach gently over a low heat for about 10 minutes until opaque and cooked. Then transfer to an ovenproof dish using a slotted spoon or a fish slice. Discard the poaching liquid.

2 To make a cheese sauce, melt the butter in a large pan, then remove it from the heat and stir in the flour to form a roux. Pour in a little milk taken from the 1.2 litres (2 pints), then put the pan back on the heat and slowly add the rest of the milk, stirring all the time. Switch to a balloon whisk and whisk the sauce over a low heat for about 5 minutes until it is smooth. Remove the pan from the heat once again and add the cheese and mustard. Stir thoroughly and season.

3 Meanwhile, trim the rough stalks from the kale and roughly chop the leaves. Place in a saucepan of boiling water and cook for about 5 minutes until nearly soft. Drain and add to the salmon. Combine gently.

4 Mix together the creamed horseradish and cheese sauce, pour over the salmon, and bake for about 15 minutes until golden.

braised oxtail

This traditional British dish is rich and hearty. For the best flavour, make it a day in advance and reheat to serve.

🥣 25 MINS PLUS CHILLING   🍲 3 HRS PLUS REHEATING

SERVES 4

1.5kg (3lb 3oz) oxtails, in large pieces

plain flour, to coat and toss

salt and freshly ground black pepper

3-4 tbsp beef drippings or vegetable oil

1 large onion, roughly chopped

1 large carrot, cut into chunks

1 large celery stick, cut into chunks

1 large parsnip, cut into chunks

85g (3oz) swede, cut into chunks

750ml (1¼ pints) hot beef stock

150ml (5fl oz) red wine or port

1 bouquet garni, made with 1 bay leaf and 2-3 sprigs each of thyme, parsley, and rosemary

1 Preheat the oven to 160°C (325°F/ Gas 3). Coat the oxtail in flour seasoned with pepper. Melt the dripping in a heavy flameproof casserole and brown the oxtail (fry in batches). Remove to a dish.

2 Toss the vegetables in flour, then brown them too (adding more dripping, if needed). Pour in 300ml (10fl oz) of the stock and stir to scrape up the bits from the bottom of the pan. Return the oxtail to the casserole, pour in the wine, and add the bouquet garni. Cover the pan tightly. Bring to the boil, then transfer to the oven to cook for 2½–3 hours. Remove from the oven and allow to cool, then refrigerate overnight.

3 Next day, remove the excess fat from the surface and add the remaining stock. Reheat in the oven at 180°C (350°F/Gas 4) for 30 minutes. Serve with mashed potato.

chinese roast duck

It is the aromatic seasoning made from a range of Oriental spices and other flavourings that gives the universally popular Chinese roast duck its particular flavour. The seasoning is spooned into the duck's body cavity and then the bird is roasted for several hours, during which time the seasoning imbues the duck with its flavour.

🥣 45 MINS PLUS AIR-DRYING AND STANDING   🍲 1 HR 45 MINS - 2 HRS

SPECIAL EQUIPMENT ▪ bamboo skewer

SERVES 4

1 duck, about 2.25kg (5lb) total weight

1 tbsp maltose or honey

For the aromatic seasoning

1 tsp Szechuan peppercorns

2 tbsp ground bean sauce or black bean sauce

1 tbsp Chinese rice wine or dry sherry

2 tsp caster sugar

½ tsp five-spice powder

2 tbsp light soy sauce

1 tsp sunflower oil

3 garlic cloves, finely chopped

2.5cm (1in) piece of fresh root ginger, peeled and finely chopped

4 spring onions, trimmed and sliced, plus extra to serve

small bunch of coriander, leaves chopped, plus extra sprigs for garnish (optional)

1 Rinse the duck inside and out with cold water and pat dry with kitchen paper. Pull away and discard any fat from the body cavity. Tie heavy string several times around the flap of skin at the neck opening. Half-fill a wok with water and bring to the boil. Immerse the duck in the water and use a ladle to pour water over the breast for 1 minute until the duck skin becomes taut. Remove the duck and pat dry with kitchen paper. Hang the duck by the string in a cool place for about 2 hours, until the skin is dry.

2 For the aromatic seasoning, heat a wok over a medium heat. Add the peppercorns and cook, stirring, for 1–2 minutes, until they smoke slightly. Transfer to a mortar and pound to a coarse powder. Put the powder in a bowl with the bean sauce, rice wine or dry sherry, sugar, five-spice powder, and soy sauce. Stir together.

3 Reheat the wok over a medium heat until very hot. Drizzle in the oil and heat until the oil is very hot. Add the garlic, ginger, and spring onions, and stir-fry for about 30 seconds, until fragrant. Add the sauce mixture and the coriander. Bring to the boil, then reduce the heat to low, and simmer for about 1 minute. Transfer to a bowl and let it cool.

4 About 45 minutes before roasting the duck, put a bamboo skewer into a bowl of water and let it soak. Preheat the oven to 200°C (400°F/Gas 6). Spoon the seasoning into the body cavity. Overlap the skin to close the cavity and thread the skewer 2–3 times from the top of the cavity through both layers of skin, then through the tail. Tie string around the tail and the top of the skewer. Set the duck, breast-side up, on a rack in a roasting tin. Roast for 15 minutes.

5 Meanwhile, combine the maltose or honey and 4 tbsp boiling water in a small bowl. Remove the duck from the oven and brush the maltose all over the skin. Reduce the oven temperature to 180°C (350°F/Gas 4) and continue roasting for 1½–1¾ hours, brushing every 15 minutes with the maltose mixture, until dark brown and the leg meat feels soft.

6 Transfer the duck to a chopping board and let it stand for about 15 minutes, then remove the string and skewer. Set a sieve over a bowl. Pour the seasoning from the duck cavity into the sieve. Skim off and discard the fat; reserve the liquid. Carve the duck and chop the meat into 2.5cm (1in) pieces. Arrange on a warmed platter, pour over the seasoning, and decorate with sliced spring onions and coriander sprigs, if using. Serve immediately.

squash, spinach, and horseradish bake

The ever-popular butternut squash has a starring role in this baked dish, ably assisted by colourful spinach leaves.

 10 MINS   🍲 30 MINS

SERVES 4

2 handfuls of spinach leaves, rinsed and drained

1 small to medium butternut squash, halved, deseeded, peeled, and thinly sliced

2 garlic cloves, grated or finely chopped

300ml (10fl oz) double cream

2 tsp freshly grated horseradish (or 3–4 tsp creamed horseradish)

salt and freshly ground black pepper

1 Preheat the oven to 200°C (400°F/Gas 6). Put the spinach in a pan with a little water (the water clinging to the leaves should be enough) and cook for a few minutes until just wilted. Alternatively, put in a microwave-proof bowl, cover loosely, and wilt in the microwave. Drain and squeeze out the excess water. Set aside.

2 Put the squash and garlic in a wide pan, pour over the cream, and simmer gently over a low heat for 10 minutes. Remove the squash with a slotted spoon and layer it in an ovenproof dish with the wilted spinach.

3 Stir the grated or creamed horseradish into the cream in the pan, then pour the mixture over the squash. Season with salt and lots of pepper. Cover with foil and roast in the oven for 20 minutes.

variation

swiss chard and pumpkin bake

Prepare in the same way, but use 200g (7oz) shredded Swiss chard instead of spinach and ½ small pumpkin for the butternut squash. Add a good grating of nutmeg instead of the horseradish at step 3.

shepherd's pie

A perennial favourite, shepherd's pie never fails to please, especially during winter. Perfect comfort food.

🥣 30 MINS   🍲 1 HR 30 MINS   ❄️ FREEZABLE

SERVES 4

550g (1¼lb) floury potatoes, peeled

large knob of butter

salt and freshly ground black pepper

3 tbsp olive oil

2 onions, diced

3 carrots, diced

550g (1¼lb) minced lamb

3 garlic cloves, chopped

1 tsp dried oregano

600g can chopped tomatoes

125g (4½oz) frozen peas

1 Preheat the oven to 180°C (350°F/Gas 4). Cook the potatoes in a pan of boiling salted water for 15–20 minutes until tender. Drain, then mash well. Add the butter and mash again until creamy. Season with salt and pepper, then set aside.

2 Meanwhile, heat the oil in a heavy-based pan over a medium heat, add the onions and carrots, and cook for 5 minutes, or until the onions are starting to soften. Add the lamb and cook, stirring constantly, for 10 minutes, or until no longer pink. Add the garlic and oregano, cook for 1 minute, then stir in the tomatoes and bring to the boil.

3 Add the peas, season well, then bring to the boil before lowering the heat. Simmer for 20 minutes, stirring occasionally. Pour a layer of the lamb sauce into individual serving dishes and top with the mashed potato. Bake in the oven for 30–35 minutes until brown on top and piping hot.

roast pork with bacon and chicory

Chicory wrapped in bacon rashers is a very satisfying foil to roast pork. This generous all-in-one recipe will give you plenty of leftovers – perfect for sandwiches the next day.

🥣 10 MINS PLUS RESTING   🍲 2 HRS

SERVES 4

- 1.8kg (4lb) loin of pork or boneless rolled shoulder
- ½ tbsp olive oil
- 1 tbsp salt
- 400g (14oz) shallots, large ones halved
- 150ml (5fl oz) dry cider
- 4 heads of chicory, trimmed
- 12 streaky bacon rashers

1 Preheat the oven to 240°C (475°F/ Gas 9). Rub the pork all over with the oil, then smother with the salt. Put in the oven to cook for 15–20 minutes, or until the skin is crispy. Remove the tin from the oven and reduce the oven temperature to 180°C (350°F/Gas 4).

2 Lift the pork up, place the shallots underneath, then sit the pork down on top of them. Drizzle over the cider and return to the oven to cook for 1¾ hours. Meanwhile, wrap the chicory evenly in the bacon and add to the tin for the last 40 minutes of cooking.

3 Remove the pork and keep it warm while it rests for at least 20 minutes. Carve the roast and serve with the chicory and other accompaniments of your choice.

variation

roast pork with bacon and celery hearts
Prepare in the same way, but use 400g (14oz) pickling onions instead of shallots. Instead of chicory, blanch 2 halved celery hearts in boiling water for 2–3 minutes, drain, wrap in the bacon, and proceed as in the original recipe.

pork chops with apple and baby onions

A stuffing piled on top of pork chops before roasting them not only enhances their flavour, but also prevents the chops from drying out in the oven: a win-win situation.

🥣 15 MINS   🍲 35 MINS

SPECIAL EQUIPMENT ▪ food processor

SERVES 4

- 2 slices of white bread
- handful of sage leaves
- 1 small onion, roughly chopped
- salt and freshly ground black pepper
- 4 x pork loin chops, about 2cm (¾in) thick and about 125g (4½oz) each
- 12 baby onions or shallots, large ones halved
- 3 cooking apples, peeled and roughly chopped
- 2 tbsp demerara sugar
- drizzle of olive oil
- handful of rosemary sprigs

1 Preheat the oven to 200°C (400°F/ Gas 6). Put the bread, sage, and onion in a food processor and blitz until you have a crumb mixture. Spread out on a baking tray and put in the oven for 5 minutes, or until golden. Return to the food processor and blitz again until finely ground. Season well.

2 Sit the chops in a roasting tin and add the baby onions. Add the apples and sprinkle them with the sugar, then drizzle over a little oil. Add the rosemary and sprinkle over a pinch of salt, some pepper, and the golden breadcrumb mixture.

3 Put in the oven to roast for 30–35 minutes, or until the meat is cooked through and the onions are beginning to brown. Turn the chops halfway through cooking. Serve with some creamy mashed potato.

Season's best **pomegranates**

Considered a superfood, the leathery skin of a pomegranate hides many "arils", each comprising a small, edible seed in a sac of ruby-red or white sweetly tart juice held by a bitter, white pith. Widely cultivated in many countries, it is at its best in early winter through to spring. Enjoy as a snack or scatter the arils over salads, or with chicken, duck, or pork. Try the juice in marinades and syrups.

Native to Iran, pomegranates are grown in Mediterranean-type climates around the world, mainly America, the Middle East, India, and Spain.

The calyx end is strikingly shaped like a crown.

Wonderful This is a leading Californian variety with a signature crimson colour, abundant juice, a sweet flavour, and glowing red arils. It is a top choice for both eating and juicing.

Middle Eastern pomegranate
The Middle East is a major exporter of pomegranates, both whole fruit and processed seeds. They have been grown there for thousands of years.

Packs of ready-prepared arils are sold separately for use in salads, desserts, and for quick snacking.

essentials
varieties available
Available as whole fruit, fresh, ready-prepared seeds in packs, and as juice. Also look for pomegranate molasses and Grenadine syrup.

buy Choose glossy fruit that feels heavy for its size. Avoid any that look dry or damaged.

store Whole fruit can be kept in the fridge for a few weeks. Packs of ready-prepared arils can be refrigerated for a few days, or frozen to be used for juice.

cook Add the juice or arils to salads, desserts, soups, stews, and sauces.

recipe ideas
Middle Eastern oranges p475

Shredded turkey, mint, and pomegranate salad p373

Turkish lamb and pomegranate pilaf p373

how to cut and prepare pomegranate
This delicious fruit has a tough skin and requires patience when preparing; however, it is worth the effort. Make sure you remove all traces of the bitter white membrane.

1 Slice off the top of the pomegranate with a sharp knife. Slice into quarters, following the lines of arils.

2 The seeds are in clusters divided by a thin membrane. Pick out the seeds from each quarter.

chicken and orange tagine

The flavours in this tagine are a harmonious blend of citrus and spice. If you can't find the spice mix ras-el-hanout, use a pinch each of ground cinnamon and grated nutmeg instead.

🥣 **20 MINS**   🍲 **1 HR 45 MINS**   ❄ **FREEZABLE**

SERVES 4

8 chicken thighs, with skin on

1 tsp ras-el-hanout spice (optional)

salt and freshly ground black pepper

1–2 tbsp olive oil

1 red onion, finely chopped

2 tsp coriander seeds, half of them crushed

2 green chillies, deseeded and finely chopped

3 garlic cloves, finely chopped

2 oranges, segmented and juice reserved

400g can chopped tomatoes

900ml (1½ pints) hot chicken or vegetable stock

handful of coriander, roughly chopped

1 Preheat the oven to 190°C (375°F/ Gas 5). Smother the chicken with the ras-el-hanout spice mix, if using, and season well with salt and pepper. Heat half the oil in a large flameproof casserole or tagine over a medium-high heat and cook the chicken (in batches, if necessary) for 6–8 minutes until golden. Remove and set aside.

2 Heat the remaining oil in the casserole over a medium heat, add the onion, and cook for 3–4 minutes until soft. Season with salt and pepper, stir through the coriander seeds, chillies, and garlic, and cook for a further minute. Add the orange juice, increase the heat, and let the sauce simmer for a minute, then return the chicken to the casserole together with its juices.

3 Add the tomatoes and a little of the stock and bring to the boil, then pour in the remaining stock and boil for 1–2 minutes. Reduce the heat, cover with the lid, and put in the oven for 1½ hours. Check occasionally that it's not drying out, and top up with a little hot water, if needed. Add the orange segments for the last 30 minutes of cooking. Stir in most of the coriander and serve with couscous, with the remaining coriander sprinkled over.

shredded turkey, mint, and pomegranate salad

Pomegranate molasses as well as seeds is used in this salad. The fragrant molasses has a tangy flavour and is essential in Middle Eastern cuisine. Find it in specialist food stores.

🥣 **15 MINS**

SERVES 4

large handful of watercress

large handful of radicchio

300g (10oz) cooked turkey breast, sliced

1 red onion, finely sliced

handful of mint leaves

seeds from 1 pomegranate

For the dressing

3 tbsp extra virgin olive oil

1 tbsp lemon juice

1 tbsp pomegranate molasses

pinch of ground cinnamon

salt and freshly ground black pepper

pinch of sugar (optional)

1 Arrange the watercress and radicchio on a serving plate and top with the turkey. Scatter over the onion, mint leaves, and the pomegranate seeds.

2 In a bowl, whisk together the oil, lemon juice, pomegranate molasses, and cinnamon. Season to taste with salt and pepper, adding some sugar, if you like. Drizzle the dressing over the salad and serve.

turkish lamb and pomegranate pilaf

Fragrant and full of colour, this pilaf has complex layers of flavour. Swap in different fruits and nuts for variety – dates, sultanas, and almonds are often used in Turkish cuisine.

🥣 **15 MINS**   🍲 **1 HR**

SERVES 4-6

2 tbsp olive oil, plus extra for drizzling

675g (1½lb) lamb leg, cut into bite-sized pieces

1 onion, finely chopped

salt and freshly ground black pepper

3 garlic cloves, finely chopped

1 green chilli, deseeded and finely sliced

1 tsp dried mint

1 tsp ground cinnamon

60g (2oz) golden sultanas or use regular sultanas

350g (12oz) easy-cook basmati rice

900ml (1½ pints) hot lamb stock

60g (2oz) hazelnuts, toasted and roughly chopped

small handful of dill, finely chopped

seeds from 1 pomegranate

75g (2½oz) feta cheese, crumbled (optional)

1 Heat the oil in a large flameproof casserole over a medium-high heat, add the lamb (in batches, if necessary), and cook for 6–8 minutes until browned on all sides. Remove and set aside.

2 Add the onion to the casserole and cook over a medium heat for 3–4 minutes until soft. Season with salt and pepper, stir in the garlic, chilli, mint, and cinnamon, and cook for another 2 minutes. Stir in the sultanas.

3 Stir through the rice and turn it, so all the grains are coated and the juices soaked up. Return the lamb to the casserole, pour over the stock, and reduce to a simmer. Partially cover and cook for 30–40 minutes, topping up with a little more hot stock if it begins to dry out. Taste and season, then stir through the hazelnuts and dill, and scatter with the pomegranate seeds. Top with crumbled feta, if using, and serve with warm pitta bread and a lightly dressed, crisp green salad.

corned beef hash with horseradish

An economical classic that could evoke the winter dishes of childhood. Creamed horseradish adds a kick to this simple recipe.

🥄 10 MINS   🍲 25 MINS   ❄ FREEZABLE

SERVES 4

1 tbsp olive oil

1 onion, finely chopped

pinch of salt

1 garlic clove, grated or finely chopped

675g (1½lb) potatoes, peeled and cut in chunks

3 large carrots, finely diced

450ml (15fl oz) hot beef stock

250g can corned beef, roughly chopped

2-3 tsp creamed horseradish

splash of Worcestershire sauce (optional)

pickled red cabbage, to serve

1 Heat the oil in a large frying pan over a low heat. Add the onion and a pinch of salt and sweat for about 5 minutes until soft and translucent. Next, add the garlic, potato, and carrot and sweat for about 5 minutes. Pour in a little of the stock and bring to the boil. Stir through the corned beef and creamed horseradish and mix well.

2 Add the remaining stock, reduce the heat slightly, and simmer gently for about 15 minutes, until the potatoes and carrots are cooked, stirring occasionally so that it doesn't stick, and to break up the chunks of corned beef. Taste and season, if needed. Add the Worcestershire sauce and stir through (if using). Serve hot with pickled red cabbage.

celeriac soufflé pie

A hearty, tasty warmer. Also try parsnips instead of celeriac.

🥄 40 MINS PLUS CHILLING   🍲 50 MINS

SPECIAL EQUIPMENT ▪ 20cm (8in) flan tin ▪ ceramic baking beans

SERVES 4

175g (6oz) wholemeal or spelt flour

salt and freshly ground black pepper

1 tbsp caraway seeds

75g (2½oz) cold butter, diced

85g (3oz) Cheddar cheese, grated

3 eggs, separated

1 celeriac, about 450g (1lb), peeled and cut into chunks

60g (2oz) butter

4 tbsp milk

4 streaky bacon rashers, diced

2 tbsp snipped chives

1 Mix the flour, salt, and caraway seeds in a bowl. Rub in the butter until the mixture resembles breadcrumbs. Stir in the cheese. Mix 3 tbsp cold water with 1 egg yolk and stir into the flour mixture to form a firm dough, adding more water if necessary. Knead gently on a lightly floured surface, then wrap with oiled cling film and chill for at least 30 minutes.

2 Meanwhile, cook the celeriac in boiling salted water until tender. Drain and return to the pan. Dry out briefly over a gentle heat. Mash with the butter and milk. Dry-fry the bacon and add to the pan with fat. Beat in the remaining 2 egg yolks and chives. Season well.

3 Preheat the oven to 200°C (400°F/ Gas 6). Roll out the pastry and use to line the flan tin, pressing it into the corners. Trim away the excess and prick the bottom all over with a fork. Line the pastry shell with greaseproof paper and fill with ceramic baking beans. Bake for 10 minutes until the edges are golden. Remove the beans and paper and return to the oven for 5 minutes to crisp. Remove from the oven and set aside.

4 Whisk the 3 egg whites until stiff. Mix 1 tbsp into the celeriac mixture. Fold in the remainder with a metal spoon. Spoon into the pastry case and bake for 25 minutes until risen, just set, and golden. Serve hot.

belly pork and squash

No meat performs better when slow cooked than tender pork.

🥄 30 MINS   🍲 2 HRS 15 MINS - 2 HRS 45 MINS

SERVES 4-6

1 tbsp olive oil

700g (1lb 9oz) pork belly

salt and freshly ground black pepper

1 onion, finely chopped

3 garlic cloves, finely chopped

3 sage leaves, finely chopped

1 sprig of rosemary

1 butternut squash, peeled, deseeded, and cut into cubes

100ml (3½fl oz) dry sherry

1.2 litres (2 pints) hot vegetable stock

1 Preheat the oven to 160°C (325°F/ Gas 3). Heat half the oil in a large flameproof casserole over a medium-high heat. Season the pork belly with salt and pepper and add it, skin-side down, to the casserole. Cook for about 10 minutes, or until it begins to colour and become crispy. Remove from the casserole and set aside.

2 Heat the remaining oil in the casserole over a medium heat, add the onion, and cook for 3-4 minutes until soft. Stir in the garlic, sage, and rosemary, followed by the squash, and turn over the ingredients to coat. Pour in the sherry, increase the heat, and let it bubble for a minute.

3 Return the pork belly to the casserole, add the stock, and bring to the boil. Reduce to a simmer, cover with the lid, and put in the oven for 2-2½ hours. Check occasionally that it's not drying out, topping up with a little hot water if needed. Slice or cut the pork into bite-sized pieces and serve in warmed shallow bowls together with the squash and its juices. Serve with crusty bread.

ham hock with red cabbage

Slow-cooked sweet cabbage is the perfect complement to ham, and with the addition of spices and dried fruit, the humble piece of meat is transformed. Ham hocks are also known as knuckles.

🥣 20 MINS   🍲 3 HRS

SERVES 4–6

2 ham hocks, about 1.35kg (3lb) each

1 small red cabbage, cored and finely shredded

2 onions, sliced

4 garlic cloves, finely chopped

a few sprigs of thyme

60g (2oz) raisins

pinch of grated nutmeg

pinch of ground cinnamon

300ml (10fl oz) white wine vinegar

600ml (1 pint) hot vegetable stock

salt and freshly ground black pepper

1 Preheat the oven to 160°C (325°F/ Gas 3). Sit the ham hocks in a large heavy-based pan and cover with water. Bring to the boil, then reduce to a simmer, partially cover, and cook gently for 1 hour. Remove the hams and reserve the ham stock, if you wish to use it instead of the vegetable stock (it can be salty). When the hams are cool enough to handle, remove the skin and discard, then sit the hams in a large flameproof casserole.

2 Add all the other ingredients to the casserole, using either the stock or the cooking liquid, and tuck the hams in neatly. Season with salt and pepper, cover, and put in the oven for 2 hours. Check occasionally that it's not drying out, topping up with a little hot water if necessary.

3 Remove the hams, shred the meat, and stir it into the casserole. Serve with baked or roast potatoes.

variation

ham hock with white cabbage and celery

At step 2 add 1 small shredded white cabbage instead of red, and 2 chopped celery sticks along with the other onions, garlic, and thyme. Omit the raisins, nutmeg, and cinnamon and add 1 tbsp caraway seeds. Cook as before. Serve with plain boiled potatoes.

roast leg of pork with orange

This is easy to adapt for a cooked ham or gammon on the bone (bake for 1 hour only). It is also excellent cold, so it is worth cooking even if you don't have a crowd to feed.

🥣 20–25 MINS   🍲 3 HRS 30 MINS – 4 HRS

SERVES 8-10

1 leg of pork, about 4.5kg (10lb) in weight

8 oranges

1 tbsp Dijon mustard

175g (6oz) dark soft brown sugar

20 cloves

small bunch of watercress

For the sauce

4 tbsp Grand Marnier

½ tsp grated nutmeg

½ tsp ground cloves

1 Preheat the oven to 180°C (350°F/Gas 4). Wipe the pork with kitchen paper, then set it in a roasting tin. Halve 6 of the oranges and squeeze out the juice. There should be about 500ml (16fl oz).

2 Pour some of the orange juice over the pork and roast in the oven for 3–3½ hours, pouring more orange juice over every 30 minutes or so to keep it moist. Slice the remaining oranges, discarding any pips.

3 To test if the pork is cooked, insert a metal skewer for 30 seconds near the centre of the leg; it should be warm to the touch when withdrawn. A meat thermometer should show 77°C (170°F).

4 Take the pork from the oven and let it cool slightly. Increase the heat to 200°C (400°F/Gas 6). Cut through the skin around the bone end of the joint. With a knife, peel the skin from the fat, starting from the wider end of the joint.

5 Mix the mustard and sugar together. Spread and press over the pork. Overlap the orange slices over the joint and stud each one with a clove. Roast for 30–45 minutes, basting with the juices every 10 minutes. Transfer to a warmed serving platter. Remove the orange slices and arrange next to the pork. Cover with foil and keep warm.

6 Pour the Grand Marnier into the roasting tin. Bring to the boil and whisk to dissolve the juices. Add the nutmeg and cloves and mix them in. Transfer to a sauce boat.

7 Carve the pork and serve on warmed plates with the orange slices, adding a little watercress, if you like. Serve the sauce separately.

jamaican-style fish with sweet potatoes

In Jamaica, typical West Indian fish species such as snapper and tilapia would be used for this dish, but coley, pollack, and sustainable cod are good seasonal choices.

🥣 15 MINS   🍲 30 MINS

SERVES 4

1 tsp allspice

1 tsp paprika

5cm (2in) piece of fresh root ginger, peeled and finely sliced

2 red chillies, deseeded and finely chopped

1 tbsp olive oil

salt and freshly ground black pepper

4 x 200g (7oz) fillets of firm-fleshed white fish, such as haddock, hake, or sustainable cod

4 sweet potatoes, peeled and cut into bite-sized pieces

small handful of coriander, finely chopped

1 Preheat the oven to 190°C (375°F/Gas 5). Mix the allspice, paprika, ginger, and chillies with the olive oil. Add a pinch of salt and lots of pepper. Smother the fish with most of the spice mixture and set aside. Toss the sweet potatoes with the remaining spice mixture and place in a roasting tin. Put in the oven to roast for 15 minutes.

2 Add the fish to the roasting tin and roast for 15 minutes, or until the potatoes are cooked – the fish will be cooked by then as well. Sprinkle with coriander and serve.

cheesy swiss chard crêpes

Most greens can be substituted for the chard in this recipe.

🥣 **1 HR PLUS STANDING**   🍲 **30-35 MINS**

SERVES 6

1 quantity pancake batter (p147)

3-4 tbsp vegetable oil

For the filling

750g (1lb 10oz) Swiss chard

30g (1oz) butter

2 garlic cloves, finely chopped

3 shallots, finely chopped

85g (3oz) soft goat's cheese

125g (4½oz) feta cheese

salt and freshly ground black pepper

pinch of grated nutmeg

For the cream sauce

250ml (9fl oz) milk

30g (1oz) butter

2 tbsp plain flour

120ml (4fl oz) double cream

pinch of grated nutmeg

30g (1oz) Gruyère cheese, grated

1 First make the crêpes as on p147 to make a total of 12. Pile them on a plate so they stay moist and warm.

2 Cut off the chard leaves and cut the stalks into 1cm (½in) slices. Boil the leaves in salted water for 2–3 minutes until tender. Drain, then chop.

3 Heat the butter in a frying pan. Add the garlic and shallots, and cook until soft but not browned. Add the chard stalks and sauté for 3–5 minutes, stirring. Add the leaves and sauté for 2–3 minutes, stirring, until all moisture has evaporated. Take the pan off the heat and crumble in the goat's cheese, then the feta. Add salt, pepper, and a pinch of nutmeg. Stir to mix, then set aside.

4 Preheat the oven to 180°C (350°F/ Gas 4). Butter a baking dish. To make the sauce, scald the milk in a pan. Melt the butter in another pan over a medium heat. Whisk in the flour and cook for 30–60 seconds, until foaming.

5 Remove from the heat, cool slightly, then whisk in the milk. Return to the heat and whisk until it boils and thickens. Whisk in the cream. Season with salt, pepper, and nutmeg, and simmer for 2 minutes. Keep warm.

6 Put 2 spoonfuls of filling on one half of the paler side of a crêpe. Fold the crêpe in half, then in half again, to form a triangle. Arrange in the dish, then continue. Spoon over the sauce. Sprinkle with the Gruyère. Bake for 20–25 minutes, until bubbling and brown. Serve hot from the dish.

beef with soy, lime, and a grapefruit and ginger salsa

The winter citrus salsa is spiced up with fiery chilli to add a refreshing sweet-hot dimension to this dish.

🥣 **10 MINS**   🍲 **15 MINS**

SERVES 4

1 tbsp groundnut oil or sunflower oil

1 red onion, cut into 8 wedges

675g (1½lb) rump steak, cut into strips

1 red chilli, deseeded and finely sliced into strips

splash of dark soy sauce

juice of 1 lime

1 tbsp runny honey

200g (7oz) chestnut mushrooms, cleaned and sliced

small handful of coriander

For the grapefruit and ginger salsa

2 grapefruit, segmented and chopped

2.5cm (1in) piece of fresh root ginger, grated

1 red chilli, deseeded and finely chopped

pinch of sugar (optional)

1 First, make the salsa. Put all the ingredients in a bowl, stir, and taste. Add a little sugar, if you wish. Set aside.

2 Heat the oil in a wok over a high heat until hot. Add the onion and stir-fry for about 5 minutes until soft, before adding the beef strips and chilli. Continue to stir-fry for another 5 minutes or so, keeping everything moving in the wok. Add the soy, lime juice, and honey, and keep stir-frying.

3 Throw in the mushrooms and stir-fry for a few minutes until they are soft and begin to release their juices.

4 To serve, pile the coriander on top of the beef and serve immediately with the grapefruit salsa and rice or noodles.

mustard chicken casserole

Chicken and mustard is a classic combination – and in this recipe, mustard is mixed with honey for a sweet marinade. If you have the time, let the chicken marinate for a few hours.

🥣 **10 MINS PLUS MARINATING**   🍲 **1 HR 45 MINS**
❄️ **FREEZABLE**

SERVES 4-6

2 tbsp wholegrain mustard

1 tbsp English mustard

2 tbsp runny honey

8 chicken thighs, with skin on

salt and freshly ground black pepper

2 tbsp olive oil

2 onions, roughly chopped

300g (10oz) parsnips, roughly chopped

1 tbsp thyme leaves

900ml (1½ pints) hot vegetable or chicken stock

small bunch of flat-leaf parsley, finely chopped

1 Preheat the oven to 160°C (325°F/Gas 3). Mix together the mustards in a bowl and stir in the honey. Season the chicken thighs well with salt and pepper, then smother them with the mustard mixture. Cover and leave to marinate for at least 30 minutes and up to 2 hours.

2 Heat half the oil in a large flameproof casserole over a medium-high heat and add the chicken thighs, a few at a time. Cook for 6–10 minutes until golden – be careful, as the honey may cause them to blacken quickly. Remove and set aside.

3 Heat the remaining oil in the casserole over a medium heat, add the onions, and toss them around the casserole to coat in any juices. Stir to scrape up the sticky bits from the bottom, then add the parsnips and thyme. Pour in the stock, bring to the boil, then reduce to a simmer. Return the chicken to the casserole together with any juices, nestling them in between the parsnips and making sure they are covered in liquid. Season, cover, and put in the oven for 1½ hours. Check occasionally that it's not drying out, and top up with a little hot water, if needed. Add the parsley, taste, and season. Serve with steamed leeks or greens.

turkey and cranberry casserole

This festive stew is an excellent use for leftover turkey.

🥣 **15 MINS**   🍲 **1 HR 15 MINS - 1 HR 45 MINS**   ❄️ **FREEZABLE**

SERVES 4-6

2 large turkey breasts

salt and freshly ground black pepper

2-3 tbsp olive oil

4 sausages, sliced

1 red onion, finely chopped

3 garlic cloves, finely chopped

250g (9oz) chestnut mushrooms, quartered

a few sprigs of rosemary

1 tbsp Dijon mustard

250ml (9fl oz) red wine

600ml (1 pint) hot chicken stock

handful of fresh cranberries

250g (9oz) fine green beans, trimmed

1 Preheat the oven to 160°C (325°F/Gas 3). Season the turkey and heat half the oil in a flameproof casserole over a medium-high heat. Cook the turkey in the casserole for 6–8 minutes; remove and set aside.

2 Heat the remaining oil in the casserole and cook the sausage for 3–4 minutes until it starts to colour. Add the onion, and cook for 2–3 minutes until soft. Stir through the garlic, mushrooms, rosemary, and mustard, cook for a minute, then increase the heat and add the wine. Let the sauce bubble for a minute, add the stock, and bring to the boil.

3 Return the turkey to the casserole, add seasoning, and stir through the cranberries. Cover with the lid and put in the oven for 1–1½ hours. Check occasionally that it's not drying out, topping up with a little hot water, if needed. Add the beans for the last 15 minutes of cooking. Remove the rosemary and the turkey breasts and shred the meat with a fork. Return the meat to the casserole and stir in. Serve with creamy mashed potatoes.

stuffed roast goose

A rich roasted goose is a traditional treat at Christmas time.

🥣 **40 MINS PLUS RESTING**   🍲 **3 HRS**

SERVES 6-8

4.5kg (10lb) goose with giblets

4 onions, finely chopped

10 sage leaves, chopped

50g (1¾oz) butter

115g (4oz) fresh breadcrumbs

salt and freshly ground black pepper

1 egg yolk

2 tbsp plain flour

tart apple sauce, to serve

1 Preheat the oven to 230°C (450°F/Gas 8). Remove excess fat from inside the goose. Prick the skin. Make a stock with the giblets, reserving the liver.

2 Boil the onions and chopped liver in a little water for 5 minutes, then drain. Mix with the sage, butter, and breadcrumbs, and season. Bind with the egg. Stuff loosely into the neck end of the goose and sew or secure with a skewer. Any leftover stuffing can be cooked separately in a small roasting tin. Cover the wings and drumsticks with foil.

3 Place the goose upside down on a rack in a deep roasting tin. Roast for 1 hour, turning the goose over after 30 minutes. Drain and reserve the fat in the roasting tin. Cover the goose with foil, lower the heat to 190°C (375°F/Gas 5), and roast for 1½ hours. Drain the fat. Remove the foil and roast for a final 30 minutes. Transfer to a serving dish and let it rest for 30 minutes.

4 For the gravy, simmer the reserved giblet stock. Heat 3 tbsp of goose fat in a pan, stir in the flour, and cook for 5 minutes over a low heat. Slowly whisk in the hot stock to thicken the gravy. Add the gravy to the roasting tin after removing the fat, stirring up the brown juices. Strain the gravy.

5 Carve the goose and serve with the gravy, stuffing, and a tart apple sauce.

festive wild rice salad

This tastes even better after standing for a few hours, so it is an ideal buffet party dish. You can prepare the wild rice salad a day ahead and keep it, covered, in the fridge. Let it come to room temperature before adding the turkey and serving.

🥣 **30-35 MINS PLUS STANDING**   🍲 **45 MINS - 1 HR 15 MINS**

SERVES 4

salt and freshly ground black pepper

200g (7oz) wild rice

85g (3oz) fresh cranberries

25g (scant 1oz) sugar

30g (1oz) pecans

julienned zest and juice of 1 small orange

2 tbsp cider vinegar

1 shallot, very finely chopped

4 tbsp vegetable oil

200g (7oz) sliced, cooked turkey breast

1 Put 750ml (1¼ pints) water in a saucepan with ½ tsp salt and bring to the boil. Stir in the rice, cover, and simmer for about 1 hour, or until tender. Drain, cool, then tip into a large bowl. Set aside.

2 Preheat the oven to 190°C (375°F/Gas 5). Spread the cranberries in a baking dish, sprinkle with the sugar, and bake in the heated oven for 10–15 minutes, until they start to pop. Let cool in the dish. Set aside.

3 Spread the pecans on a baking sheet and bake for 5–8 minutes, stirring occasionally, until toasted, then coarsely chop.

4 Bring a small saucepan of water to the boil and add the julienned orange zest. Simmer for 2 minutes, then drain and finely chop. Set aside.

5 Put the orange juice, vinegar, shallots, salt, and pepper into a bowl. Gradually whisk in the oil so the dressing emulsifies and thickens

slightly. Taste for seasoning. Add the cranberries, leaving their juice behind, and stir.

6 If necessary, remove the skin from the cooked turkey breast. Add the pecans, orange zest, and two-thirds of the dressing to the rice. Toss and let stand for 1 hour, to let the flavours combine. Taste for seasoning. To serve, transfer the rice salad to a platter, arrange the turkey on top, and spoon over the remaining cranberry dressing.

Season's best **turkey**

Mostly reared for Thanksgiving and Christmas in winter, with some in spring for Easter, turkey is a popular choice because of its unique flavour. It is a good, low-fat source of protein. Choose free-range birds, such as bronze turkeys, for ethical reasons and for better flavour. Cranberries are a favourite pairing, but it is also great with sweet spices, fragrant herbs, chestnuts, mushrooms, and citrus.

The breast has tender, white meat; good cooked any way.

Turkey (whole) Whole birds can be very large. It is best to start roasting them breast-down to ensure the white meat stays succulent and that the thicker bone areas cook through.

The leg and thigh have dark meat; roast, stew, or casserole.

Diced turkey Leg meat is darker than breast meat, but when slowly cooked, is very succulent. It is best suited to stews and pies, or for mincing.

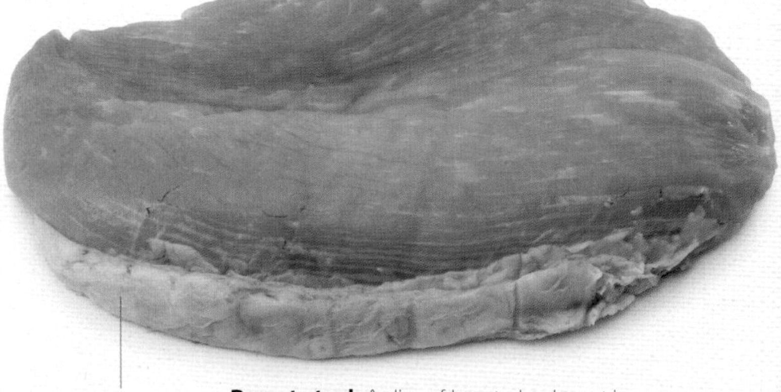

The wing has high bone-to-meat ratio; good stewed or casseroled.

Breast is the whitest and most tender meat on a turkey.

Breast steak A slice of lean turkey breast is good for poaching, grilling, or frying. If skinless, it may be called a breast fillet. When sliced or beaten out very thinly it is called an escalope. It can also be diced or sliced for stir-frying.

Leg One of the cheapest cuts, the leg comprises the thigh and the drumstick (or, from a very large bird, just the drumstick to serve several people). It can be roasted, but is often better stewed or braised.

Turkey drumstick has darker meat and includes some sinew.

Bard with bacon or baste with butter to prevent drying.

Boneless breast joint A tender joint for roasting. One breast makes a slim joint; both breasts together are plumper. The two boneless breasts sold joined, but untied, is called a butterfly, which you can stuff and tie yourself.

how to carve a turkey

This technique is suitable for turkey and other plump-breasted poultry, such as chicken or pheasant. Before carving, let the roasted bird rest a while in a warm place (on a plate to collect any juices). This relaxes the flesh, softens it, and makes it easier to carve. Use a sharp carving knife and fork to make the process of carving easier.

1 Cut through the leg joint, then cut it in half to separate the drumstick from the thigh. Repeat on the other side.

2 To remove the breast, slice down along a side of the breastbone, cut through the joint, repeat the other side.

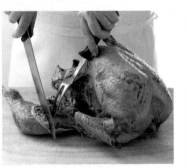

3 Cut the breast portions in half on a slight diagonal, leaving a good piece of breast meat attached to the wings.

4 To carve the breast meat only, make a horizontal cut above the wing. Continue to slice along the same line.

essentials
cuts available
Whole birds, breast steak, boneless breast joint, crown, large turkey drumstick with or without thigh, wings, diced meat, mince, sausages. Also available smoked.

buy Sold both fresh and frozen, whole or in pieces. For roasting, select one with a plump breast.

store Remove giblets and store separately. Whole birds and pieces will keep well in the bottom of the fridge for several days, completely wrapped.

cook Grill, fry, or stir-fry breast cuts; these and legs can also be stewed. Diced turkey can be stewed or stir-fried, or grilled or fried on skewers. Use mince for burgers, or as a lean substitute for beef in made dishes.

preserve Freeze fresh meat.

recipe ideas
Roast turkey with parsley and onion stuffing p382

Turkey and cranberry casserole p378

Turkey broth p362

Turkey escalopes stuffed with prunes and pecans p382

roast turkey with parsley and onion stuffing

The classic dish at Christmas, this recipe is too good to save for only once in the season. Try stuffing the turkey cavity with 4 lemon halves to add a zesty flavour to the meat.

🥣 15 MINS   🍲 3 HRS 20 MINS

SERVES 8

250g (9oz) butter

3 onions (1 finely chopped, 2 quartered)

125g (4½oz) white breadcrumbs

handful of flat-leaf parsley, finely chopped

salt and freshly ground black pepper

4kg (9lb) turkey

1 First, make the stuffing. Melt half the butter in a pan over a low heat, add the chopped onion, and sweat gently until soft. Remove from the heat, stir through the breadcrumbs and parsley, season, and set aside to cool. Preheat the oven to 200°C (400°F/Gas 6). Sit the turkey in a large roasting tin and season, inside and out. Spread the remaining butter over the skin. Stuff the onion quarters into the body cavity and the stuffing into the neck end. Roast for 20 minutes, then reduce the oven temperature to 190°C (375°F/Gas 5).

2 Cover the turkey loosely with foil and roast for 20 minutes per 450g (1lb), plus 20 minutes. Baste every hour with juices from the tin. Pierce the bird with a skewer. If the juices run clear, it is ready; if not, cook for a little longer. Remove the foil for the last 10–15 minutes.

3 Remove the turkey from the tin and put on a large warmed plate. Cover with foil and leave to rest in a warm place for 15 minutes. Serve slices of turkey with gravy, roast potatoes, cranberry sauce, and seasonal vegetables.

variation

roast turkey with sage and bacon stuffing

For the stuffing, prepare in the same way, but add 2 streaky bacon rashers, finely diced, with the onion. Use 115g (4oz) wholemeal breadcrumbs instead of white, and a handful of fresh sage instead of the parsley. Season and use as before.

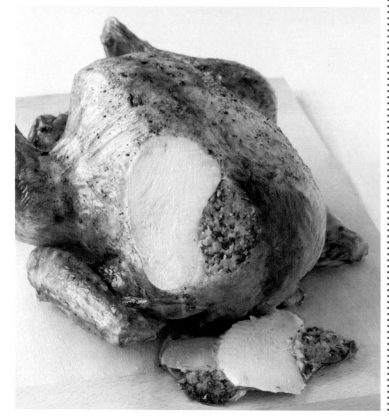

warm turkey and chickpea salad

A creative alternative to cold turkey on Boxing Day, this salad is light and healthy – great when you're feeling a bit guilty about the previous day's excesses!

🥣 15 MINS   🍲 10 MINS

SERVES 4

400g can chickpeas, drained and rinsed

1 tbsp olive oil

pinch of mild paprika

juice of 1 lemon

salt and freshly ground black pepper

350g (12oz) leftover roast turkey, sliced or roughly shredded

handful of dill, finely chopped

1 Put the chickpeas in a pan and pour over the oil, add the paprika and lemon juice, and season well with salt and pepper. Simmer very gently over a low heat for 5–8 minutes, until the chickpeas have softened slightly and warmed through.

2 To serve, toss the chickpeas with the leftover turkey, taste, and season again if needed. Scatter over the dill and serve warm with a fresh green salad or some wilted spinach.

variation

warm white bean and turkey salad

Make in the same way but use a 400g can cannellini beans instead of chickpeas. Add 1 large crushed garlic clove to the beans when simmering, and add a small handful each of chopped fresh flat-leaf parsley and coriander instead of the dill.

turkey escalopes stuffed with prunes and pecans

While you can buy ready-prepared turkey escalopes, they are very easy to make from the breasts. Serve these sweetened versions with sautéed potatoes and wilted spinach.

🍽 **15 MINS**   🍲 **15–20 MINS**

SERVES 4

2 skinless turkey breasts, about 400g (14oz) each

large handful of pitted prunes, chopped

handful of roasted pecan nuts, finely chopped

handful of flat-leaf parsley, chopped

1 tbsp olive oil

1 Preheat the oven to 200°C (400°F/ Gas 6). Cut each turkey breast in half and sandwich the 4 pieces between sheets of cling film. Pound them with a meat hammer or the edge of a rolling pin until they are an even thickness of about 5mm (¼in). Remove the cling film and slice the breasts in half so that you now have 8 escalopes.

2 Mix the prunes and nuts with the parsley in a bowl, then spoon the mixture into the middle of each turkey escalope. Roll up from one narrow end and secure with a cocktail stick.

3 Sit the turkey rolls in a roasting tin, drizzle with the oil, and roast in the oven for 15–20 minutes, until cooked through. Serve with sautéed potatoes and wilted spinach.

variation

pork escalopes with tangerine, prunes, and chestnuts

Prepare in exactly the same way, but use 4 small pork leg steaks instead of the turkey breasts. Beat out as before. For the stuffing, use the grated zest and chopped segments of 1 tangerine instead of half the prunes, and a handful of cooked, peeled chestnuts instead of the pecans. Add a good pinch of ground cinnamon with the chopped parsley.

baked turkey rolls filled with chestnuts and mushrooms

Catch fresh chestnuts at the end of their season by combining them with apricots, parsley, and delicate turkey breast in this impressive yet simple dish.

🍽 **20 MINS**   🍲 **40 MINS**

SPECIAL EQUIPMENT ▪ blender or food processor

SERVES 4

550g (1¼lb) turkey breasts, cut into 7.5cm (3in) strips

salt and freshly ground black pepper

100g (3½oz) ready-cooked chestnuts

2 garlic cloves, grated or finely chopped

small handful of flat-leaf parsley, finely chopped

75g (2½oz) dried apricots

300g (10oz) chestnut mushrooms

½ tsp dried thyme

4 tbsp olive oil

1 Preheat the oven to 180°C (350°F/ Gas 4). Season the turkey strips with a little salt and pepper and set aside. Meanwhile, put the chestnuts, garlic, and parsley in a blender or food processor and blitz for 10 seconds. Add the apricots and mushrooms and blitz for a further 5 seconds. Add the thyme and 3 tbsp of the oil and blitz for 5 seconds, or until you have a chunky paste. Season well with salt and pepper.

2 Place 1 tbsp of the mixture on each turkey strip and carefully roll it up. Place the rolls join-down in a baking dish, making sure they are quite tightly packed. Drizzle over the remaining oil, cover with foil, and bake in the oven for 30 minutes. Remove the foil and cook for a further 10 minutes, or until brown. Serve with a crisp green salad.

variation

baked turkey rolls with celery, chestnuts, and chanterelles

Prepare in the same way, but blitz a roughly chopped celery stick in the food processor with the chestnuts. Substitute 2 tbsp raisins for the apricots, and use 140g (5oz) each of chanterelle mushrooms and cup mushrooms, instead of chestnut ones.

squash, sage, and blue cheese risotto

Blue cheese and sage are a winning winter combination. Cut the squash into equal-sized pieces to help it cook evenly.

🥣 15 MINS   🍲 30 MINS

SERVES 4

1 butternut squash, halved, deseeded, peeled, and cut into bite-sized pieces

pinch of chilli flakes

2 tbsp olive oil

1.2 litres (2 pints) light vegetable stock

knob of butter

1 onion, finely chopped

salt and freshly ground black pepper

2 garlic cloves, grated or finely chopped

4 sage leaves, torn

350g (12oz) risotto rice, such as Arborio

1 large glass of dry white wine

75g (2½oz) Gorgonzola or similar blue cheese

1 Preheat the oven to 200°C (400°F/Gas 6). Put the squash in a roasting tin, sprinkle over the chilli flakes, and drizzle over 1 tbsp of the oil. Mix together, using your hands. Roast in the oven for about 15 minutes until golden and beginning to soften.

2 Meanwhile, pour the stock into a large pan and heat to a gentle simmer. Heat the remaining oil and a knob of butter in a large non-stick frying pan over a low heat. Add the onion and a pinch of salt, and sweat for 5 minutes until the onions are soft and translucent. Stir through the garlic and sage leaves, and cook for a few seconds more.

3 Next, stir through the rice, making sure that the grains are completely coated. Increase the heat to medium-high, pour in the wine, and let it simmer for a couple of minutes until the alcohol has evaporated.

4 Reduce the heat slightly and add the simmering stock a ladleful at a time, stirring frequently with a wooden spoon; when each addition of stock has been absorbed, add some more. Continue like this for about 20 minutes until the rice is al dente and creamy. Use more or less stock as required. Stir through the roasted squash and the Gorgonzola cheese, season with black pepper, and serve immediately.

garbure

This winter vegetable and pancetta one-pot recipe from southwest France is best made the day before and reheated.

🥣 40 MINS   🍲 1 HR

SERVES 4–6

100g (3½oz) lardons or diced pancetta

1 Spanish onion, finely chopped

3 garlic cloves, grated or finely chopped

1 leg confit of duck

1.5 litres (2¾ pints) chicken stock

1 small Savoy cabbage, core removed and leaves cut into 2.5 x 7.5cm (1 x 3in) strips

1 large carrot, sliced

1 celery stalk, diced

1 leek, cleaned and sliced

1 large floury potato, peeled and diced

salt and freshly ground black pepper

1 tsp pimentón picante or hot smoked paprika

½ tsp ground cumin

2–3 sprigs of thyme

2–3 sprigs of flat-leaf parsley, plus 1 tbsp finely chopped parsley, to garnish

250g (9oz) can haricot beans, drained, rinsed, and drained again

1 Put a large, deep, heavy-based casserole pan over a moderate heat, add the lardons or pancetta, and fry, stirring frequently, for 2–3 minutes or until crisp and cooked through. Remove with a slotted spoon and drain on kitchen paper. Add the onion and garlic to the pan, reduce the heat a little, and cook, stirring frequently, for 5–8 minutes or until softened.

2 Pick the meat from the duck leg, discarding the skin and bones but reserving the fat, and cut into shreds. Stir into the onion and garlic, then add the stock, cabbage, carrot, celery, leek, and potato. Season lightly with salt and more generously with pepper, then add the pimentón or paprika, cumin, thyme, and parsley. Bring to a simmer, cover, reduce the heat a little, and cook, stirring occasionally, for 30 minutes.

3 Lift out the thyme and parsley. Lightly mash the beans in a bowl, then stir them into the soup and continue cooking until the vegetables are tender. Taste and season. To serve, stir in the reserved lardons or pancetta and 1 tbsp of the duck fat, then sprinkle with the parsley.

kichidi

A warming Indian lentil dish with spiced butternut squash.

🥣 15 MINS   🍲 50 MINS   ❄ FREEZABLE

SERVES 4

1 butternut squash, about 700g (1lb 9oz), halved and deseeded

½ tsp garam masala

salt and freshly ground black pepper

2 tbsp olive oil

100g (3½oz) basmati rice

100g (3½oz) pink or red lentils

5cm (2in) piece of fresh root ginger, peeled and grated

2 tbsp ghee or clarified butter

2 tsp cumin seeds

½ tsp red chilli flakes

juice of 1 lime

3 tbsp chopped coriander

2 tbsp unsalted butter

1 Preheat the oven to 200°C (400°F/Gas 6). Put the squash halves in a roasting tin, cut side up, sprinkle with the garam masala, season, and drizzle with the oil. Cover with foil and roast for 45 minutes, or until meltingly tender. Leave to cool, then scoop out the flesh, lightly crush it with a fork, and set aside.

2 Meanwhile, combine the rice and lentils in a large saucepan and cover with 2 litres (3½ pints) water. Add the ginger, bring to the boil, then simmer for about 30 minutes until the grains have broken down. Add more water if needed. Stir in the squash.

3 Heat the ghee in a separate pan and fry the cumin and chilli for about 30 seconds until darker in colour. Tip the spices and ghee into the rice and lentils and stir, seasoning well. Stir in the lime juice and coriander. Serve with a generous dollop of butter in the centre of each helping.

pasta and mussel salad

The spiral fusilli pasta absorbs this gorgeous, tart dressing wonderfully, though hollow shells or macaroni would be good too. The pasta perfectly complements the texture of the mussels. This can be made 1 day ahead, covered, and refrigerated. When juicing your lemons, if you first roll them on a hard surface, you will find that you are able to extract more juice.

🥣 30–35 MINS   🍲 8–10 MINS

SERVES 4–6

juice of 2 lemons (about 75ml/2½fl oz)

4 shallots, finely chopped

3 garlic cloves, finely chopped

salt and freshly ground black pepper

175ml (6fl oz) olive oil

bunch of tarragon, leaves picked and finely chopped

bunch of parsley, leaves picked and finely chopped

1kg (2¼lb) mussels, scrubbed and debearded (discard any that do not close when tapped) (p364)

175ml (6fl oz) dry white wine

250g (9oz) fusilli pasta

3 spring onions, trimmed and sliced

1 Whisk together the lemon juice, half the shallots, garlic, salt, and pepper. Gradually whisk in the oil, so the dressing emulsifies and thickens slightly. Whisk in the herbs. Taste for seasoning and set aside.

2 Scrape each mussel with a small knife to remove any barnacles, then detach and discard any weed or "beard". Scrub under cold, running water; discard any with broken shells or those that do not close when gently tapped.

3 Put the wine, remaining shallots, and plenty of black pepper in a large saucepan. Bring to the boil and simmer for 2 minutes. Add the mussels, cover, and cook over a high heat for 4–5 minutes, stirring occasionally, just until the mussels open.

4 Transfer the mussels to a large bowl, discarding the cooking liquid and any that have not opened. Leave until they are cool enough to handle.

5 With your fingers, remove the mussels from their shells, reserving 4–6 mussels in their shells. Pull off and discard the rubbery ring from around each shelled mussel and put them in a large bowl.

6 Briskly whisk the herb vinaigrette and pour it over the mussels.

7 Stir gently, so all the mussels are well coated with dressing. Cover and refrigerate, while cooking the pasta.

8 Cook the pasta in a large pan of boiling salted water for about 8–10 minutes, or until it is tender but still al dente. Stir occasionally to keep from sticking. Drain, rinse with cold water, and drain again.

9 Tip the pasta into the bowl of mussels and dressing. Sprinkle the spring onions over the pasta, add salt and pepper, toss well, and taste for seasoning. Arrange on 4–6 plates. Garnish each serving with a reserved mussel in its shell, adding a lemon wedge and tarragon sprig, if you like.

Season's best **celeriac**

The thick, rough skin of this bulbous corm conceals white flesh that tastes more strongly of celery than celery itself. The peak season is late autumn through winter. It has a creamy texture when cooked, which makes it perfect for puréeing. It also makes delicious low-carbohydrate chips. Try it with other roots, mayonnaise, citrus, or walnuts. It is also good with fish and seafood.

Celeriac grows best in cool temperate regions but cannot stand harsh frosts. When harvested in early winter, if undamaged, it can be stored well right through to spring.

Celeriac What it lacks in looks, celeriac makes up with great flavour. It has a thick, gnarled skin that needs peeling thickly before use.

The best celeriac is firm and wrinkle-free. Old corms are tough and can be tasteless.

essentials
varieties available

Corms vary in size from a tennis ball to a saucer.

buy Choose roots that are at least the size of a small grapefruit. They should feel heavy and be firm to the touch, especially at the top where the leaves emerged.

store Keep for up to 2 weeks, unpeeled, in a paper bag in the vegetable drawer of the fridge, but is best used as fresh as possible.

cook Steam, boil, braise, roast, fry, or use in soups and stews. After boiling until tender, purée and mix with an equal amount of mashed potato. Add diced celeriac with celery to poultry stuffings. Eat raw in salads.

preserve Pickle alone or with other vegetables.

recipe ideas

Beef and celeriac casserole with stout and anchovies p387

Celeriac rémoulade with carrot salad p406

Celeriac soufflé pie p374

Chicken broth with celeriac and orange p450

Chicken with garlic and spiced celeriac p387

Griddled sweet potato and celeriac p395

how to prepare celeriac

Unlike some vegetables, it is important to peel thickly to remove all traces of dark skin from the celeriac. Always place it in a bowl of acidulated water (water with 1 tbsp lemon juice added) after cutting until ready to use, as it discolours quickly.

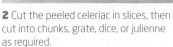

1 Holding the celeriac firmly on a board, thickly peel the corm to remove all gnarled skin using a sharp chef's knife.

2 Cut the peeled celeriac in slices, then cut into chunks, grate, dice, or julienne as required.

chicken with garlic and spiced celeriac

Celeriac is such a versatile root vegetable. Spiced with curry powder and served with tender chicken, this recipe allows its texture and flavour to come to the forefront.

 25 MINS   45 MINS

SERVES 4

8 chicken thighs, with skin on

salt and freshly ground black pepper

2 tbsp olive oil

4 whole bulbs of garlic, unpeeled, tops sliced off

4 large potatoes, peeled and chopped into bite-sized cubes

1 large celeriac or 2 small celeriac, peeled and chopped into bite-sized pieces

1-2 tsp mild curry powder

1 Preheat the oven to 200°C (400°F/ Gas 6). Season the chicken well with salt and pepper. Put half the oil in a large roasting tin and heat on the hob over a high heat. When very hot, add the chicken pieces, skin-side down, and cook for 5–8 minutes, or until browned all over, then remove the tin from the heat.

2 Add the garlic and toss with the oil. Toss the potatoes and celeriac with the remaining oil and curry powder, season well with salt and pepper, and add to the tin.

3 Put in the oven to roast for 45 minutes, or until the chicken and potatoes are cooked and golden. Give the potatoes and celeriac a turn halfway through, then keep an eye on them to check they don't burn. Serve with wilted spinach.

variation

chicken with garlic, preserved lemons, and pumpkin

Prepare in the same way, but substitute ½ pumpkin (about 750g /1lb 10 oz), deseeded, peeled, and cut into chunks for the celeriac; add 2 preserved lemons, cut in slices, to the tin. Use 1–2 tsp ground cumin instead of curry powder.

beef and celeriac casserole with stout and anchovies

A hearty stew, perfect for Sunday lunch. Stout helps to tenderize the beef and adds a malty flavour to the stock.

30 MINS   2 HRS   ❄ FREEZABLE

SERVES 4

1½ tbsp olive oil

550g (1¼lb) stewing steak or braising steak, cut into bite-sized pieces

1 onion, finely chopped

handful of fresh thyme sprigs

4 salted anchovies

½ large celeriac, peeled and cut into bite-sized pieces

½ 500ml bottle stout

600ml (1 pint) hot vegetable stock

salt and freshly ground black pepper

3 medium potatoes, peeled and cut into chunky pieces

1 Preheat the oven to 180°C (350°F/ Gas 4). Heat half the oil in a large cast-iron pan or flameproof casserole, add the meat, and cook over a medium heat, stirring occasionally, for 10 minutes, or until browned all over. Remove with a slotted spoon and set aside. Heat the remaining oil in the pan, add the onion and thyme, and cook over a low heat for 6–8 minutes, or until soft.

2 Stir in the anchovies, then stir in the celeriac and cook for 5–8 minutes. Add a little of the stout and stir to scrape up all the sticky bits from the bottom of the pan. Add the remaining stout and the stock, season with salt and pepper, then return the meat to the pan, cover with a lid, and put in the oven for 1 hour.

3 Add the potatoes, together with a little hot water if the casserole looks dry. Cook for a further 30 minutes. Serve immediately with chunks of crusty white bread.

variation

beef and carrot casserole

Prepare in the same way but substitute 4 roughly chopped carrots for the celeriac. Add the carrots to the casserole in step 2 after the anchovies, then continue as in the original recipe.

venison, shallot, and chestnut hotpot

Lean venison, sweet chestnuts, dried mushrooms, and shallots together make a rich, robust casserole full of flavour.

🥣 30 MINS 🍲 2 HRS 15 MINS ❄ FREEZABLE

SERVES 4

2 tbsp plain flour

2 tbsp thyme leaves

salt and freshly ground black pepper

550g (1¼lb) boned leg or shoulder of venison, cut into bite-sized pieces

knob of butter

2 tbsp olive oil

125g (4½oz) bacon lardons or sliced pancetta

125g (4½oz) shallots, peeled and left whole

1 glass of red wine

50g (1¾oz) dried mushrooms, such as shiitake, oyster, or porcini, soaked in 300ml (10fl oz) warm water for 20 minutes

125g (4½oz) ready-cooked chestnuts

500ml (16fl oz) hot vegetable stock

3 sprigs of rosemary

1 Preheat the oven to 150°C (300°F/Gas 2). Put the flour, thyme, and some salt and pepper in a mixing bowl, add the venison pieces, and toss well to coat them in the seasoned flour. Heat the butter with 1 tbsp of the oil in a cast-iron pan, add the venison, and cook over a medium heat, stirring frequently, for 6–8 minutes, or until it begins to colour a little. Remove with a slotted spoon and set aside. Add the lardons or pancetta to the pan and stir for 5 minutes, or until brown and crispy. Remove with a slotted spoon and set aside.

2 Add the remaining oil to the pan, then add the shallots and cook over a low-medium heat for 8 minutes, or until they are soft and turning golden. Return all the meat to the pan, season with black pepper, then add the wine and boil for 2 minutes while you stir to scrape up the crispy bits from the bottom of the pan.

3 Drain the mushrooms (reserving the liquid) and stir into the pan. Strain the reserved liquid and add it to the pan, too. Stir through the chestnuts, pour in the stock, then add the rosemary. Cover with a lid and put in the oven to cook for 2 hours, or until the meat is tender, topping up with hot water if necessary.

beef and parsnip casserole

This is a warming dish with tender beef and sweet parsnips. Choose parsnips that are about the size of a large carrot with firm unblemished flesh for the best flavour.

🥣 30 MINS 🍲 1 HR 45 MINS ❄ FREEZABLE

SERVES 4

1½ tbsp olive oil

1 onion, finely chopped

2 tbsp chopped thyme

2 garlic cloves, grated or finely chopped

salt and freshly ground black pepper

550g (1¼lb) braising steak, cut into bite-sized pieces

2 large carrots, roughly chopped

3 small parsnips, roughly chopped

750ml (1¼ pints) hot beef stock

knob of butter

200g (7oz) button mushrooms, any large ones halved

1 Preheat the oven to 180°C (350°F/Gas 4). Heat the oil in a cast-iron pan or flameproof casserole, add the onions, and cook over a low heat for 6–8 minutes, or until soft and translucent. Stir in the thyme and garlic and season well with salt and pepper. Add the steak and cook, stirring often, for 10 minutes, or until sealed. Add the carrots, parsnips, and stock. Bring to the boil, then reduce to a simmer, cover with a lid, and put in the oven to cook for 1 hour.

2 Just before the hour is up, melt the butter in a small frying pan, add the mushrooms, and cook, stirring, for 5–8 minutes, or until golden. Add the mushrooms to the casserole and cook for a further 30 minutes, topping up with hot stock or water if it begins to look dry. Serve while piping hot.

variation

venison and artichoke casserole

Prepare in exactly the same way, but use 550g (1¼lb) diced venison haunch instead of beef, and substitute 350g (12oz) Jerusalem artichokes, scrubbed or peeled and cut in chunks, instead of the parsnips. Add 3 tbsp port to the casserole with the stock.

duck with turnips and apricots

Sweet Madeira wine adds a wonderful flavour to the sauce in this dish. The recipe is suitable for wild or domestic duck.

🥣 **20 MINS PLUS STANDING**   🍲 **1 HR 30 MINS – 2 HRS**

SERVES 4

4 portions of duck

salt and freshly ground black pepper

1 tbsp vegetable oil

15g (½oz) butter

2 tbsp plain flour

175ml (6fl oz) dry white wine

500ml (16fl oz) hot chicken stock, plus more if needed

1 bouquet garni (made with 5-6 sprigs of parsley, 2-3 sprigs of thyme, and 1 bay leaf)

2 shallots, finely chopped

12-16 pickling onions, peeled and left whole

500g (1lb 2oz) turnips, peeled and roughly chopped

1 tsp granulated sugar

4 tbsp Madeira wine

175g (6oz) ready-to-eat dried apricots

1 Preheat the oven to 180°C (350°F/ Gas 4). Season the duck. Heat the oil and butter in a large flameproof casserole over a low heat and add the duck, skin-side down. Cook for 20-25 minutes until it has browned and the fat has rendered. Turn over and cook for only about 5 minutes until browned.

Remove and set aside, draining and reserving the duck fat. Heat 2-3 tbsp of the duck fat in the casserole. Add the flour and cook, stirring constantly, for 1-2 minutes until lightly browned but not burnt. Stir in the white wine, hot stock, bouquet garni, shallots, and seasoning, and bring to the boil. Return the duck to the casserole, cover with the lid, and cook in the oven for 40-45 minutes.

2 Meanwhile, heat 1-2 tbsp of the duck fat in a heavy-based pan over a medium heat. Add the onions, turnips, sugar, and seasoning and cook, stirring occasionally, for 5-7 minutes until the vegetables begin to caramelize. Add to the casserole with the Madeira wine and apricots and top up with hot water if necessary. Cover with the lid and return to the oven to cook for another 20-25 minutes until the duck and vegetables are tender. Skim off any fat from the surface, remove the bouquet garni, taste, and add more seasoning, if needed. Serve on warmed plates with wide noodles.

pork with potatoes and mushrooms in wine

An all-in-one dish for relaxed weekend entertaining that needs only minimal preparation.

🥣 **20 MINS**   🍲 **1 HR 45 MINS**

SERVES 6

1.35kg (3lb) boneless shoulder of pork, skin scored

sea salt

1kg (2¼lb) potatoes, peeled and halved, or large ones quartered

1 tbsp olive oil

a few sprigs of rosemary

350ml (12fl oz) dry white wine

250g (9oz) button mushrooms

300ml (10fl oz) hot vegetable stock

1 Preheat the oven to 220°C (425°F/ Gas 7). Sit the pork in a large roasting tin and rub the skin all over with sea salt, ensuring it gets into all the cuts. Toss the potatoes in the oil, season with sea salt, and add to the tin along with the rosemary. Roast in the oven for 20 minutes, or until the pork skin is crispy.

2 Meanwhile, heat the wine in a pan over a low heat until warm, then spoon it over the meat. Add the mushrooms, pour in the stock, then turn the oven down to 180°C (350°F/Gas 4) and cook for 1 hour.

3 Reduce the oven temperature to 150°C (300°F/Gas 2) and cook for a further 30 minutes, or until the potatoes are meltingly soft and the liquid has almost disappeared. Remove from the oven and discard the rosemary. Keep warm while the pork rests for 15 minutes. Then slice the pork and serve with the potatoes and mushrooms, and some fresh crusty bread on the side.

spicy pork with caraway seeds and cabbage

Pork can take the powerful flavours of spices and other strong ingredients well. Here, chilli adds heat while caraway seeds give a sharp aromatic flavour with sweet undertones.

🥄 10 MINS   🍲 2 HRS 30 MINS

SPECIAL EQUIPMENT ▪ food processor

SERVES 4

handful of thyme sprigs, leaves only

2 garlic cloves, finely chopped

1 tbsp olive oil

1 tsp chilli flakes

1.1kg (2½lb) pork belly, skin scored

salt and freshly ground black pepper

250ml (9fl oz) dry cider

½ Savoy cabbage, halved, cored, and shredded

knob of butter

½ tsp caraway seeds

1 Preheat the oven to 220°C (425°F/Gas 7). Put the thyme, garlic, oil, and chilli flakes in a food processor and blitz to a paste, then rub the paste over the pork flesh (but not the skin). Sit the pork in a roasting tin, skin-side up, and rub the skin with salt, ensuring it gets into all the cracks. Cook in the oven for 30 minutes, or until the skin is golden.

2 Reduce the oven temperature to 180°C (350°F/Gas 4). Pour the cider around the pork, then cover with foil, securing it around the edges of the tin, and cook for 2 hours.

3 Just before the 2 hours are up, put the cabbage in a pan of boiling salted water, and cook for 4–6 minutes, or until soft. Drain, then toss with the butter, caraway seeds, and a pinch of black pepper. Transfer to a large shallow serving bowl.

4 Slice or cut the pork into bite-sized pieces and arrange on top of the cabbage along with the juices. Serve with a spoonful of chilli jelly on the side and some fresh crusty bread.

roast sweet potato and chilli tortilla

Their creamy texture and mild flavour make sweet potatoes versatile enough for savoury dishes and desserts. A little chilli helps to cut through their spicy-sweet flavour in this tortilla.

🥄 15 MINS   🍲 45 MINS

SERVES 4–6

550g (1¼lb) sweet potatoes, peeled and cut into 2cm (¾in) cubes

1 tsp chilli flakes

5 tbsp olive oil

2 onions, finely chopped

6 eggs

salt and freshly ground black pepper

1 Preheat the oven to 200°C (400°F/Gas 6). Put the sweet potatoes on a non-stick baking tray, add the chilli flakes and 2 tbsp of the oil, and mix well. Roast in the oven for 30 minutes, or until they start to brown, turning occasionally.

2 Meanwhile, put the remaining oil in a deep frying pan, add the onions, and fry over a medium heat for 5 minutes, or until soft and translucent. Add the sweet potato, combine well, and leave to cool.

3 Break the eggs into a mixing bowl, season with salt and pepper, and beat well with a fork. Pour onto the potato and onion mixture, combine well, then pour the mixture into an oven-proof frying pan and cook over a low heat for 10 minutes, or until the egg is beginning to set. Transfer the pan to the oven and cook for a further 10 minutes, or until the top is golden. Turn out onto a plate and serve with a mixed salad.

variation

roast celeriac and leek tortilla

Make in the same way, but use 550g (1¼lb) celeriac, peeled and cut in 2cm (¾in) cubes, instead of the sweet potatoes. Sprinkle with 1 tsp chopped fresh rosemary instead of the chilli flakes before roasting. Substitute 1 chopped leek for one of the chopped onions, and fry in the same way at step 2, then continue the recipe as before.

beef and herb potato pie

This reliably good recipe is an update of a French classic.

🍲 45–50 MINS   🍲 1 HR 30 MINS

SPECIAL EQUIPMENT ▪ food processor

SERVES 6

75ml (2½fl oz) olive oil

1 large onion, diced

4 garlic cloves, 2 of the cloves finely chopped and 2 cloves left whole

1kg (2¼lb) minced beef

salt and freshly ground black pepper

400g can chopped tomatoes

250ml (8fl oz) beef stock

125ml (4fl oz) dry white wine

1kg (2¼lb) potatoes, peeled and each cut into chunks

handful of basil leaves

handful of flat-leaf parsley leaves

250ml (9fl oz) milk, plus more if needed

1 Heat one-third of the oil in a sauté or frying pan. Add the onion and cook, stirring, for 3–5 minutes until soft but not brown. Add the chopped garlic, beef, salt, pepper, and tomatoes. Reduce the heat and simmer very gently for 10–12 minutes, stirring occasionally, until the meat is brown. Stir in the stock and wine. Simmer for 25–30 minutes until most of the liquid has evaporated and the meat is still moist.

2 Boil the potatoes in a saucepan until tender. Meanwhile, blitz the herbs, the 2 whole garlic cloves, and the remaining oil to a purée in a food processor. Drain the potatoes, return them to the pan, mash them, and add the herb purée. Scald the milk in a small pan and gradually beat it into the potatoes over a medium heat. Stir for 2–3 minutes until the potatoes just hold a shape. Season to taste.

3 Preheat the oven to 190°C (375°F/Gas 5). Brush a large shallow baking dish with oil. Spoon the meat and any liquid into the dish and cover completely with an even layer of the herb potatoes. Smooth the top with the back of a spoon, then make a scalloped pattern with the tip of a dessert spoon or the tines of a fork. Dip the spoon or fork into a bowl of hot water, set close to hand, once or twice during the process so the potato does not stick to it. Bake in the oven for 35–40 minutes until the top is golden brown and the edges are bubbling with gravy. Serve immediately on warmed plates.

chicken salad with carrot and apple relish

A delicious instant salad. If you cook the chicken fresh, poach 2 skinless chicken breasts with seasoning in a shallow pan with stock or water for 8 minutes or until tender, then drain.

🍲 15 MINS

SERVES 4

2 handfuls of spinach leaves, rinsed

350g (12oz) cooked chicken, any skin removed, cut into bite-sized pieces

50g (1¾oz) pine nuts, toasted

1 tbsp olive oil

juice of ½ lemon

For the carrot and apple relish

2 carrots

2 sweet red eating apples

2 preserved lemons, finely chopped

small handful of sultanas

salt and freshly ground black pepper

1 For the carrot and apple relish, grate the carrots into a mixing bowl. Quarter and core the apples, then grate them into the bowl with the carrot. Add the preserved lemons and sultanas and mix together. Season with salt and pepper.

2 Lay the spinach leaves in a large shallow salad bowl or plate and top with the chicken pieces and toasted pine nuts. When ready to serve, drizzle over the oil and lemon juice and sprinkle with a pinch of salt. Serve with the carrot and apple relish.

variation

turkey salad with celeriac and orange relish

For the relish, grate ½ small celeriac instead of the carrots and toss immediately in 1 tsp lemon juice. Add the segments from 2 oranges instead of the grated apple, 2 tsp capers instead of the preserved lemons, and a small handful raisins. Season. Use cooked turkey instead of chicken (either poached turkey breast or leftover roast). Sprinkle with 50g (1¾oz) roughly chopped walnuts instead of the pine nuts. Dress as before.

belly pork and prunes

Dried fruit works well with a fatty meat such as pork belly; it creates a delicious, sweet sauce that cuts through the meaty richness. The earthiness of celeriac is a great addition.

🥄 15 MINS　　🍲 3 HRS – 3 HRS 30 MINS

SERVES 4-6

1 tbsp olive oil

1.1kg (2½lb) pork belly, cut into bite-sized pieces

salt and freshly ground black pepper

1 onion, finely sliced

3 garlic cloves, finely chopped

1 tbsp sherry vinegar

120ml (4fl oz) white wine

900ml (1½ pints) hot vegetable stock

140g (5oz) soft prunes, finely chopped

6 sage leaves, finely shredded

600g (1lb 5oz) celeriac, peeled and chopped into bite-sized pieces

1 Preheat the oven to 160°C (325°F/ Gas 3). Heat half of the oil in a large flameproof casserole over a high heat. Season the pork belly with salt and pepper, add it (in batches, if necessary), skin-side down, and cook until it turns golden and begins to crisp a little. Remove the pork and sit it on kitchen paper to drain.

2 Heat the remaining oil in the casserole over a medium heat, add the onion, and cook for 3–4 minutes until soft. Then stir in the garlic and cook for 1 more minute. Increase the heat and add the sherry vinegar, letting it simmer for 2–3 minutes. Pour in the wine and continue to boil for a few more minutes until the alcohol evaporates.

3 Add the stock and stir to scrape up the bits from the bottom of the casserole. Return the pork to the casserole and stir in the prunes, sage, and celeriac. Bring back to the boil, cover, and put in the oven for 2½–3 hours. Check occasionally that it's not drying out, topping up with a little hot water, if needed. Taste and season more, if needed, and serve with creamy mashed potatoes.

beef and anchovy casserole

Serve this deep-flavoured stew on cold days. The anchovies will melt into it and the redcurrant jelly adds a distinctive sweetness. It is delicious over mashed or baked potatoes.

🥄 20 MINS　　🍲 2 HRS 15 MINS – 2 HRS 45 MINS

SERVES 4-6

4 tbsp olive oil, plus extra if necessary

knob of butter

12 baby onions, peeled

a few sprigs of thyme

salt and freshly ground black pepper

1.1kg (2½lb) chuck beef, cut into chunky cubes

1 tbsp plain flour, seasoned with salt and pepper

2 leeks, trimmed and sliced

pinch of ground allspice

250ml (9fl oz) red wine

6 anchovy fillets in oil, drained and chopped

1 tbsp small capers

800ml (1 pint 7fl oz) hot beef stock

1-2 tbsp redcurrant jelly

1 Preheat the oven to 160°C (325°F/ Gas 3). Heat 2 tbsp of the oil and the butter in a large flameproof casserole over a medium heat, then add the onions, thyme, and salt and pepper. Cook for about 10 minutes until the onions start to soften and turn translucent. Remove with a slotted spoon and set aside.

2 Toss the beef in the seasoned flour. Add more oil to the casserole, increase the heat to medium-high, and cook the beef in batches for a few minutes on each side until browned all over. Remove and set aside. Add a little more oil, stir in the leeks and allspice, and cook for about 5 minutes. Also remove and set aside.

3 Add the wine and bring to the boil, stirring to scrape up the bits from the bottom of the casserole. Let it simmer for a few minutes, then stir through the anchovies, capers, stock, and redcurrant jelly. Bring to the boil, then reduce to a simmer, return the meat, leeks, and onions to the casserole and season again if you wish. Cover with the lid and cook in the oven for 2–2½ hours until the beef is tender. Check occasionally that it's not drying out and top up with a little hot water, if needed. Serve while piping hot.

cauliflower curry

Potatoes and cauliflower are tumbled in a tikka coconut sauce in this simple and economical dish.

🥄 15 MINS　　🍲 1 HR

SERVES 4-6

1 tbsp vegetable oil

1 onion, roughly chopped

salt and freshly ground black pepper

5cm (2in) piece of fresh root ginger, peeled and finely chopped

3 garlic cloves, finely chopped

2 green chillies, deseeded and finely chopped

2 tbsp medium-hot tikka curry paste

400g can chickpeas, drained and rinsed

400ml can coconut milk

600ml (1 pint) hot vegetable stock

3 potatoes, peeled and cut into bite-sized pieces

1 cauliflower, cut into bite-sized florets

1 Heat the oil in a large heavy-based pan over a medium heat, add the onion, and cook for 6–8 minutes until soft. Season, stir through the ginger, garlic, and chillies, and cook for 2–3 minutes. Stir in the tikka paste, chickpeas, coconut milk, and stock, and bring to the boil. Reduce to a simmer and cook gently, partially covered with the lid, stirring occasionally, for 30 minutes.

2 Bring another large pan of salted water to the boil. Add the potatoes and cook for 15 minutes, or until just beginning to soften. Remove with a slotted spoon and set aside. Put the cauliflower in the boiling water and cook for about 5 minutes, then drain.

3 Tip the potato and cauliflower into the sauce and turn so they are well coated, then simmer gently for a further 15 minutes or so. Serve with some rice and naan bread.

butternut squash pasta in chilli and parmesan sauce

Ripe pumpkins and winter squashes herald the onset of early winter. This pasta dish is perfect for these cooler days, as it has the comfort of cream and the warmth of red chillies. Slow-roasting the butternut squash enhances its sweetness.

🥣 20 MINS   🍲 35 MINS

SPECIAL EQUIPMENT ▪ food processor or blender

SERVES 4

200g (7oz) butternut squash, peeled and diced (prepared weight)

1-2 tbsp extra virgin olive oil

salt and freshly ground black pepper

1 garlic clove, crushed

½ red chilli, deseeded and finely chopped

8 sage leaves

150ml (5fl oz) single cream

25g (scant 1oz) Parmesan cheese, grated, plus extra to finish

350g (12oz) conchiglie pasta

1 Preheat the oven to 200°C (400°F/ Gas 6). Place the squash in a roasting tin, toss it in a little of the olive oil, season well with salt and pepper, and roast it in the oven for 30 minutes, or until soft. Remove and set aside to cool for a few minutes.

2 Meanwhile, gently fry the garlic, chilli, and sage in a little oil in a small saucepan or frying pan for 2–3 minutes.

3 Once the butternut squash has cooled slightly, put it into a food processor or blender. Pour in the cream and add the Parmesan cheese, garlic, chilli, sage leaves, plenty of black pepper, and a little salt. Blitz to a fine purée, adding 1–2 tbsp water if it looks too thick.

4 Cook the pasta until tender, but still al dente, and drain. Reheat the sauce in the pasta pan, adding more water if it seems a little stiff. Put the pasta back in the pan and mix well, allowing the sauce to coat the pasta shells. Serve hot with plenty of fresh Parmesan cheese to finish.

variation

pumpkin farfalle with blue cheese sauce

Prepare in the same way, but use 200g (7oz) peeled and diced pumpkin instead of butternut squash. Omit the chilli, use 60g (2oz) blue cheese instead of the Parmesan, and farfalle pasta instead of conchiglie.

slow-cooked swedish red cabbage

This traditional recipe, full of big fruity flavours, has become a classic requirement for a big Christmas dinner, whether you are serving roast turkey or goose, or a vegetarian dish.

🥣 20 MINS   🍲 2 HRS

SERVES 8

50g (1¾oz) butter

25g (scant 1oz) caster sugar

1 tsp salt

6 tbsp rice wine vinegar, or white wine or cider vinegar

1 red cabbage, approx 1kg (2¼lb), finely shredded

2 apples, peeled, cored, and grated

2 heaped tbsp redcurrant jelly

1 Preheat the oven to 150°C (300°F/Gas 2). In a large, heavy flameproof casserole, heat together the butter, sugar, salt, 6 tbsp water, and the vinegar. Bring to the boil and simmer for 1 minute.

2 Fold the cabbage into the liquid and bring it back to the boil. Take the casserole off the heat and cover tightly with a double layer of foil. Fit the lid on snugly and cook in the oven for 1½ hours.

3 Remove from the oven and add the grated apples and redcurrant jelly, stirring well. Add a little more water if the cabbage looks dry. Replace the foil and the lid, and return the cabbage to the oven for a further 30 minutes. Serve warm

variation

winter braised white cabbage and celery

Prepare in the same way, but substitute 1 white cabbage (about 1kg/2¼lb) instead of the red cabbage. Add 2 chopped celery sticks, 2 thinly sliced onions, and 4 tbsp dried cranberries with the cabbage, and tuck in a bay leaf. At step 3, add the grated apples as before. Discard the bay leaf before serving.

soy and sesame-glazed sweet potatoes

The inspiration for this dish comes from a classic Japanese dish known as *daigakuimo*. It is a wonderfully simple recipe that turns the humble sweet potato into something special.

🥣 10 MINS   🍲 40 MINS

SERVES 4

2 tbsp soy sauce

2 tbsp light soft brown sugar

2 tbsp rice wine

1 tbsp sesame oil

2 garlic cloves, crushed

500g (1lb 2oz) sweet potatoes, peeled and cut into wedges

1 tbsp toasted sesame seeds

1 Preheat the oven to 200°C (400°F/Gas 6). Put all the ingredients except the sweet potatoes and sesame seeds in a small saucepan. Bring to the boil, reduce the heat, and simmer for 2 minutes.

2 Put the potato wedges on a baking tray or ovenproof serving dish and pour the sauce mixture over them, tossing well. Scatter the sesame seeds over the top and cover the baking tray or dish with foil.

3 Cook for 20 minutes, then turn the oven up to 220°C (425°F/Gas 7). Remove the foil and cook for another 20 minutes. Turn the potatoes several times while cooking until they have absorbed all the sauce and are soft, glazed, and sticky. They are superb eaten alongside a piece of grilled mackerel and some wilted greens.

griddled sweet potato and celeriac

This simple combination of vegetables makes a lovely winter side dish and is a delicious accompaniment to both roast meats and casseroles.

🥣 10 MINS PLUS COOLING 🍲 20 MINS ❄ FREEZABLE

MAKES APPROX 1kg (2¼lb)

2 small or 1 large celeriac, cut in half if small, quarters if large, and then in slices, and brushed all over with sunflower oil to prevent browning

2–3 sweet potatoes, peeled and cut into 5mm (¼in) thick slices

freshly ground black pepper

a little sweet or smoked paprika (optional)

1 Season the celeriac and sweet potato on both sides with black pepper and dust lightly with paprika, if using. Preheat a griddle pan or electric griddle and brush the vegetables with oil on both sides.

2 When the griddle is very hot, but not smoking, add a single layer of vegetables (don't overcrowd them).

Press them down firmly with a fish slice until the undersides are nicely striped. Turn the vegetables over and cook for a further 2–3 minutes until just cooked and striped. Don't overcook them, or they will become too soft. If using an electric griddle, close the lid and cook the slices for about 3 minutes.

3 Once the batch of vegetables are cooked until striped and just tender, transfer to a warm place while you cook the rest of the slices, reheating the griddle between each batch. Then serve all the slices piping hot.

mixed vegetable purée

This purée is a great topping for cottage pie or bobotie, a South African baked curried meat dish. It also makes a delicious accompaniment to meat or poultry.

🥣 30 MINS 🍲 30–40 MINS ❄ FREEZABLE

SPECIAL EQUIPMENT ▪ food processor or hand-held blender

MAKES APPROX 1.8kg (4lb)

1 swede

450g (1lb) carrots

2 sweet potatoes

2 large turnips or 1 celeriac

salt and freshly ground black pepper

60g (2oz) unsalted butter

1 Peel and chop all the vegetables into evenly sized chunks or thick slices. Place in a large saucepan of cold water with a little salt. Bring to the boil, reduce the heat slightly, part-cover, and simmer for 20–25 minutes, or until all the vegetables are really tender. Drain well.

2 Purée the vegetables in a food processor or with a hand-held blender. Alternatively, use a potato ricer or mash thoroughly by hand with a potato masher.

3 Return the purée to the pan and add the butter and a good grinding of pepper. Heat gently, beating well until the butter is absorbed. Then use to top a pie before baking.

brussels sprouts with chestnuts and pancetta

A perfect foil to a Christmas meal. Although some people dislike Brussels sprouts, it is hard to find someone who doesn't like them when treated in this manner.

🥣 10 MINS 🍲 10 MINS

SERVES 4

400g (14oz) Brussels sprouts, washed and trimmed

knob of butter

100g (3½oz) pancetta, diced

100g (3½oz) chestnuts, cooked, peeled, and roughly chopped

1 tsp grated lemon zest

sea salt and freshly ground black pepper

1 Boil the Brussels sprouts in plenty of salted water for 5–7 minutes, depending on their size, until they are just tender, but not overcooked. Then drain well.

2 Melt the butter in a large frying pan or wok and fry the pancetta for 3–4 minutes until crispy. Add the Brussels sprouts, chestnuts, and lemon zest, and cook for 2 minutes until everything is heated through.

3 Season well with pepper and a little sea salt, to taste (you may not need much, as the pancetta can be very salty) and serve hot.

variation

brussels sprouts with whole chestnuts and sausages

Cook 400g (14oz) Brussels sprouts as before. Drain. Meanwhile, fry 225g (8oz) cocktail sausages for 4–5 minutes until cooked through. Drain on kitchen paper. Wipe out the pan and melt 60g (2oz) butter. Add 250g (9oz) cooked, peeled chestnuts and toss in the butter until heated through and lightly golden. Add 2 tsp chopped thyme. Toss again, add the sprouts and the sausages, and toss to heat through as before. Season to taste and serve.

Season's best **cabbages and brussels sprouts**

All cabbages and Brussels sprouts are brilliant raw and cooked. Brussels are traditional for the festive season but are good through to early spring. Cabbages are best in winter but varieties are available all year. Red and white ones are good with fruits, nuts, and seeds; green ones and sprouts with nuts or curry pastes and are particularly good with pork products and celery.

Cabbages and Brussels sprouts are hardy brassicas grown in temperate zones all over the world in different soils and are staples of the diets of many countries.

The steamed leaves make excellent wrappers for many savoury fillings.

Savoy cabbage The attractively crinkled leaves are more loosely wrapped round the head than those of other cabbages and are more full-bodied in flavour.

Brussels sprouts These grow on stalks, traditionally maturing from the base up. Modern hybrids mature all at the same time. The green tops are also eaten.

Red cabbage Offering beautiful and vibrant colour, red cabbage is sweeter than white but the leaves are tougher, so they take longer to cook.

Look for tight, small heads, with no yellow outer leaves.

The large outer leaves are excellent for blanching and stuffing; the heart is tender and sweet.

Round cabbage Also known as ball-head cabbage, this can be eaten raw and cooked, as most varieties of cabbage, but best suits stir-frying and braising.

White cabbage Also known as Dutch cabbage, this makes a firm head of tightly packed leaves with a solid core. It has a sweet taste and keeps particularly well.

Pointed cabbage This is also known as spring cabbage since it grows right through winter and spring into summer, when others are not available.

how to core and shred cabbage
This technique applies to all varieties. For the most efficient control and action when shredding, anchor the point of the knife on the cutting board, raising and lowering the blade through the cabbage. Guide the blade with the knuckles of your other hand, keeping your fingers tucked away.

1 Hold the head of cabbage firmly on the cutting board and use a sharp knife to cut it in half, straight through the stalk end.

2 Cut the halves again through the stalk lengthways and slice out the core from each quarter.

3 Working with each quarter at a time, place the wedge cut-side down. Cut across the cabbage, creating shreds.

red cabbage and bacon salad

A hearty salad for winter, the contrasts in taste, texture, and colour are wonderful.

🥣 20–25 MINS PLUS MARINATING   🍲 5 MINS

SERVES 6

½ head red cabbage (about 750g/1lb 10oz), cored and finely shredded

4 tbsp red wine vinegar

250g (9oz) lardons or thick streaky bacon rashers

leaves from 1 small cos lettuce, chopped

85g (3oz) Roquefort cheese, crumbled

For the vinaigrette

4 tbsp red wine vinegar, plus more if needed

1 tbsp Dijon mustard

salt and freshly ground black pepper

175ml (6fl oz) olive oil

1 For the vinaigrette, combine the vinegar, mustard, and a pinch of salt in a mixing bowl. Grind in the black pepper. Gradually whisk in the oil so the vinaigrette emulsifies and thickens. Then taste for seasoning.

2 Transfer the shredded cabbage to a large bowl. Boil the vinegar in a small saucepan, then pour over the cabbage and toss. Pour 2 litres (3½ pints) boiling water over and let

stand for 3–4 minutes, until slightly softened. Drain thoroughly, then return it to the large bowl. Toss the cabbage with enough vinaigrette to moisten it well. Taste for seasoning, adding more vinegar if necessary. Cover and marinate for 1–2 hours.

3 If using bacon rashers, cut into strips about 10 minutes before serving. Fry the lardons or bacon strips in a frying pan, stirring occasionally, for 3–5 minutes, or until crisp and the fat is rendered. Then spoon the hot bacon and its pan juices over the cabbage, reserving some bacon pieces for garnish, and toss them together.

4 Arrange a bed of lettuce on each of 6 plates. Spoon the remaining dressing over the lettuce. Mound the red cabbage and bacon mixture over the top. Top the salads with the crumbled blue cheese and reserved bacon and serve at once.

sweet and sour cabbage

This is a warming, slightly spicy alternative to the more traditional slow-cooked red cabbage. It is cooked on the hob (rather than baked in the oven) in just over 1 hour.

🥣 15 MINS   🍲 1 HR 15 MINS

SERVES 8

1 tbsp olive oil

1 large red cabbage, outer leaves removed, halved, and finely shredded

2 red-skinned eating apples, cut into bite-sized pieces

5cm (2in) piece of fresh root ginger, peeled and finely sliced

200ml (7fl oz) balsamic vinegar

2 tbsp soft brown sugar

salt and freshly ground black pepper

1 Put the oil in a large heavy-based pan, add the cabbage, apple, and ginger, and cook on a low heat for 10 minutes, or until the ingredients begin to soften and reduce down.

2 Add the balsamic vinegar and sugar, bring to the boil, then cover and simmer for 40–60 minutes, or until the cabbage is soft. Stir occasionally so it doesn't stick. Season well with salt and pepper and serve with roast pork or pork chops.

variation

hot and spicy white cabbage
Prepare in the same way, but use a white cabbage instead of red cabbage. Add 2 unripe pears instead of apples. Use 100ml (3½fl oz) white pickling vinegar and 300ml (10fl oz) water instead of balsamic, and add 2–3 dried red chillies to the mix along with a large handful of sultanas and a bouquet garni. When cooked, discard the chillies and bouquet garni before serving.

creamy coleslaw

This salad makes a generous quantity for a party, or the recipe can easily be halved. This version of the old favourite is pepped up with caraway seeds, soured cream, and mustard.

15-20 MINS PLUS CHILLING

SPECIAL EQUIPMENT ▪ mandoline ▪ food processor

SERVES 8-10

500g (1lb 2oz) carrots, trimmed

1 white cabbage, about 1.35kg (3lb), trimmed and cut into quarters with the core removed

2 tbsp sugar

salt and freshly ground black pepper

250ml (9fl oz) soured cream

175ml (6fl oz) cider vinegar

2 tsp mustard powder

2 tsp caraway seeds

250ml (9fl oz) mayonnaise

1 onion, finely diced

1 Using the coarse side of a grater, grate the carrots and leave in a bowl of iced water for half an hour so they crisp up. Drain very well, then wrap in a clean tea towel and shake to remove all the excess water.

2 Shred the cabbage leaves into a large bowl using a mandoline, discarding any thick ribs. Alternatively, shred the cabbage quarters in a food processor, using the slicing blade.

3 Put the sugar, salt, pepper, soured cream, and cider vinegar in a mixing bowl. Add the mustard powder and caraway seeds, then add the mayonnaise and whisk to combine. Taste for seasoning. Put the onion, carrot, and cabbage in a bowl and pour the dressing over. Stir until coated. Cover and refrigerate for at least 4 hours, so the flavours mellow.

4 Remove the coleslaw from the refrigerator and stir it once more to redistribute the dressing (you may find it has sunk to the bottom of the bowl in the refrigerator). Taste for seasoning, then serve chilled.

leeks vinaigrette

This simple, elegant dish should be prepared with the freshest leeks you can find. They can be left to marinate in the vinaigrette, covered and refrigerated, for up to 1 day.

15-20 MINS PLUS MARINATING   **15-25 MINS**

SERVES 4-6

6 leeks, about 1kg (2¼lb) total weight

salt and freshly ground black pepper

3 tbsp white wine vinegar

1 tsp Dijon mustard

175ml (6fl oz) vegetable oil

2 shallots, finely chopped

1 egg

5-7 sprigs of parsley, leaves picked and finely chopped

1 Trim the leeks, discarding the roots and green tops. Slit lengthways, leaving the leeks attached at the root end. Wash thoroughly, fanning them out under cold, running water. Divide into 2 bundles and tie them together at each end with kitchen string. Fill a wide, shallow pan with salted water and bring to the boil. Add the leeks and simmer for about 10 minutes, or until just tender.

2 Meanwhile, whisk together the vinegar, mustard, salt, and pepper in a mixing bowl. Gradually whisk in the oil so the vinaigrette emulsifies and thickens slightly. Whisk in the shallots, then taste for seasoning.

3 Test whether the leeks are tender by piercing with the tip of a small knife. Drain in a colander, remove the strings, pat dry with kitchen paper, and cut on the diagonal into 7.5cm (3in) lengths. Lay the leeks in a dish and pour over the vinaigrette. Cover and refrigerate for 1 hour or longer, if you have enough time. Then bring back to room temperature while you hard-boil and shell the egg.

4 Divide the leeks between plates. Cut the egg in half and separate the yolk from the white. Chop the white finely. Work the yolk through a sieve set over a small bowl with a spoon. Then sprinkle the leeks with parsley, the egg white, and yolk, and serve.

variation

leeks hollandaise

Cook the leeks in the same way, drain, and place in a serving dish. To make a quick Hollandaise, whisk 3 eggs in a small saucepan with 3 tbsp lemon juice. Gradually whisk in 175g (6oz) melted butter until blended. Whisk over a low heat until thickened. Do not boil. Season and pour Hollandaise over the leeks. Garnish as before.

parsnip and parmesan bread

A perfect combination of flavours to serve with a bowl of warming soup on a cold winter's day.

🥄 20 MINS   🍲 50 MINS   ❄ FREEZABLE

MAKES 1 LOAF

300g (10oz) plain flour

100g (3½oz) wholemeal self-raising flour

1 tsp bicarbonate of soda

50g (1¾oz) Parmesan cheese, finely grated

salt and freshly ground black pepper

150g (5½oz) parsnip, coarsely grated

300ml (10fl oz) buttermilk

1 Preheat the oven to 220°C (425°F/Gas 7). Line a baking tray with baking parchment. In a bowl, mix together the flours, bicarbonate of soda, and Parmesan cheese together with some salt and pepper. Roughly chop the grated parsnip to reduce the size of the shreds. Add it to the bowl, mixing it in well.

2 Make a well in the centre of the dry ingredients and gently stir in the buttermilk, bringing the mixture together to form a loose dough.

Use your hands to bring the mixture together into a ball, then turn it out onto a floured work surface and knead for 2 minutes until it forms a smooth dough. You may need to add a little extra flour at this stage.

3 Shape the dough into a round, about 15cm (6in) in diameter. Slash a cross in the top of the dough with a sharp knife to allow the bread to rise easily when baking.

4 Place the dough on the baking tray and cook in the middle of the oven for 30 minutes to create a good crust. Reduce the temperature to 200°C (400°F/Gas 6) and bake for 20 minutes until well risen, golden brown, and a skewer inserted into the middle emerges clean. Transfer to a wire rack and allow it to cool for at least 20 minutes before serving.

patatas bravas

This classic tapas dish features cubes of potatoes mixed with a spicy sauce. Be generous with the flat-leaf parsley as it looks great and adds contrasting taste and texture.

🥄 15 MINS   🍲 1 HR

SERVES 4

6 tbsp olive oil

700g (1lb 9oz) white potatoes, peeled and cut into 2cm (¾in) cubes

2 onions, finely chopped

1 tsp dried chilli flakes

2 tbsp dry sherry

grated zest of 1 lemon

4 garlic cloves, grated or finely chopped

200g can chopped tomatoes

small handful of flat-leaf parsley, chopped

salt and freshly ground black pepper

1 Preheat the oven to 200°C (400°F/Gas 6). Heat half the oil in a non-stick frying pan, add the potatoes, and cook, turning frequently, over a low heat for 20 minutes, or until starting to brown. Add the onions and cook for a further 5 minutes.

2 Add the chilli, sherry, lemon zest, and garlic, and allow to reduce for 2 minutes before adding the tomatoes and parsley. Season with salt and

pepper, combine well, and cook over a medium heat for 10 minutes, stirring occasionally.

3 Add the remaining oil, place all the ingredients in a shallow baking dish, and cook in the oven for 30 minutes, or until cooked. Serve hot with a selection of tapas dishes.

variation

potato, celery, and parsnip bake

Prepare in the same way, but cook a combination of 350g (12 oz) potatoes and 350g (12oz) parsnips, both peeled and cut into 2 cm (¾in) cubes, instead of all potatoes, and add 2 thinly sliced celery sticks at the same time. Add the zest of an orange instead of lemon, and 2 tbsp chopped fresh thyme as well as the parsley.

sweet potato and rosemary rolls

The gentle scent of rosemary and chunks of sweet potato in the dough make these rolls something special.

🥣 20 MINS 🍲 20-25 MINS ❄️ FREEZABLE

MAKES 8

300g (10oz) plain flour, plus extra if necessary

100g (3½oz) wholemeal self-raising flour

1 tsp bicarbonate of soda

salt and freshly ground black pepper

140g (5oz) sweet potato, peeled and grated

1 tsp finely chopped rosemary

250ml (9fl oz) buttermilk

1 Preheat the oven to 220°C (425°F/ Gas 7). Line a baking tray with baking parchment. In a bowl, mix together the flours and bicarbonate of soda, together with some salt and pepper. Roughly chop the grated potato to reduce the size of the shreds. Add it to the bowl with the rosemary, mixing it in well.

2 Make a well in the centre of the dry ingredients and gently stir in the buttermilk, bringing the mixture together to form a loose dough.

Use your hands to bring the mixture together into a ball, then turn it out onto a floured work surface and knead for 2 minutes until it forms a smooth dough. You may need to add a little extra flour at this stage.

3 Divide the dough into 8 equal pieces and shape them into tight rounds. Flatten the tops and cut a cross in the centre of each roll with a sharp knife, to help the rolls to rise easily when baking.

4 Place the rolls onto the baking tray and cook in the middle of the oven for 20-25 minutes until well risen and golden brown. Transfer to a wire rack and cool for at least 10 minutes before serving. These are particularly delicious eaten still warm.

gratin of swiss chard with haricots and pancetta

This rich, warming dish uses only the leaves of chard. Cut up the colourful stems, steam briefly, and serve alongside.

🥣 10 MINS PLUS SOAKING 🍲 1 HR 20 MINS PLUS RESTING

SPECIAL EQUIPMENT ▪ 1.5-litre (2¾-pint) gratin dish ▪ food processor

SERVES 4-6

400g (14oz) dried haricot or canellini beans, soaked overnight

200g (7oz) pancetta, diced

2 tbsp extra virgin olive oil

4 garlic cloves, crushed

400g (14oz) Swiss chard, destalked and finely shredded

600ml (1 pint) double cream

sea salt and freshly ground black pepper

100g (3½oz) white bread

60g (2oz) Parmesan cheese, grated

8 basil leaves

1 Preheat the oven to 200°C (400°F/ Gas 6). Drain the soaked beans, put them in a large pan of water, and bring to the boil. Turn down to a strong simmer and skim off any foam that has collected on the surface. Continue to cook for around 40 minutes or until soft.

2 In another large, deep-sided pan, cook the pancetta in the oil for 3–4 minutes until it is golden brown. Add the garlic and continue to cook for up to 30 seconds, being careful not to burn the garlic. Remove the garlic and pancetta from the oil and set aside. Add the chard to the oil in the pan and cook, stirring, for about 1 minute until it has collapsed, but is still al dente.

3 Add the pancetta, garlic, and cooked beans to the chard. Mix well, stir in the cream, and season.

4 Tip everything into the gratin dish. Top with breadcrumbs made by blitzing the white bread, Parmesan cheese, and basil in a food processor. Cook at the top of the oven for 30 minutes until golden brown. Leave the gratin to rest for 10 minutes before serving.

sausage and chestnut stuffing

You can buy ready-prepared chestnuts in packets, or if you want to prepare your own, boil or roast them in a hot oven for 15–20 minutes, let them cool, and then peel them.

🥣 10 MINS   🍲 20 MINS

SERVES 4

1 tbsp olive oil

1 onion, chopped

salt and freshly ground black pepper

6 pork sausages, skinned

250g (9oz) ready-cooked chestnuts, chopped

small handful of flat-leaf parsley

1 Heat the oil in a frying pan over a medium heat, add the onion, and cook for 3–4 minutes until the onion is soft. Season with salt and pepper, and set aside to cool.

2 Put the sausagemeat in a bowl and add the chestnuts, parsley, and cooled onion. Mix together and season with salt and pepper.

3 Use the mixture to stuff the neck of a turkey, or spread it out under the skin of a whole chicken. Alternatively, roll the mixture into balls and roast in a preheated 200°C (400°F/Gas 6) oven for about 20 minutes, or fry in a little oil until cooked through and golden.

variation

chestnut and celery stuffing
Cook the onion in the same way, but add 1 finely chopped celery stick at the same time. Stir in 115g (4oz) fresh breadcrumbs instead of the sausagemeat, then add the chopped chestnuts, a handful of fresh chopped thyme, and the parsley as before. Add a beaten egg to bind, and season well.

dauphinoise potatoes

Creamy and garlicky potatoes are an ideal accompaniment for any roast dish. If you have a mandoline, it is the perfect piece of equipment for cutting the potatoes into thin slices.

🥣 20 MINS   🍲 1 HR 45 MINS

SPECIAL EQUIPMENT ▪ 2.3-litre (4-pint) shallow ovenproof dish

SERVES 4

900g (2lb) waxy potatoes, peeled and cut into slices 3mm (⅛in) thick

300ml (10fl oz) double cream

300ml (10fl oz) milk

salt and freshly ground black pepper

3 garlic cloves, grated or finely chopped

1 Preheat the oven to 180°C (350°F/ Gas 4). Put the potatoes, cream, and milk in a large pan, and season with salt and pepper. Bring to the boil, then cover and simmer for 10–15 minutes, or until the potatoes begin to soften.

2 Using a slotted spoon, transfer the potatoes to the ovenproof dish. Sprinkle over the garlic and season well with salt and pepper. Strain the cream and milk mixture, then pour over the potatoes. Cover the dish with foil, then put in the oven to cook for 1 hour. Remove the foil and cook for a further 30 minutes, or until the top has begun to turn golden.

variation

potato and leek gratin
Follow step 1, but use 750g (1lb 10oz) potatoes. Meanwhile, sauté 2 sliced leeks in 30g (1oz) butter for 4–5 minutes until soft. Transfer half the potatoes to the ovenproof dish at step 2, then cover with a layer of all the leeks. Sprinkle over a handful of grated Gruyère cheese and half the garlic. Add the remaining potatoes, then sprinkle over another handful of grated Gruyère and the remaining garlic and continue as before.

salsify fritters

Salsify is a root vegetable that looks a little like a carrot and is cooked in exactly the same way. Serve these tasty Mediterranean fritters as an easy side dish with meat or fish.

🥣 10 MINS   🍲 25 MINS

MAKES 4

400g (14oz) salsify, peeled and cut into small, equal-sized pieces

50g (1¾oz) butter

1 garlic clove, crushed

freshly ground black pepper

1 tbsp plain flour

1 tbsp olive oil

1 Add the salsify to a pan of boiling salted water and cook for about 20 minutes, or until beginning to soften. Drain well.

2 Mash the salsify, then add half the butter, all the garlic, and some black pepper, and mash again. Divide into four and shape each portion into a cake.

3 Toss the cakes in the flour to coat lightly. Heat the oil with the remaining butter in a non-stick pan, add the cakes, and cook for about 2 minutes, or until the underside is golden. Flip over and cook the other side for about 2 minutes. Serve hot.

potato and horseradish mash

While potatoes are a fine addition to almost any main course, combining them with hearty kale, bacon, and spicy horseradish adds tons of flavour. Mashed potato also works well.

🥣 **15 MINS**　　🍲 **30 MINS**

SERVES 4

450g (1lb) floury potatoes, peeled and roughly chopped

1 tbsp olive oil

knob of butter

200g (7oz) bacon rashers, chopped

3 tsp creamed horseradish

salt and freshly ground black pepper

250g (9oz) curly kale, cooked and chopped

1 Boil the potatoes in a pan of salted water for 15–20 minutes until soft. Drain, then cut into bite-sized pieces, or mash, if you like.

2 Heat the oil and butter in a large non-stick frying pan over a medium heat. When the butter has melted, add the bacon. Fry for 5–6 minutes until golden and crispy.

3 Tip in the potatoes and stir through. Add the horseradish cream and season with salt and pepper. Stir through the curly kale until everything is combined. Cook for a few minutes until lightly golden and a little crispy.

variation

potato, celeriac, and sprouts sauté

Prepare in the same way, but use 1 large potato and ½ small celeriac, peeled and cut into chunks, instead of all potatoes. Boil and drain the vegetables, then crush (don't mash). Meanwhile, boil 250g (9oz) sliced Brussels sprouts until cooked; drain. Cook the bacon as before. Omit the horseradish. Add the potato and celeriac mix and the Brussels sprouts. Stir, season well, and fry as before.

sweet potato paratha

These flatbreads are so quick to make, it's worth doubling up and freezing half layered between greaseproof paper.

🥣 **20 MINS PLUS RESTING**　　🍲 **15–20 MINS**　　❄️ **FREEZABLE**

MAKES 4

300g (10oz) chapatti flour

salt

50g (1¾oz) unsalted butter, melted and cooled

For the stuffing

250g (9oz) sweet potato, peeled and diced

1 tbsp sunflower oil, plus extra for brushing

½ red onion, finely chopped

2 garlic cloves, crushed

1 tbsp finely chopped red chilli, or to taste

1 tbsp finely chopped fresh root ginger

2 heaped tbsp chopped coriander

½ tsp garam masala

1 To make the dough for the paratha, sift the flour and ½ tsp salt into a bowl. Add the butter and 150ml (5fl oz) water, and bring the mixture together to form a soft dough. Knead for 5 minutes, then let the dough rest, covered, for 1 hour.

2 To make the stuffing, boil or steam the sweet potato for about 7 minutes until tender. Drain it well. Heat the oil in a frying pan over a medium heat, add the red onion, and cook for 3–4 minutes until soft. Add the garlic, chilli, and ginger, and continue to cook for 1–2 minutes.

3 Add the cooked onion mixture to the sweet potato and mash well. Add the coriander, garam masala, and a good seasoning of salt, and beat until smooth. Set aside to cool.

4 When the dough has rested, divide it into 4 pieces. Knead each piece and roll it out into a circle, around 10cm (4in) in diameter. Put a quarter of the stuffing in the middle. Pull the edges up around it, forming a purse shape.

5 Pinch the edges together to seal in the stuffing, turn the dough over, and roll it out into a circle, about 18cm (7in) in diameter, taking care not to roll too hard. If the filling bursts out, wipe it off and pinch the dough together to reseal the paratha.

6 Heat a large cast-iron frying pan or griddle over a medium heat. Fry the parathas for 2 minutes on each side, turning occasionally to make sure they are well cooked and browning in places. Once they have cooked on each side once, brush the surface with a little oil before turning them again. Serve immediately alongside a curry, or as a light lunch dish with a green salad.

carrot and beetroot salad with balsamic vinaigrette

This richly-coloured salad is not just pretty; it's also packed with beneficial antioxidants. Choose young, fresh vegetables for the best flavour for a raw salad such as this.

30 MINS   **3-4 MINS**

SERVES 4-6

600g (1lb 5oz) carrots, trimmed and scrubbed

1 bunch of beetroots, about 600g (1lb 5oz), peeled and halved

50g (1¾oz) sunflower seeds or pumpkin seeds

1 tsp soy sauce (optional)

small bunch of flat-leaf parsley, chopped, or salad cress, snipped

salt and freshly ground black pepper

For the vinaigrette

6 tbsp extra virgin olive oil, plus 1 tsp for toasting the seeds

60ml (2fl oz) balsamic vinegar

1 garlic clove, crushed (optional)

1 Coarsely grate the raw carrots and beetroots and combine in a large bowl. For the vinaigrette, put the 6 tbsp oil, vinegar, and garlic (if using) in a screw-top jar, put the lid on tightly, and shake.

2 Gently heat the remaining 1 tsp olive oil in a small frying pan and toast the seeds for 3–4 minutes over a moderate heat, stirring frequently to prevent sticking. Add the soy sauce at the end of cooking (if using). Most of the soy sauce will evaporate, leaving a salty taste and extra browning for the seeds.

3 Add the parsley or cress to the carrot and beetroot. Shake the vinaigrette again, pour over the vegetables, then season to taste. Toss the salad gently, scatter the toasted seeds over, and serve.

carrot and shredded cabbage with peanuts

This Thai-style salad proves that winter recipes can be fresh and light. With its salty-sweet flavours and zingy lime and chilli dressing, it enlivens grilled chicken or fish.

15 MINS

SERVES 4

2 eating apples

4 carrots, grated

1 small white cabbage, shredded

small handful of sunflower seeds

small handful of salted peanuts or dry-roasted peanuts

For the dressing

1 tbsp light soy sauce

1 tbsp fish sauce (nam pla)

1 green chilli, deseeded and finely chopped

1 garlic clove, grated or finely chopped

juice of 2 limes

1-2 tsp caster sugar

small handful of coriander, finely chopped

salt and freshly ground black pepper

1 To make the dressing, put all the dressing ingredients in a small bowl, except the salt and pepper, and mix thoroughly until the sugar has dissolved. Taste, and season with

salt and pepper as needed, then taste again. If it needs sweetening, add more sugar; if it needs saltiness, add a little more fish sauce (nam pla).

2 Quarter and core the apples, then chop into bite-sized pieces. Put in a bowl with the carrots, cabbage, and sunflower seeds. Toss well. Drizzle over the dressing and toss together so that everything is well mixed. Transfer to a serving dish and scatter over the peanuts.

variation

carrot and noodle salad

Cook 200g (7oz) thin rice noodles, drain, rinse with cold water, and drain again. Use these instead of the shredded cabbage. Continue as in the original recipe, but transfer to individual serving bowls instead of one large bowl and offer some sweet chilli sauce to drizzle over.

horseradish sauce

Serve this hot sauce with beef, ox tongue, sausages, beetroots, and salted or smoked fish. The horseradish root should not be cooked or it will lose its pungency.

5 MINS PLUS MATURING   **10-15 MINS**

MAKES ABOUT 350ml (12fl oz)

300ml (10fl oz) white wine vinegar

1 bay leaf

12 peppercorns

2 tbsp caster sugar

2 cloves

8 tbsp double cream at room temperature, plus extra for serving (optional)

150g (5½oz) horseradish, grated

salt

1 Put the vinegar, bay leaf, peppercorns, sugar, and cloves in a small saucepan. Bring to the boil, stirring until all the sugar has dissolved, and then boil rapidly for about 5 minutes until the volume has reduced by half. Stir in the cream and boil for 1 minute.

2 Strain the liquid through a sieve into a bowl. Allow it to cool, then stir in the grated horseradish and season with salt.

3 Spoon the sauce into sterilized jars with non-metallic or vinegar-proof lids, top with waxed paper discs, seal, label, and store in a cool, dark place for up to 2 months. Thin with a little extra cream, if needed, when serving.

Season's best **carrots**

Their exceptional flavour, versatility, and the promise of good health make carrots extremely popular. As well as the familiar long, orange variety, they may be cylindrical, stubby, round, or finger-size, and purple, yellow, dark red, or white, with a sweet, refreshing taste and aroma. Maincrop are best in autumn and early winter; young finger and bunched ones in spring and summer. They are great with sweet spices and other roots, or glazed with orange juice and honey.

The sweet orange carrot was developed by the Dutch in the 16th century in honour of their king. Many varieties are now cultivated worldwide in countries with mild temperatures.

essentials
varieties available

Many varieties of young finger, bunched, maincrop, chantenay, purple, white, and round carrots.

buy The green tops should be fresh and bright; if trimmed, there should be no mould on the top. They should smell fresh and be firm. Avoid any sprouting thin white rootlets.

store Twist off any green tops and leave unwashed for up to 2 weeks in a cool, dark place. If washed and trimmed, store in the fridge for up to 1 week.

cook Eat raw, or roast, boil, braise, steam, sauté, or stir-fry. Use in soups, stews, casseroles, cakes, and breads.

preserve Pickle with other vegetables, or use to make a sweet jam or conserve.

recipe ideas

Caramelized carrots p406

Carrot and coriander relish p420

Carrot and shredded cabbage with peanuts p404

Purple carrot The original wild carrots of Afghanistan were purple. New strains have regained the colour that supplies beneficial anthocyanin and lycopene along with rich carrot flavour.

These carrots are purple outside and orange in the centre.

Chantenay They are short and stubby when fully grown. Their flavour is extraordinarily rich and there is no need to peel them before use.

Leaves should be bright green and fresh.

They have a classic cone shape.

how to make carrot batonnets

Batonnets are ideal for crudités, steaming, or stir-frying. They are about 5mm (¼in) wide and 5–6cm (2–2½in) long. Any straight vegetable can be cut to this shape.

1 Peel each carrot and cut in half crossways. Cut into 5mm (¼in) thick slices with a mandolin or a large, sharp chef's knife.

2 Stack the slices in their natural order. Trim off the rounded sides to make a neat block. Slice lengthways into strips of equal width.

Bunched carrot These delicious, sweet, fragrant carrots are perfect for scrubbing and grating raw, or for cooking lightly.

celeriac rémoulade with carrot salad

Both salads can be prepared and tossed in their dressings up to 1 day ahead of eating them. Once made, cover them and store in the fridge. The flavours will mellow and deepen.

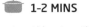 25–30 MINS PLUS CHILLING  1–2 MINS

SERVES 6

For the carrot salad

3 tbsp cider vinegar

1 tsp sugar

salt and freshly ground black pepper

75ml (2½fl oz) light olive oil

500g (1lb 2oz) carrots, coarsely grated

90g (3oz) raisins

For the celeriac salad

1 celeriac, about 750g (1lb 10oz) in weight

175ml (6fl oz) mayonnaise

2 tbsp Dijon mustard, or to taste

1 For the carrot salad, whisk the vinegar with the sugar and some salt and pepper. Gradually whisk in the oil, so the vinaigrette emulsifies and thickens slightly. Taste for seasoning. Add the carrots and the raisins. Toss everything together and taste for seasoning. Cover and refrigerate for at least 1 hour.

2 For the celeriac salad, place the celeriac on a chopping board and slice away all the thick, knobbly peel. Cut into thin slices, then into fine, even strips. Put the celeriac strips in a saucepan of cold, salted water and bring to the boil. Simmer for 1–2 minutes until tender, but still al dente, then drain.

3 Mix the mayonnaise and mustard with some salt and pepper in a bowl. Taste, adding more mustard if you like. Add the celeriac, toss, then taste for seasoning. Cover and refrigerate for at least 1 hour. Arrange the celeriac and carrot salads in individual bowls and serve.

caramelized carrots

Caramelizing carrots in a pan with butter and demerara sugar results in a glorious glossy finish and a slightly nutty flavour. Steam cabbage leaves or leeks to serve alongside.

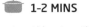 10 MINS  25 MINS

SERVES 4

1.1kg (2½lb) carrots

50g (1¾oz) butter

sprinkling of demerara sugar

handful of flat-leaf parsley, finely chopped (optional)

1 Peel and trim the carrots. Cut them in half lengthways and then in half again to make chunky batons. Cook them in a pan of lightly salted water for 10–15 minutes, or until nearly cooked, then drain.

2 Return the carrots to the pan with the butter, sugar, and parsley, and cook over a medium heat, stirring occasionally, for 10 minutes or until the carrots start to caramelize. Sprinkle with parsley, if using. Serve with roast chicken or beef.

variation

fragrant honeyed mixed roots

Prepare in the same way, but use a mixture of 350g (12oz) carrots, 350g (12oz) parsnips, and 350g (12oz) celeriac, all peeled and cut into batons, instead of all carrots. Cook in the same way at step 1. At step 2, add 1 tbsp clear honey instead of the sugar and cook as before, but sprinkle over the chopped leaves of 2 large sprigs of rosemary whilst cooking. Garnish with parsley as before (optional).

roasted squash with sage and onion

Roasting vegetables to serve alongside roast meat is one of the easiest ways for cooking a side dish. Add some whole cloves of garlic for an even greater flavour.

 15 MINS 🍲 40 MINS

SERVES 4

1 butternut squash, halved, deseeded, peeled, and cut into wedges

2 red onions, cut into eighths

handful of sage leaves, finely chopped

pinch of dried chilli flakes (optional)

salt and freshly ground black pepper

1-2 tbsp olive oil

1 Preheat the oven to 200°C (400°F/ Gas 6). Put the squash, onions, sage, and chilli flakes, if using, in a large roasting tin and season well with salt and pepper. Add the oil and combine all the ingredients with your hands.

2 Put the tin in the oven to roast for 30–40 minutes, or until the squash is cooked and golden. Serve with roast chicken or pork.

variation

roasted sweet potato and celeriac with garlic and herbs

Prepare in the same way, but use 1 sweet potato and 1 small celeriac, both peeled and cut into chunks, instead of the squash. Omit the onions and sprinkle the vegetables with 2 finely chopped garlic cloves and 2 tbsp each of chopped fresh thyme, sage, and parsley. Cook as before.

squash with chestnuts and cranberries

This is a great recipe for any festive occasion. Combining sweet squash and tart cranberries in an unusual and successful way, it's an eye-catchingly colourful seasonal dish.

🥣 15 MINS 🍲 35 MINS

SERVES 4

1-2 tbsp olive oil

knob of butter

pinch of allspice

pinch of ground cinnamon

1 butternut squash, halved, deseeded, peeled, and cut into bite-sized pieces

salt and freshly ground black pepper

200g (7oz) ready-cooked chestnuts

50g (1¾oz) fresh cranberries

caster sugar, to taste (optional)

1 Preheat the oven to 200°C (400°F/ Gas 6). Heat the oil and butter in a large frying pan over a medium heat. Add the allspice, cinnamon, and squash, season well with salt and pepper, and cook, stirring occasionally, for 15 minutes or until the squash begins to soften. Add a little more oil, if needed.

2 Add the chestnuts and stir so they are coated with the oil. Cook over a low heat for 5–10 minutes, then add the cranberries and cook for 5 more minutes.

3 Taste and season again, if needed, adding a little sugar if the cranberries are too tart (cook until the sugar has dissolved). Serve with roast chicken or turkey.

orange and chocolate tiramisu

You'll love this clever, seasonal version of the classic tiramisu dessert. Here coffee is substituted by orange juice and an orange-based liqueur complements the flavour.

20 MINS PLUS CHILLING

SPECIAL EQUIPMENT ▪ 2-litre (3½-pint) serving dish ▪ electric hand whisk

SERVES 8

20–24 sponge fingers

200ml (7fl oz) orange juice

2 tbsp Grand Marnier or Cointreau

2 large eggs, separated

25g (scant 1oz) icing sugar, sifted

500g (1lb 2oz) mascarpone cheese

grated zest of 1 orange

75g (2½oz) orange-flavoured chocolate, finely grated

1 Arrange the sponge fingers in the base of the serving dish. Drizzle with the orange juice and Grand Marnier or Cointreau and set aside while the biscuits soak up the liquid.

2 Put the egg yolks and icing sugar in a large bowl and beat with a wooden spoon until smooth and creamy. Beat in the mascarpone cheese until smooth. Put the egg whites in a mixing bowl and whisk with an electric hand whisk until soft peaks form. Fold into the mascarpone mixture along with the orange zest.

3 Pour the mixture over the sponge fingers and smooth the top. Cover and chill for at least 4 hours or overnight. To serve, decorate with the grated chocolate.

variation

pear, coffee, and walnut tiramisu

Drizzle the sponge fingers with 200ml (7fl oz) strong black coffee and 2 tbsp brandy instead of the orange juice and orange liqueur. Make the mascarpone topping as in step 2, omitting the orange zest, then fold in 2 peeled, cored, and chopped ripe pears. Finish as in the recipe at step 3, but decorate with 3 tbsp finely chopped walnuts instead of the chocolate.

orange and pistachio swiss roll

The delicate flavours of pistachio nuts and orange flower water used here give a traditional recipe a modern twist.

20 MINS ▪ **15 MINS**

SPECIAL EQUIPMENT ▪ 32.5 x 23cm (13 x 9in) Swiss roll tin ▪ electric hand whisk

SERVES 8

3 large eggs

100g (3½oz) caster sugar, plus extra for sprinkling

salt

75g (2½oz) self-raising flour

grated zest of 2 oranges, and 3 tbsp juice

2 tsp orange flower water (optional)

200ml (7fl oz) double cream

75g (2½oz) unsalted pistachio nuts, chopped

icing sugar, for dusting

1 Preheat the oven to 200°C (400°F/Gas 6). Line the tin with parchment. Set a bowl over a pan of simmering water. Add the eggs, sugar, and a pinch of salt, and whisk with an electric hand whisk for 5 minutes until thick and creamy. Remove the bowl from the pan and whisk for another 1–2 minutes until cool. Sift in the flour, then add half the orange zest, and 1 tbsp of juice. Fold together, pour into the tin, and bake for 12–15 minutes until firm to the touch.

2 Sprinkle a sheet of baking parchment with caster sugar. Turn out the cake onto the parchment. Leave to cool for 5 minutes, then peel off the parchment from the cake and discard. Sprinkle with the orange flower water if using.

3 Make an indent along one short side, about 2cm (¾in) from the edge, with the back of a knife. Using the indent to start it off, roll up the cake around the sugared parchment. Leave to cool.

4 Whip the cream and fold in the pistachios and the remaining orange zest and juice. Unroll the cake, discard the parchment, and spread the cream filling evenly over the surface. Roll up the cake again and place, joint downwards, on a serving plate. Dust with icing sugar just before serving.

pear cake

Fresh pear, yogurt, and almonds make this a very moist cake.

40 MINS ▪ **45–50 MINS** ▪ **FREEZABLE**

SPECIAL EQUIPMENT ▪ 18cm (7in) round springform cake tin

SERVES 6–8

100g (3½oz) unsalted butter, softened

75g (2½oz) light soft brown sugar

1 egg, lightly beaten

125g (4½oz) self-raising flour

1 tsp baking powder

½ tsp ground ginger

½ tsp cinnamon

grated zest and juice of ½ orange

4 tbsp Greek-style yogurt

25g (scant 1oz) ground almonds

1 large or 2 small pears, peeled, cored, and sliced

For the topping

2 tbsp flaked almonds, lightly toasted

2 tbsp demerara sugar

1 Preheat the oven to 180°C (350°F/Gas 4). Grease the tin and line with parchment. Whisk together the butter and sugar until light and fluffy. Beat the egg into the creamed mixture.

2 Sift together the flour, baking powder, ginger, and cinnamon, and gently fold into the batter. Fold in the orange zest and juice, yogurt, and the ground almonds. Pour half the batter into the tin. Top with the pears and cover with rest of the batter.

3 In a small bowl, toss together the flaked almonds and demerara sugar. Sprinkle over the top of the cake and bake for 45–50 minutes until a skewer comes out clean. Leave the cake for about 10 minutes, then turn it out onto a wire rack to cool.

chocolate orange truffle cake

Beneath the rich chocolate ganache topping lies a layer of chocolate sponge cake flavoured with Grand Marnier. Orange zest sprinkled over the top is the perfect finishing touch. Make sure you leave at least 6 hours' chilling time.

🥣 **35–40 MINS PLUS CHILLING**　　🍲 **40 MINS**

SPECIAL EQUIPMENT ▪ 25cm (10in) round cake tin ▪ electric hand whisk ▪ 23cm (9in) round springform cake tin

SERVES 10–12

100g (3½oz) plain flour

30g (1oz) cocoa powder, plus 3 tbsp to decorate

salt

4 eggs

140g (5oz) caster sugar

60g (2oz) butter, melted and cooled

4–5 tbsp Grand Marnier

grated zest of 3 oranges

For the chocolate ganache

375g (13oz) plain chocolate, cut into large chunks

375ml (13fl oz) double cream

3 tbsp Grand Marnier

1 Preheat the oven to 220°C (425°F/ Gas 7). Butter the 25cm (10in) cake tin and line the bottom with baking parchment. Butter the parchment. Sprinkle in 2–3 tbsp flour, and turn the tin to coat the bottom and side; tap the tin upside down to remove excess flour.

2 Sift together the flour, cocoa powder, and a pinch of salt. Put the eggs in a large bowl and beat with an electric hand whisk for a few seconds. Add the sugar and continue beating for about 5 minutes, until the mixture leaves a ribbon trail when the beaters are lifted.

3 Sift about a third of the flour and cocoa mixture over the egg mixture and fold together. Add another third of the flour and cocoa mixture and fold together in the same way.

Add the remaining flour and cocoa mixture and the butter, and fold them in gently, but quickly.

4 Pour the mixture into the prepared tin, then gently tap the tin on the work surface to level the mixture and knock out any large air bubbles. Bake for about 40 minutes, until the cake has risen and is just firm to the touch. Turn the cake out onto a wire rack. Peel off the paper and leave to cool.

5 Trim the cooled cake to fit the 23cm (9in) springform tin. Lightly butter the bottom and side. Transfer the trimmed cake to the tin. Sprinkle the Grand Marnier evenly over the top, cover, and set aside.

6 For the chocolate ganache, put the chocolate in a large bowl. Heat the cream until almost boiling, then pour it over the chocolate. Stir until the

chocolate has melted. Allow to cool, stirring occasionally. Add the Grand Marnier and gently stir until blended. Using the electric hand whisk, beat the chocolate ganache for 5–10 minutes, until fluffy. Do not overbeat, or it will be very stiff. With a rubber spatula or a wooden spoon, turn out the chocolate ganache on top of the cake and smooth the surface. Cover with cling film and chill for at least 6 hours, until firm.

7 Just before serving, take the cake from the fridge. Stand it on top of a bowl, then release the side of the tin. Carefully remove the base of the tin, using a palette knife. Place the cake on a wire rack with a baking sheet beneath. Sift cocoa powder over the top, using a stencil if you like, then transfer to a serving plate and sprinkle with the orange zest.

apple, sultana, and pecan cake

If you like a healthier cake, this is an excellent choice. It uses little fat and is packed full of fruit and nuts, making it a wholesome yet delicious choice.

🥄 25 MINS   🍲 30–35 MINS

SPECIAL EQUIPMENT ▪ 23cm (9in) round springform cake tin

SERVES 10-12

50g (1¾oz) shelled pecan nuts

200g (7oz) apples, peeled, cored, and finely diced

150g (5½oz) light soft brown sugar

250g (9oz) self-raising flour

1 tsp baking powder

2 tsp cinnamon

salt

3½ tbsp sunflower oil

3½ tbsp milk

2 eggs

1 tsp vanilla extract

50g (1¾oz) sultanas

whipped cream or icing sugar, to serve (optional)

1 Preheat the oven to 180°C (350°F/Gas 4). Grease the cake tin with butter and line the base with baking parchment. Place the nuts on a baking sheet and toast them in the oven for 5 minutes until crisp. Allow to cool, then roughly chop.

2 Mix the apples and sugar together in a large mixing bowl. Sift over the flour, baking powder, cinnamon, and a little salt, and fold in. Then whisk together the oil, milk, eggs, and vanilla extract in a jug.

3 Pour the milk into the cake mixture and stir until well combined. Fold in the pecans and sultanas, and pour the mixture into the prepared tin.

4 Bake in the centre of the oven for 30–35 minutes until a skewer comes out clean. Leave to cool for a few minutes in the tin, then turn out onto a wire rack and remove the baking parchment. Serve warm with whipped cream as a dessert, or cooled and dusted with icing sugar.

normandy pear tart

This frangipane-filled fruit tart is a signature dish of Normandy, France, where wonderful pears are grown.

🥄 40–45 MINS PLUS CHILLING   🍲 37–45 MINS

SPECIAL EQUIPMENT ▪ 23–25cm (9–10in) round loose-bottomed fluted tart tin ▪ food processor ▪ electric hand whisk

SERVES 6-8

375g (13oz) ready-made sweet shortcrust pastry

125g (4½oz) whole blanched almonds

125g (4½oz) unsalted butter, softened

100g (3½oz) caster sugar

1 egg, plus 1 egg yolk

3 tbsp kirsch

2 tbsp plain flour, sifted

3-4 ripe pears, peeled, cored, and cut into wedges

juice of 1 lemon

150g (5½oz) apricot jam

1 Grease the tart tin with butter. Roll out the pastry on a floured surface to a large circle, 5cm (2in) larger than the tin, and use to line the tin, pressing it into the corners. Trim away the excess and prick the bottom all over with a fork.

2 Preheat the oven to 200°C (400°F/Gas 6). Grind the almonds to a fine powder in a food processor.

3 To make the frangipane, put the butter and sugar in a mixing bowl and whisk with an electric hand whisk for 2–3 minutes until pale and creamy. Gradually add the egg and egg yolk, beating well after each addition. Add 1 tbsp kirsch, then gently stir in the almonds and flour until well blended.

4 Spoon the frangipane into the pastry shell and spread it with a palette knife. Toss the pear wedges in the lemon juice, then place the pears in a spiral pattern on top of the frangipane. Set the tin on a baking sheet and bake in the oven for 12–15 minutes. Reduce the heat to 180°C (350°F/Gas 4) and bake for a further 25–30 minutes, until the frangipane sets. Remove from the oven and leave to cool.

5 To make a glaze, melt the jam and 2 tbsp kirsch or water in a pan, then work it through a sieve set over a bowl. Unmould the tart, brush the glaze over the pears and frangipane, and serve.

classic apple crumble

This is one of the easiest and most satisfying of desserts. It makes the most of tart cooking apples, which develop a beautifully fluffy texture and milder taste when baked.

🥣 15 MINS 🍲 30 MINS ❄️ FREEZABLE

SPECIAL EQUIPMENT ▪ 1.2-litre (2-pint) ovenproof dish

SERVES 4

3 large Bramley apples, peeled, cored, and roughly chopped

50–75g (1¾–2½oz) caster sugar (depending on the tartness of the apples)

For the crumble topping

50g (1¾oz) butter, diced

125g (4½oz) plain flour

125g (4½oz) golden caster sugar or caster sugar

1 Preheat the oven to 190°C (375°F/ Gas 5). To make the crumble, place the apples and sugar in a pan with a tiny amount of water. Simmer gently until the apples begin to break down, but don't let them get too soft. Then transfer the apple mixture to an ovenproof dish.

2 To make the crumble topping, place the butter and flour in a mixing bowl. Using your fingertips, rub the butter into the flour until the mixture resembles breadcrumbs. Add the sugar and rub it in using the same method. Sprinkle the crumble on top of the apple and bake for 30 minutes, or until the topping is golden brown. Serve while still hot.

pistachio and orange biscotti

These fragrant biscotti are delicious served either with coffee or dipped in a glass of sweet dessert wine.

🥣 15 MINS 🍲 40–45 MINS ❄️ FREEZABLE

MAKES 25–30

100g (3½oz) whole pistachios, shelled

225g (8oz) self-raising flour

100g (3½oz) caster sugar

grated zest of 1 orange

2 eggs

1 tsp vanilla extract

50g (1¾oz) unsalted butter, melted and cooled

1 Preheat the oven to 180°C (350°F/ Gas 4). Spread the pistachios on an unlined baking sheet and bake in the oven for 5–10 minutes. Allow to cool, then rub in a clean tea towel to remove the skins and roughly chop.

2 Mix the flour, sugar, zest, and nuts together in a mixing bowl. In a separate bowl, whisk the eggs and vanilla extract with the butter. Then mix the wet and dry ingredients together to form a dough.

3 Turn the dough out onto a floured work surface and form into 2 logs, each 20cm (8in) x 7.5cm (3in). Place them on a baking sheet lined with silicone paper and bake for 20 minutes in the centre of the oven. Allow to cool slightly, then cut diagonally into 3–5cm (1¼–2in) thick slices with a serrated knife.

4 Return to the oven to bake for another 15 minutes, turning them after 10 minutes, until golden and hard to the touch. Then remove from the oven and allow to cool.

variation

tangerine and almond biscotti

Prepare in exactly the same way but use 100g (3½oz) roughly chopped blanched almonds instead of pistachios and the finely grated zest of 2 tangerines instead of the orange. Add 1 tsp natural almond extract instead of vanilla.

lemon tart

With its zesty lemon filling and buttery pastry base, this classic tart is always guaranteed to taste good.

🥣 **20 MINS PLUS CHILLING**   🍲 **55 MINS**

SPECIAL EQUIPMENT ▪ 20cm (8in) round loose-bottomed fluted tart tin ▪ ceramic baking beans ▪ food processor (optional)

SERVES 8

125g (4½oz) cold butter, diced

175g (6oz) plain flour

75g (2½oz) ground almonds

juice of 4 lemons, finely grated zest of 1 lemon

75g (2½oz) caster sugar

3 large eggs

175ml (6fl oz) double cream

1 Preheat the oven to 200°C (400°F/Gas 6). Put the butter and flour in a mixing bowl. Using your fingertips, rub the butter into the flour until the mixture resembles breadcrumbs. Alternatively, use a food processor. Stir in the almonds, then stir in enough ice-cold water (about 3 tbsp), so the mixture comes together to form a dough. Roll the pastry out on a lightly floured work surface to a large circle about 3mm (⅛in) thick and use to line the tart tin, pressing it into the corners. Trim away any excess around the edges, prick the bottom all over with a fork, then chill in the fridge for 30 minutes.

2 Line the pastry case with greaseproof paper and fill with ceramic baking beans. Bake in the oven for 15 minutes, then remove the paper and beans and return to the oven for a further 5 minutes, or until the pastry is cooked through. Set aside while you make the filling, and turn the oven down to 150°C (300°F/Gas 2).

3 Put the lemon juice and sugar in a mixing bowl and stir together until the sugar has dissolved. Then mix in the eggs and lemon zest. Stir in the cream and pour into the pastry case. Bake for 35 minutes, or until just set – the tart should wobble in the middle slightly when you shake the tin. Leave to cool, then chill until ready to serve. Serve with single cream.

lemon sorbet

Lemon sorbet is an international classic; light and refreshing at the end of a meal or between courses.

🥣 **20 MINS PLUS CHILLING AND FREEZING**   ❄ **FREEZABLE**

SPECIAL EQUIPMENT ▪ ice cream maker

MAKES ABOUT 750ml (1¼ PINTS)

6 large lemons, preferably unwaxed

250g (9oz) sugar

1 large egg white

1 Use a vegetable peeler to remove the peel thinly in strips from 3 of the lemons. Make sure you don't take any white pith or the sorbet will be bitter. Put the sugar, strips of lemon peel, and 250ml (9fl oz) water in a pan and bring to the boil. Boil for 5 minutes to make a syrup. Remove from the heat and allow to cool.

2 Squeeze the juice from all of the lemons and pour into a measuring jug. Add enough water to make the juice up to 400ml (14fl oz). Mix with the cooled syrup, then cover and chill in the fridge overnight.

3 Strain the mixture into an ice cream maker and follow the instructions for freezing. When the sorbet mixture starts to look icy, lightly beat the egg white just to loosen it and add to the mixture. When the sorbet is firm, transfer to the freezer for storage. If not using an ice cream maker, pour the mixture into a container, cover, and still-freeze for 1–2 hours, or until about 2.5cm (1in) of the mixture is frozen around the sides. Whisk to break up the ice particles, then cover and return to the freezer. After about 30 minutes, whisk again until smooth, then fold in the egg white. Continue freezing the sorbet until firm.

4 Half an hour before serving, transfer the sorbet to the fridge to soften slightly, then serve.

spiced quince dulce de leche pie

You can use a can of ready-made dulce de leche instead of boiling your own if you prefer.

🥣 **20 MINS**   🍲 **3 HOURS**

SERVES 6

400g can sweetened condensed milk

2 large quinces (about 225g/8oz), scrubbed

1 tbsp lemon juice

60g (2oz) caster sugar

1 star anise

grated zest of 1 lemon (optional)

1 ready-made sweet shortcrust pastry case

300ml (10fl oz) double cream, whipped

1 tsp ground cinnamon

1 Put the unopened can of condensed milk in a large saucepan and cover it with water. Bring to the boil, reduce the heat, cover, and simmer gently for 3 hours, topping up with more boiling water as necessary. Remove and leave to cool in the water.

2 Whilst it is simmering, put the quinces in the pan too, and blanch for 2 minutes (it makes them easier to peel). Remove with a slotted spoon and place in a bowl of cold water. Drain, peel, quarter, and core. Place in a bowl of water with the lemon juice to prevent browning as you prepare.

3 In a separate pan, put the sugar and 300ml (10fl oz) water, and heat gently until the sugar dissolves. Lift the quinces out of the water, place in the syrup with the star anise, cover, and poach gently for about 30 minutes until tender. Set aside to cool in the syrup, then drain, chop, and gently toss in the lemon zest, if using.

4 Put the pastry case on a serving plate. Spoon the dulce de leche in it and level the surface. Arrange the quinces in a single layer on top. Smother with the whipped cream and dust with a little ground cinnamon. Chill until ready to serve.

cold lemon soufflé

This sharp yet sweet dessert is cool, light, and fluffy.

🥄 **35–40 MINS PLUS CHILLING**　　🍲 **15–20 MINS**

SPECIAL EQUIPMENT ■ 1-litre (1¾-pint) soufflé dish
■ electric mixer or electric hand whisk

SERVES 8

10g (¼oz) powdered gelatine

4 large lemons

4 eggs, separated, plus 2 egg whites

250g (9oz) caster sugar

250ml (9fl oz) double cream

2 tbsp caster sugar

1 Cut a piece of foil, 5cm (2in) longer than the circumference of the soufflé dish, fold in half lengthways, and wrap around the dish so it stands well above the rim. Secure with tape.

2 Put 5 tsp water in a small bowl, add the gelatine, and leave for 2–3 minutes until spongy. Stand the bowl in a pan of gently simmering water and stir until the gelatine is dissolved. Do not allow to boil.

3 Meanwhile, grate the zest from 3 of the lemons, thinly pare strips of zest from the remaining lemon and reserve, then squeeze the juice from all 4 lemons. In a pan, mix the 4 egg yolks, lemon zest, lemon juice, and two-thirds of the sugar, and cook, stirring, just until the mix boils. Pour into a bowl and beat with an electric mixer or hand whisk for 5–7 minutes until light and thick. Whisk the dissolved gelatine into the lemon mix and continue whisking until cool.

4 In a bowl, whip the cream until soft peaks form, then chill in the fridge. Heat the remaining sugar with 120ml (4fl oz) water in a pan until dissolved. Boil without stirring until it reaches the hard-ball stage: to test, drop 1 tsp of the syrup into cold water. Take it between finger and thumb; it should form a firm, pliable ball.

5 While the syrup is boiling, put the 6 egg whites in a bowl and whisk until stiff peaks form. Gradually add the hot syrup, whisking constantly for 5 minutes until the meringue is cool and stiff. Set the bowl of lemon mix in a larger bowl of iced water and stir the mix gently until it thickens. Remove from the ice bath, gently fold in the chilled whipped cream, then fold in the meringue in 2 batches. Pour the soufflé into the dish and chill for at least 2 hours until firmly set.

6 Cut the reserved pared lemon zest into very fine strips. Bring a small pan of water to the boil, add the zest, and simmer for 2 minutes. Drain in a sieve, rinse with cold water, drain again, and set aside for decoration. Remove the soufflé from the fridge and allow to stand at room temperature for 30 minutes. Then sprinkle with the pared lemon zest, remove the foil collar, and serve with whipped cream.

grapefruit granita with almond biscuits

Unlike a smooth sorbet, the texture should resemble coarse snow. Whisk the granita while freezing to achieve this.

🥄 **15–20 MINS PLUS FREEZING**　　🍲 **35–40 MINS**

SERVES 4

3 grapefruit

juice of ½ lemon

50g (1¾oz) sugar, plus more to taste

85g (3oz) plain flour

15g (½oz) butter

grated zest of 1 lemon

150g (5½oz) ground almonds

125g (4½oz) caster sugar

1 tbsp brandy

1 egg, beaten

12–15 whole, blanched almonds

1 Thinly pare the zest from half a grapefruit, leaving behind the white pith, and reserve. Squeeze the juice from all the grapefruits. Strain the juice into a non-metallic bowl with the lemon juice. Add half the sugar and stir until dissolved. Freeze for 45–60 minutes until ice forms on top. Whisk to break the ice. Repeat every hour for 4–5 hours until the granita is slushy and slightly granular.

2 Preheat the oven to 180°C (350°F/ Gas 4). Butter a baking sheet and sprinkle with flour. Sift the flour into a bowl. Add the butter, lemon zest, ground almonds, sugar, brandy, and egg and stir to form a dough. Wet your hands and roll the dough into 2.5cm (1in) balls. Place on a baking sheet, leaving 2.5cm (1in) between the biscuits. Press a whole almond into each. Bake for 15–20 minutes, until light brown. Allow to cool on a wire rack.

3 With a very sharp knife, cut the pared grapefruit zest into fine julienne. In a small pan, dissolve the remaining 25g (scant 1oz) of sugar in 2 tbsp water. Add the zest and simmer for 12–15 minutes until the water has evaporated and the zest is translucent. Spread on baking parchment and allow to cool.

4 Spoon the grapefruit granita into 4 chilled glasses or bowls. Pile the candied zest on top and serve at once with the biscuits on the side.

pears poached in red wine and thyme

This impressive dinner party dessert is made with just a few simple ingredients. Prepare it a day in advance to allow the colours and flavours of the sauce to soak into the fruit.

🥄 20-30 MINS PLUS CHILLING   🍲 50 MINS

SERVES 4

750ml (1¼ pints) red wine

200g (7oz) caster sugar

2 sprigs of thyme

1 cinnamon stick

1 orange

4 firm dessert pears

1 Mix the wine, sugar, thyme, and cinnamon stick in a saucepan just big enough to hold the 4 pears. Bring to the boil and reduce to a simmer.

2 Using a peeler, remove the zest of the orange in large slivers and add to the pan. Cut the orange in half and squeeze the juice into the pan.

3 Peel the pears, leaving the stalks intact, but slicing off the base of each pear to leave a flat surface, so

it can stand upright. Add the pears to the pan, topping up with water, if necessary, to cover them. Cover with a lid and simmer over a low heat for 20 minutes, or until the fruit is soft. Leave the fruit and liquid to cool, then remove the cinnamon stick and discard. Chill in the fridge overnight.

4 Before serving, remove the pears and return the liquid to the heat in a small saucepan. Bring to the boil and simmer until it reduces to a depth of 1cm (½in), or is thickened and slightly sticky. Taste the sauce to make sure the flavours are strong, but not burnt. Strain and pour the hot sauce over the cold pears and serve with cream or ice cream.

middle eastern date cakes with pomegranate drizzle

The sharp fruitiness of the pomegranate molasses contrasts beautifully with the sweetness of dates. You can serve them plain as a sweetmeat with coffee, too.

🥄 25 MINS   🍲 4 MINS

SERVES 4

45g (1½oz) sesame seeds

175g (6oz) fresh dates, stoned and chopped

grated zest and juice of ½ orange

85g (3oz) plain flour

sunflower oil, for frying

150ml (5fl oz) crème fraîche, plus extra to serve

½ vanilla pod, scraped seeds only

1 tbsp icing sugar, sifted

3-4 tbsp pomegranate molasses

4 tbsp pomegranate seeds

1 Heat a large frying pan and toast the sesame seeds, stirring until golden. Immediately tip out of the pan into a bowl. Add the dates, orange zest, and juice to the bowl and stir in the flour to form a firm dough.

2 Using wet hands, roll the mixture into 16 small ovals (date-shaped).

3 Heat about 5mm (¼in) oil in the frying pan over a medium heat and fry the little cakes for about 2 minutes each side until golden brown. Drain on kitchen paper.

4 Mix the crème fraîche with the vanilla seeds and icing sugar until well blended.

5 Arrange the little cakes on serving plates. Drizzle the pomegranate molasses over and around the cakes and scatter with the pomegranate seeds. Add a dollop of vanilla crème fraîche on the side and serve.

chocolate mousse with cinnamon pears

Pears and chocolate go extremely well together. You could use diced poached pears, but this is a quick way of making the dessert using fresh ones tossed in a little cinnamon sugar.

🥣 25 MINUTES PLUS CHILLING

SERVES 6

3 ripe pears

1 tsp lemon juice

1 tbsp icing sugar

1 tsp ground cinnamon

For the mousse

150g (5½oz) dark chocolate

3 eggs, separated

150ml (5fl oz) double cream

115g (4oz) caster sugar

1 tbsp brandy

grated chocolate, to decorate

1 Peel, halve, and core the pears. Dice, then toss with the lemon juice, icing sugar, and cinnamon. Divide between 6 wine goblets or small serving dishes.

2 Place the chocolate in a small heatproof bowl set over a pan of simmering water (the base of the bowl must not touch the water) and heat until mostly melted.

3 Meanwhile, in a clean mixing bowl, whisk the egg whites until peaking. Next, whip the cream in a separate bowl, then the egg yolks and sugar in a third bowl until thick and pale. Remove the chocolate from the heat, stir to melt completely, then stir in the brandy. Add this mixture to the egg yolks and sugar and gently fold in. Next, fold in the cream, and, finally, the egg whites.

4 Spoon the mousse over the pears and chill to firm. Decorate with a little grated chocolate before serving.

hazelnut, chocolate, and orange tart

With a base made of pasta frolla, an Italian sweet pastry, this is a most delicious recipe for a special occasion. The tart contains a richly flavoured filling of ground hazelnuts, plain chocolate, and orange zest, all topped with a chocolate glaze.

45–50 MINS PLUS CHILLING   **35–40 MINS**

SPECIAL EQUIPMENT ▪ 23cm (9in) round fluted springform tin ▪ food processor

SERVES 6–8

For the pasta frolla dough

150g (5½oz) plain flour,
  plus more if needed

75g (2½oz) unsalted butter,
  softened

50g (1¾oz) caster sugar

¼ tsp salt

grated zest of 1 orange

1 egg

For the filling

pared zest of 2 oranges

125g (4½oz) hazelnuts

100g (3½oz) caster sugar

150g (5½oz) unsalted butter

2 tsp plain flour

2 egg yolks, plus 1 egg

60g (2oz) plain chocolate, grated

For the chocolate glaze

125g (4½oz) plain chocolate

75g (2½oz) unsalted butter, diced

2 tsp Grand Marnier

1 For the dough, sift the flour onto a work surface and make a well in the centre. Put the rest of the ingredients into the well and work with your fingertips until thoroughly mixed. Work in the flour until coarse crumbs form, then press into a ball. If it is sticky, work in a little more flour. Lightly flour the work surface and knead the dough for 1–2 minutes until very smooth. Shape into a ball, wrap tightly, and chill for about 30 minutes until firm.

2 Brush the tin with melted butter. Lightly flour a work surface, roll the dough into a 28cm (11in) round and use it to line the tin, pressing it into

the corners. Trim away the excess. With your thumbs, press the dough evenly up the sides of the tin to increase the height of the rim. Prick the bottom all over with a fork, then chill for 15 minutes until firm.

3 Meanwhile, bring a pan of water to the boil, add the pared orange zest, and simmer for 2 minutes. Drain, rinse with cold water, drain again, and coarsely chop two-thirds of it.

4 Preheat the oven to 180°C (350°F/ Gas 4). For the filling, spread the nuts on a baking sheet and toast in the oven for 6–15 minutes (watch them closely) until lightly browned. Rub in a tea towel to remove the skins and set aside to cool. Leave the oven on.

5 Once cool, blitz the nuts with the sugar in a food processor. Beat the butter in a mixing bowl until creamy.

Add the flour and nut mix and beat until light and fluffy. Add the yolks and egg, one at a time, beating after each addition. Mix in the chocolate and chopped orange zest, then spread the filling over the pastry shell. Bake on a baking sheet for 35–40 minutes, or until a knife inserted in the centre comes out clean. Allow to cool on a wire rack.

6 For the glaze, break the chocolate into chunks and heat in a bowl set over a pan of hot water (the base of the bowl must not touch the water) until melted. Gently stir the butter into the chocolate in 2–3 batches. Add the Grand Marnier, then let cool to tepid. Unmould the tart and spread the glaze over the top. Slice the remaining cooked orange zest into fine julienne strips and use to decorate the top.

dried apples

Dried fruits make healthy, additive-free snacks and are an excellent addition to muesli, baked pies, and lamb, pork, or vegetarian dishes. Apples are ideal fruits to oven-dry.

🥣 **15-20 MINS PLUS DRYING AND COOLING** ❄ **FREEZABLE**

MAKES APPROX 115-225g (4-8oz)

1kg (2¼lb) ripe apples

2 tbsp lemon juice or ½ tsp citric acid

1 Briefly wash the apples in cold water, then core and slice them into 3–5mm (⅛–¼in) rings. If using windfalls, cut away any bruised, damaged, or soft parts first. Discard the outer rings that have the most skin on them.

2 Add the lemon juice or citric acid to 600ml (1 pint) water in a bowl. Drop the apple slices into the bowl of acidulated water, drain on a tea towel, and place separately in a single layer on wire racks over baking trays.

Dry in the oven on the lowest setting (50–60°C/120–140°F/Gas ¼) for 8–24 hours, depending on the temperature (this can be done in stages if needed).

3 Turn the slices occasionally as they dry. They are ready when they look and feel like soft, pliable, chamois leather. (For a crunchier version, dry the slices until they are crisp). Remove from the oven, cover with kitchen paper, leave for 12–24 hours, and turn occasionally to ensure they contain as little moisture as possible (to reduce the risk of mould later on).

4 Pack into airtight jars and store in a cool, dry, dark place. Check regularly for any signs of deterioration.

cranberry jelly

This deep red, clear jelly has a tart, fruity flavour that goes perfectly with poultry, pork, sausages, and any cold meats.

🥣 **10 MINS PLUS STRAINING** 🍲 **35-45 MINS**

SPECIAL EQUIPMENT ■ preserving pan ■ jelly bag ■ sugar thermometer

MAKES 400g (14oz)

500g (1lb 2oz) cranberries

1 tbsp lemon juice

approx 500g (1lb 2oz) granulated sugar (see method)

1 Put the berries, 600ml (1 pint) water, and the lemon juice in a preserving pan or large heavy-based saucepan and bring to the boil over a medium heat. Turn the heat down, cover, and simmer for 25–30 minutes, or until the berries are tender. Remove from the heat and mash to a pulp with a potato masher or fork.

2 Tip the pulp into a jelly bag or fine sieve set over a large, clean bowl and leave to strain overnight until all the juice has dripped through.

3 Measure the strained juice and calculate the quantity of sugar – allow 450g/1lb of sugar per 600ml/1 pint of juice. Then pour the juice into the clean preserving pan, add the sugar, and stir gently until all the sugar has dissolved. Raise the heat, bring to the boil, and boil for 10–15 minutes. Then remove the pan from the heat to test for a set with a sugar thermometer, or using a wrinkle test (chill a saucer in the fridge before cooking). If using a thermometer, the temperature must reach 105°C (220°F); the mixture will also thicken around the sides of the pan, boil sluggishly, and the bubbles "plop" rather than froth. Or put 1 tsp jelly on the chilled saucer, allow to cool for a moment, then push it with a finger. If it leaves a trail and wrinkles slightly, it is set.

4 Skim off any surface scum, then ladle into warm sterilized jars, cover with waxed paper discs, seal, and label. Store in a cool, dark place and refrigerate after opening.

apple butter

This mild, soft spread, in which the subtle, sweet flavour of apples combines well with warm spices and citrus fruit, is best enjoyed on good, fresh bread or in desserts.

🥣 **15 MINS** 🍲 **2 HRS 10 MINS**

SPECIAL EQUIPMENT ■ preserving pan

MAKES APPROX 1kg (2¼lb)

900g (2lb) cooking apples, roughly chopped

juice of 1 orange

pinch of ground allspice

pinch of ground cinnamon

675g (1½lb) granulated sugar

1 Put the apples in a preserving pan or a large heavy-based saucepan and pour in 250ml (9fl oz) water. Bring to the boil and simmer the apples for about 10 minutes, or until soft.

2 Sieve the fruit in batches and collect the juice and purée in a clean bowl. Put this mixture back into the pan and add the orange juice, spices, and sugar. Cook on a low heat, stirring until all the sugar has dissolved.

3 Bring the mixture back up to the boil and simmer gently for about 2 hours, or longer if needed, until the mixture thickens. Stir occasionally so that it doesn't catch on the bottom of the pan.

4 The butter is ready when it is thick enough to rest on the back of a spoon without running off, or a wooden spoon drawn across the bottom of the pan leaves a clear trail. It should now be a soft, moist, spreadable paste.

5 Ladle into warm sterilized jars. Cover with discs of waxed paper, seal, and label. Store in a cool, dark place and refrigerate after opening.

pumpkin and orange spiced jam

This orange-scented jam with a subtle, spiced flavour is tasty on toast and also with savoury foods like tangy blue cheese.

🥣 20 MINS   🍲 30–40 MINS

SPECIAL EQUIPMENT ▪ preserving pan ▪ sugar thermometer

MAKES APPROX 2kg (4½lb)

1.35kg (3lb) pumpkin, peeled, deseeded, and cut into small pieces

2 cooking apples, peeled and chopped into small pieces

1.35kg (3lb) granulated sugar

juice of 1 lemon

juice of 1 orange

pinch of cinnamon

pinch of grated nutmeg

1 Put the pumpkin and apple in a preserving pan or a large heavy-based saucepan. Pour in 60ml (2fl oz) water (or enough to stop the pumpkin catching and burning), bring to the boil, then reduce to a simmer and cook for 10–20 minutes, or until the pumpkin is soft. Mash roughly with a potato masher or fork, keeping a few chunks of pumpkin whole.

2 Add the sugar, lemon and orange juice, cinnamon, and nutmeg and stir until all the sugar has dissolved. Then bring to the boil and cook at a rolling boil for 15–20 minutes, or until the jam begins to thicken. Remove the pan from the heat to test for a set with a sugar thermometer, or using a wrinkle test (chill a saucer in the fridge before cooking). If you use a thermometer, the temperature must reach 105°C (220°F); the mixture will also thicken around the sides of the pan, boil sluggishly, and the bubbles "plop" rather than froth. Or put 1 tsp jam on the chilled saucer, allow to cool for a moment, then push it with a finger. If it leaves a trail and wrinkles slightly, it is set.

3 Ladle into warm sterilized jars, cover with waxed paper discs, seal, and label. Store in a cool, dark place and refrigerate after opening.

orange marmalade

This marmalade has a sweeter finish than the classic Seville version. The oranges need long cooking to soften the peel.

🥣 20 MINS   🍲 1 HR 25 MINS – 1 HR 40 MINS

SPECIAL EQUIPMENT ▪ muslin ▪ preserving pan ▪ sugar thermometer

MAKES APPROX 450g (1lb)

1kg (2¼lb) large sweet oranges, scrubbed, with stalks removed

2 lemons

1kg (2¼lb) granulated sugar

1 Halve the oranges and lemons, squeeze the fresh juice into a jug, and reserve it in the fridge. Put the pith and pips in the centre of a muslin square and tie into a bundle with a length of string. Put the citrus shells and 1.2 litres (2 pints) water in a preserving pan. Add the bag of pith and pips, bring to the boil, half cover, and simmer for 1 hour, or until soft.

2 Tip the ingredients into a large colander over a bowl to collect the liquid and scoop out the mush from the shells with a spoon. Using a sharp knife, slice the citrus peel into evenly sliced thick or thin strands, depending on how you like it. Use as much or as little lemon peel as you wish.

3 Add the liquid, sliced peel, reserved fruit juice, and sugar to a preserving pan. Heat gently, stirring until the sugar has dissolved, turn up the heat, and boil rapidly for 5–20 minutes until a set is achieved. Remove the pan from the heat to test for a set with a sugar thermometer, or using a wrinkle test (chill a saucer in the fridge before cooking). If you use a thermometer, the temperature must reach 105°C (220°F); the mixture will also thicken around the sides of the pan, boil sluggishly, and the bubbles "plop" rather than froth. Or put 1 tsp marmalade on the chilled saucer, allow to cool for a moment, then push it with a finger. If it leaves a trail and wrinkles slightly, it is set.

4 Skim off any surface scum, leave for 10–15 minutes, then stir and ladle into warm sterilized jars. Cover with waxed paper discs, seal, and label. Store in a cool, dark place and refrigerate after opening.

cranberry and apricot chutney

This colourful chutney-cum-relish is a tangy alternative to cranberry sauce. It's quicker to make than other chutneys.

🥣 10–15 MINS PLUS MATURING 🍲 40–45 MINS

SPECIAL EQUIPMENT ▪ food processor ▪ preserving pan

MAKES APPROX 1.25kg (2¾lb)

350g (12oz) cranberries

2 cooking apples, about 350g (12oz), peeled, quartered, and cored

225g (8oz) dried apricots

1 onion, about 175g (6oz), roughly chopped

1cm (½in) piece of fresh root ginger, peeled and grated

175g (6oz) light soft brown sugar

175ml (6fl oz) apple cider vinegar

zest and juice of 1 orange

1 cinnamon stick

¼ tsp ground coriander

¼ tsp ground cumin

¼ tsp dried chilli flakes

sea salt

1 Put the cranberries, apples, and apricots in a food processor with the onion and ginger. Pulse lightly until finely chopped, then place in a preserving pan or a large heavy-based, stainless steel saucepan and add the rest of the ingredients.

2 Bring slowly to the boil, stirring until the sugar has dissolved. Reduce the heat to a gentle simmer and cook gently, uncovered, for 30–35 minutes, or until the cranberries have softened and burst and are thick and pulpy. A wooden spoon drawn across the base of the pan should leave a clear trail. Stir frequently towards the end of cooking so the chutney doesn't burn.

3 Remove the cinnamon stick and spoon into warm sterilized jars with non-metallic or vinegar-proof lids, making sure there are no air gaps. Cover each pot with a waxed paper disc, seal, and label. Leave to cool, then store in the fridge to mature for at least 2 weeks before opening. Once opened, keep refrigerated.

cranberry sauce with port

A fruity cranberry sauce is a traditional – and essential – accompaniment to poultry. This quick and easy recipe includes port or wine for added depth of flavour.

🥣 5 MINS 🍲 20 MINS

SERVES 4

225g (8oz) cranberries

4 tbsp port wine or red wine

75g (2½oz) sugar

1 Put the cranberries in a wide saucepan and pour over the port or red wine. Bring to the boil, then cover with a lid and simmer gently for 10–15 minutes, or until the berries start to soften and pop. Then squash them in the pan with the back of a spoon to your desired consistency.

2 Stir in the sugar a little at a time, tasting as you go, until it has dissolved and the sauce is the right flavour. Serve in a small dish with roast turkey or chicken.

variation

cranberry sauce with orange

For a fruitier flavour, add the finely grated zest and juice of 1 orange with the cranberries in step 1. Omit the alcohol and continue as in the original recipe.

cranberry and orange butter

Use this fruit butter as a savoury accompaniment or sweet spread, or eat with freshly shelled nuts.

🥣 10 MINS 🍲 50 MINS ❄ FREEZABLE

SPECIAL EQUIPMENT ▪ preserving pan

MAKES APPROX 800g (1¾lb)

450g (1lb) cranberries

approx 350–450g (12oz–1lb) granulated sugar (see method)

approx 15g (½oz) butter (see method)

juice and 1 tsp grated zest of 1 large sweet orange

1 Put the cranberries and 300ml (10fl oz) water into a preserving pan or a large heavy-based saucepan, cover, and bring to the boil, keeping the lid on until the cranberries have all popped. Then remove the lid and simmer the berries for 10 minutes, or until they are soft. Then mash the berries to a pulp with a potato masher or fork.

2 Sieve the fruit in batches and collect the juice and purée in a clean bowl. Measure the purée and for every 600ml/1 pint of purée, allow 350g/12oz of sugar and 15g/½oz butter; if the pulp seems very tart, allow 450g/1lb of sugar. Put the purée, sugar, butter, and orange juice and zest back in the preserving pan and cook over a medium heat. Stir gently until the sugar has dissolved.

3 Bring the ingredients to the boil, then simmer gently, stirring often, for about 40 minutes, or until the mixture has reduced to a soft, moist, spreadable paste. A wooden spoon drawn across the bottom of the pan should leave a clear trail. Ladle the mixture into warm sterilized jars, cover with waxed paper discs, seal, and label. Store in a cool, dark place and refrigerate after opening.

Season's best **cranberries**

Cranberries are available from autumn but are at their peak in winter and range alluringly in colour from bright light red to dark crimson. The hard waxy berries have a mouth-puckering sour taste when raw so need plenty of sweetening, but they make delicious juice, as well as sauces and relishes for meat, poultry, and game. They are often teamed with the flavours of orange and port or red wine.

Cranberries are commercially cultivated in North America, Britain, and Northern Europe. They grow on dwarf shrubs or trailing vines. The fruit is initially white and turns red when ripe.

Cranberry The fruit is high in pectin so when cooked quickly with sugar, it sets like conserve. Rich in vitamin C, it tops the list of health-promoting antioxidant berries.

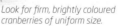

Look for firm, brightly coloured cranberries of uniform size.

essentials
varieties available
Common cranberry, small cranberry, and large American Cranberry.

buy They are at their peak in winter, when shiny and red. Avoid bags containing squashy or shrivelled fruit.

store Keep in a closed plastic bag in the fridge for up to 2 weeks. Or freeze, and cook from frozen.

cook Stew for sauces and desserts. Add to tarts, pies, muffins, cakes, and parfaits, as well as pâtés and stuffings for poultry and meat.

preserve Make jelly, dry, or bottle in syrup.

recipe ideas
Cranberry and apricot chutney p418

Cranberry and orange butter p418

Cranberry jelly p416

Squash with chestnuts and cranberries p407

Turkey and cranberry casserole p378

how to make a simple cranberry sauce
Cranberry sauce is the traditional accompaniment to festive birds, particularly turkey for Thanksgiving and Christmas. It is also a favourite with baked gammon and pork.

1 Put 225g (8oz) cranberries in a pan with 300ml (10fl oz) water or orange juice and 115g (4oz) sugar.

2 Bring to the boil and simmer gently until the fruit "pops". Tip into a bowl and leave to cool.

cider

Use any apples, including windfalls, to make cider. Generally, the sweeter the apple, the sweeter the cider.

🥣 1 HR – 1 HR 30 MINS PLUS FREEZING, STRAINING, BREWING, AND MATURING

SPECIAL EQUIPMENT ▪ food processor or fruit juicer ▪ jelly bag or muslin ▪ sterilized funnel ▪ sterilized demijohn ▪ sterilized siphon ▪ hydrometer

MAKES APPROX 4 LITRES (7 PINTS)

3.5kg (7–8lb) apples, or 4 litres (7 pints) apple juice

100g (3½oz) unrefined cane sugar

5g (⅛oz) champagne yeast

1 Ensure that the fruit is in good condition and, if using windfalls, cut away any badly bruised parts. Put all the apples in the freezer overnight to soften them by breaking down their fibrous cell walls.

2 Allow the apples to thaw thoroughly and then blitz to a pulp in small batches using a food processor. If you have an electric fruit juicer, simply juice the fresh apples instead.

3 Strain the pulp through a jelly bag or clean, muslin-lined sieve set over a large clean bowl. Leave to strain until you have 4 litres (7 pints) of juice. Measure the gravity of the strained juice with a hydrometer. If it is not in the range of 1,035–1,050, gradually dilute with water until it falls within this range. Add the sugar to the juice, stir well, and pour the juice into a demijohn using a funnel. Add the yeast and leave for 2 days at room temperature (15–25°C/59–77°F) with cotton wool in the top of the demijohn as a seal.

4 When the frothing has reduced, fit the airlock and pour water into it. The liquid should start to fizz. Leave the cider to ferment for 2 weeks or longer until the airlock has stopped bubbling.

5 Siphon the cider into sterilized bottles using a siphon, leaving 2cm (¾in) of space at the top. Seal the bottles and leave them for approximately 3 months in a dark place (a cupboard is fine) at room temperature before opening.

mulled pears

Use just-ripe, slightly firm pears for this recipe; over-ripe fruit will become unpalatably soft. Wine alone isn't strong enough to preserve the fruit, so the jars must be heat-processed too.

🥣 5 MINS   🍲 1 HR 10 MINS PLUS HEAT-PROCESSING

MAKES 1 LITRE (1¾ PINTS)

115g (4oz) granulated sugar

2 tsp lemon juice

550ml (16½fl oz) red wine, plus extra if needed

1 cinnamon stick

2 star anise

2 cloves

6 pears, peeled, cored, and halved

1 Put the sugar in a large saucepan (large enough for the pears to sit in one layer) with the lemon juice, 250ml (9fl oz) of the wine, and the spices. Bring to the boil over a medium heat, stirring until the sugar has dissolved, then boil for 2 minutes without stirring. Add the pears and cook gently for 2 minutes, turning them over once.

2 Place warm sterilized preserving jars on a cloth or wooden board. Lift the fruit out of the syrup with a slotted spoon and pack tightly into the jars without squashing it, leaving 1cm (½in) of space at the top.

3 Add the rest of the wine to the syrup. Bring back to the boil for a few seconds. Pour the syrup into a heat-proof jug (discard the cinnamon stick) and pour over the fruit. Top up with a little extra wine if needed so the fruit is completely covered. Fit the rubber band or metal lid seal and clamp on the lid. If using screw-band jars, loosen by a quarter of a turn. Then place the filled jars in a deep roasting tray lined with newspaper.

4 Put the tray of jars in the centre of the oven for 50–60 minutes to heat-process (remove the remaining air in the jars). Then remove from the oven and tighten the clips or lids (or screw on plastic screw-band lids) immediately. Leave for 24 hours, then unscrew or unclip and test the lids are firmly sealed before refastening and storing. (If using kilner jars with metal lids, you will know if you have a seal as the lid becomes slightly concave and is firm with no "give" once pressed.) Store the jars in a cool, dark place and refrigerate once open.

carrot and coriander relish

Sweet, sticky, and spicy, this relish, with its lovely hints of orange, is perfect served with a curry.

🥣 10–15 MINS PLUS MATURING   🍲 40–45 MINS

SPECIAL EQUIPMENT ▪ preserving pan

MAKES APPROX 450g (1lb)

500g (1lb 2oz) carrots, grated

1 tsp mustard seeds

2 tsp coriander seeds, crushed

1 tsp cardamom seeds (taken from pods)

2.5cm (1in) piece of fresh root ginger, peeled and grated

zest and juice of 1 orange

120ml (4fl oz) cider vinegar

125g (4½oz) granulated sugar or light soft brown sugar

1 Put the carrots in a preserving pan or a large heavy-based, stainless steel saucepan, then add the mustard seeds, coriander seeds, and cardamom seeds and stir.

2 Add the ginger and orange juice and zest, then pour in the vinegar and sugar and stir. Slowly simmer, stirring until the sugar has dissolved, then cook for 10 minutes more, stirring occasionally, until the carrots have softened. Raise the heat a little and cook for 15–20 minutes, or until most of the liquid has disappeared. Stir frequently so the mixture doesn't burn or stick on the base of the pan.

3 Ladle the relish into warm sterilized jars with non-metallic or vinegar-proof lids, seal, and label. Allow to mature for at least 1 month and refrigerate after opening.

curried apple, peach, and walnut chutney

Apples combine well with dried peaches and walnuts, which provide extra texture and flavour. If you prefer a sweeter spiced chutney, substitute mixed spice for the curry powder.

🥣 15 MINS PLUS MATURING　　🍲 1 HR 30 MINS

SPECIAL EQUIPMENT ▪ preserving pan

MAKES APPROX 1.8kg (4lb)

2 cooking apples, about 350g (12oz), peeled, quartered, cored, and cut into bite-sized pieces

1 large onion, about 225g (8oz), peeled and cut into bite-sized pieces

350g (12oz) dried peaches, cut into bite-sized pieces

175g (6oz) walnut pieces, roughly chopped

125g (4½oz) sultanas

400g (14oz) light soft brown sugar

2 tsp mild curry powder

sea salt

300ml (10fl oz) apple cider vinegar

1 Put all the ingredients in a preserving pan or large heavy-based, stainless steel saucepan. Bring slowly to the boil, stirring until the sugar has dissolved. Reduce the heat to a gentle simmer and cook for 1½ hours, or until a wooden spoon drawn across the base of the pan leaves a trail. Stir frequently towards the end of cooking so the chutney doesn't burn or stick on the base of the pan.

2 Check the seasoning and add salt or more curry powder, if needed. Simmer gently for an extra minute, stirring, to cook out the spice.

3 Spoon into warm sterilized jars with non-metallic or vinegar-proof lids, making sure there are no air gaps. Cover each pot with a waxed paper disc, seal, and label. Store in a cool, dark place for at least 1 month before using. Once opened, keep refrigerated.

red cabbage pickle

This vibrant, slightly sweet pickle is crunchy and pleasantly spiced. A wide-necked kilner jar is best for this cold pickling method so that the vegetables can fit in easily.

🥣 30 MINS PLUS STANDING AND MATURING

MAKES APPROX 1.1kg (2½lb)

675g (1½lb) red cabbage, cored and shredded

1 red onion, sliced

3 tbsp sea salt

600ml (1 pint) white wine vinegar

125g (4½oz) light muscovado sugar or caster sugar

1 tsp mustard seeds

1 tsp coriander seeds

1 Put the cabbage and onion into a large glass or ceramic bowl. Sprinkle over the sea salt and mix the ingredients together so the vegetables are well coated. Put the mixture into a colander over a bowl, sit a plate on top of the cabbage, and leave overnight for it to drain – you want to lose as much liquid from the cabbage as possible. Pour the vinegar into a large jug, add the sugar and spices, and whisk to dissolve the sugar. Cover and leave overnight too.

2 Rinse the cabbage and onion under cold water to remove the salt, then dry the vegetables thoroughly with a clean tea towel or kitchen paper.

3 Layer the vegetables in warm sterilized jars with non-metallic or vinegar-proof lids, packing them down. Stir the vinegar and pour it over the vegetables so that they are completely covered. Seal, label, and store in a cool, dark place for 1 week. Then leave in the fridge for at least 1 month before using, to allow the flavours to develop and mellow. Keep refrigerated once opened.

sauerkraut

Preserving cabbage in salt relies on its natural lactic bacteria reacting with the salt and fermenting. Home-made sauerkraut has a much better flavour than bought versions.

🥣 30–45 MINS PLUS FERMENTATION

SPECIAL EQUIPMENT ▪ food processor ▪ sterilized crock ▪ muslin

MAKES APPROX 1.35kg (3lb)

2.5–3kg (5½–6½lb) hard white or red cabbage, or half red and half white cabbage, outer leaves removed

approx 60g (2oz) coarse sea or rock salt (see method)

1 tbsp caraway seeds

1 Slice the cabbage in half, remove the core, quarter it, and finely shred it using a food processor or a sharp knife. Weigh the shredded cabbage and calculate the amount of salt you will need: approximately 60g (2oz) of salt per 2.5kg (5½lb) of cabbage.

2 Place the cabbage in a large clean bowl and sprinkle the salt evenly over it. Using your hands, work the salt thoroughly into the cabbage until it begins to feel wet. Leave for a few minutes for the salt to soften the cabbage and draw out its juices.

3 Pack into a very large sterilized crock or jar. Add 5cm (2in) of cabbage at a time and scatter with the caraway seeds. Pack each layer down with the end of a rolling pin, a large pestle, or a jam jar. Leave 7.5cm (3in) of space at the top. Add any juices from the bowl and top up with cold brine (1½ tbsp of salt to 1¾ pints of boiled water) to cover the cabbage. Put the jar on a tray, cover with clean muslin, and put a snug-fitting plate or saucer on top. Place a large jar or sandwich bag filled with water on top of the plate.

4 Leave in a well-ventilated place at room temperature (20–22°C/68–72°F) for 3–4 weeks. (Fermentation will stop and the cabbage will spoil above 24°C/76°F; if it is cooler than room temperature, the sauerkraut will take up to 5–6 weeks.) Check daily that the cabbage is submerged. Remove any scum regularly and replace with clean muslin. If the cabbage develops a pinkish hue on the surface, goes dark, or turns soft and mushy, discard the whole batch; it shouldn't be eaten. Fermentation is complete when all the bubbling has ceased. Pot up into sterilized jars, seal, and store in the fridge for 1–2 months.

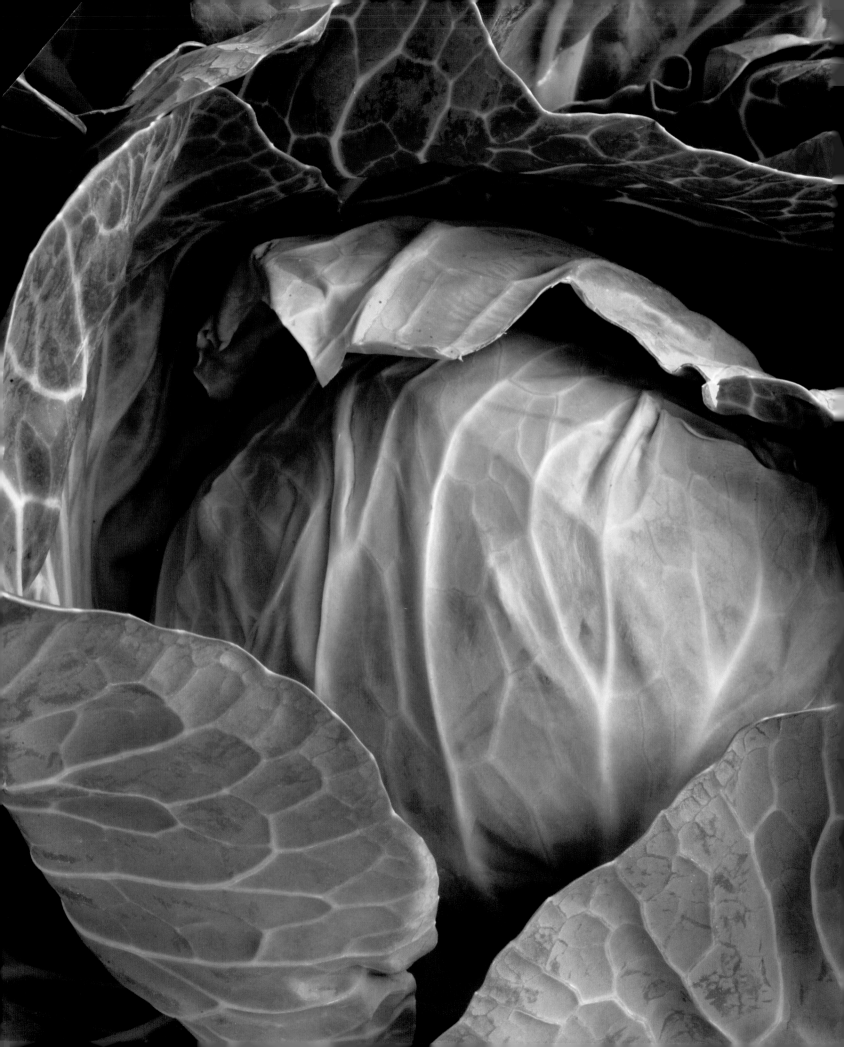

late winter

at their best

vegetables beetroot ▪ Brussels sprouts ▪ cabbages ▪ carrots (maincrop) ▪ cauliflower ▪ cavolo nero ▪ celeriac ▪ celery ▪ chicory ▪ frisée lettuce ▪ Jerusalem artichokes ▪ kale ▪ leeks ▪ mustard greens ▪ pak choi ▪ parsnips ▪ potatoes (maincrop) ▪ sprouting broccoli ▪ radicchio ▪ salsify ▪ shallots ▪ spring greens ▪ swede ▪ Swiss chard ▪ turnips

fruit avocados ▪ apples ▪ clementines ▪ dates ▪ forced rhubarb ▪ grapefruit ▪ lemons ▪ limes ▪ kiwi fruit ▪ oranges ▪ pears ▪ pomegranate ▪ satsumas ▪ tangerines

seafood abalone ▪ brill ▪ cod ▪ crayfish (farmed) ▪ dab ▪ Dover sole ▪ grey mullet ▪ haddock ▪ hake ▪ lemon sole ▪ mussels ▪ native oysters ▪ Pacific or rock oysters (farmed) ▪ rainbow trout (wild and farmed) ▪ razor clams ▪ red gurnard ▪ red mullet ▪ turbot (wild and farmed)

meat, poultry, game duck (wild and farmed) ▪ hare ▪ partridge ▪ pheasant (wild) ▪ rabbit (wild and farmed) ▪ wood pigeon (wild) ▪ venison (wild and farmed)

also available

vegetables mushrooms (cultivated) ▪ onions ▪ spinach ▪ sweet potatoes ▪ watercress **seafood** ▪ brown trout (farmed) ▪ common brown crab ▪ halibut (farmed) ▪ herring ▪ John Dory ▪ king scallops (farmed) ▪ monkfish ▪ salmon (farmed) ▪ sardines ▪ sea bass (farmed) ▪ sea bream (farmed) ▪ sea trout (farmed) ▪ whiting **meat, poultry, game** beef ▪ chicken ▪ guinea fowl (farmed) ▪ lamb ▪ pork ▪ quail (farmed) ▪ veal ▪ wild boar (farmed)

late winter recipe chooser

Split pea and bacon soup p435

Mini chicken, leek, and mushroom pies p430

Avocado, grapefruit, and Parma ham salad p432

Vegetables

Carrot
Beef and ale cobbler p451
Beef with barley and mushrooms p447
Carrot cream soup with onion and cumin p430 (v)
Braised oxtail with jerusalem artichokes p449
Carrot soup with coconut and lemongrass p438 (v)
Chicken and cornmeal cobbler p441
Creamy four root soup p432 (v)
Jerusalem artichoke soup with saffron and thyme p426 (v)
Lamb daube p456
Lamb shanks in red wine p447
Marsala chicken with pine nuts and sultanas p441
Minestrone soup p434 (v)
Pot roast smoked ham p444
Poule au pot p463
Scotch broth p435
Spiced carrot and orange cake p479 (v)
Split pea and bacon soup p435
Smoky split pea soup p435
Turkey and mushroom casserole with dumplings p446
Vegetable casserole with dumplings p464 (v)

Cabbage
Bigos p456
French cabbage soup p438
Duck legs with cabbage, pine nuts, and raisins p454
Pancetta and potatoes with red cabbage p469
Red cabbage slaw p470 (v)
Red cabbage with cider p469 (v)

Cauliflower
Braised cauliflower with chilli and coriander p448 (v)
Cauliflower soup p434 (v)
Cauliflower cheese soup p434 (v)
Haricot bean and cauliflower gratin p470 (v)

Cavolo nero
Pork with cavolo nero p445

Celeriac
Celeriac and pear coleslaw p470 (v)
Celeriac cream soup with orange and cinnamon p430 (v)
Celery and celeriac soup p428 (v)
Chicken broth with celeriac and orange p450

Creamed celeriac soup with cumin p426 (v)
Fruity lamb shanks p448
Lamb shanks in red wine p447
Lamb with roasted winter vegetables p455
Pork belly with leeks and celeriac p467

Celery
Beef with barley and mushrooms p447
Celery and apple salad with blue cheese dressing p471 (v)
Celery and celeriac soup p428 (v)
Celery, leek, and pear salad p471 (v)
Chicken and cornmeal cobbler p441
Marsala chicken with pine nuts and sultanas p441
Minestrone soup p434 (v)
Osso buco with celery, leek, and almonds p466
Poached trout salad with red grapefruit, orange, and celery p438
Roasted celery with orange and walnuts p470 (v)
Scotch broth p435
Split pea and bacon soup p435
Smoky split pea soup p435
Turkey and mushroom casserole with dumplings p446
Vegetable casserole with dumplings p464 (v)

Chicory and endives
Bistro salad with egg and lardons p439
Duck with pink grapefruit and chicory salad p442
Hunter's chicken stew p467
Pheasant with pomegranate, frisée lettuce, and leek salad p442

Jerusalem artichoke
Braised oxtail with Jerusalem artichokes p449
Jerusalem artichoke soup with saffron and thyme p426 (v)
Pot roast smoked ham p444

Kale
Beef and greens p445
Caldo verde p430 (v)
Filo pie with spicy kale and sausage p428

Leek
Beef and ale cobbler p451
Celery, leek, and pear salad p471 (v)
Creamy sweet potato and leek bake p469 (v)
Fish and leek pie p461

Leek and Cheddar cheese tart p431 (v)
Lentils with mushrooms and leeks p443 (v)
Mini chicken, leek, and mushroom pies p430
Osso buco with celery, leek, and almonds p466
Pheasant with pomegranate, frisée lettuce, and leek salad p442
Pork belly with leeks and celeriac p467
Poule au pot p463
Sweet balsamic baby leeks p468 (v)
Vegetable casserole with dumplings 464 (v)

Onion
Lamb with red onions p455
Onion confit and Gorgonzola pizza p465 (v)
Onion tart p431 (v)
Red onion marmalade p482 (v)
Sautéed liver and onions p450
Sweet balsamic onions p468 (v)

Pak choi
Wasabi beef and pak choi p442

Parsnip
Creamy four root soup p432 (v)

Potato
Caldo verde p430 (v)
Cornish pasties p463
Duck with apple and rosemary potatoes p440
Lamb chops champvallon p464
Lamb with red onions p455
Meat and potato pie p440
Mixed vegetable caldo verde p430 (v)
Pancetta and potatoes with red cabbage p469
Perfect fish and chips p457
Pork belly with onions and potatoes p467
Potato-chive monkey bread p471 (v)
Potatoes boulangère p469 (v)

Rhubarb
Rhubarb, pear, and ginger jam p484 (v)

Shallots
Caramelized shallot tart p427 (v)
Greek stifado p444
Lamb shanks in red wine p447

Swede
Beef and vegetable chilli with guacamole p443

Cornish pasties p463
Creamy swede soup p432 (v)
Creamy four root soup p432 (v)
Mixed vegetable caldo verde p430 (v)

Sweet potato
Creamy sweet potato and leek bake p469 (v)

Turnip
Creamy four root soup p432 (v)
Mixed vegetable caldo verde p430 (v)
Poule au pot p463
Seared duck with red miso, shredded turnip, and noodles p455
Turnip soup with pimento, chilli, and noodles p439 (v)
Venison casserole with turnips and prunes p454

Fruit

Apples
Apple dumplings p480 (v)
Apple sauce p468 (v)
Apple streusel cake p480 (v)
Celery and apple salad with blue cheese dressing p471 (v)
Chicken liver and apple pâté p427
Chilli jelly p483 (v)
Cinnamon apple cake p479 (v)
Crêpes with caramelized apples and chocolate p480 (v)
Duck with apple and rosemary potatoes p440
Fruity lamb shanks p448
Pancetta and potatoes with red cabbage p469
Pork Normandy p448
Rosemary jelly p482 (v)
Toffee apple cake p481 (v)

Avocado
Avocado, grapefruit, and Parma ham salad p432
Beef and vegetable chilli with guacamole p443
Crispy bacon and avocado wraps p432
Spicy chicken, avocado, and spinach wraps p432

Dates
Banana, date, and walnut loaf **p481** ⓥ
Grapefruit
Avocado, grapefruit, and Parma ham salad **p432**
Candied citrus peel **p484** ⓥ
Crab salad with grapefruit and coriander **p438**
Duck with pink grapefruit and chicory salad **p442**
Grapefruit crème de menthe jelly **p472**
Poached trout salad with red grapefruit, orange, and celery **p438**
Three-fruit marmalade **p482** ⓥ
Lemons
Lemon cheesecake **p472**
Lemon meringue pie **p473** ⓥ
Lemon polenta cake **p475** ⓥ
Three-fruit marmalade **p482** ⓥ
Oranges, clementines, and tangerines
Beef and orange daube **p446**
Beef tagine with orange and bay leaves **p454**
Braised oxtail with clementine and star anise **p449**
Caramelized oranges and passionfruit **p475** ⓥ
Celeriac cream soup with orange and cinnamon **p430** ⓥ
Chicken broth with celeriac and orange **p450**
Chocolate orange pound cake **p478** ⓥ
Chocolate orange whoopie pies **p472** ⓥ

Clementine and whisky marmalade **p485** ⓥ
Clementines in caramel syrup **p485** ⓥ
Duck in orange sauce **p450**
Lamb daube **p456**
Middle Eastern oranges **p475** ⓥ
Mince and chickpeas cooked with orange and cinnamon **p443**
Orange and cinnamon crème brûlée **p474** ⓥ
Osso buco **p466**
Poached trout salad with red grapefruit, orange, and celery **p438**
Roasted celery with orange and walnuts **p470** ⓥ
Seville marmalade **p484** ⓥ
Spiced carrot and orange cake **p479** ⓥ
Tangerine macarons **p474** ⓥ
Three-fruit marmalade **p482** ⓥ
Pears
Celeriac and pear coleslaw **p470** ⓥ
Celery, leek, and pear salad **p471** ⓥ
Chicken in sherry with pears **p441**
Chocolate and pear tartlets **p478** ⓥ
Pear and walnut dumplings **p480** ⓥ
Rhubarb, pear, and ginger jam **p484** ⓥ
Venison casserole with pears **p452**
Pomegranates
Middle Eastern oranges **p475** ⓥ
Pheasant with pomegranate, frisée lettuce, and leek salad **p442**

Seafood
Cod
Cod and mussel chowder **p460**
Creole fish and corn stew **p461**
Fish and leek pie **p461**
Fish fingers with chunky tartare sauce **p456**
Manhattan cod and mussel chowder **p460**
Perfect fish and chips **p457**
Soupe de poissons **p426**
Crab
Crab salad with grapefruit and coriander **p438**
Mussels
Cod and mussel chowder **p460**
Manhattan cod and mussel chowder **p460**
Oysters
Grilled oysters with crème fraîche and Parmesan **p439**
Grilled oysters with Tabasco **p439**
Oysters with chilli and lime mayonnaise **p436**
Oysters with lemon and Tabasco **p436**
Oysters with shallot and vinegar dressing **p436**

Meat
Duck
Bigos **p456**
Duck in orange sauce **p450**
Duck legs with cabbage, pine nuts, and raisins **p454**

Duck with apple and rosemary potatoes **p440**
Duck with pink grapefruit and chicory salad **p442**
Seared duck with five-spice and noodles **p455**
Seared duck with red miso, shredded turnip, and noodles **p455**
Hare
Jugged hare **p444**
Puff-crusted game soup **p428**
Pheasant
Game casserole **p452**
Pheasant with pomegranate, frisée lettuce, and leek salad **p442**
Rabbit
Hunter's rabbit stew **p467**
Puff-crusted game soup **p428**
Venison
Game casserole **p452**
Puff-crusted game soup **p428**
Venison casserole with pears **p452**
Venison casserole with turnips and prunes **p454**
Venison stew **p452**

Braised oxtail with clementine and star anise p449

Hunter's chicken stew p467

Apple dumplings p480

Spiced carrot and orange cake p479

Oysters with shallot and vinegar dressing p436

Duck legs with cabbage, pine nuts, and raisins p454

jerusalem artichoke soup with saffron and thyme

Use whatever proportion of carrots and Jerusalem artichokes you have, adding up to 700g (1lb 9oz) in total. The carrots enhance the colour and sweetness of the soup.

🥣 15 MINS   🍲 35–45 MINS   ❄ FREEZABLE

SPECIAL EQUIPMENT ▪ food processor or hand-held blender

SERVES 4–6

2 tbsp virgin rapeseed oil or olive oil, plus extra to drizzle

2 onions, chopped

3 garlic cloves, chopped

350g (12oz) Jerusalem artichokes, scrubbed and roughly chopped

350g (12oz) carrots, scrubbed and roughly chopped

sea salt and freshly ground black pepper

1.2 litres (2 pints) hot vegetable stock

1 tbsp fresh thyme leaves or 1½ tsp dried thyme

large pinch (about 30 strands) of saffron

juice of ½ lemon

1 Heat the oil in a large pan over a medium heat, add the onions, and cook for 3–4 minutes until soft and translucent. Add the garlic and fry for 30 seconds, or until fragrant. Stir in the Jerusalem artichokes, carrots, and a little sea salt, then cover with a lid and sweat, stirring frequently, for 10–15 minutes, or until the vegetables are softened.

2 Add the stock, thyme, and saffron, bring to the boil, then reduce the heat and simmer for 20 minutes, or until the vegetables are thoroughly soft.

3 Remove the soup from the heat and using a food processor or hand-held blender, purée until smooth. Stir in the lemon juice and season to taste. Serve with a drizzle of oil.

variation

creamed celeriac soup with cumin

Prepare in exactly the same way, but substitute 1 small celeriac, peeled and chopped, for the Jerusalem artichokes. Add 1 tsp ground cumin when sweating the vegetables, and omit the saffron. Use fresh thyme and stir in 4 tbsp single cream just before serving.

soupe de poissons

This flavoursome fish soup needs no accompaniment, but croûtes made from baguette slices rubbed with garlic, spread with rouille, or topped with Gruyère are a tasty addition.

🥣 20 MINS   🍲 1 HR   ❄ FREEZABLE

SERVES 6

5 tbsp olive oil

4 onions, chopped

2 leeks, trimmed and chopped

1.5–2kg (3lb 3oz–4½lb) mixed fish and seafood, such as cod, mullet, cold water prawns, sole, sea bass, and salmon

1 celery stick, halved

400g (14oz) tomatoes, chopped

9 garlic cloves, crushed

5 sprigs of flat-leaf parsley

3 bay leaves

thinly pared zest of ½ orange

1 tbsp tomato purée

salt and freshly ground black pepper

pinch of saffron threads

6 croûtes, to serve

1 Heat the oil in a large heavy-based pan over a medium heat. Add the onions and leeks, and cook for about 5 minutes until just golden.

2 Scale and gut the fish. Rinse all the fish and seafood. Add to the pan and stir, then add the celery, tomatoes, garlic, parsley, bay leaves, orange zest, and tomato purée. Stir and cook for 8–10 minutes until the fish is just beginning to flake when pierced with a fork. Pour in 2.5 litres (4½ pints) hot water and season lightly with salt and pepper. Reduce the heat and simmer gently for 20 minutes.

3 Remove from the heat. Leave to cool a little, stirring and mashing down the soft fish pieces with the back of a large wooden spoon. Remove the celery, orange zest, and bay leaves. If you like, blitz the soup to a rough purée using a food processor or hand-held blender. Push the soup through a sieve into a clean saucepan. Return the soup to a simmer over a moderate heat.

4 Soften the saffron in a ladleful of the soup, then stir into the rest of the soup in the pan. Adjust the seasoning. Ladle the soup into warmed bowls and serve hot, with croûtes.

caramelized shallot tart

The allium family is indispensible to most cooks, yet we rarely find ways of allowing onions and shallots to take centre stage. This simple recipe gives shallots a starring role.

🥣 **20 MINS PLUS CHILLING**　　🍲 **45 MINS**

SPECIAL EQUIPMENT ▪ food processor

SERVES 4–6

25g (scant 1oz) butter

2 tbsp extra virgin olive oil

400g (14oz) shallots, split in half lengthways

2 tbsp balsamic vinegar

a few sprigs of thyme

For the pastry

150g (5½oz) plain flour

sea salt

75g (2½oz) butter

1 For the pastry, combine the flour, a pinch of sea salt, and the butter in a food processor and mix to form fine breadcrumbs. With the motor running, add cold water, 1 tbsp at a time, until the pastry starts to stick together. Form the pastry into a ball, wrap it in cling film, and leave it in the fridge to chill for 30 minutes.

2 Preheat the oven to 200°C (400°F/Gas 6). In a large, ovenproof frying pan, melt the butter with the oil over

a medium heat. Put the shallots in, cut-side down, and cook very gently for 10 minutes until they are browned. Turn them over and cook for another 5 minutes. Add the balsamic vinegar and 2 tbsp water, then remove from the heat. Tuck the sprigs of thyme between the shallots.

3 Roll out the pastry into a circle a little larger than the frying pan. Lay the pastry over the shallots, trim, and tuck it in. Transfer the pan to the oven and cook for 30 minutes until the pastry is golden brown.

4 Remove the pan from the oven and bang it gently to loosen the shallots. Run a knife around the edges of the pastry, then put a large plate over the pan and quickly turn it over. Serve warm with a green salad.

chicken liver and apple pâté

Topped with golden slices of caramelized apple, these individual pâtés make an elegant first course.

🥣 **30-35 MINS PLUS CHILLING**　　🍲 **12-15 MINS**

SPECIAL EQUIPMENT ▪ food processor ▪ 6 ramekins

SERVES 6

3 dessert apples

250g (9oz) butter

salt and freshly ground black pepper

500g (1lb 2oz) chicken livers, trimmed

4 shallots, finely diced

2 garlic cloves, finely chopped

4 tbsp Calvados or cognac

2 tbsp caster sugar

6 slices of wholemeal bread

6 sprigs of mint, to serve (optional)

1 Core, peel, and dice 2 of the apples. Melt 2 tbsp of the butter in a frying pan. Add the diced apples, salt, and pepper. Sauté, stirring frequently, for 5–7 minutes until tender. Transfer to a bowl with a slotted spoon.

2 Melt another 2 tbsp of the butter in the pan. Add the chicken livers and season. Fry, stirring, for 2–3 minutes, until brown. Tip in the shallots and garlic, and cook for 1–2 minutes until slightly soft. Increase the heat to

medium-high. Pour the Calvados into the pan and bring to the boil. Hold a lit match to the pan's side to set the alcohol alight. Baste the chicken livers for 20–30 seconds until the flames subside. Set aside to cool.

3 Blitz the mixture in a food processor until almost smooth. Wipe out the frying pan. Cream 150g (5½oz) of the butter in a bowl until soft. Add the livers and the sautéed apples. Mix, season, and spoon into the ramekins. Smooth the tops, cover, and chill for 2–3 hours.

4 Core the remaining apple and slice into 6 rings. Melt the remaining butter in the pan. Add the apple, sprinkle with half the sugar, and fry for 2–3 minutes each side, until caramelized. Meanwhile, toast the slices of bread. Set a caramelized apple slice and a sprig of mint, if liked, on top of each pâté and serve with the toast.

filo pie with spicy kale and sausage

If you don't have kale to hand, other winter greens work well.

🥣 35–40 MINS   🍲 45–55 MINS

SPECIAL EQUIPMENT ▪ 28cm (11in) round springform cake tin

SERVES 6

200g (7oz) unsalted butter

250g (9oz) sausagemeat

3 onions, finely chopped

750g (1lb 10oz) kale, shredded

½ tsp ground allspice

salt and freshly ground black pepper

2 eggs, beaten

500g packet of filo pastry

1 Heat 30g (1oz) of the butter in a pan, add the sausagemeat, and cook, stirring, until brown. Transfer to a bowl, leaving the fat behind. Add the onions to the pan and cook until soft. Add the kale, cover, and cook until wilted. Uncover and cook for 5 minutes, stirring so the moisture evaporates.

2 Return the sausagemeat to the pan with the allspice and stir into the kale mixture. Season to taste. Remove from the heat and let cool completely. Stir in the eggs. Preheat the oven to 180°C (350°F/Gas 4). Melt the remaining butter in a pan; brush the tin with a little butter. Lay a damp tea towel on the work surface. Unroll the filo onto the towel, then using the tin as a guide, cut through the pastry sheets with a 7.5cm (3in) border. Cover the sheets with a second damp towel.

3 Put 1 filo sheet on top of a third damp towel and brush with butter. Transfer to the cake tin, pressing it well into the side. Butter another filo sheet and put it in the tin at a right angle to the first. Continue buttering and layering until half the filo is used, alternating layers at right angles.

4 Spoon the filling into the case. Butter another sheet of filo and cover the filling. Top with the rest of the filo, buttering each sheet. Fold the overhanging dough over the top and drizzle with the remaining butter. Bake the pie in the oven for 45–55 minutes until golden. Let cool slightly, then cut into wedges.

puff-crusted game soup

You can buy ready-diced mixed game, which includes furred game and pigeon, or use diced venison, rabbit, or hare.

🥣 20 MINS   🍲 1 HR 20 MINS   ❄ FREEZABLE

SPECIAL EQUIPMENT ▪ 4 deep, ovenproof soup cups

SERVES 4

large knob of butter

175g (6oz) diced game meat, cut into small pieces

1 red onion, chopped

2 tbsp plain flour

900ml (1½ pints) hot beef stock

1 tbsp redcurrant jelly

3 chestnut mushrooms, halved and sliced

1 tbsp chopped sage

4 tbsp ruby port

salt and freshly ground black pepper

1 sheet ready-rolled puff pastry, thawed if frozen

1 egg, beaten

1 Melt the butter in a saucepan over a medium heat. Add the meat and onion and cook for about 5 minutes, stirring until browned.

2 Blend in the flour and cook for 1 minute. Remove from the heat, gradually stir in the stock, add the redcurrant jelly, and bring to the boil, stirring. Add the mushrooms, sage, port, and season with salt and pepper. Return to the boil, reduce the heat, cover, and simmer very gently for 1 hour, stirring occasionally until rich and really tender. Taste and adjust the seasoning if necessary.

3 Meanwhile, preheat the oven to 220°C (425°F/Gas 7). Cut four circles from the pastry slightly larger than the soup cups, and brush with the beaten egg. Stand the soup cups on a baking sheet. Brush the edges with more beaten egg. Ladle in the soup. Top with the circles of pastry, pressing down lightly with a fork around the edge to secure. Make a small slit in the top of each pie lid with a sharp knife to allow the steam to escape. Bake in the oven for about 15 minutes, or until puffy, crisp, and golden brown. Allow to cool for 3–5 minutes before serving.

celery and celeriac soup

This earthy soup combines mildly nutty celeriac and the more assertive celery to create a fragrant, satisfying winter warmer.

🥣 15 MINS   🍲 20 MINS   ❄ FREEZABLE

SPECIAL EQUIPMENT ▪ blender or food processor

SERVES 4

1 tbsp sunflower, groundnut, or mild olive oil

60g (2oz) butter, half diced and chilled

500g (1lb 2oz) celeriac, peeled and chopped

1 large head of celery, cored and chopped

1 floury potato, peeled and chopped

sea salt and freshly ground black pepper

1 litre (1¾ pints) hot light vegetable or chicken stock

4 slices walnut bread, lightly toasted, to serve

1 Put the oil and the unchilled butter in a large frying pan over a medium heat. Add the celeriac, celery, and potato. Stir well for 2–3 minutes, then reduce the heat a little. Add 3–4 tbsp water and season lightly. Partly cover with a lid and leave to stew gently until very soft. Stir the vegetables occasionally and keep the heat low.

2 Pour the soup into a blender or food processor and blitz until smooth. Return to the pan and add the stock. Season with sea salt and pepper, stir briskly to blend, and bring to a simmer over a medium heat, stirring frequently. Reduce the heat a little and leave to simmer for 10–15 minutes, still stirring occasionally. Taste and adjust the seasoning.

3 Just before serving, whisk in the remaining chilled, diced butter. Serve hot with toasted walnut bread.

Season's best **winter leafy greens**

Asian greens is the catch-all name for a number of different brassicas, such as pak choi and the leafy mustard greens, all with varying degrees of pepperiness. Kale (both red and green) has descended from the wild cabbages of southern Europe; and dark green cavolo nero initially came from Italy. Both have a chewy texture and a slightly bitter, cabbagey flavour. Enjoy all with garlic, soy sauce, chilli, ginger, and nuts.

Cavolo nero and kale, with their sturdy leaves, are popular crops thriving in cold to warm climates. Peppery Asian greens are originally from that continent, but today grow worldwide.

Curly kale Exceptionally nutritious, the leaves of curly kale have a rich, robust flavour and coarse texture. Boil or steam until tender and bright green. Overcooked, they turn grey.

essentials
varieties available

Red and dark green curly kale, dark green cavolo nero, and various Asian greens such as pak choi (bok choy), joy soy, mustard spinach, leaf mustard.

buy Look for firm stalks and fresh-looking leaves. Avoid any that are yellowing, limp, or have brown spots.

store Best eaten fresh, or store unwashed in a plastic bag in the fridge for 3–4 days. Kale becomes bitter if stored too long. Do not put near fruits that give off ethylene gas, such as apples, or the leaves will turn yellow.

cook Boil, steam, braise, stir-fry, or add to soups and stews.

preserve Blanch and freeze.

recipe ideas

Beef and greens p445

Filo pie with spicy kale and sausage p428

Wasabi beef and pak choi p442

Cavolo nero Also known as Tuscan black cabbage or Dinosaur kale, this member of the kale family is a popular gourmet vegetable. The puckered leaves have a rich, strong flavour. Lightly steam, or sauté.

Pak choi (Bok choy) Also known as Chinese white cabbage, the crunchy, mild-flavoured stalks are almost sweet, while the leaves taste slightly mustardy.

Small heads are delicious braised whole; larger ones shredded and stir-fried, or added to soups and stews.

mini chicken, leek, and mushroom pies

Small in size but big in taste, these delicious morsels contain a creamy filling of winter produce flavoured with garlic and wine. Choose a small leek for a sweeter flavour.

🍲 **15 MINS**   🍲 **50 MINS**   ❄ **FREEZABLE**

SPECIAL EQUIPMENT ▪ 6cm (2½in) and 5cm (2in) biscuit cutters ▪ 12-hole mini muffin tin

MAKES 12

1 tbsp olive oil

25g (scant 1oz) butter

1 small carrot, finely chopped

1 small celery stick, finely chopped

1 small leek, white part only, trimmed and finely chopped

1 small garlic clove, grated or finely chopped

100g (3½oz) chestnut mushrooms, diced

250g (9oz) skinless chicken breasts, diced

1 tbsp chopped thyme leaves

grated zest of ½ lemon

3 tbsp dry white wine

120ml (4fl oz) double cream

salt and freshly ground black pepper

1½ sheets ready-rolled puff pastry

1 egg, lightly beaten, for egg wash

mixed green leaves and herbs, to serve

1 Heat the oil and butter in a frying pan over a low heat. Add the carrot and celery, and gently sweat for about 5 minutes until soft. Add the leek and sweat for a few more minutes until softened. Stir in the garlic and cook for 30 seconds, before adding the mushrooms. Cook, stirring occasionally, for a further 5 minutes.

2 Increase the heat slightly and add the chicken, thyme, lemon zest, and white wine. Cook, stirring occasionally, for 15–20 minutes. Pour in the cream and season with salt and pepper. Continue to cook for about 5 minutes until thickened slightly. Leave to cool.

3 Preheat the oven to 200°C (400°F/ Gas 6). Lightly oil the muffin tin. Using the larger biscuit cutter, cut 12 circles from the puff pastry and line the holes in the prepared muffin tin. Spoon the chicken mixture into the pastry shells. With the small biscuit cutter, cut 12 circles from the puff pastry and use them to cover each of the chicken pies. Gently press the edges together to seal. Brush the tops with the egg wash, and bake for 15–20 minutes, until golden brown. Serve hot with a mixed-leaf salad.

carrot cream soup with onion and cumin

Pushing this colourful, zingy soup through a sieve with a wooden spoon to make it super smooth may seem fiddly, but it does wonders for the texture and is well worth the effort.

🍲 **20 MINS**   🍲 **30 MINS**   ❄ **FREEZABLE**

SPECIAL EQUIPMENT ▪ blender or food processor

SERVES 6

2 tbsp sunflower, groundnut, or mild olive oil

2 large Spanish onions, coarsely chopped

1 tsp cumin seeds

1 tsp ground cumin

1kg (2¼lb) carrots, coarsely chopped

sea salt and freshly ground black pepper

grated zest and juice of 1 small unwaxed orange

120ml (4fl oz) single cream

1 tbsp finely chopped flat-leaf parsley

1 Heat the oil in a large frying pan over a medium heat, add the onion, cumin seeds, and ground cumin, and cook for 3–4 minutes or until soft. Add the carrots and 1.5 litres (2¾ pints) water, then season lightly with sea salt and pepper. Reduce the heat, cover, and simmer for 20 minutes, or until the carrots are very tender. Turn off the heat and allow to cool a little.

2 Pour the soup into a blender or food processor and process until smooth. Place a sieve over a saucepan (or the frying pan if possible) and pour the soup into the sieve, pushing it through with the back of a wooden spoon.

3 Taste and adjust the seasoning. Stir in the orange zest and juice. Reheat until piping hot and stir in the cream, then the parsley. Season with a little extra pepper and serve hot.

variation

celeriac cream soup with orange and cinnamon

Prepare in the same way but substitute 1 large celeriac for the carrots. Add the grated zest and juice of 1 large orange (instead of a small one). Omit all the cumin but add a cinnamon stick and a bay leaf when cooking. Discard before puréeing. Stir in finely chopped coriander instead of parsley.

caldo verde

A traditional Portuguese soup, caldo verde – meaning "green soup" – is made from kale (in Portugal called "galega" cabbage) and potatoes. It is fabulous comfort food.

🍲 **10 MINS**   🍲 **20 MINS**   ❄ **FREEZABLE**

SERVES 4

4 floury potatoes, peeled and cut into chunks

salt and freshly ground black pepper

500g (1lb 2oz) kale, leaves pulled from the core and very finely sliced

2 tbsp olive oil

1 Put the potatoes in a saucepan with 2.4 litres (4 pints) water and add a little salt. Bring to the boil, then reduce the temperature and simmer for about 15 minutes, or until tender. Mash the potatoes lightly with a fork, leaving them in the water.

2 Cook the kale in a pan of boiling water for 3–4 minutes. Drain and stir into the potato broth with the oil. Simmer for 1–2 minutes. Season with salt and pepper and serve hot.

variation

mixed vegetable caldo verde

Make in the same way but use 2 potatoes, 1 turnip and ½ swede, peeled and cut in chunks instead of 4 potatoes. Serve sprinkled with grated Parmesan.

onion tart

An onion tart is very simple fare made with a minimal number of ingredients. Don't hold back on the seasoning, which helps to bring out the flavour of the onions even more. The addition of paprika in this version brings added colour as well as flavour.

🥣 **15 MINS**   🍲 **55 MINS**   ❄ **FREEZABLE**

SPECIAL EQUIPMENT ▪ 20cm (8in) round fluted tart tin ▪ ceramic baking beans

SERVES 6

1 tbsp olive oil

4 onions, sliced

1 tbsp plain flour

300ml (10fl oz) milk

2 tsp mild paprika

salt and freshly ground black pepper

300g (10oz) ready-made shortcrust pastry

1 egg, lightly beaten, for egg wash

1 Preheat the oven to 200°C (400°F/Gas 6). Heat the oil in a large, non-stick, heavy-based pan over a low heat. Add the onions and sweat very gently for about 15 minutes until soft and translucent. Keep stirring throughout, so that the onions don't stick or brown.

2 Remove from the heat and stir in the flour with a wooden spoon. Add a little of the milk and stir until combined. Return the pan to the heat and keep adding the milk, slowly and gradually, stirring continuously as the mixture thickens. Add 1 tsp of the paprika and season well with salt and pepper. Remove from the heat and set aside.

3 Roll out the pastry on a floured work surface and use to line the tart tin. Trim away any excess, line the pastry shell with greaseproof paper, and fill with the ceramic baking beans. Bake in the oven for 15–20 minutes until the edges of the pastry are golden. Remove the beans and paper, brush the bottom of the shell with a little of the egg wash, and return to the oven for a couple of minutes to crisp. Reduce the oven temperature to 180°C (350°F/Gas 4).

4 Carefully spoon the onion mixture into the pastry shell and sprinkle with the remaining paprika. Return the pie to the oven and bake for 15–20 minutes until lightly golden. Serve warm with a green salad.

variation

leek and cheddar cheese tart
Prepare in exactly the same way, but use 3–4 leeks thinly sliced, instead of the onions, and add 60g (2oz) strong Cheddar cheese to the leek mixture with the paprika, at the end of step 2.

avocado, grapefruit, and parma ham salad

Great flavour and texture contrasts with the sweet and silky Parma ham against the bitter rocket and sharp grapefruit.

🥣 25–30 MINS

SERVES 4

½ small onion, grated

3 tbsp red wine vinegar

1 tbsp honey

½ tsp mustard powder

¼ tsp ground ginger

salt and freshly ground black pepper

150ml (5fl oz) vegetable oil

1 tbsp poppy seeds

4 grapefruit

2 avocados

juice of 1 lemon

175g (6oz) rocket leaves

125g (4½oz) Parma ham, cut into 2.5cm (1in) strips

1 For the vinaigrette, put the onion, vinegar, honey, mustard powder, ginger, salt, and pepper into a bowl and whisk. Gradually whisk in the oil, so the vinaigrette emulsifies and thickens. Stir in the poppy seeds and taste for seasoning.

2 With a vegetable peeler, peel half of the zest from 1 grapefruit, leaving behind the white pith. Cut into very fine julienne strips. Half-fill a small saucepan with water and bring to the boil. Add the grapefruit julienne, simmer for 2 minutes, drain, and set aside.

3 Slice off the top and base of the grapefruit. Cut away the zest, pith, and skin, following the curve of the fruit. Holding each grapefruit over a bowl, cut out the segments, cutting between the membranes. Release the segments into the bowl. Discard any seeds, cover, and refrigerate.

4 Halve the avocados and remove the stones, then peel the skin. Cut into slices lengthways and place in a bowl. Pour over the lemon juice and toss the avocado to prevent it from browning. Briskly whisk the dressing. Toss the rocket leaves with one-third of it, then divide between 4 plates. Arrange the grapefruit, Parma ham, and avocado on top. Spoon over the remaining vinaigrette and sprinkle with grapefruit julienne.

creamy swede soup

As a strictly cold-season vegetable, swede stores up a lot of starch in the edible root base. It is this, combined with honey and cream, that gives this rich, wintry soup its velvety texture.

🥣 10 MINS   🍲 40–50 MINS   ❄ FREEZABLE

SPECIAL EQUIPMENT ▪ blender or food processor

SERVES 4–6

25g (scant 1oz) butter

2 onions, chopped

750g (1lb 10oz) swede (trimmed weight), cut into cubes

sea salt and freshly ground black pepper

1 litre (1¾ pints) hot vegetable stock

1 tbsp honey

½ nutmeg

150ml (5fl oz) single cream, plus extra to garnish

1 Melt the butter in a large pan over a medium heat, add the onions, and fry for 6–8 minutes or until lightly golden. Stir in the swede and a pinch of sea salt, cover with a lid, and cook for 10 minutes, stirring frequently. Pour in the stock, add the honey, and bring to the boil. Grate the nutmeg over the soup as it boils, then lower the heat and simmer for 20–30 minutes, or until the swede is completely soft.

2 Cool briefly, then blitz in a blender or food processor until smooth and velvety. You may need to do this in batches. Season with sea salt and pepper, then stir in the cream. Serve each bowlful with a swirl of cream and a good grinding of black pepper.

variation

creamy four root soup

Prepare in exactly the same way but use 1 small swede, 2 turnips, 1 parsnip, and 1 large carrot instead of all swede.

crispy bacon and avocado wraps

Avocado flesh can turn an unattractive shade of brown very quickly, so it is always worth tossing the peeled flesh in lemon juice as quickly as possible to prevent this from happening.

🥣 5 MINS   🍲 10 MINS

SERVES 4

225g (8oz) thick back bacon rashers

1 avocado

juice of 1 lemon

freshly ground black pepper

3–4 tbsp mayonnaise

4 flour tortillas

handful of cos lettuce leaves, shredded

1 Fry the bacon in a heavy-based frying pan over a medium-high heat until golden and crispy.

2 Halve the avocado and remove the stone, then peel the skin. Cut into slices and place in a bowl. Pour over the lemon juice and toss the avocado to prevent it from browning. Add plenty of black pepper and stir in the mayonnaise.

3 Fill the tortillas with the bacon and shredded cos lettuce and top with the avocado in mayonnaise. Then roll up the tortillas and serve immediately.

variation

spicy chicken, avocado, and spinach wraps

Prepare in the same way but substitute 225g (8oz) diced cooked chicken for the bacon. Use a handful of spinach leaves instead of cos lettuce and sprinkle each wrap with a pinch of dried chilli flakes before rolling up.

Season's best **avocado**

Also called avocado pears because of their shape, avocados are at their best in the winter months and into spring. They are loaded with potassium, fibre, and exceptional levels of monosaturated fat (the good kind). They have a mild, somewhat nutty, flavour and a smooth, oily texture. Good flavour pairings include Parma ham, prawns, tomatoes, grapefruit, lime, pineapple, sugar, and balsamic vinegar.

Unlike most fruits, avocados ripen off the tree. Originally native to Central America and the Caribbean, there are over 500 cultivars planted worldwide.

essentials
varieties available

Hass, Fuerte, and Sharwill are the most popular varieties.

buy The shiny, green varieties, like Fuerte, should "give" slightly when gently squeezed. Others, like Hass, must be black and should "give" slightly at the stalk end but not feel too soft.

store Unripe at room temperature. If ripe, keep in the fridge and eat in a day or two.

cook Eat raw; cook, stuffed and baked, or in a soup.

preserve Mash the flesh with lemon juice, then freeze.

recipe ideas

Avocado and spinach soup
p16

Avocado, grapefruit, and Parma ham salad p432

Crispy bacon and avocado wraps p432

Unlike the Hass variety, the skin of Fuerte is smooth and remains green when ripe.

The pebbly skin becomes almost black as the fruit ripens.

Fuerte An easy-peeling variety with a mild flavour and creamy, pale yellow flesh that slices well. It is ideal for salads and salsas.

Hass This variety is a good choice for dips and spreads. The creamy flesh is silky smooth and the flavour wonderfully rich and nutty.

how to stone and peel avocado

Using a knife to remove the avocado stone is clean, quick, and surprisingly easy. The avocado must be just ripe to taste rich and luxurious. If underripe, the flesh is tough and slightly bitter. If overripe, it becomes black and "soapy". Rub the flesh with lemon afterwards to prevent it from browning.

1 With a chef's knife, slice straight into the avocado, cutting all the way around the stone. Gently twist the halves in opposite directions and separate.

2 Strike the cutting edge of your knife into the stone and lift the knife (wiggling if necessary) to remove it from the avocado.

3 Use a spatula to remove the flesh cleanly from the skin if you want to keep it whole. Cut into slices or wedges, or mash for dips and spreads.

minestrone soup

This is a hearty cold-weather version of the Italian soup, using a base of sweet carrot and aromatic celery.

🥣 10 MINS 🍲 40 MINS

SERVES 4

1 tbsp olive oil

1 onion, finely chopped

salt and freshly ground black pepper

1 tsp dried oregano

4 carrots, finely diced

4 celery sticks, finely diced

3 garlic cloves, grated or finely chopped

1 small glass of red wine

1 tbsp tomato purée

400g can whole plum tomatoes, chopped

600ml (1 pint) hot vegetable stock

200g (7oz) pasta, such as macaroni or vermicelli

handful of flat-leaf parsley, finely chopped

Parmesan cheese, grated, to garnish

1 Heat the oil in a large pan over a medium heat, add the onion, and cook for 3–4 minutes, or until soft and translucent. Add a pinch of salt, the oregano, and stir through the carrots and celery. Sweat gently for about 10 minutes until softened.

2 Stir through the garlic and cook for a few seconds more. Pour in the wine, increase the heat, and let it boil for 1–2 minutes until the alcohol has evaporated. Stir through the tomato purée and season well with salt and pepper. Add the canned tomatoes and vegetable stock. Bring to the boil, reduce the heat slightly, and simmer for about 20 minutes, topping up with hot water if the minestrone gets too thick (but don't make it too thin).

3 Meanwhile, cook the pasta in a large pan of boiling salted water for about 12 minutes, or until it is tender but still al dente. Drain, and chop if large. Add the pasta to the soup. Sprinkle over the parsley and serve hot with a bowl of Parmesan cheese for sprinkling over the top.

cauliflower soup

Ensure you cut off all the green leaves of the cauliflower because they can make this soup taste a little bitter.

🥣 15 MINS 🍲 40 MINS ❄ FREEZABLE

SPECIAL EQUIPMENT ▪ blender or food processor

SERVES 4

1 tbsp olive oil

1 onion, finely chopped

salt and freshly ground black pepper

1 large garlic clove, grated or finely chopped

2 celery sticks, finely chopped

1 bay leaf

2 potatoes, peeled and cut into bite-sized chunks

750ml (1¼ pints) hot vegetable stock

1 cauliflower, trimmed and cut into florets

drizzle of double cream, to serve (optional)

1 Heat the oil in a large pan, add the onion, and cook over a low heat for 6–8 minutes, or until soft and translucent. Season well with salt and pepper, then add the garlic, celery, and bay leaf and cook for 5 minutes, or until the celery begins to soften. Stir in the potatoes and cook for 5

minutes, then pour in the stock, bring to the boil, and cook for 15 minutes, or until the potatoes are nearly soft.

2 Add the cauliflower and cook for 10 minutes, or until it is soft but not watery. Remove the bay leaf and discard, then transfer the soup to a blender or food processor and blitz until smooth. Add a little more hot stock if it seems too thick. Taste, and season with salt and pepper if needed. To serve, drizzle with double cream, if using, and serve with fresh crusty bread.

variation

cauliflower cheese soup

Use only 500ml (16fl oz) stock in step 1. Purée with 250ml (9fl oz) milk and return to the pan. Stir in 2 large handfuls grated strong Cheddar cheese. Thin with a little more milk if too thick. Reheat but do not boil.

scotch broth

The traditional ingredients of a Scotch broth are lamb and barley, both of which feature prominently in this recipe. Barley needs a good hour of cooking to become sufficiently tender.

🥣 **20 MINS**　🍲 **1 HR 45 MINS**　❄ **FREEZABLE**

SERVES 4

225g (8oz) neck of lamb

salt and freshly ground black pepper

1 tbsp olive oil

1 small onion, finely chopped

2 carrots, finely chopped

2 celery sticks, finely chopped

1.2 litres (2 pints) hot chicken stock

115g (4oz) pearl barley

handful of curly parsley, finely chopped

1 Put the lamb in a large pan, cover with cold water, and season with salt and pepper. Bring to the boil, then reduce the heat and simmer for 30 minutes, or until cooked. Remove with a slotted spoon, leave to cool slightly, then shred and set aside. Reserve the cooking liquid.

2 Heat the oil in a large pan, add the onion, and cook over a medium heat for 3–4 minutes until soft and translucent. Add the carrots and celery, and cook over a very low heat for 10 minutes. Strain the reserved liquid, then add to the pan and pour in the stock. Season with salt and pepper, then add the pearl barley and bring to the boil. Reduce the heat to low and simmer for 1 hour, or until the pearl barley is cooked. Top up with hot water if it begins to dry out too much.

3 Stir through the parsley, then season again with salt and pepper if needed. Serve with fresh crusty bread.

split pea and bacon soup

Root vegetables from storage are invaluable during the cold winter months for heartwarming soups like this. Split peas take a long time to cook, so start early or use a slow cooker.

🥣 **15 MINS**　🍲 **2 HRS 15 MINS**　❄ **FREEZABLE**

SPECIAL EQUIPMENT ▪ blender or food processor

SERVES 4

2 tbsp olive oil

200g (7oz) bacon or pancetta, chopped into bite-sized pieces

1 onion, finely chopped

salt and freshly ground black pepper

2 celery sticks, finely chopped

2 carrots, finely chopped

300g (10oz) yellow split peas

900ml (1½ pints) hot vegetable stock

1 Heat half the oil in a large heavy-based pan over a medium heat, add the bacon or pancetta, and cook, stirring occasionally, for 5 minutes, or until crispy and golden. Remove with a slotted spoon and set aside. Heat the remaining oil in the pan, add the onion, and cook over a low heat for 6–8 minutes, or until soft and translucent. Season with salt and pepper, then add the celery and carrots, and cook on a low heat for 5 minutes.

2 Add the split peas and stock, and bring to the boil slowly. Cover with a lid, reduce to a simmer, and cook for 2 hours, or until the peas are tender. Check occasionally and top up with hot water if the soup begins to look too thick. Transfer to a blender or food processor and blitz until smooth. Return to the pan. Add the bacon or pancetta and season with salt and pepper. Reheat then serve with fresh crusty bread.

variation

smoky split pea soup

Omit the bacon. Cook the onion in the 2 tbsp olive oil and continue the recipe as before but add 1 tsp smoked paprika at step 2. Meanwhile, dry-fry 115g (4oz) finely diced chorizo. Ladle the soup in bowls and garnish with a small spoonful of the fried chorizo.

oysters with chilli and lime mayonnaise

An oyster knife is essential when shucking these shellfish. It will have a sturdy handle and a point at the end of the blade.

🥣 15 MINS

SPECIAL EQUIPMENT ▪ oyster knife

SERVES 4-6

2 small red chillies, deseeded

1 garlic clove, grated or finely chopped

salt and freshly ground black pepper

1 egg yolk

175ml (6fl oz) light olive oil

juice of 1 lime

24 oysters in their shells

rock salt, to serve

1 To make the chilli and lime mayonnaise, pound the chillies, garlic, and a good pinch of salt to a paste with a pestle in a mortar. Spoon the paste into a large bowl, then add the egg yolk. Stir thoroughly with a wooden spoon or whisk until smooth.

2 Gradually add the oil, drop by drop, whisking continuously, ensuring it is absorbed completely before making the next addition. Once the mixture starts to thicken, add the oil in a slow, thin drizzle. When a third of the oil has been combined, start adding the lime juice a little at a time. Keep adding and whisking until everything is well incorporated. Season with black pepper, cover with cling film, and chill until needed.

3 To prepare the oysters, discard any that have opened or do not close tightly straight away, when tapped on the work surface. Use an oyster knife, and hold the oysters over a bowl as you open them. Carefully shuck the oysters one by one (p437), catching any liquid in the bowl and transferring the opened oysters in their shells and their liquid to the fridge as you go.

4 Put a layer of rock salt on a platter to keep the oysters level. Arrange the open oysters in their shells on top of the salt and spoon over the chilled oyster liquid. Add a little chilli and lime mayonnaise over the top of each oyster and serve immediately.

oysters with shallot and vinegar dressing

Take great care when shucking an oyster as the knife can slip all too easily. For safety's sake, wrap your knife-free hand in a thick tea towel to protect it, should the worst happen.

🥣 15 MINS

SPECIAL EQUIPMENT ▪ oyster knife

SERVES 4-6

24 oysters in their shells

crushed ice

4 tbsp red wine vinegar

1 large or 2 small shallots, very finely chopped

1 To prepare the oysters, discard any that have opened or do not close tightly straight away, when tapped on the work surface. Use an oyster knife, and hold the oysters over a bowl as you open them. Carefully shuck the oysters one by one (p437), catching any liquid in the bowl and transferring the opened oysters in their shells and their liquid to the fridge as you go.

2 Arrange the oysters on an oyster plate with ice, or pack 4 serving dishes with lots of crushed ice and place the oysters on top.

3 Mix the vinegar and shallots together and put into a small dish. Place in the centre of the oysters – or the middle of the table – and serve.

variation

oysters with lemon and tabasco

Shuck the oysters as directed and serve on crushed ice with lemon wedges and Tabasco sauce on the side. Allow your guests to choose their preferred dressing or to eat the oysters unadorned.

Season's best **oysters**

Oysters are a delicacy and differ in flavour and shell colour, depending on their location. Mostly found in temperate coastal waters, they are harvested from the wild from autumn to spring, and farmed all year. Oyster tasting is an art, with many gourmet terms for its varied flavours. Pair raw oysters with shallots, red wine, vinegar, Tabasco, and lemon juice; cooked oysters go well with anchovy essence, butter, cream, and spinach.

Native oysters have an oval, scaly shell, intense taste, and firm texture.

Pacific oyster The taste of this widely cultured oyster varies enormously, depending on where it is grown. Flavours range from smoky, grassy, and acidic, through to milky and creamy. Usually graded by weight, a fair size would be 115g (4oz), or 11cm (4½in). Store the oysters cup-side down to prevent their natural juices escaping.

Native oyster Also called the European flat oyster, it is often served raw on a bed of crushed ice, dressed with lemon juice, Tabasco, and shallot vinegar. Graded by size, from 1 to 4, the largest "royals" can reach 10cm (4in).

Pacific oysters are larger and less expensive than native ones and grow quicker.

The meat of the Pacific oyster is a delicate beige in colour, with a smooth, creamy texture.

essentials
varieties available

The two main varieties, wild and farmed, are Native and Pacific oysters.

buy They should be shut tight and undamaged and smell pleasantly of the sea.

store Keep in the fridge, rounded sides down. Eat on the day of purchase.

cook Usually eaten *au naturel*, or fry, poach, grill, or bake.

preserve Can be frozen in their half shells and juice, but only if very fresh.

recipe ideas

Grilled oysters with crème fraîche and Parmesan p439

Oysters with chilli and lime mayonnaise p436

Oysters with shallot and vinegar dressing p436

how to shuck an oyster

Fresh oysters are tightly closed and hard to open without an oyster shucking knife. When shucking oysters, always protect the hand holding the oyster with a towel or oven glove, in case the knife slips while applying pressure to prise off the top shell. Holding the oyster flat on a towel will help prevent the deliciously briny liquid from spilling out.

1 Insert the tip of an oyster knife into the hinge to open the shell. Keep the blade close to the top of the shell so the oyster is not damaged. Cut the muscle and lift off the top shell.

2 Detach the oyster from the bottom shell by carefully sliding the blade of the knife beneath the oyster. They can be served raw on the half shell (scrub the shells thoroughly before opening), or removed and cooked.

crab salad with grapefruit and coriander

White crabmeat comes from the claws and legs of a crab. It has a delicate flavour and is low in fat, in contrast to brown crabmeat from the body, which has a higher fat content.

🥣 **10 MINS**

SERVES 4

350g (12oz) cooked fresh or canned white crabmeat, drained

handful of baby salad leaves

handful of coriander leaves

2 pink grapefruits, peeled, segmented, and any pith removed

For the dressing

3 tbsp olive oil

1 tbsp white wine vinegar

a pinch of sugar

salt and freshly ground black pepper

1 In a small bowl or jug, whisk together the dressing ingredients. Season with salt and pepper.

2 Mix the crabmeat with a drizzle of the dressing. Divide the salad leaves and half of the coriander leaves among 4 serving plates, and scatter over the grapefruit segments.

3 When ready to serve, drizzle the salad with the remaining dressing. Divide the crabmeat among the plates, spooning it neatly on top of the leaves. Scatter over the remaining coriander and serve immediately.

variation

poached trout salad with red grapefruit, orange, and celery
Poach 4 trout fillets in water, in a shallow frying pan for about 5 minutes until cooked through. Drain, flake the fish, discarding the skin, and leave to cool. Prepare the salad in exactly the same way, but use 1 red grapefruit and 1 large orange instead of the 2 pink grapefruits. Scatter 2 chopped celery sticks over the salad leaves and omit the coriander.

carrot soup with coconut and lemongrass

This spicy, exotically flavoured carrot soup makes an elegant starter. Serve it with lime wedges on a plate alongside, so that the guests can adjust the flavour to their liking.

🥣 **15 MINS**   🍲 **35 MINS**   ❄ **FREEZABLE**

SPECIAL EQUIPMENT ▪ blender or food processor

SERVES 4

2 tbsp vegetable oil or sunflower oil

1 onion, chopped

1 lemongrass stalk, trimmed and tough outer leaves removed

2 garlic cloves, chopped

2 tsp finely grated root ginger

1 tbsp red Thai curry paste

450g (1lb) carrots, sliced

900ml (1½ pints) hot vegetable stock

3 kaffir lime leaves

165ml can coconut milk

salt and freshly ground black pepper

lime wedges, to serve

1 Heat the oil in a large pan, add the onion, and cook for 3–4 minutes until the onion is soft. Meanwhile, finely chop the lemongrass, then add to the pan along with the garlic and ginger, and fry for 2 minutes. Add the curry paste and fry for 1 minute, stirring all the time, then add the carrots and fry for 2 minutes. Pour in the stock, add the lime leaves, and simmer for 20–25 minutes, or until the carrots are tender.

2 Remove from the heat and discard the lime leaves. Pour in the coconut milk, then pour the soup into a blender or food processor, and process until smooth. The soup shouldn't be too thick – dilute with more stock if it is. Season to taste, then serve with a grating of black pepper and lime wedges.

french cabbage soup

This chunky country soup takes only minutes to prepare and makes a good light supper or lunch dish. For a meat-free option, leave out the lardons or diced bacon.

🥣 **15 MINS**   🍲 **30 MINS**   ❄ **FREEZABLE**

SERVES 4

1 tbsp olive oil

100g (3½oz) small lardons, or diced bacon

1 Spanish onion, finely chopped

1 garlic clove, crushed

1 large Savoy cabbage, halved, cored, and leaves cut into shreds

salt and freshly ground black pepper

3 sprigs of parsley

croûtons, to garnish (optional)

1 Heat the oil in a large heavy-based casserole over a medium heat. Add the lardons (setting aside 2 tbsp to finish), onion, and garlic. Fry, stirring frequently, for 3–4 minutes or until the onion and garlic start to colour. Add the cabbage shreds, reserving a handful to finish. Stir well and season lightly with salt and generously with black pepper. Continue frying for 2–3 minutes, stirring occasionally.

2 Boil about 900ml (about 1½ pints) water in a kettle. Pour the boiling water over the vegetables and lardons, stir well, and add the parsley. Cover, reduce the heat a little, and simmer for about 20 minutes, stirring occasionally.

3 Meanwhile, place a non-stick frying pan over a medium heat. Add the reserved lardons and fry until crisp and golden. Then add the reserved cabbage shreds and fry them until they have wilted, stirring frequently. Season with a little black pepper.

4 Taste the soup and adjust the seasoning. Lift out the parsley. Ladle into individual bowls and scatter over the fried bacon and cabbage mixture. A few croûtons, if using, scattered across the surface provide a nice finishing touch.

turnip soup with pimento, chilli, and noodles

A light, colourful soup with quite a chilli kick. Larger turnips have a stronger flavour, which is perfect for this dish. Don't use the delicate baby ones.

🥣 **10 MINS** | 🍲 **30 MINS** | ❄ **FREEZABLE**

SERVES 4–6

1 onion, finely chopped

2 good-sized turnips, peeled and diced

½ tsp crushed dried chillies

1 green jalapeño chilli, deseeded and cut into thin rings

2 star anise

2 tsp tomato purée

900ml (1½ pints) hot vegetable stock or light chicken stock

1 slab dried, thin Chinese egg noodles

1 preserved pimento, drained and diced

soy sauce

freshly ground black pepper

small handful of coriander leaves, torn

1 Put the onion, turnips, chillies, star anise, tomato purée, and stock in a saucepan and bring to the boil. Lower the heat, partially cover with the lid, and simmer gently for 30 minutes, or until the turnips are really tender. Discard the star anise.

2 Meanwhile, put the noodles in a bowl, cover with boiling water, and leave to stand for 5 minutes, stirring to loosen, then drain. Stir the noodles into the soup, along with the pimento. Season to taste with soy sauce and black pepper, then stir in half the coriander. Ladle into warmed soup bowls, top with the remaining coriander, and serve.

grilled oysters with crème fraîche and parmesan

These are deliciously rich, so you can get away with serving only 3 oysters per person. Serve straight away while still piping hot or the oysters will lose their succulence.

🥣 **20 MINS** | 🍲 **1 MIN**

SPECIAL EQUIPMENT ▪ oyster knife

SERVES 4

12 large oysters

Tabasco sauce

300ml (10fl oz) crème fraîche

3 tbsp snipped chives

15g (½oz) Parmesan cheese, grated

15g (½oz) natural dried breadcrumbs

1 To prepare the oysters, discard any that have opened or do not close tightly straight away when tapped on the work surface. Use an oyster knife, and hold the oysters over a bowl as you open them. Carefully shuck the oysters one by one (p437), catching any liquid in the bowl and transferring the opened oysters in their shells and their liquid to the grill rack.

2 Preheat the grill. Add a few drops of Tabasco sauce to each oyster. Mix the crème fraîche with the chives and spoon over. Mix the Parmesan and breadcrumbs together and sprinkle over each oyster. Grill for about 1 minute until the cheese is bubbling. Serve straight away.

variation

grilled oysters with tabasco

Prepare in the same way but add a few drops of Tabasco to each shucked oyster and sprinkle with a mixture of snipped chives and chopped coriander. Top with the crème fraîche and Parmesan as before.

bistro salad with egg and lardons

Frisée lettuce belongs to the endive family, its bitterness is offset by the saltiness of bacon and the unctuous texture of a perfectly poached egg.

🥣 **5 MINS** | 🍲 **10 MINS**

SERVES 4

4 eggs

1 tbsp lemon juice

6 tbsp extra virgin olive oil

2 thick slices of bread, crusts cut off and bread diced

1 garlic clove, halved

5mm (¼in) slice fresh root ginger, peeled (optional)

115g (4oz) smoked lardons

½–1 frisée lettuce, torn

3 sprigs of thyme, leaves picked

small handful of flat-leaf parsley

small handful of coriander leaves

1 small red onion, thinly sliced

For the dressing

2 tbsp red wine vinegar

¼ tsp dried chilli flakes

2 tsp Worcestershire sauce

¼ tsp caster sugar

sea salt and freshly ground black pepper

1 Poach the eggs in gently simmering water with the lemon juice for about 3 minutes. Scoop out and put straight into cold water.

2 Heat 1 tbsp of the oil in a frying pan. Add the bread, garlic, and ginger, if using, tossing and stirring until golden. Drain the croûtons on kitchen paper. Discard the garlic and ginger.

3 In the same pan, dry-fry the lardons until crisp and golden. Drain on kitchen paper.

4 Put the lettuce in a salad bowl and tear in the herbs. Add the onion, separated into rings, lardons, and croûtons. Add the remaining 5 tbsp of the oil to a pan with the dressing ingredients. Heat gently, stirring. Pour over the salad and toss. Arrange the salad into individual bowls and top each with a poached egg.

meat and potato pie

Cook this warming winter pie either in a large dish or as individual portions to be eaten with steamed cabbage.

🥄 15 MINS   🍲 1 HR 30 MINS   ❄ FREEZABLE

SPECIAL EQUIPMENT ▪ 1.2-litre (2-pint) pie dish or 4 small individual pie dishes

SERVES 4

3 potatoes, peeled and cut into bite-sized pieces

675g (1½lb) braising steak, chopped into bite-sized pieces

1 tbsp olive oil, plus extra for braising

1 onion, finely chopped

1 tbsp plain flour

1 tbsp Worcestershire sauce

450ml (15fl oz) hot beef stock

salt and freshly ground black pepper

300g (10oz) ready-made puff pastry

1 egg, lightly beaten, for egg wash

1 Cook the potatoes in a pan of boiling salted water for 15–20 minutes until soft. Drain and set aside. Put the meat in a large frying pan with a drop of oil, and cook over a high heat for 5–8 minutes until browned all over. Remove with a slotted spoon and set aside.

2 Using the same pan, heat the oil over a low heat. Add the onion and cook gently for about 5 minutes until soft and translucent. Stir in the flour

and continue to cook for a further 2 minutes. Increase the heat a little and add the Worcestershire sauce and stock. Bring to the boil, reduce the heat, and return the meat to the pan. Cover and simmer for about 30 minutes, stirring occasionally. Stir through the potato and season well.

3 Meanwhile, preheat the oven to 200°C (400°F/Gas 6). Spoon the meat into the pie dish or small dishes. On a floured work surface, roll out the pastry until 5cm (2in) larger all around than the top of the pie dish. Cut out a strip of pastry about 2.5cm (1in) in from the edge. Wet the edge of the pie dish with a little water; fit the pastry strip all the way around, and press down firmly. Brush the pastry collar with a little of the egg wash, then top with the pastry lid. Trim the excess and pinch the edges to seal. Brush the top of the pie with the egg wash and make 2 slits with a sharp knife to allow steam to escape. Bake for about 30 minutes until puffed and golden. Serve hot.

duck with apple and rosemary potatoes

Potatoes roasted with sprigs of rosemary are a most flavourful combination. Make sure the sprigs are small, though, or they can become a little woody when cooked.

🥄 20 MINS   🍲 40–60 MINS

SERVES 4

4 large duck legs

salt and freshly ground black pepper

550g (1¼lb) potatoes, peeled and cut into chunks

3 red-skinned apples, halved, cored, and roughly chopped

a few sprigs of rosemary

drizzle of olive oil

1 Savoy cabbage, halved, cored, and leaves roughly chopped

pinch of dried chilli flakes (optional)

redcurrant jelly (optional)

1 Rub the duck legs generously with salt and pepper. Set aside for 30 minutes, if you have the time – it will help crispen up the skin. Otherwise, cook straight away.

2 Preheat the oven to 200°C (400°F/ Gas 6). Heat a large frying pan, add the duck, and cook for 8–10 minutes,

or until golden all over. Using a slotted spoon, transfer the duck to a large roasting tin. Add the potatoes and apples, scatter over the rosemary, drizzle with the oil, season, then combine well using your hands. Place in the oven and cook for about 40–60 minutes until the duck is crispy and the potatoes are golden. You may need to turn the potatoes halfway through cooking.

3 Meanwhile, put the cabbage in a pan of boiling salted water and cook for 4–5 minutes, or until it is cooked but still al dente. Drain and keep warm. Add to the roasting tin for the last 10 minutes of cooking, tucking it in and around the duck. Sprinkle with chilli flakes, if using. Transfer to a serving dish and serve with redcurrant jelly, also if using.

chicken and cornmeal cobbler

Cover the dish with foil if the top is browning too quickly.

🥣 20 MINS   🍲 1 HR 45 MINS   ❄ FREEZABLE

SPECIAL EQUIPMENT ▪ 4cm (1½in) biscuit cutter

SERVES 4

1 tbsp olive oil

3 skinless chicken breasts, cut into bite-sized pieces

salt and freshly ground black pepper

1 red onion, finely sliced

2 celery sticks, roughly chopped

1 glass of red wine

2 large carrots, roughly chopped

450ml (15fl oz) hot vegetable stock

75g (2½oz) plain flour

150g (5½oz) cornmeal

25g (scant 1oz) butter

small handful of flat-leaf parsley, chopped

splash of milk

1 small egg yolk, lightly beaten

1 Heat half the oil in a large, shallow flameproof casserole over a medium heat. Season the chicken, then cook for 10 minutes or until lightly golden, turning occasionally. Remove with a slotted spoon and set side.

2 Preheat the oven to 180°C (350°F/ Gas 4). Heat the remaining oil in the pan over a low heat, then add the onions and cook for 6–8 minutes until soft. Add the celery and cook for 5 minutes, or until soft. Pour in the wine, increase the heat, and boil for 2 minutes while the alcohol evaporates. Add the carrots, return the chicken to the pan, and season well. Pour in the stock and cook over a low heat for 1 hour, uncovered, stirring occasionally, or until all the ingredients are tender. Top up with hot water if necessary.

3 Meanwhile, put the flour, cornmeal, and a pinch of salt in a large bowl. Rub in the butter with your fingertips until you have a breadcrumb texture. Stir through the parsley, then add the milk a little at a time until the dough comes together. Form into a ball and rest it in the fridge for 20 minutes. Flatten on a floured work surface, then roll it out with a rolling pin. Cut out about 18 rounds using the cutter, and add to the casserole, brushing with egg yolk. Cook in the oven for 30 minutes until the cobblers are golden and the casserole hot.

marsala chicken with pine nuts and sultanas

Marsala wine is a fortified wine similar to port or sherry. It adds body as well as flavour, complementing the sultanas.

🥣 15 MINS   🍲 45 MINS

SERVES 4

2 tbsp olive oil

8 chicken pieces, such as thighs and breasts with skin on

1 onion, finely chopped

2 carrots, finely chopped

2 celery sticks, finely chopped

300ml (10fl oz) Marsala wine

salt and freshly ground black pepper

50g (1¾oz) pine nuts, toasted

50g (1¾oz) sultanas

handful of flat-leaf parsley, finely chopped

1 Heat the oil in a large cast-iron pan or casserole over a medium heat. Add the chicken pieces and cook for about 8 minutes until golden all over. Remove from the pan and set aside.

2 Reduce the heat to low. Add the onion, carrots, and celery to the pan, and sweat gently for a few minutes until soft. Pour in the Marsala wine and season with salt and pepper.

Return the chicken to the pan and simmer gently for about 30 minutes, topping up with water a little at a time if it begins to dry out – but don't add too much, because it should be fairly dry and the water will only dilute the flavour.

3 Stir through the pine nuts and sultanas, and cook for a few minutes more. Just before serving, stir through the parsley. Serve with a dressed green salad and fresh crusty bread.

variation

chicken in sherry with pears
Prepare in the same way, but use 150ml (5fl oz) medium-dry sherry and 150ml (5fl oz) chicken stock instead of the Marsala. Omit the pine nuts and sultanas. Melt a knob of butter and fry 2 unripe pears, peeled, cored, and diced, until lightly golden. Stir into the sauce just before serving.

duck with pink grapefruit and chicory salad

The flavours of a winter citrus salad with chicory and fennel give a refreshing sweet-sour edge to roasted duck breast.

🥣 10 MINS   🍲 25 MINS

SERVES 4

knob of butter

4 duck breasts, about 150g (5½oz) each, skin on and scored in a crisscross pattern

handful of rosemary sprigs

2 tbsp balsamic vinegar

1 head of chicory, leaves separated

1 fennel bulb, trimmed and finely sliced

2 pink grapefruits, peeled and segmented

salt and freshly ground black pepper

1 Preheat the oven to 200°C (400°F/ Gas 6). Melt the butter in a large non-stick frying pan over a high heat, then add the duck breasts, skin-side down, and the rosemary. Sear the duck for 2–3 minutes on each side until golden all over. Increase the heat, add half of the balsamic vinegar, and let it simmer for a few minutes, scraping up any bits from the bottom of the pan with a wooden spoon.

2 Transfer the duck and its vinegar juices to a roasting tin and roast in the oven for 15–20 minutes, until the duck is cooked to your liking.

3 Meanwhile, prepare the salad. Mix together the chicory and fennel, add the grapefruit segments, and toss gently. Drizzle over the remaining balsamic vinegar and season with salt and pepper. Slice each duck breast into two and serve with the salad.

variation

pheasant with pomegranate, frisée lettuce, and leek salad

Prepare in exactly the same way, but use 4 pheasant breasts instead of duck. Use half a small frisée lettuce, torn into pieces, instead of the chicory and 2 chopped baby leeks instead of the fennel. Scatter with the seeds from 1 pomegranate instead of the grapefruit.

wasabi beef and pak choi

Japanese wasabi paste, a type of hot mustard, is extremely strong, so you only need a little of it to lift the flavour of grilled beef steak.

🥣 10 MINS   🍲 10 MINS

SERVES 4

3 tbsp olive oil

2 tsp wasabi paste

4 sirloin steaks, about 200g (7oz) each

200g (7oz) pak choi, cut lengthways into 8 pieces

5 garlic cloves, grated or finely chopped

1 tbsp dark soy sauce

salt and freshly ground black pepper

1 Mix 1 tbsp of the oil with the wasabi paste in a shallow bowl. Coat the sirloin steaks completely in the mix, ensuring a thin, even covering.

2 Heat half the remaining oil in a frying pan over a medium-high heat, and fry the steaks for 2–3 minutes on each side for medium-rare, or 5 minutes on each side for well done. Remove to a plate, then leave to rest in a warm place for 5 minutes.

3 Heat the last of the oil in the pan over a low heat, add the pak choi and fry, turning once or twice, for 1–2 minutes. Add the garlic and soy sauce and fry for 1 minute, or until the pak choi has just wilted. Cut the steak into 1cm (½in) slices, season, and serve with the pak choi.

lentils with mushrooms and leeks

Lentils and mushrooms are both meaty, tasty ingredients that give this quick vegetarian dish depth and flavour. Use dried puy lentils instead of canned, for added texture.

🥄 10 MINS 🍲 25 MINS ❄ FREEZABLE

SERVES 4

1 tbsp olive oil

1 onion, finely chopped

1 bay leaf

salt and freshly ground black pepper

2 garlic cloves, grated or finely chopped

3 leeks, trimmed and sliced

2 tsp Marmite or Vegemite, or a splash of light soy sauce

225g (8oz) chestnut mushrooms, halved, or quartered if large

400g can green lentils or puy lentils, drained and rinsed

300ml (10fl oz) hot vegetable stock

handful of curly-leaf parsley, leaves picked and finely chopped

1 Heat the oil in a large frying pan over a low heat. Add the onion, bay leaf, and a little salt, and cook for 5 minutes until the onion is soft and translucent. Add the garlic and leek and stir through the Marmite, Vegemite, or soy sauce. Cook for a further 5 minutes until the leeks begin to soften.

2 Add the mushrooms and cook until they release their juices – you may need to add a little more oil if necessary. Season well with salt and pepper, then stir through the lentils and hot stock. Bring to the boil, reduce the heat, and simmer gently for 15 minutes.

3 Remove from the heat and stir in the parsley. Taste and season again if needed. Serve with some roasted tomatoes and fresh crusty bread.

mince and chickpeas cooked with orange and cinnamon

In place of canned chickpeas, try dried ones for a fuller flavour. Soak them in cold water for 8–10 hours, then boil for 1–2 hours to soften them.

🥄 10 MINS 🍲 20 MINS

SERVES 4

1 tbsp olive oil

1 red onion, finely chopped

2 garlic cloves, grated

2.5cm (1in) piece of root ginger, peeled and grated

a pinch of ground cinnamon

salt and freshly ground black pepper

675g (1½lb) minced beef

grated zest and juice of 1 orange

400g can chickpeas, drained and rinsed

150ml (5fl oz) hot vegetable stock

1 Heat the oil in a large pan over a medium heat, add the onion, and cook for about 5 minutes until the onion is soft and translucent. Add the garlic, ginger, and cinnamon, and season with salt and pepper. Stir in the beef and cook for a few minutes until the meat is no longer pink.

2 Add the orange zest and juice together with the chickpeas and stock and bring to the boil. Reduce the heat, cover, and simmer gently for about 15 minutes, stirring occasionally. Serve on a bed of rice, or with boiled new potatoes and steamed green beans.

variation

beef and vegetable chilli with guacamole

Prepare in exactly the same way, but add ¼ small swede, finely diced, and 2 carrots, finely diced, with the onion. Use 1 tsp ground cumin instead of the ginger and 1 tsp dried oregano instead of the cinnamon. Substitute 2 tbsp tomato purée for the orange zest and juice, and a 400g can drained red kidney beans for the chickpeas. Mash a ripe avocado with a squeeze of lime juice and spoon on top of the chilli before serving.

pot roast smoked ham

Knuckle or ham hock is amazing value and tasty, too. The Jerusalem artichokes add a nutty, creamy texture, but if they're not available you can use parsnips instead.

🥄 25 MINS   🍲 3 HRS 15 MINS   ❄️ FREEZABLE

SERVES 4-6

2 smoked ham hocks (knuckles), about 1.35kg (3lb) each

1 bay leaf

1 tbsp olive oil

1 onion, finely chopped

salt and freshly ground black pepper

3 garlic cloves, finely chopped

a few sprigs of thyme

3 carrots, chopped

225g (8oz) Jerusalem artichokes, peeled and sliced

125g (4½oz) yellow split peas

100ml (3½fl oz) dry cider

900ml (1½ pints) hot vegetable stock

1 Put the ham hocks and bay leaf in a large heavy-based pan, cover with water, and cook for about 2 hours, skimming away any scum that comes to the top of the pan. Remove the hams and when cool enough to handle, peel away the skins and discard. Set the hams aside. (You can reserve the stock and use it if you wish, but it can be salty.)

2 Preheat the oven to 180°C (350°F/ Gas 4). Heat the oil in a large flameproof casserole over a medium heat, add the onion, and cook for 3–4 minutes until soft. Season with salt and pepper, stir through the garlic, thyme, carrots, and artichokes and cook for a few more minutes. Stir through the split peas to coat. Increase the heat and pour in the cider, let it bubble for a minute, then add the stock and bring to the boil. Reduce to a simmer and add the hams to the casserole, tucking them down as much as possible.

3 Cover and put in the oven for about 1 hour, or until the split peas are soft. Check occasionally that it's not drying out too much, topping up with hot water if needed. By now the ham meat should slide easily off the bone, so remove it with a fork and stir it into the casserole. Taste and season if necessary, and serve with some fresh crusty bread.

greek stifado

Stifado is a rich mix of beef and onions in a red wine sauce.

🥄 30 MINS   🍲 2 HRS 15 MINS   ❄️ FREEZABLE

SERVES 4-6

3 tbsp olive oil

1.1kg (2½lb) chuck steak, cut into bite-sized pieces

salt and freshly ground black pepper

175ml (6fl oz) red wine

2 tbsp red wine vinegar

1 cinnamon stick

1 tsp ground cloves

½ tsp grated nutmeg

3 garlic cloves, finely chopped

4 tomatoes, roughly chopped

1 tbsp tomato purée

600ml (1 pint) hot vegetable stock

a few sprigs of thyme

knob of butter

500g (1lb 2oz) shallots, peeled and left whole

1 Preheat the oven to 180°C (350°F/ Gas 4). Heat 2 tbsp of the oil in a large flameproof casserole over a medium-high heat. Add the meat, season with salt and pepper, and cook for 6 minutes, or until lightly browned. Increase the heat and add the wine and vinegar. Cook for a couple of minutes, then stir in the cinnamon stick, cloves, nutmeg, and garlic and cook for a further minute.

2 Add the tomatoes, tomato purée, and then the stock. Bring the sauce to the boil, then add the thyme, cover with the lid, and cook in the oven for about 1 hour. Check occasionally that it's not drying out, topping up with a little hot water if needed.

3 Heat the remaining oil with the butter in a heavy-based pan over a medium heat, add the shallots, and cook for 6–8 minutes until golden. Stir the onions into the stew, cover, and return to the oven. Reduce the temperature to 160°C (325°F/Gas 3) and cook for a further hour, checking occasionally that it's not drying out. Remove the cinnamon and thyme, and serve with mashed potatoes or baby roast potatoes with rosemary.

jugged hare

This traditional, rich, blood-thickened stew can also be made with venison. In France, it is called a civet.

🥄 40 MINS PLUS MARINATING   🍲 2-3 HRS

SERVES 6

2 tbsp wine vinegar

1 hare, about 2-3kg (4½-6½lb) total weight, prepared and jointed (liver and blood reserved)

60g (2oz) butter

250g (9oz) unsmoked lardons, or diced salt pork

15 baby onions or small shallots, peeled and left whole

2 tbsp plain flour

300ml (10fl oz) red wine

600ml (1 pint) chicken stock

salt and freshly ground black pepper

For the marinade

1 onion, sliced

bunch of fresh herbs

½ glass white wine

½ glass wine vinegar

½ glass olive oil

1 Stir the vinegar into the blood and set aside in a covered dish with the liver. Put the hare joints in a bowl. Mix the marinade ingredients and pour over the meat. Cover and leave in a cool place for 12-24 hours, turning the joints over once or twice.

2 Remove the joints and pat dry with kitchen paper; reserve the marinade. Melt the butter in a large pan and cook the lardons and onions. Add the joints and brown gently all over. Blend in the flour. Pour in the wine and stock. Season, bring to the boil, reduce the heat, cover, and simmer for 2-3 hours until tender.

3 Mash the liver into the blood with 2-3 tbsp of the reserved marinade and pass through a fine sieve. Add to the stew and keep stirring as the sauce thickens. Do not allow it to boil. Taste, add more salt, pepper, and marinade if needed, and serve.

beef and greens

Tender beef with robust kale is a great combination. The chilli hint is subtle, but there is just enough to add interest to the dish, while the anchovies are added to enrich the sauce.

🥣 15 MINS 　 🍲 2 HRS 45 MINS 　 ❄ FREEZABLE

SERVES 6

3–4 tbsp olive oil

1.25kg (2¾lb) chuck beef, cut into bite-sized pieces

salt and freshly ground black pepper

1 tsp paprika

1 tbsp plain flour

2 onions, roughly chopped

3 garlic cloves, finely chopped

1 green chilli, deseeded and finely chopped

8 salted anchovies

4 large carrots, roughly chopped

250ml (9fl oz) red wine

900ml (1½ pints) hot beef or vegetable stock

4 large potatoes, peeled and roughly chopped

200g (7oz) curly kale, stems trimmed and leaves roughly chopped

1 Preheat the oven to 160°C (325°F/Gas 3). Heat 1 tbsp of the oil in a large flameproof casserole over a medium heat. Season the meat with salt, pepper, and paprika, and sprinkle over the flour. Add the beef pieces to the casserole (in batches and with extra oil, if necessary) and cook for 5–8 minutes until they are browned all over. Remove with a slotted spoon and set aside.

2 Add the remaining oil to the casserole, add the onions, and cook for 3–4 minutes until soft. Then stir in the garlic, chilli, and anchovies, and cook for a minute. Add the carrots and cook for a further 2–3 minutes.

3 Pour in the wine and bring to the boil, stirring and scraping up the bits from the bottom of the casserole. Pour in the stock and bring back to the boil. Add the meat and potatoes, cover, and cook in the oven for 1½ hours.

Check occasionally that it's not drying out, topping up with a little hot water if needed. Add the kale and cook for a further 1 hour, again checking that it doesn't dry out too much. Serve while piping hot with some crusty bread.

variation

pork with cavolo nero

Prepare in the same way, but use 1kg (2¼lb) diced pork instead of beef. Add 250ml (9fl oz) white wine instead of red, and use 200g (7oz) shredded cavolo nero instead of the kale.

beef and orange daube

Boef en daube is a classic beef stew in red wine from Provence in France. It is enhanced with the tang of orange zest and enriched with anchovies that "melt" into the sauce.

🥣 30 MINS   🍲 2 HRS   ❄️ FREEZABLE

SERVES 4

2 tbsp olive oil

500g (1lb 2oz) stewing steak, such as chuck steak or silverside, cut into bite-sized pieces

½ tbsp plain flour

salt and freshly ground black pepper

1 bay leaf

25g (scant 1oz) butter

2 onions, finely sliced

zest and juice of 1 orange

6 salted anchovies, finely chopped

150ml (5fl oz) red wine

550g (1¼lb) chestnut mushrooms, quartered

600ml (1 pint) hot vegetable stock

small handful of thyme, finely chopped

1 Preheat the oven to 150°C (300°F/Gas 2). Heat 2 tbsp of the oil in a cast-iron pan over a medium heat, toss the meat in the flour, season well with salt and pepper, then add to the pan with the bay leaf and stir. Cook, stirring occasionally, for 8–10 minutes, or until the meat is no longer pink. Add the butter and cook for 5 minutes, or until the meat is golden. Remove with a slotted spoon and set aside.

2 Add the remaining oil to the pan, then add the onions and cook over a low heat for 6–8 minutes, or until soft. Add the orange zest, raise the heat a little, then add the orange juice and stir to loosen all the sticky bits from the bottom of the pan.

3 Stir in the anchovies, then add the wine and simmer over a high heat for 2 minutes. Stir in the mushrooms, add the stock and thyme, and season with salt and pepper. Return the steak to the pan, cover with a lid, then put in the oven for 2 hours, or until the meat is meltingly tender.

turkey and mushroom casserole with dumplings

A filling stew with porcini mushrooms, celery, and carrots.

🥣 30 MINS PLUS SOAKING   🍲 1 HR 30 MINS   ❄️ FREEZABLE

SERVES 4

25g (scant 1oz) dried porcini mushrooms

knob of butter

1 tbsp olive oil

675g (1½lb) turkey breast, cut into bite-sized pieces

1 onion, finely chopped

2 garlic cloves, grated or finely chopped

1 bay leaf

a few sprigs of rosemary, roughly chopped

salt and freshly ground black pepper

3 carrots, cut into chunky pieces

3 celery sticks, cut into chunky pieces

1 tbsp plain flour

100ml (3½fl oz) dry sherry

600ml (1 pint) hot chicken stock

small handful of flat-leaf parsley, finely chopped (optional)

For the dumplings

225g (8oz) self-raising flour

125g (4½oz) shredded suet

1 tbsp dried oregano

1 Put the porcini in a bowl, cover with 300ml (10fl oz) hot water, and leave to soak for 30 minutes. Preheat the oven to 200°C (400°F/Gas 6). Heat the butter and half the oil in a cast-iron pan, add the turkey, and cook over a medium heat, turning the pieces frequently, for 5–8 minutes or until golden all over. Remove with a slotted spoon and set aside.

2 Heat the remaining oil in the pan, add the onions, and cook for 6–8 minutes, or until soft and translucent. Stir in the garlic, bay leaf, and rosemary and season with salt and pepper, then add the carrots and celery and cook for 5 minutes. Stir through the flour and cook for 2 minutes.

3 Raise the heat, add the sherry, and boil for a few minutes stirring continually until the alcohol evaporates, then pour in the stock. Drain the porcini (reserving the liquid) and add to the pan. Strain the soaking liquid, then add this as well. Return the turkey to the pan, cover, and put in the oven for 1 hour.

4 Meanwhile, make the dumplings. Put the flour, suet, and oregano in a mixing bowl with a pinch of salt, then add about 150ml (5fl oz) cold water a little at a time, until the mixture forms a dough. Flour your hands and shape the dough into 16 dumplings. Add these to the pan for the last 30 minutes of cooking. To serve, sprinkle over the parsley, if using.

beef with barley and mushrooms

Barley adds body and an earthy flavour to this dish. If you can find them, use wild mushrooms as a treat.

🥣 30–35 MINS　　🍲 2 HRS 15 MINS – 2 HRS 30 MINS

SERVES 6

1½ tbsp vegetable oil

675g (1½lb) braising steak, in 5cm (2in) dice

2 large onions, thinly sliced

salt and freshly ground black pepper

1 bouquet garni (5–6 sprigs of parsley, 2–3 sprigs of thyme, and 1 bay leaf)

1 litre (1¾ pints) beef stock, plus more if needed

1 large carrot, sliced

2 celery sticks, peeled and sliced

100g (3½oz) pearl barley

250g (9oz) mushrooms, trimmed and sliced

2 sprigs of flat-leaf parsley, leaves picked and finely chopped (optional)

1 Preheat the oven to 180°C (350°F/Gas 4). Heat the oil in a casserole on top of the stove until hot. Add half the beef (it should sear when it hits the pan) and brown well. Transfer to a bowl. Brown the remaining beef in the same way.

2 Add the onions with a little salt and pepper. Cook over a medium heat, stirring for 5–7 minutes, until lightly browned. Return the beef and add the bouquet garni, salt, and pepper. Pour in the stock and stir.

3 Cover the casserole and transfer to the heated oven. Cook, stirring occasionally, for about 1½ hours, then add the carrots, celery, and barley. Stir in more stock or water, if necessary, to keep the casserole moist.

4 Cover and continue cooking for 40–45 minutes longer, until the meat and vegetables are tender when pierced. The barley should be tender, but still slightly chewy. Stir in the mushrooms about 10 minutes before the end of the cooking time.

5 Discard the bouquet garni and taste the stew for seasoning. Serve in warmed individual bowls, sprinkled with the parsley, if using, and some fresh crusty bread.

lamb shanks in red wine

Perfect for a chilly day. You will need to start this dish at least 1 day ahead to have enough time to marinate the lamb.

🥣 50 MINS PLUS MARINATING　　🍲 2 HRS 45 MINS

SERVES 6

2 tsp black peppercorns, crushed

2 tsp juniper berries, crushed

4 shallots, roughly chopped

2 garlic cloves, peeled

2 onions, quartered

2 carrots, roughly sliced

1 bouquet garni (5–6 sprigs of parsley, 2–3 sprigs of thyme, and 1 bay leaf)

2 tbsp red wine vinegar

750ml (1¼ pints) dry red wine

6 lamb shanks, total weight 1.8kg (4lb), trimmed of excess fat and sinew

3 tbsp vegetable oil

30g (1oz) plain flour

750ml (1¼ pints) beef stock, plus more if needed

salt and freshly ground black pepper

30g (1oz) butter

1 celeriac, about 500g (1lb 2oz), diced

250g (9oz) mushrooms, quartered

3 tbsp redcurrant jelly

1 Put the peppercorns, juniper berries, shallots, garlic, onions, carrots, bouquet garni, and vinegar in a pan. Add the red wine, bring to the boil, and simmer for 2 minutes. Transfer to a shallow dish and set aside to cool completely. Once the marinade is cold, add the shanks and coat in the mix. Cover and refrigerate, turning occasionally, for 1–2 days.

2 Preheat the oven to 180°C (350°F/Gas 4). Dry the shanks on kitchen paper. Reserve the bouquet garni. Drain the vegetables in a sieve over a bowl. Reserve the vegetables and marinade separately. Heat half the oil in a casserole, add half the shanks, and brown well over a high heat for 3–5 minutes. Repeat with the other shanks. Add the vegetables and cook for 5–7 minutes until they start to brown. Add the flour and stir for 3–5 minutes. Add the reserved marinade, then the lamb with any juices, bouquet garni, stock, salt, and pepper. Cover and cook in the oven for 2–2¼ hours, until tender. Add more stock if needed.

3 Melt the butter in a frying pan, add the celeriac, season, and cook until tender. Transfer to a bowl. Add the mushrooms to the pan and repeat. Transfer the shanks to a plate and keep warm. Ladle the sauce into a sieve over a large pan, reserving some shallot and carrot. Press the rest with a ladle to extract the juices.

4 Whisk the redcurrant jelly into the sauce with plenty of black pepper. Bring to the boil and simmer for 20–30 minutes, until reduced by half. Add the celeriac, mushrooms, reserved carrot and shallot, and shanks. Heat until very hot, about 5–10 minutes, and serve.

braised cauliflower with chilli and coriander

A few spices can turn the humble cauliflower into something far more interesting. This dish can be served simply with some buttery basmati rice or as part of an Indian meal.

🥣 10 MINS   🍲 10 MINS

SERVES 4

400g (14oz) cauliflower, outer leaves removed, chopped into small florets

2 dried red chillies

1 tsp cumin seeds

2 tbsp sunflower oil

1 tsp black mustard seeds

½ tsp turmeric

2 garlic cloves, crushed

knob of butter

sea salt

2 tbsp coriander leaves, finely chopped

1 Blanch the cauliflower in salted boiling water for 1–2 minutes, drain, and rinse under cold water.

2 Grind together the chillies and cumin seeds in a mortar and pestle until roughly crushed. Heat the oil in a large, deep frying pan or wok,

and add the chilli and cumin seeds, mustard seeds, turmeric, and garlic. Cook gently for 1 minute until the mustard seeds start to pop.

3 Add the cauliflower and enough water so that it covers the bottom of the pan (about 6 tbsp). Bring the water to the boil and cover the pan or wok. Turn the heat down and simmer the cauliflower for 3–5 minutes, until almost cooked through.

4 Uncover the pan or wok and turn up the heat. Allow the water to cook off, turning the cauliflower all the time. When all the water has evaporated (about 5–6 minutes), add the butter and mix well until it melts. Season with sea salt and sprinkle with coriander before serving.

fruity lamb shanks

Lamb works very well with fruit, and the prunes and apple in this recipe are no exception. They add a piquant flavour.

🥣 15 MINS   🍲 3 HRS 15 MINS   ❄ FREEZABLE

SERVES 4

4 tbsp olive oil

4 lamb shanks

1 tbsp plain flour

250ml (9fl oz) white wine

1 large onion, sliced

salt and freshly ground black pepper

3 garlic cloves, finely chopped

1 tsp fennel seeds

a few sprigs of thyme

2 bay leaves

1 celeriac, peeled and chopped into bite-sized pieces

1 cooking apple, peeled, cored, and diced

200g (7oz) soft prunes, stoned and left whole

175ml (6fl oz) fresh orange juice

900ml (1½ pints) hot vegetable stock

1 Preheat the oven to 150°C (300°C/ Gas 2). Heat half the oil in a large flameproof casserole over a medium-high heat. Toss the shanks in the flour. Cook one or two at a time in the oil until golden on all sides, then set aside in a bowl. Add the wine to the casserole, increase the heat, let it simmer, and pour over the lamb. Wipe the casserole with kitchen paper.

2 Heat a little more oil over a medium heat, add the onion, and cook for 3–4 minutes until soft. Season with salt and pepper, then stir through the garlic, fennel seeds, thyme, bay leaves, and celeriac, and cook for about 5 minutes, adding more oil if necessary, until just turning golden. Add the apple and prunes, season, and cook for 1–2 minutes. Return the lamb shanks and sauce to the casserole, add the orange juice and stock, and bring to the boil.

3 Reduce to a simmer, cover, and cook in the oven for 3–3½ hours until the lamb falls off the bone, topping up with a little hot water if needed. Serve with creamy mashed potatoes.

pork normandy

This casserole of tart Bramley apples and creamy, mustardy pork makes a welcome change from heavy wintry stews.

🥣 30 MINS   🍲 1 HR

SERVES 4

1 tbsp olive oil

knob of butter

675g (1½lb) lean pork, cut into bite-sized pieces

1 onion, finely chopped

1 tbsp Dijon mustard

2 garlic cloves, grated or finely chopped

3 sticks of celery, finely chopped

3 carrots, finely chopped

½ tbsp rosemary leaves, finely chopped

1 large Bramley apple, peeled and roughly chopped

150ml (5fl oz) dry cider

100ml (3½fl oz) double cream

150ml (5fl oz) hot light chicken stock

½ tsp black peppercorns

1 Preheat the oven to 180°C (350°F/ Gas 4). Heat the oil and butter in a cast-iron pan, add the pork, and cook

over a medium heat for 6–8 minutes, or until golden brown on all sides. Remove with a slotted spoon and set aside.

2 Add the onions and cook over a low heat for 5 minutes, or until soft and translucent. Stir in the mustard, add the garlic, celery, carrots, and rosemary, and cook over a low heat, stirring often, for 10 minutes or until tender. Add the apple and cook for a further 5 minutes.

3 Pour in the cider, then raise the heat and boil for 1–2 minutes while the alcohol evaporates. Return the pork to the pan and pour in the cream and stock. Stir in the peppercorns, bring to the boil, then cover with a lid and put in the oven to cook for 1 hour, or until the sauce has reduced and the pork is tender. Serve with fluffy rice or creamy mashed potato.

braised oxtail with clementine and star anise

Rich and robust, oxtail makes an interesting change to beef, and braising it very slowly tenderizes it to the full. Prunes and clementines are a tasty addition to this stew, as their fruity sweetness and texture complement the meat.

🥣 20 MINS   🍲 3 HRS 15 MINS   ❄ FREEZABLE

SERVES 4–6

2 oxtails, about 1.35kg (3lb) each, cut into bite-sized pieces

salt and freshly ground black pepper

2 tbsp olive oil

2 red onions, sliced

3 garlic clove, finely chopped

pinch of dried chilli flakes

350ml (12fl oz) red wine

4 star anise

handful of black peppercorns

1 bay leaf

8 soft prunes, stoned and chopped

900ml (1½ pints) hot beef stock

4 clementines or 2 oranges, peeled and sliced into rings

small bunch of curly parsley leaves, finely chopped

1 Preheat the oven to 150°C (300°F/ Gas 2). Season the oxtail with salt and pepper. Heat half the oil in a large flameproof casserole over a medium heat, then add the meat in batches and fry for 8–10 minutes until browned on all sides. Remove with a slotted spoon and set aside.

2 Heat the remaining oil in the casserole over a medium heat, add the onions, and cook for 3–4 minutes to soften. Stir through the garlic and chilli flakes, then pour in the wine and let it simmer for about 5 minutes until slightly reduced. Return the meat to the casserole and add the star anise, peppercorns, bay leaf, and prunes, and pour over just enough stock to cover the meat.

3 Bring to the boil, then reduce to a simmer, add the remaining stock, cover, and put in the oven for about 3 hours. Check occasionally that it's not drying out, and top up with a little hot water if needed. Add the clementines or oranges for the last 30 minutes of cooking, and leave the casserole uncovered to allow the liquid to thicken slightly. Stir it occasionally to keep the oxtail moist and coated with the gravy. When ready, the meat will fall away from the bone. Remove the bone and discard it together with the bay leaf and star anise. Serve on a bed of pasta, sprinkled with the parsley.

variation

braised oxtail with jerusalem artichokes

Prepare in the same way, but add 250g (9oz) Jerusalem artichokes, scrubbed or peeled and cut into chunks, and 2 sliced carrots to the mixture before cooking. Omit the star anise, chilli flakes, and clementines. Add 1 tbsp brandy with the red wine. Cook as before, but serve spooned over fluffy mashed potatoes instead of the pasta.

sautéed liver and onions

This delicious recipe is a classic Venetian dish. The sweet, caramelized onions are the star of this meal and can be cooked the night before if you want to get ahead.

🥣 15–20 MINS   🍲 1 HR

SERVES 6

90ml (3fl oz) olive oil

1kg (2¼lb) large onions, sliced

salt and freshly ground black pepper

750g (1lb 10oz) calf's liver

For the mashed potatoes

635g (1lb 6oz) potatoes, peeled

4 tbsp milk

60g (2oz) butter

1 Heat two-thirds of the oil in a frying pan. Add the onions and a little salt and pepper and cover with foil. Cook over a low heat, stirring occasionally, for 25–30 minutes until very soft.

2 Remove the foil from the onions, increase the heat to medium-high, and cook, stirring constantly, for 5–7 minutes until caramelized and golden but not burned. Transfer to a bowl with a slotted spoon, leaving any excess oil in the pan.

3 Meanwhile, cut the potatoes into pieces. Put in a saucepan of salted water, cover, and bring to the boil. Simmer for 15–20 minutes until tender. Drain thoroughly and mash with a potato masher. Heat the milk in a small saucepan, add the butter, season, and mix. Gradually add the hot milk to the potatoes, beating until light and fluffy. Taste for seasoning and keep warm.

4 Slice the liver about 5mm (¼in) thick and season. Add the remaining oil to the frying pan and heat over a high heat. Add half the liver and cook for 45–60 seconds on each side, until just browned; the liver should be pink in the centre. Transfer to a plate and keep warm. Repeat with the rest of the liver. Return the onions to the pan with all the liver and stir quickly over a high heat for 30–60 seconds until very hot. Season with salt and pepper and serve at once on warmed plates with the mashed potatoes.

duck in orange sauce

A superb French classic of rich wild duck with a bitter orange sauce. It also works well with domestic duck.

🥣 10 MINS   🍲 2 HRS

SERVES 4

60g (2oz) butter

75g (2½oz) plain flour

1 litre (1¾ pints) hot game stock

1 wild duck, about 1kg (2¼lb)

2 Seville (bitter) oranges

50g (1¾oz) sugar

3 tbsp red wine vinegar

1 Melt the butter in a saucepan. When it turns golden brown, stir in the flour. Gradually whisk in the stock until smooth. Bring to the boil, then reduce the heat and simmer for about 1 hour, or until reduced by half.

2 Meanwhile, preheat the oven to 200°C (400°F/Gas 6). Prick the skin of the duck with a fork and season with salt, place breast-side down on a rack in a roasting tin, and roast in the oven for 30 minutes. Turn the duck over and roast for a further 30 minutes. Remove from the oven and, when cool enough to handle, remove the legs and breasts. Slice the breast meat and joint the legs, if desired. Then set aside in a warm place to rest.

3 Use a peeler to pare the zest off the oranges and cut it into fine strips. Blanch in boiling water for 5 minutes, then drain; reserve the zest. Squeeze the juice from the oranges.

4 Heat the sugar in a small saucepan until it melts and starts to caramelize. Add the vinegar (add with caution, as it can spit) and dissolve the caramel – this takes a few minutes. Add to the thickened game stock together with the orange juice and stir to mix. Add most of the strips of orange zest, reserving the rest as a garnish.

5 Warm the duck pieces gently in the orange sauce, being careful not to overcook them. Garnish with the remaining orange zest before serving.

chicken broth with celeriac and orange

This main meal soup has a great balance of flavours of earthy celeriac, chicken, and aromatic orange giving an extra tang.

🥣 15 MINS   🍲 1 HR   ❄ FREEZABLE

SERVES 4–6

1 tbsp olive oil

1 onion, finely chopped

1 bay leaf

salt and freshly ground black pepper

2 garlic cloves, finely chopped

zest of 1 orange and juice of ½ orange

a few sprigs of oregano, leaves picked

1 celeriac, peeled and cut into small chunks

1 litre (1¾ pints) hot chicken stock

4 skinless chicken breasts

4 sprigs of flat-leaf parsley, finely chopped, to serve

1 Heat the oil in a large heavy-based pan over a medium heat, add the onion and bay leaf, and cook for 3–4 minutes until the onion begins to soften. Season with salt and pepper, then add the garlic, orange zest, and oregano leaves, and cook for a few seconds. Stir in the celeriac and orange juice, scraping up the bits from the bottom of the pan. Then pour in the stock, add the chicken breasts, and bring the broth to the boil.

2 Reduce to a simmer and cook gently for 20–30 minutes, or until the chicken breasts are cooked. Remove the chicken with a slotted spoon and set aside until cool enough to handle, then shred into chunky pieces using your hands or two forks.

3 Continue simmering the stock for a further 15 minutes or so, topping up with a little hot water if needed. Taste and adjust the seasoning if needed and remove the bay leaf. Return the shredded chicken to the pan and stir. Serve in warmed bowls, garnished with parsley.

beef and ale cobbler

Making use of a host of winter vegetables, this hearty cobbler is great for feeding a crowd. The filling can be prepared days ahead and the whole dish needs no additional attention once it has gone into the oven.

🥣 40 MINS 　　 🍲 2 HRS 30 MINS - 3 HRS 15 MINS 　　 ❄ FREEZABLE

SPECIAL EQUIPMENT ▪ 5cm (2in) pastry cutter

SERVES 4

4 tbsp olive oil

2 onions, finely chopped

1 celery stick, finely diced

1 leek, finely sliced

150g (5½oz) button mushrooms, wiped, halved or quartered, if needed

600g (1lb 5oz) stewing steak, such as chuck, cut into 3cm (1¼in) chunks

2 tbsp plain flour

sea salt and freshly ground black pepper

500ml (16fl oz) dark ale, such as stout or porter

300ml (10fl oz) beef stock

1 bouquet garni

1 tbsp sugar

2 large carrots, cut into 2cm (¾in) chunks

For the cobbler

300g (10oz) self-raising flour

1 tsp baking powder

½ tsp salt

125g (4½oz) unsalted butter, chilled and diced

1 tbsp finely chopped flat-leaf parsley

3 tbsp horseradish sauce or horseradish cream

2-4 tbsp milk

1 egg, beaten, for glazing

1 In a large ovenproof casserole, heat 2 tbsp of the oil and fry the onion, celery, and leek for about 5 minutes until soft and translucent. Add the mushrooms and fry for 3-4 minutes until they begin to colour in places. Remove the vegetables with a slotted spoon and set aside.

2 Toss the steak in 2 tbsp seasoned flour. Heat the remaining oil in the casserole and fry the meat, a few pieces at a time, until browned on all sides. Remove the meat as it cooks and add it to the vegetables. Return the meat to the casserole with the vegetables, and cover with the ale, stock, the bouquet garni, sugar, and carrots, and bring to the boil. Reduce the heat to its lowest setting, cover, and cook for 2-2½ hours, until the meat is tender. Check it from time to time and add a little water if it is drying out.

3 Preheat the oven to 200°C (400°F/ Gas 6). Sift together the flour, baking powder, and salt. Using your fingertips, rub in the butter until the mixture resembles fine crumbs. Add the parsley. Whisk the horseradish sauce and milk, and use it to bind the dry ingredients to form a soft dough.

4 Roll out the dough on a floured work surface to about 2cm (¾in) thick. Using a pastry cutter, cut out circles. Re-roll the offcuts and re-cut until the dough is used up. When the stew is cooked, remove the bouquet garni and top the stew with the disks of cobbler dough. Overlap them slightly so that there are very few gaps where the filling can be seen.

5 Brush the cobbler tops with beaten egg and bake in the middle of the oven for 30-40 minutes until the pastry is puffed up and golden brown. Remove the casserole dish from the oven and let the stew rest for 5 minutes before serving.

venison stew

This recipe uses fresh and dried mushrooms for added flavour.

🥣 **15 MINS PLUS MARINATING**　🍲 **2 HRS 15 MINS**

SERVES 4–6

500ml (16fl oz) red wine

3 tbsp olive oil

1 tbsp crushed juniper berries

2 sprigs of rosemary

1.1kg (2½lb) venison, cut into bite-sized pieces

2 tbsp plain flour, seasoned

1 onion, roughly chopped

200g (7oz) pancetta, diced

30g (1oz) dried porcini mushrooms, soaked in warm water for 30 minutes

zest of 1 orange, coarsely chopped

900ml (1½ pints) hot vegetable stock

knob of butter

250g (9oz) chestnut mushrooms, halved

salt and freshly ground black pepper

1 Mix the wine, 2 tbsp oil, the juniper berries, and 1 sprig of rosemary in a large bowl. Immerse the meat in the marinade, cover, and refrigerate for 1 hour or overnight. Drain the meat, reserving the liquid and rosemary. Heat the remaining oil in a large flameproof casserole over a medium-high heat. Toss the venison in the flour and cook in batches until golden. Remove and set aside.

2 Reduce the heat, add the onion and pancetta, and cook for 5 minutes. Drain the porcini and strain the juice; add them and a little juice to the casserole with the orange zest, wine marinade, and rosemary. Add the stock and boil. Add the meat, reduce to a simmer, cover, and cook on a low heat for 1½–2 hours until tender. Top up with the reserved porcini juice or hot water to keep the meat covered. Heat the butter in a frying pan, cook the chestnut mushrooms until golden, then stir into the stew for the last 30 minutes. Taste and season, if needed. Serve with polenta.

game casserole

A highly flavoured stew with mushrooms, celery, and carrots.

🥣 **30 MINS**　🍲 **1 HR 15 MINS**　❄ **FREEZABLE**

SERVES 4

675g (1½lb) (boned weight) mixed game, such as pheasant, venison, and duck, cut into bite-sized pieces

plain flour, for dusting

salt and freshly ground black pepper

1 tbsp olive oil

1 tbsp brandy

1 onion, finely chopped

2 garlic cloves, grated or finely chopped

2 celery sticks, finely diced

2 carrots, finely diced

1 bouquet garni

275g (9½oz) chestnut mushrooms, quartered

1 glass of dry white wine

2 tsp redcurrant jelly

750ml (1¼ pints) hot chicken stock

1 Preheat the oven to 180°C (350°F/ Gas 4). Dust the meat lightly with a little flour, then season well with salt and pepper. Heat half the oil in a cast-iron pan, add the meat, and cook over a medium heat, stirring occasionally, for 6–8 minutes, or until browned on all sides. Remove with a slotted spoon and set aside.

2 Add the brandy to the pan and stir to deglaze, then add the rest of the oil, if needed, and the onions, and cook over a low heat for 6 minutes, or until soft. Stir in the garlic, celery, carrots, and bouquet garni and cook over a low heat, stirring occasionally, for 8 minutes, or until tender.

3 Stir in the mushrooms, then increase the heat, add the wine, and allow to boil for 2 minutes while the alcohol evaporates. Stir in the redcurrant jelly, then pour in the stock. Cover with a lid and put in the oven to cook for 1 hour, or until the meat is tender. Top up with hot water during the cooking if needed. Serve with creamy mashed potato.

venison casserole with pears

Pear makes the perfect partner to venison. This stew is tasty served with steamed Savoy cabbage with butter.

🥣 **30 MINS PLUS MARINATING**　🍲 **1 HR 45 MINS**

SERVES 6

2 tsp black peppercorns, crushed

2 tsp juniper berries, crushed

4 shallots, roughly chopped

2 garlic cloves, peeled and left whole

2 onions, quartered

2 carrots, roughly sliced

1 bouquet garni

2 tbsp red wine vinegar

750ml (1¼ pints) dry red wine

1kg (2¼lb) stewing venison (leg or shoulder), fat trimmed, cut into 4cm (1½in) cubes

3 tbsp vegetable oil

30g (1oz) plain flour

750ml (1¼ pints) hot beef stock

salt and freshly ground black pepper

4 ripe pears, peeled, cored, and chopped

3 tbsp redcurrant jelly

1 Put the spices, vegetables, bouquet garni, vinegar, and wine in a pan and bring to the boil, then simmer for about 2 minutes. Transfer to a shallow dish and leave to cool. Add the venison, stir to coat evenly, cover, and refrigerate for 6–8 hours, turning the meat occasionally.

2 Preheat the oven to 180°C (350°F/ Gas 4). Remove the venison and pat dry with kitchen paper. Strain the marinade, reserving the bouquet garni, vegetables, and marinade. Heat half the oil in a large flameproof casserole over a high heat, add the venison, and cook in batches for 3–5 minutes until brown all over. Transfer to a bowl. Heat the remaining oil over a medium heat, add the reserved vegetables, and cook for 5–7 minutes. Add the flour and cook, stirring, for 3–5 minutes until it has been absorbed. Stir in the marinade, venison, bouquet garni, stock, and seasoning. Cover and cook in the oven for 1¼–1½ hours until tender. Stir in the pears and redcurrant jelly, cook for 6–8 minutes until the pears are tender, and serve.

Season's best **venison**

Venison is the meat of all species of deer. They are hunted wild in season, which varies according to breed and gender, but most are available from autumn through to late winter. Deer are also responsibly farmed. Dark red, the meat is extremely lean, so much lower in saturated fat than most meat. Its coarse texture and mild, sweet flavour work well with cream, ginger, fennel, cabbage, pears, chocolate, and red wine for warming seasonal dishes.

Fillet or tenderloin The boned-out saddle (back) yields the loin and fillet muscles. These two prime cuts are often confused in recipes, with the loin erroneously called fillet, but cooking times are very different, as loin is at least twice as thick as fillet; also, the cuts from different species vary in size.

The fillet muscle tapers at one end; the other end may have a thicker muscle attached. The loin muscle does not taper.

Diced venison Stir-fry, grill, or stew diced haunch. Diced shoulder and shin are best stewed, but should not be mixed together as they cook differently.

Rolled haunch (leg) The haunch from small species of deer may be roasted whole or boned, or sliced into steaks. Larger haunches can be cooked on the bone, but are usually parted into individual muscles or pavés. These may be rolled and tied for roasting, or sliced into steaks.

Venison haunch is as lean as skinless chicken. Roasts should be served pink or they will be dry.

essentials

cuts available

Cuts include haunch/back leg, saddle, loin (whole and steaks), fillet/tenderloin, shoulder, shin, mince, sausages.

buy Avoid any excessively dark, bruised meat. Prime cuts come from the haunch and saddle. Allow about 175g (6oz) of boneless meat per portion.

store If pre-packed, follow the storage instructions. If not, keep covered on a plate at the bottom of the fridge for up to 4 days.

cook Prime cuts can be eaten raw as carpaccio. Roast prime joints and fry steaks, then rest them well to serve pink. Shoulder from young and small deer can also be roasted. Braise or stew venison from older deer and all forequarter cuts; joints to be braised should be larded. Use minced venison for burgers and meatballs, pasta sauces, pies, and other made dishes.

preserve Smoke and freeze fresh meat.

recipe ideas

Venison, shallot, and chestnut hotpot p388

Venison stew p452

Venison Wellingtons p282

Viltgryta p314

duck legs with cabbage, pine nuts, and raisins

Duck legs are very succulent with lots of tasty meat on them. They can, however, be fatty so the addition of redcurrant jelly and raisins helps balance this. Pine nuts give an added twist.

🥄 15 MINS 🍲 2 HRS 30 MINS

SERVES 4-6

6 duck legs

2 red onions, roughly chopped

2 garlic cloves, finely chopped

a few sprigs of thyme

1 bay leaf

1 tbsp redcurrant jelly

600ml (1 pint) hot chicken stock

salt and freshly ground black pepper

30g (1oz) raisins

30g (1oz) pine nuts, toasted

1 Savoy cabbage, cored and chopped into eighths

1 Preheat the oven to 180°C (350°F/Gas 4). Heat a large flameproof casserole over a medium heat, add the duck legs, and cook for 15-20 minutes, turning them as you go, until they begin to turn golden. Remove them from the casserole, set aside, and pour off any fat.

2 Add the onions, garlic, thyme, and bay leaf and cook for 5 minutes, then add the redcurrant jelly and cook for a few more minutes. Return the duck legs to the casserole and nestle them into the onion mixture, skin-side up. Pour over the stock, bring to the boil, then reduce to a simmer. Season with salt and pepper, cover with the lid, and put in the oven for 2 hours. Check occasionally that it's not drying out, topping up with a little hot water if needed.

3 Add the raisins, pine nuts, and cabbage to the casserole for the last 30 minutes of cooking. Discard the bay leaf, taste, and adjust the seasoning. Serve with creamy mashed potatoes and some chilli jelly on the side.

beef tagine with orange and bay leaves

Sweet, slightly acidic orange cuts through the richness of the beef in this robust Middle Eastern-style dish and blends beautifully with cinnamon and nutmeg spices.

🥄 30 MINS 🍲 1 HR 30 MINS ❄ FREEZABLE

SERVES 4

1½ tbsp olive oil

675g (1½lb) stewing steak, cut into bite-sized pieces

salt and freshly ground black pepper

1 small glass of dry white wine

2 bay leaves

900ml (1½ pints) hot vegetable stock

2 sticks of cinnamon

a pinch of grated nutmeg

400g can chickpeas, drained and rinsed

1 orange, peeled and sliced into rings

2 tbsp chopped coriander

1 Preheat the oven to 180°C (350°F/Gas 4). Heat the oil in a large cast-iron pan or flameproof casserole, add the meat, season with salt and pepper, and cook over a medium heat, stirring occasionally, for 10 minutes, or until brown on all sides. Carefully add the wine – it will spit – then stir the meat around the pan and allow the liquid to boil for 1–2 minutes while the alcohol evaporates.

2 Add the bay leaves, then pour in the stock. Add the cinnamon and nutmeg, and season again with salt and pepper. Bring to the boil, add the chickpeas, then cover with a lid and put in the oven to cook for 1 hour. Add the orange and cook for a further 30 minutes. Then stir through the chopped coriander and serve with fresh crusty bread.

variation

venison casserole with turnips and prunes

Prepare in the same way, but use 675g (1½lb) diced venison haunch instead of beef, 1 small glass of red wine instead of white, and add 2 diced turnips to the browned meat. Add 8 halved and stoned prunes instead of the orange rings.

lamb with red onions

Red onions have a distinctive red-purple skin and are sweeter and milder than white onions. Choose firm bulbs with even-coloured skins and no signs of sprouting or dampness.

🍲 20 MINS 🍲 2 HRS

SERVES 4

8 red onions, quartered

3 tbsp olive oil

900g (2lb) potatoes, peeled and quartered

salt and freshly ground black pepper

2 tbsp mint sauce

900g (2lb) lamb fillet

1 tbsp balsamic vinegar

1 Preheat the oven to 180°C (350°F/ Gas 4). Put the onions in a large roasting tin and toss with 1 tbsp of the oil. Add the potatoes, toss with the onions, then season well with salt and pepper.

2 Mix the remaining oil with the mint sauce and use to coat the lamb. Add the lamb to the roasting tin, drizzle over the balsamic vinegar, and put in the oven to roast for 1½–2 hours.

3 Remove the lamb and keep warm while it rests for 15 minutes. Slice and serve with the red onion and potato mixture.

variation

lamb with roasted winter vegetables
Prepare in the same way, but use 2 red onions, quartered, 1 small celeriac, 1 small sweet potato and 2 potatoes, peeled and cut in bite-sized chunks instead of all potatoes. Use 2 tbsp redcurrant jelly instead of mint sauce to coat the lamb.

seared duck with five-spice and noodles

Duck breasts make a quick mid-week supper. This dish of rich, spicy duck and noodles is sharpened by fresh orange juice.

🍲 10 MINS 🍲 20 MINS

SERVES 4

4 duck breasts, about 150g (5½oz) each, skin on and scored in a crisscross pattern

2–3 tsp five-spice paste

knob of butter

2 tbsp freshly squeezed orange juice

1 tsp soft brown sugar

250g packet ready-to-wok noodles

handful of coriander, finely chopped

1 Rub the duck breasts in the five-spice paste. Melt the butter in a frying pan over a medium-high heat. Add the duck breasts, skin-side down, and cook for 10 minutes until the skin is golden and crisp. Pour out the fat, turn the breasts over, and cook on the other side for 8 minutes.

2 Remove the meat, cut into slices, and arrange on a warm plate. Pour away any remaining fat, then add the orange juice to the pan along with

the sugar. Simmer for a minute or two, stirring to scrape up the bits from the bottom of the pan.

3 Add the noodles and toss them in the sauce for a couple of minutes. Remove from the heat and stir through the coriander. Serve immediately with the warm duck.

variation

seared duck with red miso, shredded turnip, and noodles
Mix 2 tsp red miso paste with 2 tsp clear honey and a small, crushed garlic clove. Melt a knob of butter over a medium-high heat and fry the duck breasts, skin-side down, for 8–9 minutes. Turn over and cook for a further 7–8 minutes. Brush the miso glaze all over the duck breasts and brown each side for a minute or two. Add a splash of water with the orange juice at step 2 and add a finely shredded turnip with the noodles.

fish fingers with chunky tartare sauce

This familiar family favourite is fresh, simple, and tasty. The fish stays moist and succulent inside its crispy coating, while the tartare sauce adds a little bit of crunchy tang.

🥣 15 MINS   🍲 10 MINS   ❄️ FREEZABLE

SERVES 4

675g (1½lb) thick white fish fillets (loin works best), such as haddock, sustainable cod, or pollack, skinned

1-2 tbsp plain flour

1 egg, lightly beaten

115g (4oz) fresh breadcrumbs, toasted

60g (2oz) Parmesan cheese, finely grated

salt and freshly ground black pepper

3 tbsp tartare sauce

1 tsp capers, rinsed, drained, and chopped

3 gherkins, drained and finely chopped

1 Preheat the oven to 200°C (400°F/ Gas 6). Cut the fish fillets into thick, even strips about 2.5cm (1in) wide; you should end up with about 20 fingers of fish.

2 Tip the flour and egg onto separate plates. Mix the breadcrumbs with the Parmesan cheese and season with salt and pepper. Dredge the fish in the flour, then dip in the egg to coat. Use the breadcrumb mixture to coat each of the fish fingers. Make sure that you coat them well, as it protects the fish while it's cooking.

3 Sit the fish fingers on a lightly oiled baking tray and bake in the oven for 5–8 minutes on each side until golden and cooked through. (Alternatively, you can shallow-fry them in a little sunflower oil if you prefer.)

4 Tip the tartare sauce into a bowl and stir through the capers and gherkins. Serve immediately with the hot fish fingers.

lamb daube

Choose a robust wine that you would happily drink for this lamb daube, and serve the dish with mashed potatoes.

🥣 45-50 MINS PLUS MARINATING   🍲 4 HRS

SERVES 4-6

900g (2lb) boned lamb shoulder, cut into large cubes

300g (10oz) piece of smoked streaky bacon, cut into 5mm (¼in) lardons

400g can chopped tomatoes

2 onions, sliced

2 carrots, sliced

175g (6oz) mushrooms, trimmed and sliced

140g (5oz) pitted green olives

250ml (9fl oz) hot beef stock

For the marinade

1 orange, zest peeled in wide strips

2 garlic cloves, finely chopped

500ml (16fl oz) red wine

2 bay leaves

10 peppercorns

3-4 sprigs each of rosemary, thyme, and parsley

2 tbsp olive oil

salt and freshly ground black pepper

1 Combine the marinade ingredients, except the oil, in a bowl. Add the lamb and mix well. Pour the oil on top and season. Cover and chill in the fridge for 2 hours, or 12 hours if time permits.

2 Preheat the oven to 150°C (300°F/ Gas 2). In a large pan of boiling water, blanch the bacon for 5 minutes. Drain and rinse with cold water. Remove the lamb and dry on kitchen paper. Strain the marinade and reserve it, the bay leaves, and the zest. Put the bacon in a casserole, add the lamb, layer the tomatoes and onions on top, and add the carrots, mushrooms, and olives. Pour in the marinade and stock, season with black pepper, and add the bay leaves and zest. Bring to the boil, cover, and cook in the oven for 3½–4 hours. Add a little hot water if needed. Then remove the bay leaves and zest and serve.

bigos

A Polish dish that includes a variety of meats and cabbage.

🥣 40 MINS   🍲 2 HRS   ❄️ FREEZABLE

SERVES 4

1 small Savoy cabbage, cored, ribs removed, and leaves shredded

salt and freshly ground black pepper

500g (1lb 2oz) sauerkraut, drained

100g (3½oz) smoked bacon, diced

200g (7oz) smoked Polish sausage, sliced

200g (7oz) duck breast or lean venison, cubed

1 large red onion, diced

1 garlic clove, crushed

150g (5½oz) chestnut mushrooms, sliced

½ tsp smoked paprika

1 bay leaf

½ tsp juniper berries

1 tsp dried marjoram

½ tsp caraway seeds, crushed using a pestle and mortar

200ml (7fl oz) red wine

250ml (9fl oz) beef stock

1 Put the cabbage in a large casserole. Cover with boiling water, season, and simmer for 10 minutes. Drain and reserve. Repeat with the sauerkraut, simmering for 5 minutes only. Drain, reserving the sauerkraut and cooking liquid.

2 Fry the bacon in a frying pan over a medium heat until crisp. Remove to a plate lined with kitchen paper. Repeat with the sausage and duck. Fry the onion, garlic, and mushrooms until soft; return the fried meats to the casserole. Stir in the paprika, bay leaf, juniper berries, marjoram, and caraway seeds. Pour in the wine and stock, cover, and simmer for 1 hour.

3 Add the cabbage, cover, and cook for 10 minutes. Stir in the sauerkraut and add some or all of the reserved cooking liquid (so the mixture is like a thick soup). Simmer for 15 minutes, then serve very hot.

perfect fish and chips

Cod in a light beer batter has an extra crispy and delicious crust. Double-fried chips are fluffy within and crisp without. The traditional accompaniment is tartare sauce and the recipe here beats anything you can buy in a jar.

🥄 45-50 MINS PLUS STANDING   🍲 20-25 MINS

SPECIAL EQUIPMENT ▪ deep-fat fryer ▪ electric hand whisk or mixer

SERVES 4

6 potatoes, total weight about 750g (1lb 10oz), peeled

vegetable oil for deep-frying

30g (1oz) plain flour

salt and freshly ground black pepper

4 skinned cod fillets, total weight 750g (1lb 10oz)

1 lemon, cut into wedges, to serve

For the tartare sauce

120ml (4fl oz) mayonnaise

1 hard-boiled egg, coarsely chopped

1 tsp drained capers, chopped

2 gherkins, coarsely chopped

1 small shallot, finely chopped

2-3 sprigs of parsley, leaves picked and chopped

2-3 sprigs of chervil or tarragon, leaves picked and chopped

For the batter

1½ tsp dried yeast (or 9g/⅓oz fresh yeast)

150g (5½oz) plain flour

1 tbsp vegetable oil

175ml (6fl oz) bitter ale

1 egg white

1 For the tartare sauce, mix together the mayonnaise, egg, capers, gherkins, shallot, and herbs, and taste for seasoning. Cover and chill in the fridge until ready to serve.

2 Square off the sides and ends of the potatoes with a knife and cut lengthways into 1cm (½in) sticks. Soak in a bowl of cold water for 30 minutes to remove the starch. Meanwhile, sprinkle the yeast over 4 tbsp warm water and let stand for about 5 minutes until dissolved.

3 For the batter, sift the flour and a little salt into a large bowl and make a well in the centre. Add the yeast

mixture, oil, and two-thirds of the beer; stir to form a smooth paste. Stir in the remaining beer, but don't overmix. Let the batter stand in a warm place for 30-35 minutes until thick and frothy.

4 While the batter is standing, heat the vegetable oil in a deep-fat fryer until it is at 180°C (350°F) on an oil thermometer. Drain the potatoes, transfer to kitchen paper, and pat dry. Dip the empty frying basket in the hot oil (to prevent the potatoes sticking). Lift the basket out of the oil, add the potatoes, and deep-fry for 5-7 minutes, until just tender when pierced with the tip of a knife and starting to brown. Lift out and let drain over the deep fryer, then tip onto a plate lined with kitchen paper.

5 Heat the oil to 190°C (375°F). Put the flour on a plate and season with salt and pepper. Coat the fish with the flour, patting them with your

hands so they are evenly coated. Whisk the egg white in a medium metal bowl with an electric hand whisk or mixer until stiff peaks form. Fold the whisked egg white into the batter with a wooden spoon. Using a 2-pronged fork, dip a piece of fish in the batter, coat it thoroughly, then hold it over the bowl briefly so excess batter can drip off. Deep-fry the fish until golden brown and crisp, about 6-8 minutes depending on the thickness of the fillets. Transfer to a baking sheet lined with kitchen paper, cover with foil, and keep warm. Repeat with the rest of the fish.

6 Put the partially cooked chips back in the frying basket and deep-fry for 1-2 minutes more until very hot and golden brown. Drain on kitchen paper. Serve with lemon wedges, accompanied by the tartare sauce.

Season's best **cod**

Caught throughout the cold waters of the Atlantic and Pacific, cod is an important commercial white fish. As it has been over-fished in some areas, choose line-caught ones from sustainable stocks (they will be clearly marked). Renowned for its succulent, chunky flakes with a sweet, seafood flavour, cod is famously fried in batter with chips, but also tastes excellent with tomatoes, peppers, olives, garlic, sweetcorn, cheese, and bacon.

Look out for the three-fin dorsal pattern that is typical of the Gadidae family.

Atlantic cod Also known as codling, sprag, or scrod, Atlantic cod is one of the largest members of the Gadidae family. It is identified by a white lateral line, green-yellow marbled skin that fades to white on the belly, and a square tail. Delicious grilled, fried, poached, baked, or cooked in soups, stews, and curries.

Atlantic cod has white flesh with a firm texture that chunks and flakes well.

Cod steak Cod steaks or cutlets are thick slices cut across the backbone, from the widest part of the fish. They can be stuffed, then poached, baked, or grilled.

how to make goujons

Goujons are small strips of fish, coated with egg and breadcrumbs, then fried. Try a few as a starter with tartare sauce or serve as a main course instead of battered larger fillets.

1 Choose thick cod fillets (or other sustainable white fish). Skin them, if necessary, then cut into finger-length strips.

2 Put some seasoned flour in a bowl, beaten egg in another, and fresh breadcrumbs in a third. Dip each strip in the flour, egg, and crumbs to coat.

3 Heat about 1cm (½in) sunflower, corn, or groundnut oil in a pan and fry the strips, a few at a time, until crisp and golden. Drain on kitchen paper.

The cheeks, considered a delicacy, are sold ready prepared and can be poached or fried.

Pacific cod Also known as Alaska cod, grey cod, true cod, or treska brown, it has dark mottled skin and a pale belly. It can grow to over 2m (6 ½ft) and is an excellent all-round fish.

Pacific cod fillet is firm, sweet, and well flavoured.

essentials

varieties available

Atlantic and Pacific cods are usually sold in fillets or steaks (fresh and smoked). The head, cheeks, and roe (fresh and smoked) are also available.

buy Choose firm, moist flesh that smells of the ocean but not too "fishy". Avoid any that are slimy, discoloured, or dying.

store Best eaten on the day of purchase but can be stored, wrapped in the fridge, for up to 24 hours.

cook Deep- or pan-fry fillets in batter or breadcrumbs; poach in stock, wine, or milk; use chopped flesh for soup or chowder; stuff and bake, grill, or poach steaks.

recipe ideas

Cod and mussel chowder p460

Fish fingers with chunky tartare sauce p456

Perfect fish and chips p457

White fish with spinach and pine nuts p169

cod and mussel chowder

A hearty dish from New England laden with chunks of cod and potatoes, and mussels to add colour and flavour. Traditionally, all this chowder needs with it is some oyster crackers, or serve it with crusty whole-wheat or rustic bread.

🥣 45-50 MINS   🍲 55-60 MINS

SERVES 4

1 large potato, about 250g (9oz) total weight, peeled and diced

750ml (1¼ pints) fish stock

1 bay leaf

4 tbsp white wine

85g (3oz) streaky bacon rashers, diced

1 onion, finely chopped

1 celery stick, peeled and finely chopped

1 small carrot, finely chopped

1 tsp dried thyme

30g (1oz) plain flour

500g (1lb 2oz) mussels, scrubbed and debearded (discard any that do not close when tapped) (p364)

500g (1lb 2oz) skinned cod fillets, cut into 2.5cm (1in) pieces

120ml (4fl oz) double cream

salt and freshly ground black pepper

3 sprigs of dill, leaves picked and finely chopped

1 As soon as you have diced the potato, put it in a bowl of cold water so it doesn't discolour. Then put the fish stock and bay leaf into a large saucepan and pour in the wine. Bring to the boil and simmer for 10 minutes until very hot and all the flavours have combined.

2 Put the bacon in a casserole and cook, stirring occasionally, for 3–5 minutes until crisp and the fat is rendered. Add the onion, celery, carrot, and thyme. Cook, stirring, for 5–7 minutes until soft. Sprinkle the flour over the casserole and cook, stirring, for a minute. Add the hot fish stock mixture to the casserole and bring to the boil, stirring until the liquid thickens slightly.

3 Drain the potato and add it to the casserole. Simmer, stirring occasionally, for about 40 minutes until the potato is very tender. Remove the casserole from the heat.

With a fork, crush about a third of the potato against the side of the casserole, then stir to combine.

4 Return the casserole to the heat and tip in the mussels. Simmer for 1–2 minutes until the shells start to open. Stir in the cod and simmer for a further 2–3 minutes until the fish just flakes easily. Do not continue to cook or the fish will start to break apart. Pour in the cream and bring just to the boil. Taste for seasoning, adding salt and pepper to taste.

5 Discard the bay leaf and any mussels that have not opened, and warn your guests to do the same if they come across any firmly shut shellfish. Ladle the chowder into warmed soup bowls and sprinkle each with some dill. Serve very hot. Accompany with oyster crackers, crumbled into each bowl or fresh crusty bread.

variation

manhattan cod and mussel chowder

This adds tomatoes for a colourful finish. Peel, deseed, and coarsely chop 550g (1¼lb) tomatoes, or use a 400g can of tomatoes. If tomatoes are not ripe and in season, canned are usually the better choice. Also finely chop 2 garlic cloves. Make the chowder as directed in step 1, using double the amount of wine, 1½ tsp dried thyme, and half the plain flour. Add the garlic and 1 tbsp tomato purée with the onion, celery, and carrots. Add the tomatoes together with the potatoes in step 3; do not crush any of the potatoes. Omit the double cream, sprinkle with chopped thyme, and serve with crusty wholemeal bread.

fish and leek pie

The subtle, sweet flavour of leeks are a great match for fish.

🥣 **15 MINS** 🍲 **50 MINS** ❄ **FREEZABLE**

SPECIAL EQUIPMENT ▪ 1.2-litre (2-pint) pie dish

SERVES 4

1 tbsp olive oil

1 onion, finely chopped

salt and freshly ground black pepper

4 leeks, finely sliced

1 tsp plain flour

150ml (5fl oz) cider

handful of flat-leaf parsley, finely chopped

150ml (5fl oz) double cream

675g (1½lb) white fish, such as cod or pollack, cut into chunks

300g (10oz) ready-made puff pastry

1 egg, lightly beaten, for egg wash

1 Preheat the oven to 200°C (400°F/Gas 6). Heat the oil in a large frying pan over a low heat. Add the onion and a little salt, and cook gently for about 5 minutes until soft and translucent. Add the leeks and continue to cook gently for about 10 minutes until softened. Remove from the heat, stir in the flour, and add a little of the cider. Return to the heat, pour in the remaining cider, and cook for 5–8 minutes until thickened. Stir through the parsley and cream, then spoon the mixture into a pie dish with the fish. Combine gently, and season well with salt and pepper.

2 Roll out the pastry on a floured work surface, so it is about 5cm (2in) larger all round than the top of the pie dish. Cut out a strip of pastry about 2.5cm (1in) in from the edge to make a collar. Wet the edge of the pie dish with a little water, fit the pastry strip all the way around the edge of the dish, and press down firmly. Brush the pastry collar with a little egg wash, then top with the pastry lid. Trim away the excess and pinch together the edges to seal. Using a sharp knife, make 2 slits in the top to allow steam to escape.

3 Brush the top of the pie with the egg wash and bake in the oven for 20–30 minutes until the pastry is puffed and golden. Serve the pie hot.

creole fish and corn stew

This chunky fish and vegetable winter stew has great texture. If you can't get hold of creamed sweetcorn, use a can of regular sweetcorn and blend it in the food processor.

🥣 **15 MINS** 🍲 **1 HR 15 MINS** ❄ **FREEZABLE**

SERVES 4-6

2 tbsp olive oil

1 onion, finely chopped

3 garlic cloves, finely chopped

3 celery sticks, finely chopped

3 carrots, finely chopped

1 tsp dried oregano

a few sprigs of thyme, leaves picked

1 tsp cayenne pepper (use less if you don't like it too hot)

400g can creamed sweetcorn

400g can sweetcorn, drained

900ml (1½ pints) hot vegetable stock

salt and freshly ground black pepper

2 potatoes, peeled and diced into bite-sized pieces

200g (7oz) cooked, peeled cold water prawns, chopped

300g (10oz) coley, pollack, or cod, skinned and cut into chunky pieces

splash of Tabasco sauce (optional)

1 Heat the oil in a large heavy-based pan over a medium heat, add the onion, and cook for 3–4 minutes until soft. Then stir through the garlic, celery, and carrot, and cook on a gentle heat for a further 5 minutes, or until the carrot is soft.

2 Stir through the herbs and cayenne pepper, then add both cans of sweetcorn and the stock. Season well with salt and pepper, bring to the boil, reduce to a simmer, and cook gently, partially covered, for 30–40 minutes. Add the potatoes and cook for a further 15 minutes.

3 Add the prawns and fish to the pan and simmer gently for 6–10 minutes, until the fish is opaque and cooked through. Taste and season further, if necessary, and stir in the Tabasco sauce, if using. Ladle into warmed bowls and serve with some crusty bread.

Season's best **swede and turnip**

The large, hardy swede has a deep, rich, earthy-sweet flavour, while turnips are smaller, white inside, and have a strong taste, faintly resembling mustard. In season throughout winter, they are excellent at the beginning of the year when other crops are scarce. They pair well with lamb, beef, game, offal, sausages, other root vegetables, cream, mushrooms, and sweet spices.

Root-like members of the cabbage family, swedes and turnips are widely grown staple crops in the cooler parts of temperate zones around the world.

Swede A heavy vegetable with tough outer skin, it needs peeling thickly before use. Its colour and flavour intensify when cooked, but it is also delicious grated raw for winter salads.

White turnip Pure white, round turnips, such as the Tokyo Cross (pictured here), have a mild flavour and a crunchy, juicy texture, much like a radish, so are particularly good grated in salads.

Purple turnip The familiar top-shaped turnip is usually purple fading to white at the root. When small in size the flavour is sweet and delicate.

Distinctive white and pinkish-purple skin.

essentials
varieties available

Large swede with purple and white or yellow skin; purple and white turnips of varying sizes, including baby turnips – tiny specimens to cook whole.

buy Choose roots without any rot, pits, or scars.

store Uncut, they will keep well in the vegetable drawer of the fridge for 3–4 weeks; wrap a cut swede in cling film and store for up to 1 week.

cook Grate raw, boil, steam, bake, roast, deep-fry as chips, or add to soups and stews.

preserve Use diced small in pickles and chutneys.

recipe ideas

Creamy swede soup p432

Poule au pot p463

Turnip soup with pimento, chilli, and noodles p439

cornish pasties

Swede lends sweetness and bulk to these traditional savoury pasties. Worcestershire sauce adds depth of flavour.

🥄 **20 MINS PLUS CHILLING**　　🍲 **40-45 MINS**

MAKES 4

100g (3½oz) lard, chilled and diced

50g (1¾oz) unsalted butter, chilled and diced

300g (10oz) plain flour, plus extra for dusting

½ tsp salt

1 egg, beaten, for glazing

For the filling

250g (9oz) beef skirt, trimmed, cut into 1cm (½in) cubes

80g (2¾oz) swede, peeled, cut into 5mm (¼in) cubes

100g (3½oz) waxy potatoes, peeled, cut into 5mm (¼in) cubes

1 large onion, finely chopped

splash of Worcestershire sauce

1 tsp plain flour

sea salt and freshly ground black pepper

1 In a mixing bowl, rub the lard and butter into the flour to resemble fine crumbs. Add the salt and enough cold water to bring the mixture together into a soft dough. Knead briefly on a lightly floured work surface, then wrap in cling film and chill for 1 hour.

2 Preheat the oven to 190°C (375°F/ Gas 5). Mix all the filling ingredients in a bowl and season well.

3 Roll the pastry out to a thickness of 5mm (¼in) on a floured work surface. Using a side plate or saucer, cut 4 circles from the dough. Fold the circles in half, then flatten them out again. Pile one-quarter of the filling into each circle, leaving a 2cm (¾in) border. Brush the border with a little beaten egg, pull both edges up over the filling, and press together to seal. Crimp the sealed edge with your fingers to form a decorative ridge. Brush beaten egg all over the pasties.

4 Bake in the centre of the oven for 40–45 minutes until golden brown. Allow to cool for at least 15 minutes before eating warm or cold.

poule au pot

This classic French dish is a complete meal in itself.

🥄 **1 HR**　　🍲 **1 HR 15 MINS - 1 HR 30 MINS**

SPECIAL EQUIPMENT ▪ trussing string ▪ muslin

SERVES 4-6

1 onion, trimmed and peeled

1 clove

1 large chicken, about 2kg (4½lb)

salt and freshly ground black pepper

1 bouquet garni

4 litres (7 pints) chicken stock, plus more if needed

1kg (2¼lb) leeks, trimmed, cut lengthways, and sliced

375g (13oz) carrots, sliced

375g (13oz) turnips, diced

2 hard-boiled eggs, shelled

juice of ½ lemon

1 tsp Dijon mustard

2 tbsp dry white wine

250ml (9fl oz) vegetable oil

1 tbsp drained capers, finely chopped

3 gherkins, finely chopped

5-7 sprigs of parsley, finely chopped

1 small bunch of chives, finely snipped

60g (2oz) vermicelli

1 Stud the onion with the clove. Put the chicken in a casserole, season, and add the bouquet garni and onion. Cover three-quarters of the chicken with stock. Bring to the boil, cover, and simmer for 45 minutes.

2 Put the leeks on a piece of muslin and tie securely to make a bundle. Repeat with the carrots and turnips in separate muslin. Add to the chicken and pour in more stock to cover. Cover and simmer for 25–30 minutes.

3 To make the sauce gribiche, separate the hard-boiled yolks and whites by pulling them apart. Cut the whites into strips and finely chop. Sieve the yolks into a bowl using the back of a spoon. Add the lemon juice, mustard, salt, pepper, and wine, and whisk until combined. Gradually pour in the oil, whisking constantly. Add the egg whites, capers, gherkins, and herbs, and whisk to combine.

4 Carve the chicken, cover the pieces with foil, and keep warm. Remove the vegetables from the broth and keep warm. Strain the broth into a pan and simmer for 10–20 minutes. Skim off the fat and taste for seasoning. Add the vermicelli and cook according to packet instructions.

5 Unwrap the vegetables, discarding the muslin, and add them and the chicken to the broth. Stir and remove from the heat. Serve in bowls with the sauce gribiche in a separate bowl.

lamb chops champvallon

This is a classic French recipe where lamb chops are cooked with potatoes and herbs: good winter warming fare.

🥣 25-30 MINS   🍲 2 HRS - 2 HRS 15 MINS

SPECIAL EQUIPMENT ▪ 23 x 32cm (9 x 13in) baking dish

SERVES 6

6 lamb loin chops (about 1kg/2¼lb), each 2.5cm (1in) thick, trimmed

salt and freshly ground black pepper

1 tbsp vegetable oil

500g (1lb 2oz) onions, thinly sliced

1.1kg (2½lb) baking potatoes, peeled and cut into very thin slices

leaves from 1 small bunch of thyme, plus a few sprigs for garnish

3 garlic cloves, finely chopped

1 litre (1¾ pints) hot chicken or beef stock, plus more if needed

1 Trim off any excess fat from the lamb chops and season both sides with salt and pepper. Heat the oil in a large frying pan over a high heat, add the chops, and cook for 1–2 minutes on each side until well browned. Remove to a plate and set aside.

2 Pour off all but about 1 tbsp of fat from the pan. Add the onions and cook over a medium heat for 3–4 minutes, until soft and translucent. Remove the pan from the heat.

3 In a large bowl, gently stir the potato slices with the softened onions, thyme leaves, and season with salt and pepper.

4 Preheat the oven to 180°C (350°F/ Gas 4) and brush the baking dish with oil. Spread half the potato mixture in the dish and sprinkle with the garlic.

5 Arrange the chops on top of the potatoes. Cover with the remaining potato mixture, placing the slices neatly in rows. Pour over enough stock to come just to the top of the potatoes. Bake, uncovered, for 2 hours, or until the lamb and potatoes are tender when pierced.

6 Divide the chops, potatoes, and onions among 6 warmed plates and spoon over a little cooking liquid. Decorate with a sprig of thyme and serve immediately.

vegetable casserole with dumplings

Dumplings are the perfect addition to a casserole or stew, as they make the dish a complete meal. For variety, add other herbs, such as thyme or tarragon to the parsley in the mixture.

🥣 25 MINS   🍲 1 HR 15 MINS   ❄️ FREEZABLE

SERVES 4-6

1 tbsp olive oil

1 onion, roughly chopped

salt and freshly ground black pepper

3 garlic cloves, finely chopped

pinch of dried chilli flakes

2 leeks, trimmed and thickly sliced

3 carrots, roughly chopped

2 celery sticks, roughly chopped

1 tbsp plain flour

900ml (1½ pints) hot vegetable stock

400g can haricot beans, drained and rinsed

a few sprigs of rosemary

225g (8oz) self-raising flour

115g (4oz) vegetable suet

2 tbsp finely chopped flat-leaf parsley

1 Preheat the oven to 160°C (325°F/Gas 3). Heat the oil in a large flameproof casserole over a medium heat, add the onion, and cook for 3–4 minutes until soft. Season with salt and pepper, then stir through the garlic and chilli flakes. Add the leek, carrots, and celery, and continue cooking for a further 10 minutes, stirring occasionally, until softened. Stir in the plain flour, then gradually stir in the stock. Add the haricot beans and rosemary. Bring to the boil, then reduce to a simmer, cover, and put in the oven for 1 hour, checking on the liquid level as it cooks and topping up with hot stock if needed.

2 While this is cooking, prepare the dumplings. Mix together the self-raising flour, suet, and parsley, and season well. Add about 120ml (4fl oz) cold water to form a soft, slightly sticky dough, trickling in more water if it seems too dry. Form into 12 balls and drop them into the stew for the last 30 minutes of cooking. Push them down a little so they are just immersed and cover with the lid. Remove the lid for the final 10 minutes, or until the dumplings are browned. Remove the rosemary, ladle the casserole into warmed bowls, and serve with crusty bread.

onion confit and gorgonzola pizzas

Onions and Gorgonzola are delicious together, topping a crust made crunchy with fine yellow cornmeal or polenta.

🥣 40-45 MINS PLUS RISING 🍲 35-40 MINS

MAKES 6

250g (9oz) unbleached strong white flour, plus more if needed

1½ tsp fast-action yeast

2 tbsp olive oil

75g (2½oz) fine yellow cornmeal or polenta

175g (6oz) Gorgonzola cheese, cut into slices

For the onion confit

2 tbsp olive oil

750g (1lb 10oz) red onions, thinly sliced

2 tsp sugar

salt and freshly ground black pepper

4 tbsp red wine

5-7 sprigs of oregano, leaves picked and chopped, plus reserve some to serve

1 Sift the flour into a bowl and add the yeast. Stir in the oil and enough warm water (about 150ml/5fl oz) to form a soft, but not sticky, dough. Knead gently on a lightly floured surface for several minutes until smooth and elastic. Return to the bowl, cover with oiled cling film, and leave to rise in a warm place for about 40 minutes until the dough has doubled in size.

2 For the onion confit, heat the oil in a frying pan over a medium heat. Add the onions and sugar, and season with salt and pepper. Cook for 5-7 minutes, stirring often, until the onions are soft and lightly brown. Add the wine and continue cooking until it has evaporated. Reduce the heat, press a piece of foil on top of the onions, and cover with a lid. Cook, stirring occasionally, for 15-20 minutes, or until the onions are soft enough to cut with a spoon. Let cool. Stir in the chopped oregano leaves.

3 Preheat the oven to 230°C (450°F/ Gas 8). Put 2 baking sheets on separate racks in the bottom half of the oven to heat. Cut 6 x 23cm (9in) squares of foil and sprinkle each generously with the cornmeal or polenta.

4 Turn out the dough onto a floured surface and knock it back by re-kneading briefly. With your hands, roll the dough into a cylinder about 5cm (2in) in diameter. Cut the cylinder in half, then cut each half into 3 equal pieces. Shape the pieces of dough into balls.

5 Roll out a ball of dough into an 18cm (7in) round. Transfer the round to 1 of the squares of foil. Repeat to shape the remaining dough. If you like, press up the edges of the rounds with your fingertips to form shallow rims. Spread the rounds with the onion confit.

6 Top the rounds with slices of the cheese and leave them in a warm place for about 15 minutes, until the dough is puffed. Bake the pizzas, on the foil, on the baking sheets, for 15-20 minutes until lightly browned and crisp. Switch the baking sheets after 7 minutes so the pizzas brown evenly. Serve the pizzas hot from the oven. Brush the crusts with oil and top them with the reserved oregano leaves.

osso buco

Winter citrus lends a delicious fragrance to this Italian classic, which is served with a zesty gremolata. A saffron and Parmesan risotto is the traditional accompaniment. Ask your butcher for a hindleg of veal as they are meatier than the front legs.

🥄 30-35 MINS   🍲 1 HR 45 MINS - 2 HRS 15 MINS

SERVES 4-6

30g (1oz) plain flour

salt and freshly ground black pepper

4-6 pieces of veal shin on the bone (about 1.8kg/4lb)

2 tbsp vegetable oil

30g (1oz) butter

1 carrot, thinly sliced

2 onions, finely chopped

250ml (9fl oz) white wine

400g can Italian plum tomatoes, drained and coarsely chopped

1 garlic clove, finely chopped

grated zest of 1 orange

120ml (4fl oz) hot chicken or veal stock

For the citrus gremolata

small bunch of flat-leaf parsley, leaves picked and finely chopped

grated zest of 1 lemon

1 garlic clove, finely chopped

1 Preheat the oven to 180°C (350°F/ Gas 4). Put the flour on a large plate, season with salt and pepper, and stir to combine. Lightly coat the veal pieces with the seasoned flour.

2 Heat the oil and butter in a large flameproof casserole over a medium heat, add the veal pieces (in batches and with extra oil, if necessary), and brown thoroughly on all sides. Transfer to a plate with a slotted spoon and set aside.

3 Add the carrot and onions to the casserole and cook, stirring occasionally, until soft. Add the wine and boil until reduced by half. Stir in the tomatoes, garlic, and orange zest, and add seasoning. Lay the veal on top and pour over the stock. Cover and put in the oven for 1½-2 hours until very tender. Check occasionally that it's not drying out, topping up with a little hot water if needed.

4 For the gremolata, mix the parsley, lemon, and garlic in a small bowl. To serve, put the veal on warmed plates, spoon the sauce on top, and sprinkle with the gremolata.

variation

osso buco with celery, leek, and almonds

Prepare in the same way, but substitute 1 sliced leek for one of the onions, and add 2 chopped celery sticks to the mixture at the beginning of step 2. Use an Italian red wine, such as Chianti, instead of the white wine and add a pinch of sugar in step 3. Prepare the gremolata for garnish, but add a small handful of toasted, flaked almonds to the mix.

pork belly with onions and potatoes

The secret behind a crisp piece of crackling is rubbing plenty of salt and oil into the skin and then cooking the meat at a high temperature for its first 20 minutes in the oven.

🥄 **25 MINS**   🍲 **2 HRS 10 MINS**

SERVES 4

500g (1lb 2oz) piece of pork belly

sea salt and freshly ground black pepper

3 tbsp olive oil

2 onions, cut into eighths

2 large potatoes, peeled and cut into wedges

125g (4½ oz) button chestnut mushrooms, halved

150ml (5fl oz) white wine

2 garlic cloves, chopped

2 tsp chopped thyme

300ml (10fl oz) hot vegetable stock

1 Preheat the oven to 220°C (425°F/ Gas 7). Score the skin of the pork belly deeply, then rub ½ tsp sea salt and 1 tbsp of the oil into it. Transfer to a baking tray and place in the oven for 20 minutes, or until the skin has crisped up. Remove from the oven and reduce the temperature to 170°C (340°F/Gas 3½).

2 Heat the remaining oil in a frying pan over a medium heat, add the onions and potatoes, and cook for 10 minutes, stirring constantly. Add the mushrooms and cook for 5 more minutes. Then add the wine and cook for 2 more minutes. Transfer the mixture to a large baking dish, add the garlic, thyme, stock, and black pepper, and combine well. Nestle the pork in the mixture, ensuring the crackling is not covered, and roast in the oven for 1½ hours.

3 Allow to rest for 10 minutes, then cut the pork into 4 pieces with scissors and serve with steamed broccoli.

variation

pork belly with leeks and celeriac

Prepare in exactly the same way, but use 3 leeks, cut in chunks, instead of the onions, and a large celeriac, peeled and cut in chunks, instead of the potatoes. Cook for 5 minutes only at step 2.

hunter's chicken stew

In Italy, this dish is called *alla cacciatora*, meaning "hunter's style". Chicory, with its slight bitterness, makes a flavoursome addition and must be added towards the end of cooking.

🥄 **20–25 MINS**   🍲 **45–60 MINS**   ❄ **FREEZABLE**

SERVES 4

1.5kg (3lb 3oz) chicken, jointed into 8 pieces

salt and freshly ground black pepper

4 tbsp olive oil

1 onion, chopped

4 garlic cloves, finely chopped

a sprig of rosemary

1 bay leaf

4 tbsp dry white wine

120ml (4fl oz) hot chicken stock

2 heads of chicory, trimmed, leaves separated, and roughly chopped

1 Season the chicken all over with salt and pepper. Heat half the oil in a large flameproof casserole over a medium heat, add the thighs and drumsticks skin-side down, and cook for about 5 minutes until they begin to brown. Add the breast pieces and cook gently for 10–15 minutes until very brown. Turn and brown the other side. Reduce the heat.

2 Add the onion and garlic, stir, and continue cooking gently for 3–4 minutes until they are soft. Season with salt and pepper, then stir in the rosemary, bay leaf, wine, and stock. Cover and simmer for 15–20 minutes until tender.

3 Add the chicory for the last 5 minutes of cooking, return the lid, and cook gently until the chicory has just softened. Discard the bay leaf and rosemary from the sauce, taste, and add seasoning if needed. Spoon out into warmed bowls and serve with crusty bread.

variation

hunter's rabbit stew

Prepare in exactly the same way, but use a jointed rabbit instead of the chicken. Add a finely chopped carrot with the onion and garlic, use red wine instead of white, and 2 heads of either red chicory or radicchio instead of the chicory.

sweet balsamic onions

Baby onions are also known as button or pearl onions. They are really immature onions kept small by dense planting. Braising them in balsamic vinegar keeps them sweet and moist.

🥣 10 MINS   🍲 35 MINS

SERVES 4

3 tbsp olive oil

400g (14oz) baby onions, peeled and left whole

3 garlic cloves, finely sliced

3 tbsp balsamic vinegar

salt and freshly ground black pepper

drizzle of olive oil or chilli oil, to serve

1 Preheat the oven to 180°C (350°F/Gas 4). Heat the oil in a deep frying pan over a low heat, add the onions, and cook, stirring frequently, for 15 minutes, or until evenly brown.

2 Transfer the onions to a small baking dish, packing them in tightly. Sprinkle with the garlic and spoon over the balsamic vinegar. Season well with salt and pepper, and bake for 20 minutes, stirring every 5 minutes. Serve hot or cold with a good drizzle of olive oil or chilli oil and some fresh crusty bread and cheese.

variation

sweet balsamic baby leeks

Use 225g (8oz) baby leeks, trimmed but left whole, instead of the baby onions. Fry them in 45g (1½oz) butter instead of the oil for 2 minutes only, turning once or twice until lightly golden and softening. Transfer to a baking dish and add a small handful of chopped walnuts, a bay leaf, and 3 tbsp white balsamic condiment instead of the balsamic vinegar. Season. Cook as before but no need to turn. Serve hot or cold.

apple sauce

The perfect accompaniment to pork, no matter how the meat is cooked. While traditionally served with a roast joint, apple sauce is just as good with cold meat or pork chops.

🥣 10 MINS   🍲 10 MINS   ❄ FREEZABLE

SERVES 4

450g (1lb) cooking apples, peeled, cored, and quartered

2–3 tbsp sugar (depending on the tartness of the apples)

1 Put the apples in a pan, sprinkle over 1 tbsp water, then add the sugar. Cover and cook on a low heat for 10 minutes, or until the apples have begun to break down.

2 Stir with a wooden spoon until the sauce reaches your preferred consistency – either a smooth purée or more chunky. Taste and add more sugar, if required. Serve warm or cold with roast pork.

pancetta and potatoes with red cabbage

Here is a speedy side dish that would happily accompany any casserole or stew – and as it includes potatoes it is very filling as well. Even better, you can reheat it the next day.

 10 MINS   15 MINS

SERVES 4

knob of butter

1 tbsp olive oil

3 cooked potatoes, peeled and cut into cubes

salt and freshly ground black pepper

175g (6oz) pancetta, diced

200g (7oz) red cabbage, lightly cooked and shredded

2 eating apples, peeled, cored, and chopped

1 Heat the butter and oil in a large frying pan over a medium-high heat. Add the potatoes and sauté for 5–10 minutes until golden and crispy, adding more oil if needed. Season with salt and pepper, then push the potatoes to one side of the pan.

2 Add the pancetta and cook until crispy. Then stir through the cabbage and apples. Cook until well combined and the apple is golden. Season again, if needed, and serve while hot.

red cabbage with cider

Red cabbage is transformed when slow cooked, becoming sweet and tender. Add a handful of sultanas, if you wish, for extra flavour, and serve with couscous or sausages.

15 MINS   1 HR – 1 HR 30 MINS

SERVES 4

½ red onion, sliced

1 large red cabbage (about 1kg/2¼lb), cored and shredded

1 apple, cored (but not peeled) and finely chopped

1 tsp five-spice powder

salt and freshly ground black pepper

300ml (10fl oz) dry cider

1 Put the onion, cabbage, apple, and five-spice powder into a large heavy-based pan, and season well with salt and pepper. Turn to mix everything together.

2 Pour in the cider and stir, then cover with the lid and cook on a low heat for 1–1½ hours, stirring occasionally. Taste and season as needed.

potatoes boulangère

Perfect for a cold winter's night, these garlicky and finely sliced potatoes are baked in the oven. The end result is a moist and tender side dish to accompany any main course.

25 MINS   1 HR

SPECIAL EQUIPMENT ▪ shallow 2.3-litre (4-pint) ovenproof dish

SERVES 4–6

50g (1¾oz) butter

6 onions, sliced

900g (2lb) potatoes, peeled and cut into 5mm (¼in) slices

3 garlic cloves, sliced

750ml (1¼ pints) hot vegetable stock or chicken stock

salt and freshly ground black pepper

1 Preheat the oven to 200°C (400°F/Gas 6). Melt the butter in a large pan over a low heat, add the onions, and cook, stirring often, for 10 minutes, or until soft and translucent. Add the potatoes, garlic, and stock, and season with salt and pepper. Stir well, then cover with a lid and simmer for 5–6 minutes, or until the potatoes start to soften.

2 Transfer the mixture to the ovenproof dish and cook for 40–50 minutes, or until the potatoes are tender and most of the stock has been absorbed. Serve with roast beef.

variation

creamy sweet potato and leek bake

Prepare in the same way, but use the white part of 3 leeks, sliced, in place of 4 of the onions, 900g (2lb) sweet potatoes, peeled and sliced, instead of ordinary ones, and use 450ml (15fl oz) stock and 300ml (10fl oz) double cream instead of all stock.

roasted celery with orange and walnuts

An unusual way to cook celery. Here the heart is quartered and roasted with orange and walnuts. Delicious served with roast chicken, pork, or a piece of grilled halibut or monkfish.

🥄 **10 MINS**   🍲 **55 MINS**

SERVES 4

4 celery hearts, trimmed and quartered

zest and juice of 1 orange

extra virgin olive oil, for drizzling

knob of butter, melted

1 tsp caster sugar

a sprig of thyme, leaves picked and chopped

handful of walnuts, chopped

sea salt and freshly ground black pepper

1 Preheat the oven to 200°C (400°F/ Gas 6). Put the celery hearts in a roasting tin and add the orange zest and juice. Drizzle with a little oil and the butter. Sprinkle over the sugar, thyme, and walnuts. Season with sea salt and pepper to taste.

2 Cover the roasting tin tightly with foil and cook in the oven for 40 minutes. Remove the foil and leave in the oven to brown for a further 15 minutes until tender and glazed. Serve hot or warm.

red cabbage slaw

This crisp, crunchy, colourful salad goes particularly well with cold meats and jacket baked potatoes, but is also delicious with cheeses and crusty bread for a light lunch.

🥄 **15 MINS**

SERVES 6

½ small red cabbage, finely shredded

2 celery sticks, chopped

½ small red onion, thinly sliced

1 red and 1 green eating apple, cored and diced (leaving the skins on)

large handful of raisins

large handful of walnuts, roughly chopped

For the dressing

6 tbsp double cream

2 tsp light soft brown sugar

½ tsp Dijon mustard

salt and freshly ground black pepper

2 tbsp red wine vinegar

1 Mix all the salad ingredients together in a salad bowl.

2 To make the dressing, lightly whip the cream with the sugar. Whisk in the mustard and a little salt and pepper. Whisk in the vinegar to form a thick pouring consistency.

3 Pour over the salad. Toss well. Any leftover salad will keep in the fridge for 2–3 days.

variation

celeriac and pear coleslaw

Use ½ small white cabbage instead of red, ½ small celeriac, grated instead of the celery sticks. And 2 large carrots, grated and 2 diced pears instead of the apples. Substitute peanuts for the walnuts. Make the dressing as before.

haricot bean and cauliflower gratin

This gratin is a complete meal in itself, although you may like to serve it with some lightly steamed leafy greens, such as cavolo nero, mustard greens, or kale.

🥄 **10 MINS**   🍲 **30 MINS**

SERVES 4

knob of butter

1 tbsp plain flour

300ml (10fl oz) milk

pinch of paprika

salt and freshly ground black pepper

125g (4½oz) strong Cheddar cheese, grated

2 tsp Dijon mustard

1 head of cauliflower, broken into florets

400g can haricot beans, drained and rinsed

1 Preheat the oven to 200°C (400°F/ Gas 6). To make the cheese sauce, melt the butter in a pan over a low heat. Remove from the heat and stir in the flour with a wooden spoon until smooth. Add a little of the milk

and stir until smooth. Return to the heat and slowly add the remaining milk, stirring continuously. Keep stirring for 5–10 minutes until the sauce has thickened.

2 Remove from the heat, sprinkle in the paprika, and season well with salt and pepper. Add 75g (2½oz) of the cheese and the mustard and stir them into the sauce. Set aside.

3 Bring a pan of salted water to the boil, add the cauliflower, and cook for about 10 minutes until soft. Drain.

4 Put the cauliflower in an ovenproof dish with the haricot beans and toss together. Pour over the sauce and top with the remaining cheese. Cook in the oven for 10–15 minutes until golden and simmering. Serve hot.

potato-chive monkey bread

This bread made of mashed potato has a soft crust.

🥣 50-55 MINS PLUS RISING   🍲 40-45 MINS

SPECIAL EQUIPMENT • 1.7-litre (3-pint) ring mould

MAKES 1

250g (9oz) potatoes, cut into large pieces

2½ tsp dried yeast, or 15g (½oz) fresh yeast

125g (4½oz) unsalted butter, plus more for greasing

1 large bunch of chives, snipped

2 tbsp sugar

2 tsp salt

425g (15oz) unbleached strong white flour, plus more if needed

1 Boil the potatoes, drain, reserving 250ml (9fl oz) of the cooking liquid, and mash well. Let the reserved liquid and potatoes cool. In a small bowl, sprinkle the yeast over 4 tbsp lukewarm water. Let it stand for 5 minutes until dissolved, stirring once.

2 Melt half the butter in a pan. Put the potatoes, cooking liquid, dissolved yeast, and melted butter into a large bowl. Add the chives, sugar, and salt, and mix. Add half the flour and mix well with your hands. Add the remaining flour, 60g (2oz) at a time.

3 Knead the dough on a floured work surface until it is smooth and elastic and forms a ball. Wash out the bowl and brush with melted butter. Put the dough in the bowl and flip until lightly buttered. Cover with a damp tea towel and leave in a warm place for 1–1½ hours, or until doubled in size.

4 Brush the ring mould with melted butter. Melt the remaining 60g (2oz) butter and pour it into a shallow dish. Turn the dough onto a lightly floured work surface and knead just to knock out the air. Cover and let it rest for about 5 minutes. Make 30 or so walnut-sized balls of dough, toss in melted butter, and transfer to the mould. Cover the mould with a dry tea towel and let rise in a warm place until the mould is full. Preheat the oven to 190°C (375°F/Gas 5).

5 Bake for 40–45 minutes, until golden brown and the bread starts to shrink from the side of the mould. Let it cool slightly on a wire rack, then carefully unmould.

celery and apple salad with blue cheese dressing

In this salad, the strong tastes of celery and bitter leaves more than hold their own against the pungency of a blue cheese dressing, with the walnuts adding crunch and texture.

🥣 10 MINS   🍲 2 MINS

SPECIAL EQUIPMENT • food processor

SERVES 4

8 tbsp or 60g (2oz) chopped walnuts

300g (10½oz) blue cheese, such as Dolcelatte or Gorgonzola

4 tbsp cider vinegar

4 tbsp hazelnut oil or walnut oil

freshly ground black pepper

4 celery sticks, trimmed and sliced diagonally into 1cm (½in) slices

2 green apples, cored and cut into thin wedges

4 large handfuls of watercress or rocket

sea salt

1 Dry-fry the walnuts for a couple of minutes in a frying pan or wok until they are golden and crispy. Set aside and leave to cool.

2 In a food processor, mix together 100g (3½oz) of the blue cheese, vinegar, oil, and a good grinding of

black pepper. Blitz to a smooth, creamy dressing, which should have thick pouring consistency. Add up to 1 tbsp cold water to thin the dressing a little if it is too thick.

3 Put the celery, apples, and watercress or rocket in a large bowl, and mix well. Coat the salad with the dressing and check it for seasoning. Top with the walnut pieces and the rest of the blue cheese, crumbled or diced into bite-sized pieces.

variation

celery, leek, and pear salad
Use pecan nuts instead of walnuts. Substitute 1 small leek, thinly sliced for 2 of the celery sticks and 2 firm pears for the apples. Dress as before.

lemon cheesecake

This cold-set cheesecake needs no baking and so produces a lighter, more delicate result.

🥣 **30 MINS PLUS CHILLING**

SPECIAL EQUIPMENT ▪ 23cm (9in) round springform cake tin

SERVES 8

250g (9oz) digestive biscuits

100g (3½oz) unsalted butter, diced

4 gelatine leaves, roughly cut up

grated zest and juice of 2 lemons, plus thinly pared zest, to garnish

350g (12oz) cream cheese

200g (7oz) caster sugar

300ml (10fl oz) double cream

1 Line the cake tin with baking parchment. Put the biscuits in a bag and crush to crumbs with a rolling pin. Melt the butter in a pan, then add the crushed biscuits, mixing well to combine. Press the biscuit mixture firmly into the base of the tin using a wooden spoon. Transfer to the fridge to chill.

2 In a small heatproof bowl, soak the gelatine leaves in the lemon juice for 5 minutes to soften them. Place the bowl over a pan of hot water and stir until the gelatine melts. Set aside to cool.

3 Beat together the cream cheese, sugar, and lemon zest in a bowl until smooth. In a separate bowl, whisk the double cream to soft peaks.

4 Beat the gelatine mixture into the cream cheese mixture, stirring well to combine. Then gently fold the whisked cream into the cheese mixture. Be careful not to lose volume.

5 Tip the cheese mixture onto the chilled biscuit base and spread evenly. Smooth the top with a damp palette knife or the back of a damp spoon. Chill for at least 4 hours or overnight.

6 To serve, run a sharp, thin knife around the inside of the tin. Gently transfer the cheesecake to a plate, making sure you remove the baking parchment. Garnish with the thinly pared lemon zest.

chocolate orange whoopie pies

A whoopie pie is two small cakes sandwiching a creamy filling. Rich, dark chocolate combined with the zesty tang of orange is a classic combination and used here to full advantage.

🥣 **40 MINS**　🍲 **12 MINS**

MAKES 10

275g (9½oz) unsalted butter, softened

150g (5½oz) light soft brown sugar

1 large egg

2 tsp vanilla extract

grated zest and juice of 1 orange

225g (8oz) self-raising flour

75g (2½oz) cocoa powder

1 tsp baking powder

150ml (5fl oz) whole milk or buttermilk

2 tbsp Greek-style yogurt or thick natural yogurt

200g (7oz) icing sugar

1 Preheat the oven to 180°C (350°F/ Gas 4). Line several baking sheets with baking parchment. Cream 175g (6oz) of the butter and the brown sugar until fluffy. Beat in the egg and 1 tsp of the vanilla extract, and add the zest. In a bowl, sift the flour, cocoa powder, and baking powder. Mix the dry ingredients and the milk into the batter in alternate spoonfuls. Fold in the yogurt.

2 Place 20 heaped tablespoons of the mixture onto the baking sheets, leaving space between them. Dip a spoon in warm water and use the back to smooth the surface of the cake mounds. Bake for 12 minutes until risen. Leave to cool slightly, then transfer to a wire rack.

3 For the buttercream, blend the remaining butter and vanilla extract with the icing sugar and orange juice, loosening with a little water. Spread 1 tbsp of the filling onto the flat side of each cake half and sandwich together with the remaining halves.

grapefruit crème de menthe jelly

Crème de menthe works fantastically with the bitter taste of grapefruit. This fruit jelly makes a really refreshing dessert with a dollop of crème fraîche.

🥣 **15 MINS PLUS STANDING AND SETTING**

SERVES 4

2 white grapefruit

30g (1oz) caster sugar, plus extra for frosting

1 egg white, lightly beaten

1 sachet powdered gelatine

450ml (15fl oz) clear apple juice

4 tbsp crème de menthe

1 Peel and segment the grapefruit (p474). Put the fruit in a bowl and squeeze the membranes over the fruit to extract all the juice, then discard. Sprinkle the sugar over the grapefruit, stir, and leave to stand for an hour, if possible, to allow the juice to run.

2 Frost the rims of 4 wine goblets: dip them in the egg white, then in caster sugar, and leave to set.

3 Meanwhile, put the gelatine in a small bowl with 2 tbsp water. Leave to soften for 5 minutes, then stand the bowl in a pan of gently simmering water and stir until the gelatine has completely dissolved. Stir into the apple juice. Add the crème de menthe.

4 Put the grapefruit slices in the wine goblets. Strain the remaining grapefruit juice into the apple juice mixture. Stir, then pour over the fruit and chill until set.

lemon meringue pie

With the sharpness of lemon combined with a smooth vanilla meringue topping, it is no wonder this pie is a family favourite.

🥣 30 MINS PLUS CHILLING   🍲 40–50 MINS

SPECIAL EQUIPMENT ▪ 23cm (9in) round loose-bottomed fluted tart tin ▪ ceramic baking beans

SERVES 8

400g (14oz) ready-made sweet shortcrust pastry

6 eggs, at room temperature, separated

3 tbsp plain flour

3 tbsp cornflour

400g (14oz) caster sugar

1 tbsp grated zest and juice of 3 lemons

45g (1½oz) butter, diced

½ tsp cream of tartar

½ tsp vanilla extract

1 Preheat the oven to 200°C (400°F/ Gas 6) and lightly butter the tin. Lightly flour a work surface and roll out the pastry. Use it to line the tin.

2 Line the pastry case with baking parchment, then fill with ceramic baking beans. Place on a baking tray and bake for 10–15 minutes, or until the pastry looks pale golden. Lift off the paper and beans, return the pastry shell to the oven, and bake for 3–5 minutes until golden. Reduce the temperature to 180°C (350°F/ Gas 4). Leave to cool slightly in the tin.

3 Put the egg yolks in a bowl and lightly beat. Combine the flour, cornflour, and 225g (8oz) of the sugar in a saucepan. Slowly add 350ml (12fl oz) water and heat gently, stirring, until the sugar dissolves and there are no lumps.

Increase the heat slightly and cook, stirring, for 3–5 minutes, or until the mixture starts to thicken.

4 Beat several spoonfuls of the hot mixture into the egg yolks. Pour this mixture back into the pan and slowly bring to the boil, stirring constantly. Boil for 3 minutes, then stir in the lemon zest and juice together with the butter. Continue boiling for a further 2 minutes, or until the mixture is thick and glossy, stirring constantly and scraping down the sides of the pan as necessary. Remove the pan from the heat; cover to keep warm.

5 Whisk the egg whites in a large clean bowl until foamy. Sprinkle over the cream of tartar and whisk.

Continue whisking, adding the remaining sugar, 1 tbsp at a time. Add the vanilla extract with the last tablespoon of the sugar, whisking until the meringue is thick and glossy.

6 Place the pastry case on a baking tray, pour in the lemon filling, then top with the meringue, spreading it so it completely covers the filling right up to the pastry edge. Take care not to spill it over the pastry, or the tart will be difficult to remove from the tin after baking.

7 Place in the oven and bake for 12–15 minutes, or until the meringue is lightly golden. Transfer to a wire rack and leave to cool completely, before removing from the tin and serving.

tangerine macarons

Sharp, zesty tangerines are used here, rather than oranges, to counter-balance the sweetness of the meringues.

🥄 30 MINS   🍲 18-20 MINS

SPECIAL EQUIPMENT ▪ blender or food processor ▪ piping bag fitted with a 1cm (½in) plain nozzle

MAKES 20

200g (7oz) icing sugar

75g (2½oz) ground almonds

2 tsp grated zest and 1 tbsp tangerine juice

2 large egg whites, at room temperature

75g (2½oz) granulated sugar

3-4 drops orange food colouring

50g (1¾oz) unsalted butter, softened

1 Preheat the oven to 150°C (300°F/Gas 2). Line 2 baking sheets with baking parchment. Draw 40 x 3cm (1¼in) circles on the parchment with a pencil, leaving a 3cm (1¼in) gap between each one. Blitz half the icing sugar with the ground almonds in a blender or food processor until finely mixed. Add 1 tsp of the tangerine zest and blitz briefly once more.

2 In a bowl, whisk the egg whites to form stiff peaks. Add the granulated sugar, a little at a time,

whisking well with each addition. Whisk in the food colouring. Fold in the almond mixture, a spoonful at a time. Transfer to the piping bag and pipe meringue into the centre of each circle.

3 Bake in the middle of the oven for 18-20 minutes until the surface is set firm. Leave the macarons to cool on the baking sheets for 15-20 minutes and then transfer to a wire rack to cool completely.

4 For the filling, cream together the remaining icing sugar and tangerine zest with the butter and tangerine juice until smooth. Transfer into the (cleaned) piping bag, using the same nozzle. Pipe a blob of icing onto the flat side of half the macarons, and sandwich with the other half. Serve the same day, or the macarons will start to go soft.

orange and cinnamon crème brûlée

In this dessert, translated as "burnt cream", a rich custard is sprinkled with sugar and then grilled for a few minutes.

🥄 15-20 MINS PLUS CHILLING   🍲 30-35 MINS

SPECIAL EQUIPMENT ▪ electric hand whisk ▪ 1.5-litre (2¾-pint) gratin dish

SERVES 8

1 cinnamon stick, snapped in half

1 litre (1¾ pints) whipping cream

grated zest of 1 orange

8 egg yolks

200g (7oz) granulated sugar

1 Preheat the oven to 190°C (375°F/Gas 5). Put the cinnamon in a pan. Warm over a low heat for 40-60 seconds, until you can smell the spice. Let cool slightly, then add the cream and orange zest. Bring just to the boil. Remove from the heat, cover, and let the cream infuse for 10-15 minutes.

2 Put the yolks and a third of the sugar in a large bowl. Mix with an electric hand whisk. Slowly pour the cream mixture into the egg yolks, whisking constantly. Ladle the mixture through a large sieve into the gratin dish. Fold an old, clean tea towel and put it on the bottom of a roasting tin. Then set the gratin dish on the towel.

3 Pour hot water into the roasting tin to come about halfway up the sides of the gratin dish. Bring the water to the boil on top of the stove, then move to the oven. Bake for 30-35 minutes, until a thin skin forms and the cream is almost firm when the dish is moved from side to side. Remove from the tin, let cool to room temperature, then chill for 3-8 hours.

4 Heat the grill to hot. Sprinkle the remaining sugar over the surface of the cream. Half-fill a roasting tin with cold water and set the gratin dish in it. Add some ice cubes to the water to keep the custard cool. Grill for 3 minutes, until the sugar melts and caramelizes on top. Let cool a few minutes so the caramel becomes crisp, then serve.

lemon polenta cake

Polenta makes a rich, moist cake with a great lemon flavour. This recipe is also a good wheat-free option.

🥄 **30 MINS** 🍲 **50-60 MINS** ❄️ **FREEZABLE**

SPECIAL EQUIPMENT ▪ 23cm (9in) round springform cake tin ▪ electric hand whisk

SERVES 6-8

175g (6oz) unsalted butter, softened

200g (7oz) caster sugar

3 large eggs, beaten

75g (2½oz) coarse yellow cornmeal or polenta

175g (6oz) ground almonds

grated zest and juice of 2 lemons

1 tsp baking powder

crème fraîche, to serve (optional)

1 Preheat the oven to 160°C (325°F/ Gas 3). Grease the cake tin and line the base with baking parchment. Cream the butter and 175g (6oz) of the sugar with an electric hand whisk until fluffy. Pour in the beaten eggs, a little at a time, whisking after each addition. Gently fold in the cornmeal or polenta and the almonds using a metal spoon. Fold in the lemon zest and baking powder.

2 Scrape the mixture into the prepared tin and smooth the surface with a palette knife. Bake for 50–60 minutes until springy to the touch and a skewer inserted in the centre comes out clean. It will not rise much. Leave the cake in the tin for a few minutes until cool enough to handle.

3 Heat the lemon juice and the remaining sugar in a small pan over a medium heat until the sugar has dissolved. Remove from the heat.

4 Turn the cake out onto a wire rack, baked side upwards. Retain the parchment. Using a thin skewer or cocktail stick, poke holes in the top of the cake while still warm. Pour the hot lemon syrup, a little at a time, over the surface of the cake. Remove the parchment and serve at room temperature on its own or with crème fraîche.

middle eastern oranges

Slices of fresh orange are made more exotic with rosewater, pomegranate seeds, and pistachio nuts.

🥄 **15 MINS**

SERVES 4

4 oranges

1-2 tbsp clear honey

2 tbsp rosewater

a good pinch of ground cinnamon

seeds from 1 pomegranate

small handful of chopped pistachio nuts (optional)

handful of mint leaves, to decorate

1 Slice the top and bottom from each orange and place them on a chopping board. Carefully slice off the skin and pith, leaving as much flesh as possible, and following the sides of the orange so you keep the shape of the fruit. Slice the oranges horizontally into thin strips, discarding any pips as you come across them, then arrange the orange slices on a serving platter. Pour over any juice that remains on the chopping board.

2 Drizzle with the honey and rosewater, and sprinkle with the cinnamon. Scatter with the pomegranate seeds and pistachio nuts, if using, then decorate with the mint leaves and serve.

variation

caramelized oranges and passion fruit

Put 60g (2oz) sugar in a saucepan with 2 tbsp water. Stir, then heat gently without stirring, until the sugar melts. Boil rapidly until a rich golden brown. Remove from the heat and add 2 tbsp water. Stir over a gentle heat until the caramel dissolves, then leave to cool. Prepare the dish in the same way, but drizzle with the caramel instead of honey, omit the rosewater, and scatter with passion fruit seeds instead of pomegranate.

Season's best **oranges, tangerines, clementines, and grapefruit**

Best in winter, these members of the citrus family are rich in vitamin C and help to detoxify the body. Oranges vary widely in size, thickness of skin, and taste; the smaller, sweeter mandarin is a popular variety, which also includes tangerines, satsumas, and clementines. Grapefruit are grown in clusters like outsized yellow grapes. They all team well with chocolate, rich meats, poultry and game, cheeses, and other fruits.

Oranges, grapefruit, and other citrus are grown in the Mediterranean and subtropical regions worldwide, especially Spain, the US, Brazil, China, Japan, South Africa, Israel, and Mexico.

Clementine This is among the smallest of the mandarin citrus family and looks like a bright orange golf ball, with thin, shiny skin, a delicate membrane, and hardly any seeds. The juice has a sweet, elusive fragrance with a tangy edge.

how to segment an orange

This technique is the quickest, easiest way to segment an orange, leaving the flesh pith-free.

1 With a sharp knife, slice away the top and bottom of the orange, then work around the fruit, slicing away the skin and pith.

2 Slice between each segment, leaving the thin layer of membrane behind until you have cut out all the segments.

Tangerine A classic small-seeded citrus with a good fragrance, sweet or sharp flavour, and a pebbly skin.

The Jaffa is a good winter orange with bright orange-coloured flesh.

Jaffa The nearly seedless Jaffa has pale, thick skin that is easily removed. The flesh is sweet, crisp, and juicy with an intense orange flavour. It is excellent to eat and to use for candied peel dipped in chocolate.

Bitter orange Unlike sweet oranges, bitter varieties such as the Seville are unpleasant to eat raw. However, they are the classic marmalade orange because of their acidity, thick peel, and numerous seeds that help the preserve to set. The Seville has a very short, early season.

Their juice and zest can also be used to make tangy sauces for rich meats, game, and duck.

Pink grapefruit Varieties such as the popular Pink Marsh tend to have thicker skin than white grapefruit, and often have a longer shelf life. Add them to a fruit compôte or a savoury salad.

The flesh is juicy, sharp, and slightly bitter.

White grapefruit The fruit tends to have thin, pale yellow skin, a narrow layer of pith, and few seeds. It makes excellent grapefruit marmalade. Varieties such as Marsh are notable for tender and generally extremely juicy, pale yellow flesh.

The pale, coral-coloured flesh has no seeds and is full of sweet juice.

Red grapefruit The brightly coloured flesh of varieties such as Ruby Red and Rio Red is juicy, tart-sweet, and almost seedless. Use in compôtes and salads and for juice.

The smooth, thin skin has a reddish tinge.

Navel orange Second only to the Valencia in commercial importance, the deliciously sweet Navel orange is seedless with a thick skin. These oranges are excellent for eating, juicing, and cooking.

essentials
varieties available
Navel, Jaffa, Valencia, blood, and bitter (Seville being the most common) oranges; pink, white, and red grapefruit; mandarins, tangerines, clementines, and satsumas.

buy Choose fruit with bright, taut, and glossy skin. It should feel heavy for its size and smell aromatic. Avoid if dry or mouldy, or has brown marks.

store Keep in a cool place in a fruit bowl, or uncovered in the fridge, for up to 2 weeks; use before the skin shrivels.

cook Peel and segment to eat alone or in salads and compôtes. Juice for drinks, jellies, and sorbets. Poach the fruit whole (peeled). Use the grated zest and juice to flavour casseroles, sauces, cakes, and biscuits. Grill grapefruit halves.

preserve Marmalade; bottle in syrup or alcohol. Candy, or dry the peel. Freeze peeled segments and slices, or whole.

recipe ideas
Beef tagine with orange and bay leaves p454

Seville marmalade p484

Tangerine macarons p474

chocolate orange pound cake

Candied orange peel adds great flavour to this loaf cake.

🥄 2 HRS PLUS CANDYING PEEL   🍲 50-60 MINS

SPECIAL EQUIPMENT ▪ 900g (2lb) loaf tin ▪ electric hand whisk

SERVES 6-8

2 oranges, peel removed and juice of 1 orange

125g (4½oz) plain flour

3 tbsp cocoa powder

1 tsp baking powder

salt

175g (6oz) unsalted butter

200g (7oz) caster sugar

3 eggs

60g (2oz) icing sugar

1 Candy the peel as in the recipe on p484. Allow 24 hours or more for drying. Reserve several pieces for decoration and finely chop the rest.

2 Preheat the oven to 180°C (350°F/ Gas 4). Butter, line, and flour the loaf tin. Sift the flour into a bowl with the cocoa powder, baking powder, and a pinch of salt. In another bowl, cream the butter and sugar with an electric hand whisk until light and fluffy. Add the eggs, one by one, beating thoroughly after each addition. Stir in the chopped candied orange peel.

3 Lightly fold in the flour and cocoa powder. Transfer the mixture to the prepared loaf tin. Tap the tin on a work surface to level the surface, and bake for 50-60 minutes, until it shrinks slightly from the sides of the tin and a skewer inserted in the centre comes out clean.

4 Run a knife around the sides of the tin to loosen the cake, invert the tin, and transfer the cake to a wire rack. Keep a baking sheet below the rack to catch any drips from the icing later. Remove the baking parchment. Leave the cake to cool completely.

5 Sift the icing sugar into a small bowl and slowly stir in enough of the orange juice to make a soft paste. Place the bowl in a saucepan of hot (not simmering) water and heat until the icing is warm and pours easily from the spoon. Drizzle the icing over the cake. Finely slice the reserved candied peel and use to top the cake. Leave to stand for about 1 hour, until the icing has set. Serve in slices.

chocolate and pear tartlets

For the best result, ensure your pears are fully ripe and juicy.

🥄 30-35 MINS   🍲 25-30 MINS

SPECIAL EQUIPMENT ▪ 8 x 10cm (4in) round fluted tartlet tins

MAKES 8

melted butter, for greasing

350g (12oz) ready-made sweet shortcrust pastry

150g (5½oz) plain chocolate, finely chopped

1 egg

125ml (4½fl oz) single cream

2 large ripe pears

1-2 tbsp caster sugar, to sprinkle

1 Brush the insides of the tartlet tins with melted butter. Group 4 of the tartlet tins together with their edges nearly touching. Sprinkle a work surface lightly with flour. Divide the pastry in half and roll 1 piece out to 3mm (⅛in) thick. Roll the pastry loosely round the rolling pin and drape it over the 4 tins to cover them.

2 Tear off a small piece of pastry from the edge, form it into a ball, dip it in flour, and use it to push the pastry into the tins. Roll the rolling pin over the tops of the tins to cut off excess pastry. Roll up the trimmings with the other piece of pastry and repeat with the remaining tins.

3 Preheat the oven to 200°C (400°F/ Gas 6). Heat a baking sheet on a shelf near the bottom of the oven. Sprinkle the chocolate into each tartlet shell.

4 To make the custard, whisk the egg and cream until thoroughly mixed. For an extra-smooth custard, run the mixture through a sieve. Spoon 2-3 tbsp of the custard over the chocolate in each tartlet shell.

5 Peel the pears, cut them in half, and remove the cores. Cut each pear half into very thin slices widthways. Arrange the slices on the custard so they overlap. Press them down very lightly into the custard, so it will bake up around the fruit, then sprinkle each tartlet evenly with the sugar.

6 Place the tartlet tins on the heated baking sheet. Bake for 10 minutes, then reduce the heat to 180°C (350°F/Gas 4) and continue baking for 15-20 minutes until the pastry is golden and the custard has set.

7 Leave the tartlets to cool slightly. Once cool enough to handle, carefully unmould them and place the tartlets on individual plates to serve.

cinnamon apple cake

This recipe is rather like making a sweet toad-in-the-hole. It can be served warm as a dessert with custard or cream, or left to cool and sliced to serve with coffee.

🥣 30 MINS　🍲 25-30 MINS

SPECIAL EQUIPMENT ▪ electric hand whisk ▪ 24cm (9½in) large square baking tin

SERVES 8-12

3-4 cooking apples (depending on size)

1 tbsp lemon juice

3 eggs

250g (9oz) caster sugar

115g (4oz) butter, diced

6 tbsp milk

4 tbsp single cream

200g (7oz) plain flour

1 tbsp baking powder

2 tsp ground cinnamon

1 Preheat the oven to 200°C (400°F/Gas 6). Butter a large baking tin, about 24cm (9½in) square, and dust with flour.

2 Peel, core, quarter, and slice the apples, and put in a bowl of water with lemon juice to prevent browning.

3 Whisk the eggs and 225g (8oz) of the sugar with an electric hand whisk until thick and pale, and leaves a trail when the beaters are lifted out of the mixture.

4 Put the butter, milk, and cream in a pan and heat gently until the butter melts, then bring to the boil. Remove the pan from the heat and allow to cool briefly, then stir into the egg mixture. Sift the flour and baking powder over the surface, and fold in with a metal spoon. Pour into the prepared tin.

5 Drain the apples and arrange them attractively over the batter. Mix the remaining sugar with the cinnamon, and sprinkle over. Bake for 25–30 minutes until golden and cooked through. Leave to cool in the tin, then cut into squares.

spiced carrot and orange cake

Grated carrots really help keep this cake moist and add flavour, too. But it's the mixed spice that makes this cake just a little bit different from standard carrot cake recipes.

🥣 20 MINS　🍲 30 MINS　❄ FREEZABLE

SPECIAL EQUIPMENT ▪ 20cm (8in) square cake tin ▪ electric hand whisk

MAKES 16

175g (6oz) self-raising flour

1 tsp ground cinnamon

1 tsp mixed spice

½ tsp bicarbonate of soda

100g (3½oz) light soft brown sugar or dark soft brown sugar

150ml (5fl oz) sunflower oil or light olive oil

2 large eggs

75g (2½oz) golden syrup

125g (4½oz) carrots, coarsely grated

zest of 1 orange

For the icing

75g (2½oz) icing sugar

100g (3½oz) cream cheese, at room temperature

1-2 tbsp orange juice

zest of 1 orange, plus extra to decorate (optional)

1 Preheat the oven to 180°C (350°F/Gas 4). Line the base and sides of a cake tin with baking parchment. In a large bowl, mix together the flour, spices, bicarbonate of soda, and sugar. In another bowl, mix the oil, eggs, and syrup together, then combine with the dry ingredients. Stir in the carrots and orange zest, transfer to the tin, and level the top. Bake for 30 minutes, or until firm to the touch. Leave to cool in the tin for 5 minutes, then cool completely on a wire rack.

2 For the icing, sift the icing sugar into a bowl, add the cream cheese, orange juice, and orange zest, and whisk with an electric hand whisk until the mixture becomes thick. When the cake is cool, spread the icing over the top. Decorate with extra orange zest, if using, and cut into 16 squares, to serve.

apple dumplings

Change the cinnamon in these apple dumplings for grated nutmeg or mixed spice if you like, and use orange zest instead of lemon for a slightly sweeter finish.

 20 MINS 🍲 30–40 MINS

SERVES 4

225g (8oz) self-raising flour, sifted

115g (4oz) vegetable suet

1 tsp ground cinnamon, plus extra to serve

grated zest of 1 lemon

4 cooking apples, peeled and cored

1 tbsp demerara sugar

60g (2oz) golden sultanas

icing sugar, to serve

1 Preheat the oven to 180°C (350°F/ Gas 4) and lightly grease a baking sheet. To make the suet pastry, put the flour, suet, cinnamon, and lemon zest into a bowl. Slowly trickle in about 100ml (3½fl oz) cold water and mix together until it forms a dough.

2 Roll out the pastry on a floured work surface and cut out 4 circles, large enough to cover each apple. Sit an apple on each round, sprinkle the demerara sugar into the holes where the apples were cored, and add the

sultanas to each. Brush the edges of the pastry with water and bring them together at the top, pinching the dough firmly to secure it in place.

3 Turn the apples over so their sealed side is face down. If you have any pastry left over, you could fashion leaves and stalks for the dumplings. Sit the dumplings on the baking sheet and cook in the oven for 30–40 minutes until golden. Sprinkle the dumplings with icing sugar and ground cinnamon, and serve with cream, custard, or ice cream.

variation

pear and walnut dumplings
Prepare in the same way, but use 4 slightly unripe pears instead of apples. Peel and cut out a 2cm deep hole in the core ends. Mix 25g (scant 1oz) finely chopped walnuts with 1 tbsp golden syrup and use to stuff the pears, then wrap in pastry and bake.

crêpes with caramelized apples and chocolate

These thin French pancakes are surprisingly easy to make.

🥣 15 MINS 🍲 20 MINS

SPECIAL EQUIPMENT ▪ electric hand whisk

SERVES 4–6

50g (1¾oz) plain flour

salt

1 egg, lightly beaten

150ml (5fl oz) milk

142ml carton double cream

knob of butter

2–3 tbsp golden caster sugar, depending on the sweetness of the apples

4 pink-skinned eating apples, sliced

vegetable oil

125g (4½oz) dark chocolate, grated

1 Sift the flour into a mixing bowl with a little salt and make a well in the centre. Put the egg and a little of the milk in the well. Using a wooden spoon, gradually stir the egg mixture, gradually incorporating the flour and the rest of the milk. Then whisk the mixture with a balloon whisk to remove any lumps. Chill in the fridge for 15 minutes, if you have time.

2 Put the cream in a bowl and whisk with an electric hand whisk until lightly whipped. Put the butter and sugar in a frying pan over a low heat and stir until the sugar has dissolved. Add the apples and toss well. Cook for 5–10 minutes, or until caramelized, then set aside and keep warm.

3 In a small, flat frying pan or pancake pan, heat a drizzle of oil on a high heat, swirling it around the pan, then tipping it out. Stir the batter, then spoon 2 tbsp of it into the pan, swirling it around so it reaches the edges. Cook for a couple of minutes, then pull up the edges with a palette knife. Turn the crêpe over and cook the other side for 1 minute. Slide it out onto a warmed plate and repeat until all the batter is cooked.

4 To serve, pile some of the apple mixture and a dollop of cream onto each crêpe, fold, and top with plenty of dark chocolate shavings.

apple streusel cake

A delicious apple cake with a crunchy cinnamon topping.

🥣 20 MINS 🍲 1 HR 15 MINS

SPECIAL EQUIPMENT ▪ 20cm (8in) round loose-bottomed or springform cake tin ▪ electric hand whisk

SERVES 8

125g (4½oz) plain flour

125g (4½oz) butter, softened

125g (4½oz) caster sugar

1 tsp ground cinnamon

2 large eggs, lightly beaten

½ tsp vanilla extract

1 Bramley apple, peeled, cored, and cut into chunks

50g (1¾oz) sultanas

For the streusel topping

75g (2½oz) butter, diced

100g (3½oz) plain flour

25g (scant 1oz) ground almonds

1 tsp ground cinnamon

50g (1¾oz) caster sugar or light soft brown sugar

1 Preheat the oven to 180°C (350°F/ Gas 4). Lightly grease and line the base of the cake tin with baking parchment. Sift the flour into a bowl, add the butter, sugar, cinnamon, eggs, and vanilla, and mix with an electric hand whisk until pale and creamy. Spoon into the tin, level the top, and scatter with the apple and sultanas.

2 For the topping, rub the diced butter and flour in a bowl with your fingertips to resemble breadcrumbs. Add the almonds, cinnamon, and sugar. Scatter on top of the cake and level it, pressing down slightly. Bake for 1¼ hours, or until a skewer inserted into the cake comes out clean (it may be damp from the fruit). Leave to cool in the tin for 20 minutes. Serve warm, or cool completely.

banana, date, and walnut loaf

Rich dates lend extra decadence to the banana loaf – the medjool variety are truly flavoursome. For added sweetness, use really ripe bananas with a brown speckled skin.

🥣 **20 MINS**   🍲 **1 HR 15 MINS**   ❄️ **FREEZABLE**

SPECIAL EQUIPMENT ▪ 18 x 9cm (7 x 3½in) 2lb loaf tin ▪ electric hand whisk

SERVES 8–10

100g (3½oz) butter, softened

100g (3½oz) caster sugar

2 large eggs

225g (8oz) self-raising flour, sifted

2 bananas, about 300g (10oz) in total, unpeeled

100g (3½oz) stoned dates (medjool are best), chopped

50g (1¾oz) walnuts, roughly chopped

1 tsp baking powder

1 Preheat the oven to 180°C (350°F/ Gas 4). Line the loaf tin with baking parchment. Put the butter and sugar in a mixing bowl and beat with an electric hand whisk until pale, light, and fluffy. Add the eggs one at a time, beating well as you do so, and add 1 tbsp of the flour after each one to stop the mixture from curdling.

2 Peel and mash the bananas in a small bowl with a fork, then stir into the loaf mixture along with the chopped dates and walnuts. Fold in the remaining flour and the baking powder, then spoon the mixture into the tin. Smooth the top, pressing well into the corners. Bake in the oven for 1–1¼ hours, or until risen and firm to the touch. If the top of the cake starts to brown too much before it is fully cooked, cover with foil. Leave to cool in the tin, then cut into slices.

toffee apple cake

Caramelizing the apples before baking them in the cake gives them a wonderful toffee apple taste.

🥣 **30 MINS**   🍲 **50–55 MINS**   ❄️ **FREEZABLE**

SPECIAL EQUIPMENT ▪ 23cm (9in) round springform cake tin ▪ electric hand whisk

SERVES 8–10

200g (7oz) unsalted butter, softened, plus extra for greasing

50g (1¾oz) caster sugar

250g (9oz) apples, peeled, cored, and diced

150g (5½oz) light soft brown sugar

3 eggs

150g (5½oz) self-raising flour

1 heaped tsp baking powder

whipped cream or icing sugar, to serve (optional)

1 Preheat the oven to 180°C (350°F/ Gas 4). Grease the tin and line the base with baking parchment. Put 50g (1¾oz) of the butter and the caster sugar in a large frying pan and heat gently until melted and golden brown. Add the diced apple and fry gently for 7–8 minutes until it starts to soften and caramelize.

2 Put the rest of the butter and the brown sugar in a bowl and whisk with an electric hand whisk until pale and creamy. Add the eggs one at a time, beating well after each addition. Sift the flour and baking powder together and gently fold into the mixture.

3 Remove the apples with a slotted spoon, reserving the pan with the juices. Scatter the apples over the base of the tin. Spoon the batter on top, place the tin on a baking tray, and bake in the centre of the oven for 40–45 minutes. Leave to cool for a few minutes, then turn out onto a wire rack.

4 Put the pan with the juices back on a low heat, and heat gently. Put the cake on a plate, make holes in it with a fine skewer or a wooden cocktail stick, and pour over the apple syrup, letting it soak in. Serve warm with whipped cream, or cooled and dusted with icing sugar, if using.

rosemary jelly

This aromatic, robust rosemary jelly is fantastic with lamb.

🥣 **10 MINS PLUS STRAINING**   🍲 **1 HR 20 MINS – 1 HR 50 MINS**

SPECIAL EQUIPMENT ▪ preserving pan ▪ jelly bag or muslin
▪ sugar thermometer

MAKES APPROX 2kg (4½lb)

large handful of rosemary sprigs

900g (2lb) cooking apples, roughly chopped (reserve the cores and pips)

approx 900g (2lb) granulated sugar

juice of 1 lemon

1 Preheat the oven to 150°C (300°F/ Gas 2). Strip off the rosemary leaves (reserve the stalks), scatter onto a baking sheet, and bake in the oven for 30–40 minutes to dry out.

2 Put the apples, cores, and pips in a preserving pan or large heavy-based saucepan. Pour in 1.2 litres (2 pints) water and add the rosemary stalks. Simmer for 30–40 minutes until the apples are mushy. Mash with a potato masher or fork, spoon the pulp into a jelly bag set or muslin-lined sieve over a large bowl, and leave to strain overnight. Measure the juice and calculate the sugar: for every 600ml (1 pint) juice use 450g (1lb) sugar.

3 Put the juice, sugar, lemon juice, and dried leaves back in the pan and cook over a medium heat, stirring until the sugar has dissolved. Bring to the boil and cook at a rolling boil for 20 minutes, or until the jelly reaches the setting point. Remove the pan from the heat to test for a set with a sugar thermometer, or wrinkle test (chill a saucer in the fridge before cooking). If you use a thermometer, the temperature must reach 105°C (220°F); the mixture will also thicken around the sides of the pan, boil sluggishly, and the bubbles "plop" rather than froth. Or put 1 tsp jelly on the chilled saucer, allow to cool for a moment, then push it with a finger. If it leaves a trail and wrinkles slightly, it is set. Leave to stand for 10 minutes.

4 Ladle into warm sterilized jars, cover with waxed paper discs, seal, and label. Store in a cool, dark place and refrigerate after opening.

red onion marmalade

This delicious marmalade made with sweet, sticky onions is perfect served with cold meats and cheese.

🥣 **20 MINS PLUS MATURING**   🍲 **1 HR 10 MINS**

SPECIAL EQUIPMENT ▪ preserving pan

MAKES APPROX 675g (1½lb)

2 tbsp extra virgin olive oil

1kg (2¼lb) red onions (approx 6), peeled, halved, and sliced

sea salt and freshly ground black pepper

150ml (5fl oz) red wine

3 tbsp balsamic vinegar

3 tbsp white wine vinegar

6 tbsp light soft brown sugar

1 Heat the oil in a preserving pan or a large heavy-based stainless steel saucepan. Add the onions, a little sea salt, and some pepper. Cook over a low to medium heat for about 30 minutes until the onions soften and turn translucent, stirring occasionally; slow cooking is essential at this point.

2 Raise the heat a little, add the wine and vinegars, and stir to combine. Bring to the boil, then reduce the heat, stir in the sugar, and cook on a low heat, stirring occasionally, for another 30–40 minutes until most of the liquid has evaporated.

3 Remove the pan from the heat. Taste and adjust the seasoning as necessary, although the flavours will mature with time. Spoon into warm sterilized jars with non-metallic or vinegar-proof lids, making sure there are no air gaps. Cover with waxed paper discs, seal, and label. Store in a cool, dark place for at least 1 month to allow the flavours to develop. Refrigerate after opening.

three-fruit marmalade

Combining three fruits results in a lovely balance of flavours, good colour, and a good set.

🥣 **25 MINS**   🍲 **1 HR 50 MINS**   ❄ **FREEZABLE**

SPECIAL EQUIPMENT ▪ preserving pan ▪ food processor ▪ muslin
▪ sugar thermometer

MAKES APPROX 2.25kg (5lb)

1 grapefruit, washed

1 orange, washed

2 lemons, washed

1.35kg (3lb) granulated sugar

1 Halve the fruit, squeeze to extract the juice, and strain the juice into a preserving pan or a large heavy-based saucepan, reserving the pips. Scrape any soft flesh from the citrus shells and add to the pan. Scoop out the membranes and white pith from the shells and gather with the pips in the muslin. Pull up the ends to make a bag and tie it with string.

2 Thinly shred the fruit peel and cut into short lengths, or finely chop in a food processor. Add to the pan with 1.7 litres (3 pints) water and the muslin bag. Bring to the boil, reduce the heat, and simmer for 1½ hours, or until the peel is really soft and the liquid has reduced by half.

3 Squeeze the bag against the side of the pan to extract the liquid, then discard. Add the sugar and stir until dissolved. Bring to a rapid boil and cook for 15 minutes, or until the setting point is reached. Remove the pan from the heat to test for a set with a sugar thermometer, or using a wrinkle test (chill a saucer in the fridge before cooking). If you use a thermometer, the temperature must reach 105°C (220°F); the mixture will also thicken around the sides of the pan, boil sluggishly, and the bubbles "plop" rather than froth. Or put 1 tsp marmalade on the chilled saucer, allow to cool for a moment, then push it with a finger. If it leaves a trail and wrinkles slightly, it is set.

5 Skim off any scum. Leave to stand for 10 minutes, then stir well and ladle into warm sterilized jars, cover with waxed paper discs, seal, and label. Store in a cool, dark place and refrigerate after opening.

chilli jelly

This red-flecked, jewel-like jelly can be served with almost any savoury dish from cheese to lamb to give it a fiery kick. Use sour cooking apples (which have the most pectin) and add 1–2 tsp chilli flakes depending on how hot you like it.

🥄 **30 MINS PLUS STRAINING**　　🍲 **50-60 MINS**

SPECIAL EQUIPMENT ▪ jelly bag or muslin ▪ preserving pan ▪ sugar thermometer

MAKES APPROX 450g (1lb)

675g (1½lb) cooking apples, skin on, chopped (reserve the cores and pips)

approx 675g (1½lb) granulated sugar

juice of 1 lemon

1-2 tsp chilli flakes

1 Put the apples, cores, and pips in a preserving pan or large heavy-based saucepan. Pour in 1.7 litres (3 pints) cold water, bring to the boil, and simmer for 30–40 minutes, or until the apples are mushy. Mash with a potato masher or a fork, spoon the pulp into a jelly bag or muslin-lined sieve set over a large bowl, and leave to strain overnight. Don't be tempted to squeeze the pulp mixture if you want a crystal-clear jelly.

2 Measure the juice and calculate the sugar: for every 600ml (1 pint) juice use 450g (1lb) sugar. Pour the juice into the pan, bring to the boil, then add the sugar and lemon juice. Stir until the sugar has dissolved, then bring to a rolling boil and cook for 20–30 minutes, or until the jelly reaches the setting point. Remove the pan from the heat to test for a set with a sugar thermometer, or using a wrinkle test (chill a saucer in the fridge before cooking). If you use a thermometer, the temperature must reach 105°C (220°F); the mixture will also thicken around the sides of the pan, boil sluggishly, and the bubbles "plop" rather than froth. Or put 1 tsp jelly on the chilled saucer, allow to cool for a moment, then push it with a finger. If it leaves a trail and wrinkles slightly, it is set. Leave to stand for 10 minutes.

4 Skim off any surface scum, then stir in the chilli flakes. Ladle into warm sterilized jars, cover with discs of waxed paper, seal, and label. Store in a cool, dark place and keep refrigerated after opening.

candied citrus peel

Home-made candied peel has much more flavour than bought varieties, is preservative-free, and is a delicious addition to cakes or desserts, or as a sweetmeat with coffee.

🥣 **15 MINS PLUS DRYING** 🍲 **1 HR 50 MINS**

MAKES APPROX 225g (8oz)

1 large or 2 small grapefruit, plus 1 pink grapefruit or 1 pomelo (or a mixture of all three), washed

granulated sugar – for quantity, see method

caster sugar, for coating

1 Score the surface of each piece of fruit into quarters with a sharp knife, then carefully remove the peel. Weigh the pieces of peel all together. Put the peel in a heavy-based saucepan, cover with water, and cook gently for up to 1 hour until soft, changing the water 2 or 3 times.

2 Drain the peel and scrape out any ragged or inner pulp from the inside of the shells. Either leave the peel in quarters, or cut into thick strips.

3 Use the same weight of sugar to peel. Put the prepared peel and sugar into a snug-fitting pan, barely cover with water, set over a low heat, and stir to dissolve the sugar. Bring to the boil and simmer very gently for 45 minutes, or until the peel is translucent and has absorbed nearly all the syrup.

4 Remove the peel from the pan and spread it out on trays lined with baking parchment. Leave at room temperature for 24 hours or longer to dry out.

5 Dip each piece of dried peel in a bowl of caster sugar until it is thoroughly coated. Place the sugared candied peel in a sterilized jar and seal. Store in a cool, dry place.

rhubarb, pear, and ginger jam

A great combination of flavours and textures makes this jam a little bit more special than most.

🥣 **15–20 MINS** 🍲 **25–30 MINS**

SPECIAL EQUIPMENT ▪ preserving pan ▪ sugar thermometer

MAKES APPROX 1kg (2¼lb)

675g (1½lb) rhubarb, rinsed and chopped into 2.5cm (1in) pieces

2 pears, peeled, cored, and chopped

800g (1¾lb) granulated sugar

juice of 1 lemon

juice of ½ orange

2 balls of stem ginger, finely chopped

1 Put the rhubarb, pears, and sugar in a preserving pan or a large heavy-based saucepan. Stir, then add the lemon juice, orange juice, and ginger. Cook on a low heat, stirring until all the sugar has dissolved.

2 Raise the heat, bring to the boil, and cook at a rolling boil for 15–20 minutes, or until the mixture reaches the setting point. Remove the pan from the heat to test for a set with a sugar thermometer, or using a wrinkle test (chill a saucer in the fridge before cooking). If you use a thermometer, the temperature must reach 105°C (220°F); the mixture will also thicken around the sides of the pan, boil sluggishly, and the bubbles "plop" rather than froth. Or put 1 tsp jam on the chilled saucer, allow to cool for a moment, then push it with a finger. If it leaves a trail and wrinkles slightly, it is set.

4 Ladle into warm sterilized jars, cover with discs of waxed paper, seal, and label. Store in a cool, dark place, and refrigerate after opening.

seville marmalade

This makes an authentic, bitter-sweet marmalade.

🥣 **45 MINS** 🍲 **1 HR 20 MINS – 1 HR 30 MINS**

SPECIAL EQUIPMENT ▪ muslin ▪ preserving pan ▪ sugar thermometer

MAKES APPROX 1kg (2¼lb)

1kg (2¼lb) Seville oranges, scrubbed in hot water, with stalk ends removed

1 large lemon, washed

1.1kg (2½lb) granulated sugar

1 Cut the fruit in half, squeeze the juice into a jug, and reserve in the fridge. Gather the pith and pips in muslin, pull up the ends to make a bag, and tie it with string.

2 Put the citrus shells, bag of pith and pips, and 1.7 litres (3 pints) water in a preserving pan or large heavy-based saucepan. Bring to the boil, half-cover, and simmer for 1 hour, or until the shells are soft (not mushy). Tip into a large sieve or colander over a bowl and press lightly to extract the liquor. Scoop excess mush from inside the cooked shells with a spoon and discard. Slice the peel into thick or thin strands, or coarse or fine chunks.

3 Put the liquor, peel, and fruit juice back in the pan. Add the sugar, heat gently, stir until the sugar dissolves, and boil rapidly for 5–15 minutes, or until the setting point is reached. Remove the pan from the heat to test for a set with a sugar thermometer, or a wrinkle test (chill a saucer in the fridge before cooking). If you use a thermometer, the temperature must reach 105°C (220°F); the mixture will also thicken around the sides of the pan, boil sluggishly, and the bubbles "plop" rather than froth. Or put 1 tsp marmalade on the chilled saucer, allow to cool for a moment, then push it with a finger. If it leaves a trail and wrinkles slightly, it is set. Leave to settle for a few minutes.

4 Skim off any scum, then stir and ladle into warm sterilized jars. Cover with waxed paper discs, seal, and label. Store in a cool, dark place and refrigerate after opening.

clementines in caramel syrup

You can also use other soft citrus fruits for this recipe.

🥣 10 MINS 🍲 15 MINS PLUS HEAT-PROCESSING

SPECIAL EQUIPMENT ▪ screw-band jar or kilner jar

MAKES 1 LITRE (1¾ PINTS)

175g (6oz) granulated sugar

10 small clementines, peeled, with the white pith scraped off with a knife

1 Put the sugar and 100ml (3½fl oz) cold water in a medium saucepan. Stir well, then heat without stirring or boiling until the sugar has dissolved. Bring to a rapid boil and cook for 5–10 minutes, or until a rich golden brown. Pour in 200ml (7fl oz) hot water, stir until the caramel dissolves, then bring the syrup back to the boil.

2 Preheat the oven to 150°C (300°F/Gas 2). Stand a warm sterilized jar on a roasting tray lined with newspaper. Pack the fruit tightly into the jar without squashing it, leaving 1cm (½in) of space at the top. Fill to the brim with the hot syrup. Tap the jar down lightly on the work surface and swivel to and fro to remove any air pockets. Add extra syrup if needed so the fruit is completely covered. Fit the rubber band or metal lid, seal, and clamp on the lid. If using screw-band jars, loosen by a quarter of a turn.

3 Put the jars in the oven for 30–40 minutes to heat process (remove remaining air), then remove from the oven and tighten the clip or lid (or screw-on plastic screw-band lid) immediately. Leave for 24 hours, then unscrew or unclip and test the lid is firmly sealed before refastening and storing. (If using a kilner jar with metal lids, you will know if you have a seal as the lid becomes slightly concave and is firm with no "give" once pressed.) Store in a cool, dark place and refrigerate after opening.

clementine and whisky marmalade

The flavour of whisky in this marmalade greatly enhances those of the citrus fruits. Clementines aren't too high in pectin or acid, so lemon juice helps the set.

🥣 10 MINS 🍲 55 MINS – 1 HR 5 MINS

SPECIAL EQUIPMENT ▪ food processor ▪ preserving pan ▪ sugar thermometer

MAKES APPROX 1kg (2¼lb)

900g (2lb) clementines, scrubbed, rinsed, and halved, with pips removed

juice of 2 large lemons

900g (2lb) granulated sugar

1–2 tbsp whisky, or use brandy

1 Either put the clementines in a food processor and pulse until shredded but not turned to mush, or squeeze the juice by hand and finely shred the skins with a sharp knife. Put the chopped fruit in a preserving pan or a large heavy-based saucepan. Pour in 900ml (1½ pints) water and bring to the boil, then simmer for 30 minutes or longer, until the rind has softened.

2 Add the lemon juice and sugar and cook on a low heat, stirring until the sugar has dissolved. Bring to the boil, then keep at a rolling boil for 20–30 minutes, or until the setting point is reached. Remove the pan from the heat to test for a set with a sugar thermometer, or a wrinkle test (chill a saucer in the fridge before cooking). If you use a thermometer, the temperature must reach 105°C (220°F); the mixture will also thicken around the sides of the pan, boil sluggishly, and the bubbles "plop" rather than froth. Or put 1 tsp marmalade on the chilled saucer, allow to cool for a moment, then push it with a finger. If it leaves a trail and wrinkles slightly, it is set. Leave to settle for a few minutes.

4 Stir in the whisky, then ladle into warm sterilized jars. Cover with waxed paper discs, seal, and label. Store in a cool, dark place and refrigerate after opening.

index

acknowledgments

Dorling Kindersley would like to thank:

Ian O'Leary for new photography; Jane Bamforth, Claire Tennant-Scull, and Diana Vowles for additional copy editing; Jane Bamforth, Jan Stevens, Clare Greenstreet, and Ann Reynolds for recipe testing; Dorothy Kikon, Martha Burley, and Elizabeth Yeates for proofreading; Michele Clarke for the index; Steve Crozier and Tom Morse for image retouching; David Roberts and Rob Laidler for the recipe database; Alison Shaw and Elizabeth Yeates for editorial assistance; Mandy Earey and Anne Fisher for design assistance; and Alicia Ingty and Neha Ahuja for their valuable input.